D1504932

People CMM®
Second Edition

A Framework for Human Capital Management

Bill Curtis

William E. Hefley

Sally A. Miller

♦♦Addison-Wesley

Upper Saddle River, NJ • Boston • Indianapolis • San Francisco
New York • Toronto • Montreal • London • Munich • Paris • Madrid
Capetown • Sydney • Tokyo • Singapore • Mexico City

CarnegieMellon
Software Engineering Institute

The SEI Series in Software Engineering ■ Human Capital Management

Many of the designations used by manufacturers and sellers to distinguish their products are claimed as trademarks. Where those designations appear in this book, and the publisher was aware of a trademark claim, the designations have been printed with initial capital letters or in all capitals.

CMM, CMMI, Capability Maturity Model, Capability Maturity Modeling, Carnegie Mellon, CERT, and CERT Coordination Center are registered in the U.S. Patent and Trademark Office by Carnegie Mellon University.

ATAM; Architecture Tradeoff Analysis Method; CMM Integration; COTS Usage-Risk Evaluation; CURE; EPIC; Evolutionary Process for Integrating COTS Based Systems; Framework for Software Product Line Practice; IDEAL; Interim Profile; OAR; OCTAVE; Operationally Critical Threat, Asset, and Vulnerability Evaluation; Options Analysis for Reengineering; Personal Software Process; PLTP; Product Line Technical Probe; PSP; SCAMPI; SCAMPI Lead Appraiser; SCAMPI Lead Assessor; SCE; SEI; SEPG; Team Software Process; and TSP are service marks of Carnegie Mellon University.

Special permission to reproduce the People Capability Maturity Model, Version 2.0 (CMU/SEI-2001-MM-001), © 2001 by Carnegie Mellon University, has been granted by the Software Engineering Institute.

Cataloging-in-Publication Data is on file with the Library of Congress.

ISBN-13: 978-0-321-55390-4
ISBN-10:   0-321-55390-X
Text printed in the United States on recycled paper at Hamilton Printing Co. in Castleton, New York.
First printing, July 2009

This book is dedicated to our families:

- *Janell, Crystal, and Catherine Curtis*
- *Nancy, Peter, Susan, Jennifer, and Daniel Hefley*
- *My extended family, especially my children,
  Todd Miller and Kerry Beck*

*We trust that the benefits of this model to others
will justify the continued family sacrifices we have made.*

Contents

Preface

The Need for an Agile Workforce

Organizations are now competing in two markets, one for their products and services and one for the talent required to produce or perform them. An organization's success in its business markets is determined by its success in the talent market. At the very time that business markets are fluctuating, talent markets seem to be shrinking. As the knowledge required to build products and to deliver services increases, the retention of experienced employees becomes critical to improving productivity and time to market. In areas such as software development and nursing, the shortage of talent is so great that companies are beginning to offer incentives that were once available only to executives or professional athletes. In every domain of business, executives know that their ability to compete is directly related to their ability to attract, develop, motivate, organize, and retain talented people.

Yet the people-related challenges of the business stretch far beyond recruiting and retention. Competing for talent and recruiting the best is not enough, and focusing just on winning the "talent wars" can be damaging to the organization [Pfeffer 01]. As agility in responding to continual change in technological and business conditions has become critical to success, organizations must strive to create learning environments capable of rapidly adjusting to the changes engulfing them. A critical component of agility is a workforce with the knowledge and skills to make rapid adjustments and the willingness to acquire new competencies. In fact, an agile workforce may reduce some of the stress currently being experienced as a talent shortage.

Organizations have attempted to apply many different techniques in their efforts to move toward strategic human capital management. They combine downsizing with restructuring, apply reengineering or process improvement, clearly communicate the organization's mission, improve information sharing, institute employee involvement programs, establish formal complaint-resolution procedures, institute gain-sharing or other incentive plans, emphasize the importance of training the workforce, formalize performance management and feedback processes, perform job or work analysis and design, support job rotation, begin to establish team-based work designs, retrain employees to meet changing demands, provide flexible work arrangements, address diversity issues, conduct formal mentoring programs, and align business and human resource strategies [Becker 96, Becker 98, Mirvis 97]. What many organizations lack is a framework for implementing these advanced practices.

People Capability Maturity Model Framework

The People Capability Maturity Model (People CMM) is a tool to help you successfully address the critical people issues in your organization. The People CMM employs the process maturity framework of the highly successful *Capability Maturity Model for Software* (SW-CMM) [Carnegie Mellon University 95] as a foundation for a model of best practices for managing and developing an organization's workforce. Version 2 of the People CMM was designed to be consistent with CMMI [CMMI 00, Chrissis 06]. The Software CMM and, more recently, CMMI-DEV have been used by software organizations around the world to guide dramatic improvements in their ability to enhance productivity and quality, reduce costs and time to market, and increase customer satisfaction. Based on the best current practices in fields such as human resources, knowledge management, and organizational development, the People CMM guides organizations in improving their processes for managing and developing their workforce. The People CMM helps organizations characterize the maturity of their workforce practices, establish a program of continuous workforce development, set priorities for improvement actions, integrate workforce development with process improvement, and establish a culture of excellence. Since its release in 1995, thousands of copies of the People CMM have been distributed, and it is used by small and large organizations in many industries and market sectors worldwide—Pfizer, Intel, IBM, Boeing, BAE SYSTEMS, Accenture, Tata Consultancy Services, Ericsson, Samsung, Lockheed Martin, Club Mahindra, HCL, Novo Nordisk, and Pershing, to name a few.

The People CMM consists of five maturity levels that establish successive foundations for continuously improving individual competencies, developing effective teams, motivating improved performance, and shaping the workforce an organization needs to accomplish its business plans. Each maturity level is a well-defined evolutionary plateau that institutionalizes new capabilities for developing the organization's workforce. By following the maturity framework, an organization can avoid introducing workforce practices that its employees are unprepared to implement effectively.

Structure of This Book

This book describes the People CMM, the practices that constitute each of its maturity levels, and information on how to apply it in guiding organizational improvements. It describes an organization's capability for developing its workforce at each maturity level. It describes how the People CMM can be applied as a standard for assessing workforce practices and as a guide in planning and implementing improvement activities. This book provides guidance on how to interpret its practices. It also presents case studies of organizations that have used the People CMM.

The first part of the book describes the rationale and evolution of the People CMM, the concepts of process maturity, the structure of the model, and how to interpret and apply the model's practices; case studies of results are also here. The second part of the book contains the practices of the People CMM—the individual, managerial, and organizational practices that contribute to maturing workforce capability. These practices describe an evolutionary improvement path from ad hoc, inconsistently performed practices, to a mature, disciplined, continual development of a workforce having the workforce competencies needed to excel at performing the organization's mission. The third and final part of this book contains the appendices. Each part is described in the following section.

The Content of the People CMM

Part One, The People Capability Maturity Model Overview: Background, Concepts, Structures, and Usage, consists of ten chapters.

- Chapter 1, The Process Maturity Framework, offers a broad view of the model; describes how the People CMM establishes an integrated system of workforce practices that matures through increasing alignment with the organization's business objectives, performance, and changing needs; and provides background on the process maturity framework adopted by the People CMM.

- Chapter 2, Increasing Organizational Capability through the People CMM, describes the maturity levels, or evolutionary plateaus, at which the organization's practices have been transformed to achieve a new level of organizational capability, and presents a description of the characteristic behaviors of organizations at each maturity level.

- Chapter 3, People CMM Process Areas, introduces the process areas in the model.

- Chapter 4, The Architecture of the People CMM, describes the components of the model, including maturity levels, goals, and practices, which ensure that the implementation of process areas is effective, repeatable, and lasting. It introduces the typographical conventions used throughout the model.

- Chapter 5, Relationships among Process Areas, addresses common areas of concern that the People CMM was designed to address and how these areas transform as the organization transitions to higher levels of organizational capability.

- Chapter 6, Interpreting the People CMM, provides insight into the meaning of the model for your organization.

- Chapter 7, Using the People CMM, explains the ways in which your organization can use the model.

- Chapter 8, Using SCAMPI with People CMM, explains the ways in which your organization can perform People CMM-based appraisals of your organization's practices using the SCAMPI appraisal method.

- Chapter 9, Experience with the People CMM, presents data regarding experiences with the People CMM.

- Chapter 10, Case Studies in Applying the People CMM, examines several case studies.

Part Two, Process Areas of the People Capability Maturity Model, describes the practices that correspond to each maturity level in the People CMM. It is an elaboration of what is meant by *maturity* at each level of the People CMM and a guide that can be used for organizational improvement and appraisal. For those who want to get a quick sense of the practices, without the rigor to apply them, an abridged version of the practices is provided in Appendix D.

Each maturity level provides a layer in the foundation for continuous improvement of the organization's workforce capability. Achieving each level of the maturity model institutionalizes different components, resulting in an overall increase in the workforce capability of the organization. Each process area comprises a set of goals that, when satisfied, stabilize an important component of workforce capability. Each process area is described in terms of the practices that contribute to satisfying its goals. The practices describe the infrastructure and activities that contribute most to the effective implementation and institutionalization of the process area.

Each section in Part Two presents the process areas within each of these maturity levels:

- The Managed Level: Maturity Level 2
- The Defined Level: Maturity Level 3
- The Predictable Level: Maturity Level 4
- The Optimizing Level: Maturity Level 5

The four appendices of the People CMM are as follows.

- Appendix A, References, provides full citations to any information cited in the People CMM.
- Appendix B, Acronyms, spells out the acronyms used in the People CMM.
- Appendix C, Glossary of Terms, defines the terms that are not adequately defined in the context of this model by the *Webster's American English* dictionary.
- Appendix D, Practice-to-Goal Mappings for People CMM Process Areas, describes the maturity levels and the process areas that correspond to each maturity level of the People CMM, and the purpose, goals, and practices of each process area. This view of the model is convenient when you want to quickly understand the content and flow of large portions of the model or if you are intimately familiar with it.

Changes in the Second Edition

Based on continuing feedback and experience from use around the globe in many industries and settings, this second edition of the People CMM has been prepared. The second edition is an update to the People CMM, Version 2. This second edition updates informative material within the People CMM and its subpractices and provides new information regarding the continuing global use of the People CMM.

Informative materials updated in this edition include the content of many practices in the People CMM. These changes are emphasized at the higher levels of organizational and workforce capability, as experience with the use of the People CMM has provided additional insights into the successful implementation of these high-maturity practices. Process areas whose informative materials have been significantly enhanced were updated based on many experiences in implementing the People CMM, especially in high-maturity organizations. These process areas are Competency Integration, Quantitative Performance Management, and Organizational Capability Management at the Predictable Level, and Continuous Capability Improvement at the Optimizing Level. Additionally, the informative material for Verifying Implementation Practices has been enhanced in many process areas.

Since the release of the first edition, use of the People CMM around the world has increased substantially. A new Chapter 10 has been added to this edition to present eight case studies of People CMM adoption across a number of industries, ranging from hospitality and services to high technology and pharmaceuticals. Chapter 8 has also been added to describe the Standard CMMI Appraisal Method for Process Improvement (SCAMPI) with People CMM. SCAMPI with People CMM is the only appraisal method supported by the SEI for use with the People CMM.

Audience

This book is addressed to anyone involved in the workplace, but especially those responsible for developing and implementing human capital management strategies and plans in their organizations, managing or developing the workforce, implementing advanced workforce practices, nurturing teams, and transforming organizational culture. It is especially useful for businesses undergoing critical organizational changes, such as downsizing, a merger, rapid growth, and change of ownership, or just surviving and thriving in today's tumultuous business conditions. It contains useful information for managers and supervisors who want guidance for managing their people, providing opportunities for individual development and growth, and effectively managing their knowledge assets. This book will help individuals trying to improve the workforce practices of their organizations, as well as those attempting to appraise the maturity of these practices in organizations. This book will provide guidance for chief resource officers (CROs), human resources professionals and their organizations, and others looking to make or strengthen the connections between human resources functions and those in the workforce—individuals seeking growth and future opportunities, front-line managers seeking to effectively motivate and retain their workforce, and executive management seeking to address workforce issues in the face of changing demographics, labor markets, and business changes.

This book complements Watts Humphrey's *Managing Technical People* [Humphrey 97a] by formalizing and expanding the maturity framework described in that book. It also complements *CMMI®, Second Edition* [Chrissis 06], by addressing the workforce improvement practices necessary to ensure long-term continual improvement in software and systems organizations. While the People CMM complements CMMI, its applicability has been proven to not be limited to systems or software-intensive organizations, as it has been applied in many industry sectors including hospitality, construction, banking, financial and insurance, energy and utilities, pharmaceuticals, business process outsourcing, high tech, information technology (IT), consulting services, government agencies, and not-for-profits. The People CMM practices have been applied in many organizations and can be applied in any organization, regardless of its business focus, size, or location.

This book does not describe all of the work being done by the authors or the Software Engineering Process Management Program of the Software Engineering Institute (SEI) at Carnegie Mellon University. For instance, the SEI supports a People CMM Lead Appraiser Track within the SEI Appraisal Program to ensure an adequate supply of experts for conducting SCAMPI with People CMM Appraisals. The SEI Appraisal Program oversees the quality and consistency of the SEI's process appraisal technology and encourages its effective use. The Standard CMMI Appraisal Method for Process Improvement (SCAMPI) is designed to provide benchmark-quality ratings relative to CMMI models. SCAMPI with People CMM appraisals are designed to provide benchmark organizational ratings relative to the People CMM.

For further information regarding the SEI, its work, or any of its associated products contact:

SEI Customer Relations
Software Engineering Institute
Carnegie Mellon University
4500 Fifth Ave.
Pittsburgh, PA 15213-2612 USA
Tel: +1-412-268-5800
Fax: +1-412-268-6257
E-mail: customer-relations@sei.cmu.edu
URL: www.sei.cmu.edu, and http://seir.sei.cmu.edu/seir

The SEI maintains a listing of authorized People CMM Lead Appraisers on its Web site—www.sei.cmu.edu/cmm-p/directory.html. For more information about the People CMM Lead Appraiser Track within the SEI Appraisal Program or training on the People CMM contact:

SEI Customer Relations
Software Engineering Institute
Carnegie Mellon University
4500 Fifth Ave.
Pittsburgh, PA 15213-2612 USA
Tel: +1-412-268-5800
Fax: +1-412-268-6257
E-mail: customer-relations@sei.cmu.edu
URL: www.sei.cmu.edu, and http://seir.sei.cmu.edu/seir

Dr. Bill Curtis, P.O. Box 126079, Fort Worth, Texas 76126-0079 USA (+1-817-228-2994); e-mail: curtis@acm.org.

Dr. Bill Hefley, Pinnacle Global Management, LLC (+1-724-935-8177); e-mail: BHefley@pinnacle-global.com.

Feedback Information

The People CMM is a living document, shaped by the needs of organizations' rapidly evolving workplaces. More than 400 change requests helped shape this version of the People Capability Maturity Model.

The SEI continues to solicit feedback from its customers. We are very interested in your ideas for improving these products. You can help. For information on how to provide feedback, see the SEI Web site, www.sei.cmu.edu/cmm-p/version2/index.html.

Acknowledgments

Leadership in Process Improvement

The People Capability Maturity Model (People CMM) draws on the topics of Capability Maturity Models, benchmark high-performance workforce practices, and organizational improvement to increase an organization's workforce capability; and presents a documented roadmap for organizational improvement.

For his contributions and guidance as the leader of the Capability Maturity Models (CMM) project at the Software Engineering Institute (SEI), his broad contributions to our ongoing discussions regarding the evolving drafts of the People CMM, and his continuing support for the People CMM efforts, we thank Dr. Mike Konrad. Watts Humphrey contributed to many discussions that led to the development and refinement of the model. The extraordinary efforts of Mark Paulk in the development of the Capability Maturity Model for Software established a world-class standard and enabled the People CMM to build on these efforts. We thank them for their contributions.

Sponsorship

We acknowledge Watts Humphrey, Ron Radice, and, especially, Bill Peterson for their foresight in providing sponsorship for this work. These gentlemen, along with Bill Curtis, have led the software process efforts at the SEI and have ensured that the process is viewed in the broad sociotechnical context in which it must be instantiated and executed—a context that involves a dynamic workforce, capable of improving and growing.

We especially thank Bill Peterson, the current manager of the Software Engineering Process Management (SEPM) Program at the Software Engineering Institute, for his continued facilitation and guidance of this work. We would also like to thank Miriam F. Browning (U.S. Army), LTG Otto Guenther (U.S. Army, Ret.), and Cynthia Kendall (Office of the Assistant Secretary of Defense C^3I) for providing the original sponsorship from the U.S. Department of Defense (DoD) necessary to complete Version 1 of the People CMM.

Reviewers

We would like to thank the many people who have been involved in the development of the People CMM. This effort could not have been accomplished without the expertise they lent to refine the model. We thank the more than 1,500 members of the People CMM Correspondence Group who contributed their time and effort to provide insightful comments and recommendations.

We would also like to thank those who took time to provide substantial comments on the various drafts of the People CMM. Individuals who provided ongoing feedback regarding Version 2 include Ajay Batra (Quality Assurance Institute (India) Ltd.), Judah Mogilensky (Process Enhancement Partners, Inc.), Raghav Nandyal (SITARA Technologies Pvt. Ltd.), and John Vu (The Boeing Company).

We also thank Charlie Ryan and Gian Wemyss of the SEI for their review and expert advice on the SCAMPI with People CMM appraisal method section. We also acknowledge the efforts of Ron Radice in leading the first pilot SCAMPI with People CMM appraisal, and documenting the results of that appraisal [Radice 05c].

Implementers

Finally, we would like to thank those who have worked with us to further prove out the concepts of the People CMM in the real world—our students and colleagues who have applied these principles in their workplaces, and the People CMM Lead Assessors and SCAMPI with People CMM Lead Appraisers who have worked with organizations to apply the model and to evaluate and benchmark their workforce practices. A current list of the SCAMPI with People CMM Lead Appraisers can be found on the SEI's Web site (www.sei.cmu.edu/cmm-p/directory.html).

We would like to thank especially those numerous individuals and organizations from the United States, India, Canada, the Netherlands, Germany, China, Australia, Denmark, England, Korea, Malaysia, Latvia, and the Philippines who have used the People CMM to guide and conduct organizational improvement activities. Since its release in 1995, thousands of copies of the People CMM have been distributed, and it has been used worldwide by small and large commercial organizations and by government organizations. Adoption rates for the People CMM have been high among high-maturity organizations that are also using CMMI-DEV or the SW-CMM. High-maturity organizations using the People CMM include Tata Consultancy Services, Infosys, and Wipro—the winner of the Institute of Electrical and Electronics Engineers (IEEE) Computer Society Award for Software Process Achievement in 2003 [Radice 05a, Curtis 03, Subramanyam 04]. High-maturity organizations using the People CMM in the United States include Lockheed Martin, Boeing, and AIS—the winner of the 1999 IEEE Computer Society/SEI Software Process Achievement Award [Lockheed 99, Vu 01, Ferguson 99, Paulk 01a, Seshagiri 00]. A survey of high-maturity software organizations showed that more than 40% of these Level 4 and Level 5 organizations were also using the People CMM [Paulk 01b]. Numerous organizations have found that the People CMM can help to support and sustain their CMMI capabilities. Recent work at the SEI has identified six frameworks that are most often being used in multimodel improvement settings: CMMI, ISO (all ISO standards as a group), Six Sigma, ITIL, eSCM, and the People CMM.

We would also like to thank Accenture, Jack Anderson (Intel), Ajay Batra (Quality Assurance Institute (India) Ltd.), Dr. Palma Buttles-Valdez (now with the SEI, formerly with TeraQuest), Ken Foster (The Boeing Company), Dr. Gargi Keeni (Tata Consultancy Services), Nina Modi (Tata Consultancy Services), Ranjit Narasimhan (HCLT BPO), Ron Radice (Software Technology Transition), A.P. Rao (HCLT BPO), Girish Seshagiri (Advanced Information Services), Teresa A. Suganski (Pfizer), Torben Thorhauge (Novo Nordisk Information Technology A/S), Srinivas Thummalapalli (Sumantrana Advisory Services Pvt Ltd.), and John Vu (The Boeing Company) for their support in supplying data regarding their experiences and outcomes with the People CMM.

A second kind of implementer has been valuable to us—our editor at Addison-Wesley, Peter Gordon. Those who have assisted us in preparing this book—John Fuller and Julie Nahil, both of Addison-Wesley, and Audrey Doyle—ably guided us through the preproduction and production processes.

Michael Zuccher's contributions in managing the SEI's Software Engineering Information Repository (SEIR)—http://seir.sei.cmu.edu/seir—and especially the People CMM components of this repository have supported many people in understanding and using the People CMM. His unique contributions are greatly appreciated.

We greatly appreciate the efforts of Marlene MacDonald and Dr. Palma Buttles-Valdez for their tireless operational support.

PART ONE

The People Capability Maturity Model Overview: Background, Concepts, Structure, and Usage

This overview presents an introduction to the People Capability Maturity Model (People CMM) and the background for developing such a model. It describes the concepts of a maturity framework and how this framework can be applied to developing the workforce capability of an organization. The structure of the People CMM is described. In addition, advice for interpreting and using the People CMM and its practices is provided to help an organization apply the People CMM in its setting. Benefits from applying the People CMM are described and several case studies are presented.

1

The Process Maturity Framework

When human capital owners [employees] have the upper hand in the market, they do not behave at all like assets. They behave like owners of a valuable commodity....They are investors in a business, paying in human capital and expecting a return on their investment.

[Davenport 99]

As other sources of competitive success have become less important, what remains as a crucial differentiating factor is the organization, its employees, and how it works.

[Pfeffer 94]

Successful firms will be those most adept at attracting, developing, and retaining individuals with the skills, perspectives, and experience necessary to drive a global business.

[Ulrich 98]

Companies like to promote the idea that employees are their biggest source of competitive advantage. Yet the astonishing reality is that most of them are as unprepared for the challenge of finding, motivating, and retaining capable workers as they were a decade ago.

[McKinsey 08a]

What distinguishes human capital and human capital measurement from human resource management is the emphasis on the value of people and what they produce, rather than a focus on the HR function itself.

[CIPD 06]

There is ... a growing body of evidence linking effective high performance HCM [human capital management] practices to the financial performance of the organisation. In particular there is a high degree of empirical support for the need for strong consistency among HCM practices to achieve good results; it is the combination of practices that matters rather than simply doing one or two well.

[DTI 03]

1.1   Organizational Maturity

The People Capability Maturity Model (People CMM) is a proven set of human capital management practices that provide an organizational change model through an evolutionary framework based on a system of workforce practices. It is designed on the premise that improved workforce practices will not survive unless an organization's behavior changes to support them. The People CMM provides a roadmap for transforming an organization by steadily improving its workforce practices. As do all Capability Maturity Models, the People CMM consists of five maturity levels, or evolutionary stages, through which an organization's workforce practices and processes evolve. At each maturity level, a new system of practices is added to those implemented at earlier levels. Each overlay of practices raises the level of sophistication through which the organization develops its workforce. Within this environment, individuals experience greater opportunity to develop and are more motivated to align their performance with the objectives of the organization.

From the perspective of the People CMM, an organization's maturity is derived from the workforce practices routinely performed inside it, and the extent to which these practices have been integrated into an institutionalized process for improving workforce capability. In a mature organization, responsible individuals perform repeatable workforce practices as ordinary and expected requirements of their positions. The more mature an organization, the greater its capability for attracting, developing, and retaining the talent it needs to execute its business.

The People CMM is a process-based model; it assumes that workforce practices are standard organizational processes that can be improved continuously through the same methods that have been used to improve other business processes. The People CMM is constructed from workforce practices and process improvement techniques that have proven effective in many organizations. A unique characteristic of the People CMM is its staged framework for introducing and steadily improving successful workforce practices, effectively transforming the capability of the organization through increased organizational maturity.

Any Capability Maturity Model derived from Humphrey's process maturity framework integrates principles from three domains: the targeted domain of processes, total quality management (TQM) practices, and organizational change. First, a CMM is designed to help an organization adopt best practices in a targeted domain. The People CMM targets workforce management processes, while other models, such as CMMI [Chrissis 06], focus on system and software engineering processes. Second, processes in the targeted domain are continuously improved to become more effective and predictable using total quality management concepts pioneered by Deming, Juran, Crosby, and others. Third, the CMM constitutes a unique approach to organizational development that introduces these practices in stages (maturity levels) to create a succession of changes in the organization's culture.

Changing an organization's culture through staged improvements to its operating processes is a unique approach to organizational development. These cultural changes provide much of the CMM's power for implementing lasting improvements and distinguish it from other quality and process improvement standards. Although many process standards can transform an organization's culture, few include a roadmap for implementation. Consequently, organizations often fail to implement the standard effectively because they attempt to implement too much too soon and do not lay the right foundation of practices.

The culture of an organization is reflected in the shared values and resultant patterns of behavior that characterize interactions among its members. Successful improvement programs guided by the People CMM change the fundamental attributes of its culture—its practices and behaviors. As an organization adopts the practices that satisfy the goals of the People CMM's process areas, it establishes the shared patterns of behavior that underlie a culture of professionalism dedicated to continuous improvement. Not surprisingly, most organizations report dramatic cultural changes as they progress through the People CMM's maturity levels.

1.2   What Is the People CMM?

The People Capability Maturity Model (People CMM) is a proven set of human capital management practices that provide a roadmap for continuously improving the capability of an organization's workforce. The People CMM refers to these practices as *workforce practices.* Since an organization cannot implement all of the best workforce practices in an afternoon, the People CMM introduces them in stages. Each progressive level of the People CMM produces a unique transformation in the organization's culture by equipping it with more powerful practices for attracting, developing, organizing, motivating, and retaining its workforce. Thus, the People CMM establishes an integrated system of workforce practices that matures through increasing alignment with the organization's business objectives, performance, and changing needs.

The People CMM was first published in 1995 [Curtis 95] and updated in 2001 [Curtis 02a]. This Second Edition updates informative material within the model, and provides new information regarding the global use of the People CMM. Since its release in 1995, the People CMM has successfully guided workforce improvement programs in many industries and geographies around the world. The People CMM book has been in print in the United States and elsewhere since its release in 2001. Although the People CMM has been designed primarily for application in knowledge-intense organizations, with appropriate tailoring it can be applied in almost any organizational setting. Additional information regarding application of the People CMM is provided in Chapters 7 and 8; Chapters 9 and 10 provide insights and case studies from the use of the People CMM.

The People CMM's primary objective is to improve the capability of the workforce. Workforce capability can be defined as the level of knowledge, skills, and process abilities available for performing an organization's business activities. Workforce capability indicates an organization's

- readiness for performing its critical business activities,
- likely results from performing these business activities, and
- potential for benefiting from investments in process improvement or advanced technology.

In order to measure and improve capability, the workforce in most organizations must be divided into its constituent workforce competencies. Each workforce competency represents a unique integration of knowledge, skills, and process abilities acquired through specialized education or work experience. Strategically, an organization wants to design its workforce to include the various workforce competencies required to perform the business activities underlying its core competencies [Prahalad 90]. Each of these workforce competencies can be characterized by its capability—the profile of knowledge, skills, and process abilities available to the organization in that competency.

The People CMM describes an evolutionary improvement path from ad hoc, inconsistently performed workforce practices, to a mature infrastructure of practices for continuously elevating workforce capability. The philosophy implicit in the People CMM can be summarized in the ten principles shown in Figure 1.1.

The People CMM is an evolutionary framework that guides organizations in selecting high-priority improvement actions based on the current maturity of their workforce practices. The benefit of the People CMM is in narrowing the scope of improvement activities to those vital few practices that provide the next foundational layer for developing an organization's

---

1. In mature organizations, workforce capability is directly related to business performance.

2. Workforce capability is a competitive issue and a source of strategic advantage.

3. Workforce capability must be defined in relation to the organization's strategic business objectives.

4. Knowledge-intense work shifts the focus from job elements to workforce competencies.

5. Capability can be measured and improved at multiple levels of the organization, including individuals, workgroups, workforce competencies, and the organization.

6. An organization should invest in improving the capability of those workforce competencies that are critical to its core competency as a business.

7. Operational management is responsible for the capability of the workforce.

8. The improvement of workforce capability can be pursued as a process composed from proven practices and procedures.

9. The organization is responsible for providing improvement opportunities, and individuals are responsible for taking advantage of them.

10. Because technologies and organizational forms evolve rapidly, organizations must continually evolve their workforce practices and develop new workforce competencies.

FIGURE 1.1
The principles underlying the People CMM

workforce. By concentrating on a focused set of practices and working aggressively to install them, organizations can steadily improve their workforce and make lasting gains in their performance and competitiveness.

The People CMM has proven successful because it allows organizations to characterize the maturity of their workforce practices against a benchmark being used by other organizations. Many workforce benchmarks focus on employee attitudes and satisfaction rather than workforce practices. Although attitudes and satisfaction are important predictors of outcomes such as turnover, they do not always provide the guidance necessary for identifying which practices should be improved next. In contrast, the staged framework of the People CMM helps organizations prioritize their improvement actions. In addition, since the People CMM treats workforce development as an organizational process, improved workforce practices are easier to integrate with other process improvement activities.

1.3   Factors Driving the Demand for the People CMM

Forty years ago people feared that technology would reduce the need for educated workers, thereby leaving large segments of the population unemployed. The opposite occurred. In fact, the demand for educated workers exceeds the supply. In the knowledge economy, companies are competing in two markets, one for its products and services and one for the talent required to develop and deliver them. In periods of low unemployment, the talent market is all the more competitive, while in periods of high unemployment, downsizing, and retrenching, organizations strive to retain their very best personnel. Recruiting and retention are as important as production and distribution in the corporate business strategies of knowledge-intense companies. Although most companies understand the importance of attracting and retaining talent, many lack a coherent approach to achieving their talent goals, irrespective of whether these talent goals are focused on supporting a rapidly growing organization or one that is challenged with retaining its core abilities in the face of downward economic pressures. Further, most organizations lack a vision for how to integrate a system of practices to achieve their workforce objectives.

The practices required to attract, develop, and retain outstanding talent have been understood for decades. In his acclaimed book, *The Human Equation,* Jeffrey Pfeffer of the Stanford Graduate School of Business identified seven principles of workforce management that distinguished the companies that had exhibited the largest percentage stock market returns over the past quarter century [Pfeffer 98]. These principles include

1. employment security,
2. selective hiring of new personnel,
3. self-managed teams and decentralization of decision making,
4. comparatively high compensation contingent on organizational performance,
5. extensive training,
6. reduced status distinctions and barriers, and
7. extensive sharing of financial and performance information.

These principles characterize organizations that no longer expect employees merely to execute orders, but rather to act as independent centers of intelligent action coordinated toward a common purpose. Deep technical and business knowledge is required to make rapid decisions that are not only correct, but also consistent with decisions made by colleagues. Recruiting for outstanding technical talent is critical, but it is not enough because business knowledge can be developed only within an organization. Thus, the development and coordination of a modern workforce requires an integrated set of practices that address attracting, developing, organizing, motivating, and retaining outstanding individuals.

The need for these practices today is highlighted as organizations struggle to deal with a number of workforce issues. These include not only developing appropriate plans for the future workforce and recruiting and retaining appropriately skilled and knowledgeable staffs, but also doing so in the face of labor scarcity, where the number of qualified people available never seems to reach the demand; in the face of a changing workforce, where in many regions of the globe there is both an aging or "graying" of the workforce and an increase in the number of millennials or Generation Y employees seeking greater work-life balance, as organizations struggle to retain their workforce, reach and attract sufficient numbers of new workers, and make appropriate use of retirees or older workers; and in conditions demanding increased organizational capabilities for human capital management to support employee development and retention [Martin 08, Martin 07, McKinsey 08b]. These needs are driven by a workforce that must be nimble and agile to adapt in the face of a rapidly changing business environment, a labor environment where lifelong employment may no longer be the norm and organizations which demonstrate limited collaboration and workforce planning across business units have line managers who believe these issues are solely the responsibility of the human resources function, and have to adapt to recruiting and developing staff at experience levels different from their traditional entry-level hires. While organizations and their leaders globally are deeply concerned about the intensifying competition for talent, few companies make it an integral part of a long-term business strategy and focus enough on retaining strategic competency capabilities, even in the face of business downturns, and many even try to cut costs over the short term or raise their short-term earnings by cutting talent development or retention expenditures [McKinsey 08b, Reich 08].

Senior management views workforce effectiveness issues as important in delivering business results in 84% of organizations, but in only half of those organizations is it perceived that managers devote sufficient time to fundamental people management practices, and repeated studies over more than a decade have shown that only slightly more than one-fifth of Human Resources' time is spent on strategic work, with the largest percentage of Human Resources' time spent on being an administrator of human resource activities [Ringo 08, Lawler 03, Lawler 06]. In many organizations, Human Resources is not perceived as a strategic partner of the business [Lawler 06]. Addressing the organization's workforce issues requires more than that; it has been shown to require an integrated *human capital management* (HCM) perspective on the organization, its workforce, and the best ways to manage the workforce to obtain long-term results. HCM is an approach to people management (or workforce management) that treats it as a high-level strategic issue and seeks systematically to analyze, measure, and evaluate how people policies and practices create value [Kingsmill 03]. HCM approaches should be treated as a high-level strategic issue rather than an operational matter "to be left to the human resources function."

An example of an organization moving toward a human capital perspective is the U.S. government. Four human capital challenges facing the federal government have been identified:

1. Leadership, continuity, and succession planning
2. Strategic human capital planning and organizational alignment
3. Acquiring and developing staffs whose size, skills, and deployment meet agency needs
4. Creating a results-oriented organizational culture

Additionally, the Government Accountability Office has identified critical success factors that address each of these pervasive challenges, as shown in Figure 1.2. Human capital reform actions, such as the *Chief Human Capital Officers Act of 2002* [US 02], call for systems and standards for

1. aligning human capital strategies of government agencies with the missions, goals, and organizational objectives of those agencies,
2. integrating these human capital strategies into the budget and strategic plans of the agencies,
3. closing skill gaps in mission-critical occupations,
4. ensuring continuity of effective leadership through implementation of recruitment, development, and succession plans,
5. sustaining a culture that cultivates and develops a high-performing workforce,
6. developing and implementing knowledge management strategies supported by appropriate investment in training and technology, and
7. holding managers and Human Resources officials accountable for efficient and effective human resource management.

The benefit of better workforce practices has been demonstrated empirically in numerous studies [Amit 99, Appleby 00, Becker 98, Birdi 08, Bontis 02, Delaney 96, DTI 03, Hassan 06, Huselid 95, Kling 95, Labor 93, Lawler 01, Mavrinac 95, Shih 06, Tzafrir 06, Verburg 07, Wall 05]. Organizations that make better use of their resources are more able to employ these resources to execute their business strategies [Amit 99]. Organizations that employ an integrated human resources strategy represent a significantly higher proportion of world-class companies [Appleby 00]. In some cases, even mere reputation signals regarding an organization's human resources practices have been positively associated with increases in share prices [Hannon 96]. Welbourne and Andrews examined 136 nonfinancial organizations that first offered their stock (i.e., made their initial public offerings) on the U.S. stock market in 1988 [Welbourne 96]. They looked at the value these firms placed on their employees, and determined that the value of human resources is indeed positively and significantly related to a firm's survival. The average survival probability for all organizations in the study was 0.70. Organizations that placed a high level of value on their employees had a 0.79 probability of survival, and firms who placed less value on their employees had a survival probability of only 0.60. When considering employee compensation and rewards, an organization that had high levels of employee value and employee compensation and rewards increased its survival probability to 0.92, while firms that scored low on both measures lowered

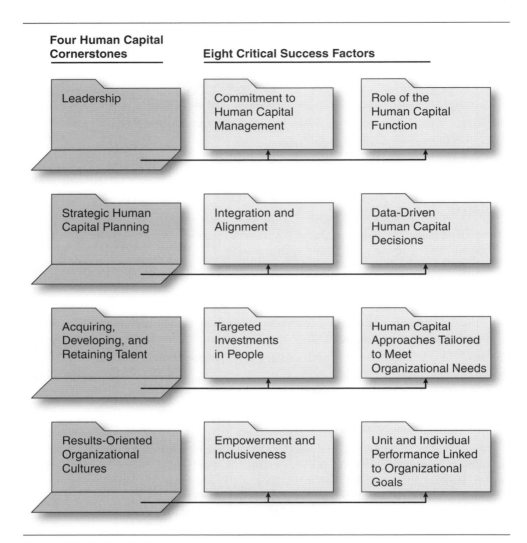

FIGURE 1.2
Critical success factors for managing human capital strategically
Source: [GAO 02]

their chance of organizational survival to 0.34. Thus, workforce practices were shown to have a significant effect on the survival of these firms.

Analysis of several samples throughout the 1990s shows strong support for a very positive relationship between high-performance workforce practices and an organization's financial performance [Becker 98]. This research shows that a one standard deviation improvement of a firm's workforce practices resulted in approximately a 20% increase in shareholder value and a significant reduction in voluntary departure rates. A study of work-force practices in almost 1000 firms across all major industries showed that "a one standard deviation increase in use of such practices is associated with...a 7.05 percent decrease in turnover [i.e., employee departure rate] and, on a per employee basis, US $27,044 more in sales and US $18,641 and US $3,814 more in market value and profitability, respectively" [Huselid 95]. Companies with the best workforce practices have been shown to outperform other firms in growth of profits, sales, earnings, and dividends [Hansen 89, Kravetz 88].

These practices are usually considered integral to a TQM program, and are included as criteria in quality models such as the Malcolm Baldrige National Quality Award (MBNQA) [Baldrige 01] or the European Foundation for Quality Management (EFQM) Excellence Model [EFQM 99]. Research into the MBNQA has indicated that the inclusion of human re-source management is critical in the cause-and-effect chain starting with strategic planning [Wilson 00]. This research has shown that the strategic planning factor in the MBNQA in-fluences human resource management, which in turn influences process management, which directly influences both financial results and customer satisfaction. Thus, human resource management is an indirect link to these key external performance measures.

Over the past several decades, business books and the trade press have flooded man-agers with workforce practices, each demonstrated to produce benefits in at least some ap-plications. These practices include competency modeling, 360° performance reviews, Web-enabled learning, knowledge management, team building, cool space, participatory de-cision making, incentive-based pay, mentoring, meeting management, and empowered work. Many of these practices have been actively applied for over a decade. Nevertheless, many or-ganizations have moved slowly on improving their workforce practices or have failed to suc-cessfully implement the necessary holistic system of workforce practices.

If these practices have been well known for a decade or more, why have so many orga-nizations failed to implement them? The fundamental impediments have been a lack of man-agement commitment and a piecemeal, unintegrated approach to adoption. Consequently, the People CMM was designed to integrate workforce practices into a system and involve man-agement early in their deployment. The People CMM presents the development of a capable workforce as a process with well-understood practices that can be implemented in stages as the organization matures.

1.4   What Is the Process Maturity Framework?

The original concept for a process maturity framework was developed by Watts Humphrey and his colleagues at IBM in the early 1980s. In his 27 years at IBM, Humphrey noticed that the quality of a software product was directly related to the quality of the process used to de-velop it. Having observed the success of total quality management in other parts of industry, Humphrey wanted to install a Shewart-Deming improvement cycle (Plan-Do-Check-Act) into a software organization as a way to continually improve its development processes. However, organizations had been installing advanced software technologies for a decade using methods akin to the Shewart-Deming cycle without much success. Humphrey real-ized that the Shewart-Deming cycle must be installed in stages to systematically remove impediments to continuous improvement. Humphrey's unique insight was that organizations had to eliminate implementation problems in a specific order if they were to create an environment that supported continuous improvement guided by Deming's principles.

The staged structure that underlies the maturity framework was first elaborated by Crosby in *Quality Is Free* [Crosby 79]. Crosby's quality management maturity grid describes five evolutionary stages in adopting quality practices in an organization. This framework was adapted to the software process by Ron Radice and his colleagues working under the direction of Humphrey at IBM Corporation [Radice 85]. Crosby's original formulation was that the adoption of any new practice by an organization would occur in five stages: the organization would become aware of the new practice, learn more about it, try it in a pilot implementation, deploy it across the organization, and achieve mastery in its use.

The original formulation of the maturity framework in IBM [Radice 85] adopted Crosby's approach of evolving each process through these five stages. However, Humphrey realized organizations were not succeeding in long-term adoption of improved software development practices when they applied this maturity framework to individual practices or technologies. Humphrey identified serious impediments to long-term adoption that had to be eliminated if improved practices were to thrive in an organization. Since many of these problems were deeply ingrained in an organization's culture, Humphrey realized that he had to formulate an approach that addressed the organization, not just its individual processes.

Humphrey wanted software organizations to continually improve their software development processes, and he wanted these improvements to be based on statistical information about how each critical process was performing. However, he had observed that improved software development practices did not survive unless an organization's behavior changed to support them. Consequently, he designed the process maturity framework to enable an organization to achieve a state of continuous process improvement in five stages. Because of this staging, the process maturity framework is more than a process standard comprising a list of best practices. Rather, it integrates improved practices into a staged model that guides an organization through a series of cultural transformations, each of which supports the deployment of more sophisticated and mature processes.

Through software process assessments, workshops, and extensive review, the SEI evolved Humphrey's process maturity framework into the *Capability Maturity Model for Software* (SW-CMM) [Carnegie Mellon University 95]. Version 1 of the *Capability Maturity Model for Software* was released after extensive national review in August 1991, and Version 1.1 [Paulk 93a, 93b] was released in January 1993. A more recent version that integrates CMM-based approaches for improving both software and systems engineering processes, CMM Integrated (CMMI) [CMMI 00], was first released in late 2000, and most recently updated in 2006 [Chrissis 06].

Over a dozen years of experience with the People CMM demonstrates that this process maturity framework is also applicable to the management and improvement of workforce practices within an organization. The following paragraphs describe this process maturity framework.

At the first level of maturity, the Initial Level, an organization has no consistent way of performing its work. Since most work processes are ad hoc, they are constantly reinvented on each project, and frequently appear chaotic. Without well-understood ways of conducting their work, managers have no reliable basis for estimating the effort required to complete a project. In a rush to meet overly aggressive deadlines, the project staff begins cutting corners on sound practices and making mistakes that are not detected until it is much more time consuming and costly to remove them than to have prevented them. As a result, projects lose control of their schedule, costs, and product quality. Since work is chronically overcommitted in low-maturity organizations, their results depend largely on the skills of exceptional individuals and on excessive overtime. Executives in these organizations often hail their people as their most important asset, belying the fact that immature organizations have few assets or processes that add value to the efforts of their people.

A fundamental premise of the process maturity framework is that a practice cannot be improved if it cannot be repeated. In an organization's least mature state, proven practices are repeated only sporadically. The most common impediment to repeatability is a committed delivery date that hard-working staffs cannot meet regardless of how sophisticated their skills or technology or how intense their efforts. Other particularly wicked impediments are uncontrolled requirements changes that devastate the original planning. The first step in helping an organization improve its maturity is focused on helping organizations remove the impediments that keep them from repeating successful software development practices.

At the second level of maturity, organizations must establish a foundation on which they can deploy common processes across the organization. Before being able to successfully implement many advanced practices, management must first establish a stable environment in which to perform professional work. They must ensure that people are not constantly rushing about pell-mell, cutting corners, making mistakes due to hasty work, and fighting the fires that characterize overcommitted organizations. Until basic management control of daily work is established, no organization-wide practices have a chance of being deployed successfully because no one has the time to master them. The primary objective of a Maturity Level 2 environment is to enable people to repeat practices they have used successfully. To enable this repeatability, managers must get control of commitments and baselines. The effort to establish a repeatable capability is the effort to establish basic management practices within each unit or project. Only when this management discipline is established will the organization have a foundation on which it can deploy common processes.

At the third level of maturity, the organization identifies its best practices and integrates them into a common process. Once people are able to perform their work using practices they have found to work, the organization has the ability to identify which practices work best in its unique environment. These practices are documented and integrated into a common process in which the entire organization is then trained. Measures of the critical practices in this process are defined and collected into a repository for analysis. When the organization defines a standard process for performing its business activities, it has laid the foundation for a professional culture. Most organizations report the emergence of a more common culture as they achieve Maturity Level 3. This culture is based on common professional practices and common beliefs about the effectiveness of these practices.

At the fourth level of maturity, the organization begins managing its processes through the data that describes its performance. The performance of the organization's critical processes is characterized statistically so that the historical performance of the process can be used to predict and manage its future performance. The premise underlying this quantitative management is that if a well-understood process is repeated, you should get essentially the same result. If the result obtained deviates significantly from the organization's experience, the cause needs to be determined and corrective action taken if necessary. Since business processes are now managed by numbers rather than just by milestones, the organization can take corrective action much earlier. When the organization's processes are managed quantitatively, its performance becomes much more predictable. When the organization can characterize the performance of its processes quantitatively, it has profound knowledge that can be used to improve them.

At the fifth and highest level of maturity, the organization uses its profound, quantitative knowledge to make continuous improvements in its processes. Based on its data, the organization can identify which processes can benefit most from improvement actions. These improvements can involve actions ranging from adjustments to processes to the deployment of new technologies. In addition, the organization uses its data to identify its most persistent defects. The root causes of these defects are analyzed and actions are taken to eliminate their occurrence. Managing technological and process change becomes standard organizational processes and process improvement throughout the organization becomes perpetual. Since the organization has competent people performing trusted processes, it empowers people throughout the organization to attempt continuous improvements to their work processes and to propose organizational changes for improvements that would appear to have the broadest benefits.

In the abstract, the maturity framework builds an environment in which

- practices can be repeated,
- best practices can be transferred rapidly across groups,
- variations in performing best practices are reduced, and
- practices are continuously improved to enhance their capability.

The process maturity framework assumes that each practice has a risk to its successful adoption that is directly related to the maturity of the organization's existing base of practices. One important premise of the model is that sophisticated practices should not be attempted until the foundation of practices required to support them has been implemented. Thus, the practices at each level of maturity prepare the organization to adopt practices at the next level. This staging of process maturity levels is unique in the organizational change literature and provides much of the framework's power for improving organizations.

1.5   Why Did the People CMM Emerge in the Software Industry?

The process maturity framework was designed for application to practices that contribute directly to the business performance of an organization, that is, to the organization's capability for providing high-quality products and services. As use of the SW-CMM began to spread in the early 1990s, software organizations began to request similar guidance for improving their workforce practices. This led to the development of the People CMM [Curtis 95]. Since the capability of an organization's workforce is critical to its performance, the practices for managing and developing them are excellent candidates for improvement using the maturity framework. Thus, the People CMM has been designed to increase the capability of the workforce, just as the SW-CMM increased the capability of the organization's software development processes.

Knowledge is the raw material of software development. Although software tools can help record and manage knowledge, they do not create or apply it. Perhaps no industry in history has been as knowledge intense as software development, an industry whose only product is proceduralized knowledge. Not surprisingly, the level of talent on a software project is often the strongest predictor of its results [Boehm 81], and personnel shortfalls are one of the most severe project risks [Boehm 87]. Performance ranges among professional software engineers routinely exceed 20 to 1 [Curtis 81, Sackman 68, Valett 89]. Although the presence of an extraordinary individual on a project can have dramatic impact, there are not enough "wizards" to staff more than a handful of the projects in most organizations [Curtis 88].

Much of a professional software developer's time is spent learning through such activities as reading manuals, discussing design issues with colleagues, building prototypes to test ideas, and attending organized learning experiences such as seminars and conferences. The pace of technical change and the depth of knowledge required to implement complex systems require extensive investment in personal learning. Increasing the capability of software developers is necessary to

- meet growing demand for software while faced with a talent shortage,
- master the accelerating pace of change in technology, programming languages, and business applications, and
- increase the reliability of software systems, especially in life-critical and business-critical applications.

A serious shortage of software professionals, which grew dramatically during the 1990s, exacerbates these problems. Initially, the availability of offshore software talent to support outsourcing of software development or to apply themselves as visiting workers quelled the perceived talent crisis. By the late 1990s, however, turnover rates among software companies in countries such as India had risen to as much as 30% annually as these companies began to compete for increasingly scarce talent within their borders [Embar 01, Paulk 01a]. The shortage became even more pronounced when considering the needs for available talent with skills in the latest technologies. The shortage of software talent has created a number of problems, including

- high turnover,
- loss of critical system knowledge,
- escalating salaries and benefits,
- staffing shortfalls,
- increased workloads, overtime, and stress,
- decreased family/work-life balance,
- increasing product and service costs, and
- unfinished work.

Until the talent shortage of the 1990s, the software industry largely ignored workforce issues. Rather, continual cost and schedule overruns on projects and critical system failures dominated the attention of software executives. Attempts to fix the "software crisis" with better technology yielded disappointing results through the 1970s and 1980s. By the mid-1980s, the software industry realized that its primary problem was a lack of discipline, both in project management and in software development practices. Since the beginning of the 1990s, the SW-CMM has guided many software organizations in improving their management and development processes. Even during the early stages of adopting the SW-CMM, the software community realized the process maturity framework constituted a unique approach to organizational development that could be applied in areas other than software development.

While assessing their software development practices, many organizations found that they also suffered serious shortcomings in workforce management. These workforce-related problems included inadequate training, inaccurate performance feedback, crowding, lack of career opportunities, and noncompetitive compensation. Many software organizations discovered that improvements to their development practices required significant changes in the way they managed people, changes that were not fully accounted for in the SW-CMM. Most improvement programs were focused on process or technology, not people. In response to requests from many software organizations, the SEI initiated a project to produce a model for improving workforce practices guided by the principles underlying the process maturity framework. This model was Version 1 of the People CMM, which was first released in 1995 [Curtis 95]. The development of the People CMM, Version 1, was supported by the U.S. government with broad participation from industry globally. Anticipating the emergence of human capital, information technology workforce, and workforce aging issues [Walker 01, McClure 02], senior leaders in the Army's Chief Information Office and Office of the Assistant Secretary of Defense sponsored development of the People CMM. The leaders in these organizations were working to proactively address the human capital management needs of their organizations by supporting this work.

1.6   How Is the People CMM Being Applied?

Following six years of use of the People CMM, Version 2 was released [Curtis 02a]. During this period, the People CMM was in use around the globe by many organizations. These included companies such as Boeing, Ericsson, Lockheed Martin, Novo Nordisk IT A/S, and Tata Consultancy Services [Curtis 00, Keeni 00b, Martín-Vivaldi 99, Miller 00, Vu 01]. Since its release in 2001, printed editions of the People CMM have been available in Japan [Curtis 03a], China [Curtis 03b], and India [Curtis 02b, Curtis 07]. It has also been translated into Kannada, the state language of Karnataka, India. Several books and research theses at both the masters and doctoral levels have been written, building on the People CMM [Nandyal 03, Curley 04, Dahmann 03, Josko 04, Vaz 04, Wademan 05, Wheeler 06].

Today, the People CMM has been applied in numerous industries and types and sizes of organizations around the globe. Industries using the People CMM range from high-tech and information technology companies, to pharmaceuticals and hospitality, to construction and government agencies. A partial list of the types of organizations using the People CMM is

Organization Types

Business Process Outsourcing	Information Technology
Hospitality	Consulting
Construction	Defense Contractors
Insurance	Pharmaceuticals
Government Agencies	Defense Agencies
Energy/Utilities	Software Development
Banking/Financial Services	Management Information Systems

FIGURE 1.3
Types of organizations around the world using the People CMM

shown in Figure 1.3. Chapters 7 and 8 provide additional details about using the People CMM, and Chapters 9 and 10 provide examples and experiences from organizations using the People CMM to improve their workforce capability.

The People CMM has also been used to support and sustain the attainment of CMMI maturity levels [Buttles 08, Muralidharan 04, Nandyal 06, Radice 05a, Radice 05b, Subramanyam 04, Wemyss 07]. By building competencies and a workforce that can successfully execute and manage its processes, the People CMM establishes a foundation for building a culture that values process and that facilitates the implementation of CMMI. Additionally, the People CMM strengthens and greatly extends the people and culture dimensions that the CMMI model framework touches on only lightly. Integrating the People CMM with process maturity frameworks, such as CMMI, speeds the emergence of a capable workforce having a culture that is required to enable and sustain institutionalized process improvements.

Based on continuing feedback and experience from use around the globe in many industries and settings, this Second Edition of the People CMM has been prepared. The Second Edition is an update to the People CMM, Version 2. This Second Edition updates informative material within the People CMM and its practices and provides new information regarding the continuing global use of the People CMM.

2

Increasing Organizational Capability through the People CMM

2.1 Maturity Levels in the People CMM

A Capability Maturity Model (CMM) is constructed from the essential practices of one or more domains of organizational process. The People CMM concerns the domain of workforce management and development. A CMM describes an evolutionary improvement path from an ad hoc, immature process to a disciplined, mature process with improved quality and effectiveness.

Capability Maturity Model (CMM)	A Capability Maturity Model is an evolutionary roadmap for implementing the vital practices from one or more domains of organizational process (see Appendix C for definitions of terms).

All CMMs are constructed with five levels of maturity. A maturity level is an evolutionary plateau at which one or more domains of the organization's processes have been transformed to achieve a new level of organizational capability. A maturity level consists of related practices for a predefined set of process areas that improve the organization's overall performance. Thus, an organization achieves a new level of maturity when a system of practices has been established or transformed to provide capabilities and results the organization did not have at the previous level. The method of transformation is different at each level, and requires capabilities established at earlier levels. Consequently, each maturity level provides a foundation of practices on which practices at subsequent maturity levels can be built. In order to be a true CMM, the maturity framework underlying a model must use the principles established in the process maturity framework for transforming the organization at each level.

Maturity Level	A maturity level represents a new level of organizational capability created by the transformation of one or more domains of an organization's processes.

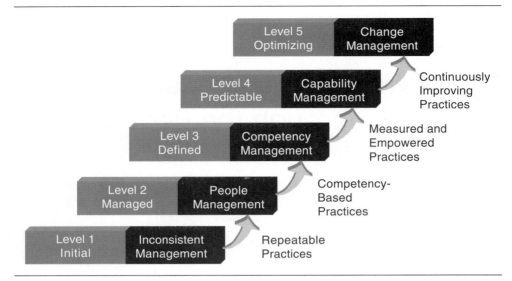

FIGURE 2.1
The five maturity levels of the People CMM
Source: Adapted from Humphrey [1989] and Carnegie Mellon University [1995] with permission.

The People CMM applies the principles of the process maturity framework to the domain of workforce practices. Each of the People CMM's five maturity levels represents a different level of organizational capability for managing and developing the workforce. Each maturity level provides a layer in the foundation for continuous improvement and equips the organization with increasingly powerful tools for developing the capability of its workforce. The nature of the transformation imposed on the organization's workforce practices to achieve each level of maturity is depicted in Figure 2.1.

2.2 Behavioral Characteristics of Maturity Levels

The People CMM stages the implementation of increasingly sophisticated workforce practices through these maturity levels. With the exception of the Initial Level, each maturity level is characterized by a set of interrelated practices in critical areas of workforce management. When institutionalized and performed with appropriate regularity, these workforce practices create new capabilities within the organization for managing and developing its workforce.

2.2.1 The Initial Level: Maturity Level 1

Organizations at the Initial Level of maturity usually have difficulty retaining talented individuals. Even though many low-maturity organizations complain about a talent shortage, the inconsistency of their actions belies whether they actually believe it [Rothman 01]. Low-maturity organizations are poorly equipped to respond to talent shortages with anything other than slogans and exhortations. Despite the importance of talent, workforce practices in low-maturity organizations are often ad hoc and inconsistent. In some areas, the organization has not defined workforce practices, and in other areas, it has not trained responsible individuals to perform the practices that exist. Organizations at the Initial Level typically exhibit four characteristics:

1. Inconsistency in performing practices
2. Displacement of responsibility
3. Ritualistic practices
4. An emotionally detached workforce

Generally managers and supervisors in low-maturity organizations are ill prepared to perform their workforce responsibilities. Their management training is sparse and, when provided, tends to cover only those workforce practices with the greatest legal sensitivity. The organization may typically provide forms for guiding workforce activities such as performance appraisals or position requisitions. However, too often little guidance or training is offered for conducting the activities supported by these forms. Consequently, managers are left to their own devices in most areas of workforce management.

Low-maturity organizations implicitly assume that management skill either is innate or is acquired by observing other managers. However, if managers are inconsistent in managing their people, nascent managers will be learning from inconsistent role models. Management capability should ultimately be defined as a competency, just like other critical skill sets that are required by the organization. However, in launching People CMM-based improvements, managers must be held accountable for performing basic workforce practices even though their personal methods for performing them may differ.

Since low-maturity organizations rarely clarify the responsibilities of managers, inconsistencies are to be expected. Consequently, the way people are treated depends largely on personal orientation, experience, and the individual "people skills" of their managers, supervisors, or team leaders. Although some managers perform their workforce responsibilities diligently, others perform some workforce activities with little forethought and ignore other responsibilities altogether. Studies have consistently shown that one of the major causes for voluntary turnover is related to individuals' relationships with their managers or supervisors [Buckingham 99].

Managers in low-maturity organizations rarely share a common vision about the fundamental responsibilities of management. They perceive management to be about producing results, not about producing people who produce results. Although managers in low-maturity organizations accept responsibility for the performance of their unit, many do so without understanding how to manage the collective performance of those in the unit. In particular, they often lack skill and place little emphasis on evaluating and improving the capability and performance of people who report to them.

Many managers in low-maturity organizations consider workforce activities to be "administrivia"—something less than the real work of managers. As a consequence of this attitude, workforce activities such as performance appraisals and job candidate interviews are often performed hastily without adequate preparation. Responsibility for other workforce practices such as recruiting for open positions and identifying training needs are displaced to Human Resources or other staff groups. This displacement reflects a refusal to accept personal responsibility for the capability of the unit or the people in it. These actions are characteristic of managers who have not been properly prepared for their responsibilities in managing people.

If an organization does not establish clear policies for managing its workforce, it should not be surprised when some managers hold attitudes more characteristic of an era when unskilled workers were considered interchangeable. Although these attitudes are counterproductive in knowledge-intense organizations, many managers have come from educational environments where they focused intently on developing their own skills and were not rewarded for developing the skills of others. From the perspective of the People CMM, individuals own responsibility for developing their knowledge and skills. However, managers own responsibility for ensuring that the people in their unit have the skills required to perform their work and for providing opportunities to develop these skills.

In immature organizations, many workforce practices are performed with little or no analysis of their impact. Recruiting campaigns, classroom training, and bonuses are among the many practices that are performed more as a ritual of organizational life than as processes that have been designed to achieve specific and measurable results. In the worst case, the failure to evaluate workforce practices ensures the failure to detect occasions when their impact is counterproductive to their intended effect. Consequently, ritualism can be as damaging to organizational effectiveness as inconsistency.

When an organization fails to proactively develop its workforce, career-oriented people pursue their own agendas. Mediocre performance and high turnover are typical when organizations provide few financial or career incentives for individuals to align themselves with the organization's business objectives. Loyalty declines when individuals do not perceive the organization to be a vehicle by which they will achieve their career aspirations. In these circumstances individuals perceive the organization as an opportunity for developing specific skills that, once developed, will be used to pursue career opportunities elsewhere.

Constant churn in the workforce diminishes its capability. Although some turnover, or voluntary attrition, may be necessary or even beneficial, high turnover limits the level of skill available in the workforce, thereby limiting an organization's ability to improve its performance. Improvement programs guided by the People CMM are often initiated when an organization faces a talent shortage exacerbated by an inability to attract or retain talented individuals. The first step in changing this state of affairs is to get managers to take responsibility for the capability and development of those who report to them.

2.2.2   The Managed Level: Maturity Level 2

The workforce practices implemented at the Managed Level focus on activities at the unit level. The first step toward improving the capability of the workforce is to get managers to take workforce activities as high-priority responsibilities of their job. They must accept personal responsibility for the performance and development of those who perform the unit's work. The practices implemented at Maturity Level 2 focus a manager's attention on unit-level issues such as staffing, coordinating commitments, providing resources, managing performance, developing skills, and making compensation decisions. Building a solid foundation of workforce practices in each unit provides the bedrock on which more sophisticated workforce practices can be implemented at higher levels of maturity.

An important reason to concentrate initially on practices at the unit level is founded on the frequent failure of organization-wide improvement programs. These programs often fail because they were thrust on an unprepared management team. That is, managers were struggling with problems that were not addressed by organizational changes. They often lacked the experience and skill needed to implement sophisticated practices. Consequently, Maturity Level 2 focuses on establishing basic practices in units that address immediate problems and prepare managers to implement more sophisticated practices at higher levels. It is difficult to implement organization-wide practices if managers are not performing the basic workforce practices required to manage their units.

Focusing at the unit level first also establishes a foundation in managing performance that can be enhanced with more sophisticated practices at higher levels. If people are unable to perform their assigned work, sophisticated workforce practices will be of little benefit to individuals or the organization. In a Maturity Level 2 organization, managers are vigilant for problems that hinder performance in their units. Frequent problems that keep people from performing effectively in low-maturity organizations include

- Work overload
- Environmental distractions
- Unclear performance objectives or feedback
- Lack of relevant knowledge or skill
- Poor communication
- Low morale

The effort to ensure that workforce practices are performed in each unit begins when executive management commits the organization to continuously improve the knowledge, skills, motivation, and performance of its workforce. Executive management manifests these commitments in policies and provides the resources needed to support unit-level implementation of basic workforce practices. Executive management reinforces this commitment by performing basic workforce practices with their immediate reports and by subsequently holding all managers accountable for the performance of workforce practices in their respective units.

Through policies and accountability, executive management communicates that managers are to accept personal responsibility for ensuring that workforce practices are implemented effectively in their units. Individuals responsible for performing workforce practices are expected to develop repeatable methods for activities such as interviewing job candidates or providing performance feedback. Although managers may perform workforce activities differently, people in a unit are able to develop consistent expectations about how they will be treated. In addition, the regularity with which practices are performed in each unit, regardless of the method or style, is the first step in creating greater consistency across the organization.

In applying the People CMM, it is important to distinguish between management and managers. There are responsibilities that need to be managed and there are people called managers, but there is no required one-to-one mapping between them. Although we often refer to "managers" in describing responsibilities for workforce practices at Maturity Level 2, these practices could be performed by team leaders, human resources specialists, trainers, peers, or others depending on how responsibilities are allocated within the organization. At any level of maturity, some, perhaps many, workforce practices may be performed by individuals or groups who are not "managers." As the organization matures beyond Maturity Level 2, an increasing number of workforce practices will be performed by someone other than a manager.

As an organization achieves Maturity Level 2, units become stable environments for performing work. Units are able to balance their commitments with available resources. They can manage their skill needs, both through acquiring people with needed skills and through developing the skills of those already in the unit. Managers are focused on managing individual performance and coordinating individual contributions into effective unit performance. At Maturity Level 2, an organization's capability for performing work is best characterized by the capability of units to meet commitments. This capability is achieved by ensuring that people have the skills needed to perform their assigned work and that performance is regularly discussed to identify actions that can improve it. Measurements of status and performance of these workforce activities provide management with a means of monitoring and ensuring appropriate performance of workforce practices.

One of the first benefits organizations experience when they implement improvements guided by the People CMM is a reduction in voluntary turnover. At Maturity Level 2, the People CMM addresses one of the most frequent causes of turnover—poor relations with the immediate supervisor. When people begin to see a more rational work environment emerge in their unit, their motivation to stay with the organization is enhanced. As their development needs are addressed, they begin to see the organization as a vehicle through which they can achieve their career objectives.

2.2.3   The Defined Level: Maturity Level 3

Organizations at the Managed Level find that, although they are performing basic workforce practices, there is inconsistency in how these practices are performed across units and little synergy across the organization. The organization misses opportunities to standardize workforce practices because the common knowledge and skills necessary to conduct its business activities have not been identified. At Maturity Level 2, units are identifying critical skills to determine qualifications for open positions, evaluate training needs, and provide performance feedback. However, there is no requirement at Maturity Level 2 for identifying common attributes among these skills across units or for determining the practices that are most effective in developing them.

Once a foundation of basic workforce practices has been established in the units, the next step is for the organization to develop an organization-wide infrastructure building on these practices that ties the capability of the workforce to strategic business objectives. The primary objective of the Defined Level is to help an organization gain a competitive advantage by developing the various competencies that must be combined in its workforce to accomplish its business activities. These workforce competencies represent the critical pillars that support the strategic business plan; their absence poses a severe risk to strategic business objectives. In tying workforce competencies to current and future business objectives, the improved workforce practices implemented at Maturity Level 3 become critical enablers of business strategy.

The concept of workforce competencies implemented in the People CMM differs from the concept of "core competency" popularized by Prahalad and Hamel [Prahalad 90]. *Core competency* refers to an organization's combination of technology and production skills that create its products and services and provide its competitive advantage in the marketplace. In the People CMM, workforce competencies reside one level of abstraction below an organization's core competency, as shown in Figure 2.2. Each *workforce competency* represents a distinct integration of the *knowledge, skills, and process abilities* required to perform some of the business activities that contribute to an organization's core competency. The range of workforce competencies an organization must integrate depends on the breadth and type of business activities that comprise its core competencies. Therefore, these workforce competencies are a strategic underpinning of the organization's core competencies.

By defining process abilities as a component of a workforce competency, the People CMM becomes linked with the process frameworks established in other CMMs and with other process-based methods, such as business process reengineering. A process ability is demonstrated by performing the competency-based processes appropriate for someone at an individual's level of development in the workforce competency. To define the process abilities incorporated in each workforce competency, the organization defines the competency-based processes that an individual in each workforce competency would be expected to perform in accomplishing his or her committed work. Within a workforce competency, a competency-based process defines how individuals apply their knowledge, perform their

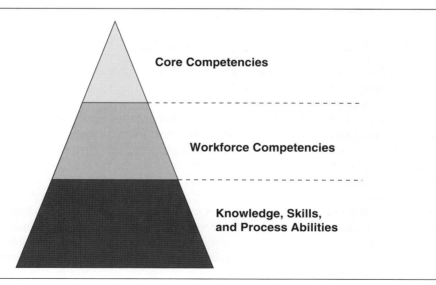

FIGURE 2.2
Hierarchy of competency abstractions

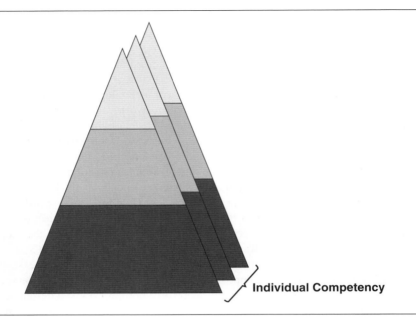

Individual Competency

FIGURE 2.3
Individual competency comprises the knowledge, skills, and process abilities an individual possesses

skills, and apply their process abilities in the context of the organization's defined work processes. Individual competency denotes the combination of knowledge, skills, and process abilities an individual possesses, which may be related to performing tasks or roles for the organization, as shown in Figure 2.3.

At Maturity Level 3, the organization builds an organization-wide framework of workforce competencies that establishes the architecture of the organization's workforce. Each workforce competency is an element of the workforce architecture, and dependencies among competency-based processes describe how these architectural elements interact. Thus, the architecture of the workforce must become an element of the strategic business plan. Workforce practices become mechanisms through which this architecture is continually realigned with changes in business objectives. The architecture of the organization's workforce must evolve as business conditions and technologies change.

Because workforce competencies are strategic, the organization must develop strategic workforce plans for ensuring the required capability in each of its current or anticipated workforce competencies. These plans identify the actions to be taken in acquiring and developing the level of talent needed in each workforce competency. The People CMM makes no assumption about whether the organization sustains these workforce competencies internally or acquires them through partnerships, alliances, independent contracting, or outsourcing.

The members of the organization's workforce who share the knowledge, skills, and process abilities of a particular workforce competency constitute a competency community. The aggregated level of knowledge, skills, and process abilities available in a competency community determines an organization's capability in that workforce competency. The capability of an organization's business processes is, in part, determined by the extent to which competency communities can translate their collective knowledge, skills, and process abilities into work performance. Maturity Level 3 establishes the infrastructure for defining measures of capability, in preparation for capability being quantitatively managed at Maturity Level 4.

At the Defined Level, the organization adapts its workforce practices to its business needs by focusing them on motivating and enabling development in its workforce competencies. Once workforce competencies are defined, training and development practices can be more systematically focused on developing the knowledge, skills, and process abilities that compose them. Further, the existing experience in the workforce can be organized to accelerate the development of workforce competencies of people of lesser skill and experience. Graduated career opportunities are defined around increasing levels of capability in workforce competencies. The graduated career opportunities motivate and guide development of individuals. The organization's staffing, performance management, compensation, and other workforce practices are adapted to motivate and support development in workforce competencies.

When the processes to be performed by each workforce competency are defined, the organization has a new foundation for developing workgroups. Competency-based processes form a basis for defining workgroup roles and operating processes. Rather than relying only on the interpersonal coordination skills developed at Maturity Level 2, workgroups can now organize themselves by tailoring and applying standard competency-based processes. The ability to use defined processes simplifies coordination in the workgroup, since it no longer rests solely on the interpersonal skills of group members to determine how to manage their mutual dependencies.

Competent professionals demand a level of autonomy in performing their work. To best use the abilities of competent professionals, the organization must create an environment that involves people in decisions about their business activities. Decision-making processes are adjusted to maximize the level of competency applied to decisions, while shortening the time required to make them. Individuals and workgroups are given the business and performance information they need to make competent decisions. A participatory culture enables an organization to gain maximum benefit from the capability of its workforce competencies while establishing the environment necessary for empowering workgroups.

A common organizational culture typically develops as the organization achieves the Defined Level. This culture is best described as one of professionalism, since it is built from common understanding of the knowledge and skills that need to be developed to achieve superior levels of performance and a definition of the competency-based processes that such individuals perform. Since these workforce competencies are strategic to the business, the organization reinforces their importance by developing and rewarding them. As a result, the entire workforce begins to share responsibility for developing increasing levels of capability in the organization's workforce competencies. The workforce practices that were implemented at Maturity Level 2 are now standardized and adapted to encourage and reward growth in the organization's workforce competencies.

2.2.4   The Predictable Level: Maturity Level 4

An organization at the Defined Level has established an organizational framework for developing its workforce. At the Predictable Level, the organization manages and exploits the capability created by its framework of workforce competencies. This framework is sustained through formal mentoring activities. The organization is now able to manage its capability and performance quantitatively. The organization is able to predict its capability for performing work because it can quantify the capability of its workforce and of the competency-based processes they use in performing their assignments.

There are at least three ways in which the framework of workforce competencies enables the organization to more fully use the capabilities of its workforce. First, when competent people perform their assignments using proven competency-based processes, management trusts the results they produce. This trust enables the organization to preserve the results of performing competency-based processes and develop them as organizational assets to be reused by others. In essence, people trust the asset because they trust the methods through which it was produced. When these assets are created and used effectively, learning spreads rapidly through the organization and productivity rises when reuse replaces redevelopment.

Second, this trust also gives managers the confidence they need to empower workgroups. Managers will transfer responsibility and authority for committed work into workgroups only if they believe the members of the workgroup are competent to perform the work and use processes that have been proven effective. When the organization achieves Maturity Level 3, the conditions required for empowerment—competent people, effective processes, and a participatory environment—are established. In achieving Maturity Level 4, management senses less risk in empowering workgroups and is willing to delegate increasingly greater levels of authority for managing day-to-day operations and for performing some of their own workforce practices. Increasingly free of managing operational details, managers at Maturity Level 4 are able to turn their attention to more strategic issues.

Third, when members of each workforce competency community have mastered their competency-based processes, the organization is able to integrate different competency-based processes into a single multidisciplinary process. At Maturity Level 3, individuals performing different competency-based processes manage their mutual dependencies by defining points of coordination. However, their competency-based work is performed largely in isolation, independent of each other's competency-based processes. However, when competency-based processes have been institutionalized, the organization can begin to integrate different competency-based processes into a multidisciplinary process that better integrates the work of several workforce competencies. An example would be the integration of software and hardware design processes into a single product design process in which the different competency-based processes are interwoven at every point where they share a potential dependency. Such multidisciplinary processes have proven to accelerate business results.

In addition to exploiting the possibilities enabled by the competency framework, the organization begins to manage its capability quantitatively. Within each unit or workgroup, the performance of competency-based processes most critical for accomplishing business objectives is measured. These measures are used to establish process performance baselines that can be used to manage competency-based processes and assess the need for corrective action. The creation and use of these baselines and associated measures is similar to the methods that underlie Six Sigma programs [Harry 00, Pande 00]. Although Six Sigma techniques can be used at any level of maturity, the full sophistication of a Six Sigma approach is best enabled at Maturity Level 4. Members of a competency community have immediate data for evaluating their performance and deciding on the need for corrective actions. The immediate availability of process performance data also contributes to the rationale for empowering workgroups to manage their business activities.

The organization uses the data generated by competency-based processes to establish process capability baselines for its critical competency-based processes. These baselines can be used for planning, for targeting improvements, and for predicting the organization's capacity for work. The organization evaluates the impact of workforce practices and activities on the capability of competency-based processes and takes corrective action when necessary. Process capability baselines and associated analyses are used as inputs for workforce planning.

The combined availability of workforce capability baselines and process capability baselines for competency-based processes enables both unit and organizational performance to become more predictable. These data allow management to make more accurate predictions about performance and better decisions about tradeoffs involving workforce capability or process performance issues. The quantitative management capabilities implemented at Maturity Level 4 provide management with better input for strategic decisions, while encouraging delegation of operational details to people close to the processes.

2.2.5   The Optimizing Level: Maturity Level 5

At the Optimizing Level, the entire organization is focused on continual improvement. These improvements are made to the capability of individuals and workgroups, to the performance of competency-based processes, and to workforce practices and activities. The organization uses the results of the quantitative management activities established at Maturity Level 4 to guide improvements at Maturity Level 5. Maturity Level 5 organizations treat change management as an ordinary business process to be performed in an orderly way on a regular basis.

Although several individuals may be performing identical competency-based processes, they frequently exhibit individual differences in the methods and work styles they use to perform their assignments. At Maturity Level 5, individuals are encouraged to make continuous improvements to their personal work processes by analyzing their work and making necessary process enhancements. Similarly, workgroups are composed of individuals who have personalized work processes. To improve the capability of the workgroup, each person's work processes must be integrated into an effective operating procedure for the workgroup. Improvements at the individual level should be integrated into improvements in the workgroup's operating process. Mentors and coaches can be provided to guide improvements at both the individual and workgroup levels. Simultaneously, the organization continually seeks methods for improving the capability of its competency-based processes.

Although individuals and workgroups continually improve their performance, the organization must be vigilant to ensure that performance at all levels remains aligned with organizational objectives. Thus, individual performance must be aligned with the performance objectives of the workgroup and unit. Units must ensure their performance is aligned with the objectives of the organization. At Maturity Level 5, the process performance data collected across the organization is evaluated to detect instances of misalignment. Further, the impact of workforce practices and activities is evaluated to ensure that they encourage rather than discourage alignment. Corrective action is taken to realign performance objectives and results when necessary.

Inputs for potential improvements to workforce practices come from many sources. They can come from lessons learned in making improvements to the workforce activities in a unit, from suggestions by the workforce, or from the results of quantitative management activities. The organization continually evaluates the latest developments in workforce practices and technologies to identify those developments with the potential to contribute to the organization's improvement objectives. Data on the effectiveness of workforce practices that emerged from quantitative management activities are used to analyze potential performance improvements from innovative workforce practices or proposed changes to existing practices. Innovative practices that demonstrate the greatest potential for improvement are identified and evaluated in trial applications. If they prove effective, they are deployed throughout the organization.

The workforce capability of Maturity Level 5 organizations is continually improving. This improvement occurs through both incremental advances in existing workforce practices and adoption of innovative practices and technologies that might be expected to have a dramatic impact. The culture created in an organization routinely working at the Optimizing Level is one in which everyone strives to improve his or her own capability, and contributes to improvements in the performance of the workgroup, the unit, and the organization. Workforce practices are honed to support a culture of performance excellence.

3

People CMM Process Areas

3.1   Process Area

Each maturity level of the People CMM, with the exception of the Initial Level, consists of three to seven process areas. Each process area identifies a cluster of related practices that, when performed collectively, achieve a set of goals considered important for enhancing workforce capability. Each process area organizes a set of interrelated practices in a critical area of workforce management, such as staffing, compensation, or workgroup development. Each of these areas constitutes an important organizational process. The process areas at each level of maturity create a linked system of processes that transform the organization's capability to manage its workforce.

Process Area	A cluster of related practices that, when performed collectively, satisfy a set of goals that contribute to the capability gained by achieving a maturity level.

Process areas identify the capabilities that must be institutionalized to achieve a maturity level. They describe the practices that an organization should implement to improve its workforce capability.

3.2   The Process Areas of the People CMM

The process areas in each of the five maturity levels of the People CMM are displayed in Figure 3.1.

3.2.1   The Initial Level: Maturity Level 1

The Initial Level of maturity contains no process areas. Although workforce practices performed in Maturity Level 1 organizations tend to be inconsistent or ritualistic, virtually all of

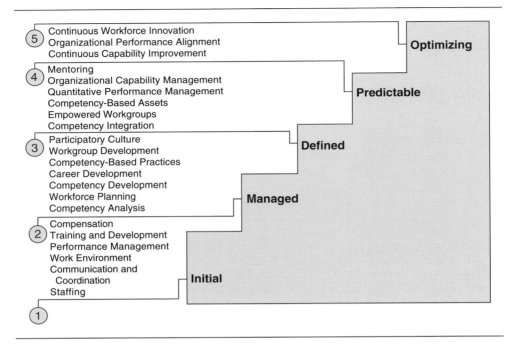

FIGURE 3.1
Process areas of the People CMM

these organizations perform processes that are described in the Maturity Level 2 process areas. Some of these processes may be legally mandated. Organizations that do not achieve the goals of each of the Maturity Level 2 process areas are performing as Maturity Level 1 organizations.

3.2.2   The Managed Level: Maturity Level 2

To achieve the Managed Level, Maturity Level 2, managers begin to perform basic people management practices—such as staffing, managing performance, and adjusting compensation—as a repeatable management discipline. The organization establishes a culture focused at the unit level for ensuring that people are able to meet their work commitments. In achieving Maturity Level 2, the organization develops the capability to manage skills and performance at the unit level. The process areas at Maturity Level 2 are Staffing, Communication and Coordination, Work Environment, Performance Management, Training and Development, and Compensation. These six process areas are described briefly in the following paragraphs. High-level relationships among these process areas are depicted in Figure 3.2.

Staffing

The purpose of Staffing is to establish a formal process by which committed work is matched to unit resources and qualified individuals are recruited, selected, and transitioned into

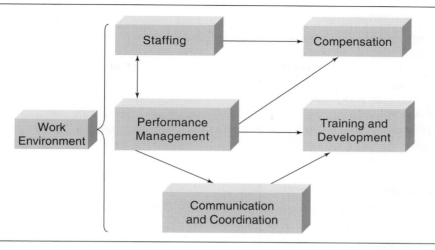

FIGURE 3.2
Relationships among Maturity Level 2 process areas

assignments. Staffing is positioned as the primary process area at Maturity Level 2 because staffing decisions provide an organization's greatest opportunities to influence performance. All other practices designed to improve the capability of the workforce must start from the baseline of talent brought into positions in the organization. Managers balance the unit's work commitments with its available staff, since few organizational processes are able to demonstrate their potential benefits in organizations that are chronically overworked. Managers take responsibility for recruiting talent for open positions and they coordinate with organizational recruiting activities, both internally and externally focused. A formal selection process is developed to ensure thorough and fair evaluation of the skills and qualifications of each candidate. Mechanisms are established for transitioning people into new positions, among assignments, or if necessary, out of the organization.

Communication and Coordination

The purpose of Communication and Coordination is to establish timely communication throughout the organization and to ensure that the workforce has the skills to share information and coordinate activities efficiently. This process area establishes a culture for openly sharing information and concerns across organizational levels and among dependent units. Prior to having the defined processes that aid the development of workgroups at Maturity Level 3, workgroup performance depends on people having the skills required to coordinate their activities and manage shared dependencies. Prior to the availability of defined processes, the interpersonal communication and coordination skills need to be developed to provide a foundation for the structured development of workgroups at higher levels. Communication and Coordination establishes the basis for developing and empowering workgroups.

Work Environment

The purpose of Work Environment is to establish and maintain physical working conditions and to provide resources that allow individuals and workgroups to perform their tasks efficiently without unnecessary distractions. The work environment must be managed to ensure it supports the committed work of those in the organization. This process area focuses on both the resources provided for performing work, and the physical conditions in which the work is performed. Management must balance expenditures on resources and environment with justifications based on the work being performed. Managers monitor resource needs and environmental conditions that affect their unit and mitigate problems judged to present serious risks to health, safety, or efficiency.

Performance Management

The purpose of Performance Management is to establish objectives related to committed work against which unit and individual performance can be measured, to discuss performance against these objectives, and to continuously enhance performance. The primary focus of Performance Management is on the continual discussion about the performance of work to identify ways to improve it. Discussions of performance focus not only on the individual, but also on work processes, resources, and any other issues that can be addressed to improve performance. The discussion of performance occurs in the context of the measurable objectives individuals or workgroups are trying to achieve. These objectives are linked to committed work. The primary role of performance appraisal is to record the results of performance for use as input to decisions about adjustments to compensation, personal development planning, staffing, promotion, and other workforce activities. Performance problems are managed and resolved. Outstanding performance is recognized.

Training and Development

The purpose of Training and Development is to ensure that all individuals have the skills required to perform their assignments and are provided relevant development opportunities. The primary focus of Training and Development is on removing the gap between the current skills of each individual and the skills required to perform their assignments. Each unit develops a training plan to ensure that all individuals have the skills required by their assignments. Once individuals have the necessary skills to perform current assignments, they may focus their development activities on other objectives.

Compensation

The purpose of Compensation is to provide all individuals with remuneration and benefits based on their contribution and value to the organization. The organization must formulate a compensation strategy that motivates and rewards the skills and behaviors the organization considers vital to its success. Compensation represents the only process area at the Managed Level whose execution is coordinated by actions at the organizational level. Compensation must be coordinated primarily through centralized activity in order to establish a sense of equity in the system. Once the workforce perceives the system to be equitable, it can be adjusted to motivate the development of necessary skills and better alignment of individual performance with that of the workgroup, unit, or organization.

Periodic adjustments to compensation are reviewed to ensure they are equitable and consistent with the organization's strategy and plan.

3.2.3   The Defined Level: Maturity Level 3

To achieve the Defined Level, Maturity Level 3, the organization identifies and develops the knowledge, skills, and process abilities that constitute the workforce competencies required to perform its business activities. The organization develops a culture of professionalism based on well-understood workforce competencies. In achieving Maturity Level 3, the organization develops the capability to manage its workforce as a strategic asset. The process areas at Maturity Level 3 are Competency Analysis, Workforce Planning, Competency Development, Career Development, Competency-Based Practices, Workgroup Development, and Participatory Culture. These seven process areas are described briefly in the following paragraphs. High-level relationships among these process areas are depicted in Figure 3.3.

Competency Analysis

The purpose of Competency Analysis is to identify the knowledge, skills, and process abilities required to perform the organization's business activities so that they may be developed and used as a basis for workforce practices. The organization maintains descriptions of the knowledge, skills, and process abilities that comprise each workforce competency. These descriptions are maintained and available in an organizational repository. These descriptions

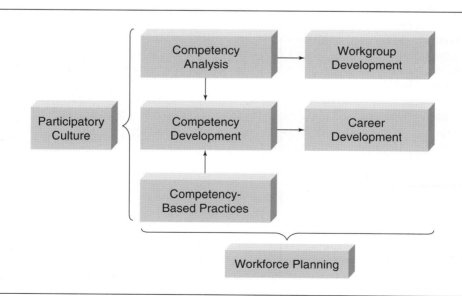

FIGURE 3.3
Relationships among Maturity Level 3 process areas

are periodically reassessed to ensure they remain current with the organization's technologies and business activities. The work processes used by capable individuals in each workforce competency are defined and updated as necessary. The People CMM refers to these work processes as competency-based processes, since they rely on individuals in the workforce within a specific area of competency as having the necessary knowledge, skills, and process abilities to successfully carry out these competency-based processes. Competency information regarding an individual's capability in the workforce competencies relevant to that individual's work or career is collected and maintained. From this competency information, resource profiles of the organization's level of capability in each of its workforce competencies can be determined.

Workforce Planning

The purpose of Workforce Planning is to coordinate workforce activities with current and future business needs at both the organizational and unit levels. Workforce Planning ties the organization's workforce activities directly to its business strategy and objectives. Through workforce planning, the organization identifies the workforce it needs for its current and future business activities and plans the actions to be taken to ensure the required workforce is available when needed. Strategic workforce plans provide those responsible for workforce activities in units with a reference for ensuring that they perform their responsibilities with an understanding of how the unit's workforce activities contribute to the business.

Competency Development

The purpose of Competency Development is to enhance constantly the capability of the workforce to perform its assigned tasks and responsibilities. The workforce competencies identified in Competency Analysis and the needs identified in Workforce Planning provide the foundations for the organization's competency development program. Graduated training and development opportunities are designed to support development in each of the organization's workforce competencies. Individuals pursue competency development opportunities that support their individual development objectives. The organization uses the experience of its workforce to develop additional capability in each of its workforce competencies through practices such as mentoring. Mechanisms are established to support communication among the members of a competency community.

Career Development

The purpose of Career Development is to ensure that individuals are provided opportunities to develop workforce competencies that enable them to achieve career objectives. A personal development plan is created and periodically updated for each individual. Opportunities for training and other career-enhancing activities are made available. Progress against development plans is tracked. Graduated career opportunities and promotion criteria are defined to motivate growth in the organization's workforce competencies. Promotion activities are performed on a periodic and event-driven basis. Individuals are periodically counseled about career options, and opportunities for advancement are communicated to them.

Competency-Based Practices

The purpose of Competency-Based Practices is to ensure that all workforce practices are based in part on developing the competencies of the workforce. The staffing, performance management, compensation, and related workforce practices established through performing the activities of process areas at the Managed Level must be adjusted to support the organization's focus on developing workforce competencies. Workforce activities that had focused primarily on unit concerns at the Managed Level are reoriented to include concerns that are strategic to shaping the organization's workforce and the workforce competencies it needs. As a result of incorporating an organizational orientation in the performance of workforce activities, the performance of activities should become more consistent across units.

Workgroup Development

The purpose of Workgroup Development is to organize work around competency-based process abilities. As used in the People CMM, a *workgroup* is a collection of people who work closely with each other on highly interdependent tasks to achieve shared objectives. Work and workgroups are designed to maximize the interdependency of tasks in the workgroup and to minimize dependencies with other workgroups. Workgroups tailor competency-based processes for use in planning and performing their business activities. Workgroups tailor the defined roles incorporated in the processes and assign them to workgroup members. Responsible individuals manage workgroup performance and track the status of work. When a workgroup's business activities are complete, it is disbanded through an orderly process that preserves its assets, completes required workforce activities, and ensures appropriate work assignments for each of its departing members.

Participatory Culture

The purpose of a Participatory Culture is to enable the workforce's full capability for making decisions that affect the performance of business activities. Establishing a participatory culture lays the foundation for high-performance workgroups. Establishing a participatory culture begins with giving individuals and workgroups information about organizational and unit performance and how their performance contributes, in addition to information they need to perform their committed work. Individuals and workgroups use defined processes to make decisions and resolve conflicts and disputes.

3.2.4   The Predictable Level: Maturity Level 4

To achieve the Predictable Level, Maturity Level 4, the organization quantifies and manages the capability of its workforce and competency-based processes, in addition to exploiting the opportunities afforded by defined workforce competencies. The organization creates a culture of measurement and exploits shared experience. At Maturity Level 4, the organization has the capability to predict its performance and capacity for work. The process areas at Maturity Level 4 are Competency Integration, Empowered Workgroups, Competency-Based Assets, Quantitative Performance Management, Organizational Capability Management, and Mentoring. These six process areas are described briefly in the following paragraphs. High-level relationships among these process areas are depicted in Figure 3.4.

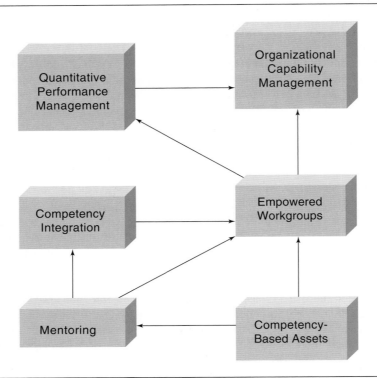

FIGURE 3.4
Relationships among Maturity Level 4 process areas

Competency Integration

The purpose of Competency Integration is to improve the efficiency and agility of interdependent work by integrating the process abilities of different workforce competencies. Competency Integration interweaves different competency-based processes to achieve a seamless process-based interaction among individuals from different competency communities. These integrated competency-based processes provide more tightly woven interactions to allow problems among product, service, and work dependencies to be identified and corrected quickly. Competency Integration involves analyzing work to identify opportunities to integrate the processes used by different workforce competencies. These integrated competency-based processes are defined and work situations are tailored for their use. Workforce practices and activities such as staffing, performance management, compensation, and the work environment are adjusted to support multidisciplinary work using integrated competency-based processes.

Empowered Workgroups

The purpose of Empowered Workgroups is to invest workgroups with the responsibility and authority to determine how to conduct their business activities most effectively. Empowerment involves delegating responsibility and authority for work results to a workgroup and training its members in the skills and processes required for working in an empowered environment. Empowered workgroups are managed as an entity, rather than as individuals. The work environment is adjusted to support empowered performance by workgroups. Empowered workgroup members accept increasing responsibility for the performance of workforce practices such as recruiting, selection, performance management, reward, training, development, and compensation activities that are appropriate to the structure and function of the empowered workgroup. Workgroup performance and contributions to it are considered in making individual compensation decisions, as well as in recognizing and rewarding outstanding performance.

Competency-Based Assets

The purpose of Competency-Based Assets is to capture the knowledge, experience, and artifacts developed in performing competency-based processes for use in enhancing capability and performance. A competency-based asset captures knowledge, experience, and artifacts developed in performing competency-based processes in an organization. A competency-based asset is a bundle of information or an artifact that has been prepared in standard format and made available for widespread use. As an organizational asset, it becomes a component of one or more workforce competencies. Competency-Based Assets involves encouraging individuals and workgroups to capture and share the information and artifacts developed from performing competency-based processes. Selected bundles of information or artifacts are organized into competency-based assets that can be reused in performing business activities. Workforce practices and activities are adjusted to encourage both the development and use of competency-based assets.

Quantitative Performance Management

The purpose of Quantitative Performance Management is to predict and manage the capability of competency-based processes for achieving measurable performance objectives. Individuals and workgroups determine which competency-based processes contribute most to achieving unit objectives and set measurable objectives for the performance of these processes. Committed work is estimated and planned using process performance baselines developed from past performance of the relevant competency-based processes. A quantitative performance management strategy is developed for identifying, measuring, and analyzing the performance of the competency-based processes that most contribute to achieving unit objectives. Performance data are collected and analyzed according to the strategy. The performance of competency-based processes is brought under quantitative control. Corrective actions are taken when the performance of competency-based processes deviates significantly from performance objectives.

Organizational Capability Management

The purpose of Organizational Capability Management is to quantify and manage the capability of the workforce and of the critical competency-based processes it performs. The organization's capability in a specific workforce competency is assessed from the number of individuals in a competency community and the aggregated level of knowledge, skill, and process ability that they possess. Data regarding competency development trends are defined and collected, and trends are compared to objectives in the strategic workforce plan. The organization evaluates the impact of its workforce practices on capability in each of its workforce competencies. Organizational Capability Management also involves characterizing the process capability of critical competency-based processes through process performance baselines and quantitative performance models. These capability results are used in planning and managing the performance of competency-based processes. The impact of workforce practices on the capability and performance of competency-based processes is quantified and managed and the results of these analyses are used in organizational decisions. The results of these analyses are used in adjusting workforce practices to improve their impact on performance and results.

Mentoring

The purpose of Mentoring is to transfer the lessons of greater experience in a workforce competency to improve the capability of other individuals or workgroups. Mentoring relationships are designed to accomplish specific objectives. At the Defined Level, mentoring and coaching is informal, and the knowledge and skills imparted by mentors are defined more by their experience and judgment than by a documented combination of knowledge, skills, and process abilities to be imparted. At Maturity Level 4, mentoring activities are organized around the knowledge, skills, and process abilities to be imparted. Mentoring activities are also used to deploy competency-based assets. Criteria are developed for selecting mentors and training them for their assignments.

3.2.5   The Optimizing Level: Maturity Level 5

To achieve the Optimizing Level, Maturity Level 5, everyone in the organization is focused on continuously improving his or her capability and the organization's workforce practices. The organization creates a culture of product and service excellence. At Maturity Level 5, the organization continuously improves its capability and deploys rapid changes for managing its workforce. The process areas at Maturity Level 5 are Continuous Capability Improvement, Organizational Performance Alignment, and Continuous Workforce Innovation. These three process areas are described briefly in the following paragraphs. High-level relationships among these process areas are depicted in Figure 3.5.

Continuous Capability Improvement

The purpose of Continuous Capability Improvement is to provide a foundation for individuals and workgroups to continuously improve their capability for performing competency-based processes. Continuous Capability Improvement involves enterprise-wide support for

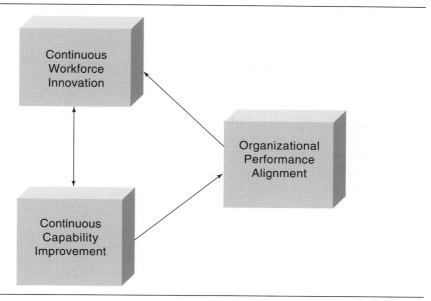

FIGURE 3.5
Relationships among Maturity Level 5 process areas

individuals and workgroups as they focus on improving their capability in the performance of competency-based processes. Individuals focus on the capability of their personal methods for performing competency-based processes. They engage in learning activities to improve their personal work processes. Workgroups focus on improving the capability and performance of their operating processes by continuously improving the integration of the personal work processes performed by workgroup members.

Organizational Performance Alignment

The purpose of Organizational Performance Alignment is to enhance the alignment of performance results across individuals, workgroups, and units with organizational performance and business objectives. Organizational Performance Alignment builds on the analyses of competency-based processes initiated in the Quantitative Performance Management and Organizational Capability Management process areas. Those analyses focused narrowly on process performance; analyses of performance alignment expand this focus to evaluate how the various components of performance fit together across workgroups, units, and the entire organization. Practices in this process area knit together a complete picture of performance within the organization and how workforce practices and activities affect the integration of its various business activities. These analyses allow management to align performance across the entire enterprise and to use workforce activities strategically to achieve organizational business objectives.

Continuous Workforce Innovation

The purpose of Continuous Workforce Innovation is to identify and evaluate improved or innovative workforce practices and technologies, and implement the most promising ones throughout the organization. Responsible individuals are continually encouraged to make improvements to their performance of workforce activities. A group is assigned responsibility for coordinating continuous improvements to the organization's workforce practices. Recommendations for adopting innovative or improved workforce practices can come as lessons learned while improving the performance of workforce activities, as suggestions from the workforce, or as analyses of best practices at other organizations. The most promising innovations are evaluated in trial use and, if successful, are implemented across the organization. The effectiveness of these improved practices is evaluated quantitatively and the results are communicated to the workforce.

4

The Architecture
of the People CMM

4.1 Structural Components of the People CMM

This chapter describes the structure of the People CMM. It describes the model's structure, the maturity levels, the process areas that correspond to each maturity level of the People CMM, and the goals and practices in each process area. The glossary in Appendix C contains definitions of terms described in this and other sections. Understanding the meaning of the structural components of the People CMM is crucial to using the information in Part Two effectively.

The relationships among the structural components of the People CMM are illustrated in Figure 4.1. Organizational capability describes the level of knowledge, skills, and process abilities in the organization's workforce and the ability of the workforce to apply them to improve business performance. Organizational capability contributes to an organization's performance and its ability to achieve business objectives. It is an important predictor of business performance. While not a structural component found in the People CMM, an organization's workforce capability is indicated by its maturity level.

The components of the structure of the People CMM include the following:

- Maturity levels
- Process areas
- Goals
- Practices

The architectural structure of the People CMM is depicted in Figure 4.1. Practices represent guidelines for achieving process area goals, which in turn describe the objectives and scope of a process area. Process areas contribute the means by which the organization is transformed at each maturity level to produce a new organizational capability. Each of these components is described in the following sections. Chapter 5 addresses the interpretation of these components.

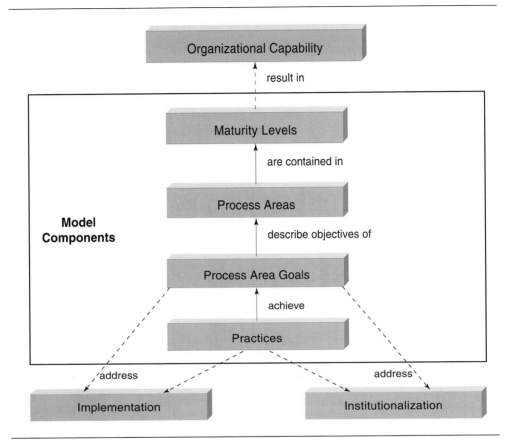

FIGURE 4.1
Structure of the People CMM

4.2   Maturity Levels

The People CMM consists of five maturity levels that lay successive foundations for continuously improving talent, developing an effective workforce, and successfully managing the human capital of an organization. Each *maturity level* is a well-defined evolutionary plateau that establishes and institutionalizes a level of capability for improving the organization's workforce. The five maturity levels provide the top-level structure of the People CMM.

Each maturity level is composed of several process areas. Each process area contains a set of goals that, when satisfied, establish that process area's ability to affect workforce capability. Process areas and their goals are described in the following sections. The maturity levels are measured by the satisfaction of a predefined set of the process areas and their goals at each maturity level. Maturity levels are used to characterize organizational improvement relative to a set of process areas, which provide an indication of an organization's workforce capability.

4.3   Process Areas

Each *process area* organizes a set of interrelated practices in a critical area of workforce management, such as staffing, compensation, or workgroup development. Each of these areas constitutes an important organizational process. The process areas at each level of maturity create a linked system of processes that transform the organization's capability for managing its workforce.

Process Area	A cluster of related practices that, when performed collectively, satisfy a set of goals that contribute to the capability gained by achieving a maturity level.

Each process area contains a set of goals that, when satisfied, establish that process area's ability to affect workforce capability. Process areas identify both the capabilities that must be institutionalized to achieve a maturity level and the practices that an organization should implement to improve its workforce capability.

As introduced in Chapter 3, there are 22 process areas in the five maturity levels in the People CMM. With the exception of the Initial Level (Maturity Level 1), each maturity level is composed of several process areas. Process areas have been defined to reside at a single maturity level. Figure 4.2 shows each of these 22 process areas and their respective maturity levels. For example, one of the process areas for Maturity Level 2 is Performance Management.

Each process area contains

- the purpose statement of the process area,
- a brief description of the process area,
- the goals for the process area, and
- the practices of the process area.

Purpose Statement

The purpose statement describes the purpose of each process area. The purpose statement is an informative model component.

For example, the purpose statement of the Workforce Planning process area is "The purpose of Workforce Planning is to coordinate workforce activities with current and future business needs at both the organizational and unit levels."

Description

The description section of each process area presents the major concepts covered in the process area. The process area description is an informative model component.

An example from the description section of the Staffing process area is "Staffing involves processes related to balancing the workload with available resources, recruiting, selecting among candidates for open positions, entering or leaving the organization, and transitioning into new positions."

Maturity Level	Focus	Process Areas
5 **Optimizing**	Continuously improve and align personal, workgroup, and organizational capability	Continuous Workforce Innovation Organizational Performance Alignment Continuous Capability Improvement
4 **Predictable**	Empower and integrate workforce competencies and manage performance quantitatively	Mentoring Organizational Capability Management Quantitative Performance Management Competency-Based Assets Empowered Workgroups Competency Integration
3 **Defined**	Develop workforce competencies and workgroups, and align with business strategy and objectives	Participatory Culture Workgroup Development Competency-Based Practices Career Development Competency Development Workforce Planning Competency Analysis
2 **Managed**	Managers take responsibility for managing and developing their people	Compensation Training and Development Performance Management Work Environment Communication and Coordination Staffing
1 **Initial**	Workforce practices applied inconsistently	

FIGURE 4.2
Process areas of the People CMM

4.4   Goals

A goal describes the unique characteristics that must be present to satisfy the purpose of the process area. Goals are used in appraisals to help determine whether a process area is satisfied.

Each process area contains three to five goals stating the objectives it was designed to accomplish. These goals constitute the requirements an organization should satisfy in implementing the workforce practices in a process area. Collectively they indicate the scope, boundaries, and intent of the process area. Goals apply to only one process area.

Process Area Goal	An organizational state to be achieved by implementing the practices of a process area.

Goals apply to only one process area and address the unique characteristics that describe what must be implemented to satisfy the purpose of the process area. The goals of a process area summarize the states that must exist for that process area to have been implemented and institutionalized. "Implemented and institutionalized" implies that these states have been implemented in an effective and lasting way. Each process area contains a number of implementation goals and a single institutionalization goal. An example of an implementation goal from the Performance Management process area is "The performance of committed work is regularly discussed to identify actions that can improve it." The institutionalization goal from the Performance Management process area is "Performance Management practices are institutionalized to ensure they are performed as managed processes."

The extent to which the goals have been accomplished is an indicator of the level of capability the organization has established and institutionalized at that maturity level, that is, its workforce capability. When the goals of all process areas at a maturity level and lower levels have been satisfied, the organization will have achieved the maturity level and established a new level of capability in managing its workforce. The path to achieving this new level of workforce management capabilities is indicated by the set of goals associated with each process area. The goals of a process area summarize a state that exists when an organization has implemented the practices of that area. Analysis of goal achievement can be used to determine whether an organization has effectively implemented a process area. A process area has not been satisfactorily implemented until all its goals accurately describe the organization's behavior or state of affairs.

Goals are the model components that must be achieved by an organization's planned and implemented processes. The statement of each goal is a required model component. Only the statement of the goal is a required model component. The goal identifier, which is the word "goal" followed by the goal number, is considered an informative model component. Required components are essential to achieving process improvement in a given process area. They are used in appraisals to determine process area satisfaction and organizational process maturity. As required model components, goals are used in appraisals to determine whether a process area is satisfied.

In adapting the practices of a process area to a specific unit, the amount of success in satisfying the goals can be used to determine whether the adaptation is a reasonable rendering of the practices. Similarly, when appraising or evaluating alternative ways to implement a process area, the goals can be used to determine if the alternative practices satisfy the intent of the process area.

4.5   Practices

Each process area is described in terms of the *practices* that contribute to satisfying its goals. The practices, when collectively addressed, accomplish the goals of the process area. The workforce practices in each process area provide guidance for improving an organization's capability to manage and develop its workforce. These practices have been selected for inclusion because they contribute to satisfying process area goals. However, they constitute neither an exclusive nor an exhaustive list of the practices an organization might implement in pursuing the goals of a process area. Nevertheless, when the recommended workforce practices are performed collectively, the organization should achieve the collective states described by the goals of the process area.

Practice	A subprocess of a process area that contributes to achieving a process area goal.

Treating workforce practices as subprocesses highlights the importance of integrating them into an effective process, rather than mandating their performance as mindless bureaucracy. When workforce practices are treated as processes, the entire paraphernalia of process analysis and improvement becomes available for implementing and improving workforce practices. The People CMM is a process-based approach to staging the implementation and improvement of workforce practices.

"Practices" is used throughout the People CMM to refer to standard, defined workforce management processes. These processes may be defined at various organizational levels and varying degrees of formality, depending on the practice and its associated maturity level. "Activities" refer to actions taken by individuals, in workgroups or units, or by the organization to implement these practices.

A practice is the description of an activity that is considered important in achieving the specific goal to which it is mapped. The practices describe the activities expected to result in achievement of the goal of a process area. For example, a practice from the Performance Management process area is "Performance objectives based on committed work are documented for each individual on a periodic or event-driven basis."

Practices are expected model components. Expected components describe the practices an organization that is achieving a set of goals will typically implement. Only the statement of the practice is an expected model component. The practice identifier, which is a word that indicates the practice type followed by a number, subpractices, and any supplementary information associated with the practice, are considered informative model components.

The practices are meant to guide individuals and groups implementing improvements or performing appraisals. Either the practices as described, or acceptable alternatives to them, must be present in the planned and implemented processes of the organization before goals can be considered satisfied. The practices state the fundamental policies, procedures, and activities to be established for the process area. The practices describe "what" is to be done, but they should not be interpreted as mandating "how" the goals should be achieved. Alternative practices may accomplish the goals of a process area. The practices should be interpreted rationally to judge whether the goals of the process area are effectively, although perhaps differently, achieved.

In each process area, the practices describe the activities and infrastructure that contribute most to the effective implementation and institutionalization of the process area. Figure 4.3 depicts the mapping of practices to goals. Some of these practices in each process

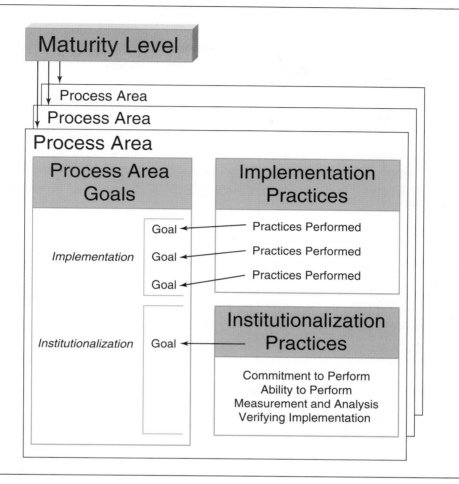

FIGURE 4.3
Implementation and institutionalization practices mapped to process area goals

area implement workforce practices, and are mapped to implementation goals. Other practices establish the support needed to institutionalize their performance, and are mapped to a single institutionalization goal in each process area. Thus, the practices in each process area are organized to address implementation and institutionalization of the expected state described by the goals. This organization groups the practices in a sequence that is helpful for organizations using them. A focus on both implementation and institutionalization of a process area ensures that the effect of the process area on organizational capability is effective, repeatable, and lasting.

Appendix D provides a detailed mapping of the practices of the People CMM to the goals of each process area. These practice-to-goal mappings can be used to help comprehend the structure of the model, to guide the implementation of improvement activities, and to evaluate the satisfaction of goals during an appraisal. These mappings suggest the strongest relationships between practices and goals.

4.5.1   Implementation Practices

In each process area, the implementation practices are grouped into the *Practices Performed* category. The Practices Performed in each process area describes practices that should typically be implemented to achieve the goals of the process area. Practices Performed is the largest category of practices because they describe the expected implementation of the process areas.

4.5.2   Institutionalization Practices

Institutionalization practices are practices that help to institutionalize the implementation practices in the organization's culture so that they are effective, repeatable, and lasting. These institutionalization practices, taken as a whole, form the basis by which an organization can institutionalize the implementation practices (described in the Practices Performed of the process area). Institutionalization practices are as important as implementation practices because they address what must be done to support and institutionalize the process areas.

The institutionalization practices are organized into four categories. The *Commitment to Perform* and *Ability to Perform* practices describe prerequisites for implementing each process area. *Measurement and Analysis* and *Verifying Implementation* practices determine if prerequisites have been met and processes have been institutionalized. The categories of institutionalization practices contained in each process area are as follows.

Commitment to Perform

Commitment to Perform describes the actions the organization must take to ensure that the activities constituting a process area are established and will endure. Commitment to Perform typically involves establishing organizational policies, executive management sponsorship, and organization-wide roles to support practices to develop workforce capability.

Ability to Perform

Ability to Perform describes the preconditions that must exist in the unit or organization to implement practices competently. Ability to Perform typically involves resources, organizational structures, and preparation to perform the practices of the process area.

Measurement and Analysis

Measurement and Analysis describes measurements of the practices and their analysis. Measurement and Analysis typically includes examples of measurements that could be taken to determine the status and effectiveness with which the Practices Performed have been implemented. These examples are not intended to be prescriptive or exhaustive. The organization's workforce activities or other sources [Becker 01, Boudreau 07,

Cascio 08, Cascio 00, Fitz-enz 95, Fitz-enz 09, Gates 02, Gates 03, Gates 08, Holbeche 01, Kingsmill 03, Mayo 01, Ulrich 97, Yeung 97] can provide applicable measures.

Verifying Implementation

Verifying Implementation describes the steps to ensure that the activities are performed in compliance with the established policies and procedures. Verification typically encompasses objective reviews and audits by executive management and other responsible individuals.

4.5.3   Practice Statements

Each practice consists of a single sentence, often followed by a detailed description. The practice identifier, which is a word indicating the practice type followed by a number, is considered an informative model component. Practices are presented in a hierarchical format, as shown in Figure 4.4, which depicts an example page of practices from a process area. The practices include the following.

Practice Statement

The practices state the fundamental policies, procedures, and activities for the process area. They are identified in bold and are numbered within each category of practices. For example, the first practice in Practices Performed is identified as Practice 1, and the first practice in the Ability to Perform category is identified as Ability 1.

Subpractices

Subpractices, also known as subordinate practices, are listed beneath the practice statements. Subpractices describe activities one would expect to find implemented for the practice. Subpractices are detailed descriptions that provide guidance for interpreting and implementing the practices. The subpractices can be used to help determine whether the practices are implemented satisfactorily. Subpractices are informative model components that help model users understand the goals and practices and how they can be achieved. Subpractices may be worded as if prescriptive, but are actually an informative component in the model that provides details that help model users get started in thinking about how to approach practices and goals. Subpractices are detailed descriptions that provide guidance for interpreting practices. For example, a subpractice from the Performance Management process area is "Performance objectives for each individual are drawn from and are consistent with their work commitments."

Supplementary Information

Supplementary information includes notes (or elaborations), examples, and references. Supplementary information are informative model components.

A note is text that can accompany nearly any other model component. It may provide detail, background, or rationale. Notes may include definitions of terms. Terms are italicized in a note to indicate the first use of the term. Definitions are provided in the note, and also in the Glossary in Appendix C.

An example is a component comprising text and often a list of items, usually in a box, that can accompany nearly any other model component and provides one or more examples to clarify a concept or described activity. Examples provide informative assistance in

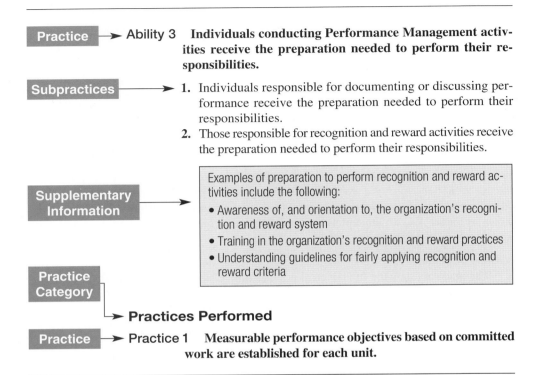

FIGURE 4.4
Examples of Practice Statements

interpreting a practice. References are informative model components that direct the user to additional information in this or a related process area.

A reference is a pointer to additional or more detailed information in related process areas and can accompany nearly any other model component.

Supplementary information appears in shaded boxes following the practices or subpractices. The following is an example of a note, or an elaboration, which also contains a reference.

> Refer to Appendix D for the *Practice-to-Goal Mappings,* which illustrate the relationships between the practices of each of the 22 process areas in the People CMM and the relevant process area goals. The specific practice-to-goal mappings can be used for comprehending the structure of the model, for guiding the implementation of improvement activities, and for evaluating the satisfaction of goals during an appraisal.

4.6   Required, Expected, and Informative Components

Each component of the People CMM can be classified as either a required component, an expected component, or an informative component.

Required model components describe what an organization must achieve to satisfy a process area. Goals are required model components that are to be achieved by implementing improved workforce processes. Required components are essential contributors to the organizational capability achieved at the maturity level where its process area is located. Goals are used in appraisals to determine process area achievement and organizational maturity.

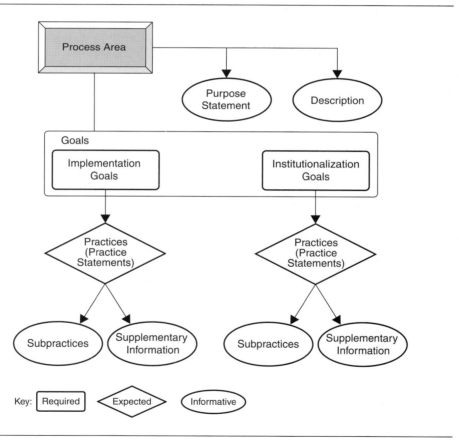

FIGURE 4.5
Relationships of model components in the People CMM

Practices are *expected model components.* Expected components describe the practices an organization will typically implement to achieve the process area goals. They are meant to guide individuals and groups in implementing improvements or performing appraisals. Either the described practices, or acceptable alternatives to them, must be present with a reasonable frequency of implementation of the practice before goals can be considered achieved. Only the statement of the practice is an expected model component. Any supplementary information associated with the practice is considered *informative model components.*

Supplementary information, such as subpractices, notes, and references, are *informative model components* that help those using the People CMM understand the goals and practices and how they can be achieved. Informative components provide details that help explain or elaborate approaches to implementing and institutionalizing the practices and goals.

The model components can be summarized to illustrate their relationships, as shown in Figure 4.5.

This chapter has presented the structure of the People CMM. Chapter 6 provides guidance on interpreting the model.

5

Relationships among Process Areas

5.1   A System of Related Practices

The People CMM describes a system of practices. It helps an organization develop a vision of how to integrate a system of practices to achieve its workforce objectives and provides the framework to guide implementation of those practices. These practices guide the development of a human capital management framework for the organization.

Each maturity level of the People CMM, with the exception of the Initial Level, consists of three to seven process areas. Each process area identifies a cluster of related practices that, when performed collectively, achieve a set of goals considered important for enhancing workforce capability. Each process area organizes a set of interrelated practices in a critical area of workforce management, such as staffing, compensation, or workgroup development. Each of these areas constitutes an important organizational process. The process areas at each level of maturity create a linked system of processes that systematically implement and transformationally improve the organization's capability to manage and empower its workforce. At each maturity level, the organizational focus builds on that deployed at the lower levels. For example, as an organization moves toward implementing the Maturity Level 3 practices, the organizational focus shifts from stabilizing local work units and ensuring they can meet their performance requirements at Maturity Level 2 to focusing on the organization and meeting its strategic workforce needs and performance requirements at Maturity Level 3.

Process areas identify the capabilities that must be institutionalized to achieve a maturity level. They describe the practices that an organization should implement to improve its workforce capability. For example, the process areas at Maturity Level 2 comprise a system of interrelated workforce practices that typically reflect a near-term cycle, perhaps a fiscal year or other short-term planning cycle. They provide for ongoing feedback about performance, as well as training and development to enable individuals to perform in their assigned positions. This cycle may relate to specific workforce practices, such as budgetary concerns, workload planning, periodic review of individual accomplishments, or compensation adjustments. At higher levels of maturity, the planning cycles may be more strategic, driven from evolving business conditions, longer-range business plans, or strategic workforce plans to shape the human capital needed by the organization.

5.2   Process Area Threads in the People CMM

Process areas in the People CMM reside at a single maturity level. However, some process areas are linked across maturity levels by common areas of concern that the People CMM was designed to address. These links cause workforce practices established at a maturity level to be transformed by one or more process areas at higher maturity levels. For instance, the Training and Development practices that were established at Maturity Level 2 are transformed into Competency Development practices at Maturity Level 3. Four areas of concern are addressed by process areas linked across maturity levels in the People CMM:

1. Developing individual capability
2. Building workgroups and culture
3. Motivating and managing performance
4. Shaping the workforce

The conceptual structure of the People CMM is a matrix that crosses the primary areas of concern in managing the workforce with the organizational transformations associated with the maturity levels. The areas of concern constitute objectives that the People CMM was designed to address. These objectives are addressed in a different way at each maturity level. The maturity levels represent substantive changes in how the organization addresses these areas of concern. The cultural shift achieved at each maturity level is attained by transforming the organization's workforce practices to support the objectives of the new level. The four areas of concern, and the process areas linked across maturity levels to address them, are displayed in Figure 5.1.

5.2.1   Developing Individual Capability

The effort to develop individual capability begins at the Managed Level by identifying and addressing the immediate training needs of people in each unit (Training and Development). If individuals have the knowledge and skill required to perform their committed work, then they can use training opportunities to develop skills for possible future assignments. The focus at Maturity Level 2 is on ensuring that individuals have the skills to accomplish their committed work.

At the Defined Level, the focus shifts from the skills needed in individual units to concern for the workforce competencies the organization needs to accomplish its current and strategic business objectives. The organization identifies the knowledge, skills, and process abilities that constitute its workforce competencies (Competency Analysis). It then establishes an organization-wide development program to help individuals gain capability in the workforce competencies most relevant to their assignments and careers (Competency Development).

Maturity Levels	People CMM Threads			
	Developing Individual Capability	Building Workgroups and Culture	Motivating and Managing Performance	Shaping the Workforce
5 Optimizing	Continuous Capability Improvement		Organizational Performance Alignment	Continuous Workforce Innovation
4 Predictable	Competency-Based Assets Mentoring	Competency Integration Empowered Workgroups	Quantitative Performance Management	Organizational Capability Management
3 Defined	Competency Development Competency Analysis	Workgroup Development Participatory Culture	Competency-Based Practices Career Development	Workforce Planning
2 Managed	Training and Development	Communication and Coordination	Compensation Performance Management Work Environment	Staffing

FIGURE 5.1
Process threads in the People CMM

At the Predictable Level, the organization establishes mechanisms for exploiting the opportunities created by the formation and organization of its workforce competencies. For instance, the results of performing competency-based processes are preserved as assets that can be used to transfer knowledge and capability to others who share the workforce competency (Competency-Based Assets). Mentors use competency-based assets and other competency development materials to achieve defined objectives while assisting those with less experience to develop their capability (Mentoring).

At the Optimizing Level, the focus shifts to continuous improvement of an individual's capability. People can initiate an individual program to continuously improve the personal work processes through which they perform competency-based processes (Continuous Capability Improvement). People are empowered to make changes in their personal work processes that they believe will improve their performance. The lessons they learn can be recommended to the organization for incorporation into defined competency-based processes.

5.2.2 Building Workgroups and Culture

The effort to improve coordination and interaction among people begins at the Managed Level with a focus on improving interpersonal communication skill (Communication and Coordination). People develop more effective methods for coordinating dependencies in their work and for conducting meetings. These are the initial skills required for developing effective workgroups. In the absence of defined processes, the organization's ability to manage dependencies in its business activities depends on the interpersonal skills of its employees. The focus at Maturity Level 2 is on coordination among individuals in units to establish a local capability to manage dependencies in committed work.

Practices at the Defined Level establish an organizational capability for coordinating work dependencies that is built on the foundation afforded by the coordination skills of individuals. At Maturity Level 3, the organization seeks to reduce the coordination burden on its workforce by defining the work processes used in each workforce competency. A competency-based process defines how individuals in a specific workforce competency apply their knowledge, perform their skills, and apply their process abilities in the context of an organization's defined business processes. These competency-based processes also provide the next foundation for developing workgroups. That is, a workgroup's operating processes are composed in part from competency-based processes and the roles defined for performing them (Workgroup Development). In addition, the organization develops a participatory culture by increasing the availability of information for making decisions and involving the workforce in decisions that affect their work (Participatory Culture). A participatory culture allows the organization to gain its fullest benefit from the capability of its workforce and establishes the foundation for empowerment.

At the Predictable Level, the organization begins to exploit the capabilities offered by its foundation of competency-based processes. When each competency community has defined and mastered its work processes, the organization can move beyond coordinating work dependencies through the formally defined interfaces among competency communities that were established at Maturity Level 3. At Maturity Level 4, the organization integrates and interweaves the competency-based processes of different workforce competencies into a multidisciplinary process to increase the efficiency with which they manage work dependencies (Competency Integration). When managers trust the capability of both the people and the competency-based processes they are using, they are ready to empower workgroups. The organization empowers workgroups with the autonomy to manage their work processes and perform some of their workforce activities (Empowered Workgroups).

At the Optimizing Level, workgroups continually improve their operating processes by improving the integration of the personal work processes used by their workgroup members (Continuous Capability Improvement). Lessons learned in improving a workgroup's operating processes are reviewed to determine if they constitute improvements to be adopted in the competency-based processes of one or more workforce competencies. Thus, practices at Maturity Level 5 seek to continually improve the integration and performance of work among individuals and workgroups.

5.2.3   Motivating and Managing Performance

At the Managed Level, the practices for motivating and managing performance are focused on individual performance in the context of the unit's committed work. Each unit establishes an environment that has adequate work resources and does not impede or distract from job performance (Work Environment). Performance objectives are established at both unit and individual levels (Performance Management). Periodic discussions are held about the performance of work to identify opportunities to improve it. Unacceptable performance is managed and recognition is provided for outstanding performance. A compensation strategy is defined that includes performance in making adjustments in compensation (Compensation). The compensation must be evaluated and adjusted for equity to ensure it provides a credible foundation for motivating performance and growth.

At the Defined Level, performance is managed in part as a level of capability in a workforce competency. The capability of a workforce competency community is defined in relation to levels of knowledge, skill, and process ability. The workforce practices established at the Managed Level are adapted to motivate the development of additional capability in one or more workforce competencies (Competency-Based Practices). In particular, the compensation system is adjusted to include growth in workforce competencies as a consideration in making adjustments to compensation. In addition, the organization establishes a set of graduated career opportunities designed to motivate and reward people for developing additional capability in their chosen workforce competencies (Career Development).

At the Predictable Level, the organization understands and controls performance quantitatively. Since the members of each competency community are performing similar competency-based processes, the organization can quantify the capability of these processes and compare current performance to past results (Quantitative Performance Management). This ability to quantify performance allows individuals and workgroups to develop quantitative expectations about their future performance that can be used for both planning and managing work. Individuals and workgroups use the measures emerging from the performance of their competency-based processes to evaluate their performance against expected results at the process event level. Analyzing these measures against past process performance affords greater prediction of future results and tighter control when corrective action needs to be taken.

At the Optimizing Level, the organization uses its quantitative process performance results to ensure that performance at all levels of the organization is aligned with organizational business objectives (Organizational Performance Alignment). Performance data is used to evaluate whether performance is aligned across individuals, workgroups, and units. The effect of workforce practices on performance is evaluated quantitatively to ensure these practices are motivating aligned performance. When necessary, corrective action is taken to bring performance objectives, quantitative process results, and the impact of workforce practices into alignment with organizational objectives.

5.2.4   Shaping the Workforce

The effort to shape the workforce to meet business needs begins at the Managed Level by establishing basic practices for recruiting, selecting among job candidates, and orienting people into new assignments (Staffing). The practices implemented at Maturity Level 2 help shape the workforce at the unit level by ensuring that people have the skills to perform the unit's committed work.

At the Defined Level, the organization begins shaping the workforce by identifying the workforce competencies required to achieve its strategic business objectives. The organization develops a strategic workforce plan by identifying the level of capability it needs in each workforce competency (Workforce Planning). Within each workforce competency, the organization plans for the workforce activities required to meet its capability objectives. Units are expected to contribute to accomplishing these strategic plans as they conduct their workforce activities. Thus, at Maturity Level 3, workforce activities established in the units at Maturity Level 2 are performed with an understanding of how they contribute to strategic objectives at Maturity Level 3.

At the Predictable Level, the organization quantifies the capability of its workforce and uses these data to manage its development (Organizational Capability Management). The organization tracks progress toward targeted capability levels in each of its workforce competencies and takes corrective action where necessary. The organization quantitatively evaluates the impact of its workforce practices on achieving the strategic workforce objectives established in its workforce plans.

At the Optimizing Level, the organization continually searches for innovative practices or technologies to improve the capability and motivation of its workforce (Continuous Workforce Innovation). Innovative practices or technologies are selected and evaluated in trial applications to determine if they can make measurable improvements. The organization has developed standard mechanisms for deploying changes and improvements across the organization. Thus, the continuous improvement of workforce capability is institutionalized at Maturity Level 5.

6

Interpreting the People CMM

6.1 Interpreting the Practices

Each process area in the People CMM describes a set of practices that, when implemented, accomplish the goals outlined for that process area. The intention in defining these practices is not to require or espouse a specific method of performing workforce practices, organizational structure, separation of responsibilities, or management approach. Rather, the intention is to describe the essential elements of an effective program for developing and motivating the workforce. The practices are intended to communicate principles that apply to a variety of organizations, are valid across a range of typical business activities, and will remain valid over time. Therefore, the approach is to describe the principles and leave implementation decisions up to each organization, according to its culture and its staff.

In describing practices, the People CMM seeks to delineate the "what" and not the "how." These practices describe the "whats" in broad terms so that organizations are left great leeway in creatively implementing the "hows." For example, the People CMM might indicate that individual performance should be reviewed periodically. However, it would not specify how often, what dimensions should be reviewed, who provides input, or how a performance discussion should be performed. Decisions about how practices should be implemented are left up to the organization.

Although the practices described in the People CMM are meant to be independent of any particular implementation, examples of specific practices are consistently used in elaborating the practices to improve clarity. These examples typically list numerous methods for implementing a practice or numerous issues an organization may have to address in implementing a practice. These examples are not intended to be prescriptive or exhaustive; however, they are merely included to provide informative assistance in interpreting a practice.

To provide workforce practices that apply to a wide range of situations, some of the practices are stated without many implementation details to allow flexibility. Throughout the practices, nonspecific phrases like "affected individuals," "adequate," "as appropriate," and "as needed" are used. The use of such nonspecific terms allows the widest possible interpretation and application of the practices. In many cases, examples are provided for nonspecific terms, at least for the first use of the term. These phrases may have different meanings for two organizations, for two units in a single organization, or for one unit at different points in its life cycle. Each unit or organization must interpret these nonspecific phrases for its own situation. These nonspecific phrases are used so that goals and practices can be interpreted in light of an organization's business objectives. Certain phrases and conventions are used to provide continuity and consistency among the process areas. The major phrases and conventions are described, arranged by category of practice, in the following sections.

6.1.1   Commitment to Perform

The Commitment to Perform practices describe the activities the organization must perform to ensure that the practices of a process area are established and will endure.

Policy

Policy statements generally refer to establishing, maintaining, and following a written, organizational policy for the practices of that process area. This emphasizes the connection between organizational commitment and the practices performed in workgroups and units. Policies typically do not provide implementation details, but merely commit the organization to comply with a set of guiding practices and behaviors in the area covered by the policy.

Organizational Coordination

An organizational role(s) is assigned responsibility for coordinating activities at the organizational level. This coordination role may involve defining common procedures; assisting units in defining their own procedures; reviewing unit-level activities for compliance with laws, regulations, policies, and the like; collecting and sharing experience across the organization; or providing advice, when asked. In some cases, these responsibilities for organizational coordination may be divided across multiple groups, such as competency ownership teams with responsibilities for organization-wide coordination within each workforce competency community.

6.1.2   Ability to Perform

The Ability to Perform practices describe the preconditions which must exist for the process area to be implemented and institutionalized.

Resources and Funding

An Ability to Perform practice reflects the need for adequate *resources* and *funding* for the activities covered by the process area. These resources and funding generally fall into five categories: adequate personnel, adequate funding, adequate time, access to special skills, and access to tools. Tools that may be of use in performing the activities of the process area are listed as examples. The term *funding* is used, rather than *budgets,* to emphasize that having a budget is not sufficient; funding should be appropriately expended on the intended purposes.

Preparation to Perform Responsibilities

The People CMM addresses an individual's preparation to perform the practices relevant to assigned responsibilities. This context is somewhat broader than might normally be considered when using the term *training*. Training is provided to make an individual or workgroup proficient through specialized instruction and practice. Training may include informal, as well as formal, vehicles for transferring knowledge and skills to the staff. While many organizations use classroom training to build the knowledge, skills, and process abilities of their employees, the People CMM also accommodates other techniques, including facilitated video, computer-aided instruction, mentoring and apprenticeship programs, guided self-study, and knowledge gained from experience. Preparation to perform one's responsibilities can be gained through training, mentoring, prior experience, or other forms of learning, but the individuals must possess the knowledge, skills, and process abilities necessary to perform their responsibilities.

Orientation

In some process areas, the members of the workforce need to understand the practices that will affect them, such as in Compensation and Performance Management. *Orientation* is used broadly to indicate that the level of knowledge or skills being transferred is less than would be expected to be transferred to someone who was being prepared to perform the practices. Orientation is an overview or introduction to a topic for people who oversee, work with, or are affected by the individuals responsible for performing in the topic area.

Defined and Documented

At Maturity Levels 3, 4, and 5, the workforce practices to be implemented must be *defined and documented* so that consistency can be achieved across the organization in implementing workforce practices. Thus, at Maturity Level 3 workforce practices begin to be treated as standard organizational processes.

Prerequisite Items

Some process areas require documents or materials to exist as inputs for the practices to be performed. For example, workforce competency descriptions and competency-based processes are prerequisites for Competency Development. In keeping with the People CMM philosophy of highlighting the vital few practices, not all prerequisite items are listed for each process area. The People CMM incorporates practices only for prerequisites that have been found to be particularly critical for implementing the process area.

6.1.3 Practices Performed

In contrast to the institutionalization practices, Practices Performed shows great structural variability, because the implementation activities for the process area vary in level of detail, organizational focus (e.g., unit or organization), and need for planning and documentation. The following are some generalizations.

Plans

Plans require management commitment, from the standpoint of both creating them and ensuring that they are followed. The practice for a plan requires that it be developed or revised and that the activities of the process area be based on it. Certain practices call for establishing and maintaining a strategy. For example, at Maturity Level 4, process areas that implement quantitative management activities only on selected practices require a quantitative management strategy. The practice for such a strategy also requires that it be developed or revised and that the activities of the process area be based on it.

According to a Documented Procedure

A *documented procedure* is usually necessary so that the individuals responsible for a task or activity are able to perform it repeatedly. Documented procedures are critical for learning from experience. Unless the procedures are documented, it is difficult for someone to determine exactly how results were achieved and what might bring better results. When used as a component of preparing responsible individuals, documented procedures contribute to greater consistency in learning and performing a workforce practice. The formality and level of detail of a documented procedure can vary significantly, from a hand-written desk procedure for a responsible individual, to a formal standard operating procedure used throughout the organization. The formality and level of detail depend on who will perform the task or activity (e.g., individual or workgroup), how often it will be performed, the importance and intended use of the results, the maturity level of the organization, and the intended recipients of the results.

Establish and Maintain

The People CMM includes practices and goals that *establish and maintain* specified artifact(s). This phrase connotes a meaning beyond its component terms; it includes its use and documentation as well as periodic updating. For example, "The organization establishes and maintains a documented policy for conducting its Performance Management activities" means that not only must a policy be formulated and documented, but also it must be used throughout the organization, and periodically reviewed and updated to remain current with the organization's changing conditions.

6.1.4   Measurement and Analysis

The Measurement and Analysis practices describe basic measurement activities that are necessary to determine status related to the Practices Performed. Measurements that are inherently part of the activities of the process area are described in the informative material included in the Practices Performed.

Status

Some measures need to be taken to indicate the implementation status of the practices the organization has chosen to implement to comply with its policy in a particular area. These measures typically concern such issues as the level or frequency of performance, the effort or cost of performance, and the breadth of the organization through which the practices have been implemented. They are measures that support management's tracking of compliance and performance.

Effectiveness

Some measures are collected to evaluate the *effectiveness* of the practices in use. In many cases, effectiveness measures are not collected for Maturity Level 2 process areas because differences among units in how practices are implemented will make it difficult to perform effectiveness analyses. However, the greater organization-wide consistency in implementing practices at Maturity Levels 3 through 5 provide a more effective foundation for evaluating the efficiency of the practices implemented. These measures allow an organization to determine whether corrective actions or improvements need to be made to practices to achieve fuller benefit from their implementation.

Aggregation of Unit Measures to the Organizational Level

Some information needs to be aggregated and analyzed at the organizational level in order to support the goals of a process area. For instance, compensation information needs to be aggregated and analyzed at the organizational level to support the organization's efforts in establishing and maintaining equity in its compensation system.

6.1.5   Verifying Implementation

The Verifying Implementation practices generally relate to verifying compliance with organizational policies and oversight by executive management.

Verifying Compliance

A responsible individual should verify that responsible individuals are performing appropriate practices in compliance with the organization's policies and stated values, and that these activities comply with relevant laws and regulations. This responsibility is a process assurance function that reports compliance to executive management and can identify needs for corrective action.

Executive Management Reviews

The primary purpose of periodic reviews by executive management is to provide awareness of, and insight into, workforce activities at an appropriate level of abstraction in a timely manner. The time between reviews should meet the needs of the organization and may be lengthy, as long as adequate mechanisms for reporting exceptions are available. The scope and content of executive management reviews will depend on which executive is involved in the review. Reviews by the executive responsible for all human resource activities of an organization are expected to occur on a different schedule, and address different topics, from a review by the chief executive of the organization. Executive management reviews would also be expected to cover different topics, or similar topics, at a higher level of abstraction than unit-level reviews.

Audit of Data Definitions and Use

The purpose of periodic audits of data definitions and use is to provide assurance that these data are defined appropriately, and that they are being used in the performance of workforce activities and are being protected according to organizational policies. Organizations may have to comply with privacy, security, or confidentiality requirements around certain human resources, workforce planning, performance, or competency data. Periodic audits provide mechanisms to ensure the correct definition and use of data.

6.2   Organizational Roles and Structure

Although the People CMM recommends practices that are independent of specific organizational structures and models, its practices consistently use terminology related to organizational structure and roles that may differ from those implemented in any specific organization. The following sections describe the various concepts related to organizational roles and structures that are necessary for interpreting the practices of the People CMM.

6.2.1   Organizational Roles

A *role* is a cluster of defined responsibilities that may be assumed by one or more individuals. A one-to-one correspondence between roles and individuals is not necessary. One person could perform multiple roles, or one individual could perform each role. Various individuals are responsible for an organization's workforce activities. These individuals include executive managers; managers at all levels, including workgroup leaders, line managers, and matrix managers; the individuals themselves; and the human resources function. The following descriptions of roles are frequently used in the practices.

Executive Manager
> An executive manager fulfills a management role at a level high enough in an organization that the primary focus is the long-term vitality of the organization, rather than operational issues related to specific products and services. An executive manager provides and protects resources for long-term improvement of the workforce processes. *Executive management,* as used in the People CMM, can denote any manager who satisfies the preceding description, up to and including the head of the whole organization. As used in the practices, the term *executive management* should be interpreted in the context of the process area and the units and organization under consideration. The intent is to include specifically those executive managers who are needed to fulfill the leadership and oversight roles essential to achieving the goals of the process area.

Manager
> A manager fulfills a role that encompasses providing technical and administrative direction and control to individuals performing tasks or activities within the manager's area of responsibility. The traditional functions of a manager include planning, resourcing, organizing, directing, and controlling work within an area of responsibility.

Individuals, Workforce
> Several terms are used in the People CMM to denote the individuals who perform the various roles required to execute the business of the organization. *Individuals* are those who are the focus or recipients of workforce practices and activities. Thus, while the people who report to a manager are the "individuals" affected by the workforce activities the manager performs, the manager is an "individual" affected by the workforce activities performed by the manager's supervisor. The *workforce* refers to the collection of individuals that comprise the organization. Since most managers are themselves

individuals affected by the workforce activities of their managers, managers are included when *workforce* is used. In some practices, the term *individuals* is meant to identify specific people in the organization when used in qualified and bounded expressions such as "responsible individuals," or "individuals responsible for improving."

Organizational Role(s) Assigned Responsibility for Processes

At the Managed Level, organizational role(s) are assigned responsibility for assisting and advising units in performing the practices of each process area. At the Defined Level and beyond, organizational role(s) are assigned responsibility for coordinating activities in a process area or a workforce competency across the organization. These responsible individuals, whether they are process owners or competency managers, may be members of the human resources function or they may be designated members of the organization itself. Regardless of their placement in the organizational structure, these individuals exercise organization-wide responsibilities for their assigned processes or workforce competencies. Examples of individuals who might be assigned responsibility for process- or competency-related activities include the following:

- Members of the human resources function
- Members of a training or development function
- Organizational competency management group

Human Resources Function, Member of the Human Resources Function

The human resources function is the collection of responsibilities in an organization that coordinates workforce practices and activities at the organizational level. They typically focus on devising practical, effective ways to manage employer-employee relations. Their responsibility is directed toward, but not limited to, the recruiting, selection, hiring, and training of employees and the formulation of policies, procedures, and relations with employees or their representatives. Generally, the concerns of the human resources function encompass recruiting and hiring practices, benefits, classification and compensation, employment, performance management, labor relations, staff services, and training and development, as well as facilitating the development of improved workforce practices. The scope of the responsibilities of the human resources group depends largely on the size and type of business of the organization. In the People CMM, the term *human resources* is intended to imply any staff function responsible for the implementation of workforce practices in a particular area of concern, even if the responsible individual(s) does not reside in a Human Resources department. The human resources function also shares the responsibility for verification and measurement of the organization's workforce activities with management and serves in a quality assurance role for the organization's workforce processes.

Throughout an organization's process improvement efforts, the human resources function maintains these common administrative roles. However, some aspects of the role of the human resources function change as the organization and its staff change as a result of improvements in workforce capabilities. For example, as the organization's workforce capability increases, the human resources function shares with management and individuals the responsibility for process and individual improvement.

6.2.2   Organizational Structure

The People CMM does not specify organizational structure. It uses an organization's existing structure and provides a framework for the organization to improve its capability to make use of and develop its workforce, thus improving its workforce capability. For example, the People CMM does not dictate an organizational structure or placement for the human resources function. See Section 6.2.1 for a discussion of the roles that may influence the organizational structure of the human resources function. Other organizational factors, such as those discussed in Section 6.6.1, affect the size and structure of the human resources function.

The fundamental concepts of organization, unit, and workgroup must be understood to properly interpret the practices of the People CMM. The following paragraphs define the use of these concepts in the People CMM.

Organization

An *organization* is an entity in a company or other collective structure (e.g., major sector of a corporation, government agency, branch of service, or nonprofit entity). It has an identifiable executive manager(s) who has the responsibility for the operations, practices, and performance of the organization. Most frequently, an organization is contained within a single site and has a local human resources function, but this is not always true. An organization is the entity in which an improvement program is applied.

Unit

A *unit* is a single, well-defined organizational component (e.g., a department, a section, a project, etc.) within an organization that typically has an individual who is assigned management or supervisory responsibility for its activities. The term *unit* is used to refer to any organizational entity that is accountable to a specified individual (usually a manager) responsible for accomplishing a set of performance objectives that can be met only through collective action. A workgroup may constitute the lowest-level unit, but the lowest-level units often consist of several workgroups. *Unit* is a recursive concept; units may be composed from other units cascading down the organization. For instance, a division may be a unit consisting of departments, each of which may be a unit consisting of programs, each of which may be a unit consisting of projects, and so on.

Workgroup

A *workgroup* is a collection of people who work closely with each other on highly interdependent tasks to achieve shared objectives. A workgroup reports to a responsible individual who may be involved in managing its day-to-day activities. In the People CMM, an *empowered workgroup* refers to a workgroup that is granted a level of autonomy in managing and performing its work and may perform some of its own workforce practices. Not all workgroups develop into empowered workgroups.

Empowered Workgroup

An *empowered workgroup* is a workgroup whose members exercise considerable autonomy in managing and conducting their business activities. They may also be granted a level of responsibility for performing some of the workforce activities internal to the workgroup.

6.3   Implementation Issues

6.3.1   Time Horizons

A variety of time scales are present within the practices of the People CMM. Some practices require awareness of ongoing performance, while others address performance or review cycles that may be monthly, quarterly, or annual. Time cycles for unit performance are typically cycles of one year or less, while time cycles or planning horizons for competency-based human capital management are typically much longer, stretching to three to five years. Many of the practices at the Managed Level are often implemented in shorter cycles, such as a fiscal year or operational budget cycles, while higher maturity practices may be implemented over a longer period of time, such as the strategic planning horizon for workforce plans.

6.3.2   Levels of Organizational Structure

Practices are implemented at, and involve individuals from, different levels of organizational structure in the organization. Some practices are implemented by, or are the responsibility of, individuals, while others are unit-level practices. Other practices cut across competencies or across the entire organization. It is important to understand the organizational levels involved, and to appropriately plan implementation and institutionalization support for each affected level. These considerations also apply in performing SCAMPI with People CMM appraisals, as appraisal teams will encounter mixed goals [Radice 05c], where the appraisal evidence will come from multiple levels of the organization's structure.

6.3.3   Evolving Practice Implementations across Maturity Levels

The organization's implementations of practices evolve at different maturity levels. A practice that is implemented within a process area at a given maturity level will transform or be implemented in a more robust manner at a higher maturity level. For example, many fundamental human resources practices are implemented at the Managed Level. In the Competency-Based Practices process area at the Defined Level many of these practices are enhanced to address the issues of workforce competencies and competency development. Figure 6.1 presents a view of how practices transform in the Developing Individual Capability process area thread.

6.3.4   Implementing a System of Practices

The People CMM describes a system of practices. It has been noted that "it is the combination of practices that matters rather than simply doing one or two well" [DTI 03]. This stems from a stream of research in human resources that suggests that "bundles" of interrelated and internally consistent practices are necessary to improve organizational performance. In fact,

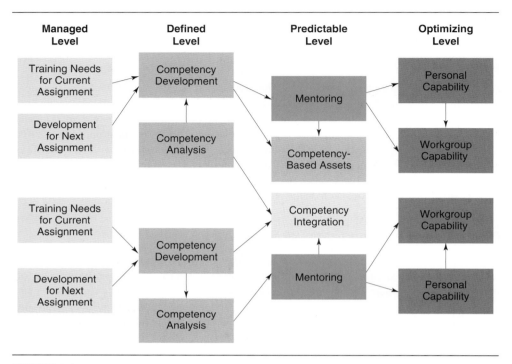

FIGURE 6.1
Developing competency and capability across maturity levels

these practices are necessary to reinforce each other, and to build complementary capabilities in the organization. The maturity levels of the People CMM are one form of bundle of related practices that reinforce each other, sustain development of workforce capability, and have been shown to lead to improved performance. While implementers can pick and choose the practices they wish to implement, the full power of the combinations of practices comes from implementing a set of consistent and coherent practices.

6.4   Institutionalization Issues

Capability Maturity Models are unique among process standards in providing guidance for institutionalizing the practices recommended in the model. The history of improvement programs is replete with failures that were caused when the performance of improved practices decayed over time. This decay often occurred because the organization had not provided the support necessary to sustain the use of the practices over time or through changes in executives, in managers, or in business conditions. The People CMM provides categories of practices that establish the conditions required to institutionalize practices: Commitment to Perform, Ability to Perform, Measurement and Analysis, and Verifying Implementation. Some of these practices exhibit different attributes at different maturity levels.

6.4.1   Executive Management Responsibilities

A common reason why workforce development or human capital management programs fail is lack of executive management leadership. That being said, those responsible for facilitating these programs are often hard-pressed to specify exactly what they expect from executives. This section addresses 12 critical actions executive management should take to ensure the success of People CMM-based improvement programs.

1. **Take personal responsibility.** Executives do not deliver products or services to customers. Managers and their staffs do that. Executives build organizations that deliver products and services to customers, and this responsibility cannot be delegated. At the core of Watts Humphrey's Process Maturity Framework that underlies the People CMM is a unique model of organizational change and development. Since the responsibility for organizational transformation rests in the executive office, the People CMM is a tool for executives to use in improving the performance of their workforce. The People CMM will transform not only workforce practices, but also the organization's culture and the way business results are attained. Executives should not launch a People CMM-based improvement program until they are willing to become personally accountable for its success—or failure.

2. **Set realistic goals.** Executives must initiate improvement actions with a clear statement of the issues driving change and the objectives to be achieved. Slogans such as "Level 2 by quarter 2" do little more than reinforce the poor methods for setting performance objectives that Level 2 was designed to eliminate. If the objectives are unrealistic, the improvement program will be just one more of the organization's failed initiatives. The improvement program must model the behaviors it wants the organization to adopt, especially well-analyzed performance objectives for committed work. Schedules for attaining maturity levels should result from performance objectives that balance the committed work underlying workforce development with the resources and time required to achieve them. Rewards and bonuses should be based on the accomplishment of the committed work, rather than arbitrary dates for appraisal results.

3. **Establish a People CMM-based improvement program.** People CMM-based organizational transformation must be managed, as would any successful project. Executives must assign responsibility for managing the program, provide funding and resources, expect periodic status reports, and measure results. People assigned to lead various components of the improvement program must be good role models. Executives should ask frequent questions about plans for the improvement program and the assumptions underlying them. The competency descriptions, competency-based process diagrams, workforce planning templates, workforce measures, and other artifacts produced through the improvement program become organizational assets. They should be treated as products, albeit for internal use, and be produced with the same discipline used in producing any other product.

4. **Manage change.** How many initiatives can dance on the head of a unit manager? Many organizations have multiple improvement programs underway simultaneously. In the initial stages of these programs, the unit manager is the person most affected and often is inundated by the number of changes required. Executives must determine the amount of change the organization can absorb, prioritize the changes to be made, and shield the organization from improvement overkill. The good news is that some improvement programs such as Six Sigma, CMMI, and the People CMM can be synthesized and managed in an integrated manner, since they evolved from the concepts initiated by Shewhart and Deming.

5. **Align management.** Human Resources and related groups have little power to enforce improvements or change management behavior. If middle managers resist adopting better workforce practices, only executives can force them to align with the program. Executives must build consensus among managers on the objectives and tactics for implementing improved workforce practices and hold them accountable for achieving these objectives. Measuring the progress of the improvement program and the underlying workforce practices gives visibility to support this accountability. In particular, middle managers must help build the skills of the unit managers who report to them to effectively implement the organization's workforce practices.

6. **Align incentives.** Executives must ensure that incentives are aligned with the planned objectives of the improvement program and do not send mixed messages about the behaviors the organization values. Incentives must shift from rewarding those who achieve business results at the expense of the workforce, to rewarding those most effective at achieving results through developing the skills and competencies of their people. Rewards should go to those who are strong role models of developing the people who report to them. Incentives must send a message that management values contributions to building a capable workforce just as much as it values individual performance.

7. **Establish policies and empower Human Resources.** Policies that merely regurgitate goals from People CMM process areas represent a lost opportunity for executives to communicate their expectations for behavior in their organizations. Once policies are established, executives need visibility into the organization's compliance. Human Resources and related groups have influence only to the extent that executives attend to their status reports and address noncompliance. One great value of a human resources function is their ability to mentor unit managers and others on how to perform workforce practices that truly support compliance. Thus, they both audit and aid compliance.

8. **Focus on performance.** If a People CMM-based improvement program is initiated with a focus on a process area such as Staffing, then only managers who have open positions will be engaged. However, all unit managers are responsible for the performance of those who report to them. By focusing on Performance Management early, the improvement program not only engages all unit managers, but also begins to see benefits from improved performance. This early focus on performance emphasizes that People CMM-based improvement must ultimately be evaluated against organizational performance.

9. **Involve the workforce.** The People CMM begins the empowerment of the workforce by involving them in setting performance objectives at the Managed Level, and it in-

creases their responsibility at each subsequent maturity level. Executives must understand and encourage this cultural transition. They must also ensure that the workforce is involved in analyzing and defining workforce competencies since they are the best source for identifying and updating the knowledge, skills, and process abilities required. In addition, the insights of the workforce are critical in determining what development help they need and what types of incentives are the most motivating. The workforce is also a critical contributor in performing trial implementations of proposed improvements to workforce practices.

10. **Review status.** Executives own the organization's rate of improvement. Business reviews should focus not only on work status and financial results, but also on the progress being made in adopting workforce practices and of any impending issues or risks. Executives emphasize their commitment to improved workforce practices through active engagement in reviews and use of measurements. Consequently, they should add indicators of relevant workforce practices to their dashboards.

11. **Replace laggards.** Human Resources and related groups own responsibility for assisting improvement of workforce practices with the innovators, early adopters, and early and late majorities. Executives own the problem of laggards, especially if they are in management. For an improvement program to succeed, executives must be willing to remove even friends for failure to make progress. Successful organizational change programs often end up with different management teams than the ones they started with.

12. **Never relent.** True leadership begins under stress. With all the pressures generated by demanding business schedules and cost cutting, executives must nevertheless stand firm in driving the improvements to the workforce practices that they know the organization needs. If they relent under pressure, the organization learns the art of excuses. The ultimate appraisal of workforce capability or organizational maturity is determined by which practices the organization refuses to sacrifice under grinding pressure.

Executives can assume other responsibilities in supporting improvement of their workforce practices. Nevertheless, these 12 responsibilities have proven critical since they require executive authority and represent acts of leadership around which the People CMM-based improvement program can galvanize. Executives with little experience in organizations with disciplined workforce practices are understandably concerned about risking their career on practices that have not contributed significantly to their advancement. Fortunately, there is a growing body of data and community of mature organizations to attest that faith in People CMM-based practices is well placed. It does not take leadership to follow the trodden path. It takes leadership to pursue the promise of new ways, develop enhanced managerial competencies, and develop new levels of workforce capability.

6.4.2   Maturity Level 2 Procedures versus Maturity Level 3 Defined Practices

At Maturity Level 2, the practice in Commitment to Perform (typically Commitment 1) that concerns establishing an organizational policy describes high-level guidance for conducting the practices performed in the process area. The policy often mandates that procedures be developed for implementing the practices of a process area and it may indicate some of the functions or activities to be covered in the procedures. However, it does not specify the details of the procedures to be developed for implementing the practices in the process area. Different managers or units may implement the practices in different ways using different procedures, provided that the procedures they use comply with the guidance provided in the policy.

At Maturity Levels 3, 4, and 5, the final practice included in the Ability to Perform category indicates that the practices and procedures to be implemented should be defined and documented. The objective is to specify these practices as standard organizational processes that can be learned and applied consistently by any responsible individual in the organization. The transition from Maturity Level 2 to high levels of maturity involves evolving from local procedures within units to standard organizational processes, practices, and procedures. Procedures mandated by policies at Maturity Level 3 (Commitment to Perform) would typically be implemented at the organizational level and would become part of the defined and documented practices provided to responsible individuals as guidance in performing their workforce activities.

6.4.3   Defined, but Not Quantified or Optimized

The People CMM describes a system of practices that are required by the institutionalization goal to be defined and documented. The institutionalization goal in each process area at Maturity Levels 4 and 5 requires that the practices implemented in achieving the goals of the process area be "performed as defined organizational processes" (a Maturity Level 3 attribute), but not quantified for predictability or optimized through continual improvement.

At Maturity Level 4, the organization is able to predict its capability for performing work because it can quantify the capability of its workforce and of the competency-based processes they use in performing their assignments. The practices that are quantified at Maturity Level 4 are most frequently competency-based processes. Some workforce practices may be quantified in order to determine their effect on the capability of the workforce or of the competency-based processes being performed. However, this quantification is not required of all workforce practices, only those most likely to affect capability results. The selection of these workforce practices is best handled through selection procedures in the relevant Practices Performed, rather than as a requirement in the institutionalization goal.

At Maturity Level 5, some workforce practices may be selected for improvement. However, not all workforce practices are required to undergo continual improvement. Therefore, the goals of the process areas at Maturity Levels 3, 4, and 5 require that practices be defined. However, further improvement of these practices through quantification or optimization is the province of actions taken in the Practices Performed at Maturity Levels 4 and 5 to achieve the implementation goals of the process areas.

6.5   Maturity Level Concerns

The process areas within the maturity levels are composed of systems of practices that describe an evolution of organizational capability. Understanding these relationships and how lower maturity practices provide a foundation for higher maturity practices is essential in applying the People CMM.

6.5.1   Maturity Level 3 Is Enough!

Section 3.2 describes the evolution of the organization's capability as it matures. Some organizations have chosen to end their maturity growth at the Defined Level. That is, they believe they have achieved a stable operating state after having defined their workforce competencies.

However, Maturity Level 3 is not a stable state. Without constant updating and renewal, the definition of the organization's workforce competencies will become obsolete, and responsible individuals will stop using them when performing workforce activities. This degrades the organization's capability back to the Managed Level, and eventually it may devolve to the Initial Level. The organization and its business environment constantly change. The maturity level most capable of helping the organization manage change is the Optimizing Level, where change management is treated as a standard business process. The decision about which maturity level to attain is an executive management decision, but management should not be deceived that the organization has achieved a steady operating state at any level.

Continuing to pursue higher levels of maturity can be a natural outcome of achieving a level and wondering how to exploit the opportunities for improved results. Once an organization achieves Maturity Level 2, managers will start requesting standard descriptions of skills for position descriptions, for assessing training needs, for evaluating performance, and for similar responsibilities. These standard descriptions are exactly what Competency Analysis provides and it saves managers time in performing their workforce activities, while providing excellent reference material on career and promotional opportunities to the workforce. Similarly, once the workforce is using competency-based processes, the next logical steps are to measure and ultimately improve them. When the organization is focused on business benefit, it typically finds that higher levels of maturity allow it to better exploit the opportunities afforded by accomplishments at lower maturity levels.

6.5.2   Level Fever

One of the great dangers in using Capability Maturity Models as guides for improvement is "level fever." When an organization succumbs to level fever, attaining the maturity level becomes more important than achieving the business benefits attained through improved practices. Consequently, preparing for a formal appraisal becomes more important than ensuring that the practices implemented provide useful results.

Striving for a level has both benefits and risks. Since the attainment of a maturity level represents a significant achievement for the organization, everyone is motivated to implement the full set of improved practices. The exhilaration of achieving a level motivates the organization to pursue the next level. However, the organization must ensure that the practices implemented in pursuit of higher maturity levels are creating beneficial changes. Otherwise, the organization is adding bureaucracy that will have to be dismantled eventually.

Level fever is most often created when maturity level designations become part of business or contract award evaluations. The use of maturity ratings has been confined mostly to the use of the CMM for Software (SW-CMM) or CMM Integrated (CMMI) to evaluate the capability of software or system development contractors. However, the People CMM may become part of a competitive evaluation process when the capability and longevity of a workforce are critical to contract success, such as in outsourcing.

When maturity ratings are part of the competitive evaluation process, tremendous pressure is placed on an appraisal team. Weaknesses or opportunities for improvement that should have been raised in the appraisal may get suppressed because of the substantial revenues at stake. Weak practices can be evaluated as strengths so as not to affect the eventual maturity rating. Under these circumstances, maturity ratings can lose their credibility, and concerns over weak appraisals may incorrectly get translated into concerns regarding the validity of the People CMM as a guide for improvement.

A better use of maturity models for evaluating suppliers treats the model as a method for risk analysis. That is, the contracting organization evaluates candidate suppliers against the process areas at a targeted maturity level and compares their profiles of strengths and weaknesses against the goals of each process area. The contracting organization then determines which supplier's profile of practices presents the fewest risks, and incorporates these results as input into the contract award decision. Thus, the maturity profile, not the maturity level, is included with cost and other important decision criteria. In fact, the winning supplier can be given an incentive in the contract to make improvements to the weaknesses identified in an appraisal.

6.5.3   Skipping Maturity Levels

Some organizations try to skip to higher maturity levels by implementing measurement, empowerment, or continuous improvement practices without building the infrastructure of practices provided by lower maturity levels of the model. Although skipping levels is tempting, experience indicates that it usually leads to a failed improvement program. In fact, it can actually damage the organization if the workforce builds expectations for changes that are not fully deployed when the program unravels.

Consider a situation in which an organization is trying to implement a sophisticated compensation scheme to tie bonuses to business results at the team, unit, and organizational levels. If the organization has not established a foundation of equitable compensation, measurable performance objectives, timely performance feedback, and open communication of business results, the scheme risks failure.

Similarly, consider an organization that declares its intention to empower teams. If managers have not developed trust in the capability of the people and the processes they are using, managers will continue to exert control over matters that workgroups believe are under their authority. These situations create frustration and cynicism in the workforce. These problems could have been avoided by first developing the foundation of lower maturity practices required to make the higher maturity practices credible and effective.

Skipping levels is counterproductive because each maturity level forms a necessary foundation upon which the next level can be built. The People CMM was designed to develop the supporting foundation needed to ensure that higher-level practices can achieve their full impact on improving workforce capability. Processes without the proper foundation fail at the very point they are needed most—when under stress—and they provide no basis for future improvement.

6.5.4   Ignoring Process Areas

Some organizations may want to declare a process area as being nonapplicable in their environments. Process areas should not be dropped from concern hastily. In the extreme, this practice can result in dropping process areas that the organization finds difficult to implement, regardless of the implications for other process areas or for the organization's benefits from their ongoing improvement program. Because these process areas form systems of mutually supporting practices, it is difficult to identify which process area is an obvious candidate for being ignored.

As an example, consider the Competency Integration process area at the Predictable Level. The Competency Integration process area is focused on improving the efficiency and agility of interdependent work by integrating the process abilities of different workforce competencies. An organization might argue that it has only one area of workforce competency and, therefore, Competency Integration is irrelevant to its business practices. However, such organizations often integrate people from their support staffs into workgroups dominated by a single workforce competency. For instance, a marketing person may be integrated with a service delivery group. If these situations are frequent, the collective implementation of practices in Competency Integration may offer substantial improvements in operational costs, productivity, or cycle time.

In general, all process areas should be treated as relevant to an organization unless no appropriate application can be found for the practices of the process area. Such an analysis should consider the process area not only as a stand-alone entity, but also in terms of related process areas. The threads that link process areas across maturity levels were presented in Figure 5.1. Ignoring a process area may put the effectiveness of other higher-maturity process areas in its thread at risk by removing critical foundational practices. Similarly, the effectiveness of other process areas at the same maturity level may be affected because, when a process area is ignored, a critical component of the system of practices typically installed at that maturity level is missing. For example, Competency Analysis is not only essential to support the implementation of other Defined Level process areas, such as Workforce Planning, Competency Development, Career Development, and Competency-Based Practices, but it also provides a foundation for practices at higher maturity levels, including Competency-Based Assets and Continuous Capability Improvement. The People CMM is designed as a system of practices, and the integrity of the system is critical to its successful implementation.

6.5.5   Implementing Practices out of Maturity Level Sequence

Although skipping entire maturity levels will eventually hamper an improvement program, the model does not restrict an organization from implementing a workforce practice at a maturity level higher than the level currently being pursued. If the organization believes that it can derive substantial benefit from a practice several levels higher because it addresses immediate needs or problems, then the organization might elect to proceed with implementation. However, the organization must be cautious of the risks introduced by the absence of any foundational practices at lower levels on which the higher maturity practice might have ordinarily been built.

The maturity levels in the People CMM describe characteristic patterns of practices and behaviors. Each level forms a foundation on which an organization can build workforce practices effectively and efficiently at succeeding maturity levels. However, an organization can occasionally benefit from implementing processes described at a higher maturity level even though it has not satisfied all the process areas at a lower maturity level. Once the foundation of supporting practices has been laid, a high-maturity practice has a much higher likelihood of successful deployment, even if other lower maturity practices are still being implemented. That is, if practices critical to the performance of the higher maturity practice have not been implemented, then its effectiveness may be at risk.

Even if the foundational practices are in place, a high-maturity practice may also be at risk if the culture has not evolved sufficiently to provide enduring support for the practice. For instance, practices involving the type of empowerment instituted at Maturity Level 4 may be at risk if the prevailing culture is shaped by trying to implement basic management responsibility and control at Maturity Level 2. For this reason, organizations should be conservative in the number of high-maturity practices it introduces out of order. Failed practices cast doubt over the effectiveness of the entire improvement program.

The People CMM should not be interpreted as prohibiting practices or activities from higher maturity levels that the organization finds beneficial. For example, workgroup empowerment practices are not discussed in the People CMM until the Predictable Level, yet organizations at the Initial Level may have implemented self-managed teams for some activities. Similarly, a less mature organization may be able to train its workforce in areas that would correspond to workforce competencies (Defined Level), provide team-based incentives (Predictable Level), or use formal mentoring programs (Predictable Level). The organization should evaluate the effectiveness of these practices in light of the risks created by and cracks in the foundation of practices that should be implemented to support them.

If the organization sees the opportunity to benefit from a higher maturity practice and can support its performance, then the organization should implement it. However, the ability to implement practices from higher maturity levels does not imply that maturity levels can be skipped without risk. There is risk in implementing practices without the proper foundation being developed at lower maturity levels. For example, the team-building literature contains many examples of programs to empower teams that failed [Mohrman 95]. Some of these failures occurred because the foundation in communication skills, participatory culture, and adjustments to compensation practices had not been properly developed. Similarly, many innovative motivational practices fail to work effectively in an environment where there are no objective performance criteria or where basic performance management practices are performed inconsistently. Likewise, rushing to implement skills-based management systems that constitute an implementation of the organization's workforce competencies at the Defined Level can prove ineffective when the organization has no history of identifying skill needs for training or selection at the Managed Level.

The maturity framework as represented in the People CMM is a resilient and proven guide for improving an organization's capability. It must be implemented with common sense and good management judgment. It is intended to be neither exclusive nor exhaustive in guiding improvements to workforce practices. Its guidance must be adapted to each organization, but its principles have proven effective over a large range of organizational types and sizes.

6.5.6   Implementing People CMM Practices with CMMI Continuous Representation

The People CMM is presented only in a staged representation [Chrissis 06]. After lengthy review of the literature and experience gathered from implementers of programs to improve workforce practices, it was determined that these programs often fail when workforce practices are not introduced as a system of practices or in reinforcing bundles, but rather are deployed in isolation. Studies have indicated that "it is the combination of practices that matters rather than simply doing one or two well" [DTI 03]. For instance, efforts to install empowered teams are likely to fail if compensation practices continue to reward individual performance without recognizing contributions to team performance and team success.

While CMMI can be implemented using a continuous representation, the People CMM, because of its interconnected systems of practices, should only be used in implementing practices in a staged representation. While specific higher-level process areas can be implemented or appraised for implementation progress separately, the People CMM is intended to be implemented maturity level by maturity level. Research has shown that successful human capital implementations require the concurrent implementation of "bundles" of related practices. These concepts are captured within the People CMM as process areas within a specific maturity level.

Although skipping entire maturity levels will eventually hamper an improvement program, the model does not restrict attention to specific process areas that may be important to the organization., as long as there is recognition that failure to successfully implement supporting (or interconnected) process areas may degrade or impact successful implementation of a desired outcome.

Workforce issues identified in CMMI may cause adjustments to the implementations of workforce practices from the People CMM so that the organization may take full advantage of the power of both frameworks—CMMI and the People CMM. These workforce issues may also point out opportunities where the organization needs to implement a set of related practices across a given People CMM maturity level in order to better sustain the accomplishments driven by CMMI-based process improvements. Organizations should remember that the goal of software process improvement is often not to improve process, but to provide business benefits [Staples 08].

6.6   Applying Professional Judgment

Professional judgment is critical to informed use of the People CMM. A model is a simplified representation of the world. Capability Maturity Models (CMMs) contain the essential elements of effective processes for one or more disciplines. Like other CMMs, the People CMM provides high-level guidance for developing the organization's process (i.e., "what" should be implemented), but it does not provide a detailed description of the practices the organization will implement (i.e., "how" it should be implemented in any given organizational setting). A CMM specifies the practices that could be implemented to achieve its goals, but it does not specify details about how these practices should be implemented in the organization.

6.6.1   Organizational Factors

Organizational factors, such as size, regional and organizational culture, and business objectives, must be considered when implementing and institutionalizing the practices of the People CMM. When applying the People CMM in a particular context, a reasonable interpretation must be made of how these practices might be implemented. The People CMM must be interpreted flexibly when applying it to smaller organizations or unusual business circumstances so that unreasonable or needlessly bureaucratic activities are not implemented. For instance, small organizations may implement the practices without the infrastructure that large organizations need. A small organization may have one individual filling the multiple roles of president, regional sales manager, human resources manager, product evangelist, and janitor; in a larger organization, one or more specialists may fill each of these roles.

Another organizational factor that should be considered when using the People CMM as guidance or in an appraisal setting is the composition of the workforce. Individuals have many different relationships with an organization. Some are full-time employees, others may be part-time or casual employees, other individuals may be contractors or other forms of affiliates, and other individuals may be on loan or visiting from another organization. In applying the practices to these various categories of individual, decisions must be made about how to appropriately apply these practices to all individuals in each of these categories. For some individuals, such as certain contract employees, selected practices relating to their training and development, as well as practices relating to their compensation, may not be the responsibility of the organization that they are currently supporting, but rather are the responsibility of their originating organization.

Professional judgment must be used when interpreting the practices and how they contribute to the goals of a process area. In particular, the process areas may map in complex ways to the practices and associated activities in an organization. The process areas describe a set of interrelated objectives that all organizations should achieve, regardless of their size, locations, or products. The practices contained in process areas constitute recommendations for achieving the objectives that have proven effective in many types of organizations, and therefore are expected to work in most organizations that implement the People CMM. Although process areas depict behavior that should characterize any organization, the practices of the People CMM must be interpreted in light of an organization's structure, the nature of its workforce, the organization's business environment, and other circumstances.

6.6.2   Goodness of Workforce Practices

Since there are several ways to implement most workforce practices, should the "goodness" of a workforce practice be evaluated during an appraisal of an organization's workforce practices? The People CMM does not place "goodness" requirements on workforce practices, although it does establish minimal criteria for a "reasonable" practice in some situations. The objective of the People CMM is to implement practices that provide a foundation for systematic improvement of organizational capability and performance over time, based on the organization's business needs. When such practices are put into place, the organization adjusts them to improve their effectiveness. These adjustments must be performed with an understanding of how the practices work in a particular business context, rather than by an externally imposed notion of "goodness."

"Goodness" is a matter of both interpretation and degree. Complying with a reasonable practice does not necessarily imply that the practice is efficient in achieving its purpose or that the unit or organization is guaranteed good performance. There may be many factors influencing both organization and unit success whose impact masks the benefit of a workforce practice. For example, a successful unit that builds a product no one buys is a business failure, regardless of how well the workforce is trained. Accordingly, we discourage evaluation of a workforce practice for "goodness," because it is beyond the scope of most appraisal teams to make that judgment.

What, then, are the criteria for a *reasonable* workforce practice? A reasonable practice is one that contributes to building workforce capability under most circumstances. For example, if a manager took people in the unit out for a beer after work on Fridays to implement a practice for seeking their opinions on working conditions (which is a practice that might support the goals of the Communication and Coordination process area) would that constitute a reasonable practice? It could certainly be documented and consistently followed. Some might argue that it is effective for loosening people up to talk about things that concern them. However, "taking the unit out for a beer" would typically not be judged a reasonable practice for seeking input on working conditions, because in many locations it leaves the organization legally liable if a participating member of the unit were to have an automobile accident on the way home. Since many people like to go straight home after work or do not drink, going for a beer after work may not guarantee that everyone has had an opportunity to express opinions on working conditions. Professional judgment is necessary to make such distinctions about the reasonableness of a practice.

Nothing in the People CMM is intended to restrict or override sound executive judgment in designing and managing an organization. The People CMM is designed as a tool that guides the implementation of practices to assist the organization in achieving its business objectives. Organizations will always live in the midst of tension between implementing the full set of practices described in the People CMM and tailoring what they feel to be a minimally adequate set of practices for their organization. The resolution of this tension lies in the goals of each process area. Goals are the requirements, and organizations should insist on implementing an adequate set of practices for achieving the goals. The practices included in the People CMM provide a description of the practices they would expect to find in a reasonable, adequate set.

7

Using the People CMM

7.1 Uses of the People CMM

The People CMM helps organizations to

- characterize the maturity of their workforce practices,
- guide a program of continuous workforce development,
- set priorities for improvement actions,
- integrate workforce development with process improvement, and
- establish a culture of professional excellence.

The value of the People CMM is in the way that organizations use it. The People CMM can be applied by an organization in three primary ways:

1. As a guide in planning and implementing improved human capital management practices
2. As a guide for improving organizational standards
3. As a standard for analyzing and appraising an organization's implemented workforce practices

The People CMM is being used around the globe. The Version 1 technical report was first released in 1995 [Curtis 95]. The first edition of the People CMM book, containing Version 2 of the model, has been published in English [Curtis 02a], and in two editions in India [Curtis 02b, Curtis 07], in China [Curtis 03b], and in Japan [Curtis 03a]. The People CMM has been translated into Japanese, Spanish, and Kannada, the language in the state of Karnataka in India, where Bengaluru (formerly Bangalore) is located.

The types of organizations that have used the People CMM are shown in Figure 7.1. These organizations range in size from small organizations of fewer than 100 individuals, to organizations spanning the globe and employing approximately 29,000 individuals at locations in 32 countries across 5 continents [Radice 05a, Radice 05c].

Organization Types

Business Process Outsourcing	Information Technology
Hospitality	Consulting
Construction	Defense Contractors
Insurance	Pharmaceuticals
Government Agencies	Defense Agencies
Energy/Utilities	Software Development
Banking/Financial Services	Management Information Systems

FIGURE 7.1
Types of organizations using the People CMM

7.1.1   Early Uses of the People CMM

Because much of the early experience in applying the People CMM was in the software and information technology industries, this section highlights numerous examples from those industries. However, the lessons learned in these industries should be relevant to most other segments of industry and government as well. Since its release in 1995, the People CMM has been used throughout the United States, Canada, Europe, Asia, Africa, Australia, and India to guide and conduct organizational improvement activities. It has been used worldwide by both small and large commercial organizations, and by government organizations. As of 2001, adoption rates for the People CMM appeared to be highest in India, where high turnover and increasing salary pressures are forcing software organizations to address workforce issues. In India, the People CMM has been referred to as the "weapon of choice against the brain drain" [Crane 01].

Organizations in North America, Europe, and Australia that have used the People CMM include Lockheed Martin [Lockheed 99], Boeing [Porter 01, Vu 01], BAE SYS-TEMS[Chaffee 96], Ericsson [Martín-Vivaldi 99], IBM Global Services [Paulk 01a, 01b], Novo Nordisk IT A/S (NNIT) [Curtis 00], Citibank, the U.S. Army, and Advanced Information Services Inc. (AIS), the winner of the 1999 Institute of Electrical and Electronics Engineers (IEEE) Computer Society/SEI Software Process Achievement (SPA) Award [Ferguson 99; Paulk 01a, 01b; Seshagiri 00].

7.1.2   People CMM Use and Appraisals in Recent Years

Use of the People CMM continues across the globe. Formal organizational assessments and appraisals using the People CMM as a benchmark have been conducted in the United States, Asia, Europe, and Australia. People CMM appraisals have been conducted in the United States, India, Canada, the Netherlands, Germany, China, Australia, Denmark, England, Korea, Malaysia, and the Philippines.

Organizations that have used the People CMM to implement improvement typically point to one or more of several major reasons to initiate these efforts.

- The organization wanted to establish a baseline understanding of its workforce practices to enable appropriate improvement or to meet specified organizational objectives, such as becoming or being recognized as an "Employer of Choice."

- The organization needed to cope with the results of an organizational merger, transition, or change in ownership by providing insights into workforce-related issues arising from this organizational change. In many of these cases, the organization is dealing with issues arising from blended cultures and previously divergent workforce practices, and wishes to examine the current capability of the organization in light of its merged policies, procedures, and processes.

- The organization was working to sustain or accelerate attainment of higher maturity levels via solid workforce practices. Often these organizations are dealing with sustaining organizational process improvement activities, such as attaining and sustaining higher CMMI levels, integrating multiple organizational functions (e.g., systems, software, hardware, financial), and aligning the performance of multiple teams, perhaps cross-functional or multidisciplinary project teams.

- The organization is using competency systems to ensure the availability of a skilled and capable workforce.

- The organization is working to sustain or enhance its performance with a focus on future workforce needs and capabilities to meet its strategic plan.

- The organization is using competency systems to ensure the availability of a skilled and capable workforce, develop competent replacements for an aging workforce, and support retention of corporate knowledge assets.

- The organization is updating lapsed or expired People CMM appraisal results. With the introduction of the SCAMPI with People CMM appraisal method, appraisal results now have a limited duration before they lapse.

A number of case studies of People CMM adoption and use are presented in Chapter 10. In addition to the reasons outlined in the preceding list, some of the reasons for applying the People CMM that are seen in these cases or other adoption experiences include the following.

- In an organization that had long experience in using the People CMM in support of its improvement activities, along with using the SW-CMM and CMMI in its software and engineering organizations, there was a desire in its services units to ensure that the internal standards they were establishing for managing their service development and service delivery activities were consistent with the People CMM.

- Another organization with a similar history of implementing successful process improvements across its business chose to implement a series of People CMM appraisals to ensure consistency of the implementations of its human resources practices across its global sites.

- The organization wanted to deploy an internal quality management system that was consistent with global best practices and standards. It also wanted to utilize the People CMM to not only sustain its process improvement efforts, but also serve as the basis for its integrated human resources processes.

■ The organization implemented internal appraisals of its human resources practices to ensure that its practices were serving to drive innovation and effectively use its workforce competencies, by preparing the people with improved knowledge and skills, and with the ability to be agile and adapt and innovate in their business.

7.2   Approaches Taken in Applying the People CMM

The People CMM provides a framework that can be applied to developing an organization's workforce capability. It provides a description of the workforce practices that might be expected to be in place in an organization to achieve a set of goals for organizational improvement. When implemented and institutionalized in an organization, these workforce practices and activities are not decontextualized, theoretical practices, but become intertwined in the strategy and performance of the organization. A recent business novel [Kishore 08] describes how to blend various strategy and improvement frameworks in the context of an organization that is struggling to align its organizational strategy and performance management systems to survive.

Organizations have chosen to apply the People CMM for a variety of purposes. The following paragraphs introduce the most common of these uses and identify the case studies in Chapter 10 that demonstrate these uses.

7.2.1   Driving Internal Human Capital Management Improvement

Based on mandates and goals to transform organizations, human capital managers are being asked to

■ craft organizational strategies that address development and management of the workforce,

■ establish human capital management plans,

■ become data-driven about their workforce management, and

■ become results-oriented [Miller 06].

Many organizations have difficulty accomplishing these objectives because of their current management control systems. Organizations are using the People CMM as the framework to establish workforce plans to ensure that they have, retain, and grow the appropriately skilled workforce. This enables these organizations to become forward-looking, rather than dealing only with information from the past. Pfizer is an example of such an organization.

7.2.2   Supporting Internal Processes and Standards

Other organizations are using the People CMM as guidance in developing their own internal processes and standards for human capital systems. Some of these organizations may choose to be appraised against the People CMM, while others are using the People CMM for requirements to guide the development and improvement of their internal processes and standards. Organizations such as Ericsson and Intel are examples of such organizations.

7.2.3   Supporting Increased Business Capability

Many organizations are highly dependent on their workforce to achieve business capability and deliver customer satisfaction. Organizations that seek to improve delivery capability or sustain continual innovation have found the People CMM to be a mechanism to ensure these transformations. Organizations such as HCLT BPO and Mahindra Resorts have found that a People CMM-based focus on developing workforce competencies and enabling innovation in the workforce support increased customer satisfaction.

7.2.4   Sustaining High Performance

Adoption rates for the People CMM have been high among high-maturity organizations that are also using CMMI or the SW-CMM. The People CMM has been shown to support and sustain CMMI implementation [Buttles 08, Wemyss 07]. High-maturity organizations using the People CMM include Tata Consultancy Services (TCS), Infosys, and Wipro—the winner of the IEEE Computer Society/SEI Software Process Achievement (SPA) Award in 2003 [Radice 05a, Curtis 03, Subramanyam 04]. High-maturity organizations using the People CMM in the United States include Lockheed Martin, Boeing, and AIS—the winner of the 1999 IEEE Computer Society/SEI Software Process Achievement Award [Lockheed 99, Vu 01, Ferguson 99, Paulk 01a, Seshagiri 00]. A survey of high-maturity software organizations showed that more than 40% of these Level 4 and Level 5 organizations were also using the People CMM [Paulk 01b], although not all of these organizations had yet chosen to engage in a formal People CMM appraisal. Recent work at the SEI has identified six frameworks that are most often being used in multimodel improvement settings: CMMI, ISO (all ISO standards as a group), Six Sigma, ITIL, eSCM, and the People CMM.

When an organization achieves Level 3 or higher in CMMI, it is easier to integrate the People CMM activities simultaneously with process improvements, since many of the higher level process issues have been incorporated into People CMM practices. As organizations progress with multiple Capability Maturity Models, they find that they are able to develop interlinked architectures for both their business processes and the workforce competencies required to perform these processes. When implemented effectively, these architectures enable effective execution of the organization's business strategy.

7.3   The IDEAL Life Cycle Model for Improvement

Humphrey [97a] describes the use of the People CMM in an organizational improvement program. The following section shows how the People CMM can be used to support such an improvement program. It introduces the People CMM as a source of guidelines for improving the capability and readiness of an organization's workforce in the context of the Initiating, Diagnosing, Establishing, Acting, and Learning (IDEAL) model for process improvement. This chapter presents the IDEAL approach [Gremba 97], provides an introduction to two ways that organizations can use the People CMM, and discusses issues in implementing a People CMM-based improvement program.

The IDEAL model is an improvement model that serves as a roadmap for initiating, planning, and guiding improvement actions. This model for improvement programs is grounded in several years of experience with and lessons from software process improvement programs. This model is a life cycle for organizing the phases of an improvement program. The IDEAL model defines a systematic, five-phase, continuous process improvement approach, with a concurrent sixth element addressing the project management tasks that span the five phases. Figure 7.2 depicts five phases and relevant tasks of the IDEAL life cycle for an improvement program:

1. Initiating—establish support and responsibilities for improvement
2. Diagnosing—identify the problems to be solved
3. Establishing—select and plan specific improvement activities
4. Acting—design, pilot, implement, and institutionalize improvements
5. Learning—identify improvements in IDEAL-based activities

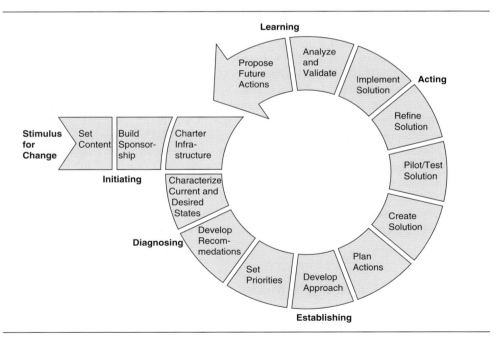

FIGURE 7.2
The IDEAL model

7.4   The People CMM as a Guide for Improving Workforce Practices

The People CMM provides guidance for implementing practices in an organization. Two levels of guidance are provided by the People CMM.

1. Maturity levels and process areas within each maturity level provide guidance on a strategy for developing the organization over time.

2. Practices within the process areas provide guidance on practices that the organization can employ to solve explicit problems or decrease shortcomings in its workforce practices.

In providing guidance, the People CMM does not specify the explicit workforce practices to be implemented. Rather, it sets a framework for selecting and tailoring practices to the organization's history, culture, and environment. There are many professional sources that describe specific methods for workforce practices such as performance management, workgroup development, and training. When implementing workforce practices and activities in an organization, the practices and activities adopted should be tailored to fit that organization's needs and culture. As described in Section 4.6, practices in the People CMM are expected model components. While the People CMM describes the practices that an organization that is achieving a set of goals will typically implement, it does not prescribe how they must be implemented in an organization. The culture of the organization, as well as the regional or national culture where the organization is located, should be considered when implementing workforce practices. Studies have shown that performance is higher when practices are congruent with the national culture [Newman 96].

Deploying improved workforce practices can be accomplished best as a component of a change management, or organizational improvement, program. The People CMM does not provide guidance on how to implement the improvement program itself. The People CMM is a roadmap for organizational growth and can be implemented with a model of how to conduct an improvement program. A model for conducting improvement programs, the IDEAL model, was presented in Section 7.3.

In addition to providing guidance, the People CMM can be used as a tool to support verifying or validating improvement efforts. One way to do so is to apply the People CMM as a benchmark to compare against planned workforce practices and activities. AT&T's experiences with the People CMM provide an example of such use. Within AT&T, an internal team was chartered to develop and propose a human resources plan that would address the competency needs of their business. This team was focused on developing an "integrated approach to recruiting, developing, and motivating" AT&T staff [Yochum 96]. The People CMM was used to validate the team's planned efforts.

Another way that the People CMM can be used to guide and check progress of improvements is as a measurement of progress. One example of the People CMM's use as a key measure of progress in organizations is in a Balanced Scorecard framework [Kaplan 92]. The Balanced Scorecard framework is being applied by AIS to "communicate, implement, and manage the AIS business strategy" [Seshagiri 00]. AIS established five categories of strategic objectives in its Balanced Scorecard framework: financial, or how should the organization appear to its shareholders; customer, or how must the organization appear to its customers; employee, or how must the organization develop and manage its workforce; internal business process, or in which business processes must the organization excel; and learning and growth, or how must the organization sustain its ability to change and improve. Aligning each of these five strategic objectives should lead to increased organizational performance, not only against each objective, but also overall. Figure 7.3 shows the strategic alignment of these objectives.

The AIS Balanced Scorecard is shown in Figure 7.4. Of the five categories of strategic objectives in the AIS Balanced Scorecard, the People CMM has direct impact on three: employee, internal business process, and learning and growth. Highlighted portions of this scorecard show impacts of the People CMM in two ways. The first, which is circled in this figure, shows the use of results of a comparison or benchmark of organizational practices against the People CMM as a specific measurement of outcomes. The second, in italics in this figure, shows the components, outcomes, and drivers in the scorecard that are affected by practices from the People CMM. Resulting outcomes would be employee satisfaction, continual process improvement, and competency growth and alignment between individuals and the organization.

Not only can these impacts be seen in the organizational Balanced Scorecard framework, but also they can be traced into actions at the individual level to bring about performance to achieve the objectives of the Balanced Scorecard framework. At AIS, the Balanced Scorecard strategic objectives feed into the objectives for each individual in his or her assigned position. This objective setting begins a performance management cycle by establishing accountability in individual positions. The performance management cycle is closed when performance is examined and improvement goals and individual performance ratings are identified. When individual development plans are deployed across the organization, these improvement goals will feed into each individual's development plan. Thus, each individual's actions are aligned with the organization's goals to achieve the objectives set in the Balanced Scorecard framework.

The core outcomes in the Employee portion of the AIS Balanced Scorecard show the use of the People CMM in an appraisal setting. The following paragraphs describe the use of the People CMM as the basis for organizational appraisals.

FIGURE 7.3
Alignment of strategic objectives using the Balanced Scorecard

Strategic Objectives	Strategic Measurements Core Outcomes	Strategic Measurements Performance Drivers
Financial		
Consistently meet or exceed shareholder expectations for – revenue growth – profitability – return on investment	Employee target ratio of gross revenue to base salary Projects' profitability target Increase in shareholder equity	Designated expenses' target reduction in expense to revenue ratio
Customer		
Consistently meet or exceed customer expectations for – defect free and on-time delivery – value for products and services – achieving time-to-market goals	Customer responses indicating value "achieved" Statements of Work lost due to not meeting customer time-to-market goals	Defect-free deliveries On-time or ahead-of-schedule deliveries
Employee		
Consistently meet or exceed employee expectations for *– training* *– compensation* *– communication* *– work environment* *– performance management* *– career development*	**Employee responses and assessment indicating People CMM Repeatable Level Key Process Areas fully satisfied**	*Disciplined, repeatable, and stable workforce practices documented*
Internal Business Process		
Projects achieve predictable results for effort, schedule, and defects **within known range of AIS organization– defined process capability**	Projects with actual effort and schedule less than committed effort and schedule	Projects planned and managed **according to their defined process which is an approved tailoring of the AIS organization-defined process**
Engineers achieve the highest possible quality in the design, code phases of a component, module, or program	Components, modules, programs with zero integration test defects	Components with target percentage of defects removed before compile and test
AIS organization-defined process is continuously improved	New products or product enhancements with documented quality better than its predecessor	Process Improvement Proposals submitted and implemented
Learning and Growth		
Investment in people, process, and technology enables achievement of customer, employee, and shareholder satisfaction goals	*Engineers achieving training goals* *Engineers align their career goals with company goals* *Engineers improve productivity continuously*	**Engineers acquire new skills** **Engineers achieving career plans** **Engineers use the Personal Software Process**

FIGURE 7.4
AIS Balanced Scorecard   (Adapted from [Seshagiri 00] with permission.)

7.5   The People CMM as a Basis for Understanding Organizational Workforce Capability

The People CMM provides a standard against which the workforce practices of an organization can be assessed. These activities typically fit within the first two phases of the IDEAL life cycle, as follows:

1. Initiating phase
   - Set improvement context within the organization.
   - Establish sponsorship for a People CMM-based improvement program.
   - Establish a People CMM-based improvement infrastructure with responsibility for acting on results.
2. Diagnosing phase
   - Analyze or appraise the strengths and weaknesses of the organization's current workforce practices.
   - Develop improvement program recommendations.

7.5.1   People CMM-Based Appraisals

The SCAMPI with People CMM appraisal method [Wemyss 08] supports organizations in using the People CMM to guide improvements in their workforce practices. A People CMM-based appraisal is only one component of a successful improvement program. It supports organizations in appraising their current workforce management practices. It is a diagnostic tool designed to achieve the following objectives.

- Identify strengths and weaknesses in workforce practices against a community standard.
- Build consensus around the fundamental workforce problems facing the organization.
- Support prioritization of improvement needs so that the organization can concentrate its attention and resources on a few vital improvement actions.
- Galvanize the organization to take action on needed improvements immediately following the appraisal.

An appraisal is a diagnostic tool that is used to measure the capability and maturity of an organization's workforce practices. The results of an appraisal support, enable, and encourage an organization's commitment to improving its ability to attract, develop, motivate, organize, and retain the talent needed to steadily improve its organizational capability. The method helps an organization gain insight into its workforce capability by identifying the strengths and weaknesses of its current practices related to the People CMM. Results from a People CMM-based appraisal provide a snapshot of the workforce practices as actually performed across the organization. The People CMM appraisal team determines whether a practice is implemented broadly across the organization and is institutionalized. The appraisal team determines whether the goals and intent of each process area have been satisfied. The results of a People CMM-based appraisal can be presented as a profile of the organization's strengths and weaknesses against the process areas of the People CMM. The maturity level achieved by an organization is the lowest maturity level for which all of the process areas have been successfully implemented. When combined with the practices of the People CMM as guidance, the results of the appraisal indicate the practices or process areas that the organization should consider when initiating an improvement program. The method helps an organization to identify improvements that are most beneficial, given the organization's business objectives and current maturity level.

As each improvement cycle completes, it is important to begin the next cycle with a diagnosis of the organization at that point in time. The IDEAL model recognizes this as the learning phase that leads directly into the next diagnosing phase. These recurring diagnoses can serve to measure the progress and organizational learning that have been accomplished, determine the effectiveness of institutionalization of workforce practices, and identify future improvement needs. The organization's workforce practices should be reappraised periodically and action plans developed to address the appraisal findings. These periodic reappraisals should be scheduled to meet organizational business needs, the schedules of its improvement cycle(s), or as needed to ensure ongoing commitment and involvement in continual improvement.

An organization should examine its rationale for performing these reappraisals and determine whether a formal, rigorous appraisal such as a SCAMPI Class A with People CMM appraisal or a lighter-weight appraisal, based on sampling process areas and selected areas of the organization, such as a SCAMPI Class B with People CMM or a SCAMPI Class C with People CMM, will provide the best insight to support its continual improvement needs. SCAMPI with People CMM appraisals are discussed in the next chapter.

7.5.2 Organizational Analyses

To supplement SCAMPI with People CMM appraisals, other forms of analyses could be performed in an organization that is seeking to understand its workforce practices against those of the People CMM or to identify high-priority areas for improvement. Uses of these analyses are to provide a quick-look, or incremental, view of progress in implementing People CMM practices or to understand a baseline or current practice implementation. Such analyses normally require minimal days of effort; are typically based on interviews with management, the human resources function, and the workforce; and give only a snapshot of the people-related capabilities of the organization.

Several types of People CMM-based analyses can be performed. Two types of People CMM-based analyses are described in this section: baseline analyses and questionnaire-based analyses. Each of these analyses is most appropriate for distinct usage scenarios, as shown in Figure 7.5.

These People CMM-based analyses offer lightweight options to gain insights into the workforce capability of the organization. Baseline analyses can provide insights into shortfalls in the organization's implementation of the People CMM practices through a lighter-weight analysis process. Questionnaire-based analyses may be appropriate for organizations seeking to identify problem areas or to gain support for improvement, and for organizations performing an interim assessment to measure progress in an improvement program.

Characteristic

Analysis Type	Baseline Analysis	Questionnaire-Based Analysis
Usage Mode	Self-assessment, typically Initial (first-time) or Incremental (partial) Assists organization in preparing for a SCAMPI appraisal	Self-assessment, typically Initial (first-time) or Incremental (partial) Assists organization in preparing for a SCAMPI appraisal
Advantages	Organization gains insight into own capability; provides a starting point to focus on areas that need most attention; promotes buy-in and ownership of results through participation in analysis and planning; typically inexpensive; short duration; rapid feedback	Organization gains insight into own capability; focuses on areas that need most attention; promotes awareness and buy-in
Disadvantages	Risk of participant biases influencing results; not enough depth to ensure completeness; does not emphasize rigor and cannot be used for maturity level rating	Does not emphasize depth of coverage and rigor and cannot be used for maturity level rating
Sponsor	Any internal manager sponsoring an improvement effort	Any internal manager
Team Size	3–12 persons (recommended)	1–6 persons
Team Qualifications	Limited experience, except for the facilitator	Limited experience, except for the facilitator
Team Leader Requirements	Facilitator trained in the People CMM	Facilitator trained in the People CMM

FIGURE 7.5
Characteristics of People CMM analysis types

A People CMM-based analysis can be conducted by itself or combined with some other assessments of the organization, such as an employee opinion assessment or other organizational diagnostics. Both of these analyses can also assist an organization in getting ready for a SCAMPI with People CMM appraisal and they can be used as progress indicators to understand how well improved workforce practices have been implemented in the organization. The following paragraphs describe each of these analyses types.

Baseline Analyses

A baseline analysis is an organizational analysis that examines the organization's workforce activities against a benchmark standard (in this case, the People CMM), and identifies gaps or shortcomings in the implementation of the organization's workforce practices. These analyses can be performed for a variety of reasons [Byrnes 04]:

- provide an initial, detailed appraisal to baseline an improvement plan,
- provide an initial appraisal to bridge to a new maturity level, or new process areas, or new parts of an organization,

- provide a detailed look at target areas found weak in a previous appraisal—anticipating a future benchmark appraisal, or

- provide a means to gain participation in and buy-in for baselining current status and planning improvements to be implemented in a People CMM-based improvement program.

A baseline analysis is conducted as a guided workshop, led by a qualified facilitator. A People CMM Lead Appraiser or another individual with People CMM knowledge and group facilitation skills would lead participants through this workshop. The format is a combination of training and organizational analysis. It includes both training in the People CMM and a guided critique of the organization's implemented practices. This guided critique can elicit input on the extent to which practices are routinely implemented, as well as inputs on perceptions regarding the urgency for improving the implementation and institutionalization of each practice. The organization can use this information to focus its improvement activities on areas considered to be the most critical.

A baseline analysis uses the practices of the People CMM as a benchmark to compare against organizational norms. Current practices are identified and proposed improvements are developed by the team. One example of a template to support this analysis is shown in Figure 7.6. Proposed improvements are reviewed, agreed to, and prioritized by the participants. The results of the workshop can be used by an organization as a baseline for a People CMM-based improvement program.

Questionnaire-Based Analyses

A questionnaire-based analysis is an alternative approach for organizations seeking to gain insight into their workforce capability. A questionnaire-based analysis is less rigorous than an appraisal; it is based solely on the questionnaire data and does not obtain corroboration of practices from extensive interviews, as is done in a formal SCAMPI appraisal. It is best applied as an initial, first-time, or incremental (i.e., partial) selfassessment, which allows the organization to focus on areas that need the most attention. Awareness of, and buy-in to, the improvement activities are promoted through participation in the questionnaire process. A questionnaire-based analysis has proven to be less useful in providing insight into process implementation in organizations with a high level of workforce capability, as there is often less variability in the responses in an organization that has most of the People CMM practices well implemented.

Typically, questionnaire or survey participants attend a survey administration session where they receive an explanation of the People CMM and the appraisal or analysis process being followed. This session typically delivers a short presentation describing the People CMM, the purpose of the survey, and its role in the appraisal or analysis process. This information may be communicated to participants through other media, depending on the communications planned surrounding the analysis. During this session, questionnaires are distributed to participants. Although several options may be offered for completing the survey (such as in a group session, individually outside of a group session, or online), participants typically complete their questionnaires in a group session where assistance is available to help them understand the intent of the questions and to provide directions for responding. Questionnaires have been used in two versions: one for individual contributors, and another for those in managerial positions. Specialized questionnaires by role, such as competency owners or human capital managers, may also be used to gain specific insights into selected process areas.

Staffing	Current State	Proposed Improvements	Urgency/Priority
P1 Responsible individuals plan and coordinate the staffing activities of their units in accordance with documented policies and procedures.			
P2 Each unit analyzes its proposed work to determine the effort and skills required.			
P3 Individuals and work groups participate in making commitments for work they will be accountable for performing.			
P4 Each unit documents work commitments that balance its workload with available staff and other required resources.			
P6 Position openings within a unit are analyzed, documented, and approved.			
P7 Position openings within the organization are widely communicated.			
P8 Units with open positions recruit for qualified individuals.			
P9 External recruiting activities by the organization are planned and coordinated with unit requirements.			

FIGURE 7.6
Example of a People CMM baseline analysis worksheet

Responses to the questionnaire or survey are scored and compiled into summary reports, typically by a facilitator trained in the People CMM. These reports provide information about the consistency with which workforce practices are performed. For each question, the report provides both summary statistical data and any written comments related to that question. Figure 7.7 shows an example of a questionnaire report for a single question.

44. To what extent have you received the training needed to perform your work responsibilities?

12	26	109	93	41	55	5
To a very great extent	To a great extent	To some extent	To a little extent	To a very little extent	Don't know	Doesn't Apply

Comments:
"Training was provided too late to be useful"
"Training was too generic—unrelated to our applications"
"Found mentoring by senior colleagues to be more beneficial than classroom training"
"By the time the training was available I had transferred to another project and no longer needed the training I received"
"Training helped greatly, could have used more"
"Training was too introductory, I already knew what they taught"
"Why doesn't someone train my manager?"

FIGURE 7.7
Example of a People CMM questionnaire result

Responses are analyzed and a summary presentation is delivered to the organization. The data from the questionnaires can be used to understand the implementation of practices, but do not provide the same results as a full appraisal and do not constitute a basis for assigning the organization a maturity rating. Those responsible for making improvements will use the results to prioritize improvement activities and move into the Establishing phase of the IDEAL model.

Questionnaires provide an opportunity for an organization to gain insight into its implemented processes, identify applicable substantiating objective evidence, and capture comments that might be useful in understanding the implemented processes. Thus, questionnaire-based analyses may be useful for organizations that are preparing for a SCAMPI with People CMM appraisal, but that want to characterize current practice implementation and begin to collect practice implementation data to support the future planned appraisal.

7.6   Implementing a People CMM-Based Improvement Program

In the following paragraphs, an approach to conducting a People CMM-based improvement program is presented through the phases of the IDEAL model.

7.6.1   Planning and Executing the Improvement Program

People CMM-based improvement programs should be conducted as part of an overall organizational improvement strategy. Human resources professionals have emphasized that the People CMM program should not be treated as just a human resources initiative. Rather, these improvement activities should be presented as a program with ongoing involvement by operational management to improve the capability of the organization's workforce. Professionals in human resources, training, organizational development, and related disciplines have unique expertise that can assist operational managers in improving their workforce practices. Nevertheless, the responsibility for ensuring that the organization has a workforce capable of performing current and future work lies primarily with operational management. Improving the organization's workforce capability is a strategic issue which demands the attention and governance of executive management.

Once the decision to address this strategic issue of organizational improvement has been made, successful improvement programs must be run like any other project. That is, they must have senior management support, plans must be prepared, their progress must be tracked, and someone must be accountable for their performance. The IDEAL model presents a proven life cycle that can be used to manage and guide an improvement program.

As previously discussed, the first stage of IDEAL is the *Initiating* phase, wherein executive support is engaged and the infrastructure for improvement is organized. The most common reason for the failure of improvement programs is lack of executive support. An improvement program should not be initiated until executive support is ensured. The effort often begins with one or more briefings to executives. These briefings should include information about

- the benefits of People CMM-based improvements, such as reduced turnover or departure rates and greater readiness to perform organizational strategies;
- a description of the proposed responsibilities, effort, and schedule involved in the improvement program; and
- executive responsibilities under the People CMM and in supporting the improvement program.

Once executive support is ensured, the infrastructure for improvement should be organized. Several groups should be created to run the improvement program. The program should be run from an improvement group; a human capital management team; a process group, such as an enterprise process group (EPG), an organizational process group, or a process engineering group; a process management committee; or some other entity that reports to line management in the organization. If no such group exists, then one should be created explicitly for making workforce-related improvements.

This core improvement group should report to a Management Steering Committee that oversees and approves the improvement efforts. This group should have representation from both operational management and the human resources function. It should have immediate knowledge of how various workforce-related practices are being performed in the organization and a vision for improving the current practices. The steering group must also have authority to commit resources to improvement activities.

Once executive support and an infrastructure for improvement have been established, the organization then prepares to enter the *Diagnosing* phase. During this phase, the organization conducts a People CMM-based appraisal and develops the findings and recommendations. (People CMM-based appraisals are discussed in Chapter 8.) With the appraisal results in hand, the organization is ready to enter the *Establishing* phase. When moving beyond the Initial Level, many organizations have reported that two issues must be addressed:

1. Defining their workforce process as an understood system of workforce practices
2. Delivering appropriate management and supervisory training to develop skills in their workforce processes

The improvement group selects and prioritizes, during the Establishing phase, improvement actions to be implemented, and gets the Management Steering Committee to approve this strategic selection. Since the organization can absorb only a limited amount of change at one time, improvement plans may address only a limited number of improvements in any given period. Often, these include the most serious problems that should be chosen for action, as well as other improvement actions chosen because they are necessary to lay the groundwork for further improvements, or because they are "meaningful low-hanging fruit" or issues that are relatively easy to address that can be used to demonstrate the early successes of the improvement program.

An action team should then be organized to address identified problem(s). The members of the action team should be chosen to ensure that it contains expertise in both the problem and the method of solution. For instance, an action team addressing performance management in an organization should have people who understand the criteria against which performance should be measured, how to work with the workforce in analyzing job performance, the methods of evaluating job performance, what kind of recognition and rewards motivate members of the workforce, and related topics that are covered in the Performance Management process area.

One of the first duties of the team is to develop an action plan that addresses planned improvements in the problem area. Developing and tracking such an action plan is one of the distinguishing factors of successful improvement teams. Another success factor is coordinating the plans and activities of the action teams to ensure that they do not degrade the organization's existing processes or negatively affect other improvements. To ensure that the action team stays on a successful trajectory, the team should be facilitated by someone from the core improvement group.

Many People CMM improvement programs start with performance management. While some managers may not have open positions requiring staffing activities and others may not be involved in compensation decisions, all are involved in managing performance. Implementing improvements guided by the Performance Management process area has the added advantage of focusing on the relationship between managers and those who report to them that is critical for retaining employees. Performance Management is also the process area at Maturity Level 2 that is most likely to have near-term effects on productivity, quality, and efficiency, at least at the unit level. Performance management, and especially handling unsatisfactory performance, is typically one of the weakest areas in low-maturity organizations. Therefore, improvements in conducting performance management activities often yield benefits for the organization, while getting the entire management team engaged in the launch of a People CMM-based improvement effort.

Once an action team has developed a basic plan for its activities, it launches into the *Acting* phase. The action team should identify best workforce practices that are already being used in the organization and build on them. Additional practices can be identified to implement a new process that complements and builds on current best practices. Proposed workforce practices should be reviewed by the action team with those who are expected to implement them. The core implementation group and the Management Steering Group should continually review the plans, activities, and progress of the action team during this phase.

As described in the Continuous Workforce Innovation process area, the improved practices that have been defined should be tested to ensure that they work as expected before being installed across the organization. After a successful trial, the practices can be implemented across the organization and institutionalized. Institutionalization implies that there is enough infrastructure in the organization to ensure that the practices are continually practiced even with the inevitable movement of people to new responsibilities and the assignment of new people.

When an action team has completed implementing practices in its assigned areas of concern, then the organization can complete the IDEAL cycle with the *Learning* phase. In this phase, each action team assesses the lessons learned in developing and implementing its improvements, and the improvement group determines how the process of improvement efforts can be enhanced. They then begin to plan the next implementation of an IDEAL cycle to make the next round of improvements. Since executive support should remain strong if a successful implementation has been completed, the improvement team can begin to plan the next People CMM appraisal.

IDEAL is a repeating cycle that establishes a continuous improvement capability within the organization. The IDEAL cycle is an expanded version of the Shewart-Deming Plan-Do-Check-Act improvement cycle. As such, it has much in common with other total quality management improvement activities. The use of IDEAL with workforce improvements implies that many of the principles that have been used to improve other aspects of organizational life can be used to improve the development of workforce practices.

7.6.2   Integrating Maturity-Based Improvement Programs

Recent work at the SEI has identified six frameworks that are most often being used in multimodel improvement settings: CMMI, ISO (all ISO standards as a group), Six Sigma, ITIL, eSCM, and the People CMM. This section focuses on integrating maturity-based improvement programs using CMMI and the People CMM, although the People CMM can be used with other frameworks.

When introducing multiple improvement programs, the organization needs to assess the amount of change it can reasonably absorb and adjust expectations and schedules accordingly. This is especially acute at Maturity Level 2, where the individuals responsible for making the majority of the changes are unit level managers. In order not to overload these managers with change, the organization should stage the introduction of the improvement programs. Under many circumstances, unit managers should first master their process-related management skills. After acquiring sound work unit or project management skills, these managers can undertake improvements guided by the People CMM to supplement their project management activities. In fact, the People CMM relies on good process management at Level 2 to provide such inputs as work unit objectives and tasks.

The People CMM applies the essential elements of a Capability Maturity Model to the workforce practices of the organization. Therefore, organizations that have some experience in applying another process-focused CMM, such as CMMI for improving their software development processes, will find that the People CMM is compatible with an improvement philosophy they have already adopted.

There are no plans to integrate the People CMM into CMMI, either directly or by extensions. Currently, all of the CMMs that have been integrated into CMMI are concerned with behavior performed in or on behalf of projects, whereas the People CMM is concerned with behavior performed continuously throughout the organization. Nevertheless, the People CMM, Version 2, has adopted some of the advances made in the CMMI model framework to ensure that People CMM improvement programs would integrate with improvement programs guided by CMMI. The People CMM's focus on process abilities in workforce competencies at the Defined Level and quantitative performance management practices at the Predictable Level clearly supports integrating these various models [Hefley 03].

Using CMMI and the People CMM together in an improvement program begs the question of whether the organization should synchronize its maturity levels on the two models. Maturity growth on one model does not require or restrict maturity growth on the other. However, maturity growth on either model assists or accelerates maturity growth on the other. Experience has shown that applying the People CMM has accelerated or sustained other process improvement activities [Buttles 08, Muralidharan 04, Nandyal 06, Porter 01, Radice 05b, Tondon 00, Vu 01].

Both models begin at Maturity Level 2 by emphasizing the responsibility of project or unit managers for installing basic discipline in their environments. Creating this basic discipline using either model aids in creating the management attitudes that support growth in the other model. Basic management discipline will enable both the process of developing software and the process of developing the workforce.

At Maturity Level 3, the analysis of knowledge and skills and the determination of core competencies require an understanding of the work being performed. Thus, it may be best for an organization to define its software process before it begins defining the knowledge, skills, and process abilities required by the competencies involved in executing its defined organizational set of standard processes. This is an area of dependency between the two models. Certainly, the concepts of an organization-wide way of performing technical activities and of an organization's core competencies fit well together, each supporting the other's development. The People CMM activities for defining and developing workforce competencies elaborate and extend the required training program and process management activities described in CMMI.

At Maturity Level 4, the data being generated by the software process provide an excellent source of information on whether the development of knowledge and skills is effective, and where shortfalls might exist. That is, a mature software process will provide data that can be used in analyzing the trends that form the core of managing the organization's competency development and performance alignment. At the same time, the development of high-performance, competency-based teams instills the kind of empowerment and increased employee satisfaction that has been observed in high-maturity organizations [Billings 94, Carnegie Mellon University 95, Wigle 99, Yamamura 99].

At Maturity Level 5, both models emphasize establishing continuous improvement as an ordinary process. Both models also seek to engage individuals in making the continuous improvement of their own work a personal objective. Thus, at the Optimizing Level, the models begin to merge in their search for ways to improve performance continuously. At this level, the capability of the process and the capability of the workforce may be difficult to distinguish.

By building competencies and a workforce that can successfully execute and manage its processes, the People CMM establishes a foundation for building a culture that values process and that facilitates the implementation of CMMI-DEV. Additionally, the People CMM strengthens and greatly extends the people and culture dimensions that the CMMI model framework touches on only lightly. Integrating the People CMM with process maturity frameworks, such as CMMI, speeds the emergence of a capable workforce having a culture that is required to enable and sustain institutionalized process improvements. The People CMM is a comprehensive system of workforce practices that improves the quality of an organization's workforce. The benefits extend from traditional workforce measures such as employee satisfaction and retention, to performance measures that affect customer experience and loyalty. Thus, the People CMM supplements an organization's Quality Management System by improving the quality and capability of its workforce.

Since CMMI and the People CMM share similar underlying philosophies about how to change and mature an organization, it should not be surprising that they support each other at each level of maturity. The challenge for an organization initiating an improvement program that has both CMMI and People CMM components is to integrate an improvement strategy that allows improvements guided by one model to help create an environment that supports improvements guided by the other model. At the same time, the organization must always balance the amount of change being undertaken so that the workforce is not inundated with change activities that interfere with conducting the organization's business. An organization that can balance these tensions and improvement strategies will find that it has a powerful competitive advantage in a well-defined process being executed by a well-prepared and motivated workforce.

8

Using SCAMPI with People CMM

8.1 SCAMPI with People CMM Appraisal Method

Beginning in 2008, results from appraisals conducted according to the People CMM-Based Assessment Method [Hefley 98] are no longer accepted by the Software Engineering Institute (SEI), the People CMM Steward. The People CMM team at the SEI is focusing its efforts on the SCAMPI with People CMM appraisals. People CMM appraisals are now being conducted using the Standard CMMI Appraisal Method for Process Improvement (SCAMPI) with People CMM [Wemyss 08]. SCAMPI with People CMM is the only appraisal method supported by the SEI for use with the People CMM.

The Standard CMMI Appraisal Method for Process Improvement (SCAMPI) A, Version 1.2: Method Definition Document (MDD) [SCAMPI 06b] defines rules for ensuring the consistency of appraisal ratings. For benchmarking against other organizations, appraisals must ensure consistent ratings. The achievement of a specific maturity level or the satisfaction of a process area must mean the same thing for different appraised organizations.

The SCAMPI family of appraisals includes Class A, B, and C appraisal methods. SCAMPI Class A is the most rigorous method and the only method that can result in a maturity level rating. SCAMPI Class B provides options in model scope, but the characterization of practices is fixed to one defined scale and is performed on implemented practices. SCAMPI Class C provides a wide range of options, including characterization of planned approaches to process implementation according to a scale defined by the user.

As described in the SCAMPI MDD, an appraisal is an examination of one or more processes by a trained team of professionals using an appraisal reference model as the basis for determining strengths and weaknesses. An appraisal is typically conducted in the context of process improvement or capability evaluation. The term *appraisal* is a generic term used throughout the CMMI model framework to describe applications in these contexts, traditionally known as assessments and evaluations. While the appraisal modes of usage identified for the SCAMPI method include internal process improvement, supplier selection, and process monitoring, the most appropriate appraisal mode of usage for SCAMPI with People CMM is for internal process improvement. Organizations use appraisals to appraise internal processes, generally to either baseline their maturity level(s), to establish or update a process improvement program, or to measure progress in implementing such a program. Applications include measuring process improvement progress, conducting process audits, focusing on specific concerns, or appraising specific parts of the organization. SCAMPI Class A, B, or C with People CMM appraisals supplement other tools for implementing process improvement activities.

Characteristic

Appraisal Type	SCAMPI Class A with People CMM Appraisal	SCAMPI Class B with People CMM Appraisal	SCAMPI Class C with People CMM Appraisal	Multimodel Appraisal
Appraisal Class	SCAMPI Class A	SCAMPI Class B	SCAMPI Class C	SCAMPI Class A
Usage Mode	For benchmarking or process improvement. Focus is on institutionalization.	Process improvement. Focus is on deployment.	Process improvement. Focus is on approach.	For benchmarking or process improvement. Focus is on institutionalization.
Advantages	Rigorous and in-depth investigation of workforce practices.			Rigorous and in-depth investigation of practices, both for work-force practices and for the processes in the multimodel domain(s).
	Thorough coverage; strengths and weaknesses for each process area investigated; robustness of method with consistent, repeatable results; provides objective view.	Fewer resources required than Class A: people, evidence, preparation time, on-site time, and reporting. Less disruptive to the organization. Can serve as a mini Class A.	Fewer resources required than Class B: people, evidence, preparation time, on-site time, and reporting. Less disruptive to the organization. Can serve as a mini Class B.	Thorough coverage; strengths and weaknesses for each process area investigated across multiple domains; robustness of method with consistent, repeatable results; provides objective view. Requires fewer resources than separate Class A for each model: people, evidence, preparation time, on-site time, and reporting.

FIGURE 8.1
Characteristics of People CMM appraisal types

Characteristic

Appraisal Type	SCAMPI Class A with People CMM Appraisal	SCAMPI Class B with People CMM Appraisal	SCAMPI Class C with People CMM Appraisal	Multimodel Appraisal
Disadvantages	Demands significant resources. Maturity level ratings may not be needed.	No maturity level ratings. Findings not representative of entire organization. Model coverage incomplete.	No maturity level ratings. Findings not representative of entire organization. Model coverage incomplete. Limited evidence may provide misleading or inaccurate results.	Demands significant resources. Maturity level ratings may not be needed. Requires considerable experience in each domain, large team, and SCAMPI Lead Appraiser authorized in each model.
Sponsor	Executive management of the organization	Management	Management or process improvement group	Executive management of the organization
Team Size	Minimum of 4 persons	Minimum of 2 persons	Minimum of 1 person	Minimum of 4 persons per domain
Team Qualifications	Very Experienced	Experienced	Less Experienced	Very Experienced in each domain
Appraisal Team Leader Requirements	SCAMPI with People CMM Lead Appraiser	SCAMPI with People CMM Lead Appraiser or B+C Team Leader	SCAMPI with People CMM Lead Appraiser or B+C Team Leader	SCAMPI Lead Appraiser authorized in all models used

FIGURE 8.1
Continued

Several types of People CMM-based appraisals can be performed. Each type of appraisal is most appropriate for distinct usage scenarios, as shown in Figure 8.1. Key differentiating attributes for appraisal types include

- the appraisal scope,
- the degree of confidence in the appraisal outcomes,
- the generation of maturity level ratings, and
- the cost and duration of the appraisal.

Organizations planning a SCAMPI with People CMM appraisal select the type and class of SCAMPI appraisal appropriate to their needs. An organization that is committed to improvement, but that needs help in identifying improvement actions, may choose to perform a SCAMPI Class B with People CMM or a SCAMPI Class C with People CMM appraisal, rather than a formal SCAMPI Class A with People CMM appraisal. A SCAMPI Class A with People CMM appraisal may also be appropriate for such an organization because it provides the most rigorous examination of an organization's workforce practices and activities and it serves both to diagnose and to build broad buy-in for continual improvement. A SCAMPI Class A with People CMM appraisal also provides the organization with a maturity level rating. A multimodel appraisal may be performed using SCAMPI with People CMM and SCAMPI with a CMMI model.

The following paragraphs describe each of these appraisal types. They provide an overview of the SCAMPI with People CMM method, rather than details about how to enact it. These details are available in other documentation available from the SEI (www.sei.cmu.edu). The SCAMPI MDD [SCAMPI 06b] provides an overview of the appraisal method, context, concepts, and detailed activities and practices associated with each process that composes the SCAMPI method. An additional document with guidance specifically addressing the use of SCAMPI with People CMM [Wemyss 08] is also available from the SEI. The MDD and SCAMPI with People CMM guidance documents are primarily intended for SCAMPI Lead Appraisers and Team Leads authorized to perform SCAMPI with People CMM appraisals.

8.2   SCAMPI with People CMM—Class A Appraisals

The Standard CMMI Appraisal Method for Process Improvement (SCAMPI) with People CMM is designed to provide benchmark-quality maturity level ratings relative to the People CMM. A SCAMPI Class A with People CMM appraisal satisfies all of the Appraisal Requirements for CMMI (ARC) v1.2 requirements for a SCAMPI Class A appraisal [SCAMPI 06a].

The SCAMPI Class A with People CMM appraisal method is used to identify strengths, weaknesses, and appraisal ratings relative to the appraisal reference model (i.e., the People CMM). A SCAMPI Class A appraisal enables an appraisal sponsor, who is the leader within the organization who sponsors an appraisal to meet business needs, to

- gain insight into an organization's capability by identifying the strengths and weaknesses of its current processes,
- relate these strengths and weaknesses to the reference model(s),
- derive a maturity level rating,
- prioritize improvements for improvement plans, and
- focus improvement plans on improvements that correct weaknesses that generate risks or that are most beneficial to the organization given its current level of organizational maturity or workforce capability.

The SCAMPI Class A with People CMM appraisal method has two primary objectives.

1. Provide a common, integrated appraisal method capable of supporting appraisals in the context of internal process improvement.

2. Provide an efficient appraisal method capable of being implemented within reasonable performance constraints.

Characteristic	Explanation
Accuracy	Appraisal ratings are truly reflective of the organization's maturity, reflect the appraisal reference model, and can be used for comparison across organizations. Appraisal results reflect the strengths and weaknesses of the appraised organization (i.e., no significant strengths and weaknesses are left undiscovered).
Repeatability	The ratings and findings of an appraisal are likely to be consistent with those of another independent appraisal conducted under comparable conditions (i.e., another appraisal of identical scope will produce consistent results).
Cost/Resource Effectiveness	The appraisal method is efficient in terms of person-hours spent planning, preparing, and executing an appraisal. The method takes account of the organizational investment in obtaining the appraisal results, including the resources of the host organization, the impact on the appraised organization, and the appraisal team.
Meaningfulness of Results	Appraisal results are useful to the appraisal sponsor in supporting decision making.
ARC Compliance	SCAMPI Class A is a Class A appraisal method and complies with all ARC v1.2 requirements.

FIGURE 8.2
Essential characteristics of a SCAMPI Class A with People CMM appraisal

The SCAMPI Class A with People CMM appraisal method is also designed to prioritize and satisfy certain essential characteristics, as shown in Figure 8.2.

Performing appraisals efficiently involves minimizing the use of resources and the impact on appraisal teams and appraised organizations, while maintaining the essential method characteristics that ensure the high degree of accuracy required for an effective benchmarking appraisal method. Since SCAMPI Class A with People CMM is suitable for benchmarking, thus requiring high confidence in ratings, thoroughness is necessary. SCAMPI Class A with People CMM appraisals can be used to generate maturity level ratings as benchmarks to compare maturity levels across organizations. Only a SCAMPI Class A with People CMM appraisal can produce a maturity level rating. Under current SEI policies, there is a three-year maximum period of validity for results and ratings from SCAMPI Class A with People CMM appraisals. Three years after the appraisal end date, the appraisal results will expire and become invalid based on age; however, an appraisal result can become invalid for other reasons.

Organizations for which (a) generation of ratings is not required, (b) generation of a benchmark result is not required, (c) the primary application is identification of strengths and weaknesses for process improvement, and (d) efficiency of appraisal resources is a primary concern may be well advised to consider alternative appraisal types. Alternative SCAMPI with People CMM appraisal types are shown in Figure 8.1. This consideration of alternative SCAMPI with People CMM appraisal types is particularly relevant for organizations that are early in their process improvement cycle or that cannot invest in a full SCAMPI team to support a SCAMPI Class A with People CMM appraisal.

SCAMPI Class A with People CMM is an integrated appraisal method that can be applied in the context of internal process improvement. As a benchmarking method, the SCAMPI Class A with People CMM emphasis is on a rigorous method capable of achieving high accuracy and reliability of appraisal results through the collection of objective evidence from multiple sources. SCAMPI Class A with People CMM consists of three phases. Each phase is briefly described in the following subsections.

Phase 1: Plan and Prepare for Appraisal

The sponsor's appraisal objectives for performing a SCAMPI Class A with People CMM appraisal are determined in phase 1. All other planning, preparation, execution, and reporting of results proceed from this initial activity. Because of the significant investment and logistical planning involved, considerable iteration and refinement of planning activities should be expected in phase 1. In the second phase, the amount of iteration will decrease as data are collected, analyzed, refined, and translated into findings of significance relative to the model.

A team of experienced and trained personnel performs a SCAMPI Class A with People CMM appraisal over a period of time negotiated by the sponsor and the appraisal team leader. The scope of the organization to be appraised, as well as the scope of the People CMM model (process areas), must be defined and agreed to. The scope of the organization and model provides the basis on which to estimate personnel time commitments, logistical costs (e.g., travel), and overall costs to the appraised organization and of the appraisal team.

Successful application of SCAMPI with People CMM relies on adjusting the parameters of the method to the needs of the organization and to the objectives and constraints of the sponsor's organization. The sponsor's objectives largely influence appraisal tailoring decisions. The reference model scope, the size of the organizational unit, the number and characteristics of sampled units, the size of the appraisal team, and the number of interviews greatly influence things such as preparation time, time on-site, and monetary costs, and so are also major factors when choosing tailoring options. All tailoring decisions must be documented in the appraisal plan.

During the appraisal, the appraisal team verifies and validates the objective evidence provided by the appraised organization to identify strengths and weaknesses relative to the People CMM model. Objective evidence consists of documents or interview results used as indicators for implementation and institutionalization of model practices. Before the second phase begins, members of the appraised organization typically collect and organize documented objective evidence. The information-processing "engine" of the appraisal is thus fueled by the objective evidence already available, saving the appraisal team the time and effort of a discovery process.

The SCAMPI Class A with People CMM method is designed on the assumption— although not the requirement—that relevant documented objective evidence is available for review in advance. This assumption is typically discussed with the appraisal sponsor and his or her representatives during development of the appraisal plan, and a decision is made whether to conduct a verification-based or a discovery-based appraisal. While it is not absolutely required for performance of a SCAMPI Class A with People CMM appraisal, this advance preparation by the appraised organization is key to the most efficient execution of the method. Analysis of preliminary documented objective evidence provided by the appraised organization plays an important role in setting the stage for appraisal execution. If substantial data are missing at this point, subsequent appraisal activities can be delayed or even cancelled if the judgment is made that continuing appraisal activities will not be sufficient to make up for the deficiency. The decision to conduct a verification-based appraisal is revisited at a key point in the appraisal process when a review is performed to determine readiness to proceed with such an appraisal as planned. If the appraised organization has not provided documented objective evidence of sufficient quality and completeness to enable a verification-based appraisal, the appraisal plan should be updated to reflect the effort that must be undertaken for the appraisal team to search for and discover that objective evidence during the Conduct Appraisal phase, or another appraisal type should be considered.

Phase 2: Conduct Appraisal

In phase 2, the appraisal team focuses on collecting and analyzing data from the organizational unit to judge the extent to which the model is implemented. An organizational unit is the part of an organization that is the focus of an appraisal. An organizational unit operates within a coherent workforce context, a coherent process context, and a coherent set of business objectives.

Integral to a SCAMPI with People CMM appraisal is the concept of coverage, which means collecting data and information on all the People CMM practices for appropriate instances of the practice implementation within the organizational unit. Practice implementation at the organizational unit level is a function of the degree of practice implementation at various levels. Within a SCAMPI with People CMM appraisal, these levels may include the organization, units, workgroups, competencies, or individuals. The extent to which an organizational unit has implemented the People CMM Practices can be determined only by considering, in aggregate, the objective evidence of practice implementation throughout the organizational unit. During this second phase, the data-collection plan developed in phase 1 undergoes continuous iteration and refinement to obtain sufficient coverage.

Appraisal teams are obligated to seek and consider objective evidence of multiple types in determining practice implementation and goal satisfaction. The SCAMPI Class A method is data oriented in that decisions on practice implementation and goal ratings are made based on the aggregate of objective evidence available to the appraisal team. Multiple types of objective evidence must be considered, including the following.

- Documents—written information relative to the implementation of one or more model practices. These documents may include organizational policies, procedures, implementation-level artifacts, instruments (e.g., questionnaires), and presentation materials.

- Interviews—oral interaction with those implementing or using the processes within the organizational unit. Interviews are typically held with various groups or individuals, such as Human Resources, managers, and individuals.

The aggregation of objective evidence provided is used as the basis for determining practice implementation. To make reasonable judgments regarding an organization's implemented processes relative to the People CMM appraisal teams base their judgments on the collection of objective evidence for each practice applicable to process area goals within the appraisal scope. Appraisal teams compare the objective evidence collected against the corresponding practices in the People CMM. In making inferences about the extent to which practices are or are not implemented, appraisal teams draw on the entire model document to understand the intent of the model, and use it as the basis for their decisions. This comparison includes the required and expected model components (i.e., goals and practices) as well as informative material, such as model front matter, introductory text, glossary definitions, and subpractices.

The appraisal team follows a consensus-based, structured process to synthesize and transform information collected from the sources. Upon determining that sufficient coverage of the People CMM model and organizational unit has been obtained, appraisal findings and maturity level ratings may be generated. Goal ratings are determined within each process area, which collectively can be used to determine a rating for the individual process areas, as well as a maturity level rating for the organizational unit.

Goal ratings are a function of the extent to which the corresponding practices are present in the planned and implemented processes of the organization. In the People CMM, there is a direct relationship between goals and the practices that contribute toward achievement of those goals. (See Appendix D for this goal-to-practice mapping.) Goals are required model components; practices are expected model components in that alternative practices could be implemented that are equally effective in achieving the intent of the associated goals. In the SCAMPI Class A with People CMM method, a fundamental premise is that satisfaction of goals can be determined only upon detailed investigation of the extent to which each corresponding practice is implemented throughout the organizational unit.

Phase 3: Report Results

In phase 3, the appraisal team provides the appraisal findings and maturity level ratings to the appraisal sponsor and the organization. An appraisal record is generated and provided to the sponsor, documenting further information regarding the appraisal. A completed appraisal data package, which includes a subset of the contents of the appraisal record, is forwarded to the People CMM Steward. The Steward uses this data for the purposes of quality control and reporting of appraisal measures to the community.

8.3   SCAMPI with People CMM—Class B Appraisals

A SCAMPI with People CMM appraisal also can be performed as a SCAMPI Class B with People CMM appraisal or as a SCAMPI Class C with People CMM appraisal to complement the SCAMPI Class A with People CMM appraisal type. These SCAMPI Class B and Class C methods, by definition, are not suitable for benchmarking, but are tools for an organization's process improvement journey. This family of integrated SCAMPI with People CMM appraisals (SCAMPI Class A, B, and C with People CMM), using common artifacts and being upward compatible, has significant advantages as organizations pursue workforce improvement in a systematic fashion. Key differences in the requirements for SCAMPI appraisal classes are shown in Figure 8.3. Key differences in performing these three classes of SCAMPI with People CMM appraisals are in the degree of confidence in the appraisal outcomes, whether ratings are generated, and the appraisal cost and duration.

Requirements	SCAMPI Class A	SCAMPI Class B	SCAMPI Class C
Types of Objective Evidence Gathered	Documents and interviews	Documents and interviews	Documents or interviews
Ratings Generated	Goal ratings required	Not allowed	Not allowed
Organizational Unit Coverage	Required	Not required	Not required
Minimum Team Size	4	2	1
Appraisal Team Leader Requirements	Lead Appraiser	Person trained and experienced	Person trained and experienced

FIGURE 8.3
Key differences in requirements for SCAMPI appraisal classes
Source: [SCAMPI 06a]

A SCAMPI Class B with People CMM appraisal is often performed when an organization needs to accurately assess its progress toward a target maturity level. It results in detailed findings that describe the strengths and weaknesses of the organization's workforce practices relative to the People CMM, a characterization of People CMM practices, and identification of the organization's key issues with respect to successfully implementing and institutionalizing the practices of the People CMM.

The SCAMPI Class B method is based on the SCAMPI Class A method, except that it does not result in a maturity level rating. Appraisal teams for a SCAMPI Class B with People CMM can be smaller in size than for a SCAMPI Class A with People CMM appraisal. A SCAMPI Class B with People CMM requires less data—which reduces the number of artifacts that must be identified and organized before the appraisal and reduces the time and effort needed to conduct the appraisal—and does not generate or report goal or process area ratings.

8.4   SCAMPI with People CMM—Class C Appraisals

SCAMPI Class C with People CMM appraisals, the least rigorous of the SCAMPI with People CMM appraisal types, are highly flexible and can be conducted to address a variety of needs. As they are typically much shorter in duration than SCAMPI Class A and Class B appraisals, SCAMPI Class C appraisals are often performed to provide a quick gap analysis of an organization's workforce practices relative to the People CMM, to assess the adequacy of a new process before it is implemented, to monitor the implementation or implementation progress of an improved workforce practice or practices, or to determine an organization's readiness for a more robust SCAMPI Class A with People CMM or a SCAMPI Class B with People CMM appraisal.

A SCAMPI Class C with People CMM appraisal can be scoped at any level of the People CMM structure, such as a process area, a goal, or a practice. It requires less effort to complete, as the appraisal team can be as small as one person, and corroboration of data collected and validation of the findings with appraisal participants are not required. A SCAMPI Class C with People CMM appraisal has no specific requirements regarding the sources of objective evidence (i.e., artifacts and interviews). A SCAMPI Class C with People CMM appraisal could incorporate a questionnaire-based analysis.

8.5   Multimodel Appraisals

A SCAMPI Class A with People CMM appraisal can be conducted as a stand-alone appraisal, as described earlier, or as a multimodel appraisal using the People CMM and one of the CMMI models.

When a SCAMPI Class A with People CMM appraisal is conducted jointly with another SCAMPI-based appraisal, data for the People CMM-based appraisal may be gathered separately, since the unit of study is not a project, as it typically is during a process-focused appraisal. Because of its content, the People CMM focuses on organizational units such as business units, sections, and departments, and how workforce practices are conducted within these units. Because both components of a multimodel appraisal are SCAMPI-based, the SCAMPI with People CMM appraisal uses the same appraisal conventions as a SCAMPI with a CMMI model. For example, both appraisals are led by an authorized SCAMPI Lead Appraiser, are performed by a trained appraisal team, observe confidentiality regarding nonattribution of the information obtained, and interview people at various levels of the organization. The results of a SCAMPI with People CMM-based appraisal should be presented as a separate analysis of the organizational unit against the practices of the People CMM, and a separate People CMM maturity level rating should be given to indicate the workforce capability of the organization.

9

Experience with the People CMM

9.1 Adoption of the People CMM

The previous chapters addressed uses of the People CMM. This chapter presents data regarding experiences with the People CMM, and Chapter 10 examines a number of case studies of this use. As discussed in Chapter 7, the People CMM can be applied by an organization in three primary ways:

1. As a guide in planning and implementing improved human capital management practices

2. As a guide for improving organizational standards

3. As a standard for analyzing and appraising an organization's implemented workforce practices

So, if organizations are adopting the People CMM for one of these purposes, why are they doing so? What factors motivate an organization to make these changes? There are several reasons why organizations implement high-performance workforce practices, including

- improving organizational capability;

- supporting and sustaining high-maturity capability, such as CMMI implementation;

- increasing the accountability of the organization's human resource management activities;

- having failed to implement improvements or change programs for some specific issue, such as competency or skills management or increased use of teams, but finding underlying problems that prevent the success of these initiatives;

- trying to implement teams or competencies;

- communicating, and putting into routine practice, shared values regarding the workforce;

- implementing strategic imperatives, such as becoming an "Employer of Choice"; and

- meeting competitive pressures in the marketplace.

Formal organizational appraisals using the People CMM as a benchmark have been conducted in the North America, Asia, India, Europe, and Australia. From organizations that have been using the People CMM, either as a guide for improvement or as a basis for assessing organizational capability, a number of clear benefits have been seen. They are addressed in the next section.

9.2   Benefits of People CMM Adoption

The People CMM provides a framework that can be applied to developing an organization's workforce capability. It provides a description of the workforce practices that might be expected to be in place in an organization to achieve a set of goals for organizational improvement. When implemented and institutionalized in an organization, these workforce practices and activities are not decontextualized, theoretical practices, but become intertwined in the performance of the organization.

Using a model of a high-performing organization, based on organizational excellence models, such as the Malcolm Baldrige National Quality Award criteria and the EFQM Excellence Model [Baldridge 01, EFQM 99, Eskildsen 00, Wilson 00], Figure 9.1 shows these workforce practices and activities. It also shows the scope of the People CMM, and the practices that it suggests, against an overall model of organizational excellence. A similar mapping could be made to other comprehensive models of organizational performance. The People CMM addresses more than just human resource management; it also addresses aspects of process management through its focus on competency-based processes, measurement and analysis of performance extending from the individual level to aligning performance across the organization, and aspects of strategic planning as it relates to workforce and competency planning.

As the upper-right portion of Figure 9.1 indicates, benefits as outcomes or business results have been realized in three clear areas: reduced turnover, increased employee satisfaction, and reputation signals. Direct outcomes include reduction in voluntary turnover, or departure, rates and increased employee satisfaction. Organizations that use the People CMM have experienced decreases in turnover to 5% to 10% below industry average. One organization experienced a decrease to 3% compared with an industry average of 18% and an initial departure rate within this organization that approached 50%. Increased employee satisfaction is another outcome experienced by organizations. Organizations have seen an increase in employee satisfaction of two to three points or higher (on a scale from 1 to 10). The case studies in the remainder of this chapter provide detailed examples of these outcomes.

As we saw in Chapter 1, reputation signals can be quite meaningful to an organization. In some cases, they have been positively associated with increased share prices [Hannon 96]. These reputation signals have been evidenced through various communications media by different organizations. The media used by organizations to communicate their use of the People CMM include press releases, organizational Web sites, and presentations or publications. Organizations that have used press releases to announce results of organizational appraisals using the People CMM include Pershing LLC (Bank of New York Mellon), IBM Global Services India, Intelligroup, Lockheed Martin Mission Systems, and Sutherland Global Services [BNY Mellon 07, Business Line 02, Intelligroup 00, Lockheed 99, Sutherland 08]. Many organizations have used their corporate Web sites to indicate their organizational

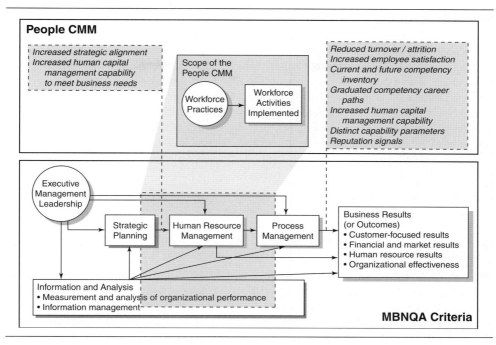

FIGURE 9.1
Results experienced from use of the People CMM

capability and their use of the People CMM. These include BAE SYSTEMS, Mastek, RS Software, and Siemens [BAE SYSTEMS 01, Mastek 01, RS 01, Siemens 01]. An example is the text on the BAE SYSTEMS Mission Solutions Web site that describes numerous organizational accomplishments:

> We achieved [Maturity] LEVEL 2 recognition when evaluated according to the standards of the Software Engineering Institute's People Capability Maturity Model (P-CMM). This model measures the effectiveness of a company's people management practices, including performance management, staffing, training and development, communications, and work environment. BAE SYSTEMS Mission Solutions is a leading proponent of instituting this model, and was the first company to conduct a P-CMM appraisal for an entire organization.
>
> [BAE SYSTEMS 01]

Numerous presentations or publications have been made by organizations using the People CMM. Some of these presentations or publications have been made by senior executives or key leaders within the organization, which can add additional credence to a reputation signal [Griffin 00, Keeni 00a, Kumar 01, Major 98, Vu 01, Yochum 96]. These signals, and their use in press releases or other marketing material, are seen by some organizations as a market differentiator that will enable them to acquire additional market share or business.

While many organizations using the People CMM are experiencing these types of outcomes, others are experiencing outcomes that affect the organization much farther up the value chain. These outcomes are shown in the upper-left portion of Figure 9.1 as increased strategic alignment. One example is the alignment that occurs at AIS using its performance management and career development activities, coupled with the organization's Balanced Scorecard, which was shown in Figure 7.4. This process was described in AIS's 1999 description of its ongoing improvement activities [Ferguson 99, Figure 21 depicts the AIS overall People Management System]. In its workforce activities, there are four outcomes from the self-evaluation and feedback process:

1. Individual improvement goals
2. Summary rating
3. Individual training goals
4. Individual-broadening assignment and activities goals

The links from the Balanced Scorecard to an individual's goals for improvement, training, and broadening assignments and activities help to align the individual's career plans with the overall company goals.

In our work with organizations, we have seen numerous other benefits arise from use of the People CMM. A brief list of some of these benefits, both tangible and intangible, includes the following:

- Developing a common language to address workforce issues, especially between human resource management and the line management
- Encouraging a "systems" perspective of workforce processes
- Providing a framework for process documentation
- Involving first-line managers as active "process owners" for their areas of responsibility
- Use of process measurements both to get an objective self-evaluation and as a scorecard
- Greater attention to effective performance feedback, often through more frequent formal performance appraisals (e.g., quarterly, every six months, and at project completion)
- Greater willingness to use documented performance improvement plans
- Explicit cascading of performance goals
- Enhanced clarity and communication about the organization's compensation philosophy or strategy
- Effective competency management implementations
- Addressing the challenge of career planning in environments where high attrition rates and high business growth are common, and individuals want to be in control of their careers
- Ability to address higher maturity issues, such as empowered workgroups, after resolving long-festering lower maturity problems, such as performance management

Some of these benefits may be internal to "just" the human resource management component of Figure 9.1, but many of them have the capability to either enable or derail effective performance in the organization. Consider just the single example of setting performance improvement plans in place. This is one of the hardest things many managers must do in their careers. Left unaddressed, however, performance problems send signals to others that can lead to decreases in employee satisfaction and retention difficulties.

9.3 Benefits Vary by Maturity Level Achieved

At the beginning of the twenty-first century, increasing numbers of organizations in North America, Europe, and Asia, especially in India, Japan, China, the Philippines, and Malaysia, have been adopting the People CMM. Organizations have been appraised at all maturity levels including Maturity Level 5 and the benefits they experienced differ by level.

Empirical results from People CMM-based improvement programs are now becoming available. The initial data suggest that well-run improvement programs are able to achieve the objectives set by the organization, with the most frequent result for organizations that achieve Maturity Level 2 being a reduction in voluntary turnover. In fact, organizations achieving People CMM Managed Level uniformly report increases in workforce morale and reductions in voluntary turnover. Often, an early benefit an organization experiences as it achieves Maturity Level 2 is a reduction in turnover. The reduction usually decreases the rate of voluntary employee departures to single digits, occasionally reducing this turnover by half or more. For instance, HCL Technologies BPO Services reported that it increased the percentage of satisfied employees from 70% to 87% and reduced employee turnover from 17% to 11% as it moved up the maturity stages to Level 3 [Rao 07]. Most organizations that have achieved Maturity Level 4 or 5 have turnover in the single digits. The turnover costs that are avoided by improved retention—hiring, training, and lost opportunity costs—often more than pay for the cost of the improvements associated with achieving Maturity Level 2. Figure 9.2 presents a sample of the voluntary turnover reductions for companies that reported achieving the Managed Level. These results are not surprising, since years of research have shown that one of the best predictors of voluntary turnover is employees' relationship with their supervisors. The primary change at Level 2 is to get unit managers to develop repeatable practices for managing their people and to ensure that the skill needs of their units are met. These skills begin building the bond between supervisors and their reports that develops a belief that the organization cares about an individual's skills and development. This belief is a critical component of the employee loyalty that reduces turnover.

At Maturity Level 3, organizations begin experiencing improved productivity through a focus on developing the workforce competencies required to conduct their business activities. For instance, Figure 9.3 compares the level of competency among the members of a software development project at Infosys (shown as the overall competency index) with the project's cost of quality (rework). Infosys reports a significant correlation of 0.45 ($p<0.05$) between these variables, indicating that 21% of the variation in the cost of quality can be accounted for by the collective competency of the team. That is, the more competent the members of team, the less rework the project will experience. Such data can then be used to relate

Company	Initial Turnover		Level 2 Turnover	
Boeing BRS	1998		1999	
	7%		5%	
Novo Nordisk	1996		2000	
	12%		8%	
GDE Systems	1996		1998	
	7.8%		7.1%	

FIGURE 9.2
Annualized voluntary turnover in organizations achieving the Managed Level
Source: [Curtis 03]

competency levels with costs which enable an organization to develop ROI models for investments in workforce development. Executives need such models to make investment decisions and balance workforce development costs with performance benefits.

At Maturity Level 3, executives see a benefit that is hard to quantify, as they become able to evaluate the viability of their strategic business objectives against the capability of their workforce. They also see the emergence of development mechanisms that they can use to prepare the workforce to meet future business challenges. At Maturity Level 3, executives use the practices recommended in the People CMM to integrate the workforce and its development to the organization's strategic business plan.

The results shown in Figure 9.3 are an example of the quantitative analyses of workforce capability implemented at Maturity Level 4 from an Infosys site that has now reached People CMM Level 5. Infosys has been assessed at People CMM Maturity Level 5 and uses data such as these for evaluating the effectiveness of its workforce management practices. Other high-maturity organizations implement similar practices, consistent with the requirements of the People CMM and the needs of their business.

At Maturity Level 4, an organization begins to achieve what Deming [Deming 86] referred to as *profound knowledge* about the impact of its workforce practices on its workforce capability and on the performance of its business processes. This knowledge enables management to make tradeoff decisions regarding investments in workforce practices. For instance, Figure 9.4 presents a comparison developed by Tata Consultancy Services regarding the percent of time spent in training and its correlation with criteria such as defects per person-hour, review efficiency, effort, and rework.

The trends in Figure 9.4 are all in a favorable direction with various measures of effort and quality decreasing, and review efficiency increasing as training time increases; however, data are needed through more quarters to determine the absolute strength of these relationships. Once the strength of these relationships is understood, and asymptotes or other important trends have been determined, then management is armed with a powerful quantitative tool to make decisions regarding the optimal investment in training. Similar mentoring data identified tradeoffs regarding sending senior people on overseas assignments versus using them as mentors at sites in India.

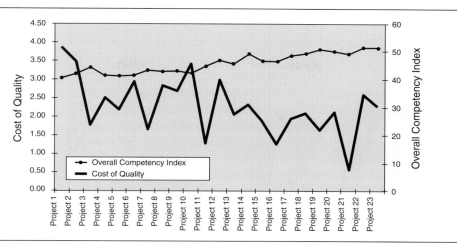

FIGURE 9.3
Correlation of competencies with cost of quality at Infosys
Source: [Curtis 03]

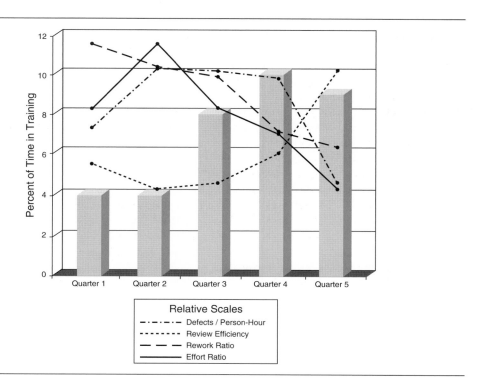

FIGURE 9.4
Relationship of percent time in training to various performance baselines at TCS
Source: [Curtis 03]

At Maturity Level 4, high-maturity organizations are able to adjust their workforce practices to achieve targeted performance objectives using their workforce. Organizations find several exceptional opportunities to increase productivity, quality, and other business results. Reusing assets created by members within a workforce competency has demonstrated remarkable productivity benefits; these assets do not have to be re-created for future use, and lessons do not have to be relearned through wasteful trial and error. The availability of performance data as processes are being performed provides opportunities for improving productivity by understanding and eliminating waste or inefficiency. Finally, integrating people with different competencies in empowered teams provides opportunities to reduce cycle times and the time it takes to reach decisions, identify defects, or resolve problems. As workgroups begin to take on more responsibility for their own management, the organization is able to flatten its hierarchy and shift management's focus increasingly from operational to strategic issues.

At Maturity Level 5, high-maturity organizations are able to experience the results of continual improvement and innovation. Individuals are empowered to manage and improve their own performance, and use these results to drive innovation and improvement in the organization and its processes. Organizations benefit from strategic adaptability and agility in managing the competencies of their workforce and continually improving their processes and capability.

10

Case Studies in Applying the People CMM

10.1 Overview of the Case Studies

The case studies presented in this chapter provide insight into the use of the People CMM by a number of organizations around the globe operating in a variety of business settings. Case studies from the Boeing Company, Pfizer Worldwide Technology, and Intel address organizations that are starting out and maturing using the People CMM as a guide. Several cases highlight the use of the People CMM in support of internal standards or an organization's use of another framework, such as CMMI. Case studies from Intel, Ericsson, and Accenture provide insights into organizations using the People CMM in this way. Application of the People CMM has been occurring in a variety of business areas, as shown in Figure 7.1. One business area where the People CMM has gained traction is in service industries, in both hospitality and business process outsourcing (BPO) settings. Case studies from Club Mahindra, a vacation resort company, and HCLT BPO, a BPO service provider, show the great applicability of the People CMM in these service industry settings. A number of high-maturity organizations have successfully integrated the People CMM into their daily activities. An example of such an organization is shown in the case study of Tata Consultancy Services (TCS).

10.2 Boeing

The Boeing Company has used the People CMM as the framework to improve workforce practices since 1997 [Vu 01]. Boeing Information Systems conducted the first multimodel assessment, using both the Software CMM and the People CMM in 1997. Boeing Information Systems began to use the People CMM as a framework to improve its workforce practices and retain skilled workers in 1997. Boeing has developed an internal capability to conduct People CMM assessments. Nineteen assessments have been completed at Boeing, including both stand-alone People CMM-Based Assessments and Joint Assessments [Vu 01].

The Boeing Company Shared Services Group Internal Computing Business Resources Support (BRS) organization has used the People CMM and the Software CMM together in their process improvement and management endeavors. This organization reports that it achieved Maturity Level 2 using the People CMM, and it was the first Boeing organization to accomplish this. This organization, the result of a merger of two organizations, has approximately 130 staff. The Business Resources Support organization had previously achieved Software CMM Maturity Level 2 with its two merged organizations in 1996 and 1997.

The management team in BRS demonstrates a philosophy of valuing employees. The management team sponsored a program to build and improve people processes in the organization using the People CMM. Even with a merger of the organization occurring, the management team saw the need to improve workforce processes along with the organization's software processes. In 1997, the organization had a departure rate of 50%. In 1998, that rate had dropped to 7%, and in 1999 it was at 3%. BRS reports that this improvement was due to the people processes implemented in the organization. As shown in Figure 10.1, BRS managers were able to spend more time managing the human capital of the organization, while increasing employee satisfaction and significantly decreasing employee turnover. Thus, BRS was able to address issues relative to both the Software CMM and the People CMM together, while experiencing decreasing employee turnover rates and improving employee satisfaction.

While managers were increasing the effectiveness of their time spent managing employees and increasing the time they spend with each employee on performance management discussions, their employees were indicating that significant improvements had occurred in the performance management activities in the BRS organization. Performance management is an area of interest, not just because of the marked improvements noted in BRS, but also because it is the process area most commonly in need of the greatest improvement in organizations striving to achieve Maturity Level 2. Figure 10.2 shows the increase in employee evaluation of performance management practices at BRS from 1996 to 1999. Also during this period, employee satisfaction rose. In 1996, BRS had an average employee satisfaction rating of only 5.7 (on a 10-point scale). By 1999, it had risen to a rating of 8.9, with no individuals expressing dissatisfaction with the organization. These results are depicted in Figures 10.1 and 10.3. During the last two years shown in Figure 10.3, the BRS unit was affected by

	Time Managing People	Employee Satisfaction	Employee Turnover
Industry	30%–60%	6.8	16%
Boeing	10%–35%	5.8	10%–15%
BRS	35%–75%	8.9	< 3%

FIGURE 10.1
Results at Boeing BRS
Note: Employee satisfaction is measured on a 10-point scale of increasing satisfaction.

Performance Management	1996	1999
Unit performance criteria	3.2	8.2
Individual performance criteria	3.1	8.6
Performance review	4.2	9.2
Focus on performance of the job	3.1	8.7
Formal performance feedback	3.2	9.2
Performance improvement	3.4	9.2
Recognition and reward	3.8	8.7

FIGURE 10.2
Performance management improvements at Boeing BRS

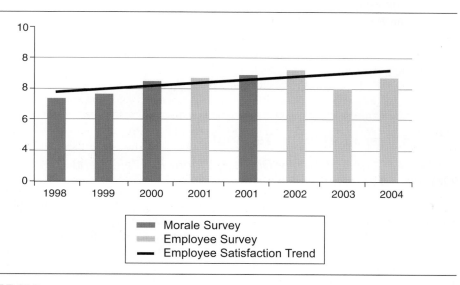

FIGURE 10.3
Employee satisfaction results at Boeing BRS and the successor organization
(IT Services, World Headquarters Support)

the Boeing merger and acquisition activities and transitioned into the IT Services, World Headquarters Support organization [Foster 05].

Boeing believes that its investments in the People CMM will help the organization improve its workforce processes, as well as attract and retain skilled workers [Vu 01]. Boeing's use of the People CMM has a scope of impact of over 6,000 employees. Within this organization, People CMM Assessments, People CMM Workshops, Readiness Reviews, and Quarterly Reviews are conducted, and qualified personnel provide training and internal consulting on the People CMM and its use. Boeing has experienced these results from applying the People CMM.

- Workforce practices have improved overall, in spite of reorganizations.
- Skills acquired and competency-related tools used can be carried into the future, enabling competency-based management and development of the workforce.
- Individuals and managers repeatedly demonstrate high quality in performing their committed work.
- Continued sponsorship for ongoing workforce improvement has been demonstrated.
- Measures of workforce practices are collected and used in managing the organization.
- Key roles throughout the organization have been identified and are qualified to support ongoing workforce practice improvement (e.g., training focal point, process owners).
- Human Resources and Finance work closely with people managers to sustain good workforce practices.
- Executive management regularly reviews workforce practices and their improvement progress [Foster 05].

10.3   Pfizer Worldwide Technology

Teresa A. Suganski, Senior Director, Worldwide Talent and Organization Capability, Pfizer

Pfizer Worldwide Technology (WT) was created in late 2006. This restructure took several independently run functions and combined them into "OneIT" in order to drive Pfizer business objectives through a strategic and aligned approach for using technology. In addition, the combined organization was designed to support a new shared services model of delivery. WT is an organization of 3,100 IT professionals who act as strategic business partners to leaders in all Pfizer divisions including Research and Development, Medical, Commercial, Manufacturing, and Corporate functions. WT supports over 90,000 colleagues in 90 countries with a mission to deliver business value and delight our business partners by transforming WT into an effective, agile organization that uses repeatable solutions, shared services, and quality-driven design.

10.3.1   Why Did Pfizer Worldwide Technology Select the People CMM?

WT leaders determined early on that a deliberate strategy was required to bring together the various legacy information technology (IT) organizations across Pfizer, and they wanted an approach that would support both the culture and the "logistics" of becoming OneIT. They decided to base their alignment approach on the People Capability Maturity Model (People CMM). The People CMM was seen as an organizational change model based on state-of-the-art workforce practices to help organizations

- develop the workforce required to execute the business strategy,
- characterize maturity of workforce practices,
- set priorities for improving workforce capability,
- integrate improvements in process and the workforce, and
- become an employer of choice.

WT selected the People CMM because it would

- align legacy IT divisions by defining a common philosophy, approach, and "language" related to workforce practices to achieve OneIT, engage colleagues, and improve overall job satisfaction;
- effectively manage talent across WT to support business strategies by creating a shared understanding of competencies and roles and by defining a common methodology for talent management and review;
- enable data reporting and analysis through the common use of systems, and make data collection and analysis the foundation for workforce development decisions;
- encourage transparency and collaboration across WT lines in the areas of performance management, talent development, compensation, portfolio management, and workforce planning and reporting; and
- provide specific measures on the utilization and effectiveness of workforce practices.

In addition, the WT leadership team appreciated that the People CMM incorporates four workforce practice themes and five levels of maturity. This meant the model would provide a framework for organizational change and development over several years, with each maturity level building an enhanced system of workforce practices added to those implemented at earlier levels. Figure 10.4 presents these levels of workforce practices enabled through implementing the People CMM.

A fundamental precept of the People CMM is that the workforce practices at each maturity level survive only if they are "institutionalized." The WT team charged with developing and implementing the People CMM within WT spent their first year focusing on the institutionalization criteria of Commitment to Perform and Ability to Perform. Commitment to Perform focuses on ensuring that documented policies or procedures were established and maintained and organizational roles were assigned the responsibility for assisting, advising, and coordinating practices. Ability to Perform focuses on ensuring that organizational roles were assigned responsibility and authority for ensuring activities are performed, practices and procedures for performing activities are documented, and colleagues conducting these activities receive the orientation and training needed.

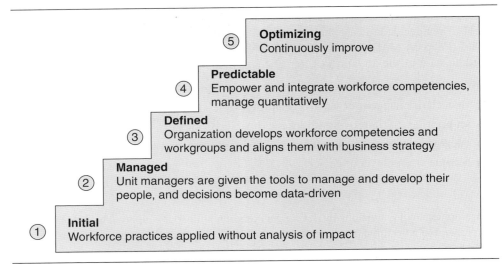

FIGURE 10.4
Progression of human capital management focus as organizations adopt higher maturity levels of the People CMM

In addition, the team developed the fundamental operating principles which would guide WT implementation of the People CMM over several years. These operating principles were as follows.

- Align with Pfizer Corporate.
- Partner with Human Resources (HR) at every opportunity.
- Use and leverage existing systems (talent planning, performance management, the HR self-service portal, Personal Profiles, and individual development plans).
- Influence enhancements.
- Push for system integration.
- Don't reinvent the wheel; "reapply with pride."
- Minimize unique IT investments: Keep maintenance at a minimum; go for a long "shelf life"; buy, don't build.
- Build over time, with minimal fanfare—no "flavor of the month."
- Develop, don't "own," tools and processes.
- Use managers and leaders to implement.

10.3.2   Development of the WT Colleague Engagement Framework

The first step in the successful implementation or "institutionalization" of the People CMM in WT was to modify it slightly to more closely align with the lexicon of Pfizer workforce practices. Pfizer adapted the names to fit its existing terms, but did not modify the practices themselves.

As indicated in Figure 10.5, the result was careful adherence to the four themes and the fundamental principles of the People CMM, combined with a more WT-specific interpretation of the workforce practices associated with each maturity level. In addition, the decision was made to refer to the People CMM as the Colleague Engagement Framework (CEF) within Pfizer Worldwide Technology.

Maturity Levels	People CMM Threads			
	Developing Roles and Competencies	Building Workgroups and Culture	Motivating and Managing Performance	Shaping the Workforce
5 Optimizing	Continuous Proficiency/Capability Improvement		Organizational Performance Alignment	Continuous Workforce Innovation
4 Predictable	Role/Competency-Based Assets	Role/Competency Integration Empowered Workgroups	Quantitative Performance Management	Organizational Proficiency/ Capability Management
3 Defined	Talent Management and Review WT Roles and Competencies	Workgroup Development Participatory Culture	Role/Competency-Based Practices Career Development	Workforce Planning and Reporting
2 Managed	Training and Development	Communication and Coordination	Performance Tools: • Goal Setting • Compensation • Performance Management • Rewards & Recognition	Staffing

FIGURE 10.5
Process threads of the People CMM as mapped to the context of Pfizer Worldwide Technology

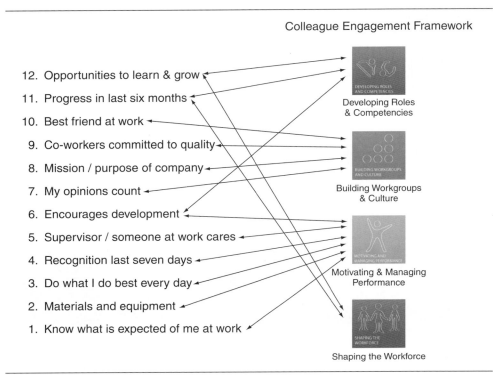

FIGURE 10.6
Progression of human capital management focus as organizations adopt higher maturity levels of the People CMM

The WT implementation team was charged by WT leadership to position and utilize the People CMM in such a way that managers developed the competencies required to build and maintain strong colleague engagement as measured by the Gallup Survey (Pfizer Colleague Engagement Survey). Figure 10.6 shows the alignment of the CEF with the components of the Colleague Engagement Survey.

10.3.3 Deployment of the WT Colleague Engagement Framework

With the workforce practices matrix in place, the WT implementation team set about addressing the issue of making the CEF accessible and easy to understand for all colleagues. The intention was to develop an innovative approach to providing easy colleague access to the workforce practices defined in the CEF while highlighting the comprehensive and highly integrated nature of the model; to stress that the workforce practices were not discrete "one-off" events, but rather a set of processes, tools, and systems, visibly and transparently "knit together." Partnering closely with WT Communications the team developed three key elements to achieve these goals: CEF Flash Simulation, CEF Portal, CEF Game.

CEF Flash Simulation

The second element developed by WT Communications and the CEF Implementation Team is a simulation that takes the graphical elements tied to the People CMM themes, as embodied in the WT CEF, and makes them "come to life." The simulation literally walks the viewer through the CEF, taking him or her on a journey through the framework with a new colleague (George) and his manager. The simulation uses the example of the Lominger competencies to illustrate how workforce practices are tied together across the People CMM themes. The tone of the simulation is decidedly nonacademic and intentionally colloquial. The simulation serves as an introduction to the concepts and basic components of the Colleague Engagement Framework utilizing color and other graphical elements to draw in and engage the viewer.

Figure 10.7 is a voiceover excerpt and visual image from the CEF Flash Simulation describing how the new employee, George, came into the WT organization.

> *Let's take a look at how the CEF would support developing a colleague within WT.*
>
> *Let's start with a new colleague named George.*
> *It's George's first day on the job, and he's headed to New Hire Training.*
> *But let's go back a bit and see how George got here.*
>
> *George's manager worked with HR and WT's Workforce Planning group to identify the need for the new, entry-level position.*
>
> *Together, they created a job description using the Automated Role Profile. That's a tool that takes into account all of the roles within WT (called the Universal Role Set), Career Ladders, Lominger Behavioral Competencies, and Technical Skills (using SFIA).*
>
> *As part of George's interview for the job, all interviewers used a behavior-based interview guide that used Lominger and SFIA as its foundation.*
>
> *George got the job, and as part of the new hire process, he and his manager completed a Lominger assessment (see the connections?). This Lominger assessment will follow George and his manager as they plan for the year.*
>
> *Together, they create George's objectives for the year.*
>
> *One of George's goals is to take the "Managing My Career" course. This will help George articulate with his manager what he's passionate about, where his skills are, and what the needs of the organization are. George will use his Lominger assessment to inform his work in the course.*

IDP

□ *Complete Individual Development Plan (IDP)*

FIGURE 10.7
The CEF Flash Simulation provides an introduction to the concepts and basic components of the Colleague Engagement Framework.

CEF Portal

The portal, which sits on the WT Web site, provides a "one-stop shop" to house all workforce practice tools and processes. The portal, shown in Figure 10.8, is organized around four graphical elements tied to the four People CMM themes and repeats the graphic for each theme in all materials and processes associated with that theme. In keeping with the guiding principles for implementation, the portal also provides links to the Pfizer systems which support the various workforce practices.

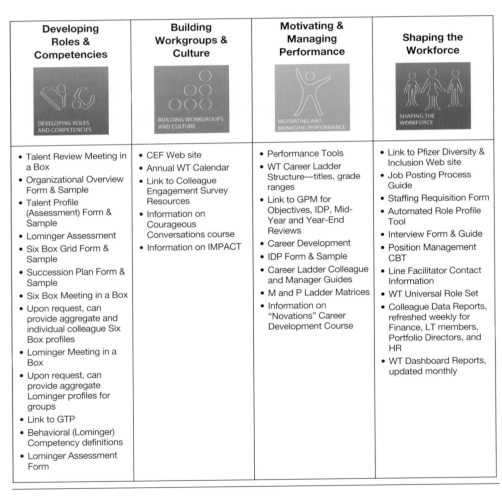

Developing Roles & Competencies	Building Workgroups & Culture	Motivating & Managing Performance	Shaping the Workforce
• Talent Review Meeting in a Box • Organizational Overview Form & Sample • Talent Profile (Assessment) Form & Sample • Lominger Assessment • Six Box Grid Form & Sample • Succession Plan Form & Sample • Six Box Meeting in a Box • Upon request, can provide aggregate and individual colleague Six Box profiles • Lominger Meeting in a Box • Upon request, can provide aggregate Lominger profiles for groups • Link to GTP • Behavioral (Lominger) Competency definitions • Lominger Assessment Form	• CEF Web site • Annual WT Calendar • Link to Colleague Engagement Survey Resources • Information on Courageous Conversations course • Information on IMPACT	• Performance Tools • WT Career Ladder Structure—titles, grade ranges • Link to GPM for Objectives, IDP, Mid-Year and Year-End Reviews • Career Development • IDP Form & Sample • Career Ladder Colleague and Manager Guides • M and P Ladder Matrices • Information on "Novations" Career Development Course	• Link to Pfizer Diversity & Inclusion Web site • Job Posting Process Guide • Staffing Requisition Form • Automated Role Profile Tool • Interview Form & Guide • Position Management CBT • Line Facilitator Contact Information • WT Universal Role Set • Colleague Data Reports, refreshed weekly for Finance, LT members, Portfolio Directors, and HR • WT Dashboard Reports, updated monthly

FIGURE 10.8
The CEF Portal provides a comprehensive interface to workforce practices within WT

Developing Roles & Competencies	Building Workgroups & Culture	Motivating & Managing Performance	Shaping the Workforce
DEVELOPING ROLES AND COMPETENCIES	BUILDING WORKGROUPS AND CULTURE	MOTIVATING AND MANAGING PERFORMANCE	SHAPING THE WORKFORCE
• Lominger Meeting in a Box • Technical (SFIA) Skill definitions • WT Universal Role Set • Automated Role Profile • New Hire Curriculum • WT Standard Processes & Tools Curriculum • Role-Based Curriculum • Competency-Based Leadership Curriculum • Training Reporting & Administration • Colleagues can view and update their training transcript • Managers can request training and gap reports for their direct reports • Training Course Development • How to create a CBT to P2L • How to add an instructor-led course to P2L • Link to P2L			•

FIGURE 10.8
Continued

CEF Game

The final element developed to introduce the Colleague Engagement Framework concepts and specific workforce practices to colleagues is a board game. As with the CEF Portal, CEF Flash Simulation, and other CEF-related internal communications, the graphical elements tied to each theme are also repeated in the board game, sending a subtle but important message that all workforce practices are tied to the CEF. Teams compete to get to the final square on the board, answering questions related to the themes and specific workforce practices. The game was designed for group play in a meeting setting, but will be adapted to allow for Web-based individual play.

10.3.4 Next Steps and Future Work in Pfizer Worldwide Technology

Over the next several years the team will focus on the remaining criteria for institutionalization, including

- measurement and analysis;
  - the creation and use of measurements in each process area to determine the status, performance, and effectiveness of practices;
  - robust analysis of WT results on the Pfizer Colleague Engagement Survey (the Gallup 12);
- confirmation/verification of implementation;
  - verification by a responsible colleague that activities are conducted according to the organization's documented policies, practices, and procedures (this colleague also will address noncompliance);
  - periodic review by executive management of the process area activities, status, and results, and subsequent resolution of any issues; and
- periodic auditing of the definition and use of measures for compliance with organizational policies.

The CEF Web site will continue to evolve, moving to a SharePoint platform which allows for a more fluid, interactive experience when accessing the site. In addition, the team will continue to work on ensuring that the CEF provides workforce practices that support the WT Strategic Business Framework.

10.4 Intel Information Technology

Jack Anderson, Chair, Innovation Management Working Group, Innovation Value Institute

Intel Information Technology (Intel IT) supports the computing needs of over 80,000 Intel employees in more than 70 sites worldwide. Intel IT sources, designs, develops, implements, and maintains the hardware, software, and IT solutions that enable the company to run effectively. The environment and supporting infrastructure is very complex, and organizational changes occur frequently to meet emerging business needs. Responding to continual change in technological and business conditions is vital to Intel's success, and has led the company to create a learning and development environment capable of adjusting to these changes.

For several years, Intel IT had conducted self-assessments using Intel corporate tools such as Safety Self-Assessment, Corporate HR Organization Health surveys, and

Self-Assessment Methodology (SAM), along with customized tools such as Intel IT's Organizational Assessment, to identify areas for improvement within the organization [Intel 03]. While organizations apply many different techniques to move toward strategic human capital management, they often lack a comprehensive framework for implementing advanced people management practices.

Until 2001, Intel IT did not have a framework that measured its workforce practices and organizational capabilities. After investigating several different ideas, Intel IT decided that the People CMM was the most appropriate model for attaining its objectives of developing a world-class workforce and organization capabilities for IT by strategically shaping its future workforce and influencing its partners and industry.

After attending the Software Engineering Institute's training on the People CMM, the Intel IT core team converted their entire assessment process into a gap analysis. Initially, the team took the official People CMM process and mapped it against the process currently used. The result was a process familiar to Intel IT employees, which enables the organization to measure progress from one assessment to the next without losing the spirit of the original SAM assessment.

The core team elected to use the practices identified in each process area of the formal assessment as their questions, and developed a scoring system that mapped to their SAM process via measures and a reporting process that resonated with leadership and organization employees.

10.4.1   Intel-Adapted People CMM Assessment Process

Intel introduced a "lite" assessment method based on the familiar SAM process that allowed the company to obtain actionable results. Intel adopted a new scoring mechanism and drafted a core team of assessors who had the best visibility into their workforce and people practices. The assessment process is an adaptation of the familiar SAM-lite process. Each assessor completes the assessment independently. A facilitator then aggregates and analyzes the results and the results are discussed in a large group consensus meeting. Figure 10.9 shows the results from the Intel-adapted People CMM assessment process. The three to five top-priority improvement solutions are then embedded into management roles.

Initially, the results showed that Intel IT had most of the Level 2 People CMM process areas under control, but had not made as much progress as it would have liked on the Level 3 process areas. Based on the results, Intel IT prioritized Training and Development and Communication and Coordination at Level 2 and most of the Level 3 process areas for investment and improvement in the following assessment period.

Performing this kind of assessment is useful in that it uses a recognized industry-standard improvement model in a very efficient way for such a large organization. Presenting data in this way can help some technical managers who have not yet gotten the message that people practices are as important as all other IT technical practices.

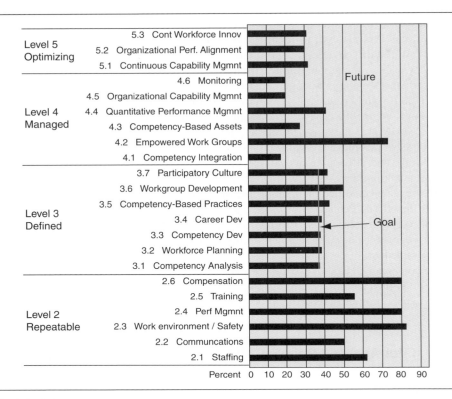

FIGURE 10.9
Results from the Intel-adapted People CMM assessment process
Source: [Curley 04] with permission

10.4.2   Developing IT People as Assets

From the People CMM Level 3 process areas, Intel chose three key elements that it considered pivotal in improving the IT people asset: organizational competency management, workforce development, and career development.

Organizational Competency Management

Competency management is concerned with defining, qualifying, and managing the current and future competencies required for the IT organization and for the enterprise as a whole. Organization-wide competency management is a process that is difficult to perform and can be easily overlooked because everybody assumes someone else is doing it. Engaging in competency management at the IT organization level ensures that the competencies you begin developing now are the ones you need in two years' time.

Workforce Development

To implement workforce development, you need a comprehensive documented process that provides IT managers with a framework for making the right staffing decisions and growing employee competencies. Workforce planning is concerned with putting the right number of people with the right knowledge, skills, experiences, and competencies in the right jobs at the right time. Workforce planning and development occurs within the context of the firm's mission, strategic plan, and budgetary resources.

Career Development

Career development initiatives should provide a mechanism for employees to manage their own careers, identify and obtain the training and experience they need to progress through the IT organization, and add value to their work. At Intel IT, this goal translates into a process with five integrated components:

- Career paths—illustrative paths for the most typical career trajectories paired with the skills required for a new position
- Job descriptions—standardized job descriptions with specifically defined competencies
- Skills Builder—a skills self-assessment tool with options to provide feedback to people on their readiness for a new position and provide recommendations for a personal development plan
- Development plans—a standardized template and development process for recording and tracking individual development plans
- Training—specific training resources organized by job type

This integrated process was supported by an intranet portal that provides these tools and services to the globally distributed workforce [Anderson 05].

Intel IT used the People CMM findings as a key input into Organizational Capability Assessments (OCAs). These OCA analyses compared a wide range of future trend information (e.g., business and technical trends, and emerging workforce demographics) with data derived from People CMM appraisals of current strengths and areas of improvement to produce an action plan that was understood and supported throughout the organization. This plan helped to improve the quality of development programs 25% over three years. It established such programs as the IT Principal Engineer Program and Technical Leadership Pipeline that will enable a strong workforce for the future.

10.4.3   Evolution of Capability Measures: From Functional Practice to Innovation

Intel IT launched the assessment of people capabilities as part of a drive to become a world-class IT organization. With strong, visionary leadership who believed IT had the ability to transform itself from a utility to a value center for the company, Intel IT initially focused on operational excellence and functional reliability. Assessments at this stage took the form of measurements of and continuous improvement for the basics, such as safety and functional performance management.

Once it showed significant improvement, the organization strove to become a recognized leader of performance demonstrating the Intel Corporate Values: Customer Orientation; Discipline; Great Place to Work (GPTW); Quality; Risk Taking; and Results Orientation. It started employing Intel's SAM methodology to measure itself. And with this came a striving goal to achieve Intel's top award for organizations, the IQA (Intel Quality Award). This serious focus required an in-depth analysis of the people side of the business, relating directly to Intel's GPTW value. And with this came the study, adaptation, and implementation of the People CMM and the ability to articulate strengths and improvement areas for the management of IT's people assets.

Once IT achieved its goal and was recognized as a role model of Intel Corporate Values with the IQA, it started to look at the next level of capability: the ability of the IT workforce to be creative, adaptive, and innovative. It looked at practices that supported Risk Taking and creative thinking. It looked at the top levels of the People CMM and assessed its systemic innovative practices for technical leadership and transformational mentoring and training. IT took a serious look at improving the innovation-enabling aspects identified in the People CMM and developed an in-depth assessment of innovation practices—the Innovation Self-Assessment—to measure strengths and improvement areas in its culture of innovation.

Over the course of three years, Intel IT achieved many of its innovation goals, including a 200% increase of patents emerging from the IT workforce, and solid improvement in employee feedback about the organization's leadership and GPTW scores. The organization has been able to share best known methods for driving innovation and has used this focus area to build partnerships with Intel customers and strategic IT partners. Intel IT has also been a co-founder of the Innovation Value Institute (IVI), a consortium of over 35 companies that have come together to improve the IT industry (for more information, visit http://ivi.nuim.ie/).

Intel IT received a great deal of value from the People CMM and the focused assessments that followed. It used them to focus on the big picture of capability rather than piecemeal improvements.

10.5   Ericsson

An example of an organization using the People CMM in support of its internal processes and standards is Ericsson. Ericsson has developed a Service Delivery Maturity Model (SDMM) for use in guiding its services business and improving service delivery performance throughout the business. The SDMM is a complex matrix model where the maturity level is viewed from three perspectives: people management, delivery performance, and organizational culture [Ericsson 08]. While meeting the unique needs of the Ericsson services business, the people management perspective of the SDMM is aligned with the workforce practices found in the People CMM. The organizational culture perspective is focused on creating service business awareness in the service delivery organization. Ericsson has deployed an internal assessment methodology to certify service business units as conforming to the SDMM, thus demonstrating internally and externally to its customers its capability as "a reliable business partner" within the organization [Ericsson 08].

10.6   Accenture

10.6.1   Process for Performance: How the People CMM Helps Organizations Achieve High Performance

Since 2001, Accenture has committed to a long-term industrialization journey across its Delivery Center Network for Technology—a part of its Global Delivery Network that performs system integration and application outsourcing work on a worldwide basis. The Accenture Global Delivery Network is a network comprising more than 50 delivery centers at carefully chosen locations across the globe. Each center is staffed by skilled professionals who form an integrated delivery network comprising over 83,000 individuals. Accenture uses a number of industry standards to guide its quality initiatives, such as Capability Maturity Model Integration (CMMI), the People Capability Maturity Model (People CMM), the Information Technology Infrastructure Library (ITIL), ISO 9001, ISO 14001, ISO 20000, ISO 27001, the eSourcing Capability Model for Service Providers (eSCM-SP), and Lean Six Sigma [Accenture 08].

Accenture has been an active user of the CMM family of models since the early 1990s. Accenture has pursued CMMI Maturity Level 5 across the entire Global Delivery Network, with approximately 90% of its delivery center employees currently working in CMMI Maturity Level 5 centers, including the Accenture delivery centers in India, China, the Philippines, Spain, and Brazil. In addition, Accenture has implemented CMMI across its entire U.S. Public Services Operating Unit and has achieved CMMI Maturity Level 4 in that organization. Accenture is also one of the few organizations in the world to have achieved People CMM Maturity Level 5. Accenture is pursuing the People CMM across its Global Delivery Network and has been independently appraised at Maturity Level 5 in centers in India, China, and the Philippines, and at Maturity Level 3 in three centers in Europe and Africa.

In undertaking this journey, Accenture selected the comprehensive People CMM as the framework of choice to benchmark its people practices. Due to the maturity of existing baseline processes, it achieved appraisal at the highest level of the model (Maturity Level 5) in its delivery centers in India in just 18 months across a workforce at that time of more than 17,000 delivery people. Maintaining the momentum, two further locations have also achieved People CMM Maturity Level 5 appraisal results as the company has undertaken a multicontinent rollout of the framework to Accenture delivery centers in North America, South America, Europe, Asia, and Africa. So why use the People CMM, and how can this framework help an organization achieve high performance?

10.6.2   Why Did Accenture Undertake the Journey?

Accenture believes that attaining higher maturity levels of the People CMM is helping it in the following ways.

- Developing distinctive capabilities—The People CMM framework enables Accenture to measure and develop capabilities on a consistent, global basis. Having distinctive capabilities is increasingly important in a competitive market.

- Reducing risk—As Accenture continues to experience rapid growth, it believes that the People CMM is considerably reducing the people dependency of its practices.

- Linking business outcomes—The People CMM practices enable the organization to gain a clearer perspective of people practices within the context of its desired business outcomes.

- Establishing a capability development framework—Motivation has been achieved by providing its employees with a structured framework on the skills they need to develop in order to be effective.

- Increasing employee engagement and attracting talent—Creating an industrialized approach to employee communication has a direct correlation to the increased engagement of Accenture's people and has served as a strong recruitment marketing tool.

10.6.3   What Differentiates Accenture's Adoption of the People CMM?

More than 35,000 employees have been impacted by the People CMM program in Accenture. The sheer geographical complexity of the implementation, zigzagging across multiple continents including North America (Canada and the United States), South America (Argentina and Mexico), Europe (Latvia, Slovakia, the United Kingdom, and Spain), Asia Pacific (China, the Philippines, and India), and Africa (Mauritius), Accenture believes that the global consistency of its existing processes and capabilities has eased the path toward accreditation.

Although the scale of the accreditation program has been considerable, staged implementation with defined targets has addressed the individual needs of specific delivery centers. For example, the company has taken into account cultural differences as well as local employment law.

For any organization experiencing rapid growth—such as the doubling of Accenture India's workforce in one year—the need to drive a measurable, repeatable, and predictable employment experience for its people as well as its procedures is a business priority. As part of Accenture's expansive plan to establish a world-class global delivery model and benchmark the services of Human Resources, the introduction of the People CMM brings people practices in line with the standards it has already achieved around delivery excellence.

Accenture believes several essential factors are influencing its People CMM achievements.

- Strong endorsement from the global leadership of its business operations, including senior executives such as the Delivery Center Network for Technology lead and the High Performance Delivery lead, provided executive-level global sponsorship for these efforts.

- Dedicated leadership, and ownership of the implementation from a business executive in each of the local delivery centers, have supported and enhanced this global sponsorship.

- Small, effective, localized teams (including representatives from Human Resources, the software engineering process team, and technology specialists) were able to implement locally a consistent set of global human resources processes.

- Sound baseline processes meant that Accenture began the accreditation process from a high level of maturity with less distance to go to achieve the set goals and objectives.

- Internally, its employees were engaged by positioning the People CMM as an improvement mechanism rather than an accreditation program. With actions and goals targeted specifically to each delivery center, the program was personalized by the teams to appeal to their local audiences.

10.6.4   What Has Accenture Achieved?

As a recent Accenture publication has shown, the development of a distinctive capability in multiplying talent can create extraordinary value and become an important and lasting source of competitive advantage that powers an organization to high performance. Adoption of the People CMM framework has helped Accenture delivery centers attain remarkable achievements in their business and workforce objectives of increased employee morale, satisfaction, and engagement; better talent management; improved workforce capability to meet business growth; and improved marketability. Samples of these achievements are shown in Figure 10.10. The People CMM framework not only has contributed toward improvements in both engagement and attrition rates within Accenture delivery centers, but also has helped the company to realize additional benefits within the various local markets.

Personal Continuous Improvement in the Philippines

One of the process areas under the People CMM framework refers to "continuous improvement." At the Accenture delivery center in the Philippines, myPod is an example of continuous personal improvement and quantifiable personal goals. myPod, shown in Figure 10.11, is aimed at encouraging innovation at an individual level, with each individual having his or her own "Pod station." This supports Accenture's global strategy that encourages innovation and high performance.

Accenture Delivery Center	Benefits	Further Outcomes
India	9% improvement in engagement in the past two years	Ranked among the top ten "Best Employers in India" conducted by *Business Today* magazine
China	7% reduction in attrition within a year	Earned an award as one of the top ten employers in China
The Philippines	16% improvement in engagement in the past two years	Achieved a 2% reduction in attrition in 18 months

FIGURE 10.10
Achievements of the People CMM initiative in Accenture global delivery centers

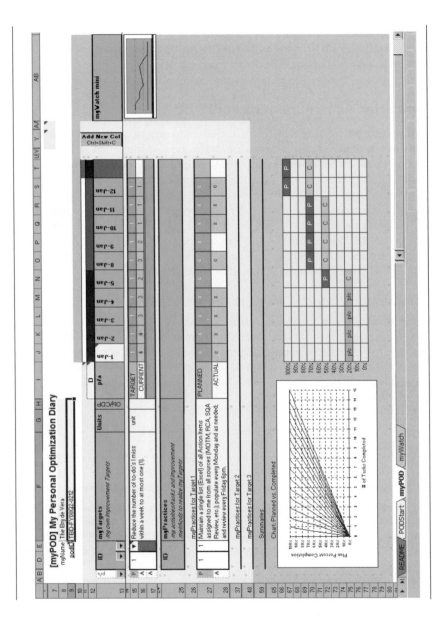

FIGURE 10.11
One view of myPod: My Personal Optimization Diary from an Accenture delivery center staff member

Top Ten Accolade for China

Accenture China earned an award in 2007 as one of the "Top 10 Best Employers in China" by global human resources consultancy Hewitt Associates. The award followed a thorough review entailing meetings, interviews, and an online survey to compare the working environments of organizations across a wide variety of industries. Commenting on the role of the People CMM implementation in gaining the award, Chi-Wei Wang, executive sponsor for the Accenture delivery centers in China, says, "The assessment process has left no stone unturned, introducing a level of rigor that is bringing significant benefits to the Accenture delivery centers in China."

10.6.5   Accenture's Commitment to High Performance

Accenture is committed to maintaining and improving practices in line with the three-year renewal and review required by the People CMM appraisal process. In a highly complex and competitive global marketplace, Accenture recognizes that the need to improve the ability to attract, develop, motivate, organize, and retain talent is stronger than ever. Being one of the first organizations to adopt the People CMM framework on this scope and scale, Accenture believes that it has demonstrated that accreditation is not a daunting and complex process, but rather an opportunity to achieve high performance across the organization.

10.7   Club Mahindra

Mahindra Holidays & Resorts India Ltd. (MHRIL) is a vacation timeshare company. To compete in its market, MHRIL decided to focus on its people as a competitive differentiator. This is a focus that could have significant impact on MHRIL, as understaffing and poor training are two of the most common people problems in the hospitality industry [Poulston 08]. Poor training has also been shown to be the cause of many other problems in the hospitality industry [Poulston 08].

A People CMM-based improvement program was initiated in 2003 to align workforce practices with the business strategy and MHRIL's existing strong commitment to service excellence. Club Mahindra implemented this People CMM program at its Varca Beach property in Goa, India [Mallick 05]. The focus of these activities was to define and begin to use the workforce competencies needed to succeed at the Goa property. Once the workforce competencies were defined, existing human resources practices were evaluated. Some of these practices satisfied the model as implemented, but some needed adjustments or updates to meet the intent of the People CMM practices. All human resources processes were upgraded to be consistent with Competency-Based Practices at People CMM Maturity Level 3. Revised workforce practices were built around the newly defined competencies to implement practices such as competency-based interviewing, competency-based appraisals, competency-based rewards and recognition schemes, and competency-based nomination to operational teams and committees. Key lessons learned from this effort were

- the importance of treating the initiative as a project;

- implementing change management activities in support of the deployment of improved workforce practices;

- planning for the involvement of all personnel, regardless of level, encompassing operational managers and staff;

- planned communications efforts to provide information and orientation to affected personnel;

- regular internal audits as well as external preassessment exercises to check and verify the effectiveness of the implementation; and

- obtaining full support and encouragement by top management, thereby providing a sense of ownership in the improvement program.

Tangible Benefits	Example Results
1. Improved customer satisfaction	• Decrease in negative remarks (12% to 7.8%) • Increase in positive remarks (66% to 74%) • Increase in members volunteering to give feedback (78% to 82%) • Increase in guest scores among all departments; for example, on the Holiday Experience Profile (HEP), the average unit score rose from 3.05 to 3.45
2. Reduced operational costs	• Recruitment costs were reduced; no longer needs to advertise in local newspaper to get applications • Attrition rate fell considerably from December 2003 (4.5%) to June 2004 (1.5%)
3. Improved objective performance scores	• Appraisal scores improved over three quarters, with greater consistency across departments
4. Established a "knowledge bank"	• Established a forum to share experiences and learn from each other on a continuing basis • Knowledge bank is updated on an event-driven basis and learnings are shared and put into practice

Intangible Benefits	Example Behaviors
1. Employee morale	• Fall in attrition rate • Better feedback on training and orientation sessions
2. Greater cross-level interaction	• Increase in voluntary participation • Constructive debates on important issues
3. Rise of participatory culture	• Increased volunteering to committees • Increased delegation in decision-making processes
4. Air of positivism and openness	• Clarity on unit processes and policies • Level of interaction during orientation sessions

FIGURE 10.12
Tangible and intangible benefits of the People CMM at Club Mahindra

As Club Mahindra achieved People CMM Maturity Level 3, its gains in employee satisfaction and retention translated into improved experiences and satisfaction for its members (customers). Club Mahindra Varca Beach in Goa experienced considerable benefits from the People CMM-based improvement program. Once better workforce development processes were in place, managers developed better people management skills. As managers' skills improved, Club Mahindra observed faster competency growth within the workforce, leading to better service quality and performance. Club Mahindra also accomplished better organizational development, leading to better workforce satisfaction that contributed to enhanced customer satisfaction. Figure 10.12 summarizes both the tangible and intangible benefits achieved by Club Mahindra.

A recent study of the relationship between human resource management (HRM) and organizational performance in the Indian hotel industry found that hotel performance is positively correlated with HRM practices [Chand 07]. Club Mahindra's experiences in implementing the People CMM underscore those findings.

10.8   HCLT BPO

Many companies outsource their business processes to an external service provider, who in turn owns, administers, and manages the selected process based on defined and measurable performance criteria. This global business process outsourcing (BPO) market is forecast to exceed $450 billion by 2012 [NelsonHall 08]. In India alone, BPO revenues are expected to reach $10.9 billion in FY2008, and the number of employed workers in BPO services is expected to exceed 704,000 [D'Monte 08]. Organizations in this marketplace are faced with a number of issues that the People CMM can help them address. Several BPO organizations have found benefits from using the People CMM, with BPO organizations achieving as high as Maturity Level 5 beginning in 2007 [HCL 07].

HCL Technologies Ltd.–BPO Services is a division of HCL Technologies Ltd., a global technology and IT enterprise. It employs over 12,800 professionals operating out of India and Northern Ireland. HCL Technologies Ltd. started its BPO operations in its N1 Center in 2001. The center began operations with telemarketing services and soon won a project of fund collections. In 2003, two U.S.-based retail clients began operations with HCL's N1 Center. One of these clients started operations in N1 with only 50 seats, and today it is one of the largest of N1's clients, with close to 600 seats. By 2007, N1 was operating out of three locations employing over 1,500 people.

10.8.1   The Need for the People CMM in the BPO Business

Based on the NASSCOM studies, the current HR trends within the BPO industry reveal that accessibility to talent is very high (at around 80% to 90% of total graduates), but only 10% to 15% of these students have the skills for direct employment without prior training. Out of this suitable pool, only about 50% are willing to join the industry. A high attrition rate of about 40% annually in the BPO industry in India was predicted to create a paucity of 300,000 BPO professionals by 2009. This shortage is expected to cause a rise in expenditures for recruitment, training, and development, potentially depriving the industry of its low-cost benefit. Managing attrition in BPOs has become a strategic priority for CEOs as it is affecting the bottom line of their organizations.

To motivate and retain employees, as well as attract talent, HCL needs to create an environment of employee engagement by offering tangible rewards, quality work opportunities, future growth opportunities, inspirational values, a good work-life balance, and improved workforce policies. Since its inception, HCL Technologies Ltd.–BPO Services has continuously adapted to changing trends in the industry. The organization has always attempted to confront the inherent industry challenges and its pull factors, while acknowledging that attrition remains a major threat. Needless to say, over the years the organization has been demonstrating a business-driven innovation in its workforce practices.

The People CMM has been identified as a global and well-structured approach for assessing and improving current people practices. The organization recognized the potential of the model, and appreciated the fact that implementation of the model would augment and enhance its existing practices and procedures.

10.8.2 The People CMM Journey at HCLT BPO

HCL Technologies Ltd.–BPO Services selected the People CMM as a business strategy to help the organization retain people and become an employer of choice. HCL believed that highly satisfied employees generate high performance, which results in higher business productivity. Figure 10.13 shows how the People CMM, with its focus on the workforce and the processes they execute, supports the business strategy linkage between talent management and business delivery at HCLT BPO.

While the Corporate Human Resources team was aware of the People CMM, its features, and its benefits, it was essential to sensitize the business leadership team of N1 on these topics. Human Resources engaged external consultants to make an initial presentation to the leadership team. Formal approval from the leadership team was obtained in early 2006 and the implementation journey began.

Executives representing Human Resources, the business, and the delivery center head collaborated to champion the initiative, establishing it as an organizational initiative. Immense support was received from the Operations department and other support functions. A dedicated Human Resources, Quality, and Operations workgroup was constituted to drive this initiative. Internal communications supported this organizational initiative. One example of these communications mechanisms is shown in Figure 10.14. A People CMM workgroup was formed with defined objectives, a roadmap, and a competency-based team structure. Domain experts for each process area were selected as process leaders based on the key functional competencies required. The process leaders were responsible for creating and documenting the policies and procedures and for implementing the workforce practices.

At the beginning of the People CMM journey, the delivery center head assigned a specific weight in the Key Result Areas (KRAs) for People CMM implementation for various roles. This was done in order to ensure involvement in and compliance to the model. The KRAs of all employees in the center were based on the Balanced Scorecard approach, touching upon all four quadrants: Learning and Growth, Internal Business Process, Customer, and Financial Perspective.

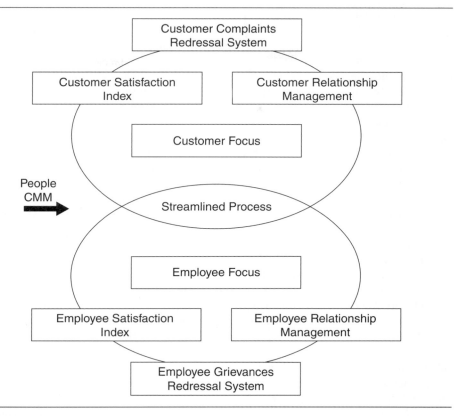

FIGURE 10.13
Business strategy linkage between talent management and business delivery at HCLT BPO

FIGURE 10.14
Internal communications supported the organizational initiative

The organization was already reasonably mature in certain workforce practices (such as Communication, Staffing, Performance Management, and Training and Development) before the People CMM journey started. But in light of the best practices in the model, all people processes and practices were reviewed, refined, and improved over a period of 15 months. In addition, key people-centric metrics were identified and tracked. This helped the organization to keep an eye on the measurement and monitoring activities that are necessary to determine the status and trends related to the people practices performed.

In the journey, HCLT BPO introduced competency-based career development discussions with the goal of providing a platform and guidance to employees for achieving their career aspirations. These discussions helped the organization to evaluate the competencies available in the internal talent pool and develop competencies required for the current and future business. At an individual level, the practice helped employees to visualize the career path available in HCL. An employee could not only grow internally in HCLT BPO, but also choose a career in another division of HCL Technologies. HCLT BPO also enhanced recruitment, transition, and training practices to specifically focus on competency-based selection and recruitment, which helped to improve the quality of new hires.

The People CMM journey initiated with the development of the HCLT BPO Competency Framework, which serves as the basis for all competency-based people practices. The wholly in-house-developed competency framework consisted of identifying the functional and behavioral competencies for each job role in each function. This was developed with the joint efforts of the competency leader and their competency team, along with all the Function Heads from the delivery center as well as Corporate. The framework details the definition of each competency and the various proficiency levels. The threshold level for each job role was also defined. The Competency Framework is being used during recruitment, training and development, performance management, career development, micro succession planning, and strategic workforce planning.

One major strength resulting is the performance evaluation structure in the delivery center. Performance management is not just an annual exercise; it is reviewed on a quarterly, monthly, weekly, and daily basis. Performance-related feedback is shared with employees on a regular basis so that corrective action can be suggested in a timely manner.

Competency communities for best-practice sharing have been formed at various levels. Centralized knowledge repositories are available for each of these forums. The company intranet is a very powerful platform for easy access to information on areas such as KRAs, competency levels, and career progression paths. Links such as "My KRA" (where an employee can view his or her KRAs), "My Competency" (where an employee can view the competencies required for his or her job, as well as current and required threshold levels), and "My Career" (which explains the qualifications, experience, competencies, performance ratings, and so on required to achieve a certain career path) are available on the intranet. This has created transparency in the system, and these tools have had a powerful positive impact on employees.

10.8.3   Return on Investment (ROI) from People CMM Implementation in HCLT BPO's N1 Center

As a result of implementing the People CMM in the HCLT BPO N1 Center, improvements were realized in several areas, as summarized in Figure 10.15. These areas included people process efficiency, employee benefits, delivery optimization, and business impact.

HCLT BPO also saw a substantial rise in Employee Satisfaction Survey scores, from 70.56% to 87%. Figure 10.16 highlights this dramatic change. A comparison of the two satisfaction surveys done within a span of six months showed an almost 16% improvement in scores. In addition, a dipstick survey resulting in an 87% score was conducted in June 2007, when the people practices up to Maturity Level 3 were successfully implemented across the delivery center and the SCAMPI Class A with People CMM appraisal was conducted.

Besides regular Employee Satisfaction Surveys, HCLT BPO conducted regular opinion polls on the intranet to gauge the effectiveness of the implementation of people practices. In addition, Open House (Town Hall) Sessions, Skip Level Meetings, and Infant Meets (for new employees) were conducted to gain an understanding of employee concerns and satisfaction.

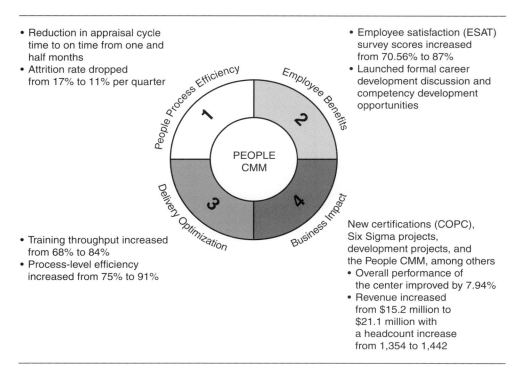

- Reduction in appraisal cycle time to on time from one and half months
- Attrition rate dropped from 17% to 11% per quarter

- Employee satisfaction (ESAT) survey scores increased from 70.56% to 87%
- Launched formal career development discussion and competency development opportunities

- Training throughput increased from 68% to 84%
- Process-level efficiency increased from 75% to 91%

New certifications (COPC), Six Sigma projects, development projects, and the People CMM, among others
- Overall performance of the center improved by 7.94%
- Revenue increased from $15.2 million to $21.1 million with a headcount increase from 1,354 to 1,442

FIGURE 10.15
Major gains from People CMM implementation at HCLT BPO

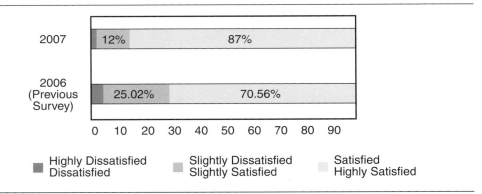

FIGURE 10.16
Employee Satisfaction Survey results

Another outstanding result of implementing the People CMM practices was a declining attrition rate in the delivery center, which is shown in Figure 10.17. The key accomplishment in attrition rate was realized by June 2007, when the monthly attrition percentage dropped to 1.74%. This is noted as the lowest attrition percentage seen in the history of HCLT BPO Services. Based solely on the savings made in FY 2006–2007 due to reduced attrition, HCLT BPO has achieved an ROI of approximately $200,000 as a result of its People CMM program.

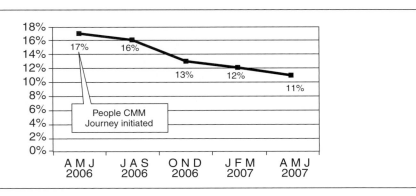

FIGURE 10.17
Employee attrition results covering the period from initiation of the People CMM implementation to appraisal

The People CMM brought to the organization a major focus on developing workforce competencies to enable employees to progress toward their career objectives and help the organization achieve talent development and engagement. With help from the competency-based reviews, the individual capability levels were assessed. Based on the workforce development plan targets and business plans, a Competency Development Plan was formed, deployed, and tracked after every quarterly review. Formal Mentoring Programs, On the Job Training, Functional Trainings, Empowerment Sessions, Behavioral Trainings, Buddy Up Programs, Competency Communities, and other development activities were delivered to develop individual capabilities. These changes impacted the satisfaction level, which increased from 60% to 83% on availability of career development opportunities.

HCLT BPO saw an improvement not only in people process efficiency, but also in employee motivation; impacts of this were also reflected in delivery process performance, and hence on the business. As a result of this, HCLT BPO saw an increase in training throughput which had an impact on the performance of the new employees going live on the floor after their new hire training. This was measured using transaction monitoring and productivity data. The process-level efficiency metric which entails average call handling time (AHT), productivity per hour, utilization, and other quality parameters increased from 75% to 91%.

10.9   Tata Consultancy Services

Tata Consultancy Services (TCS), headquartered in Mumbai, India, is a global IT services, business solutions, and outsourcing organization. TCS employs approximately 120,000 associates serving over 800 clients in 42 countries.

By 2001, thirteen of its development centers had been assessed at Maturity Level 5 on the Software CMM. In August 2001, four TCS Offshore Development Centers (at Gurgaon II and Noida in Delhi, Tidel Park in Chennai, and in Kolkata, India) became the first organizations to be assessed at Maturity Level 4 of the People CMM. These assessment results were significant because the Maturity Level 4 workforce practices and capabilities within TCS had been implemented over several years through a corporate focus on ensuring that TCS has the workforce capability it needs strategically combined with a focus in the centers on implementing the workforce practices necessary to sustain a high-maturity work environment. The four TCS centers assessed at Maturity Level 4 on the People CMM had already achieved Maturity Level 5 on the Software CMM. The high-maturity software practices that had been implemented provided a strong base for implementing high-maturity workforce practices.

TCS is the world's first organization to achieve an enterprise-wide Maturity Level 5 on CMMI and the People CMM, based on an extensive SCAMPI Class A appraisal, the most rigorous assessment methodology [Radice 05a, Radice 05c]. Key aspects underpinning the appraisal results were TCS's quality framework and strategic corporate focus on the workforce. The TCS quality framework is implemented through the TCS Integrated Quality Management System (iQMS), which integrates processes, people, and technology maturity through various established frameworks and practices, including IEEE, ISO 9001: 2000,

CMMI, the SW-CMM, the People CMM, and Six Sigma. In 2006, TCS achieved enterprise-wide certifications for ISO 9001:2000, BS 7799-2:2002, and BS 15000-1:2002. ISO 9001:2000 provides requirements for a quality management system and includes processes for continual improvement, as well as an assurance of conformity to customer and regulatory requirements. BS 7799 is a standard for Information Security Management. BS-15000 is an industry standard for IT service management. This was the largest enterprise-wide multiple certification of an IT solutions organization to date. It is TCS's second enterprise-wide achievement after it became the first company to be appraised enterprise-wide for CMMI and the People CMM at Maturity Level 5 in 2004.

TCS's strategic corporate focus on the workforce is initiated with recruiting at selected universities in India. University sources are selected based on a number of parameters including the quality of their program and graduates, library facilities, standard of entrance tests, number of full-time faculty, number of computers vis-à-vis number of students, and others. TCS maintains an internal ranking of universities and annually develops a plan targeting the number of graduates in intends to attract from each. Each development center maintains an Academic Liaison Officer who interacts with selected universities in the center's geographic region. Annually TCS interviews candidates at each selected university using teams that include both management and technical people trained in interviewing skills. The teams evaluate technical skills, attitude, and communication skills, and are empowered to make offers to candidates with the desired qualifications. Offer/join ratios are analyzed to guide changes in recruiting activities at different universities.

Upon joining TCS, new employees are sent to the corporate training center for induction training that includes preparation in technical areas, process, and interpersonal skills. During this training, dedicated resources (known as "lifeguards") are provided for every group of new hires to guide and help new entrants in their transition phase from students to professionals. At the end of more than two months of training, the new hires are tested to ensure they are capable of performing the type of work they will be assigned once allocated to a development center. These results are analyzed to provide feedback to universities on the preparation of their graduates. TCS uses these test results to occasionally revise the rankings of universities and adjust recruiting plans accordingly.

Tests are given routinely at the end of internal courses, and students are not given credit for completion of their career plans unless they achieve a minimum score. In addition, several months after people return from training, their managers are asked to rate the effectiveness with which new skills have been developed and deployed in order to provide feedback on the effectiveness of courses.

TCS has established a Manpower Allocation Task Committee with affiliates at each center to allocate talent across centers and projects. Over the past several years, TCS has consolidated multiple systems that describe knowledge and skills into one corporate Skills Management System. This system is sufficiently flexible to define the knowledge, skills, and other important attributes required by different assignments across the various centers. Thus, very different types of workforce competencies can be identified based on the specific clusters of domain knowledge and technical knowledge required for different projects. This system allows for recording an individual's level of proficiency against each component of knowledge or skill, making it a key tool for providing career paths: technical, managerial, and quality. The Manpower Allocation Task Committee uses this system to allocate talent across centers and projects to ensure that people who are completing assignments are considered for appropriate assignments elsewhere in the organization. This committee produces a list of qualified candidates from across TCS to be reviewed and evaluated by a project team to identify candidates with the best fit.

When people are assigned to a new center they are provided with induction training into the business of the center. Each project maintains an induction manual that provides several days' preparation for working on the project. TCS maintains a number of continuing education programs that consist of a mix of internal courses, computer-based training, professional certifications, university training, and knowledge-sharing sessions among communities of professionals with similar competencies. Employees are expected to spend 20 days per year in learning activities, and their individual development plans are tracked as a component of their performance objectives. The Corporate Training and Education Group develops and resources an annual training plan with inputs from each center.

On joining TCS, individuals receive formal performance feedback every two months until such time as they are confirmed to have moved beyond probationary status. After this point, performance feedback is provided twice every year on a formal basis. However, much more performance feedback occurs in discussions between project leaders and team members. As will be discussed later, project teams have taken an increasing role in managing their own performance.

To strengthen its competency development programs, TCS supports a number of mentoring programs. At the simplest level, centers provide "lifeguard" mentors to "freshers" just joining the center. Technical mentors with expertise in specific areas are selected at each center and trained to work with other professionals for six to eight weeks to ensure they learn the knowledge and skills required in their induction training plan on a project. These relationships are reviewed weekly to ensure they are making adequate progress. The Process and Quality Assurance Groups provide mentoring to managers to ensure they have all the skills required on a project startup list. These mentors work with managers at project launch and periodically throughout the project to ensure that they are developing the management skills required by their assignments.

Another source of shared learning in TCS comes through corporate and center-specific Process Asset Libraries, the e-Knowledge Management System, the Integrated Project Management System, and other knowledge repositories. These repositories house the artifacts produced to support project activities and the artifacts produced by projects that can be reused. The types of information available through these repositories include defined technical processes, project plans and process performance data from previous projects, best practices, lessons learned reports, software tools, templates for various uses, white papers on technical topics, case studies, and training material. The Internet is used to support communication among technical professionals at different sites to establish communities of competence in the various domains of TCS's business.

TCS has begun evaluating the percentage of time spent in various learning activities and their impact on outcomes and competency growth. For instance, Figure 10.18 shows the relationship between the percentage of budget devoted to training activities and the percentage spent correcting defects in one center. Root-cause analyses indicated that lack of knowledge was a major cause of defects, and training was an important mechanism for addressing this cause. As the data continue to grow, correlated trends can be identified and used to assess the

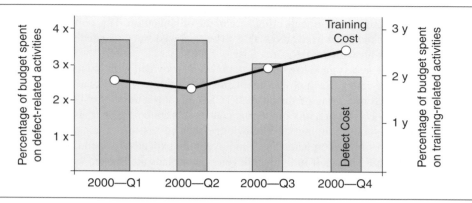

FIGURE 10.18
Relationship between training and defect costs at one TCS center

relative impact of training on defect costs and other performance issues. These relationships can be used to evaluate tradeoffs and set targets for training and other workforce practices.

Another center compared the percentage of effort devoted to mentoring with the growth of proficiency in specific areas of competency within its workforce. The analysis identified an important tradeoff between the number of senior people sent for assignments overseas and the availability of technical mentors. These analyses are typical of a Maturity Level 4 organization's ability to identify the impacts of specific workforce practices on a range of business outcomes. Maturity Level 4 organizations have moved beyond merely reporting the overall benefits of a collection of workforce practices on a global outcome such as turnover. In analyzing the effects of individual workforce practices on specific performance outcomes, managers in high-maturity organizations are better prepared to make tradeoff decisions and adjust the performance of particular workforce practices to match business costs and outcomes.

Most work at TCS is performed in projects. Since TCS has been appraised at CMMI Maturity Level 5, these projects use data on process events, such as the number and types of defects found during design or code inspections, to evaluate the effectiveness of their work. The immediate availability of performance data for their work processes has empowered project teams to manage more of their own performance. Increasingly, project teams perform root-cause analyses on their defects to identify actions that can be taken to eliminate the most common causes of defects. As a result of these root-cause analyses, teams often establish specific training plans or internal mentoring activities targeted at reducing defect types best addressed through learning activities. Having the ability to take action on their own performance coupled with involvement in selecting and inducting new members have provided critical initial steps in developing the self-management capability of project teams.

Another trend that has increased the empowerment of teams is the confluence of the Quality Management System that describes the basic technical and management processes used by all project teams and the Skills Management System that describes the knowledge, skills, and other attributes of TCS's various workforce competencies and each individual's level of proficiency in these competencies. Increasingly TCS is able to describe work as a combination of roles in a defined process and the competencies required to perform these roles. The combination of roles and competencies reduces the focus on hierarchy and increases the emphasis on capability for accomplishing assignments.

This focus on roles and competencies also facilitates integration of different competencies into project teams. Over the past several years TCS has revised its work activities to deemphasize parallel but separate work streams, and increase the joint involvement of different competencies into a common project process guided by the Quality Management System. TCS has revised its organizational structure to emphasize cross-functional cells that map technology specialties into industry segments. This integration among competencies is evident in

- greater integration of processes performed by business domain experts with those performed by software technology experts throughout the development cycle of a project,

- tighter integration of processes performed by hardware specialists with those performed by software specialists involved in data center operations, and

- greater integration of technical people with staff specialists on task committee activities.

Greater integration of different competencies has also produced greater emphasis on cross-training in multiple disciplines as a component of both individual development plans and project training plans.

One of the most critical business problems for clients who outsource their software and systems integration work to companies like TCS is the continuity and capability of the technical staff. High rates of employee departures in the staff assigned to a client's activities force the client to continually pay for the learning curves of new people rather than benefit from the growing capability of a stable staff. In addition, many clients are demanding that companies like TCS begin to perform more of their work on fixed-price contracts rather than on hourly billing. High-maturity companies prefer a higher mix of fixed-price work because they cannot be compensated fully for their enhanced capability on hourly billings. Simply stated, more capable people require fewer hours to complete their contractual commitments. However, the greater the capability of a team working against a fixed price, the greater the profit margin on the contract. TCS has even started modeling the relationship between workforce capability and projected business performance. TCS's workforce practices were implemented to address these critical issues rather than to achieve a People CMM rating. As a result, workforce practices are core to TCS's business strategy.

10.10   Conclusion

When improvements guided by the People CMM are initiated, they are sometimes perceived as a human resources program. However, organizations at higher maturity levels have uniformly found the People CMM to be a general business excellence model more than merely a human resources model. At higher maturity levels, the increasing focus on performance improvement moves a People CMM-based improvement program directly into affecting the operational performance of the unit or business. Once executives identify an organization's strategic objectives, the People CMM provides guidance that improves the organization's ability to satisfy the identified objectives through deploying a competent, capable workforce that is executing and continually improving its business processes.

PART TWO

Process Areas of the People Capability Maturity Model

Part Two describes the practices that correspond to each maturity level in the People CMM. It is an elaboration of what is meant by maturity at each level of the People CMM and a guide that can be used for organizational improvement and appraisal. For those who want to get a quick sense of the practices, without the rigor that is needed in applying them, a summary of the practices is provided in Appendix D.

Each maturity level provides a layer in the foundation for continuous improvement of the organization's workforce capability. Achieving each level of the maturity model institutionalizes a different component of workforce capability, resulting in an overall increase in the workforce capability of the organization. Each process area comprises a set of goals that, when satisfied, stabilize an important component of workforce capability. Each process area is described in terms of the practices that contribute to satisfying its goals. The practices describe the infrastructure and activities that contribute most to the effective implementation and institutionalization of the process area.

The Managed Level: Maturity Level 2

Process Areas at the Managed Level focus on establishing a foundation of basic workforce practices that can be continuously improved to develop the capability of the workforce. This foundation of practices is initially built within units to instill a discipline for managing people and to provide a supportive work environment with adequate work resources. The unit balances work commitments with available resources. Qualified people are recruited, selected, and transitioned into assignments within the unit. Performance objectives are established for committed work, and performance is periodically discussed to identify actions that can improve it. Individuals develop interpersonal communication skills to ensure that work dependencies are coordinated effectively. The knowledge and skills required for performing assignments are identified and appropriate training and development opportunities are provided. The compensation is based on an articulated strategy and is periodically adjusted to ensure equity. The process areas at Maturity Level 2 include:

	Process Areas
Staffing	159
Communication and Coordination	183
Work Environment	197
Performance Management	210
Training and Development	231
Compensation	244

Staffing

A process area at Maturity Level 2: Managed

Purpose

The purpose of Staffing is to establish a formal process by which committed work is matched to unit resources and qualified individuals are recruited, selected, and transitioned into assignments.

Description

Staffing is positioned as the primary process area at the Managed Level since staffing decisions provide an organization's greatest opportunities to influence performance. All other practices designed to improve the capability of the workforce must start from the baseline of talent brought into the organization. Few organizational processes are able to demonstrate their potential benefits in organizations that are chronically overworked because of poor staffing practices.

Staffing involves processes related to balancing the workload with available resources, recruiting, selecting among candidates for open positions, entering or leaving the organization, and transitioning into new positions.

Matching committed work to available resources begins with analyzing proposed work to determine the skills and effort required to perform it. Individuals and workgroups then make commitments based on their assessment of the effort and resources required to satisfy commitments. The unit negotiates commitments with affected parties to balance the committed work with the resources available in the unit for performing the work. These commitments are then documented so that they can be used in other business and workforce activities.

Recruiting activities begin when positions are opened. Tasks to be performed by individuals filling these open positions and the characteristics of candidates who would be capable of performing the tasks are listed. These open positions are communicated to the unit's workforce so that they can aid in recruiting and screening qualified candidates. The openings are also internally posted and communicated to external sources of qualified candidates. Responsible individuals within a unit ensure the unit is active in recruiting to meet its staffing needs. The status of recruiting activities is reviewed periodically. Lessons learned about recruiting approaches and sources are periodically assessed.

A list of qualified candidates is drawn from the results of recruiting efforts. A selection strategy is developed based on the characteristics of the position to be filled. A short list of the most qualified candidates is chosen for further consideration. The skills and experience of the candidates on the short list are thoroughly evaluated against position criteria through reference checks and other methods decided in advance. The rights and dignity of the candidates are respected throughout the selection process. Appropriate individuals in the unit participate in the selection process. Ultimately, the candidate best fitting the position criteria is selected.

The organization coordinates its activities to attract selected candidates. Transition activities are conducted to assist individuals in adjusting to their new position and to the organization, if they are a new hire. The results of the selection process are reviewed and success is measured on a periodic basis.

Outplacement activities involve determining the basis for selecting individuals to be discharged and applying these criteria consistently to all affected employees. The rights and dignity of those discharged from the organization are respected throughout the process. When individuals are discharged for unsatisfactory performance or other valid causes, the reasons are documented and discussed. When individuals voluntarily resign from the organization, the reasons for their resignation are sought and corrective actions are taken, if necessary.

Goals

Goal 1   **Individuals or workgroups in each unit are involved in making commitments that balance the unit's workload with approved staffing.**

Goal 2   **Candidates are recruited for open positions.**

Goal 3   **Staffing decisions and work assignments are based on an assessment of work qualifications and other valid criteria.**

Goal 4   **Individuals are transitioned into and out of positions in an orderly way.**

Goal 5   **Staffing practices are institutionalized to ensure they are performed as managed processes.**

Commitment to Perform

Commitment 1   **The organization establishes and maintains a documented policy for conducting its Staffing activities.**

Issues typically addressed in the policy include:

1. Staffing activities comply with the business objectives and stated values of the organization.

2. Staffing activities comply with all applicable laws and regulations.

> Examples of relevant laws and regulations include the following:
> - Requirements to verify the right to work (i.e., citizenship, work permits, etc.)
> - Regulations regarding workplace inclusiveness, such as Equal Employment Opportunity (EEO) requirements, or access for the disabled, such as the Americans with Disabilities Act (ADA) requirements
> - Other regulatory mandates, such as conflict of interest, licensing, or certification
> - National, state, and local laws and regulations

3. Individuals or workgroups in each unit are involved in making commitments for the work that they will be held accountable for accomplishing.

4. Workloads are balanced with the staff available to perform the work.

5. Responsibilities for initiating, conducting, and approving all staffing decisions are assigned.

6. Appropriate procedures are defined, documented, and used.

> These procedures are intended to define a minimal set of staffing activities. The purpose of these procedures is to keep those in units who are responsible for staffing from having to invent their own procedures. Providing standard procedures is not intended to reduce the flexibility of units to perform staffing activities best suited to their unit's needs. Using or tailoring standard procedures provides units with the guidance for conducting their staffing activities in compliance with applicable laws, regulations, and organizational policies.

> The human resources function or other appropriate professionals should review all such procedures to ensure they
> - Are consistent with relevant laws, regulations, and organizational policies
> - Respect the rights and dignity of individuals and groups

Staffing procedures are established and maintained for:

- making commitments for work to be accomplished;
- declaring positions to be open;
- documenting open position needs, including identified selection criteria;
- recruiting internal and external candidates;
- announcing the availability of positions;
- developing a list of qualified candidates;
- evaluating and selecting the candidate whose skills and other qualifications best fit the identified selection criteria of the open position;
- conducting background and reference checks;
- communicating outcomes to candidates, both positive and negative;
- handling confidential selection information;
- transferring selected internal candidates, including releasing them from their current positions;
- transitioning selected candidates into their new positions;
- orienting selected candidates to the organization;
- handling retirements;
- handling voluntary resignation;
- handling job abandonment;
- notifying the workforce about periods for outplacements and resignations;

- discharging individuals for unsatisfactory performance or cause;
- out-processing and conducting exit interviews with terminating employees;
- performing workforce reductions and outplacement; and
- ensuring appropriate distribution, use, and retention of staffing documentation, including granting access to, and ensuring confidentiality of, these staffing data.

7. The rights and dignity of individuals are to be protected during all staffing activities.

8. Reasons for voluntary separation from the organization are identified.

9. Staffing practices and activities comply with relevant laws, regulations, and organizational policies.

Commitment 2   **An organizational role(s) is assigned responsibility for assisting and advising units on Staffing activities and procedures.**

> Examples of individuals who might assist or advise units on Staffing activities and procedures include the following:
> - Human resources or other appropriate professionals
> - Workload or planning experts
> - Resource managers
> - Recruiters
> - Legal staff
> - Training and development staff

Ability to Perform

Ability 1   **Within each unit, an individual(s) is assigned responsibility and authority for ensuring that Staffing activities are performed.**

> Examples of individuals who may be assigned responsibility for various Staffing activities include the following:
> - A member of the human resources function or other appropriate professionals
> - The unit manager or assistant
> - A staffing or work allocation committee
> - A project or group leader
> - An empowered team

Ability 2   Adequate resources are provided for performing Staffing activities.

1. Documented business plans, budgets, or similar guidance are available that indicate the work to be assigned to each unit and the budget available for staffing to perform the assigned work.

2. Where feasible, experienced individuals who have expertise in Staffing methods and procedures are made available for conducting Staffing activities.

3. Resources to support Staffing activities are made available.

> Examples of resources to support Staffing activities include the following:
> - Guidelines for estimating workloads
> - Templates for job or task descriptions
> - Templates for recruiting announcements
> - Instruments used in the selection process
> - Candidate folders including resumes, recommendations, and correspondence
> - Copies of policies such as recruiting travel, relocation, benefits, and transition
> - Standard forms for documenting Staffing activities

4. Support for Staffing activities is made available.

> Examples of support for Staffing activities include the following:
> - Recruiting trips
> - Announcements and advertising, such as internal job announcements or external job advertisements
> - Candidate interview trips
> - Recruiting costs, including finder's fees or referral fees
> - Time for interviewing and evaluating candidates
> - Staff involvement in staffing processes
> - Orientation courses and materials

5. Adequate funding is provided for the approved positions within a unit.

> Adequate funding for positions involves funding for all components of compensation and any other non-Work Environment-related funding needs. Refer to Ability 2 of the Work Environment process area for information regarding resources for establishing and maintaining the work environment.

Ability 3   **Individuals performing Staffing activities receive the preparation in methods and procedures needed to perform their responsibilities.**

> Examples of methods in which individuals may receive training include the following:
> - Laws and regulations governing selection and employment
> - Position, workload, and task analysis
> - Staffing procedures required by organizational policy
> - Developing and weighting selection criteria
> - Interviewing skills
> - Selection techniques and candidate evaluation
> - Orienting and transitioning individuals into new positions

Ability 4   **Individuals participating in Staffing activities receive appropriate orientation in Staffing practices.**

> Examples of issues to be imparted through orientation include the following:
> - Laws and regulations governing staffing
> - Organizational policies governing staffing
> - Selection methods and criteria

Practices Performed

Practice 1   **Responsible individuals plan and coordinate the staffing activities of their units in accordance with documented policies and procedures.**

1. Unit staffing activities are based on the effort and skills required to accomplish the unit's committed work.

2. Unit staffing activities are planned and tracked.

3. Unit staffing activities are conducted according to the organization's documented policies and procedures.

4. Unit staffing activities are defined and conducted with the assistance and approval of human resources or other groups with organizational responsibility for staffing practices and activities.

5. Unit staffing activities are reviewed with appropriate levels of management, as required.

Practice 2 **Each unit analyzes its proposed work to determine the effort and skills required.**

> Examples of sources of a unit's proposed work include the following:
> - The organization's strategic business plan or objectives
> - Divisional or departmental business plans or objectives
> - A unit's approved business plan or objectives
> - A project's statement of work, work breakdown structure, or plan
> - Responsibilities allocated to a unit as part of a larger project or organizational undertaking
> - Anticipated flow of work
> - Standard organization-wide activities
> - A documented agreement with higher organizational levels about the type and amount of work to be undertaken

1. A unit's proposed work is analyzed to determine the types of tasks and effort required to perform them.

> Examples of factors to be considered in analyzing workload include the following:
> - Length of a workday and workweek
> - Regulations and expectations about overtime
> - Choices among methods for performing the work
> - Primary tasks that constitute the work
> - Amount of effort required to perform these tasks
> - Cognitive and physical characteristics of these tasks

2. The types of skills needed to perform proposed work are identified.

> Examples of factors this analysis should consider include the following:
> - Match of skills to required tasks
> - Experience available in needed skills
> - Typical productivity of people at different experience levels
> - Length of time typically required to fill open positions
> - Performance expectations regarding the proposed work

Practice 3   **Individuals and workgroups participate in making commitments for work they will be accountable for performing.**

1. Responsible individuals in each unit identify the scope of the proposed work to be performed and the work products or services to be produced, and communicate this information to those who will perform the work.

> The purpose of this practice is to ensure that the people doing the work have a common understanding of the work to be performed and work products to be produced.

2. Individuals are involved in reviewing the work proposed for a unit and, when appropriate, approving the inputs that initiate the work.

3. Individuals or workgroups are involved in analyzing how work should be allocated within the unit.

4. Individuals or workgroups are involved in estimating the resources, effort, and schedule required to accomplish the work that they have been allocated.

5. Individuals or workgroups negotiate to balance their workload with anticipated resources and time.

6. Individuals or workgroups establish commitments they will be held accountable for meeting.

> A *commitment* is a pact that is freely assumed, visible, and expected to be kept by all involved.

7. Individuals or workgroups participate in reviewing and approving the work commitments made by the unit.

8. Individuals or workgroups are involved in reviewing progress against commitments and, when necessary, making changes to the commitments regarding their work.

9. Individuals or workgroups participate in replanning committed work that could alter their commitments.

Practice 4   **Each unit documents work commitments that balance its workload with available staff and other required resources.**

1. Each unit's committed work incorporates, and is consistent with, the commitments established by individuals or workgroups within the unit.

2. Units make commitments for which they expect to have adequate staffing or other required resources.

> Units can make commitments for which their current staffing and other required resources are inadequate, if needed resources have been approved and are expected to be obtained in sufficient time to meet commitments. If a unit makes commitments in the absence of a plan that provides the required staffing or makes available resources in sufficient time to meet the commitments, business and workforce risks should be identified and communicated.
>
> If chronic overtime results from over-committed work, corrective action to reduce excessive overtime should be planned and tracked to closure, unless continuing overtime is acceptable to members of a unit. Even when members of a unit accept or request overtime, the levels of overtime worked should be monitored and corrective action taken.

3. Each unit's commitments are negotiated with those to whom the unit is accountable.

> Examples of those to whom the unit may be accountable include the following:
> • Management
> • A program or project
> • Other units with which the unit shares dependencies
> • Internal or external customers

4. If the number and type of staff required to accomplish the committed work are not available, potential position openings are identified.

> Refer to Practice 6 for information regarding the analysis, documentation, and approval of potential position openings.

5. If potential positions required for performing proposed work are not opened, commitments are adjusted accordingly.

6. Each unit documents its commitments to form the basis for its staffing, performance management, compensation, and other business or workforce activities.

Practice 5   Individual work assignments are managed to balance committed work among individuals and units.

1. Individual workloads are periodically evaluated to ensure they are balanced, and adjustments are made to individual commitments as needed to improve balance and avoid overload.

2. When an individual's committed work is nearing completion, opportunities are sought to apply their effort to other business activities in their current unit or in other units.

3. When individuals are responsible for committed work in several units, those to whom their responsibilities report coordinate to:

   - ensure the combined commitments do not create work overload,

   - coordinate expectations for timing of work and results,

   - resolve conflicts among work commitments, and

   - allocate the responsibilities for workforce activities involving the affected individual(s), as appropriate.

Practice 6   **Position openings within a unit are analyzed, documented, and approved.**

1. When the committed or proposed work exceeds the unit's current capacity, the unit proposes to open positions for additional staff.

2. Tasks to be performed by each open position are identified and documented.

3. Characteristics of candidates who are capable of performing the tasks involved in each open position are defined and documented.

> Examples of relevant characteristics may include the following:
> - Job-related knowledge
> - Task-related skills, including the critical skills needed by successful candidates to perform assigned tasks (*Critical skills* are those skills that, if not performed effectively, could jeopardize the successful performance of assigned tasks.)
> - Work habits
> - Ability to work in groups or teams
> - Development potential within the organization
> - Years of relevant experience
> - Related accomplishments
> - Education, as evidenced by degrees or training certificates
> - Willingness to accept the tasks, job characteristics, and work conditions of the position

4. The primary source(s) for filling each open position is determined.

> Examples of sources for filling positions may include the following:
> - Internal recruiting
> - External recruiting
> - Temporary or contract staff
> - Consultants

5. Position openings are approved according to a documented procedure based on:

   ■ increased workload,

   ■ budget,

   ■ departed staff, or

   ■ other relevant criteria.

Practice 7   Position openings within the organization are widely communicated.

1. Appropriate mechanisms are selected and used for communicating open positions.

   > Communication is intended to be made to those in the relevant population who may have the characteristics of candidates capable of performing the tasks. In some cases, the organization may focus its communications activities because the relevant candidate pool is narrow. Examples of those who may receive focused communication of position openings include the following:
   > • Potential candidates with highly specialized qualifications.
   > • Potential candidates for critical positions who have been prepared through succession planning. Refer to Practice 8 of the Workforce Planning process area for information regarding succession planning.
   > • Potential candidates internal to the organization.

2. Open positions are communicated throughout the organization so that qualified individuals can apply for the opening.

3. Open positions within a unit are regularly communicated to members of the unit so that they can assist in recruiting qualified candidates.

Practice 8   Units with open positions recruit for qualified individuals.

1. The individual(s) responsible for a unit's staffing activities coordinate actions taken to attract qualified internal and external candidates for open positions.

2. Units coordinate requirements for open positions with recruiting resources at the organizational level, if they exist, and the unit's activities are performed within the recruiting context established by the organization.

   > Each unit is responsible for meeting its commitments, and therefore is ultimately responsible for filling the positions required to perform committed work. The unit should take an active role in identifying and attracting individuals qualified to fill open positions.

3. Within the context of organizational activities, the unit takes action to use both internal and external mechanisms, as appropriate, to attract qualified individuals.

4. Individuals in a unit are encouraged to identify and attract qualified candidates for open positions, as appropriate.

Practice 9   External recruiting activities by the organization are planned and coordinated with unit requirements.

1. Responsibilities for external recruiting activities are coordinated between the unit and the organization, and recruiting activities are planned.

> External recruiting activities can be conducted either by members of the unit or by the organization, depending on the source of candidates being approached. When the organization takes responsibility for approaching a source of candidates, it should represent both current and anticipated needs of units in the organization.

2. Likely sources of candidates who are qualified for open positions are identified.

> Examples of sources for contacting likely candidates include the following:
> - Universities
> - Technical schools
> - Trade publications
> - Bulletin boards
> - Advertisements
> - Professional, trade, or honorary societies
> - Professional conferences and trade shows
> - Minority recruitment sources
> - Professional recruiters
> - Colleagues
> - Other relevant sources

3. Position openings are communicated to external sources through relevant media.

4. A designated individual(s) follows up with external sources to aid in contacting qualified candidates.

5. Interest from qualified candidates is coordinated with units that have open positions.

Practice 10   A selection process and appropriate selection criteria are defined for each open position.

1. Selection criteria are defined from:

- the tasks, job characteristics, and work conditions of the open position,
- characteristics of candidates who are capable of performing the work responsibilities of the open position,

- other skill needs of the unit or organization, and
- other staffing objectives of the organization.

2. Activities for evaluating the qualifications and fitness of each candidate against the selection criteria are defined.

> Examples of activities for evaluating candidates include the following:
> - Individual interviews
> - Group interviews
> - Formal structured interviews
> - Presentations
> - Sample tasks
> - Reviews of the candidate's portfolio
> - Selection center exercises
> - Biographical/experience inventories
> - Job-related tests
> - Other appropriate methods

3. The selection activities defined are organized into a selection process for the open position.

4. The selection activities and process are reviewed by an appropriate individual from the human resources function to ensure that they respect the rights and dignity of each candidate chosen for further consideration and that they are consistent with all laws, regulations, and organizational policies governing selection decisions.

5. The selection process is communicated to the existing workforce and candidates involved.

Practice 11   Each unit, in conjunction with its human resources function, conducts a selection process for each position it intends to fill.

1. A list of candidates for each position is drawn from recruiting activities, maintained throughout the selection process, and retained for future use.

> Examples of uses for this retained list include the following:
> - Reports of staffing activities required by laws and regulations
> - Analyses to determine the most effective sources of candidates
> - Analyzing factors influencing recruiting success and failure

2. A set of qualified candidates is invited to undergo further evaluation through the selection process.

3. The selection process is performed to generate information regarding candidates' qualifications and fitness relative to the identified selection criteria for the position.

4. Candidates are provided information regarding the tasks, job characteristics, and work conditions of the position that would help them evaluate their own suitability for the position.

5. The selected candidate's background and references are checked according to a documented procedure.

6. Appropriate members of the unit participate in the selection process and provide input to the selection decision.

7. Documentation from the selection process is systematically maintained according to a documented procedure.

> Issues covered in the procedure may include the following:
> - What information will be maintained
> - How long documentation will be maintained
> - Who has access to the documentation
> - How documents may be inspected and challenged
> - How documentation security will be maintained
> - How the documentation may be used

Practice 12   **Positions are offered to the candidate whose skills and other qualifications best fit the open position.**

1. The identified selection criteria are consistently applied to all candidates involved in the selection process.

2. All qualified candidates are compared regarding their relative fitness for the open position, and the candidate whose skills and other valid attributes best fit the open position is selected.

> Although position-relevant skills are usually the most important criteria for selecting among candidates, other valid criteria may be considered in making a decision. Examples of other valid criteria may include the following:
> - Potential learning curve in acquiring critical skills
> - Breadth of skills beyond those required by the open position
> - Experience within a particular domain of work or market segment
> - Likelihood of developing good working relationships with other members of a group or unit
> - Orientation to important business objectives
> - Potential to grow in the position or organization
> - Organizational objectives for shaping the workforce

3. Timely feedback is provided to all candidates regarding the results of the selection process.

Practice 13   **The organization acts in a timely manner to attract the selected candidate.**

1. The hiring process is designed to respond within sufficient time to attract selected candidates.

2. Within reason and fairness to the existing workforce, the hiring unit attempts to coordinate the arrangements for the position with the attributes and expectations of the selected candidate.

3. Terms of the offer are negotiated with the selected candidate in accordance with the documented policies of the organization.

> Usually, the human resources staff handles the terms of the offer. However, those in the hiring unit who are responsible for administering compensation decisions should be a party to these negotiations, since the outcome of these negotiations can create imbalances in the unit's compensation and benefits profile.

> Examples of the terms of the offer that can be negotiated include the following:
> - Job level and title
> - Salary and benefits
> - Probationary period
> - Relocation
> - Training
> - Assignment and tasks
> - Office arrangements
> - Privileges
> - Other appropriate issues

Practice 14   **The selected candidate is transitioned into the new position.**

1. Responsibilities are assigned for transition activities.

> Examples of transition activities include the following:
> - Relocation planning
> - House-hunting
> - Setting up a computing environment
> - Preparing an office and required equipment
> - Selecting an orientation mentor
> - Meeting existing members of the unit
> - Orientation to the job
> - Orientation to the organization

2. Transition activities are planned and performed.

3. When individuals transition among work assignments within the organization, workforce activities involving them are either completed or transitioned with them, as appropriate.

> Transitions among work assignments may occur within or across units. Examples of workforce activities for which responsibilities must be transitioned appropriately include the following:
> - Establishing new work commitments
> - Recording the results of performance against completed commitments
> - Orienting to new work activities or a new unit
> - Identifying training needs related to new assignments
> - Establishing new performance objectives

4. Orientation to the organization is provided to the newly assigned individual.

> Examples of information typically presented in an orientation include the following:
> - Business objectives and stated values of the organization
> - Company and organizational structure
> - The organization's business (i.e., the products, software, or services it provides)
> - Relevant policies
> - Employee benefits and services
> - Computing and information facilities
> - Other appropriate issues

5. Orientation to the unit and job responsibilities is provided to the newly assigned individual.

> Each newly assigned individual typically receives job orientation through a number of mechanisms during their transition period. These mechanisms can include the following:
> - Orientation sessions
> - Learning activities
> - On-the-job training
> - Guidance from people in the unit

Examples of information typically presented in a job orientation include the following:
- Description of initial tasks
- People in the unit
- Ordinary unit processes and procedures
- Job-related knowledge
- Location of resources, such as computing facilities, information sources, and supplies
- Upcoming events and schedules
- Other appropriate issues

Practice 15   **Representative members of a unit participate in its staffing activities.**

1. Unless their participation in specific staffing activities is inappropriate, members of the unit participate in staffing activities.

The knowledge and experience of individuals in a unit should be incorporated into the unit's staffing activities and decisions. In some cases, it may be impractical to include all members of a unit in a specific staffing activity; however, representative members should be selected to participate.

Examples of staffing activities in which members of the unit can participate include the following:
- Analyzing tasks
- Identifying characteristics of qualified candidates
- Recruiting
- Referring potential candidates
- Screening potential candidates
- Evaluating qualified candidates
- Making selection decisions
- Checking references
- Attracting selected candidates
- Mentoring or orienting newly assigned individuals
- Other relevant activities

Examples of reasons why it may be inappropriate for some or all members of a unit to participate in specific staffing activities include the following:
- Lack of knowledge required for providing useful input to a specific staffing decision
- Exposure to confidential information
- Protection of privacy
- Security

2. In some cases, members of a unit may be invited to participate in staffing activities based on relevant characteristics.

> Examples of relevant characteristics on which members of a unit might be selected to participate in staffing activities include the following:
> - Technical experience or expertise
> - Organizational tenure
> - Membership in appropriate groups
> - Knowledge of relevant laws and regulations
> - Selection by other members of the unit
> - Availability
> - Preparation for participating in staffing activities

3. Each unit periodically reviews the status of its staffing activities with all members of the unit.

4. Each unit reviews and documents lessons learned from its staffing activities.

Practice 16   Workforce reduction and other outplacement activities, when required, are conducted according to the organization's policies and procedures.

> Examples of reasons for outplacement include the following:
> - Workforce reductions
> - Workforce restructuring
> - Loss of budget or work
> - Shifts in skill needs
> - Changes in location of facilities

1. The effort and skills required to be retained following a workforce reduction or other outplacement activity are identified.

> Refer to Practice 2 for information regarding analyzing proposed work to determine the effort and skills required.

2. The criteria for retaining or releasing individuals are defined in each unit where a workforce reduction or other outplacement activities are planned.

> Examples of criteria for retaining or releasing individuals include the following:
> - Unit's activities and workload
> - Tasks to be performed
> - Job characteristics
> - Skill requirements
> - Individual performance results

> At the Managed Level, criteria may address the need for specific skills or critical skills necessary to perform planned work following a workforce reduction.

3. The identified criteria are consistently applied to all individuals subject to workforce reductions or other outplacement actions.

4. Workforce reduction activities are performed according to a documented procedure.

5. Workforce reduction and outplacement activities are reviewed to ensure that they respect the rights and dignity of each individual and that they are consistent with all applicable laws, regulations, and organizational policies governing staffing and discharge decisions.

> Various laws and regulations may affect outplacement activities. Examples of relevant laws include the following:
> - Worker Adjustment and Retraining Notification (WARN) Act in the United States
> - Consolidated Omnibus Budget Reconciliation Act (COBRA) in the United States
> - Health Insurance Portability and Accountability Act (HIPAA) in the United States
> - Transfer of Undertakings (Protection of Employment) Regulations (TUPE) in the United Kingdom
> - Acquired Rights Directive in the European Union

6. Workforce reduction and outplacement activities are communicated to those affected.

7. Individuals to be discharged from a unit are made aware of open positions within the organization, when appropriate.

8. The discharge of individuals from the organization is handled according to a documented procedure.

> Examples of issues that might be in the documented procedure include the following:
> - Methods for identifying individuals to be discharged
> - Documentation required to justify or support discharge
> - Methods for reviewing and approving discharge decisions
> - How individuals will be informed of their discharge
> - Actions to be taken during the discharge process
> - Disposition of personal and organizational property
> - Appropriate access to work premises
> - Severance package
> - Outplacement assistance

9. Communication concerning outplacement(s) is made to individuals or work-groups who might be affected by them.

> Examples of information to be communicated concerning outplacement include the following:
> - Timing of the outplacement(s) and its extent
> - Causes for the outplacement, if appropriate
> - Support being provided to outplaced individuals, if appropriate
> - In the case of multiple outplacements, the status of whether outplacements will continue or whether they have been completed

10. The secure status of essential individuals the unit or organization intends to retain is reinforced through direct communication.

> Examples of information to be communicated to those not subject to outplacement include the following:
> - Statements of job security, where appropriate
> - Strong messages of commitment to individuals or workgroups that the unit or organization intends to retain

Practice 17 **Discharges for unsatisfactory performance or other valid reasons are conducted according to the organization's policies and procedures.**

1. Individuals are informed of behaviors that could result in discharge.

> Examples of reasons for discharge could include the following:
> - Unsatisfactory performance
> - Misconduct

> Refer to Practices 10 through 12 of the Performance Management process area for information regarding communication about unsatisfactory performance.

2. Actual behaviors or performance that could result in discharge are documented and discussed with the affected individual.

3. The decision to discharge an individual is reviewed and approved by appropriate managers and the human resources function before action is taken.

4. The discharge of an individual from the organization is handled according to a documented procedure.

> Examples of issues that might be included in the procedure include the following:
> - Documentation required to justify or support discharge
> - Methods for reviewing and approving discharge decisions
> - How individuals will be informed of their discharge
> - Actions to be taken during the discharge process
> - Disposition of personal and organizational property
> - Appropriate access to work premises
> - Severance package
> - Limits on the information that can be provided about the individual's former employment

5. Communication concerning the discharge is made to individuals or work-groups who might be affected by it.

Practice 18   Causes of voluntary resignation from the organization are identified and addressed.

> Although voluntary resignation for reasons such as retirement, family move, or caring for family members may not result from organizational or unit problems, other causes, such as poor working conditions, lack of training, lack of career opportunities, unchallenging work, better compensation elsewhere, stress, or work-life balance issues, represent conditions the unit or organization should address to retain the workforce.

1. Cause(s) for voluntary resignation and improvements that could be made to the unit or organization are identified through exit interviews, personal discussions with the departing individual, or other appropriate means.

2. The departing individual may be offered an opportunity to talk with someone, other than the person to whom they have been responsible, about the causes for their voluntary departure.

> Examples of other people that the departing individual might talk with include the following:
> - A higher level manager
> - A lateral manager
> - A representative from the human resources function or another similar group
> - An ombudsman
> - A senior individual in the departing individual's unit or specialty
> - An employee committee
> - Someone identified by the departing individual

3. If appropriate, corrective actions are taken that would increase retention.

4. When trends in causes for voluntary resignation at the unit or organization levels can be identified, corrective action should be taken, if possible.

Measurement and Analysis

Measurement 1   Measurements are made and used to determine the status and performance of Staffing activities.

Examples of measurements include the following:
- Time spent establishing committed work
- Percent of commitments met
- Revisions to commitments
- Number of open positions identified
- Number of qualified candidates contacted through each recruiting source
- Percent of qualified candidates contacted directly by staff rather than through other sources
- Percentage of selected candidates accepting offers
- Cost per hire
- Success of selection methods based on performance at the end of a probationary period
- Demographics of candidates and hires, including factors such as source, age, or diversity
- Time spent on recruiting, selection, and transitioning
- Time from opening a position to filling it
- Percent of unit members involved in staffing activities
- Rate of transitioning individuals into new positions
- Number of people undergoing outplacement
- Cost of outplacement
- Percent of voluntary turnover
- Cost of replacing those who voluntarily resign

Measurement 2   Unit measures of Staffing activities are collected and maintained.

1. Units collect data as Staffing activities occur.

2. Measurements made to determine the status and performance of Staffing activities are maintained.

> Examples of reasons for maintaining measurements of Staffing activities include the following:
> - Periodic analysis to determine unit-level trends
> - Aggregating data at the organizational level to develop organizational measures
> - Analysis to determine organizational trends
> - Evaluation of organizational trends

Verifying Implementation

Verification 1   A responsible individual(s) verifies that Staffing activities are conducted according to the organization's documented policies, practices, procedures, and, where appropriate, plans; and addresses noncompliance.

These reviews verify that:

1. Staffing activities comply with the organization's policies and stated values.

2. Staffing activities comply with all relevant laws and regulations.

3. Staffing activities are performed according to the organization's documented practices and procedures.

> These reviews may use measures regarding the status and performance of Staffing activities, as well as unit measures of Staffing activities, to ensure that a comprehensive review of Staffing activities occurs. These measures provide indicators of the status and performance of Staffing activities across the units. Refer to Measurement 1 and Measurement 2 for information regarding measurement of Staffing activities.

4. Noncompliance issues are handled appropriately.

Verification 2   Executive management periodically reviews the Staffing activities, status, and results; and resolves issues.

These reviews address:

1. Progress in performing staffing activities, including:

- filling open positions,
- attracting selected candidates,
- balancing workload against work commitments, and
- performing workforce reduction and other outplacement activities.

2. Results from reviews of Staffing practices and activities.

> Refer to Verification 1 for information regarding reviews of Staffing activities to ensure adherence to the following:
> - Relevant laws and regulations
> - Organizational policies, practices, and procedures

3. Status of resolution of noncompliance issues.
4. Trends relevant to future staffing decisions and requirements.
5. Effectiveness of Staffing activities in achieving staffing results.

Communication and Coordination
A process area at Maturity Level 2: Managed

Purpose
The purpose of Communication and Coordination is to establish timely communication throughout the organization and to ensure that the workforce has the skills to share information and coordinate activities efficiently.

Description
Communication and Coordination establishes the initial basis for developing and empowering workgroups. This process area establishes a culture for openly sharing information across organizational levels and laterally among dependent units. Increasing the flow of information provides the foundation for a participatory culture and empowered workgroups. A critical attribute of this culture is that individuals can feel confident in raising concerns to management without fear of retribution.

Prior to having the benefit of defined processes, people who work together must have the skills required to coordinate their activities and manage shared dependencies. At higher maturity levels, defining competency-based processes removes some of the burden from individuals for managing dependencies by coordinating the required interactions into defined roles and tasks. Prior to the availability of defined processes, interpersonal communication and coordination skills need to be developed to provide a foundation for the structured development of workgroups at higher levels.

Establishing effective communication begins with communicating the organization's values, policies, practices, and other significant organizational information to the workforce. In addition to this top-down information, bottom-up communication is stimulated by seeking the opinions of individuals on their working conditions. Lateral communication among units begins by focusing on communication required to accomplish committed work.

In order to reinforce the importance of open communication, the organization establishes formal procedures for raising and resolving concerns. Once raised, these concerns should be tracked to closure by management to reinforce their respect for the knowledge and experience from which these concerns emerge. Eliminating fear of reprisal or retribution establishes respect for individuals as an important component of the culture.

The interpersonal communication skills necessary to maintain effective working relationships are developed. To maintain effective workgroups, interpersonal problems are addressed quickly and meetings are managed to ensure that workgroup time is used most effectively. Individuals identify dependencies in their committed work and establish agreements for coordinating their activities. Individuals monitor progress against these dependencies to ensure coordination within their workgroup.

Goals

Goal 1   Information is shared across the organization.

Goal 2   Individuals or groups are able to raise concerns and have them addressed by management.

Goal 3   Individuals and workgroups coordinate their activities to accomplish committed work.

Goal 4   Communication and Coordination practices are institutionalized to ensure they are performed as managed processes.

Commitment to Perform

Commitment 1   Executive management establishes and communicates a set of values for the organization regarding the development and management of its workforce.

Examples of workforce issues that can be addressed through the organization's values include the following:

- Implicit and explicit commitments between the organization and its workforce
- Commitment to growing skills and increasing performance
- Philosophy of career development
- Treatment of individuals
- Workforce rights
- Open communication without fear of reprisal
- Emphasis on collaboration and teamwork
- Intent to align individual, workgroup, unit, and organizational performance
- Desired cultural values and attributes
- Conflict or dispute resolution
- Workplace violence
- Respecting the rights and dignity of individuals during the performance of workforce activities
- Workforce diversity issues
- Sensitivity to and respect for diverse cultures within the workforce
- Emphasis on quality of work life (QWL) and work-life balance
- Commitment to continuous improvement of people-related activities
- Social responsibility and social accountability, addressing labor practices, human rights, child and forced labor, health and safety, collective bargaining, discrimination, disciplinary practices, working hours, and compensation [CEPAA 97, GRI 06, SA8000 08]
- Other values, as appropriate

Executive management:

1. Documents a set of values to guide people-related behavior in the organization.

2. Publicly endorses the documented values of the organization.

3. Ensures that the values are communicated to all members of the workforce.

> Examples of methods for communicating the values of the organization include the following:
> - Public display of the organization's values statement
> - Open discussion of values-related issues through appropriate communications channels
> - Inclusion of values in orientation training, management training, and other appropriate training
> - Explicitly using and applying the values when performing people-related activities
> - Referring to guiding values in explaining decisions
> - Other methods, as appropriate

4. Derives policies and procedures for workforce activities from these values.

5. Establishes mechanisms to ensure that all workforce activities comply with the organization's values.

6. Enforces corrective action when workforce activities do not comply with the values of the organization.

7. Ensures that executive decisions and actions demonstrate consistent support for the organization's values.

Commitment 2   The organization establishes and maintains a documented policy for conducting its Communication and Coordination activities.

Issues typically addressed in the policy include:

1. Relationship of the Communication and Coordination activities to the business objectives, plans, and documented values of the organization.

2. Importance of maintaining an open environment that supports communication flow in all directions.

3. Requirements for periodic communication of organization-wide information to all individuals and workgroups.

4. Requirements for developing communication skills in all individuals and workgroups.

5. Opportunities for raising and resolving concerns.

6. Importance of establishing and meeting commitments involving work dependencies.

7. Importance of ensuring that individuals understand the impact of their communication or interactions and its potential to create a hostile work environment.

> In particular, individuals should be familiarized with the types of communication or interactions that could create a hostile work environment for other members of the workforce, especially those related to issues such as harassment, discrimination, equal opportunity, workplace violence, or similar concerns.

8. Communication and Coordination activities comply with relevant laws, regulations, and organizational policies.

Commitment 3   **An organizational role(s) is assigned responsibility for assisting and advising units on Communication and Coordination activities and procedures.**

> Examples of individuals or groups who might assist and advise on Communication and Coordination activities include the following:
> - Human resources or other appropriate professionals
> - Employee communications staff
> - Training and development staff
> - Organizational development staff
> - Technical writing staff
> - Public relations staff
> - Other communications staff

Ability to Perform

Ability 1   **Within each unit, an individual(s) is assigned responsibility and authority for ensuring that Communication and Coordination activities are performed.**

Ability 2   **Adequate resources are provided for performing Communication and Coordination activities.**

1. Experienced individuals with communication or coordination expertise are made available for Communication and Coordination activities.

2. Resources for supporting Communication and Coordination activities are made available.

3. Support for implementing improvements in communication or coordination is made available.

4. Adequate funding to accomplish Communication and Coordination activities is made available.

Ability 3 **Individuals responsible for facilitating or improving Communication and Coordination activities receive the preparation needed to perform their responsibilities.**

> Examples of training related to facilitating or improving communication or coordination include the following:
> - Relevant communication or coordination methods
> - Facilitating and developing communication skills in others
> - Development of interpersonal communication skills
> - Dispute arbitration or resolution techniques
> - Planning and coordination methods
> - Meeting facilitation
> - Addressing concerns, grievances, or issues
> - Planning and executing an organizational communication strategy
> - How to use different communication media effectively

Practices Performed

Practice 1 **The workforce-related policies and practices of the organization are communicated to the workforce.**

1. Individuals and units are informed of policies and practices that affect them.

> Examples of people-related policies and practices that should be communicated include the following:
> - Hiring policies
> - Training and development policies
> - Compensation strategies
> - Career growth policies
> - Promotion and transfer procedures
> - Retraining practices
> - Procedures for raising a concern
> - Performance management practices

2. Whenever people-related policies and practices are changed, the changes are communicated to the workforce.
3. The organization periodically determines whether the workforce is aware of its people-related policies and practices.
4. When misunderstandings of the people-related policies and practices exist, corrective action is taken.

Practice 2   **Information about organizational values, events, and conditions is communicated to the workforce on a periodic and event-driven basis.**

Examples of information that is to be communicated to the workforce include the following:
- Organizational mission, vision, and strategic objectives
- Business ethics
- The organization's values
- Business plans and objectives
- Financial results and conditions
- Business performance
- Quality, productivity, cost, or time-to-market results
- Changes in organizational structure or processes
- Notable events

Examples of communication mechanisms include the following:
- Organization-wide meetings
- Staff meetings
- One-on-one meetings
- Bulletin boards
- Electronic mail announcements
- Internal publications
- Newsletters
- Memos

Practice 3   **Information required for performing committed work is shared across affected units in a timely manner.**

1. Responsible individuals in each unit:

   - identify the dependencies their committed work has created with other units,
   - agree with responsible individuals in affected units how they will share information,
   - ensure that information needed to perform committed work is shared among affected units in a timely manner,
   - ensure that affected members of their unit are receiving the information they need from sources outside the unit,
   - ensure that affected members of their unit are timely in providing needed information to those in other units, and
   - take corrective action when communication breakdowns occur.

2. When necessary, those to whom dependent units report assist in establishing the communication needed to perform committed work.

Practice 4   Individuals' opinions on their working conditions are sought on a periodic and event-driven basis.

1. Input is collected on a periodic basis.

> Examples of mechanisms for gathering opinions from individuals include the following:
> - Opinion surveys or organizational climate questionnaires
> - Interviews with a sample of the workforce
> - Discussions with management, including meetings that allow individuals to skip levels of management or to meet with management representatives, such as an ombudsman
> - Group meetings on concerns
> - Focus groups or advisory boards, composed of individuals
> - Postmortem project reviews
> - Suggestion boxes or other private means
> - Email or other electronic means
> - Other solicitations for input
> - Appraisals, such as a SCAMPI with People CMM appraisal

2. The receipt of opinions from members of the workforce is acknowledged.

3. Inputs are analyzed and results are prepared according to the topics being studied.

4. Where appropriate, the results of these analyses, decisions based on them, and actions taken are communicated to the workforce.

5. To ensure confidentiality, results are presented so that individuals or groups cannot be identified as the source of information unless they have given their permission to be identified.

Practice 5   Individuals or groups can raise concerns according to a documented procedure.

> A *concern* is an issue, state of affairs, condition, or grievance that an individual or workgroup wants the organization to address and resolve.

1. The procedure typically specifies:

   - how a concern may be raised;
   - requirements for tracking and resolving concerns that have been raised;

- how responses should be provided regarding a concern;
- how to conduct and record a meeting, if needed, to discuss possible resolutions of a concern;
- follow-on activities after problem-solving meetings; and
- how to raise a concern directly with higher management if it cannot be resolved at a lower level.

2. Individuals or groups may raise a concern to any level of management without fear of reprisal.

> Examples of mechanisms for raising a concern may include the following:
> - Submission of written concerns to an appropriate individual
> - Meetings with an appropriate individual or manager
> - Meetings with an identified neutral party or ombudsman
> - Formal grievance procedures

3. The resolution of a concern can be appealed to higher management levels.

Practice 6 **Activities related to the resolution of a concern are tracked to closure.**

1. Responsibilities are assigned for tracking the status of concerns.
2. The status of all open concerns is periodically reviewed by management.
3. When appropriate progress has not been made in resolving a concern, corrective action is taken.

Practice 7 **The interpersonal communication skills necessary to establish and maintain effective working relationships within and across workgroups are developed.**

> Examples of interpersonal skills that support working relationships include the following:
> - Interpersonal communication and dynamics
> - Active listening skills
> - Group communication and dynamics
> - Interaction protocols for specific situations
> - Problem resolution skills
> - Conflict resolution skills
> - Negotiation skills
> - Multicultural sensitivity and other diversity-related skills

1. Needs for developing interpersonal skills are identified.

> Examples of mechanisms through which the need for developing interpersonal skills can be identified include the following:
> - Self- or workgroup evaluation
> - Observation by manager, workgroup leader, or other responsible individual
> - Discussions of performance
> - Analysis indicating that an interpersonal skill, such as negotiation, is a critical component for accomplishing an individual's or workgroup's committed work

2. Methods for developing or improving interpersonal skills are identified and performed.

> Examples of methods for developing or improving interpersonal skills include the following:
> - Training or orientation
> - Mentoring or coaching
> - Facilitated group discussion or workshop

3. When appropriate, individuals are sensitized to cultural issues that would influence interpersonal or workgroup communication styles.

Practice 8   **Interpersonal problems or conflicts that degrade the quality or effectiveness of working relationships are handled appropriately.**

> Examples of appropriate ways to handle interpersonal problems include the following:
> - Improving interpersonal communication skills
> - Advising or counseling one or more individuals
> - Improving the dynamics of a group
> - Using an ombudsman, arbitrator, or facilitator
> - Reassigning one or more individuals
> - Conducting performance management actions
> - Taking disciplinary action

Practice 9   **Individuals and workgroups coordinate their activities to accomplish committed work.**

> Refer to Practice 3 of the Staffing process area for information regarding making commitments for work that individuals or workgroups will be accountable for performing.

1. Individuals and workgroups participate in making decisions about how to organize and perform their work.

2. Individuals and workgroups organize and perform their work to satisfy their commitments and dependencies.

> Refer to the Performance Management process area for information regarding establishing objectives related to committed work against which unit and individual performance can be measured, discussions of performance against these objectives, and enhancements to achieved performance.

Practice 10   Individuals and workgroups monitor and coordinate the dependencies involved in their committed work.

> Some work in a unit can be performed independently by individuals because it does not involve dependencies on the work of others in order to satisfy commitments. However, where the work is interdependent, individuals and workgroups should ensure they mutually agree to their commitments in order to coordinate their activities.

1. Committed work at the unit, workgroup, and individual levels is analyzed to identify dependencies.

2. Individuals and workgroups agree on the dependencies created by their committed work.

3. Mutually agreeable mechanisms for coordinating dependent work are established.

4. Agreements for coordinating dependent work are documented.

> Work dependencies may take many different forms. Dependencies in work may range from highly repetitive, routine activities to dependencies involving occasional results from large, nonroutine undertakings. The means for documenting dependencies can vary widely and should be matched to the characteristics of the dependency.

> Examples of appropriate forms of documenting agreements concerning dependencies include the following:
> - Plans and schedules
> - Defined processes or procedures
> - Defined roles
> - Job or position descriptions
> - Memoranda of understanding
> - Contracts
> - Defined performance objectives based on committed work

5. Individuals or workgroups communicate in advance when dependencies cannot be met.

6. When necessary, dependencies are revised through mutual agreement among affected parties.

Practice 11   Meetings are conducted to make the most effective use of participants' time.

1. Guidelines are developed for maximizing meeting efficiency based on the organization's culture and values, business processes, and the purpose of the meeting.

> Examples of topics addressed by meeting guidelines include the following:
> - Meeting purpose
> - Meeting planning
> - Meeting agenda and time management
> - Responsibilities and roles of participants
> - Attendance size and requirements
> - Meeting procedures
> - Location and room setup
> - Participation mechanisms
> - Practices for tracking action items or issues

2. Meetings are called only if they offer an adequate benefit for the time consumed; otherwise, a more efficient way to accomplish the purpose of the meeting is pursued.

3. To the extent possible, a meeting's purpose, objectives, and procedures are planned, and an agenda is distributed in advance.

4. Meetings are conducted to maintain focus on accomplishing their original purpose.

5. Meetings are conducted to encourage the participation of all who are able to make a contribution.

6. Actions to be performed following the meeting are assigned and tracked to completion.

Measurement and Analysis

Measurement 1   Measurements are made and used to determine the status and performance of Communication and Coordination activities.

> Examples of measurements include the following:
> - Use of communication media
> - Number of people trained in communication skills
> - Number of people trained in meeting management and facilitation skills
> - Results from opinion surveys
> - Number of interpersonal conflicts handled through formal mechanisms
> - Number of concerns raised
> - Number of meetings requested for expressing concerns
> - Time and effort expended to resolve concerns, grievances, or issues
> - Number of dependencies documented
> - Percent of commitments completed on time
> - Time spent in meetings
> - Meeting measures, such as percent of meetings starting and ending on time, and percent of meetings with agendas and with agendas distributed in advance
> - Rate at which meeting action items are closed

Measurement 2   Unit measures of Communication and Coordination activities are collected and maintained.

1. Units collect data as Communication and Coordination activities occur.
2. Measurements made to determine the status and performance of Communication and Coordination activities are maintained.

> Examples of reasons for maintaining measurements of Communication and Coordination activities include the following:
> - Periodic analysis to determine unit-level trends
> - Aggregating data at the organizational level to develop organizational measures
> - Analysis to determine organizational trends
> - Evaluation of organizational trends

Verifying Implementation

Verification 1   A responsible individual(s) verifies that the Communication and Coordination activities are conducted according to the organization's documented policies, practices, procedures, and, where appropriate, plans; and addresses noncompliance.

These reviews verify that:

1. Communication and Coordination activities comply with the organization's policies and stated values.

2. Communication and Coordination activities comply with all relevant laws and regulations.

3. Communication and Coordination activities are performed according to the organization's documented practices and procedures.

> These reviews may use measures regarding the status and performance of Communication and Coordination activities, as well as unit measures of Communication and Coordination activities, to ensure that a comprehensive review of Communication and Coordination activities occurs. These measures provide indicators of the status and performance of Communication and Coordination activities across the units. Refer to Measurement 1 and Measurement 2 for information regarding measurement of Communication and Coordination activities.

4. Noncompliance issues are handled appropriately.

Verification 2   Executive management periodically reviews the Communication and Coordination activities, status, and results; and resolves issues.

These reviews verify:

1. Progress in the performance of any planned communication activities.

2. Results from reviews of Communication and Coordination practices and activities.

> Refer to Verification 1 for information regarding reviews of Communication and Coordination activities to ensure adherence to the following:
> - Relevant laws and regulations
> - Organizational policies, practices, and procedures

3. Status of resolution of noncompliance issues.

4. Trends related to communication and coordination, including:

   - trends related to communication issues,
   - rate at which serious communication problems occur and are being reduced, and
   - trends related to concerns raised, including the number of concerns raised and the rate of resolving them.

5. Resolutions of concerns comply with the organization's documented policies and procedures.

6. Effectiveness of Communication and Coordination activities in achieving effective communication and coordination.

Work Environment

A process area at Maturity Level 2: Managed

Purpose

The purpose of Work Environment is to establish and maintain physical working conditions and to provide resources that allow individuals and workgroups to perform their tasks efficiently without unnecessary distractions.

Description

The work environment must be managed to ensure it supports the committed work of those in the organization. This process area focuses on both the resources provided for performing work, and the physical conditions under which the work is performed. Management must balance expenditures on resources and environment with justifications based on the work being performed. This process area reinforces management's responsibility to monitor resource needs and environmental conditions that affect the workforce's ability to perform work efficiently. Management should have plans for mitigating those problems judged to present serious risks to health, safety, or efficiency. Continual interruptions are one of the greatest impediments to efficiency in knowledge-intense environments. While distractions cannot be eliminated, attempts should be made to minimize them.

Establishing an effective work environment begins with identifying the physical environment and resources needed to perform committed work. An appropriate physical environment and personal workspace are provided for individuals and workgroups to perform their assigned responsibilities. Resources needed to perform committed work are made available in a timely manner. Improvements to the effectiveness of the work environment are identified and prioritized. Within reasonable boundaries, high priority improvements are implemented. Environmental conditions that would degrade or endanger the health or safety of the workforce are eliminated. Physical factors that would degrade work efficiency are addressed. Distractions in the work environment are identified and minimized.

Goals

Goal 1   **The physical environment and resources needed by the workforce to perform their assignments are made available.**

Goal 2   **Distractions in the work environment are minimized.**

Goal 3   **Work Environment practices are institutionalized to ensure they are performed as managed processes.**

Commitment to Perform

Commitment 1 **The organization establishes and maintains a documented policy for conducting its Work Environment activities.**

Issues typically addressed in the policy include:

1. The organization's work environment is developed to support the business objectives and stated values of the organization.

2. Laws, regulations, and organizational policies governing the work environment are communicated to the workforce, administered, and enforced.

> Guidance should be sought from human resources, legal, ergonomics and safety, or other appropriate professionals in interpreting and administering these laws and regulations since they can have serious legal implications.

> Examples of laws and regulations include the following:
> - Safety-related laws and regulations, including those of safety-related regulatory agencies such as the Occupational Safety and Health Administration (OSHA)
> - National and local building and fire codes
> - Laws and regulations providing access for the physically challenged, such as the Americans with Disabilities Act (ADA)
> - Other applicable national, state, or local laws and regulations

3. Adequate space is provided for performing assigned work.

4. Within prudent limits, the resources needed to perform assigned work are identified, prioritized, and made available.

5. Conditions that degrade the work environment are eliminated.

6. Distractions in the work environment are minimized.

7. Work Environment practices and activities comply with relevant laws, regulations, and organizational policies.

Commitment 2   An organizational role(s) is assigned responsibility for assisting and advising units on work environment-related activities, and for assuming appropriate organizational responsibilities for the physical work environment and work resources.

> Examples of individuals or groups who may assist and advise on work environment-related activities, and assume appropriate organizational responsibilities, include the following:
> - Committees on work environment conditions
> - Management or staff committees
> - Physical plant or facilities staff
> - Telecommunications staff
> - Computing facilities staff
> - Financial staff
> - Members of the human resources function or other appropriate professionals

Ability to Perform

Ability 1   Within each unit, an individual (s) is assigned responsibility and authority for ensuring that Work Environment activities are performed.

Ability 2   Within prudent limits, adequate resources are provided for performing Work Environment activities, implementing the physical environment and resources necessary to perform assigned work, and making improvements to the work environment.

> Prudent limits are those that are determined by management and are based on considerations that might include the following:
> - Responsible fiscal policies
> - Sound management of the organization's resources
> - Investment priorities
> - Resources that would be expected to be available in a professional environment
> - Resources that are available in competitors' environments
> - Benchmarks of similar work environments

1. Documented business plans, budgets, or similar guidance are available that indicate the work to be assigned to each unit and the budget available for providing a physical work environment and other work-related resources.

2. Experienced individuals who have expertise in various aspects of the work environment are available for implementing an effective work environment.

> Examples of contributions that could be made by those with special skills include the following:
> - Designing and implementing effective work environments
> - Analyzing needed resources for performing assigned work
> - Analyzing impediments in the work environment
> - Analyzing the potential benefits from automation
> - Identifying resources that would improve performance
> - Training in laws, regulations, and organizational policies governing the work environment

3. Adequate budget and resources are made available for implementing the physical environment and work resources that are needed for performing assigned work.

4. Funding to accomplish Work Environment activities is made available.

5. Adequate funding is made available for resources that would improve the work environment.

6. Support for implementing work environment improvements is made available.

Ability 3   The workforce receives the preparation needed to maintain an effective work environment.

> Examples of work environment issues to be covered with the workforce include the following:
> - Laws, regulations, and organizational policies governing the work environment
> - Procedures for handling violations of laws, regulations, and organizational policies; and the responsible individual(s) to which such issues should be reported
> - Procedures for reporting problems, acquiring or disposing of equipment, altering a workspace, or similar work environment issues
> - Health and safety procedures
> - How to use equipment or workstations

Ability 4   Those responsible for improving the work environment receive the preparation in relevant methods and procedures needed to perform their responsibilities.

> Examples of training in methods to improve the work environment include the following:
> - Detailed information regarding laws, regulations, and organizational policies governing the work environment and how they are to be interpreted
> - Remedies and procedures for handling violations of laws, regulations, organizational policies, and procedures related to the work environment
> - Methods for assessing the work environment
> - Methods for minimizing or eliminating impediments or distractions in the work environment
> - Methods for aiding task performance with technology

Practices Performed

Practice 1   The physical environment and resources required to perform committed work are identified in each unit.

> Analysis of the physical environment and work resources can be conducted at the organizational level in conjunction with analysis at the unit level. While many of the resources covered in these practices may be provided at the organizational level, the unit must be involved in comparing space and resources to committed and planned work to ensure that space and resources are adequate for performing the assigned work.

1. Work is analyzed to determine the type of physical environment and resources required to perform it.

> Examples of the resources to be considered include the following:
> - Individual workspace
> - Group workspace
> - Meeting space
> - Support or production areas
> - Telecommuting support
> - Support for remote locations
> - Storage
> - Special characteristics of physical workspaces
> - Furniture
> - Production equipment
> - Communication equipment
> - Work materials
> - Computers
> - Supplies

2. The physical environment and resources needed to perform assigned work are compared to those currently available within the unit to determine unit needs.

3. A responsible individual(s) takes appropriate action to acquire workspace or resources needed to perform assigned work.

> Examples of appropriate actions may include the following:
> - Preparing budget requests for the needed physical environment or other resources
> - Developing cost-benefit justifications for acquiring the physical environment or other resources needed
> - Coordinating actions needed to implement improvements, including documenting needed improvements, consulting with appropriate subject matter experts, and submitting purchase orders or requests for bids on improvements
> - Negotiating with those responsible for managing building or computing facilities, distributing equipment or supplies, or other work environment-related resources

4. If the physical environment or other resources needed cannot be obtained, a responsible individual(s) develops a contingency plan that articulates performance risks and coordinates its implementation with all affected parties.

Practice 2   The physical environment required to perform assigned work is provided.

1. Adequate space is provided for performing assigned work.

> Examples of space that could be important for performing assigned work include the following:
> - Individual workspaces
> - Spaces for group work
> - Public spaces, such as conference rooms and meeting spaces
> - Specialized workspaces, such as laboratories and training areas
> - Support areas for production or storage

2. To the extent possible, the physical environment is designed and organized to support efficient performance of assigned work.

3. To the extent possible, culturally important issues are considered when organizing the physical environment.

4. Characteristics of the physical environment that are important for work performance are adjusted and, if necessary, monitored.

> Examples of characteristics of the physical environment that could be important for work performance include the following:
> - Security
> - Visibility
> - Noise
> - Voice communication
> - Airborne particulates

5. When aspects of an adequate physical environment cannot be provided, a contingency action is implemented.

Practice 3   Individual workspaces provide an adequate personal environment for performing assigned work responsibilities.

Individual workspaces provide:

1. Protected private space where personal effects, work tools, and products can be secured and stored as necessary.

2. Adequate desktop space for using tools and other resources in performing tasks and storing the work products produced.

3. Adequate illumination for performing work.

4. Sufficient isolation and noise protection to support the level of concentration needed to perform individual work.

5. Sufficient space to perform work activities alone or with a limited number of colleagues, as appropriate.

Practice 4   The resources needed to accomplish committed work are made available in a timely manner.

1. Adequate physical and technical resources are provided for performing committed work.

> Examples of physical and technical resources include the following:
> - Office furniture and equipment
> - Lighting
> - Computers, workstations, or other computing equipment
> - Application software (e.g., editors, word processing and document production tools, spreadsheets, and project management tools)
> - Communications technologies, such as telephones, fax machines, modems, and electronic mail facilities
> - Communications and office equipment for remote locations or telecommuting
> - Printing and reproduction equipment
> - Documentation
> - Laboratory equipment
> - Maintenance on resources
> - Training equipment

2. Specialized resources that would normally be available for performing a specific type of work in most organizations are made available.

> For example, in a software development organization, basic computational technology resources could include the following:
> - Computers, workstations, or other computing equipment
> - Networks
> - Software development tools and environments
> - Project management tools
> - Electronic communications

3. Adequate staff support is provided.

> Examples of staff support resources include the following:
> - Business and administrative support
> - Computer support personnel
> - Technical writing and documentation support
> - Laboratory technicians
> - Clerical support

4. Resource and staff support needs are planned and provided on a periodic (e.g., annual) and event-driven (e.g., project initiation) basis.

5. When resources cannot be provided on a timely basis or at all, contingency actions are implemented.

Practice 5   Improvements are made to the work environment that improve work performance.

1. The work environment is periodically analyzed to identify changes or resources that could improve work performance.

> This analysis could be a component of the analyses performed in Practice 1.

2. Potential improvements to the work environment are prioritized.

> Complying with laws and regulations regarding access for the disabled or physically challenged, such as the Americans with Disabilities Act, or meeting ergonomic requirements may cause a higher priority to be placed on some improvements. Guidance should be sought from the human resources, facilities, legal, or other appropriate professionals in complying with such laws and regulations.

3. Within prudent limits, such as available budget, resources for high priority improvements are made available.

4. When implementing large, pervasive improvements across the workplace, improvements are planned and deployed.

5. When needed, support for or training in the use of newly deployed resources is made available.

Practice 6   Environmental factors that degrade or endanger the health or safety of the workforce are identified and corrected.

1. Responsible individuals maintain awareness of conditions in the work environment that might affect the health or safety of individuals who might be exposed to them.

> Examples of individuals who might exercise responsibility for maintaining awareness of work environment conditions include:
> - Individuals responsible for buildings, facilities, and other physical resources
> - Security staff
> - Managers, supervisors, team leaders, and others with supervisory or leadership responsibility
> - Individuals designated to monitor specific environmental conditions
> - Individuals who conduct periodic inspections of the work environment

2. Responsible individuals report work environment conditions that would degrade or endanger health or safety to individuals who can address them.

> Examples of environmental factors that degrade or endanger the health or safety of the workforce include the following:
> - Unsafe working conditions
> - Inadequate security
> - Improper ergonomics
> - Exposure to unhealthy substances
> - Poor air or water quality
> - Excessive stress

3. Responsible individuals identify and implement reasonable accommodations to protect the health or safety of the workforce while corrections are being made.

4. Responsible individuals monitor progress in correcting health or safety-related conditions to ensure they are corrected in a timely manner.

Practice 7   Physical factors that degrade the effectiveness of the work environment are identified and addressed.

1. Responsible individuals maintain awareness of the physical factors in the work environment that could degrade the performance of those exposed to these factors.

> Examples of physical factors that could degrade the effectiveness of the work environment include the following:
> - Inadequate office or meeting space
> - Poor lighting
> - Inadequate heating, ventilation, or cooling
> - Unpleasant odors
> - Vibration
> - Excessive noise
> - Crowding

2. Responsible individuals identify and take action to mitigate the effects of physical factors that could degrade the performance of individuals exposed to them.

> Examples of actions that could be taken to mitigate the effects of physical factors in the work environment include the following:
>
> - Correct the problem
> - Provide resources that reduce the impact of the problem (e.g., fans or heaters for addressing inadequate temperature control)
> - Communicate future intentions that would alleviate the problem (such as acquiring additional office space to reduce crowding)
> - Make accommodations on an individual basis that allow individuals to make reasonable adjustments that reduce the impact of problems on their personal work

3. Responsible individuals monitor the performance of affected individuals to determine if additional actions need to be taken to mitigate the impact of physical factors.

4. If it is determined that it is not possible to effectively eliminate the impact of a physical factor, alternative mitigation strategies and solutions are pursued.

Practice 8   **Sources of frequent interruption or distraction that degrade the effectiveness of the work environment are identified and minimized.**

> Examples of interruptions or distractions include the following:
>
> - Telephone calls
> - Excessive meetings
> - Poorly organized work processes
> - Unnecessary or excessive administrative tasks
> - Work that could be performed by other, more appropriate, individuals
> - Excessive socializing

Measurement and Analysis

Measurement 1 **Measurements are made and used to determine the status and performance of Work Environment activities.**

> Examples of measurements include the following:
> - Average area of individual workspaces in the work environment
> - Average area of desktop surfaces in individual or group workspaces
> - Utilization of shared public spaces, such as conference rooms
> - Number of complaints or concerns raised about the work environment
> - Number of violations of work environment laws or regulations
> - Effectiveness of improvements on performance
> - Percent of work affected by time distractions
> - Percent of time spent in meetings
> - Rate at which physical distractions are corrected
> - Investment in work environment improvements

Measurement 2 **Unit measures of Work Environment activities are collected and maintained.**

1. Units collect data as Work Environment activities occur.
2. Measurements made to determine the status and performance of Work Environment activities are maintained.

> Examples of reasons for maintaining measurements of Work Environment activities include the following:
> - Periodic analysis to determine unit-level trends
> - Aggregating data at the organizational level to develop organizational measures
> - Analysis to determine organizational trends
> - Evaluation of organizational trends

Verifying Implementation

Verification 1 **A responsible individual(s) verifies that Work Environment activities are conducted according to the organization's documented policies, practices, procedures, and, where appropriate, plans; and addresses noncompliance.**

These reviews verify that:

1. Work Environment activities comply with the organization's policies and stated values.
2. Work Environment activities comply with relevant laws and regulations.

3. Conditions in the work environment satisfy all applicable laws, regulations, and organizational policies.

4. Improvements in the work environment are deployed in a timely and effective fashion.

5. Severe, especially physical, distractions are handled in a timely manner.

6. Work Environment activities are performed according to the organization's documented practices and procedures.

> These reviews may use measures regarding the status and performance of Work Environment activities, as well as unit measures of Work Environment activities, to ensure that a comprehensive review of Work Environment activities occurs. These measures provide indicators of the status and performance of Work Environment activities across the units. Refer to Measurement 1 and Measurement 2 for information regarding measurement of Work Environment activities.

7. Noncompliance issues are handled appropriately.

8. Violations of laws and regulations are handled in a manner consistent with legal requirements.

Verification 2   Executive management periodically reviews the Work Environment activities, status, and results, including improvements to the work environment; and resolves issues.

These reviews verify:

1. Results from reviews of the work environment.

2. Status of any violations of applicable laws and regulations.

3. The amount and effectiveness of improvements made in the work environment.

4. Progress in performing Work Environment activities, including installing improvements in the work environment.

5. Results from reviews of Work Environment practices and activities.

> Refer to Verification 1 for information regarding reviews of Work Environment activities to ensure adherence to the following:
> - Relevant laws and regulations
> - Organizational policies, practices, and procedures

6. Status of resolution of noncompliance issues.

7. Trends related to work environment-related issues.

8. Effectiveness of Work Environment activities in achieving work environment results.

Performance Management

A process area at Maturity Level 2: Managed

Purpose

The purpose of Performance Management is to establish objectives related to committed work against which unit and individual performance can be measured, to discuss performance against these objectives, and to continuously enhance performance.

Description

The primary focus of performance management is on continual discussion of work performance to identify ways to improve it. Continual discussion of performance focuses not only on the individual, but also on work processes, resources, and any other issues that can be addressed to improve performance. The discussion of performance occurs in the context of measurable objectives that individuals are trying to achieve in their work. The role of performance appraisal in this orientation is primarily to record the results of performance for use as input to decisions about adjustments to compensation, personal development planning, staffing, promotion, and other workforce activities.

The process of managing performance is initiated by collaboratively defining measurable objectives for unit performance that are based on the unit's committed work. These unit objectives establish the framework in which individual performance objectives can be defined. Measurable performance objectives are defined for each individual based on their committed work, and are revised as needed. Performance objectives at the unit and individual levels are periodically reviewed to determine their continued relevance, and, if needed, they are revised.

Those responsible for performance feedback have ongoing discussions about the performance of committed work with those they are assigned to review. Continuous discussion of the performance of committed work involves mutual investigation of ways to enhance performance. Those responsible for providing performance feedback maintain an awareness of the performance of individuals and workgroups against their committed work. Accomplishments against performance objectives are periodically documented and discussed.

When they arise, performance problems are discussed and documented. If performance continues to be unsatisfactory, a performance improvement plan is developed and tracked. Employment actions may be taken based on results accomplished against the performance improvement plan.

Outstanding performance is recognized or rewarded. Reward includes special recognition outside of the compensation system for accomplishments of significant value to the organization. A recognition and reward strategy is developed and communicated to the workforce. As rewards are made, public recognition is provided to reinforce those skills or behaviors that the organization values.

Goals

Goal 1   **Unit and individual performance objectives related to committed work are documented.**

Goal 2   **The performance of committed work is regularly discussed to identify actions that can improve it.**

Goal 3   **Performance problems are managed.**

Goal 4   **Outstanding performance is recognized or rewarded.**

Goal 5   **Performance Management practices are institutionalized to ensure they are performed as managed processes.**

Commitment to Perform

Commitment 1   **The organization establishes and maintains a documented policy for conducting its Performance Management activities.**

Issues typically addressed in the policy include:

1. Performance Management activities serve business objectives and the stated values of the organization.
2. Performance is to be measured against defined objectives related to committed work.
3. The rights and dignity of each individual are respected during the conduct of all Performance Management activities.
4. Performance management information and data are confidential to the individual(s) they concern.
5. Appropriate performance management procedures are defined, documented, and used.

> The human resources function or other appropriate professionals should review all such procedures to ensure they
> - Are consistent with relevant laws, regulations, and organizational policies
> - Respect the rights and dignity of individuals and groups

Performance management procedures are established and maintained for:

- identifying those responsible for providing performance feedback,
- developing measurable performance objectives related to committed work,
- periodically discussing the performance of committed work and possible improvements,
- documenting and discussing accomplishments against performance objectives at least once during the period covered by the objectives,

- resolving disagreements about performance feedback,
- documenting development needs,
- handling performance problems,
- rewarding outstanding performance, and
- ensuring appropriate distribution, use, and retention of performance documentation, including granting access to, and ensuring confidentiality of, these performance data.

> Examples of procedural guidance on performance documentation include the following:
> - What information should be documented
> - How documentation may be used
> - How and to whom documentation should be distributed
> - Where documentation should be stored
> - How long documentation should be retained
> - Who has access to the documentation
> - How documents may be inspected and challenged
> - How documentation is to be kept secure

6. Outstanding performance is recognized and rewarded, when appropriate.

> *Recognition* is accomplished through special acknowledgments made to an individual or group for accomplishments of value to the organization. *Rewards* are provided through special recognition outside of the compensation system for accomplishments of significant value to the organization. Rewards usually consist of variable amounts of money or other considerations provided to individuals or groups at appropriate times without any prior agreement as to conditions of receipt. Rewards are distinguished from recognition in that rewards typically involve financial considerations.
>
> Recognition and rewards can be made on a periodic (e.g., annual performance awards) or occasional (e.g., project completion) basis. Recognition and rewards are made to reinforce the skills and behaviors that the organization values.

7. Appropriate recognition and reward procedures and guidelines are defined, documented, and used.

> The human resources function or other appropriate professionals should review all such procedures or guidelines to ensure they
> - Are consistent with relevant laws, regulations, and organizational policies
> - Respect the rights and dignity of individuals and groups

Recognition and reward procedures or guidelines are established and maintained for:

- identifying those responsible for recognition and reward activities,
- defining the purposes of recognition and rewards,

- defining the basis for awarding special recognition or making rewards,
- communicating the structure of the recognition and reward system to the workforce,
- recommending an individual or group for recognition or reward,
- determining appropriate recognition and rewards,
- providing recognition and reward information to individuals,
- establishing and maintaining equity in the recognition and rewards system, and
- publicizing recognition and rewards.

8. Performance Management practices and activities comply with relevant laws, regulations, and organizational policies.

Commitment 2   An organizational role(s) is assigned responsibility for assisting and advising units on Performance Management activities.

> Examples of individuals who may assist or advise units on Performance Management activities include the following:
>
> - Human resources or other appropriate professionals
> - Resource manager
> - Productivity or quality staff
> - Legal staff
> - Those with expertise in performance improvement techniques

Ability to Perform

Ability 1   Within each unit, an individual(s) is assigned responsibility and authority for ensuring that Performance Management activities are performed.

> Examples of individuals who may be assigned responsibility for various Performance Management activities include the following:
>
> - The unit manager or assistant
> - A resource manager
> - A performance committee
> - A project or workgroup leader
> - An empowered workgroup
> - A committee of peers
> - An individual
> - A member of the human resources function or other appropriate professionals

Ability 2   Adequate resources are provided for performing Performance Management activities.

1. The organization's business objectives or plans are available to support setting unit performance objectives.

2. Experienced individuals who have expertise in performance management methods are made available for guidance in these activities.

> Examples of expertise in performance management include the following:
> - Definition of performance objectives and measurement of performance related to committed work
> - Analysis of tasks and performance against committed work
> - Productivity and quality improvement methods
> - Methods for providing effective feedback
> - Methods for handling problem people
> - Reward systems
> - Laws, regulations, policies, and procedures governing performance management

3. Resources for supporting Performance Management activities are made available.

> Examples of resources to support Performance Management activities include the following:
> - Repositories of previously defined performance objectives
> - Templates with categories for recording performance information
> - Templates for capturing developmental or improvement needs information
> - Examples of documentation for performance problems
> - Standard forms for documenting performance management activities

4. Funding to accomplish Performance Management activities is made available.

5. Adequate time is allocated for participating in Performance Management activities.

6. Experienced individuals who have expertise in recognition and reward programs are made available for guiding these activities.

> Examples of contributions that could be made by those with special skills include the following:
> - Designing and revising a recognition and reward program
> - Determining criteria for making rewards
> - Participating in recognition and reward decisions

7. Resources to support recognition and reward activities are made available.

> Examples of resources to support recognition and reward activities include the following:
> - Recognition and reward guidelines
> - Repositories of previously defined recognition and reward criteria
> - Examples of documentation for recognition and rewards
> - Space for recognition announcements in bulletins and other organizational media
> - Standard forms for documenting recognition and reward activities

8. Funding to accomplish recognition and reward activities is made available.

Ability 3   Individuals conducting Performance Management activities receive the preparation needed to perform their responsibilities.

1. Individuals responsible for documenting or discussing performance receive the preparation needed to perform their responsibilities.

> Examples of relevant skills in which individuals responsible for documenting or discussing performance feedback are trained include the following:
> - Defining performance objectives related to committed work
> - Evaluating performance against committed work
> - Listening and feedback skills
> - Performance appraisal methods
> - Identifying development needs
> - Handling problem employees
> - Documenting and managing unsatisfactory performance
> - Providing recognition and rewards
> - Laws and regulations governing performance management

2. Those responsible for recognition and reward activities receive the preparation needed to perform their responsibilities.

> Examples of preparation to perform recognition and reward activities include the following:
> - Awareness of, and orientation to, the organization's recognition and reward system
> - Training in the organization's recognition and reward practices
> - Understanding guidelines for fairly applying recognition and reward criteria

Ability 4   **Individuals who participate in Performance Management activities receive appropriate orientation in Performance Management practices.**

> Examples of relevant orientation topics regarding performance management include the following:
> - Defining objectives related to committed work
> - Analyzing task and job performance
> - Conducting job performance discussions
> - Developing individual capabilities
> - Recognizing and rewarding outstanding performance

Practices Performed

Practice 1   **Measurable performance objectives based on committed work are established for each unit.**

> A *work commitment* is an agreement concerning work to be accomplished. The commitment is made to the responsible individual for whom the work is being performed or to whom the result is being delivered. A *performance objective* is a measurable attribute or result of work behavior that can be used to evaluate the performance of a unit, workgroup, or individual. Examples of sources for deriving performance objectives include the following:
> - An attribute or measure of the work performed to meet a commitment
> - The results of the work performed to meet a commitment
> - Results or benefits that accrue from meeting a commitment
> - A measurable contribution to the work performance of others
> - A level of development to be achieved
> - Results to be achieved by others for whose performance an individual is accountable

1. The unit's performance objectives are based on the unit's committed work. These performance objectives are established and maintained on a schedule that coincides with the schedule on which work commitments are made for the unit.

> Examples of measurable performance objectives based on committed work include the following:
> - Work products to be produced
> - Milestones to be met
> - Quantitative quality targets to be achieved
> - Customer/user satisfaction levels to be achieved
> - Costs to be saved
> - Cycle time to be reduced
> - Increased integration with cooperating units
> - Services to be provided
> - Business to be won

2. The unit's work commitments are consistent with the business objectives and plans of the organization.

3. All appropriate members of the unit are involved in developing the unit's performance objectives based on their involvement in making work commitments.

4. The unit's performance objectives are reviewed with and approved by those to whom the unit is accountable.

5. Approved performance objectives for the unit are documented.

6. Approved performance objectives for the unit are communicated to all members of the unit and relevant stakeholders.

Practice 2   The unit's performance objectives are periodically reviewed as business conditions or work commitments change, and, if necessary, they are revised.

1. Unit performance objectives are periodically reviewed with management or other members of the organization to determine the appropriateness of these objectives to changed business conditions or work commitments.

2. When appropriate, a unit's performance objectives are revised using appropriate procedures.

3. Revisions to the unit's performance objectives are documented.

Practice 3   Those accountable for the accomplishment of unit performance objectives track and manage unit performance.

> This practice involves performance issues at the unit level, rather than at the individual level. The issues to be addressed in this practice involve collective results across individuals that are more appropriately addressed as unit performance, rather than as individual performance. The remaining practices in this process area focus on individual performance against individual performance objectives.

1. Those responsible for unit performance maintain awareness of unit accomplishments against committed work and other aspects of unit performance.

> Examples of issues to maintain an awareness of include the following:
> - Unit performance against documented unit performance objectives
> - Accomplishment of dependencies shared with other units
> - Impediments to achieving documented unit performance objectives
> - Influence of changing business conditions or work commitments on reprioritizing documented unit performance objectives
> - Need to revise documented unit performance objectives

2. Unit progress against performance objectives is reviewed and discussed with:

   - members of the unit,
   - representatives of other units with which the unit shares performance dependencies, and
   - individual(s) to whom those responsible for unit performance report.

> Examples of performance issues to be reviewed and discussed may include the following:
> - Unit performance compared with documented objectives
> - Coordination of activities and dependencies involved in performing committed work
> - Changes in unit performance objectives
> - Perceptions of performance by others if these perceptions are relevant to performance objective

3. Opportunities to enhance unit performance are discussed and improvement actions are identified.

> Examples of topics related to performance improvement to be discussed may include the following:
> - Opportunities for improvements in processes, tools, or resources
> - Knowledge and skills needing development
> - Improvements in communication needed to perform committed work
> - Improvements in coordination of activities

4. Unsatisfactory performance against unit performance objectives is managed.

> This subpractice is focused on problems in unit performance whose causes can be attributed to factors beyond individual performance problems. Refer to Practices 10, 11, and 12 of the Performance Management process area for information regarding managing unsatisfactory performance at the individual level.

- Impediments to achieving unit performance objectives are identified.
- Corrective actions for improving unit performance are implemented.
- Changes to unit plans or objectives are documented and communicated to all affected parties.
- Corrective actions are tracked.

Practice 4   Performance objectives based on committed work are documented for each individual on a periodic or event-driven basis.

1. Each individual's performance objectives are drawn, in part, from the performance objectives of their unit.

   - The unit's performance objectives are allocated to individuals based on their responsibilities.
   - Individuals review these allocated objectives against their committed work before accepting responsibility for them.
   - Issues with any allocated performance objectives are raised and negotiated with the individual(s) responsible for the unit's performance.
   - When the unit's performance objectives are revised, each individual's allocated performance objectives are revised to remain consistent with the unit's new performance objectives and committed work.

2. The objectives for each individual's job performance are not in conflict with their unit's performance objectives.

3. Performance objectives for each individual are drawn from, and are consistent with, their work commitments.

4. Individuals participate in developing their performance objectives.

5. Individuals agree to and approve their performance objectives.

6. Individual performance objectives are documented.

Practice 5   Performance objectives for each individual are reviewed on a periodic or event-driven basis, and, if necessary, they are revised.

1. Individual performance objectives are periodically reviewed to determine their appropriateness under changing personal, workgroup, or unit conditions.

2. Performance objectives are reviewed every time personal, workgroup, or unit work commitments are revised.

3. When appropriate, the individual's performance objectives are revised using the standard procedures employed for defining their performance objectives.

4. Revisions to the individual's performance objectives are documented.

Practice 6   **Those responsible for performance management activities maintain on-going communication about the performance of committed work with those whose performance they manage.**

> Examples of methods for maintaining communication about the performance of committed work include the following:
> - Informal discussions
> - Informal performance feedback discussions
> - Periodic meetings to review progress
> - Periodic meetings to analyze how the performance of assigned responsibilities could be improved
> - Periodic meetings to document and discuss accomplishments against performance objectives

1. Various components of work performance are periodically discussed and analyzed.

2. Ways to improve the performance of committed work are periodically discussed and improvement actions are taken.

> Refer to Practice 6 of the Training and Development process area for information regarding development discussions with individuals.

> Examples of ways to improve the performance of committed work include the following:
> - Training in task-related knowledge and skills
> - Apprenticing to an experienced individual or group
> - Mentoring or coaching
> - Improved coordination with other individuals
> - Improvements in work environment conditions

Practice 7   **Those responsible for managing the performance of others maintain an awareness of accomplishments against performance objectives for each of the individuals whose performance they manage.**

> Examples of accomplishments to maintain awareness of include the following:
> - Performance against documented individual objectives
> - Individual contributions to performance against documented objectives for other individuals, their workgroup, or their unit
> - Impediments to achieving documented performance objectives
> - The influence of changing business conditions or work commitments on reprioritizing documented performance objectives
> - The need to revise documented performance objectives

Practice 8   **Potential improvements in process, tools, or resources, which could enhance an individual's performance of committed work, are identified, and actions are taken to provide them.**

> Examples of mechanisms through which improvements that could enhance work performance are identified include the following:
> - Ongoing discussion about work performance between individuals and those responsible for managing their performance
> - Group discussion of work performance
> - Problem solving sessions
> - Recommendations by a mentor, coach, or trainer
> - Process or work analysis activity
> - Management or customer reviews or feedback

Practice 9   **The accomplishments of individuals against their performance objectives are documented and discussed on a periodic or event-driven basis according to a documented procedure.**

> Accomplishments can be documented and discussed on a periodic schedule, such as annually or twice yearly, or on an event-driven basis, such as at the completion of specific committed work (e.g., end of a project). Accomplishments should be documented and discussed at least once during the period defined for a set of documented performance objectives.

> Examples of methods for documenting and discussing performance results include the following:
> - Performance appraisals
> - Peer group evaluations
> - 360° reviews
> - Performance panel reviews

1. Those responsible for documenting and discussing accomplishments against performance objectives perform these tasks according to a documented procedure.

   The procedure typically specifies:

   - how often accomplishments are reviewed against objectives,
   - how information regarding accomplishments and other aspects of performance are obtained,
   - what performance information is documented,
   - whether and how performance information is reviewed before being discussed,
   - how performance results are discussed with individuals or workgroups,
   - topics that may not be appropriate during a discussion of accomplishments and objectives
   - whether training needs or career options are discussed,
   - how unsatisfactory performance is addressed,
   - how disagreements are resolved,
   - how performance management activities are performed when individuals or those responsible for managing individuals' performance transition, and
   - to whom performance documentation is distributed.

2. The procedure for documenting and discussing accomplishments against performance objectives is communicated to all those affected by it.

3. An agreement is reached about a time for documenting and discussing accomplishments against performance objectives with each individual affected by the procedure.

4. Information about accomplishments against committed work and other aspects of performance is gathered and evaluated.

5. When individuals are responsible for committed work in several units, those to whom their responsibilities report coordinate to ensure that:

   - information about accomplishments against committed work and other aspects of performance is gathered and evaluated, and
   - any overall evaluation of performance incorporates results covering all relevant committed work.

6. If appropriate, performance documentation is reviewed with appropriate individuals prior to discussing it with those whose performance is being discussed.

> Examples of appropriate individuals for reviewing performance documentation include the following:
> - The next higher level of management
> - A representative of the human resources function or other appropriate professionals
> - Those who provided performance information
> - Stakeholders in the performance objectives

7. Accomplishments against committed work and other aspects of performance are discussed.

> Examples of topics related to performance to be discussed may include the following:
> - Individual performance compared with documented objectives
> - Special causes of performance variation, if applicable
> - Opportunities for improvements in processes, tools, or resources
> - Knowledge and skills needing development
> - Development opportunities completed
> - Career options
> - Capability on a number of predefined dimensions as evidenced in performance against objectives, demonstrated application of critical skills, or other relevant dimensions
> - Perceptions of performance by others if these perceptions are relevant to performance objectives
> - Subjective or hard to measure factors such as interpersonal skills

8. If necessary, disagreements about performance results, interpretations, or other performance feedback are discussed and raised to an appropriate entity, such as a higher level of management, the human resources function, or other appropriate professionals.

9. Skills needing development and actions to develop them are discussed.

> Refer to Practice 6 of the Training and Development process area for information regarding development discussions with individuals.

10. Unsatisfactory performance is discussed and preparations are made for follow-up actions.

11. Opportunities to enhance performance are discussed and actions are identified.

12. Accomplishments against performance objectives and other results of the performance discussion are documented and maintained in a form consistent with organizational guidance.

13. Performance documentation is used in performing other workforce activities according to documented procedures.

Examples of other workforce practices for which performance documentation provides input include the following:

- Compensation
- Recognition and rewards
- Identification of training and development needs
- Career opportunities
- Promotions
- Disciplinary action
- Outplacement

Practice 10   **If performance problems occur, they are discussed with the appropriate individual(s).**

Particularly serious problems should be brought to the attention of the human resources function or other appropriate professionals. Their guidance should be followed in handling serious problems, since actions leading to disciplinary sanctions or termination can have legal implications.

---

1. Performance problems are identified, based on appropriate performance objectives, policies, or other applicable guidelines.

2. A formal discussion concerning the performance problem is held with the individual(s).

3. Agreement is reached on:

   ■ a statement of the performance problem, and

   ■ actions or conditions that would resolve the performance problem, if implemented.

4. The results of discussions regarding the performance problem are documented.

5. Actions or results agreed to in the formal discussion concerning the performance problem are monitored.

Practice 11   Performance improvement plans are developed for resolving persistent performance problems according to a documented procedure.

> Guidance should be sought from human resources or other appropriate professionals in developing, managing, and making decisions based on performance improvement plans.

1. Performance improvement plans address:
   - the performance problem(s) that must be corrected,
   - the actions to be taken to correct the problems,
   - the results that are expected in correcting the problem(s),
   - the frequency for reviewing results against the performance improvement plan,
   - the objectives and criteria that are used in evaluating progress against the performance improvement plan,
   - the minimal acceptable performance for improvement purposes,
   - the consequences for failure to improve performance,
   - the criteria to be used to evaluate whether a different position or career option should be considered, and
   - the maximum duration for the period covered by the performance improvement plan.

2. Performance improvement plans are documented.

> The actions called out in the performance improvement plan constitute a new set of work commitments and documented performance objectives. These commitments and objectives supercede previous work commitments and performance objectives.

3. Individuals agree to their performance improvement plans.

4. The organization provides reasonable resources to assist individuals in improving performance.

Practice 12   Progress against a documented performance improvement plan is periodically evaluated, discussed, and documented.

> Guidance should be sought from the human resources function or other appropriate professionals in developing, managing, and making decisions based on comparing the accomplishments to the objectives of a performance improvement plan.

> Examples of actions that could be taken as a result of evaluating performance against a performance improvement plan include the following:
> - Continuation in current position.
> - Reassignment to another position.
> - Development actions. Refer to Practices 6 and 7 of the Training and Development process area.
> - Discharge. Refer to Practice 17 of the Staffing process area.

1. Progress is reviewed periodically throughout the period covered by the performance improvement plan.

2. Progress and discussions regarding the performance improvement plan are documented throughout the period covered by the performance improvement plan.

3. If performance deviates significantly from the objectives in the performance improvement plan, corrective action is discussed.

4. At an appropriate time, the improvement program is terminated, and decisions are made and documented based on performance against the objectives of the performance improvement plan.

Practice 13   **Guidelines for recognizing or rewarding outstanding performance are developed and communicated.**

> Rewards are distinguished from recognition in that rewards typically involve financial considerations. Recognition or rewards can be made on a periodic (e.g., annual performance awards) or occasional (e.g., project completion) basis.

1. The organization develops guidelines for providing recognition or rewards in an effort to achieve reasonable consistency across units. These guidelines typically specify:

   - The purposes for which recognition or rewards are offered.

   > Recognition or rewards are made to reinforce the skills and behaviors that the organization values.

■ What is provided as recognition or rewards.

> Examples of recognition or rewards include the following:
> - Money
> - Plaques, trophies, certificates, or citations
> - Public recognition
> - Time off
> - Special perquisites (or perks)
> - Special assignments
> - Parties or celebrations
> - Other meaningful considerations

■ The criteria on which recognition or rewards are determined.

> Examples of criteria for providing recognition and rewards include the following:
> - Exceptional individual, workgroup, or unit performance
> - Process improvement
> - Project completion
> - Exceptional quality
> - Exceeding objectives
> - Accomplishments beyond work assignments
> - Outstanding skill development
> - Outstanding service to customers

■ That those providing recognition or rewards attempt to make decisions that are consistent with other recognition and reward activities in the organization.

■ Responsibilities in recommending, approving, and administering recognition or rewards.

■ How each recognition or reward is documented.

2. The guidelines for providing recognition or rewards are consistent with the organization's compensation strategy and practices.

> Refer to the Compensation process area for information regarding compensation strategy and administration.

3. Guidelines for providing recognition and rewards are communicated.

> Examples of information that should be communicated about these guidelines include the following:
> - The different types of recognition or rewards that can be provided
> - The method for recommending an individual or group for recognition or reward
> - The method and criteria through which recognition or rewards are determined

Practice 14 **Recognition or rewards are made on an appropriate basis as events occur that justify special attention.**

1. Recognition or rewards are determined according to established guidelines.

2. Recognition or rewards are provided close in time to the performance for which they are awarded.

3. Recognition and rewards are presented to individuals or groups in a way that conveys the organization's appreciation.

4. When appropriate, recognition and rewards are made known to others in the organization in a way that highlights the behaviors or results that the organization values.

Measurement and Analysis

Measurement 1 **Measurements are made and used to determine the status and performance of Performance Management activities.**

> Examples of measurements include the following:
> - Percent of accomplished performance objectives at unit and individual levels
> - Rate of change in performance objectives during the performance period at unit and individual levels
> - Profile of performance across unit objectives
> - Profile of performance across individual objectives
> - Trends in development needs identified in discussing performance
> - Percent of the workforce with performance problems
> - Progress against performance improvement plans
> - Time spent on performance management activities
> - Number of individuals or groups whose outstanding performance was recognized
> - Number and size of rewards
> - Time from proposing a recognition or reward until it is received

Measurement 2   Unit measures of Performance Management activities are collected and maintained.

1. Units collect data as performance management activities occur.

2. Measurements made to determine the status and performance of performance management activities are maintained.

> Examples of reasons for maintaining measurements of performance management activities include the following:
>
> - Periodic analysis of performance data to identify trends
> - Periodic analysis of data comparing performance results to work commitments to identify trends
> - Periodic analysis to determine unit-level trends
> - Aggregating data at the organizational level to develop organizational measures
> - Analysis to determine organizational trends
> - Evaluation of organizational trends

Verifying Implementation

Verification 1   A responsible individual(s) verifies that the Performance Management activities are conducted according to the organization's documented policies, practices, procedures, and, where appropriate, plans; and addresses non-compliance.

These reviews verify that:

1. Performance Management activities comply with the organization's policies and stated values.

2. Performance Management activities comply with relevant laws and regulations.

3. Performance Management activities are performed according to the organization's documented practices and procedures.

> These reviews may use measures regarding the status and performance of Performance Management activities, as well as unit measures of Performance Management activities, to ensure that a comprehensive review of Performance Management activities occurs. These measures provide indicators of the status and performance of Performance Management activities across the units. Refer to Measurement 1 and Measurement 2 for information regarding measurement of Performance Management activities.

4. Actions related to the development and implementation of performance improvement plans are periodically reviewed to ensure that they conform to documented policies.

5. Actions related to recognition and reward are periodically reviewed to ensure that they conform to documented policies and guidelines and to evaluate consistency across units.

6. Noncompliance issues are handled appropriately.

Verification 2   Executive management periodically reviews the Performance Management activities, status, and results; and resolves issues.

These reviews verify:

1. Appropriateness of performance objectives defined at the unit level.

2. Status of performance problems and improvement plans.

3. Progress in performing Performance Management activities.

4. Results from reviews of Performance Management practices and activities.

> Refer to Verification 1 for information regarding reviews of Performance Management activities to ensure adherence to the following:
> - Relevant laws and regulations
> - Organizational policies, practices, and procedures

5. Status of resolution of noncompliance issues.

6. Trends related to performance.

7. Effectiveness of the performance management activities in enhancing performance.

Training and Development

A process area at Maturity Level 2: Managed

Purpose

The purpose of Training and Development is to ensure that all individuals have the knowledge and skills required to perform their assignments and are provided with relevant development opportunities.

Description

The primary focus of Training and Development is on removing the gap between the current knowledge and skills of each individual and the critical skills required to perform their assignments. Once individuals have the necessary knowledge and skills to perform current assignments, they may focus their development activities on other objectives.

Each unit identifies the critical skills required for each individual to successfully perform their assigned tasks. Critical skills are those that, if not performed effectively, could jeopardize the successful performance of these assigned tasks. Training needs related to these critical skills are identified for each individual. These training needs may address deficiencies in either the individual's knowledge or the individual's skills. Then, each unit develops a training plan based on the training needs identified for each individual within the unit. Training in critical skills is delivered in a timely manner and is tracked against the unit's training plan.

After removing the gap between the current knowledge and skills of each individual and the critical skills required to perform their assignments, other development objectives can be pursued. Development discussions are held regularly to ensure each individual recognizes the organization's interest in their professional development. These development discussions are held to discuss training needs, as well as potential next assignments, career options, and other development interests. Training and development opportunities are identified for each individual that support their individual development objectives.

Since resources and opportunities are limited in many circumstances, training and development activities should be prioritized for each individual. Training in the critical skills required to perform an individual's assigned work should take precedence over training that supports their development interests. When individuals have addressed their needs for training in critical skills, their available training time and resources can be used to pursue training or other development activities that provide preparation for future assignments, career options, or other development interests. Thus, the training and development activities identified for individuals within the scope of available time and resources may not satisfy all of their development objectives.

Goals

Goal 1   **Individuals receive timely training that is needed to perform their assignments in accordance with the unit's training plan.**

Goal 2   **Individuals capable of performing their assignments pursue development opportunities that support their development objectives.**

Goal 3   **Training and Development practices are institutionalized to ensure they are performed as managed processes.**

Commitment to Perform

Commitment 1   **The organization establishes and maintains a documented policy for conducting its Training and Development activities.**

Issues typically addressed in the policy include:

1. Training and development activities serve the business objectives and stated values of the organization.
2. Training requirements for critical skills required to perform assigned work are identified.
3. Training to support the performance of assigned responsibilities is timely.
4. Training and development opportunities are provided to support individual development needs.
5. Training time is allocated for each individual.
6. Training and Development practices and activities comply with relevant laws, regulations, and organizational policies.

Commitment 2   **An organizational role(s) is assigned responsibility for assisting and advising units on Training and Development activities and procedures.**

> Examples of individuals who might assist or advise units on Training and Development activities include the following:
> - Members of the training or development functions
> - Instructional designers
> - Members of the human resources function or other appropriate professionals
> - Appropriate managers or other appropriate personnel

Ability to Perform

Ability 1   **Within each unit, an individual(s) is assigned responsibility and authority for ensuring that Training and Development activities are performed.**

> Examples of individuals who might be assigned responsibility for various Training and Development activities include the following:
> - The unit manager or assistant
> - A training coordinator or committee
> - A project or group leader
> - An empowered team
> - A member of the human resources function or other appropriate professional

Ability 2   **Adequate resources are provided for performing Training and Development activities.**

1. When feasible, experienced individuals who have expertise in training and development methods are made available for conducting Training and Development activities.

> Examples of contributions that could be made by those with special skills include the following:
> - Assisting in analyzing critical skills
> - Providing knowledge of sources for relevant training or development opportunities
> - Applying instructional design principles
> - Conducting in-house training
> - Evaluating mastery of learning, transfer of learned skills to the workplace, and return on investments in training

2. Resources for supporting Training and Development activities are made available.

> Examples of resources for supporting Training and Development include the following:
> - Templates for critical skills or training needs analysis
> - Skill inventories
> - Job aids
> - Training roadmaps
> - Lists of training or development opportunities available
> - Resources for in-house training and development
> - Workstations and training software
> - Software and materials for developing training

3. Support for implementing Training and Development activities is made available.

> Examples of implementation support include the following:
> - Training materials
> - Guided self-study or independent study materials
> - Distance learning
> - Development or procurement of training
> - Delivery of training
> - Training facilities and equipment
> - Instructor certification (i.e., train the trainer)
> - Evaluation of the quality and effectiveness of the training
> - Maintenance of training records

4. When required, adequate facilities are made available for on-site training.

> Example characteristics of adequate training facilities include the following:
> - Freedom from distractions such as noise, unpleasant temperatures, and interruptions
> - Separation from the actual work environment
> - Sufficient space for student functions and exercises
> - Ability to simulate actual working conditions when appropriate
> - Physical resources as needed to support training, such as computers, overhead projectors, flip charts, and white boards

5. Resources are made available to support the accomplishment of each unit's training plan.

6. Funding to accomplish training and development activities is made available.

Ability 3   Training time is made available to each individual according to the organization's training policy.

> Examples of methods to determine the amount of training time to be allocated to each individual include the following:
> - Standard number of days of training that each individual should receive during a chosen time period (usually per year)
> - Existing level of skill
> - Time needed to acquire the critical skills required by an individual's current assignment
> - Time required to develop a skill
> - Time required to achieve a given proficiency level in actual working conditions
> - Time needed to prepare for potential future assignments

Ability 4   **Individuals performing Training and Development activities receive the preparation needed to perform their responsibilities.**

    1. Individuals responsible for identifying training and development needs receive the preparation needed to perform their responsibilities.

> Examples of relevant methods for identifying training and development needs in which individuals are prepared include the following:
> - Analyzing critical skills
> - Discussing potential next assignments, career options, and other development interests
> - Identifying training needs
> - Identifying training and development resources
> - Developing and tracking unit training plans

    2. Individuals who develop or provide training have the necessary training or experience required to perform their responsibilities.

Practices Performed

Practice 1   **In each unit, the critical skills required for performing each individual's assigned tasks are identified.**

> Refer to Practice 2 of the Staffing process area for information regarding identification of the skills needed to perform work.

    1. The tasks involved in performing each individual's assigned work are identified.

> Work should be analyzed to identify tasks that could jeopardize the successful performance of the assignment if these tasks are not performed well according to the task-related criteria. Examples of task-related criteria include the following:
> - Accuracy
> - Speed
> - Synchronization with other tasks

2. The critical skills needed by each individual to perform their assigned tasks are identified.

> *Critical skills* are those that, if not performed effectively, could jeopardize the successful performance of assigned tasks. Examples of critical skills include the ability to:
> - Execute specific procedures
> - Perform tasks within specific time limits
> - Perform tasks to defined accuracy
> - Use equipment safely and effectively
> - Follow instructions
> - Interpret information
> - Organize actions, material, or people

3. Communication skills required to perform assigned tasks are identified and included among critical skills.

> Examples of communication skills include the following:
> - Literacy in one or more of the languages used in the organization
> - Knowledge of local jargon or technical terms
> - Situational communication protocols
> - Oral presentation skills
> - Negotiating skills
> - Writing skills
> - Ability to use communication media

4. The critical skills needed by an individual are updated each time there is a significant change in their assigned tasks.

Practice 2   **Training needed in critical skills is identified for each individual.**

1. The knowledge and skills of each individual are evaluated against the critical skills needed to perform their assigned tasks to determine if training is needed.

> Examples of methods for evaluating training needs include the following:
> - Individual's personal assessment
> - Individual's previous experience
> - Performance feedback sessions and reviews
> - Assessment centers
> - Tests
> - Training records

2. Prior to undertaking a new assignment, an individual's knowledge and skills are assessed against the critical skills required for the new assignment to determine if training in these skills is needed.

3. The critical skill needs of each individual in a unit are identified as the gap between the knowledge and skills possessed by the individual and the critical skills needed to perform the tasks assigned to them.

> If the identification of needed knowledge and skills is made independently by a responsible individual, it should always be discussed, and modified as appropriate, during formal or informal performance feedback or development discussions with each individual.

4. The types of training needed by each individual to develop the critical skills needed to perform assigned tasks are identified.

5. If the critical skills required by assigned tasks change, an individual's training needs are reevaluated.

Practice 3   Each unit develops and maintains a plan for satisfying its training needs.

> The training needs of a unit consist of the aggregated training needs of the individuals and workgroups within the unit. Each unit's training plan consists of the training activities identified for each individual or workgroup in the unit.

The unit's training plan typically specifies:

1. Training needed by each individual or workgroup to perform their assigned responsibilities.

2. Training to be provided to individuals or workgroups to support their development interests.

3. The schedule for when training is to be provided.

4. How this training is to be provided.

> Examples of methods for delivering training include the following:
> - Classroom instruction
> - Apprenticeship or mentoring programs
> - Job rotation
> - On-the-job training
> - Cross-training positions
> - Seminars and tutorials
> - Conferences and workshops
> - Local college and university courses
> - Computer-aided instruction
> - Videotapes
> - Directed self-study courses

5. How coordination with other groups that are involved with training is to be accomplished.

> Examples of other groups that are involved with training may include the following:
> - Process or improvement group
> - Corporate training group
> - External training providers
> - Local colleges and universities

Practice 4   Individuals or groups receive timely training needed to perform their assigned tasks.

1. Training alternatives are evaluated to determine which provides the most effective mechanism for developing the required knowledge and skills.

> Examples of training alternatives include the following:
> - Classroom training
> - Distance learning
> - Mentoring
> - Apprenticeships
> - Self-paced learning courses

Training alternatives may be available from a number of sources. Examples of these sources include the following:

- The unit
- Internal training organizations
- External training providers
- Local colleges and universities

2. Training content is evaluated to ensure that it covers all the knowledge and skills needed by the individual or group to perform their assigned responsibilities.

3. Training is scheduled to provide knowledge and skills for timely application in performing assigned tasks.

4. Individuals and groups provide feedback on the quality and usefulness of the training they receive.

Practice 5   Training is tracked against the unit's training plan.

1. The unit's training activities are routinely reviewed against its training plan.

2. When training activities performed deviate significantly from the plan, corrective action is taken.

3. Completion of training activities is documented for each individual.

Practice 6   A development discussion is held periodically with each individual.

Development needs and interests may be discussed with individuals on a continuing basis; however, at a minimum, individuals should be offered an opportunity to hold a formal development discussion at least once during each period covered by the formal recording of performance results. Development discussions can be conducted:

- As part of ongoing performance feedback. Refer to Practice 6 of the Performance Management process area for information regarding maintaining ongoing communication about performance.

- In conjunction with or subsequent to providing formal performance feedback. Refer to Practice 9 of the Performance Management process area for information regarding formal performance feedback.

1. The knowledge and skills needed to enhance performance in current and future assignments are identified and discussed.

> Information about knowledge and skills needing development can come from the following:
> - Evidence from current performance
> - Changing requirements of the current assignment
> - Anticipated future assignments
> - Individual desire to know more in an area relevant to the organization
> - Recommendations from others
> - Individual desire for reassignment or advancement

2. Potential future assignments, career options, and other development interests are discussed.

3. Development activities to enhance knowledge and skills, and to prepare for future assignments and career options, are identified.

4. When training time can be allotted to support preparation for future assignments, career options, and other development interests, objectives for each individual's development are established.

> *Individual development objectives* represent a combination of development needs to enhance knowledge and skills and to prepare for future assignments and career options. Individual development objectives at the Managed Level are less formal than those objectives documented in personal development plans that will be established in the Career Development process area at the Defined Level.
>
> Individual development objectives are organized primarily around the career interests of the individual, since the organization may not be able to offer input or guidance from well-defined career paths or competency descriptions. Input for individual development objectives can be drawn from the following:
> - Needs for development of critical skills
> - Changes in work or responsibilities
> - Potential next assignments
> - Career options
> - Other development interests

Practice 7   Relevant development opportunities are made available to support individuals in accomplishing their individual development objectives.

> If an individual has the critical skills required to perform their committed work, then their allocated training time may be used to pursue development objectives relative to potential future assignments or other development objectives. Consequently, the scope of relevant learning experiences may be large and choices should to be matched to an individual's level of skill and experience. Appropriate development opportunities can be made available following a development discussion or on other occasions by supervisors or other responsible individuals. Examples of development opportunities include the following:
>
> - Courses
> - Degree or certification programs
> - Mentors or coaches
> - Special temporary assignments
> - Position or role assignments

1. Responsible individuals assist individuals in identifying development opportunities that would support their individual development objectives.

2. When possible, relevant opportunities are sought for assigning work or exposing individuals to experiences that support their individual development objectives.

Practice 8   Individuals pursue development activities that support their individual development objectives.

1. Time to pursue development opportunities is coordinated with committed work and other relevant schedules.

2. Development opportunities are accomplished according to identified objectives for each individual's objectives.

3. The accomplishment of development opportunities is tracked to ensure they are timely with respect to an individual's development objectives.

4. The impact and results of completed development activities are discussed to determine if adjustments to individual development objectives are needed.

5. The results of development activities are documented and used as input to performance management, staffing, promotion, compensation, and other workforce activities as appropriate.

Measurement and Analysis

Measurement 1 **Measurements are made and used to determine the status and performance of Training and Development activities.**

> Examples of measurements include the following:
> - Amount of training provided
> - Rate of training against stated training needs
> - Timeliness of training
> - Cost of training
> - Retention of trained skills
> - Improvements in learned skills
> - Application of learned skills or behaviors in job performance
> - Quality of training as rated in student evaluations
> - Frequency of development discussions
> - Number and type of development opportunities arranged

Measurement 2 **Unit measures of Training and Development activities are collected and maintained.**

1. Units collect data as Training and Development activities occur.

2. Measurements made to determine the status and performance of Training and Development activities are maintained.

> Examples of reasons for maintaining measurements of Training and Development activities include the following:
> - Periodic analysis to determine unit-level trends
> - Aggregating data at the organizational level to develop organizational measures
> - Analysis to determine organizational trends
> - Evaluation of organizational trends

Verifying Implementation

Verification 1 **A responsible individual(s) verifies that Training and Development activities are conducted according to the organization's documented policies, practices, procedures, and, where appropriate, plans; and addresses noncompliance.**

These reviews verify that:

1. Training and Development activities comply with the organization's policies and stated values.

2. Training and Development activities comply with relevant laws and regulations.

3. Training and Development activities are performed according to the organization's documented practices and procedures.

4. Training and Development activities are performed according to the unit's plans and selected methods.

> These reviews may use measures regarding the status and performance of Training and Development activities, as well as unit measures of Training and Development activities, to ensure that a comprehensive review of Training and Development activities occurs. These measures provide indicators of the status and performance of Training and Development activities across the units. Refer to Measurement 1 and Measurement 2 for information regarding measurement of Training and Development activities.

5. All actions related to the development and implementation of training plans are periodically reviewed to ensure they conform to documented policies.

6. Noncompliance issues are handled appropriately.

Verification 2 **Executive management periodically reviews the Training and Development activities, status, and results; and resolves issues.**

These reviews verify:

1. The amount and effectiveness of the training provided.

2. Progress in performing planned Training and Development activities.

3. Results from reviews of Training and Development practices and activities.

> Refer to Verification 1 for information regarding reviews of Training and Development activities to ensure adherence to the following:
> - Relevant laws and regulations
> - Organizational policies, practices, and procedures

4. Status of resolution of noncompliance issues.

5. Trends related to training and development needs.

6. Effectiveness of Training and Development activities in accomplishing planned training.

Compensation

A process area at Maturity Level 2: Managed

Purpose

The purpose of Compensation is to provide all individuals with remuneration and benefits based on their contribution and value to the organization.

Description

Compensation represents the only process area at the Managed Level whose execution is co-ordinated by actions at the organizational level. Compensation must be coordinated primarily through centralized activity in order to establish a sense of equity in the system. Once the workforce perceives the system to be equitable, it can be adjusted to motivate the development of needed skills and better alignment of individual performance with that of the work-group, unit, or organization. The compensation system should be designed to motivate and reward the skills and behaviors the organization considers vital to its success.

A compensation strategy is developed that states the organization's philosophy and methods for compensating individuals. This compensation strategy is periodically reviewed against business conditions and revised when necessary. The opinions and interests of the workforce are considered in shaping the compensation strategy. The strategy covers all forms of compensation to individuals, both fixed and variable, and the criteria by which compensation is determined. A compensation plan is prepared periodically to guide the administration of the compensation strategy.

Those responsible for making compensation decisions are provided guidance in administering and discussing the compensation strategy and decisions. Compensation decisions are based on criteria stated in the strategy and elaborated in the plan. Adjustments are made to an individual's compensation based on performance and other documented criteria such as skill development or promotion. Adjustments to compensation are communicated to affected individuals along with information about the basis for the adjustment.

Compensation decisions are reviewed to ensure they are equitable. They are reviewed collectively against external benchmarks to evaluate the extent to which total compensation is equitable in relation to the market. Compensation decisions are reviewed individually relative to other internal compensation decisions to ensure that compensation is equitable across the staff in relation to skills, experience, performance, and other appropriate criteria. Corrections are made to adjust inequities.

Goals

Goal 1   **Compensation strategies and activities are planned, executed, and communicated.**

Goal 2   **Compensation is equitable relative to skill, qualifications, and performance.**

Goal 3   **Adjustments in compensation are made based on defined criteria.**

Goal 4   **Compensation practices are institutionalized to ensure they are performed as managed processes.**

Commitment to Perform

Commitment 1   **The organization establishes and maintains a documented policy for conducting its Compensation activities.**

> *Compensation* is used to represent the concept of pay and guaranteed benefits. Pay includes any guaranteed fixed rate of salary or hourly wages provided to individuals, plus any variable amounts that are provided based on an existing agreement between the organization and the individual on how it is administered.

Issues typically addressed in the policy include:

1. Compensation activities serve business objectives and stated values of the organization.

2. The compensation strategy, practices, and activities comply with relevant laws, regulations, and organizational policies.

> Examples of laws and regulations with which compensation systems must comply include the following:
> - Labor-related laws and regulations, such as the Fair Labor Standards Act
> - Laws and regulations that govern equal access to the workplace, limit discrimination, and identify sexual harassment, including the Equal Employment Opportunity (EEO) laws and regulations, Older Workers Benefit and Protection Act, and Equal Pay Act
> - Retirement- and pension-related laws and regulations, such as Social Security and Medicare, COBRA, and the Employee Retirement Income Security Act
> - Consumer Credit Protection Act
> - Other applicable national, provincial, state, and local laws and regulations

3. Responsibilities for the organization's compensation strategy and plan are defined and assigned.

4. A compensation strategy is developed and periodically reevaluated.

5. Equity is established and maintained in the compensation system.

6. A compensation plan is periodically developed for administering the compensation strategy.

7. The basis for determining and adjusting compensation includes skill qualifications and performance.

8. The frequency with which compensation activities are performed is defined.

9. Responsibilities are defined for:

  ■ those who develop and administer the compensation strategy and plan.

  ■ those who make compensation decisions using the compensation strategy and plan.

10. Compensation information is confidential to the individual concerned.

11. The forms in which compensation information may be communicated, when it may be communicated, who may communicate it, and to whom it may be communicated are defined.

12. Appropriate compensation procedures are defined, documented, and used.

> The human resources function or other appropriate professionals should review all such procedures to ensure they
> - Are consistent with relevant laws, regulations, and organizational policies
> - Respect the rights and dignity of individuals and groups

Compensation procedures are established and maintained for:

  ■ making adjustments to compensation, and

  ■ ensuring appropriate distribution, use, and retention of compensation documentation, including granting access to, and ensuring confidentiality of, these compensation data.

Commitment 2 **An organizational role(s) is assigned responsibility for performing or coordinating Compensation practices at the organizational level and for assisting and advising units on Compensation activities.**

Ability to Perform

Ability 1 **Within each unit, an individual(s) is assigned responsibility and authority for ensuring that Compensation activities are performed.**

> Examples of individuals who may be assigned responsibility for various Compensation activities include the following:
> - The unit manager or other designated individual
> - A compensation and reward committee
> - A resource manager
> - A project or workgroup leader
> - An empowered workgroup
> - A member of the human resources function or other appropriate professional

Ability 2   **Adequate resources are provided for Compensation activities.**

1. Experienced individuals, who have expertise in compensation methods and procedures, are made available for guiding compensation activities

> Examples of contributions that could be made by those with special skills include the following:
> - Designing and revising the compensation system
> - Determining criteria for adjustments to compensation
> - Participating in compensation decisions

2. Resources for supporting Compensation activities are made available.

> Examples of resources include the following:
> - Spreadsheets and analysis tools
> - Compensation surveys
> - Compensation templates and guidelines

3. The available funding for the various components of compensation is determined.

4. Funding for Compensation activities is made available.

Ability 3   **Individuals performing Compensation activities receive the preparation needed to perform their responsibilities.**

1. Individuals performing Compensation activities are made aware of those components of the organization's compensation strategy that they need to understand to fulfill their responsibilities.

2. Individuals performing Compensation activities receive preparation to perform the Compensation practices needed to perform their responsibilities.

3. Individuals communicating information regarding the compensation strategy or an individual's compensation package are prepared to communicate this information appropriately.

Practices Performed

Practice 1   **An organizational compensation strategy is developed.**

The organization's compensation strategy typically includes:

1. The rationale behind the strategic decisions made in the compensation strategy.
2. The vehicles for providing compensation and how they are to be used.

> Examples of vehicles for providing compensation include the following:
> - Salary or hourly wages
> - Piece rate pay or incentives
> - Incentive pay (e.g., commissions or sales incentives)
> - Periodic bonuses
> - Profit-sharing
> - Gain-sharing
> - Health, life, or disability insurance
> - Benefits such as holidays, leave, and educational assistance
> - Daycare or childcare benefits
> - Retirement contributions
> - Stock or stock options
> - Professional society memberships
> - Company furnished resources (e.g., cars, home computers)
> - Special assignment pay

3. Definition of the recurring basis on which adjustments to compensation are made.

> Examples of the recurring basis on which adjustments to compensation are made include the following:
> - Periodic, such as annually or quarterly
> - Event-driven, such as on the completion of a project, completion of a performance period, or anniversary date of the individual in the organization
> - Other recurring bases, as defined by the organization

4. Criteria for determining and adjusting compensation.

Examples of criteria for determining and adjusting compensation may include the following:

- Current competencies and skills
- Experience
- Education completed
- Availability of skills in the market
- Job evaluation
- Job or pay bands (broadbanding)
- Individual performance and similar merit-based factors
- Team or unit performance
- Rate of change in cost of living
- Promotion
- Increase in work responsibilities
- Behaviors or activities valued by the organization
- Contribution to improvement activities
- Personal improvement relative to prior performance
- Unit or organizational performance
- Continued benefit of past contributions or performance
- Functions performed beyond assigned responsibilities
- Additional skills developed
- Leadership exercised
- Willingness to take on difficult assignments
- Position responsibilities
- Impact of position on unit or organizational performance

5. Guidelines for using different compensation vehicles and criteria in determining compensation for different positions.

6. The method(s) by which compensation decisions are made for individuals (and positions, workgroups, or units, if appropriate).

7. Methods for establishing and maintaining equity in the compensation system.

8. The frequency with which the compensation strategy needs to be reviewed.

9. Criteria for evaluating the appropriateness of the compensation strategy.

Practice 2   The organization's compensation strategy is periodically reviewed to determine whether it needs to be revised.

1. The review is organized by the individual(s) assigned responsibility for coordinating Compensation activities across the organization.

2. The compensation strategy is reviewed against its objectives and effects.

> Examples of data regarding compensation strategy effects against which the objectives of the compensation strategy should be reviewed include the following:
> - Opinions and feedback of the workforce
> - Recruiting and hiring
> - Individual, workgroup, or unit performance
> - Retention and voluntary turnover
> - Competency development
> - Career development
> - Workforce planning

3. Revision of the compensation strategy is considered when:

   - it is not having the intended motivational effect,
   - it does not reflect current business or market conditions,
   - it creates inequities,
   - it is having unintended or harmful effects,
   - current practices are not competitive with benchmark data from similar organizations, or
   - better compensation concepts have been identified.

4. The decision to revise the compensation strategy is reviewed with executive management.

Practice 3   When appropriate, the workforce provides inputs for developing or revising components of the organization's compensation strategy.

> Gathering input from individuals for developing or revising the compensation strategy is beneficial in gaining insights into the most effective compensation strategies, determining perceived fairness of the strategy, and generating buy-in and support for the strategy. Input can be gathered from individuals or from a committee representing some or all of the workforce.

> Refer to Practice 4 of the Communication and Coordination process area for information regarding seeking individuals' opinions on their working conditions.

1. The workforce can provide inputs to the compensation strategy regarding:

   - benefits and drawbacks of current compensation vehicles,
   - criteria for determining or adjusting compensation,
   - fairness of the compensation strategy, and
   - methods for administering compensation.

2. If appropriate, individuals or committees can review proposed revisions to the compensation strategy with regard to:

   - impact of proposed changes on motivation and performance,
   - fairness of proposed changes, and
   - most effective ways to initiate and administer the changes.

Practice 4   A documented compensation plan is prepared periodically for administering compensation activities needed to execute the compensation strategy.

The compensation plan typically includes:

1. The financial data needed for administering the compensation strategy and guiding compensation decisions.

   > Examples of financial data for making compensation decisions include the following:
   > - Entry level compensation for positions, grades, pay bands, or other graduated structures in the compensation system
   > - Changes in the average or total range of compensation for grades, pay bands, or other graduated structures in the compensation system
   > - Size of cost of living or other standard periodic adjustments
   > - Sizes of compensation increases and how they are to be determined from defined criteria
   > - Changes in benefits or their levels
   > - Size of bonus or incentive pool(s) and how its distribution is to be determined
   > - Pricing related to stock options

2. The schedule of events and responsibilities for those involved in administering the compensation strategy.

3. How the methods described in the compensation strategy are applied in making compensation decisions.

4. How and when the compensation decisions are reviewed.

Practice 5 **The compensation plan is designed to maintain equity in administering the compensation strategy.**

    1. The organization maintains an awareness of internal, market, and business conditions affecting compensation equity.

> Examples of methods for maintaining awareness of internal, market, and business conditions relevant to compensation include the following:
> - Market compensation surveys
> - Compensation benchmarks with local companies or industry peers
> - Information from exit interviews
> - Opinions and feedback of the workforce
> - Information from recruiting activities
> - Information from selected candidates who declined employment offers

    2. Based on market and business conditions, adjustments are made to appropriate components of compensation to ensure that these components support the level of market equity intended by the compensation strategy.

> Restoring compensation equity compared to market levels may require actions that last several months to several years.

    3. Adjustments are made to appropriate components of compensation to establish the levels of internal equity across individuals with similar position responsibilities, skills, or performance levels intended for these components by the compensation strategy.

    4. Guidance is provided for making compensation decisions that maintain the equity intended in the compensation strategy.

Practice 6 **The organization's compensation strategy is communicated to the workforce.**

    1. Information typically communicated to the workforce includes:

        ■ strategic basis and structure of the compensation strategy, and

        ■ events that result in changes to compensation.

    2. Whenever the compensation strategy is changed, the changes are communicated to the workforce.

Practice 7   **Each individual's compensation package is determined using a documented procedure that is consistent with the organization's compensation policy, strategy, and plan.**

The procedure typically specifies:

1. How financial resources are allocated to units for assignment to individual compensation packages.

2. Who makes decisions that allocate compensation resources to units and to the individual's compensation packages.

3. How criteria are applied in making decisions for individual compensation packages.

4. How compensation decisions are reviewed and approved before being communicated to individuals.

5. How compensation decisions are communicated to individuals.

6. How individuals may address issues related to their compensation packages.

Practice 8   **Compensation adjustments are made based, in part, on each individual's documented accomplishments against their performance objectives.**

1. Responsible individuals determine compensation adjustments based on criteria established in the compensation policy, strategy, and plan.

2. The documented accomplishments against performance objectives are used as part of the criteria for determining the size of the adjustment made to each individual's compensation package.

3. Responsible individuals perform adjustments to compensation in accordance with a documented procedure.

> The procedure for making adjustments to compensation would typically include the following:
> - How compensation is determined for new hires
> - How compensation is to be handled for people changing locations within an organization
> - Frequency with which scheduled adjustments to individual compensation should be considered
> - How adjustments are to be triggered by events, such as special achievements or promotions
> - How the level of adjustment is to be determined
> - The process for initiating and approving adjustments
> - How compensation decisions are to be communicated to affected individuals
> - How and when compensation decisions are to be reviewed for equity

4. Adjustments to compensation can be made on an exception basis, when required by business needs, with appropriate approval.

> Examples of exceptions for adjustments may include the following:
> - Serious inequities
> - Retention of undervalued skills

Practice 9 **Decisions regarding an individual's compensation package are communicated to the individual.**

1. Adjustments to compensation are communicated to affected individuals prior to their effective date by an individual responsible for communicating compensation information to the individual(s) affected.

2. The basis for the size of the adjustment is explained along with appropriate information from the compensation plan that provides a better understanding of the basis for the adjustment.

3. Individuals are guided to where they can obtain more information on:

   - the compensation strategy or plan,

   - tax implications of compensation decisions,

   - laws and regulations governing compensation,

   - implications about choices they make among compensation alternatives, or

   - how to raise an issue about their compensation.

Practice 10 **Responsible individuals periodically review compensation packages for those whose compensation they administer to ensure they are equitable and consistent with the organization's compensation policy, strategy, and plan.**

1. Results of compensation decisions are compared within a unit to determine if compensation is equitably related to position responsibilities, skills, and performance across the members of the unit.

2. Results of compensation decisions are compared across units to identify inequities in how compensation is being administered.

3. Results of compensation decisions are reviewed across units to identify inequities involving individuals with similar position responsibilities, skills, or performance.

Practice 11 **Action is taken to correct inequities in compensation or other deviations from the organization's policy, strategy, and plan.**

1. When inequities are identified within or across units, they are communicated both to the appropriate unit managers and to individuals responsible for coordinating Compensation activities across the organization.

2. An approach for addressing the inequity is developed that accounts for:

- fairness to the individuals involved,
- compliance with laws and regulations,
- consistency with the compensation strategy and plan,
- effect on morale and retention,
- phasing of corrective actions,
- immediate and long-term impact on the compensation strategy and procedures, and
- precedence established for later compensation decisions or actions.

3. Corrective actions to improve equity are taken and communicated to affected individuals.

Measurement and Analysis

Measurement 1 **Measurements are made and used to determine the status and performance of Compensation activities.**

> Examples of measurements include the following:
> - Growth in compensation
> - Effects of criteria on compensation
> - Compensation by position type
> - Compensation by vehicle type
> - Extent of compensation inequities
> - Timeliness and efficiency of compensation activities

Measurement 2 **Unit measures of Compensation activities are collected and maintained.**

1. Units collect data as Compensation activities occur.
2. Measurements made to determine the status and performance of Compensation activities are maintained.

> Examples of reasons for maintaining measurements of Compensation activities include the following:
> - Periodic analysis to determine unit-level trends
> - Aggregating data at the organizational level to develop organizational measures
> - Analysis to determine organizational trends
> - Evaluation of organizational trends

Measurement 3   Aggregate trends in compensation activities and decisions are measured and reviewed on a recurring basis.

1. Unit measures of compensation activities and decisions are collected and aggregated at the organizational level.

2. A historical database of compensation data is maintained.

3. Compensation data are periodically analyzed to determine trends and evaluate effectiveness.

> Examples of trends that can be reviewed include the following:
> - Compensation versus market by position
> - Workforce perceptions regarding compensation practices and equity
> - Growth in compensation over time
> - Compensation versus individual, unit, and/or organizational performance

Verifying Implementation

Verification 1   A responsible individual(s) verifies that Compensation activities are conducted according to the organization's documented policies, practices, procedures, and, where appropriate, plans; and addresses noncompliance.

These reviews verify that:

1. Compensation activities comply with the organization's policies and stated values.

2. Compensation activities comply with relevant laws and regulations.

3. Compensation activities are performed according to the organization's documented practices and procedures.

4. Compensation activities are performed according to the organization's plans and selected methods.

> These reviews may use measures regarding the status and performance of Compensation activities, as well as unit measures of Compensation activities, to ensure that a comprehensive review of Compensation activities occurs. These measures provide indicators of the status and performance of Compensation activities across the units. Refer to Measurement 1 and Measurement 2 for information regarding measurement of Compensation activities.

5. Noncompliance issues are handled appropriately.

Verification 2   **Executive management periodically reviews the Compensation activities, status, and results; and resolves issues.**

These reviews verify:

1. The structure and growth of compensation.
2. Progress in performing planned Compensation activities.
3. Results from reviews of Compensation practices and activities.

> Refer to Verification 1 for information regarding reviews of Compensation activities to ensure adherence to the following:
> • Relevant laws and regulations
> • Organizational policies, practices, and procedures

4. Status of resolution of noncompliance issues.
5. Trends related to compensation, both internal and external to the organization.
6. Effectiveness of Compensation activities in achieving their intended results.

The Defined Level:
Maturity Level 3

Process Areas at the Defined Level focus on establishing an organizational framework for developing the workforce. The organization identifies the knowledge, skills, and process abilities that underlie the workforce competencies needed to perform its business activities. The organization develops strategic plans for the workforce needed to accomplish current and future business objectives. Development opportunities are established for assisting individuals in improving their capability in these workforce competencies. Graduated career opportunities are developed around growth in one or more workforce competencies. The workforce practices implemented at Maturity Level 2 are adjusted to motivate and support development in the organization's workforce competencies. The process abilities defined for each workforce competency are used for tailoring defined processes and establishing roles that provide the next step in workgroup development. A participatory culture is established that enables the most effective use of the organization's talent for making decisions and executing work. The process areas at Maturity Level 3 include:

Competency Analysis

A process area at Maturity Level 3: Defined

Purpose

The purpose of Competency Analysis is to identify the knowledge, skills, and process abilities required to perform the organization's business activities so that they may be developed and used as a basis for workforce practices.

Description

Prahalad and Hamel [Prahalad 90] describe an organization's core competence as the combination of technology and production skills that create its products and services and provide its competitive advantage in the marketplace. Achieving and sustaining a core competence requires assembling a workforce composed of people with different types of knowledge, skill, and abilities to follow processes. Each of these different sets of knowledge, skills, and process abilities constitute a workforce competency. The range of workforce competencies needed by an organization is determined by the range of business activities that collectively constitute or support the organization's core competencies.

Competency Analysis begins by analyzing the organization's business activities to identify the workforce competencies required to perform them. These workforce competencies are each analyzed to identify their essential knowledge, skills, and process abilities. Workforce competency descriptions are periodically reassessed to ensure they remain current with the actual knowledge, skills, and process abilities required by the organization's business activities. The organization maintains a repository of these workforce competency descriptions. The competency-based processes, which are work processes used by capable individuals in each workforce competency, are defined and updated as necessary. Anticipated changes in products, services, processes, or technologies are analyzed to determine their implications for future workforce competency requirements.

Competency information regarding an individual's capability in the workforce competencies relevant to their work or career is collected and maintained. From this competency information, resource profiles of the organization's level of capability in each of its workforce competencies can be determined. Competency information is updated as necessary to keep it current.

Workforce competency descriptions and information are used to guide strategic workforce planning, support development of the organization's workforce competencies, and enable the tailoring of workforce activities across the organization. Competency descriptions and information should be used at the unit level in performing the workforce activities described in the Staffing, Training and Development, Performance Management, Competency Development, Competency-Based Practices, and other process areas. Individuals should have access to workforce competency descriptions for planning their development and career activities.

Goals

Goal 1   **The workforce competencies required to perform the organization's business activities are defined and updated.**

Goal 2   **The work processes used within each workforce competency are established and maintained.**

Goal 3   **The organization tracks its capability in each of its workforce competencies.**

Goal 4   **Competency Analysis practices are institutionalized to ensure they are performed as defined organizational processes.**

Commitment to Perform

Commitment 1   **The organization establishes and maintains a documented policy for conducting its Competency Analysis activities.**

Issues typically addressed in the policy include:

1. Workforce competency analyses serve the business objectives and stated values of the organization.

2. The workforce competencies required to accomplish the organization's business objectives (including technical, managerial, and administrative work) are identified.

3. A list of the workforce competencies on which to base workforce activities is maintained and revised, as necessary.

4. Workforce competency analyses are conducted on a periodic and event-driven basis to maintain and update the workforce competency descriptions.

5. A repository of defined workforce competency descriptions and competency information is maintained.

6. Appropriate Competency Analysis procedures are defined, documented, and used.

> The human resources function or other appropriate professionals should review all Competency Analysis procedures to ensure they:
> - Are consistent with relevant laws, regulations, and organizational policies
> - Respect the rights and dignity of individuals and groups

Competency Analysis procedures are established and maintained for:

- documenting and maintaining workforce competency descriptions,
- determining changes in workforce competency descriptions,
- controlling changes or updates to workforce competency descriptions,

- collecting and storing of competency information, and
- maintaining and using the workforce competency information repository, including who has access and for what purposes.

> Refer to Practices 6, 7, and 8 of this process area for practices regarding the development and maintenance of the organization's workforce competency information repository.

7. Competency Analysis practices and activities comply with relevant laws, regulations, and organizational policies.

Commitment 2   An organizational role(s) is assigned responsibility for coordinating Competency Analysis activities across the organization.

> Examples of individuals who might be assigned responsibility for coordinating workforce competency analysis activities include the following:
> - Members of the human resources function or other appropriate professionals
> - Members of the training or development functions
> - Organizational competency definition or competency management group
> - Committee of representatives from ownership teams for each workforce competency

Ability to Perform

Ability 1   A responsible individual(s) coordinates the Competency Analysis activities for defining, developing, and maintaining each workforce competency.

> Workforce competency analyses may involve individuals from numerous units across the organization. The individuals who conduct the initial analyses of a workforce competency may not be the same individuals who maintain the competency descriptions or coordinate development in the competency over time. Examples of individuals or groups that may be involved in defining and maintaining a workforce competency include the following:
> - Human resources or other appropriate professionals
> - An organizational competency definition or competency management group
> - Process engineering groups focused in areas of workforce competency
> - Responsible individuals housed within a functional unit devoted to a specific workforce competency (e.g., a center of excellence [CoE])
> - A group of experienced, capable individuals within the competency who form a competency ownership team

Ability 2   **Adequate resources are provided for performing Competency Analysis activities.**

1. Documentation of the organization's business activities and processes are made available for analysis.

2. Strategic and operational business objectives are made available for developing the strategic workforce plan.

3. Experienced individuals who have expertise in workforce competency analysis are made available.

> Examples of individuals who can contribute to workforce competency analysis include the following:
> - Members of the human resources function or other appropriate professionals
> - Members of the training or development functions
> - Members of quality or process improvement groups
> - Managers
> - Business strategists
> - Instructional designers

4. Resources for supporting Competency Analysis activities are made available.

> Examples of resources to support workforce competency analysis include the following:
> - Task analysis tools
> - Position analysis questionnaires
> - Skills analysis inventories
> - Process analysis instruments
> - Data collection and analysis tools
> - Knowledge acquisition or knowledge engineering tools

5. Funding to accomplish Competency Analysis activities is made available.

6. Time, resources, and access to staff for analyzing workforce competencies are made available.

Ability 3 **Individuals performing Competency Analysis activities develop the knowledge, skills, and process abilities needed to perform their responsibilities.**

1. Individuals performing Competency Analysis activities receive preparation in relevant analysis methods and techniques needed to perform their responsibilities.

2. Individuals who participate in Competency Analysis activities are provided orientation to the purpose of and methods used in the Competency Analysis activities.

> Examples of topics that might be included in the preparation of those involved in competency analysis techniques include the following:
> - Workflow and task analysis
> - Knowledge and skill analysis
> - Behavioral analysis
> - Knowledge engineering
> - Process analysis and definition

Ability 4 **The practices and procedures for performing Competency Analysis are defined and documented.**

1. Practices and procedures are defined and documented at the organizational or unit levels, as appropriate.

2. Guidelines for tailoring the practices and procedures for use in different circumstances are documented and made available, as necessary.

3. The individual(s) assigned responsibility for coordinating Competency Analysis activities across the organization ensures that defined practices and procedures are:

   - maintained under version control,

   - disseminated through appropriate media,

   - interpreted appropriately for different situations, and

   - updated through orderly methods.

4. Experiences, lessons learned, measurement results, and improvement information derived from planning and performing Competency Analysis practices are captured to support the future use and improvement of the organization's practices.

Practices Performed

Practice 1 **The workforce competencies required to perform the organization's business activities are identified.**

> A *competency* is an underlying characteristic of an individual that is causally related to effective and/or superior performance, as determined by measurable, objective criteria, in a job or situation [adapted from Spencer 93, p. 9]. This concept of a competency of an individual is different from the concept of a core competency of an organization, as formulated by Prahalad and Hamel [Prahalad 90]. The People CMM refers to the concept of a competency at the individual level as a *workforce competency* possessed by the individual. This is similar to Athey and Orth's [Athey 99] description of a competency as a set of observable performance dimensions, including individual knowledge, skills, attitudes, and behaviors, as well as collective team, process, and organizational capabilities, that are linked to high performance, and provide the organization with sustainable competitive advantage.

> A *workforce competency* represents the knowledge, skills, and process abilities needed within the workforce to perform the organization's business activities. A workforce competency can be stated at a very abstract level, such as a need for a workforce competency in software engineering or technical writing. Workforce competencies can also be decomposed to more granular abilities, such as competencies in designing avionics software, testing switching system software, or writing user manuals and training materials for reservation systems.

1. The business activities that implement the organization's mission and strategy are identified.

2. The workforce competencies the organization must develop and maintain to perform these business activities are identified.

Practice 2   Each of the organization's workforce competencies is analyzed to identify the knowledge, skills, and process abilities that compose it.

Competencies have often been treated as descriptions of effective behaviors performed as part of a job. Although these descriptions provided a starting point for discussing performance, they often did not include sufficient detail about the knowledge or specific skills an individual needed to match the behavioral descriptions in practice. The People CMM encourages analyzing the knowledge, skills, and process abilities comprising a workforce competency to the level of detail required for diagnosing development needs and appropriate activities. Thus, a workforce competency should describe its constituent knowledge, skills, and process abilities to a level sufficient for guiding development activities that enable capable performance of required job behaviors.

- *Knowledge* is the information and understanding that an individual must have to perform a task successfully.
- *Skills* are the behaviors that an individual must be able to perform in order to accomplish committed work. Skills may involve behaviors that directly accomplish the task or that provide the support of, or coordination with, others involved in accomplishing tasks.
- *Process* abilities are the capacity to perform individual skills in the specific sequencing or method used in the organization to coordinate activities among individuals or groups, and to adjust the performance of skills, as necessary, to maintain an orderly flow of work.

1. A plan is developed for analyzing workforce competencies that typically includes:

   - the competency analysis activities to be performed,
   - the schedule for competency analysis activities,
   - the individuals or groups responsible for competency analysis activities,
   - the resources and effort required, including access to the staff, and
   - the process for review and approval of the plan by all parties affected by competency analysis activities.

2. A method is selected for performing workforce competency analyses.

Examples of methods for workforce competency analysis include the following:
- Position analysis
- Critical incident interviews
- Behavioral event interviews
- Process analysis and engineering
- Task analysis
- Knowledge engineering
- Analysis of skill needs

3. The organization defines the level for decomposing the knowledge, skills, and process abilities underlying each of its workforce competencies.

> The granularity, or level of detail, of descriptions may vary across workforce competencies. One approach is for the organization to maintain high-level descriptions of the knowledge, skills, and process abilities that are generic to a workforce competency across its many applications in the organization. Organizational components at lower levels may elaborate or tailor these generic descriptions for the specific knowledge, skills, and process abilities required to perform their committed work.

4. The knowledge, skills, and process abilities required to perform committed work are defined for each workforce competency.

5. Subject matter experts are involved in analyzing the knowledge, skills, and process abilities required to perform their committed work.

6. A description of the knowledge, skills, and process abilities is defined for each workforce competency using a representation and format that is appropriate for its intended use.

7. Descriptions of workforce competencies are used for guiding workforce practices at the organizational level and within units.

Practice 3   Workforce competency descriptions are documented and maintained according to a documented procedure.

1. Workforce competency descriptions are documented and maintained to provide descriptions of the knowledge, skills, and process abilities underlying each workforce competency.

> Workforce competency descriptions vary widely based on the organization's philosophy about the most important contributors to individual performance. Many organizations have described competencies as sets of behavioral characteristics. Other organizations have focused on specific components of knowledge or elements of skill. Examples of information that may be incorporated into workforce competency descriptions include the following:
>
> - Knowledge required to perform required tasks
> - Skills required to perform required tasks
> - Competency-based processes or workflows that an individual may be expected to perform
> - Ability to perform skills within the processes or workflows defined by the organization for performing the work
> - Behavioral characteristics of how skills and processes are performed
> - Behavioral manifestations of an orientation toward the work, colleagues, or customers
> - Personality characteristics that are conducive to successful performance
> - Types or levels of knowledge, skills, and process abilities that would characterize different levels of capability in a workforce competency

> Workforce competency descriptions may include descriptions of workflows or competency-based processes that competent individuals are expected to perform. However, these process descriptions are often described separately as organizational business processes or procedures. Refer to Practice 5 for information relating to establishing and maintaining competency-based processes.

2. Workforce competency descriptions are documented and maintained according to organization standards.

> Organization standards are applied when documenting and maintaining workforce competency descriptions to ensure:
> - Consistency among the workforce competency descriptions
> - Suitability of the workforce competency descriptions for their intended use

> Examples of issues addressed by these organization standards typically include the following:
> - Format and content of workforce competency descriptions
> - Level of granularity needed to understand and describe the workforce competency
> - Storage of workforce competency descriptions in an information base that is designed for use in supporting and performing workforce activities

3. Workforce competency descriptions are controlled and maintained under version control for use in supporting and performing workforce activities.

4. Workforce competency descriptions are made available to the workforce for use in:

   - designing or tailoring workforce practices,
   - performing workforce activities, or
   - planning individual development opportunities.

Practice 4   Workforce competency descriptions are updated on a periodic and event-driven basis.

1. Workforce competencies are periodically reanalyzed to determine if they continue to reflect the knowledge, skills, and process abilities necessary to perform the organization's business activities.

> Each of the workforce competency descriptions is periodically evaluated to determine whether its level of detail is appropriate for its intended use. Workforce competency descriptions are as likely to be over-defined as they are to be under-defined. As workforce competency information begins to be collected and used, those providing and consuming this information are able to provide feedback on the appropriate granularity and structure for different workforce competency descriptions. This feedback may determine the need for, and provide insight for, adjusting organizational standards for workforce competency descriptions.

2. Changes in products, services, processes, or technology are analyzed as necessary to determine whether:

   ■ affected workforce competency descriptions need to be updated,

   ■ new workforce competencies need to be defined, or

   ■ obsolete workforce competencies need to be phased out.

3. Action is taken to update, add, or phase out affected workforce competency descriptions based on the results of periodic or event-driven reanalysis.

> Typical changes to workforce competency descriptions may include the following:
> - New knowledge and skills that must be developed or acquired
> - Changes in existing knowledge and skills
> - Knowledge and skills that are outdated or no longer needed

4. Organization standards for workforce competency descriptions are adjusted, as necessary.

5. Changes to workforce competency descriptions are incorporated according to a documented procedure and organization standards.

6. Changes to workforce competency descriptions are provided as input for developing strategic workforce plans and for planning workforce activities within units.

Practice 5   The competency-based processes to be performed by capable individuals in each workforce competency are established and maintained.

> A *competency-based process* defines how individuals within a specific workforce competency apply their knowledge, perform their skills, and apply their process abilities within the context of an organization's defined work processes. Competency-based processes are documented, trained, performed, enforced, measured, and improved over time. Possessing a process ability indicates that an individual is able to perform the competency-based processes appropriate for someone at their level of development in the workforce competency. A process ability for a particular workforce competency may represent only part of a defined organizational process, since other elements of the defined process may be performed by individuals with different workforce competencies. To define the process abilities incorporated in each workforce competency, the organization needs to have defined the competency-based processes that an individual in each workforce competency would be expected to perform in accomplishing their committed work.

> Examples of competency-based processes include the following:
>
> - The defined processes used by software developers for designing, developing, and testing a product
> - The defined processes used by a sales group for managing a sales cycle with a prospective customer
> - The defined processes used by an organization's financial group for gathering data, analyzing results, and preparing inputs for the quarterly financial report
> - The processes used by an emergency medical team in handling specific forms of trauma

1. A capability is established for defining and maintaining the processes used within each workforce competency.

> Examples of those capable of defining and maintaining competency-based processes include the following:
>
> - A corporate group, such as a quality department
> - A quality or process improvement group
> - Responsible individual(s) housed within a functional unit devoted to a specific competency
> - A group of subject matter experts within the competency who form a process or competency ownership team

2. Competency-based processes are documented and made available for guiding those developing or performing a workforce competency.

> Defined, competency-based processes should:
>
> - Be consistent with an organization standard for process representation
> - Capture the best practices from the organization's current business activities related to the workforce competency
> - Identify the behaviors expected of a capable individual
> - Describe what should be done but not precisely how to do it
> - Be tailorable for use under different conditions
> - Clarify points of coordination among individuals or roles who must cooperate to accomplish committed work
> - Be defined with the participation of capable individuals who are currently performing the processes
> - Correct gaps or weaknesses in the processes currently in use
> - Be managed and taught as a component of a workforce competency
> - Be fit for use
> - Be presented in a format that is easy to understand and use

3. Documented competency-based processes are updated on an event-driven basis to reflect:

- changes in business operations, products, or services,
- changes in other processes or development technologies,
- lessons learned from the performance of competency-based processes, or
- other process improvements.

Practice 6 **Information about the use of competency-based processes is captured and made available.**

> Refer to Practice 8 of the Competency Development process area for practices regarding the capture and use of competency-based experiences and information within a competency community.

> Examples of information that could be captured include the following:
> - Quantitative data on the use of processes
> - Quality records
> - Documentation produced through performing the processes
> - Guidelines for tailoring processes
> - Lessons learned

1. Information collected on the performance of competency-based processes is maintained in a repository for future use.

2. Lessons learned are identified that improve competency-based processes for future use.

3. Information regarding the use and performance of competency-based processes is made available.

Practice 7 **Competency information regarding the capabilities of individuals in their workforce competencies is collected and maintained according to a documented procedure.**

> *Competency information* typically describes an individual's level of capability in relation to the list of knowledge, skills, and process abilities contained in relevant workforce competency descriptions. Although competency information is typically collected at the individual level, it could be collected at other levels. For instance, competency information might be collected at the workgroup level if a particular workforce competency is a characteristic of a workgroup and would not exist as a competency of individuals acting alone.

1. This documented procedure typically specifies:

   - responsibilities for collecting and maintaining competency information,
   - what competency information is collected and maintained in the organization's workforce competency information repository,
   - how competency information is used,
   - how competency information is represented and presented,
   - how confidentiality is established and maintained for competency information,
   - what competency information is made available, if any,
   - who may have access to competency information and under what circumstances,
   - how competency information is controlled and updated,
   - how the completeness and accuracy of competency information is audited,
   - restrictions on the use of competency information, and
   - mechanisms by which individuals can review and correct their competency information.

2. Individuals participate in collecting and organizing their competency information according to the documented procedure.

> Individuals may complete their own competency information alone or in cooperation with a responsible individual, such as a supervisor, mentor, or human resources representative. Relevant information is drawn from many sources and organized into the format used for describing competencies by the organization.

> Examples of sources of information on an individual's level of capability in a workforce competency include the following:
> - Training and other development records
> - Mentoring or apprenticeship reports
> - Performance management records
> - Career planning information
> - Management assessment of knowledge, skills, and process abilities
> - Self-assessment of knowledge, skills, and process abilities
> - Peer evaluations
> - Process assessments
> - Awards and achievements
> - Professional accomplishments
> - Assessment centers
> - Information from the performance of business activities

3. The validity of an individual's competency information is established by the individual, as well as by a party responsible for verifying the accuracy of information being submitted to the organization's repository.

4. On a periodic or event-driven basis, individuals and other responsible parties review, update, and verify an individual's competency information.

Practice 8   **Current resource profiles for each of the organization's workforce competencies are determined.**

> A *resource profile* for a workforce competency represents the number of individuals at each level of capability within the workforce competency. An example of progressive levels of capability within a workforce competency may include a beginner, a novice, a journeyman, a senior practitioner, and a master or expert.

1. Competency information is aggregated at the organizational level for each of the organization's workforce competencies.

> Information to be aggregated includes measures defined in the Staffing, Training and Development, Performance Management, Competency Development, and Career Development process areas.

2. The organization uses aggregated competency information to develop a resource profile for each of the organization's workforce competencies.

> Examples of capability information that might be included in a resource profile include the following:
> - Number of individuals in each competency
> - Number of individuals at each level of capability within each workforce competency
> - Distribution of individuals at each graduated career level within each workforce competency
> - Distribution of knowledge and skill within each workforce competency
> - Number of individuals possessing specialized skills, such as experience with specific programming languages, design methodologies, or specific applications or legacy systems, within each workforce competency
> - Distribution of workforce competencies across units in the organization

3. Resource profiles are made available, as appropriate, for use in workforce planning, the analysis of workforce practices, and other workforce activities.

Practice 9   **Competency information is updated on a periodic and event-driven basis.**

1. Competency information for an individual (or other unit of analysis) may be updated as accomplishments, experience, or events justify.

2. Competency information for affected individuals should be updated as appropriate when workforce competency descriptions are modified, added, or phased out.

3. The state of the organization's competency information is periodically audited to ensure that it is maintained with appropriate currency.

Measurement and Analysis

Measurement 1   **Measurements are made and used to determine the status and performance of Competency Analysis activities within each unit and across the organization.**

> Examples of measurements include the following:
> - Amount of time or number of people involved in analyzing workforce competencies or in collecting competency information
> - Number of workforce competencies defined
> - Effectiveness of meeting milestones in analyzing workforce competencies or collecting competency information
> - Amount of competency information collected
> - Period between updates of workforce competency analyses or competency information
> - Extent to which competency information is used in designing or tailoring workforce practices and performing workforce activities

Measurement 2   **Measurements are made and used to determine the quality of workforce competency descriptions and competency information.**

> Examples of measurements of the quality of workforce competency descriptions or of competency information include the following:
> - Level of detail to which workforce competency descriptions are defined
> - Frequency and range of uses of workforce competency descriptions and competency information
> - Usability of workforce competency descriptions or competency information
> - Number of revisions made to workforce competency descriptions
> - Number of corrections made to competency information

Verifying Implementation

Verification 1 **A responsible individual(s) verifies that Competency Analysis activities are conducted according to the organization's documented policies, practices, procedures, and, where appropriate, plans; and addresses noncompliance.**

These reviews verify that:

1. Competency Analysis activities comply with the organization's policies and stated values.

2. All actions related to the development of workforce competency descriptions and the use of competency information are periodically reviewed to ensure that they conform to documented policies.

3. Competency Analysis activities comply with relevant laws and regulations.

4. Competency Analysis activities are performed according to the organization's documented practices and procedures.

5. Noncompliance items are handled appropriately.

6. Workforce competency descriptions and competency information are consistent with existing and anticipated organizational conditions and needs.

Verification 2 **Executive management periodically reviews the Competency Analysis activities, status, and results; and resolves issues.**

These reviews verify:

1. The appropriateness of workforce competency analysis activities and competency information.

2. Progress in performing Competency Analysis activities.

3. Results from reviews of Competency Analysis practices and activities.

> Refer to Verification 1 for practices regarding reviews of Competency Analysis activities to ensure adherence to the following:
> - Relevant laws and regulations
> - Organizational policies, practices, and procedures

4. Status of resolution of noncompliance issues.

5. Trends related to competency analysis.

6. Effectiveness of Competency Analysis activities in supporting workforce activities.

Verification 3   The definition and use of competency descriptions and competency information are periodically audited for compliance with organizational policies.

> Organizational policies which may apply could include human resource, human capital, information security, confidentiality, privacy, or data disclosure policies.

1. Definitions of competency description and competency information are reviewed for compliance with organizational policies.

> The data definitions define what data is to be collected, aggregated, and used. They are not the data values themselves. For example, family name or surname could be a component of a data definition, but "Smith" would be a specific data value for an instance of family name.

2. Periodic audits ensure that competency description and competency information are accessed and used in accordance with organizational policies.

> These audits may be accomplished through reviews of ongoing reporting, such as system access and use monitoring reports, and auditing to ensure compliance with relevant information security standards and organizational policies.
>
> System access and use monitoring ensures that the data are accessed only by authorized individuals, while compliance auditing ensures that these individuals perform appropriate procedures in compliance with organizational policies and standards.

Workforce Planning

A process area at Maturity Level 3: Defined

Purpose

The purpose of Workforce Planning is to coordinate workforce activities with current and future business needs at both the organizational and unit levels.

Description

Workforce Planning ties the organization's workforce activities directly to its business strategy and objectives. Through workforce planning, the organization identifies the workforce it needs for its current and future business activities and plans the actions to be taken to ensure the required workforce is available when needed. The People CMM does not make an assumption that the organization must meet all of its workforce needs from within. Workforce planning could include partnerships, alliances, acquisitions, independent contracting, and other means for ensuring that the required components of workforce competencies are provided in support of business plans and objectives. Strategic workforce plans provide those responsible for workforce activities in units with a reference for ensuring that they perform their responsibilities with an understanding of how the unit's workforce activities contribute to the business.

The workforce planning process begins by identifying the current and future workforce competency needs of the organization. These needs are assessed from anticipated future developments in the business and its products, services, markets, technologies, and business processes. The organization identifies those workforce competencies where action is needed to meet these needs. A competency development plan is created for each workforce competency identified as needing action by the organization. A strategic workforce plan is created by integrating these competency development plans and determining the organization's actions to provide the needed competencies over time. The strategic workforce plan sets long-term objectives for workforce activities at the organizational and unit levels. Performance against these plans is periodically checked and reported at the appropriate level.

As part of planning their workforce activities, units set specific objectives for contributing to the organization's strategic workforce objectives while meeting the current needs of the unit. Succession plans are developed for each critical position in the organization to ensure a continuous supply of qualified position candidates.

Goals

Goal 1   **Measurable objectives for capability in each of the organization's workforce competencies are defined.**

Goal 2   **The organization plans for the workforce competencies needed to perform its current and future business activities.**

Goal 3   **Units perform workforce activities to satisfy current and strategic competency needs.**

Goal 4   **Workforce Planning practices are institutionalized to ensure they are performed as defined organizational processes.**

Commitment to Perform

Commitment 1   **The organization establishes and maintains a documented policy for conducting its Workforce Planning activities.**

Issues typically addressed in the policy include:

1. Workforce planning serves the business objectives and stated values of the organization.

2. Units contribute to satisfying the strategic competency needs of the organization.

3. The organization's workforce competency needs can be traced to the requirements of its current and anticipated products, services, and other business activities.

4. Responsibilities involved in workforce planning are defined and assigned.

5. Appropriate procedures are defined, documented, and used for:

   - developing and updating the strategic workforce plan at an appropriate frequency,
   - creating and updating competency development plans for workforce competencies at an appropriate frequency,
   - planning workforce activities within each unit,
   - reviewing and approving workforce plans,
   - basing all relevant workforce activities on workforce plans,
   - correcting and amending workforce plans,
   - reviewing the compliance of workforce activities with workforce plans,
   - documenting workforce planning processes and results, and
   - communicating workforce plans throughout the organization.

6. Workforce Planning practices and activities comply with relevant laws, regulations, and organizational policies.

Commitment 2   An organizational role(s) is assigned responsibility for coordinating Workforce Planning activities across the organization.

> Examples of individuals who might be assigned responsibility for coordinating Workforce Planning activities include the following:
>
> - Members of the human capital management function or other appropriate professionals
> - Members of the human resources function or other appropriate professionals
> - Members of the training or development functions
> - Organizational competency definition or competency management group
> - Committee of representatives from ownership teams for each workforce competency

Ability to Perform

Ability 1   Within each unit, an individual(s) is assigned responsibility and authority for ensuring that Workforce Planning activities are performed.

Ability 2   A responsible individual(s) coordinates the Workforce Planning activities for each workforce competency.

> Workforce Planning activities in each workforce competency focus on establishing and maintaining competency development plans. Examples of individuals or groups that may be involved in defining and maintaining the competency development plan for a workforce competency may include the following:
>
> - Human resources or other appropriate professionals
> - An organizational competency definition or competency management group
> - Process engineering groups focused in areas of workforce competency
> - Responsible individual(s) housed within a functional unit devoted to a specific workforce competency (e.g., a center of excellence [CoE])
> - A group of experienced, capable individuals within the competency who form a competency ownership team

Ability 3   Adequate resources are provided for performing Workforce Planning activities.

1. Strategic and operational business objectives and plans are made available for developing workforce plans.

2. The organization's workforce competencies are identified.

> Refer to the Competency Analysis process area for information regarding developing and maintaining descriptions of workforce competencies.

3. Individuals with expertise in workforce planning and competency development are available for developing workforce plans.

> Examples of individuals with expertise in workforce planning and competency development include the following:
> - Members of the human capital management function or other appropriate professionals
> - Members of the human resources function or other appropriate professionals
> - Members of the training or development functions
> - Strategic planners
> - Subject matter or domain experts
> - Product or technology planning staff
> - Executive management

4. Resources for supporting Workforce Planning activities are made available.

> Examples of resources to support Workforce Planning activities include the following:
> - Planning tools
> - Spreadsheets
> - Effort estimating tools
> - Labor pool analyses and forecasts
> - Competency analysis tools
> - Other workforce analysis and planning tools

5. Workforce plans are made available to those responsible for planning each unit's workforce activities.

6. Funding to accomplish Workforce Planning activities is made available.

7. Time for Workforce Planning activities is made available.

Ability 4   Individuals performing Workforce Planning activities develop the knowledge, skills, and process abilities needed to perform their responsibilities.

> Examples of appropriate guidance or training that may be provided as part of this preparation may include the following:
> - Appropriate strategic assignments
> - Training in long-range workforce planning
> - Training in analyzing competency needs
> - Training in planning unit workforce activities
> - Training in planning competence development activities

Ability 5   **The practices and procedures for performing Workforce Planning are defined and documented.**

1. Practices and procedures are defined and documented at the organizational or unit levels, as appropriate.

2. Guidelines for tailoring the practices and procedures for use in different circumstances are documented and made available, as necessary.

3. The individual(s) assigned responsibility for coordinating Workforce Planning activities across the organization ensures that defined practices and procedures are:

   - maintained under version control,
   - disseminated through appropriate media,
   - interpreted appropriately for different situations, and
   - updated through orderly methods.

4. Experiences, lessons learned, measurement results, and improvement information derived from planning and performing Workforce Planning practices are captured to support the future use and improvement of the organization's practices.

Practices Performed

Practice 1   **The current and strategic workforce needs of the organization are documented.**

1. The organization's current workforce needs are documented from inputs provided by each unit that identify:

   - the number of people required to accomplish the unit's committed work compared to the number available,
   - the unit's current staffing plan or objectives,
   - the workforce competencies needed to conduct the business activities constituting these commitments compared to the unit's current capability in these workforce competencies, and
   - the unit's anticipated future commitments that have current staffing implications.

2. The strategic workforce needs of the organization are documented from inputs that anticipate the organization's future business activities.

Examples of relevant inputs concerning strategic workforce needs include the following:

- The organization's business strategies, objectives, or plans
- The organization's product and service capabilities
- The organization's competency descriptions
- Anticipated product development or service delivery technologies
- Anticipated work processes and environments
- Anticipated markets and revenues
- Data from benchmarking activities
- Anticipated changes in laws, regulations, and organizational policies

Examples of people with knowledge of the organization's future business needs include the following:

- Executive and line managers
- Experienced individuals
- Technologists
- Strategic planners
- Marketing specialists
- Human resources professionals
- Customer representatives
- External consultants

3. The organization's current capability in each workforce competency is compared to its current and strategic workforce needs to determine staffing and development requirements necessary to satisfy these current and strategic needs.

Refer to Practice 8 of the Competency Analysis process area for information regarding evaluating the organization's capability in each of its workforce competencies.

The organization's strategic workforce needs cannot be developed in a strictly top-down or bottom-up fashion. Although the organization should aggregate the anticipated competency needs of its units, significant changes in the processes or technologies used to perform work can result in units being created, eliminated, or radically reorganized. Therefore, strategic workforce planning must consist of more than a simple aggregation of each unit's needs.

4. The organization selects, from the organization's current and anticipated workforce competencies, those workforce competencies that require action be taken to meet identified staffing and development requirements.

5. The organization documents the list of selected workforce competencies requiring competency development activities in its strategic workforce plan.

Practice 2   **Measurable objectives are established for developing the organization's capability in each of its selected workforce competencies.**

> Examples of measurable objectives for capability in each of the organization's workforce competencies include the following:
> - The level of knowledge, skill, and process ability available in each of the organization's workforce competencies
> - The rate at which knowledge, skill, and process ability are acquired in each of the organization's workforce competencies
> - The deployment of workforce competencies across the organization
> - The rate at which individuals develop knowledge, skill, and process ability in multiple workforce competencies
> - The rate at which new workforce competencies can be developed and deployed across the organization

Measurable objectives for developing capability in each of the organization's workforce competencies are:

1. Derived from the strategic and operational business objectives and plans.
2. Aggregated at the organizational level into organizational objectives.
3. Reviewed and approved by the appropriate level of management.
4. Included in the appropriate competency development plans.
5. Reviewed periodically and revised, as necessary.

Practice 3   **A competency development plan is produced for each of the organization's selected workforce competencies.**

> Competency development plans can either be produced as separately documented plans for each workforce competency, or be integrated together in the organization's strategic workforce plan. In either case, the plan for each competency should be prepared by individuals with appropriate expertise in both the subject domain of the competency and the workforce activities required to develop it. Competency development plans may also be produced for workforce competencies the organization does not currently possess, but anticipates needing in the future.

1. Competency development plans for each of the organization's selected workforce competencies are developed according to a documented procedure that specifies:

   - the schedule for producing and updating the plan,
   - responsibilities for contributing to or producing the plan,

- processes to be used in producing and approving the plan, and
- the information to be included in the plan.

2. The competency development plan for each selected workforce competency is based on:

   - the competency development requirements established by comparing the organization's current level of capability in the competency with the capability needed to accomplish its currently committed work,
   - the strategic needs for this competency based on anticipated future business activities, and
   - the organization's established competency development activities.

3. The competency development plan for each selected workforce competency includes:

   - measurable objectives for developing capability in the workforce competency,
   - the number of people anticipated or required with the needed competency over the period covered by the plan,
   - how the number of people with the competency will be developed or staffed,

---

Examples of mechanisms through which people with a workforce competency can be developed or staffed include the following:
- Hiring individuals with the competency
- Acquiring an external organization with the competency
- Developing the competency through training
- Motivating the competency through career development and competency-based practices
- Bringing in consultants
- Hiring contractors with the competency
- Outsourcing the work to other firms with the competency

- the internal workforce activities needed to develop the competency,
- the competency development time typically required for individuals to achieve the required level of capability in the workforce competency,

---

The amount of competency development time needed may vary across different workforce competencies, based on the knowledge, skills, and process abilities required by the workforce competency and each individual's level of capability.

- the resources to perform the workforce activities needed for developing and maintaining the competency,

- how the competency will be maintained or enhanced over time, and

- the rate of change in the knowledge, skills, and process abilities composing this competency needed to support the organization's anticipated business activities.

4. The competency development plan for each selected workforce competency undergoes review by all affected parties.

Examples of parties affected by the development plan for a workforce competency include the following:
- Those responsible for coordinating workforce activities across the organization
- Those responsible for performing and reporting workforce activities, especially those related to competency development
- Those responsible for units or workgroups

---

5. The organization's competency development plans are incorporated into the organization's strategic workforce plan and provide input to planned workforce activities by units.

Practice 4   Competency development plans are reviewed and revised on a periodic and event-driven basis.

1. Competency development plans are periodically reviewed and revised with a frequency that matches:

- anticipated rate of significant changes in the knowledge, skills, and process abilities composing the competency,

- appropriate opportunities to assess progress in competency development and take corrective actions, or

- the need to review and revise the organization's strategic workforce plan.

2. Competency development plans are reviewed and revised on an event-driven basis when:

- rapid changes in business, technology, or other relevant conditions require changes in knowledge, skills, or process abilities composing the competency,

- changes in committed work or other business activities substantially change the staffing requirements for the competency, or

- competency development activities are failing to achieve their intended results.

3. Competency development plans are revised according to documented procedures.

Practice 5   **The organization establishes and maintains a strategic workforce plan to guide its workforce practices and activities.**

1. The strategic workforce plan is developed using a documented procedure that specifies the:

   ■ schedule for performing Workforce Planning activities,

   ■ schedule for periodically reviewing and revising the strategic workforce plan,

   ■ individuals or groups responsible for different strategic Workforce Planning activities,

   ■ resources required for the Workforce Planning activities, and

   ■ process for reviewing and approving Workforce Planning activities by all affected parties and by executive management.

2. The strategic workforce plan integrates the competency development plans for each of the organization's selected workforce competencies.

3. The strategic workforce plan documents the organization's decisions regarding the mechanisms through which workforce competencies will be developed or provided.

Examples of mechanisms for developing or providing workforce competencies include the following:

- Competency development activities for existing or new staff as defined in the competency development plans for each of the organization's selected workforce competencies. These activities may include developing specialists within the competency, providing minimal training to all individuals to achieve a base-level competency, retraining individuals or groups whose competencies may become obsolete or oversupplied, providing cross-training for selected individuals, or training selected groups within units.

- Staffing activities to reallocate or recruit individuals necessary to meet the current and strategic workforce needs of the organization. These staffing activities may include assignments to support growth in the competency, offering growth through graduated career opportunities, or recruiting individuals possessing or capable of possessing the competency at levels to support the organization's competency needs.

- Competitive sourcing activities to obtain workforce competencies from other units in the organization or from external service providers.

- Other actions, such as adjusting the compensation strategy to motivate development or retention of needed competencies.

---

4. The strategic workforce plan provides long-term requirements for growth or shrinkage in various workforce competencies and for guiding the development of competency-based practices.

5. The strategic workforce plan provides guidance for planning unit workforce activities.

6. The strategic workforce plan includes descriptions of anticipated organizational changes required to attract, develop, motivate, and retain the workforce required to execute its future business.

> Examples of organizational changes include adjustments or modifications to the following:
> - Workforce practices
> - Working conditions or arrangements
> - Learning technologies
> - Structure of the organization
> - Technologies through which work is performed
> - Location of the work

7. The strategic workforce plan includes a risk assessment of the organization's ability to attract, recruit, and retain the workforce that will be needed for conducting its future business.

8. The strategic workforce plan is reviewed and revised periodically to reflect changes in the business.

> The strategic workforce plan is intended to provide a relatively stable set of workforce objectives for the organization to pursue. Revisions to the plan most likely occur as revisions to competency development plans are made. Revisions to the strategic workforce plan typically only occur in the presence of changes in business conditions or technologies. Under such circumstances, the organization might be better served by redeveloping the plan rather than by merely revising it.

9. The strategic workforce plan provides input to the organization's business plan and strategy concerning the availability of the workforce needed to perform planned or anticipated business activities.

Practice 6   Units plan workforce activities to satisfy current and strategic competency needs.

> A unit's workforce activities may be planned at a single time and documented in a single planning document. However, different types of workforce activities within a unit may be planned at different times and be documented in different ways. Some unit-level activities may be documented in plans that are aggregated at higher organizational levels or have been decomposed to actions at lower organizational levels. Plans for different workforce activities may vary in their level of formality, detail, or format. The purpose of planning is to make units proactive in performing activities that provide for their competency needs and provide the documented information needed for strategic workforce planning and tracking at higher levels.

1. Each unit defines and documents performance objectives for:

   ■ developing the workforce competencies needed to perform its business activities,

   ■ contributing to the strategic competency development objectives of the organization, and

   ■ performing planned workforce activities that support these competence development objectives.

   > Relevant portions of the unit's performance objectives for developing workforce competencies may be included in the individual performance objectives of those responsible for performing the unit's workforce activities. The unit's performance objectives for developing competencies are reflected in the personal development plans of those whose competencies are to be developed.

2. Units plan their workforce activities to satisfy:

   ■ the current competency needs of the unit, and

   ■ their performance objectives relative to the organization's strategic workforce plan.

   > Examples of objectives for units planning their workforce activities include the following:
   > • Determining unit staffing, training, and other needs for workforce activities
   > • Aggregating planned workforce activities of the unit into the workforce plans of higher level units
   > • Contributing to the organization's understanding and planning of its overall requirements for staffing, training, and other workforce activities
   > • Implementing workforce activities that contribute to the strategic workforce objectives of the organization

3. Units plan their workforce activities with guidance from the organization that indicates:

   ■ schedules and events relevant to the unit's workforce activities,

   ■ resources available to assist in planning or performing the unit's workforce activities,

   ■ inputs from the organization's strategic workforce plan or other relevant sources,

   ■ information needed by the organization concerning the unit's workforce needs and activities, and

   ■ how planning information is to be represented and communicated.

4. Each unit's workforce activities are planned by those accountable for workforce activities within the unit, in collaboration with those responsible for coordinating unit plans with plans or activities at higher organizational levels.

5. Units identify and document their workforce requirements (e.g., staffing levels, competency needs, training requirements, etc.) for the next planning period.

6. Units identify and document unit- and organizational-level activities required to support their current and future workforce needs.

These activities include all workforce responsibilities initiated in the process areas at the Managed Level, in addition to new responsibilities developed in process areas at the Defined Level. Examples of unit-level workforce activities include the following:

- Staffing anticipated open positions
- Performance management activities
- Activities for increasing the unit's workforce competencies, in addition to any training required for performing the specific assignments made in executing the unit's business activities
- Training to be delivered
- Career development activities
- Administering compensation
- Administering recognition and rewards
- Improving the work environment
- Developing workgroups

Examples of organizational-level activities that support unit workforce activities include the following:

- Performing organizational recruiting activities
- Organizing training delivery
- Developing career opportunities
- Preparing compensation and reward plans
- Making improvements to the work environment
- Other needed workforce activities

---

7. Units identify, assess, and document the risks associated with the unit's workforce activities.

8. Plans for each unit's workforce activities and related planning data are documented and maintained.

Practice 7   Units review and revise plans for workforce activities on a periodic and event-driven basis.

1. Plans for a unit's workforce activities are periodically reviewed and revised with a frequency that matches:

    ■ the schedule for establishing work commitments and performance objectives,

    ■ appropriate opportunities to assess progress in planned unit workforce activities, or

    ■ the need to review and revise the organization's strategic workforce plan.

2. Plans for workforce activities within a unit are reviewed and revised on an event-driven basis when:

    ■ rapid changes in committed work, technology, or other relevant conditions require changes in competencies or workforce activities,

    ■ changes in committed work or other business activities substantially change staffing requirements, or

    ■ planned workforce activities are failing to achieve their intended results.

3. Where appropriate, units revise their plans for workforce activities according to documented procedures.

Practice 8   The organization develops succession plans for its critical positions.

> *Succession plans* are developed for critical positions within the organization to ensure that qualified individuals with the required knowledge, skills, and process abilities are always available to perform the position's responsibilities.

> *Critical positions* are those positions that are critical to the accomplishment of the organization's business objectives. Critical positions can include more than just executive and other senior management positions. Certain technical, operational, or business positions may also be designated as critical positions because of the difficulty in finding or developing individuals with the knowledge, skills, and process abilities to perform successfully in these positions. The organization organizes the development and career activities required to provide qualified candidates to fill critical positions.

> Characteristics of critical positions include the following:
> - Has responsibilities that are critical to business success
> - Exercises influence, control, or direction over the performance of many other individuals, workgroups, or units
> - Requires levels of knowledge, skills, or process abilities that are not readily available or easily obtained in the labor market
> - Requires levels of knowledge, skills, or process abilities that are not easily developed by most individuals in relevant workforce competencies
> - May require specialized experiences as a component of preparation for the critical position

1. Critical positions are identified.

2. Critical position profiles are developed that provide a description of each position, the competencies required to perform its responsibilities, and critical success factors.

3. A candidate pool for each critical position is developed.

4. For individuals identified through candidate pools, staffing, performance management, training, career development, and similar development activities are based, in part, on succession planning objectives.

5. The progress made by candidates in developing the workforce competencies required for critical positions is tracked.

Practice 9 **The organization's performance in meeting the objectives of its strategic workforce plan is tracked.**

1. Progress in meeting the objectives of the strategic workforce plan is reviewed periodically with executive management.

2. If results deviate significantly from the objectives documented in the strategic workforce plan, corrective action is taken.

> Examples of corrective action include the following:
> - Taking specific actions to bring results into compliance with the objectives of the strategic workforce plan
> - Reviewing unit workforce plans to ensure they support strategic objectives and revising them when necessary
> - Revising workforce objectives or tactics

Practice 10 **Progress in meeting the objectives of the competency development plan for each of the organization's workforce competencies is tracked.**

1. For each workforce competency, an individual or group is assigned responsibility for tracking performance against its competency development plan.

2. If results deviate significantly from the competency development plan for a specific workforce competency, corrective action is taken.

> Examples of corrective action include the following:
> - Taking specific actions to bring results into compliance with the objectives of the competency development plan
> - Reviewing results against unit plans or personal development plans to determine if they need to be addressed in growing the competency
> - Reviewing competency development capabilities to determine if there are issues of capacity, timeliness, or effectiveness that need to be addressed
> - Revising competency development plans

3. Progress against competency plans is reviewed on a periodic basis with executive management.

Practice 11 **Each unit's performance in conducting its planned workforce activities is tracked.**

1. Each unit periodically reviews its status in performing planned workforce activities.

2. The progress of each unit in executing its planned workforce activities is periodically reviewed at the organizational level.

3. Corrective actions are taken when results deviate significantly from a unit's objectives in performing its planned workforce activities.

> Examples of corrective action include the following:
> - Taking specific actions to bring results into compliance with the unit's workforce needs and objectives
> - Reviewing a unit's planned workforce activities against current unit performance and the organization's strategic workforce plan to determine if revisions are necessary

4. Progress in meeting each unit's objectives in its development plan is periodically reviewed with those responsible for higher level units and those responsible for workforce activities.

Measurement and Analysis

Measurement 1   Measurements are made and used to determine the status and performance of Workforce Planning activities.

> Examples of measurements include the following:
> - Time spent in organizational and unit-level workforce planning
> - Number of people involved in Workforce Planning activities
> - Effectiveness of meeting milestones in workforce planning
> - Effectiveness of achieving the objectives of the strategic workforce plan
> - Effectiveness in performing workforce activities at the organizational and unit levels
> - Number of revisions made to workforce plans
> - Length of time between workforce planning cycles

Measurement 2   Unit measures of workforce planning are collected and aggregated at the organizational level.

1. A historical database of workforce planning data is maintained.
2. Workforce planning data are periodically analyzed to determine trends.

Verifying Implementation

Verification 1   A responsible individual(s) verifies that Workforce Planning activities are conducted according to the organization's documented policies, practices, procedures, and, where appropriate, plans; and addresses noncompliance.

These reviews verify that:

1. Workforce Planning activities comply with the organization's policies and stated values.
2. Workforce Planning activities comply with relevant laws and regulations.
3. Workforce Planning activities are performed according to the organization's documented practices and procedures.
4. Noncompliance issues are handled appropriately.
5. Workforce plans are kept current and reflect existing and anticipated organizational conditions and needs.

Verification 2   **Executive management periodically reviews the Workforce Planning activities, status, and results; and resolves issues.**

These reviews verify:

1. The appropriateness of Workforce Planning activities.
2. The appropriateness of unit planning activities.
3. Progress in performing Workforce Planning activities.
4. Results from reviews of workforce plans against the organization's stated values and appropriate policies.
5. Results from reviews of Workforce Planning practices and activities.

> Refer to Verification 1 for information regarding reviews of Workforce Planning activities to ensure adherence to the following:
> - Relevant laws and regulations
> - Organizational policies, practices, and procedures

6. Status of resolution of noncompliance issues.
7. Trends in the results of planned workforce activities compared to strategic workforce objectives.
8. Effectiveness of Workforce Planning activities in achieving documented plans.

Competency Development

A process area at Maturity Level 3: Defined

Purpose

The purpose of Competency Development is to enhance constantly the capability of the workforce to perform its assigned tasks and responsibilities.

Description

The workforce competencies identified in Competency Analysis and the needs identified in Workforce Planning provide the foundations for the organization's competency development program. Development activities are designed to raise the level of knowledge, skill, and process ability in the organization's current and anticipated workforce competencies.

The organization maintains standards for the quality of the training and development activities offered to its workforce. Graduated training and development opportunities are designed to support development in each of the organization's workforce competencies. The organization ensures that information concerning competencies and development opportunities is available to the workforce. Each individual sets objectives for development in one or more of the workforce competencies of the organization and identifies development opportunities to support them. Individuals actively pursue competency development opportunities that support their development objectives.

The organization uses the experience accumulated in its workforce as an asset for developing additional capability in each of its workforce competencies. Experienced individuals are used as mentors for other individuals or workgroups. Mechanisms are established to support communication among the members of a competency community. A *competency community* is composed of the individuals who share and practice a workforce competency (based on the concept of communities of practice [Wenger 00, Wenger 98, Brown 00]). Data and other information that emerges from the performance of a competency are captured and made available for use by other members of the competency community.

Goals

Goal 1   **The organization provides opportunities for individuals to develop their capabilities in its workforce competencies.**

Goal 2   **Individuals develop their knowledge, skills, and process abilities in the organization's workforce competencies.**

Goal 3   **The organization uses the capabilities of its workforce as resources for developing the workforce competencies of others.**

Goal 4   **Competency Development practices are institutionalized to ensure they are performed as defined organizational processes.**

Commitment to Perform

Commitment 1   **The organization establishes and maintains a documented policy for conducting its Competency Development activities to develop the workforce competencies required to perform its business processes.**

Issues typically addressed in the policy include:

1. Competency Development activities serve the business objectives and stated values of the organization.

2. Activities to increase the workforce competencies of the organization supplement activities to increase the knowledge, skills, and process abilities required to perform work in each unit.

3. The organization continuously develops the knowledge, skills, and process competencies in each of its workforce competencies.

4. The organization ensures that effective methods for developing and maintaining workforce competencies are provided and used.

5. The organization uses its existing base of knowledge, skills, and process abilities to support competency development activities.

6. Progress in developing workforce competencies is tracked for:

   ■ all individuals,

   ■ each unit, and

   ■ the organization.

7. Competency Development practices and activities comply with relevant laws, regulations, and organizational policies.

> Human resources or other appropriate professionals are consulted to ensure that Competency Development activities comply with all relevant laws, regulations, and organizational policies.

Commitment 2   **An organizational role(s) is assigned responsibility for coordinating Competency Development activities across the organization.**

> Examples of individuals who might be assigned responsibility for coordinating Competency Development activities include the following:
>
> • Members of the human resources function or other appropriate professionals
> • Members of the training or development functions
> • Organizational competency management group
> • Committee of representatives from ownership teams for each workforce competency

Ability to Perform

Ability 1   Within each unit, an individual(s) is assigned responsibility and authority for ensuring that Competency Development activities are performed.

Ability 2   A responsible individual(s) coordinates the Competency Development activities for each workforce competency.

> For each workforce competency, an individual or group takes responsibility for defining a development program. The development program could be defined by a corporate group such as human resources or training, by a human resources function within the organization, by a competency ownership group composed of experts in the competency, or by a group composed of representatives both from a corporate group and experts in the competency.

Ability 3   Adequate resources are provided for performing the planned organization-wide and unit-specific Competency Development activities.

1. The organization's workforce competencies are defined.

> Refer to Practices 2 and 3 of the Competency Analysis process area for a description of the practices that produce descriptions of the process abilities of each of the organization's workforce competencies.

2. Workforce competency descriptions and competency-based processes are available for use in Competency Development activities.

> Refer to Practices 2, 3, and 5 of the Competency Analysis process area regarding practices that produce descriptions of the organization's workforce competencies and competency-based processes.

3. Experienced individuals who have expertise in developing specific competencies (i.e., specific knowledge, skills, or process abilities) are made available for assisting in the development of workforce competencies.

4. Resources for supporting Competency Development activities are made available.

> Examples of resources to support Competency Development include the following:
> - Training and tutorial materials
> - Self-study guides
> - Training facilities
> - Process descriptions and support material
> - On-the-job training aids
> - Descriptions of available training opportunities
> - Repositories for competency-based experiences and information

5. Funding to accomplish Competency Development activities is made available.

6. The organization's strategic workforce plan allocates a recommended amount of time for individuals to participate in competency development activities.

> Refer to Practices 3 and 5 of the Workforce Planning process area for information regarding planning competency development activities.

7. Each unit's workforce planning allocates a portion of each individual's time for participation in competency development activities.

> Refer to Practice 3 of the Training and Development process area, Practice 6 of the Workforce Planning process area, and Practice 5 of the Career Development process area for information regarding planning Competency Development activities.

Ability 4 **Individuals performing Competency Development activities develop the knowledge, skills, and process abilities needed to perform their responsibilities.**

1. Individuals assigned responsibility for counseling others on training and professional development have received orientation in the opportunities provided for developing workforce competencies.

2. Individuals who provide training, mentoring, or other services for developing workforce competencies have received adequate professional training in the competencies that they are responsible for developing.

Ability 5 **Individuals who participate in Competency Development activities receive appropriate orientation in Competency Development practices.**

1. Individuals receive orientation to the graduated training and development activities and learning opportunities relevant to their workforce competencies.

> Examples of means for providing this orientation include the following:
> - Orientation sessions for individuals participating within a competency community
> - Learning maps that describe the graduated training and development opportunities available in a workforce competency
> - Mentoring

2. Individuals participating within a competency community receive orientation to the purpose, membership, and mechanisms for exchange within the competency community.

> A *competency community* consists of those members of a workforce who share the common knowledge, skills, and process abilities of a particular workforce competency.

Ability 6 **The practices and procedures for performing Competency Development are defined and documented.**

1. Practices and procedures are defined and documented at the organizational or unit levels, as appropriate.

2. Guidelines for tailoring the practices and procedures for use in different circumstances are documented and made available, as necessary.

3. The individual(s) assigned responsibility for coordinating Competency Development activities across the organization ensures that defined practices and procedures are:

   ■ maintained under version control,

   ■ disseminated through appropriate media,

   ■ interpreted appropriately for different situations, and

   ■ updated through orderly methods.

4. Experiences, lessons learned, measurement results, and improvement information derived from planning and performing Competency Development practices are captured to support the future use and improvement of the organization's practices.

Practices Performed

Practice 1 **Competency development activities are based on the competency development plans within each workforce competency.**

> Refer to Practices 2, 3, 4, 5, and 10 of the Workforce Planning process area for information regarding developing, updating, and tracking competency development plans. Refer also to Practice 6 of the Workforce Planning process area for information regarding each unit's planned workforce activities to satisfy its current and strategic competency needs.

1. Competency development activities are selected and based on their support for the organization's:

   ■ competency development plans, and

   ■ objectives for developing capability in the workforce competency.

2. Competency development activities are prioritized to align with:

   ■ the organization's measurable objectives for developing capability in each of its workforce competencies,

   ■ the competency development plan for each of the organization's workforce competencies, and

   ■ cost, schedule, and other business considerations.

3. The relationship between each competency development activity and the organization's competency development plans and objectives for developing capability in the workforce competencies is documented and communicated.

Practice 2   Graduated training and development activities are established and maintained for developing capability in each of the organization's workforce competencies.

1. Graduated training and development activities for developing capability in each of the organization's workforce competencies are identified.

> Examples of competency development activities include the following:
> - Formal classroom training
> - Courses of study at educational institutions
> - Degree programs
> - Licensing or certification programs
> - Guided self-study
> - Apprenticeship or mentoring
> - Just-in-time training
> - Workgroup (or team) training and development activities
> - Knowledge repositories and tools
> - Career development planning

2. The organization establishes standards for the learning activities included in the training and development of its workforce competencies.

3. All courses, learning materials, and other development activities and artifacts are qualified against the organization's standards before being offered to the workforce.

4. Learning activities are periodically reviewed to:

   - ensure their compliance with established standards,

   - identify revisions that are needed in the standards, and

   - ensure effectiveness in developing workforce competencies.

5. Resources for delivering the training and development activities are identified and made available.

6. The training and development program is updated as changes are made to profiles of the organization's workforce competencies.

7. The graduated training and development activities in each workforce competency are communicated to those responsible for career counseling.

8. Training and development records are maintained at the organizational level.

> Refer to Practice 8 of the Competency Analysis process area for information regarding maintaining organizational competency information.

Practice 3   **The organization makes available descriptions of workforce competencies and information about development opportunities related to them.**

> Examples of vehicles for making competency descriptions and information about development opportunities available to those interested in developing additional capability in a competency include the following:
> - Career counseling or performance management sessions
> - Bulletin boards
> - Information repositories open to members of the workforce
> - Training and development documents and brochures
> - Web pages on an intranet

Practice 4   **Competency-based training and development activities are identified for each individual to support their development objectives.**

1. A responsible individual(s) helps each individual identify competency-based training and development needs and ensures that appropriate competency development activities are identified, planned, and performed.

> Personal development plans or career development activities, described in the Career Development process area, may not affect some individuals (e.g., part-time employees or contractors). However, these individuals may need to perform competency-based processes to accomplish their committed work.
>   Affected individuals create and maintain a personal development plan. Refer to Practice 5 of the Career Development process area for information regarding developing and maintaining each individual's personal development plan.

2. A responsible person counsels individuals, as needed, about available training and development in relevant workforce competencies and how development in different competencies affects career directions.

> Development in workforce competencies may be oriented toward improved capability in an individual's current assignment, as well as toward developing capability in related competencies.

3. A waiver procedure is established and used to determine when individuals already possess the knowledge, skills, and process abilities composing one or more of the organization's workforce competencies.

4. Wherever possible, assignments are identified to provide individuals with experience in using the competencies they are developing.

Practice 5   **Individuals actively pursue learning opportunities to enhance their capabilities in the organization's workforce competencies.**

1. Individuals are encouraged to take the initiative in pursuing competency development opportunities.

> The organization fosters an environment that empowers individuals to pursue development in relevant workforce competencies. Refer to the Training and Development and Career Development process areas for practices regarding each individual's role in their personal development.

2. Competency development activities are performed on a timely basis to support individual development objectives.

> Refer to Practices 6 and 7 of the Training and Development process area for information regarding the establishment of individual development objectives, and to Practice 5 of the Career Development process area for information on creating and maintain individuals' personal development plans.

3. Individuals ensure their competency information is updated when competency development activities are completed.

> Refer to Practice 7 of the Competency Analysis process area for information regarding updating each individual's competency information.

Practice 6   **Capable individuals within a competency community are used to mentor those with less capability in the competency.**

> *Mentoring* refers to a process of transferring the lessons of greater experience in a workforce competency to improve the capability of other individuals or workgroups. Mentoring should only be considered for workforce competencies in which less-capable individuals could benefit from the guidance and experience of more-capable individuals. Mentoring activities may be targeted to specific individuals, such as those new to the organization or novices in a workforce competency. In many cases at the Defined Level, participation in mentoring activities may be voluntary.

1. Within each appropriate workforce competency, mentoring is made available.

> Examples of purposes for which mentoring is made available include the following:
> - Orientation and adjustment to the organization
> - Development of specific knowledge and skills
> - Learning how to perform processes within the organization
> - Development of workforce competencies
> - Preparation of specific management or executive skills
> - One-on-one personal attention
> - Improved group effectiveness
> - Workgroup development
> - Career advice and development
> - Counseling and advice concerning problems

2. Individuals willing to act as mentors are prepared to perform their responsibilities.

   - Experienced and capable individuals are invited to volunteer to perform mentoring activities.
   - Candidate mentors are evaluated to ensure they have the required personal skills and capability in relevant workforce competencies to perform mentoring activities effectively.
   - Mentors receive training or orientation in mentoring skills.

3. Mentors and those being mentored establish arrangements for conducting their mentoring relationship.

4. Mentors provide timely feedback and guidance to those they mentor.

> Examples of issues that might be addressed when providing feedback and guidance during mentoring include the following:
> - Evaluation of work performance
> - Use of time and setting priorities
> - Interpersonal style and skills
> - Decision making
> - Knowledge, skills, or process abilities needing development
> - Barriers to job performance or career growth
> - Understanding the organization

Practice 7   The organization supports communication among those comprising a competency community.

> The members of a workforce that share the common knowledge, skills, and process abilities of a particular workforce competency constitute a *competency community*. Much competency development occurs through information exchanges among those within a competency community. When fostered, these "communities of practice" [Wenger 00, Wenger 98, Brown 00] can function as self-organizing mechanisms for sharing competency-based information and learning among members of a competency community. This form of competency development supplements other competency development activities performed in the organization.

> Examples of mechanisms for supporting communication within a competency community include the following:
> - Periodic meetings
> - Informal discussions
> - Professional activities
> - Social gatherings
> - Peer group reviews, boards, and similar activities
> - Periodic newsletters or bulletins
> - Updated technical, process, or business documentation
> - Electronic bulletin boards, web pages, and other forms of computer-mediated communication and networking
> - Information repositories

Practice 8   Competency-based experience and information is captured and made available to those within a competency community.

1. Those within a competency community identify the data, experience, and other forms of competency-related information that represent effective sources of learning for other members of the competency community.

2. Those within a competency community capture data and other forms of information that can become a source of learning for others in the competency.

3. Competency-based data and information are stored in appropriate repositories.

4. Responsible individuals periodically update and maintain the information repositories used within a competency community.

Measurement and Analysis

Measurement 1   **Measurements are made and used to determine the status and performance of Competency Development activities within each unit and across the organization.**

Examples of measurements include the following:
- Amount of time spent in developing the knowledge, skills, and process abilities underlying the organization's workforce competencies
- Number of people and amount of effort involved in developing or delivering Competency Development activities
- Amount and types of communication within a competency community
- Amount of effort spent on capturing and documenting competency-based information
- Amount of process or competency-based experience and information available in repositories
- Rate of progress in competency development activities

Measurement 2   **Measurements are made and used to determine the quality of Competency Development activities.**

Examples of measurements of the quality of Competency Development activities include the following:
- Individual ratings of the effectiveness of each competency development method
- Level of knowledge, skill, or process ability developed in each workforce competency through different development methods
- Performance-based evidence of increases in knowledge, skills, or process abilities in each workforce competency
- Results of certification programs, where appropriate
- Rate at which individuals request access to different training programs or methods

Verifying Implementation

Verification 1   A responsible individual(s) verifies that Competency Development activities are conducted according to the organization's documented policies, practices, procedures, and, where appropriate, plans; and addresses noncompliance.

These reviews verify that:

1. Competency Development activities comply with the organization's policies and stated values.
2. Competency Development practices and activities comply with relevant laws and regulations.
3. Competency Development activities are performed according to the organization's documented practices and procedures.
4. Noncompliance issues are handled appropriately.
5. Competency development methods and materials are consistent with the existing and anticipated conditions and needs of the organization.

Verification 2   Executive management periodically reviews the Competency Development activities, status, and results; and resolves issues.

These reviews verify:

1. Appropriateness of Competency Development activities at the organizational and unit levels.
2. Progress in performing Competency Development activities.
3. Results from reviews of Competency Development practices and activities.

> Refer to Verification 1 for information regarding reviews of Competency Development activities to ensure adherence to the following:
> - Relevant laws and regulations
> - Organizational policies, practices, and procedures

4. Status of resolution of noncompliance issues.
5. Trends related to competency development.
6. Effectiveness of Competency Development activities in achieving planned objectives in the organization's workforce competencies.

> Refer to Practice 10 of the Workforce Planning process area for information regarding evaluating progress in achieving objectives of competency development plans.

Verification 3   The definition and use of data on competency development are periodically audited for compliance with organizational policies.

> Organizational policies which may apply could include human resource, human capital, information security, confidentiality, privacy, or data disclosure policies.

1. Definitions of competency development data are reviewed for compliance with organizational policies.

> The data definitions define what data is to be collected, aggregated, and used. They are not the data values themselves. For example, level of knowledge, skill, or process ability developed in each workforce competency by each individual possessing this workforce competency could be a component of a data definition, but "Expert" would be a specific data value for an instance of level of knowledge, skill, or process ability developed in each workforce competency.

2. Periodic audits ensure that competency development data are accessed and used in accordance with organizational policies.

> These audits may be accomplished through reviews of ongoing reporting, such as system access and use monitoring reports, and auditing to ensure compliance with relevant information security standards and organizational policies.
>
> System access and use monitoring ensures that the data are accessed only by authorized individuals, while compliance auditing ensures that these individuals perform appropriate procedures in compliance with organizational policies and standards.

Career Development

A process area at Maturity Level 3: Defined

Purpose

The purpose of Career Development is to ensure that individuals are provided opportunities to develop workforce competencies that enable them to achieve career objectives.

Description

Career Development activities are designed to help individuals see the organization as a vehicle for achieving their career aspirations. The organization creates mechanisms through which individuals can increase their capability in their chosen workforce competency as well as their value to the organization. The organization's career development policy identifies the jobs, positions, or competencies for which Career Development activities are appropriate.

Graduated career opportunities and promotion criteria are defined to motivate growth in the organization's workforce competencies. Graduated career opportunities represent an arrangement of positions or work responsibilities that require increasing levels of capability in one or more workforce competencies. Promotions are made periodically, based on defined criteria. Graduated career opportunities are periodically evaluated to determine if they need to be updated.

Individuals in competency communities affected by career development activities periodically evaluate their capability relative to the knowledge, skills, and process abilities defined for their workforce competency. Individuals in these identified categories create and periodically update personal development plans. Progress against these plans is tracked and development opportunities are identified. Opportunities for training and other career-enhancing activities are made available. Individuals are encouraged to take an active role in defining and developing their competencies and career opportunities.

Individuals are periodically counseled about career options, and opportunities for advancement are communicated to them. An effort is made to match work assignments with career objectives. Individuals are encouraged to take the initiative in pursuing career opportunities.

Goals

Goal 1   **The organization offers career opportunities that provide growth in its workforce competencies.**

Goal 2   **Individuals pursue career opportunities that increase the value of their knowledge, skills, and process abilities to the organization.**

Goal 3   **Career Development practices are institutionalized to ensure they are performed as defined organizational processes.**

Commitment to Perform

Commitment 1   **The organization establishes and maintains a documented policy for conducting its Career Development activities.**

Issues typically addressed by the policy include:

1. Career Development activities serve the business objectives and stated values of the organization.
2. Graduated career opportunities are designed to provide growth in the workforce competencies of the organization.
3. Job types, positions, or competencies in the organization affected by Career Development practices are defined.

> Not all individuals may be affected by the organization's Career Development practices. The use of the term "affected" implies that an activity is conducted only with those individuals in positions or job types who are covered in the organization's career development policy. Examples of individuals who might not be covered by the career development policy include the following:
> - Part-time or temporary workers
> - Contractors
> - Certain positions or job types identified by the organization
> - Individuals on performance improvement plans
> - Individuals affected by impending separation or retirement from the organization

4. Documented procedures are developed to guide Career Development activities. These procedures typically specify:
   - methods for identifying career options within the organization,
   - procedures for discussing career options with each individual, and
   - frequency of discussing career options with individuals.
5. Career Development practices and activities comply with relevant laws, regulations, and organizational policies.

Commitment 2   **An organizational role(s) is assigned responsibility for coordinating Career Development activities across the organization.**

> Examples of individuals who might be assigned responsibility for coordinating Career Development activities include the following:
> - Members of the human resources function or other appropriate professionals
> - Members of the training or development functions
> - Organizational competency management group
> - Committee of representatives from ownership teams for each workforce competency

Ability to Perform

Ability 1   **Within each unit, an individual(s) is assigned responsibility and authority for ensuring that members of the unit participate, as appropriate, in Career Development activities.**

> Examples of individuals who might be assigned responsibility for various Career Development activities within a unit include the following:
> - The unit manager or other designated individual
> - A project or workgroup leader
> - A mentor or coach
> - A competency or resource manager
> - A career counselor
> - An advisory group within a competency area
> - An empowered workgroup
> - A member of the training or development staff
> - A member of the human resources function or other appropriate professionals

Ability 2   **A responsible individual(s) coordinates the Career Development activities for each workforce competency.**

> Examples of individuals or groups that may be involved in coordinating Career Development activities in a workforce competency include the following:
> - Human resources or other appropriate professionals
> - An organizational competency management group
> - Responsible individuals housed within a functional unit devoted to a specific workforce competency (e.g., a center of excellence [CoE])
> - A group of experienced, capable individuals within the competency who form a competency ownership team

Ability 3   **Adequate resources are provided for implementing Career Development activities.**

1. When feasible, experienced individual(s) with expertise in supporting Career Development activities are made available.

> Examples of contributions that can be made by those with special skills in Career Development activities could include the following:
> - Designing graduated career opportunities
> - Developing career choice guidelines
> - Assessing development and career interests
> - Providing information about career opportunities and growth within the organization
> - Updating descriptions of graduated career opportunities to reflect changes in workforce competencies or advances in work processes, products, or technologies

2. Resources for supporting Career Development activities are made available.

> Examples of resources to support Career Development include the following:
> - Guidelines on career choices in the organization
> - Graduated career opportunity descriptions
> - Career interest inventories and scales
> - Other assessment techniques and materials

3. Support for implementing Career Development activities is made available.

> Examples of implementation support include the following:
> - Maintaining career development records
> - Maintaining graduated career paths
> - Maintaining listings of open positions

4. Funding to accomplish Career Development activities is made available.

5. Adequate time is made available for participating in Career Development activities.

Ability 4   Individuals responsible for Career Development activities develop the knowledge, skills, and process abilities needed to perform their responsibilities.

1. Those responsible for designing graduated career opportunities, developing promotion criteria, or performing career assessments have received the professional training necessary to perform their responsibilities.

2. Those responsible for Career Development activities within a unit have appropriate training in the organization's graduated career opportunities in competencies relevant to the unit's workforce.

3. Those responsible for providing career advice receive preparation in:

   - assessing career interests and capabilities,
   - providing career guidance,
   - interpreting career guidance provided from other sources, and
   - interviewing, listening, and advising skills.

Ability 5   **Individuals who participate in Career Development activities receive appropriate orientation in career development opportunities and activities.**

> Examples of information that might be addressed in career development orientation include the following:
> - Topics related to the strategic workforce plan regarding the future requirements of the organization
> - Competency development planning information
> - Graduated career opportunities and promotion criteria
> - Evaluating personal capabilities in workforce competencies
> - Setting career objectives
> - Establishing and maintaining personal development plans
> - Guidance on selecting learning and development opportunities
> - How the individual can grow in their competencies

Ability 6   **The practices and procedures for performing Career Development are defined and documented.**

1. Practices and procedures are defined and documented at the organizational or unit levels, as appropriate.

2. Guidelines for tailoring the practices and procedures for use in different circumstances are documented and made available, as necessary.

3. The individual(s) assigned responsibility for Career Development activities across the organization ensures that defined practices and procedures are:

   - maintained under version control,
   - disseminated through appropriate media,
   - interpreted appropriately for different situations, and
   - updated through orderly methods.

4. Experiences, lessons learned, measurement results, and improvement information derived from planning and performing Career Development practices are captured to support the future use and improvement of the organization's practices.

Practices Performed

Practice 1 **The organization defines graduated career opportunities to support growth in the workforce competencies required to perform its business activities.**

> *Graduated career opportunities* represent an arrangement of positions or work responsibilities that require increasing levels of capability in one or more workforce competencies. Refer to Practice 3 of the Competency Analysis process area for information regarding the documentation of the organization's workforce competencies. Graduated career opportunities include not only upward promotion opportunities within the organization such as career ladders or paths, but also career lattices that provide broadening or lateral assignments to gain experience or increase the individual's capabilities in additional workforce competencies. Such opportunities may be in other units or in assignments to other organizations either in or allied with the company. An organization may have many combinations of graduated career opportunities.

> An example of a set of graduated career opportunities that involve both technical and management growth in software engineering might include a progression such as the following:
> - Support programmer
> - Software engineer
> - Senior software engineer
> - Software team leader or project manager
> - Software system architect or program manager
> - Senior consulting software engineer or division manager
> - Fellow or vice president
> - Chief scientist or executive vice president

1. The organization specifies the purposes to be achieved through establishing sets of graduated career opportunities.

> Examples of purposes for graduated career opportunities include the following:
> - Motivating individuals to develop the competencies required to execute the organization's current and future business activities
> - Ensuring growth in the organization's workforce competencies
> - Rewarding individuals for growth in workforce competencies
> - Enabling individuals to expand their ability to serve the organization when their performance and capability justify greater responsibility or influence
> - Deploying competent individuals or teams most effectively throughout the organization
> - Preparing succession for positions requiring greater competency or experience
> - Ensuring careers are aligned with business strategy and direction
> - Steadily improving the organization's performance

2. Graduated career opportunities are designed to support business strategies or needs.

> Examples of business strategies or needs that may influence the definition of career opportunities include the following:
> - Current and future products and services
> - Standard business processes and methods
> - Organizational structure and architecture
> - Corporate culture and climate
> - Availability of individuals with knowledge and skills in the organization's workforce competencies
> - Nature of the customer and business environment
> - Workforce competencies of the competition
> - Professional practices within specific knowledge and skill areas

3. Several choices of graduated career opportunities are made available for career planning.

> Examples of choices among career opportunities may include the following:
> - Technical
> - Administrative
> - Managerial
> - Sales and marketing
> - A mixture of assignments across or within several career areas

4. Criteria for advancing through graduated career opportunities are documented and communicated to the workforce.

> Examples of criteria for advancement through graduated career opportunities include the following:
> - Knowledge, skills, and process abilities required at each graduated level
> - Demonstrated performance or accomplishments required for each graduated level
> - Potential to perform responsibilities successfully at each graduated level
> - Characteristic working styles required at each graduated level
> - Demonstrated impact on the group, unit, or organization required for each graduated level
> - Potential for developing additional knowledge and skills that are required for advancement to each graduated level
> - Potential to affect others through performance of responsibilities at each graduated level

Practice 2   Career promotions are made in each area of graduated career opportunities based on documented criteria and procedures.

> Documented promotion criteria and procedures for considering the promotion of qualified individuals are defined for each workforce competency, cluster of competencies, or other career area where graduated career opportunities have been defined. These promotional criteria and procedures may differ across workforce competencies or areas of career opportunity.

The promotion procedures typically specify:

1. The bases (i.e., frequency or other criteria) for initiating promotion activities within the area.
2. How individuals may apply or be nominated for promotion consideration.
3. How criteria for promotion are developed, approved, and communicated.
4. How and by whom nominated candidates are to be evaluated.
5. How and by whom promotion decisions are made and approved.
6. Which other workforce activities or practices are activated by the promotion decisions.
7. How appeals to promotion decisions can be made and how appeals are handled.
8. How often promotion criteria and procedures are evaluated for improvements.

Practice 3   Graduated career opportunities and promotion criteria are periodically reviewed and updated.

1. Graduated career opportunities and their associated promotion criteria are periodically reviewed to ensure they are aligned with the definition of workforce competencies, the business strategy of the organization, and other relevant considerations.
2. Additions, deletions, or changes in workforce competencies are analyzed as necessary to determine whether:

   ■ affected graduated career opportunities and promotion criteria should be updated,

   ■ new graduated career opportunities and promotion criteria should be defined, or

   ■ obsolete career opportunities should be phased out or eliminated.

3. Action is taken to update, add, or phase out graduated career opportunities or promotion criteria based on the results of periodic or event-driven reanalysis.
4. Changes to graduated career opportunities are implemented and maintained under version control.
5. Changes in graduated career opportunities or promotion criteria are communicated to the workforce.

Practice 4   **Affected individuals periodically evaluate their capabilities in the workforce competencies relevant to their career objectives.**

> Examples of methods for getting periodic feedback on their capabilities in workforce competencies include the following:
> - Formal or informal performance feedback
> - Self-assessment materials or guides
> - Evaluation at the end of learning opportunities
> - Assessment centers
> - Reviews by peer or promotion panels
> - Standardized tests or evaluation techniques
> - Professional licensure or certification evaluations
> - Feedback from mentors or coaches

1. Opportunities are available to individuals for determining their capabilities in relevant workforce competencies.

2. In some instances, the organization may require an evaluation of an individual's competencies for promotion or assignment to specific positions.

3. Evaluations of an individual's capabilities on relevant workforce competencies are used as input for creating personal development plans and for identifying relevant career options.

4. Individuals are made aware of any competency information that will be entered into promotion or staffing decisions.

Practice 5   **Affected individuals create and maintain a personal development plan to
guide their training and career options.**

> Examples of information presented in a personal development plan include the following:
> - Career objectives
> - Career paths, assignments, or experiences to achieve those objectives
> - Knowledge, skills, and process abilities identified in Performance Management activities to enhance performance in the current assignment
> - Competencies and other capabilities needed to progress toward the career objectives
> - Potential next assignments
> - Competencies required for potential next assignments
> - Plans for developing the competencies required for potential next assignments
> - Individual development objectives
> - Other development activities, such as professional growth

1. The personal development plan is created jointly between an individual and the person responsible for their career guidance.

2. Career development objectives are based on the graduated career opportunities defined for the organization.

3. The personal development plan identifies training and other development activities needed to accomplish the career objectives of the individual.

4. Opportunities for personal development are identified and encouraged.

> Examples of opportunities to support personal development include the following:
> - Training
> - Activities to build new competencies
> - Certification or licensure
> - Temporary assignments
> - Involvement with task forces or committees
> - Work assignments that would support the individual's development needs
> - Other development activities, such as mentoring

5. The personal development plan is updated periodically as changes occur in:

   - the individual's career objectives,

   - the organization's business strategy or activities,

   - the definition of the organization's workforce competencies,

   - the knowledge, skills, and process abilities needed for potential future assignments, or

   - the career options available.

6. The personal development plan for some individuals may be based, in part, on succession planning objectives identified in succession planning activities.

> Refer to Practice 8 of the Workforce Planning process area for information regarding succession planning.

Practice 6 **Career options and development in the organization's workforce competencies are discussed with affected individuals on a periodic or event-driven basis.**

1. Affected individuals are made aware of the organization's graduated career development opportunities and relevant aspects of the organization's strategic workforce plan and associated competency development plans.

2. Affected individuals are counseled on how to prepare for the opportunities they wish to pursue.

3. Affected individuals periodically discuss career opportunities with those responsible for providing them with career advice.

> Examples of topics for career discussions may include the following:
> - Advice and discussion to help develop career objectives
> - Assessment of individual capabilities relevant to career objectives
> - The creation or updating of a personal development plan
> - Individual performance against personal development plans
> - The initiation, adjustment, or termination of career development activities

4. Those responsible for Career Development activities continually identify opportunities to increase the workforce competencies and other knowledge, skills, or process abilities relevant to the career objectives of the individuals they advise.

5. Progress against personal development plans and the impact and results of development activities are discussed with affected individuals.

6. Alignment of personal development plans with the organization's strategic workforce plans and competency development plans are discussed with affected individuals.

Practice 7   Affected individuals pursue training and development opportunities that enhance their career options and capabilities in the organization's workforce competencies.

1. Affected individuals are encouraged to accept responsibility for developing their capabilities and careers. They should take an active role in:

   - accomplishing the objectives set in their personal development plans,
   - identifying opportunities for development experiences, and
   - pursuing external activities or training that enhances their knowledge, skills, and process abilities.

2. Development opportunities are performed as planned in personal development plans.

3. Assignments outside of normal work responsibilities that support an affected individual's development needs are provided, as appropriate.

> Examples of assignments outside of normal work responsibilities that may support the individual's development needs include the following:
> - Special tasks and temporary responsibilities
> - Task forces or committees
> - Problem resolution teams
> - Time to pursue special interests or skills
> - Process or quality improvement activities
> - Professional activities

Practice 8   Individual development activities are tracked against personal development plans.

1. Those responsible for career discussions periodically review individual performance against personal development plans with each individual.

2. Progress against the personal development plan is discussed during periodic performance management, development, or career discussion sessions.

3. The impact and results of development opportunities completed are discussed to see whether adjustments to career objectives or individual development objectives need to be made.

4. When progress deviates significantly from the personal development plan, potential corrective actions are evaluated.

> Examples of corrective actions include the following:
> - Revising the schedule of planned development activities
> - Changing the development activities
> - Revising the career objectives or individual development objectives
> - Ensuring that development time is built into the individual's schedule

5. Individuals ensure that organizational competency records concerning their knowledge, skills, and process abilities are updated whenever they have completed significant development events or experiences.

> Refer to Practices 6, 7, and 8 of the Competency Analysis process area for information regarding the organization's workforce competency information repository.

Measurement and Analysis

Measurement 1   Measurements are made and used to determine the status and performance of Career Development activities within each unit.

Examples of measurements include the following:
- Time and resources spent in defining and updating graduated career opportunities
- Staff effort spent in career development activities
- Frequency and timeliness of career discussions
- Amount of training identified in development plans
- Number of career development plans documented
- Progress against personal development plans
- Number of applications for promotion or candidates considered for promotion
- Resources and effort spent on promotions
- Timeliness of promotion actions
- Number of promotions and rejections, and rationale
- Percent of workforce undergoing promotion consideration
- Rate of providing career development training

Measurement 2   Unit measures of Career Development status are collected and aggregated at the organizational level.

1. A historical database of Career Development data is maintained.
2. Career Development data are periodically analyzed to determine trends.

Measurement 3   Measurements are made and used to determine the effectiveness of Career Development activities.

Examples of measures of the effectiveness of Career Development activities include the following:
- Ability to attract or retain people in a workforce competency
- Number of people at different graduated career levels compared to organizational needs
- Rate at which people are progressing through graduated career levels
- Capability and demonstrated performance of people at different graduated career levels

Verifying Implementation

Verification 1   **A responsible individual(s) verifies that Career Development activities are conducted according to the organization's documented policies, practices, and procedures; and addresses noncompliance.**

These reviews verify that:

1. Career Development activities comply with the organization's policies and stated values.
2. Career Development activities comply with relevant laws and regulations.
3. Career Development activities are performed according to the organization's documented practices and procedures.
4. Career Development activities are performed according to the unit's plans and selected methods.
5. Noncompliance issues are handled appropriately.

Verification 2   **Executive management periodically reviews the Career Development activities, status, and results; and resolves issues.**

These reviews verify:

1. Progress in career development across the workforce against the business needs of the organization.
2. Progress in performing Career Development activities.
3. Results from reviews of Career Development practices and activities.

> Refer to Verification 1 for information regarding reviews of Career Development activities to ensure adherence to the following:
> - Relevant laws and regulations
> - Organizational policies, practices, and procedures

4. Status of resolution of noncompliance issues.
5. Trends related to career options and growth.
6. Effectiveness of Career Development activities in achieving planned results.

Competency-Based Practices

A process area at Maturity Level 3: Defined

Purpose

The purpose of Competency-Based Practices is to ensure that all workforce practices are based in part on developing the competencies of the workforce.

Description

The practices established through performing the activities of process areas at the Managed Level need to be adjusted to support the organization's focus on developing workforce competencies. Workforce activities that had focused primarily on unit concerns at the Managed Level are re-oriented by adjusting them to include concerns that are strategic to shaping the organization's workforce and the workforce competencies needed in the workforce. As a result of incorporating an organizational orientation in the performance of workforce activities, the performance of activities should become more consistent across units and should better support the development and retention of those workforce competencies that the organization needs.

The organization's workforce activities are performed by deploying a defined, consistent set of workforce practices that can be tailored for use with different workforce competencies. These Competency-Based Practices may also be further tailored for implementation in various units or geographic locations.

Both the organization and its units adjust recruiting practices to satisfy requirements for workforce competencies identified in the strategic workforce plan. The organization works with potential sources of qualified candidates to improve the application rate for individuals with aptitude in relevant workforce competencies. Selection methods are tailored to assess the knowledge, skills, and process abilities related to workforce competencies. Staffing decisions are based, in part, on capability in the relevant competencies that are involved both in the new position and in possible future positions.

Units develop performance objectives for contributing to long-term development in workforce competencies. Individuals incorporate competency development into their performance objectives. Periodic discussions of work performance include feedback on development and application of workforce competencies.

The organization's compensation strategy and practices are structured to motivate development in the organization's workforce competencies. Adjustments to compensation are partly based on developing and applying workforce competencies. Recognition and rewards can be provided for outstanding development or application of workforce competencies.

Goals

Goal 1   **Workforce practices are focused on increasing the organization's capability in its workforce competencies.**

Goal 2   **Workforce activities within units encourage and support individuals and workgroups in developing and applying the organization's workforce competencies.**

Goal 3   **Compensation strategies and recognition and reward practices are designed to encourage development and application of the organization's workforce competencies.**

Goal 4   **Competency-Based Practices are institutionalized to ensure they are performed as defined organizational processes.**

Commitment to Perform

Commitment 1   **Relevant organizational policies promote increased capability in the organization's workforce competencies.**

> In deploying Competency-Based Practices as organizations mature, existing policies that were put in place at the Managed Level are typically revised to address issues relevant to the competency focus of the organization's workforce practices at the Defined Level.

Issues typically addressed in these policies include:

1. Recruiting activities focus on the most likely sources of candidates with existing or potential capability in the organization's workforce competencies.

2. The organization's workforce activities are tailored to motivate and develop the organization's workforce competencies.

3. Selection activities are based, in part, on identifying candidates with the strongest capabilities and potential in the organization's workforce competencies.

4. Performance management includes activities, criteria, and feedback designed to aid development of individuals in the organization's workforce competencies.

5. Recognition and reward activities focus, in part, on motivating development and application of the organization's workforce competencies.

6. Compensation strategies focus, in part, on increasing the organization's capability in its workforce competencies.

7. Competency-based adjustments to policies, workforce practices, and workforce activities comply with relevant laws, regulations, and organizational policies.

> All competency-based adjustments to workforce practices are reviewed by a human resources or other appropriate professional to ensure their compliance with all applicable laws and regulations governing these practices, as well as the organization's policies and stated values.

Commitment 2 **An organizational role(s) is assigned responsibility for coordinating adjustments in workforce practices designed to increase the organization's capability in its workforce competencies.**

> Examples of individuals who might be assigned responsibility for coordinating adjustments in workforce practices include the following:
> - Members of the human resources function or other appropriate professionals
> - Members of the training or development functions
> - Organizational competency definition or competency management group

Ability to Perform

Ability 1 **Within each unit, an individual(s) is assigned responsibility and authority for ensuring that workforce practices and activities are designed to motivate individuals and workgroups to develop and apply workforce competencies.**

Ability 2 **A responsible individual(s) coordinates the competency-based practices and activities for each workforce competency.**

Ability 3 **Adequate resources are provided for ensuring that workforce practices and activities are designed to increase the organization's capability in its workforce competencies.**

1. The workforce competencies of the organization have been analyzed, and the organization's capability in these competencies is known.

> Refer to the Competency Analysis, Workforce Planning, and Competency Development process areas for practices that identify, plan for the development of, and develop the organization's workforce competencies.

2. Experienced individuals who have expertise in workforce practices are available for guiding adjustments that increase the organization's capability in its workforce competencies.

3. Resources for supporting workforce practices and activities that have been adjusted to increase the organization's capability in its workforce competencies are made available.

> Examples of resources that could be used to support adjusting workforce practices and activities include the following:
> - Information bases on recruiting sources
> - Selection guides and aids
> - Performance management forms and guides
> - Training materials
> - Compensation and reward guides
> - Career planning guides and tools
> - Electronic availability of information concerning competency-based workforce practices
> - Other relevant workforce assets

4. The strategic workforce plans of the organization and each unit's planned workforce activities focus on increasing the capability of the organization in its workforce competencies.

5. Funding to accomplish competency-based workforce practices and activities is made available.

6. Adequate time is made available for performing competency-based workforce practices and activities.

Ability 4 **Those responsible for competency-based workforce activities develop the knowledge, skills, and process abilities needed to perform their responsibilities.**

1. Individuals assigned responsibility for performing competency-based workforce activities receive training or orientation in the application of these practices.

2. Individuals assigned responsibility for designing and adjusting competency-based workforce practices receive training in the knowledge and skills required for performing their responsibilities.

Ability 5   **The practices and procedures for performing competency-based workforce practices are defined and documented.**

1. Practices and procedures are defined and documented at the organizational or unit levels, as appropriate.

2. Guidelines for tailoring the practices and procedures for use in different circumstances are documented and made available, as necessary.

3. The individual(s) assigned responsibility for Competency-Based Practices across the organization ensures that defined practices and procedures are:

   ■ maintained under version control,

   ■ disseminated through appropriate media,

   ■ interpreted appropriately for different situations, and

   ■ updated through orderly methods.

4. Experiences, lessons learned, measurement results, and improvement information derived from planning and performing competency-based workforce practices are captured to support the future use and improvement of the organization's practices.

Practices Performed

Practice 1   **Recruiting activities are planned and executed to satisfy the organization's requirements for workforce competencies.**

1. Recruiting activities are tailored to satisfy organizational workforce competency objectives, in addition to the specific requirements of currently open positions.

> Refer to Practice 1 of the Workforce Planning process area for information regarding identifying the workforce needs of the organization. Refer to Practices 7, 8, and 9 of the Competency Analysis process area for information regarding tracking the competencies of the workforce.

2. The organization communicates its current and anticipated requirements for workforce competencies to likely sources of qualified candidates.

> Refer to Practices 7, 8, and 9 of the Staffing process area for information regarding communication to internal and external sources of qualified candidates.

3. The organization establishes relationships with external sources willing to develop qualified candidates with the knowledge and skills that match the organization's current and anticipated competency requirements.

Examples of possible aspects of relationships with sources of qualified candidates include the following:

- Periodic recruiting trips
- Financial support for teaching, research, or collaborative projects
- Providing facilities or equipment in support of teaching or research
- Summer or part-time employment for faculty or students
- Internships
- Sabbatical opportunities for faculty
- Providing lecturers on a temporary or sabbatical basis
- Frequent interaction with educational institutions to track the development of the most qualified candidates
- Career guidance to students
- Involvement and support for professional or honorary societies
- Support for professional meetings and conferences
- Awards and other forms of recognition for outstanding students or professionals

---

Practice 2   Selection processes are enhanced to evaluate each candidate's potential for contributing to organizational and unit objectives for capability in workforce competencies.

1. Descriptions of open positions:

   - incorporate information from relevant workforce competencies,
   - describe the level of capability required in each relevant workforce competency, and
   - describe how the open position relates to career development in relevant workforce competencies.

2. In addition to the specific requirements of an open position, selection criteria are enhanced to include:

   - current capability in relevant workforce competencies,
   - potential future capability in workforce competencies, and
   - evidence of interest in developing relevant workforce competencies.

3. In addition to information about position-related knowledge and skills, selection processes are designed to produce information about each candidate's capabilities in relevant workforce competencies.

Practice 3   **Staffing decisions are made, in part, to achieve the competency development objectives of the organization and the career objectives of qualified candidates.**

1. Competency information is used to identify internal candidates for open positions or special assignments.

> Managers, human resource professionals, or others responsible for career planning can use the organization's competency information. Based on the organization's policies regarding use of personal data, different levels of information may be available to different individuals or workgroups. Support (manual or electronic) is provided for using competency information.

2. Personal development plans and career objectives are used as input when selecting among candidates for open positions.

> The selection process, especially for positions beyond entry level, involves the review of the development plans of qualified internal candidates to further develop, or broaden, their capabilities in the organization's workforce competencies. Thus, the staffing process becomes one mechanism for increasing the organization's capability in its workforce competencies.

3. Staffing decisions consider career development objectives when an open position represents a graduated career opportunity in one or more workforce competencies.

4. In addition to position responsibilities, candidates are evaluated for their potential to contribute to the organization's current and future capability requirements in workforce competencies.

5. The demonstrated capability of candidates in relevant workforce competencies is incorporated into selection decisions.

6. The demonstrated capability of individuals in relevant workforce competencies is incorporated into workforce realignment or workforce reduction decisions.

> Refer to Practice 16 of the Staffing process area for information regarding workforce reduction and other outplacement activities.

Practice 4   **Transition activities provide orientation to workforce competencies.**

1. Orientation to new positions is designed to familiarize individuals with the competencies required to perform their work assignments.

2. Orientation for individuals new to the organization is designed, in part, to inform them about the organization's workforce competencies and career development options, including:

   - the knowledge, skills, and process abilities in competencies relevant to their work,
   - development activities,
   - career opportunities, and
   - competence-related workforce practices.

Practice 5 **Work assignments are designed, in part, to enhance personal and career development objectives.**

1. Work assignments are defined in consultation with individuals assigned responsibility for the work.

2. Work assignments are defined in an agreement about the committed work that will be performed in response to the requirements of the position being filled.

3. To the extent possible, work assignments are designed to enhance:

   - the immediate development objectives in the individual's personal development plan,
   - the individual's growth in workforce competencies, and
   - the individual's career objectives.

4. The extent to which work assignments contribute to personal and career objectives is discussed during staffing, performance management, and related activities.

Practice 6 **Each unit documents performance objectives for developing workforce competencies.**

1. Each unit defines and documents performance objectives for:

   - developing the workforce competencies needed to perform its business activities,
   - contributing to the strategic competency development objectives of the organization, and
   - performing planned workforce activities that support these competence development objectives.

> Refer to Practice 3 of the Workforce Planning process area for information regarding identifying the establishment of competency development plans for selected workforce competencies. The unit-level performance objectives for developing workforce competencies should support the accomplishment of the organization's competency development plans, as well as the business needs of the unit.

2. Relevant portions of the unit's performance objectives for developing workforce competencies are included in the individual performance objectives of each person who is responsible for performing the unit's workforce activities.

3. The unit's performance objectives for developing competencies are allocated to the personal development plans of those whose competencies are to be developed.

Practice 7 **Each individual documents performance objectives for developing additional capability in the organization's workforce competencies.**

1. Objectives for developing in relevant workforce competencies are included in each individual's performance objectives.

> Example criteria to consider when selecting among workforce competencies to include in an individual's performance objectives include the following:
> - Relevance of the workforce competency to current assigned responsibilities
> - Relevance of the workforce competency to future business activities within the unit
> - Relevance of the workforce competency to the career development plans of the individual
> - Contribution to growth in the workforce competencies of the workgroup, unit, or organization
> - Importance to the organization's strategic requirements for workforce competencies

2. Some of each individual's performance objectives are drawn from their personal development plans.

> Examples of performance objectives related to individual competency and career development include the following:
> - Increasing capability in one or more of the organization's workforce competencies
> - Achieving limited capability in workforce competencies that supplement an individual's primary competencies
> - Assisting other members of the unit or organization in increasing their capability in the organization's workforce competencies

Practice 8 **Ongoing discussions of work performance include feedback on an individual's development and application of relevant workforce competencies.**

1. Those responsible for ongoing communication about an individual's work performance provide feedback concerning:

   - evidence of growing capability in relevant workforce competencies,

   - current level of capability in relevant workforce competencies, and

   - ability to apply relevant workforce competencies for improving work performance.

2. Individuals are encouraged to seek guidance from relevant sources on their development and application of workforce competencies.

> Examples of relevant sources of feedback on development and performance of competencies include the following:
> - Managers
> - Mentors or coaches
> - Trainers or performance experts
> - Senior professionals in the competency
> - Peers
> - Outside experts

Practice 9 **Each individual's performance is assessed, in part, against the objectives of their personal development plan.**

1. Each individual's success in accomplishing the objectives established in their personal development plan is evaluated when providing formal performance feedback.

2. Each individual's work performance is evaluated to assess their level of capability in relevant workforce competencies.

3. The results of each individual's work performance are evaluated to identify evidence of capability in workforce competencies not involved in his or her assigned responsibilities or performance criteria.

> Reasons for evaluating other workforce competencies include gathering information for guiding decisions about additional career options and development opportunities.

4. Information about each individual's capability in the organization's workforce competencies is documented for use in:

   - planning their development activities and career options,
   - reviewing progress in accomplishing development objectives, and
   - identifying new, or revising existing, development objectives.

> Refer to Practice 9 of the Competency Analysis process area for information regarding updating competency information.

Practice 10   **The compensation strategy is established and maintained, in part, to increase the organization's capability in its workforce competencies.**

   1.   The compensation strategy is adjusted to achieve specific objectives in developing and applying the organization's workforce competencies.

> Examples of competency objectives to be motivated by adjustments in the compensation strategy include the following:
>
> • Motivating growth in workforce competencies
> • Motivating the workforce to develop capability in scarce competencies
> • Maintaining equity in compensation among comparable capability levels across workforce competencies, and in relation to relevant labor markets
> • Attracting talent with knowledge and skills in the organization's workforce competencies
> • Retaining talent in the organization's workforce competencies
> • Motivating the use of workforce competencies to improve performance
> • Supporting others in developing and applying workforce competencies

   2.   Compensation practices are adjusted as necessary to achieve the objectives of the compensation strategy.

> Examples of compensation practices that can be adjusted to support the organization's compensation strategy include the following:
>
> • Creating salary bands across related workforce competencies for capability levels (e.g., technical associate, member of the technical staff [MTS], senior MTS, principal MTS, etc.) defined relative to the knowledge, skills, and process abilities within each workforce competency
> • Tying some compensation actions to events (rather than position changes or calendar-based actions) indicating achievement of greater capability within a workforce competency (such as receipt of a degree or professional certification)
> • Factoring into a bonus or other variable-based pay the attainment or application of greater capability in relevant workforce competencies
> • Tying the level or availability of some benefits to developing and applying greater capability in relevant workforce competencies
> • Tying stock and other incentives to developing and applying greater capability in workforce competencies

   3.   The effectiveness of the compensation strategy in improving the organization's capability in its workforce competencies is:

   ▪ periodically reviewed,

   ▪ adjusted as necessary to support capability and performance objectives, and

   ▪ revised as appropriate when intended competency development or performance results are not achieved.

Practice 11   **Compensation practices are defined to support capability objectives within each workforce competency.**

> Refer to Practice 2 of the Workforce Planning process area for information regarding establishing measurable capability objectives within each workforce competency.

1. Within each workforce competency, compensation practices are evaluated for their current and anticipated impact on:

   - strategic capability and staffing goals in the competency,
   - ability to attract and retain people with required capabilities in the competency,
   - graduated career development and promotional opportunities within the competency, and
   - increasing the impact of capability in the competency on performance.

2. Compensation practices are adjusted to support capability objectives in each workforce competency.

> Examples of adjustments to compensation practices that support capability objectives include the following:
> - Compensation actions for recruiting selected candidates with needed competencies
> - Compensation adjustments based on availability of different competencies within the local or national labor markets
> - Compensation actions based on promotion through graduated career steps within a competency
> - Compensation actions for completing specific competency development activities such as courses, degrees, or professional certifications
> - Compensation actions for applying increased capability in a competency to improve performance
> - Compensation actions for accomplishments in assisting the competency development of other individuals

3. All adjustments to compensation practices that support capability objectives in a specific workforce competency must:

   - be aligned with objectives in the strategic workforce plan;
   - be consistent with the compensation policy, strategy, and related adjustments to organization-wide compensation practices; and
   - maintain equity among workforce competencies relative to their value to the organization and availability in the marketplace.

Practice 12   **Adjustments to compensation are partly determined by each individual's development and application of relevant workforce competencies.**

1. Individuals' development and application of relevant workforce competencies is factored into decisions concerning their compensation.

> Examples of competency-based factors affecting compensation decisions include the following:
>
> - Current capability in relevant workforce competencies
> - Development of capabilities in scarce competencies
> - Market value of their capability in their competencies
> - Successful completion of personal development plan objectives
> - Ability to translate capability in workforce competencies into performance at the individual, workgroup, unit, or organizational levels
> - Contribution in helping or mentoring others to improve in the organization's workforce competencies

2. The impact on compensation of developing and applying capability in relevant workforce competencies is discussed with each individual.

3. Each individual's compensation is reviewed to ensure it is:

   - consistent with the organization's compensation policy and practices;

   - consistent with objectives documented in the organization's strategic workforce plan, the unit's planned workforce activities, and the individual's personal development plan;

   - consistent with the individual's capability in relevant workforce competencies; and

   - equitable with the compensation of other individuals possessing similar capabilities.

4. Corrective actions are taken when an individual's compensation is found to be inequitable or inconsistent with organizational policies, practices, objectives, or individual capability.

Practice 13   **Recognition and rewards for developing or applying workforce competencies are provided, when appropriate, at the individual, workgroup, or unit levels.**

1. Policies are revised to include development and application of the organization's workforce competencies as a basis for recognition or reward.

2. The level of recognition or reward is equitable with regard to the level of capability developed or applied.

Practice 14 **As the definition or requirements of its workforce competencies change, the organization reevaluates its workforce policies and practices and adjusts them, as needed.**

> Examples of adjustments to relevant policies and procedures as the competency requirements change to meet organizational needs and workforce plans include the following:
> - Adjustments to recruiting procedures to ensure selection of individuals who satisfy the organization's requirements for necessary workforce competencies.
> - Adjustments to workforce reduction procedures to ensure retention of necessary workforce competencies and appropriate outplacement of individuals not retained in their current positions or within the organization.
> - Adjustments to compensation procedures to address recruiting and retention of targeted workforce competencies.

Measurement and Analysis

Measurement 1 **Measurements are made and used to determine the status and performance of workforce practices to increase capability in the organization's workforce competencies.**

> Examples of measurements include the following:
> - Amount of time spent in tailoring workforce policies, practices, and activities to support developing and applying the organization's workforce competencies
> - Number of people involved in tailoring workforce activities to the organization's workforce competencies
> - Rate of progress in tailoring the workforce activities to focus on the organization's workforce competencies

Measurement 2   **Measurements are made and used to determine how effectively competency-based workforce practices are increasing capability in the organization's workforce competencies.**

> Examples of measurements of the effectiveness of competency-based workforce practices include the following:
> - Staff ratings of the effectiveness of competency-based workforce practices
> - Increased level of knowledge, skills, and process ability resulting from competency-based recruiting, selection, and performance management practices
> - Effectiveness of various competency development practices and activities in increasing the capability of individuals or workgroups in the organization's workforce competencies
> - Increased level of motivation and retention resulting from competency-based career planning, compensation, and reward practices
> - Indicators of the organization's increased efficiency or quality in performing competency-based workforce activities

Verifying Implementation

Verification 1   **A responsible individual(s) verifies that competency-based workforce practices are conducted according to the organization's documented policies, practices, procedures, and, where appropriate, plans; and addresses noncompliance.**

These reviews verify that:

1. Competency-based workforce practices and activities comply with the organization's policies and stated values.

2. All actions related to competency-based workforce practices and activities are periodically reviewed to ensure that they conform to documented policies.

3. Competency-based workforce practices and activities comply with relevant laws and regulations.

4. Competency-based workforce practices and activities are performed according to the organization's documented practices and procedures.

5. Noncompliance issues are handled appropriately.

Verification 2   Executive management periodically reviews the activities implementing competency-based workforce practices, their status, and results; and resolves issues.

These reviews verify:

1. The appropriateness of competency-based workforce activities at the organizational and unit levels.

2. Progress in performing competency-based workforce activities.

3. Results from reviews of competency-based workforce practices and activities.

> Refer to Verification 1 for information regarding reviews of Competency-Based Practices activities to ensure adherence to the following:
> - Relevant laws and regulations
> - Organizational policies, practices, and procedures

4. Status of resolution of noncompliance issues.

5. Trends related to competency-based workforce practices.

6. Effectiveness of competency-based workforce practices and activities in achieving planned objectives in the organization's workforce competencies.

Workgroup Development
A process area at Maturity Level 3: Defined

Purpose
The purpose of Workgroup Development is to organize work around competency-based process abilities.

Description
As used in the People CMM, a *workgroup* is a collection of people who work closely together on tasks that are highly interdependent to achieve shared objectives. A workgroup reports to a responsible individual who may be involved in managing its day-to-day activities.

Responsible individuals analyze the work within a unit or set of related units to identify the dependencies among tasks. Work can then be designed around workgroups that maximize the interdependency of tasks within the workgroup and minimize dependencies with other workgroups.

The organization defines common workgroup methods and procedures to be used in performing standard activities that occur in most groups, such as problem solving or holding meetings. The workgroup tailors these processes along with those from the workforce competencies represented in the workgroup into a process to be used in planning and performing its business activities. Workgroups tailor the defined roles that must be performed within its processes and assign them to workgroup members.

Workgroup members work with each other to coordinate dependencies and ensure adequate flow of information. They also work on developing their workgroup skills and improve the workgroup's effectiveness. When a workgroup shares dependencies with other workgroups or organizational entities, it interacts with them to define interfaces to coordinate their activities and commitments.

A responsible individual ensures the workgroup develops documented performance objectives, and that these objectives are allocated to each of its members. Responsible individuals manage workgroup performance and track the status of work. When a workgroup's business activities are complete, it is disbanded using an orderly process that preserves its assets, completes required workforce activities, and ensures appropriate work assignments for each of its departing members.

Goals

Goal 1 **Workgroups are established to optimize the performance of interdependent work.**

Goal 2 **Workgroups tailor defined processes and roles for use in planning and performing their work.**

Goal 3 **Workgroup staffing activities focus on the assignment, development, and future deployment of the organization's workforce competencies.**

Goal 4   Workgroup performance is managed against documented objectives for committed work.

Goal 5   Workgroup Development practices are institutionalized to ensure they are performed as defined organizational processes.

Commitment to Perform

Commitment 1   The organization establishes and maintains a documented policy for conducting Workgroup Development activities.

Issues typically addressed in the policy include:

1. Workgroup Development serves the business objectives and stated values of the organization.

2. Workgroup Development activities are planned within units and are included in the strategic workforce plan.

3. Workgroups are organized to perform interdependent tasks that constitute some of the organization's business activities.

4. Procedures are defined, documented, and used for guiding the organization's Workgroup Development activities.

   These procedures typically specify:

   - how work is analyzed and designed to expedite its performance in workgroups,
   - how workgroups are staffed,
   - how workgroups establish performance objectives and work commitments,
   - how workgroup skills are developed and maintained,
   - how workgroup performance is managed, and
   - how workgroups are dissolved, when appropriate.

5. Workgroup Development practices and activities comply with relevant laws, regulations, and organizational policies.

> Human resources or other appropriate professionals are consulted to ensure that Workgroup Development activities comply with all relevant laws, regulations, and organizational policies.

Commitment 2   **An organizational role(s) is assigned responsibility for coordinating Workgroup Development activities across the organization.**

Commitment 3   **Workgroup Development activities are incorporated into the organization's strategic workforce plan and the planned workforce activities within units.**

Ability to Perform

Ability 1   **Within each unit, an individual(s) is assigned responsibility and authority for ensuring that members of the unit participate in Workgroup Development activities, as appropriate.**

Ability 2   **Adequate resources are provided for performing Workgroup Development activities.**

1. The organization's workforce competencies are defined.

> Refer to Practices 3 and 5 of the Competency Analysis process area for a description of the practices that produce descriptions of the process abilities of each of the organization's workforce competencies.

2. Workforce competency descriptions and competency-based processes are available for use in Workgroup Development activities.

> Refer to the Competency Analysis process area regarding practices that produce descriptions of the organization's workforce competencies and competency-based processes.

3. Experienced individuals who have expertise relevant to Workgroup Development are made available for developing workgroups.

> Examples of individuals with expertise in Workgroup Development include the following:
> - Human resources or other appropriate professionals
> - Training or other development staff
> - Group trainers or facilitators
> - Quality or process improvement staff
> - Individuals from successful workgroups

4. Resources for supporting Workgroup Development activities are made available. The resources provided to workgroups should be:

- selected for their support of the workgroup's defined processes,

- integrated into the defined processes and other work-related activities of the workgroup, and

- consistent across dependent workgroups to the extent possible.

> Examples of resources to support Workgroup Development activities include the following:
> - Space for group meetings
> - Furniture and other physical resources for supporting workgroup meetings and activities
> - Voice and electronic communication equipment
> - Electronic access and tools for supporting virtual workgroups
> - Transportation in support of workgroup activities
> - Workgroup management tools and resources
> - Workgroup planning and estimating tools
> - Tools for managing process and role definitions

5. Funding to accomplish Workgroup Development activities is made available.

6. Adequate time is made available for training and facilitation in workgroup skills.

Ability 3 **Responsible individual(s) to whom the members of a workgroup are accountable develop the knowledge, skills, and process abilities needed to manage workgroups.**

> Examples of relevant workgroup management skills in which responsible individuals might be trained include the following:
> - Establishing performance objectives for a workgroup's committed work that are drawn from the unit's performance objectives
> - Technical and competence-based aspects of the work assigned to a workgroup
> - Competency-based roles and processes
> - Procedures for estimating, planning, and tracking group work based on defined workgroup roles and processes
> - Methods for applying workforce activities, such as staffing, performance management, recognition and reward, and competency development, to workgroups
> - Methods for managing the performance of individuals within the workgroup context
> - Methods for coaching and facilitating workgroups

Ability 4 **Workgroup members receive appropriate guidance or training in work-group skills.**

> Examples of relevant workgroup skills may include the following:
> - Workgroup formation and member selection
> - Stages of workgroup development
> - Tailoring competency-based workgroup processes
> - Role and task definition
> - Group dynamics
> - Workgroup leadership and decision making
> - Establishing and managing workgroup performance objectives
> - Workgroup communication and coordination
> - Resolving workgroup problems and conflicts
> - Cross-training in various roles and responsibilities

Ability 5 **The practices and procedures for performing Workgroup Development are defined and documented.**

1. Practices and procedures are defined and documented at the organizational or unit levels, as appropriate.

2. Guidelines for tailoring the practices and procedures for use in different circumstances are documented and made available, as necessary.

3. The individual(s) assigned responsibility for coordinating Workgroup Development activities across the organization ensures that defined practices and procedures are:

   - maintained under version control,
   - disseminated through appropriate media,
   - interpreted appropriately for different situations, and
   - updated through orderly methods.

4. Experiences, lessons learned, measurement results, and improvement information derived from planning and performing Workgroup Development practices are captured to support the future use and improvement of the organization's practices.

Practices Performed

Practice 1   The committed work within a unit is analyzed to identify its process dependencies.

    1. Those responsible for the performance of a unit analyze its committed work to identify the dependencies required to accomplish it.

> Examples of sources of dependencies in a unit's committed work include the following:
> - Competency-based process abilities of those performing the work
> - Defined workflows and other processes within the organization
> - Dependencies shared with individuals or workgroups in other units
> - Work rules captured in automated systems
> - Knowledge of those performing the unit's work

    2. The process dependencies within a unit's committed work are documented.

Practice 2   Committed work is structured to optimize the coordination and performance of interdependent work within workgroups.

    1. Committed work is organized and allocated to workgroups to:

        ■ ensure each workgroup performs a defined collection of interdependent tasks,

        ■ ensure no workgroup is assigned more work than it can accomplish,

        ■ optimize the gathering of task dependencies within a workgroup,

        ■ minimize task dependencies across workgroups, and

        ■ ensure coordination of task dependencies with workgroups in other units.

    2. Workgroups are organized to perform a defined collection of interdependent tasks.

    3. The committed work in a unit is periodically reevaluated to determine whether it continues to be allocated across workgroups in a way that optimizes the coordination and performance of interdependent work.

Practice 3   Each workgroup is formed to perform a defined set of business activities and to accomplish defined objectives.

> Workgroups are frequently composed of people from a single unit. Even when contained within one unit, workgroups may occasionally include one or two members from other units who are required for specific tasks. However, workgroups can form outside unit boundaries with members from several units. When workgroup membership extends to several units, workgroup reporting and accountability must avoid creating conflicts between individual and workgroup reporting relationships.

1. A responsible individual(s) organizes each workgroup to perform a set of defined business activities.

> Refer to Practices 9 and 13 of this process area for information regarding how workgroup performance objectives may be established and documented through the workgroup planning process, and how the workgroup establishes performance objectives with the manager or supervisor to whom it reports.

2. Each workgroup is chartered to perform a documented set of business activities and to accomplish defined objectives.

> Topics addressed in the charter for a workgroup typically include the following:
> - Workgroup purpose
> - Assigned business activities
> - Defined objectives
> - Detailed responsibilities, where applicable
> - Boundaries
> - Resources available
> - Identification of the individuals responsible for tracking and managing workgroup performance

3. Each workgroup's assigned business activities and objectives are periodically reviewed to ensure:

   - the activity of the workgroup remains aligned with its chartered business activities and objectives,
   - the workgroup's business activities and objectives remain aligned with the organization's objectives, and
   - corrective action is taken to address misalignments.

Practice 4   **Methods and procedures for performing common workgroup functions are defined and maintained for use by workgroups.**

> Although workgroups will differ in the competencies composing them and the responsibilities they are assigned, they nevertheless perform some common activities for which the organization can provide common methods and procedures. Examples of common workgroup functions performed by workgroups include the following:
> - Negotiating work commitments
> - Maintaining awareness of the status and progress of work commitments
> - Brainstorming
> - Problem solving
> - Resolving conflicts

1. Methods, procedures, and tailoring guidelines for performing common workgroup functions are established and maintained.

> Examples of artifacts to be maintained to support common workgroup methods and procedures include the following:
> - Method or procedure definitions
> - Templates and forms
> - Tailoring guidelines for use in adapting the methods and procedures for use in different types of workgroups
> - Sample artifacts produced in applying the methods and procedures
> - Materials for training the methods and procedures
> - Case studies of how the methods and procedures have been applied

2. Information regarding defined workgroup methods and procedures is communicated and made available.

> Examples of mechanisms for communicating defined workgroup methods and procedures and making them available include the following:
> - Intranet or other electronic means
> - Manuals
> - Workgroup facilitators

3. Defined workgroup methods and procedures are periodically reviewed and revised to ensure the best workgroup practices continue to be propagated throughout the organization.

Practice 5   **The competencies required to perform a workgroup's business activities are identified.**

1. Before a workgroup is formed, the workforce competencies needed to perform the workgroup's business activities are identified.

2. The workforce competencies required to perform the workgroup's business activities are documented and made available for use in staffing, performance management, training, and other workforce activities related to the workgroup.

3. The workforce competencies included in a workgroup are reevaluated whenever the processes, technologies, products, or services associated with a workgroup are significantly redefined.

Practice 6   **Staffing processes are performed to ensure that workgroups are staffed with individuals whose competencies match those needed to perform the workgroup's business activities.**

1. Individuals to whom workgroups report incorporate workforce competency information into workgroup staffing processes.

> Examples of workforce competency-related information to be incorporated into a workgroup's position descriptions, selection processes, and criteria for evaluating candidates include the following:
>
> - Workforce competencies related to the business activities assigned to the workgroup
> - Ability to work in a group environment
> - Ability to coordinate with individuals possessing other workforce competencies
> - Ability to fulfill a specific role responsibility in the workgroup, such as team leader or intergroup liaison
> - Ability to acquire additional competency related to the workgroup's business activities
> - Contribution to the individual's competency development and career objectives

2. When appropriate, workgroup members are involved in recruiting candidates with appropriate workforce competencies for open positions.

> Typically, workgroup members are involved in staffing processes and decisions. Examples of occasions when workgroup members may not be involved in staffing processes and decisions include the following:
>
> - When management is initially assigning a set of individuals to form a workgroup
> - When an individual is being assigned to perform a temporary role in the workgroup
> - When an individual with a unique competency is being assigned by another group to fill a specific competency-based role in the workgroup, such as finance or quality assurance

3. When appropriate, workgroup members are involved in executing a selection process for evaluating the competencies and other qualifications of candidates for open positions in the workgroup.

> Examples of non-competency-related information that may be incorporated into workgroup selection processes and decisions include the following:
>
> - Existing work load and time available to fulfill workgroup responsibilities
> - Anticipated fit with other members of the workgroup
> - Other organizational staffing goals

4. When appropriate, workgroup members are involved in selection decisions.

5. The workgroup is involved in orienting new members to the workgroup's processes, commitments, and other members.

Practice 7 **Workgroups tailor competency-based processes for performing their business activities.**

> In order to improve coordination within a workgroup beyond what can be achieved solely through good interpersonal skills, a workgroup must define a set of operating processes for coordinating their work. Frequently, workgroups are composed of members from a single workforce competency (e.g., a software development team, a sales team, or a financial audit team), and individual members fill roles typically structured by the process abilities defined within their competency.
>
> At the Defined Level, workgroup processes typically revolve around the process abilities within workforce competencies, and occasionally require coordinated interfaces between processes performed by individuals from different competencies.

> However, individuals from a different competency are occasionally assigned to fill a role in a workgroup. In such cases, members from a different competency often fulfill "staff" functions affiliated with the workgroup rather than functioning as integral members. For instance, a finance specialist managing the budget for a product development project plays a role primarily defined by their competency in finance. How they perform most of their processes within the workgroup is defined by the process abilities of their competency in finance. In performing their role, they coordinate their financial activities with the rest of the workgroup based on dependencies in the product development process for financial information or actions.

1. Workgroup members sharing a common workforce competency jointly:

   - analyze the workgroup's assigned responsibilities to determine activities and results for which they will most likely be accountable,

   - compare competency-based processes from their workforce competency to the activities and results for which they will most likely be accountable,

   - select among the alternatives and tailor competency-based processes to best support the workgroup's performance,

   - document the competency-based processes to be used in supporting the workgroup's performance and any tailoring required to make the processes more fit for use, and

- periodically review the tailored competency-based processes to ensure they continue to support workgroup performance and take corrective action where concerns are detected.

> When workgroup members are from different workforce competencies, individuals from each competency select and tailor processes from their workforce competency for use in guiding their contributions to the workgroup. Thus, the different members of a workgroup may be following different competency-based processes in performing their work. Each member follows the competency-based processes associated with their workforce competency.

2. When a workgroup is composed of members from different workforce competencies, they should:

   - review and agree on the competency-based processes being employed by members from each competency, and
   - mutually define interfaces between their competency-based processes for coordinating work dependencies.

3. The workgroup documents its operating processes which include:

> A *workgroup's operating processes* at the Defined Level are composed from the collection of tailored competency-based processes and common workgroup methods and procedures selected for use within the workgroup. A workgroup's operating processes are used for:
> - Guiding the activities of workgroup members
> - Orienting new workgroup members
> - Understanding and evaluating the process performance of the workgroup

   - the competency-based processes tailored by members of the workgroup from their workforce competencies,
   - mutually defined interfaces between competency-based processes, and
   - choices among common workgroup methods and procedures defined by the organization for performing common workgroup functions.

Practice 8 **Roles for performing the workgroup's operating processes are defined and allocated to individuals.**

> When a workgroup method, a procedure, or a competency-based process is too large to be performed by a single individual, it must be divided into work packages called roles. A *role* is a defined set of work tasks, dependencies, and responsibilities that can be assigned to an individual as a work package. A role describes a collection of tasks that constitute one component of a procedure or process, whereas an assignment consists of one or more roles whose performance constitutes an individual's committed work. A role is distinguished from an individual's assignment within the workgroup, which consists of performing one or more roles.

1. The roles necessary to perform the tailored competency-based processes or common workgroup methods and procedures required to accomplish a workgroup's business activities are defined.

> Descriptions of predefined roles are often incorporated into definitions of competency-based or common workgroup methods and procedures. For competency-based processes, process elements are gathered into clusters of related tasks that can be assigned as a role to one or more individuals possessing the competency. Roles defined in common workgroup methods and procedures can be assigned to any member of the workgroup trained to perform the tasks composing the role. Individuals may perform more than one role as part of their contribution to the workgroup.
>
> If roles are not defined within competency-based or common workgroup methods and procedures, then the elements of these processes must be organized into defined roles. Roles may be specific to competency-based processes or to common workgroup methods and procedures, or may be a combination of both. As the organization learns more about how these roles evolve in workgroups, it may incorporate them into the definitions of competency-based or common workgroup methods and procedures. Well-defined roles can be reused by other workgroups when performing similar processes.
>
> When some tasks required to accomplish the workgroup's committed objectives are not defined in competency-based or common workgroup methods and procedures, then they must be organized and allocated among workgroup members as individual roles.

2. Defined roles are tailored for use within the context of the workgroup's business activities.

> Examples of activities through which role descriptions are tailored and elaborated for use include the following:
> - Tailoring competency-based processes
> - Tailoring common workgroup methods and procedures
> - Workgroup planning
> - Defining workgroup or individual performance objectives
> - Reviewing individual or workgroup performance
> - Performing process analyses
> - Coordinating activities among workgroup members

3. A responsible individual(s) allocates roles among members of the workgroup.

> The individual to whom a workgroup reports is responsible for ensuring that its roles are defined and assigned appropriately. However, responsible managers can delegate this responsibility to another individual, such as a team leader or workgroup facilitator, or to the workgroup itself. Individuals should only be allocated roles they can be expected to accomplish within the limits of their competency and available effort. Examples of reasons behind role assignments to individuals may include the following:
> - Competency or experience in the tasks assigned to the role
> - Balancing of work across individuals
> - Cross-training in the workgroup's business activities
> - Competency or career development

4. Each workgroup member's assignment is documented as the combination of roles allocated to them.

> Example forms in which assignments may be documented include the following:
> - Position descriptions
> - Workgroup planning documents
> - Agreements for coordinating work dependencies
> - Performance objectives for committed work

5. A responsible individual(s) periodically analyzes the performance of workgroups to ensure that no individual is overloaded with roles.

6. A responsible individual(s) periodically analyzes the performance of workgroups to ensure defined roles are not overloaded with tasks.

Practice 9   Workgroup activities and commitments are planned.

1. Workgroups plan how they will accomplish the business activities assigned to them.

   Workgroup planning typically addresses:

   ■ performance commitments,

   ■ competency-based processes and common workgroup methods and procedures tailored for use by the workgroup,

   ■ roles to be performed,

   ■ work dependencies within the workgroup, or with other workgroups or organizational entities,

   ■ descriptions of work products or services,

   ■ schedules and budgets,

   ■ resources required,

   ■ how risks will be identified and handled,

   ■ measures of process performance, and

   ■ necessary management and support activities.

   > Examples of information from which a workgroup's plans can be developed include the following:
   > • Assigned responsibilities
   > • Descriptions of products or services
   > • Descriptions of competency-based processes or common workgroup methods and procedures
   > • Work breakdown structures
   > • Previously constructed plans by workgroups assigned similar responsibilities
   > • Historical data on workgroup and task performance

2. Members of the workgroup agree to:

   ■ their individual commitments to the workgroup,

   ■ the workgroup's commitments to other workgroups, its own unit, or other entities in the organization, and

   > When members of a workgroup individually or collectively do not believe they can accomplish the business activities assigned to them within the parameters (e.g., time, budget, quality, etc.) specified, they must negotiate work responsibilities until they arrive at commitments they believe they can meet.

- changes to individual or workgroup commitments.

> These commitments serve as the basis for establishing measurable performance objectives for the workgroup. Refer to Practice 13 for information regarding establishing the workgroup's performance objectives and tracking and managing workgroup performance against these objectives.

3. A workgroup's plan is reviewed to ensure:

   - it satisfies the responsibilities assigned to the workgroup,
   - the commitments are achievable,
   - the workgroup's dependencies with other entities in the organization are coordinated,
   - workloads are balanced across the workgroup, and
   - no individual's performance commitments to the workgroup are in jeopardy because of work commitments to this or other workgroups or organizational entities.

4. Workgroup plans are documented.

> Examples of how a workgroup's plan can be documented include the following:
> - As a separate workgroup plan
> - As a component of a project or unit plan
> - As performance objectives at the individual, workgroup, or unit levels
> - As a component of a documented workflow
> - As a contribution to the work of a unit or higher organizational entity

Practice 10   **Workgroup members establish mechanisms for communicating information and coordinating dependencies among roles.**

1. Workgroup members identify the dependencies among their role responsibilities.

2. Workgroup members agree on how they will coordinate work processes and products to satisfy their dependencies, and these agreements are documented during such activities as:

   - the tailoring of competency-based or common workgroup methods and procedures to create the workgroup's operating processes,
   - workgroup planning, or
   - the definition and allocation of roles.

3. When subsets of workgroup members are using different competency-based processes, they define interfaces between roles in different competencies to ensure the coordination necessary for meeting the workgroup's performance objectives.

4. Workgroups define methods for coordinating the flow of information required by the workgroup's operating processes and role responsibilities.

5. Workgroups determine the frequency with which meetings are needed to share information, maintain coordination, and track status.

6. Workgroup members ensure they have a common understanding of the terms and representations they use in communicating.

7. Workgroup members coordinate with each other to ensure that gaps or other problems in their workgroup's operating processes are handled.

8. Workgroups periodically review their performance to identify and correct problems such as:

   ■ breakdowns in communication and coordination of dependencies,

   ■ breakdowns, gaps, or inefficiencies in defined processes,

   ■ overloaded role responsibilities, or

   ■ workload imbalances across individuals.

Practice 11 **Skills needed to perform jointly as a workgroup using the workgroup's operating processes are developed.**

> This practice focuses on development needs specific to the workgroup in such areas as the workgroup's operating processes, the organization's common workgroup methods and procedures, workgroup dynamics, workflow, coordination, and competency-based processes defined or tailored at the workgroup level.
>
> Refer to the Competency Development process area for information focused on individual development in the organization's workforce competencies and to Practice 7 of the Communication and Coordination process area for information regarding individuals' development of interpersonal communication skills.

> Examples of the responsible individual(s) who interacts with the workgroup to manage the workgroup's development needs include the following:
> - The individual to whom the workgroup reports
> - An individual from the training or development function
> - An expert in workgroup or team development
> - An individual from the human resources function or other appropriate professionals

1. As the workgroup is initiated, a responsible individual identifies any needs for training and development, based on:

   - individual workgroup members' capability to perform the workgroup's operating processes,
   - the specific tailoring of competency-based or common workgroup methods and procedures for use within the workgroup as the workgroup's operating processes, and
   - the roles that individuals have been assigned to fulfill.

2. A responsible individual analyzes the workgroup's performance to determine its development needs.

Factors to evaluate in analyzing workgroup performance may include the following:
- Workgroup performance against objective performance criteria
- How the work is organized and carried out by the workgroup
- Peer reviews by people external to the workgroup
- Workgroup self-evaluation
- Appropriate quality and productivity metrics
- Skill development needs for existing workgroup members (both individual competency development needs and needs for development of workgroup knowledge, skills, and process abilities)
- Performance improvement against baselines
- The contribution of the workgroup to the performance of the unit and the organization

---

3. Working with a responsible individual, the workgroup documents a plan for its development activities that includes:

   - development objectives for the workgroup,
   - specific development actions to achieve these objectives,
   - the schedule for performing the unit's Workgroup Development activities, and
   - development activities that support the organization's strategic workforce plan.

4. The workgroup performs its development activities.

5. A responsible individual(s):

   - reviews the accomplishment of the workgroup's development activities and the impact of these development activities on workgroup behavior and performance,
   - documents completed development activities, and
   - recommends corrective action when development activities do not achieve their intended objectives.

Practice 12   **Workgroups that share dependencies define interfaces through which their activities and commitments are coordinated.**

1. Workgroups identify the dependencies they share with other workgroups or organizational entities.

2. Dependent workgroups or their representatives interact to:

   - plan activities that satisfy their dependencies,

   - review and agree to their mutual commitments,

   - raise and resolve issues in their work,

   - coordinate their activities as necessary,

   - jointly monitor progress toward satisfying dependencies,

   - take corrective action as necessary when dependencies are in jeopardy, and

   - improve conditions and processes that affect their mutual work.

3. Problems or issues that cannot be resolved among dependent workgroups are handled according to a documented procedure.

> Unresolved issues can be raised to management, submitted to an arbitration group, or addressed by a documented method that is appropriate to the type of issue and is approved by management. Examples of intergroup issues include the following:
> - Incompatible schedules
> - Poorly synchronized processes
> - Different rates of progress
> - Technical issues
> - Risks
> - Quality problems
> - Unplanned dependencies

Practice 13   **A responsible individual(s) tracks and manages workgroup performance.**

> Managing workgroup performance is separate from managing the performance of individual workgroup members. In practice, many of the activities for managing the performance of individuals and of workgroups may occur in close temporal proximity and may be performed by the same individual. However, workgroups need performance feedback on their performance as workgroups, on their coordination, and on their collective actions; rather than on their individual performance. This practice supplements, but does not replace, the Performance Management practices and Competency-Based Practices performed for individuals.

1. The workgroup establishes performance objectives with the manager or supervisor to whom it reports.

> Refer to Practice 9 for information regarding how these workgroup performance objectives may be established and documented through the workgroup planning process.

2. Responsible individuals ensure that:

   - each individual's performance objectives are aligned with the performance objectives of the workgroup,

   - personal development plans do not conflict with the performance objectives of the workgroup, and

   - the workgroup's performance objectives are aligned with those of other workgroups or organizational entities with which it shares dependencies.

3. The individual to whom the workgroup reports maintains an awareness of its performance.

> Examples of means to maintain awareness of workgroup performance may include the following:
> - Tracking performance against plan
> - Reviewing performance data
> - Reviewing measures of process performance
> - Maintaining awareness of technical issues and decisions
> - Reviewing risks to performance
> - Attending status review meetings
> - Reviewing individual or workgroup progress reports
> - Contacting customers of the workgroup's products or services
> - Contacting other workgroups with which it shares dependencies

4. The individual to whom the workgroup reports maintains ongoing communication with the workgroup about its performance.

> Ongoing communication about workgroup performance involves more than just formal progress review meetings, but should also consist of informal discussions of workgroup performance with some or all members. When conducted with individual members of the workgroup, a mix of individual and workgroup performance can be discussed. Other examples of mechanisms for maintaining ongoing communication with individuals within the workgroup and with the workgroup include the following:
> - Management by walking around (MBWA)
> - Workgroup staff meetings
> - Frequent informal meetings
> - Ongoing interactions with individuals and groups

5. A responsible individual(s) facilitates the workgroup in evaluating the individual and collective performance of its members.

> This responsible individual may be the individual to whom the workgroup reports or may be someone outside the group with expertise in workgroup development.

6. When workgroups share work dependencies, their mutual performance is tracked and managed by an individual(s) with responsibility for their collective performance.

> An example of a mechanism to track performance when workgroups share work dependencies is to hold status reviews of coordinated intergroup performance. When held, these status reviews of coordinated intergroup performance typically:
> - Involve all affected groups or stakeholders
> - Review technical, cost, staffing, and schedule performance against workgroup plans
> - Identify corrective actions, if necessary
> - Review coordination of dependencies between groups
> - Address conflicts and issues not resolvable at lower levels
> - Review and manage risks
> - Ensure that action items are assigned, reviewed, and tracked to closure
> - Are terminated by a summary report from each meeting which is prepared and distributed to all affected groups

7. Responsible individuals ensure that workgroups have the information they need to perform their committed work.

8. The individual to whom the workgroup reports periodically provides formal feedback to the workgroup about its performance according to a documented procedure.

> The workgroup and the individual to whom they report develop an agreement as to the method and schedule by which formal feedback is provided. Examples of vehicles through which formal feedback can be provided to workgroups include the following:
> - Formal progress reviews
> - 360° review by stakeholders in the workgroup performance
> - Workgroup performance reviews scheduled separately from progress reviews

9. The individual to whom the workgroup reports works with the workgroup to discuss and resolve problems.

> Examples of problems to be resolved include the following:
> - Resource allocation issues
> - Internal workgroup conflicts
> - Breakdowns in coordination with other workgroups or units
> - Overloaded assignments
> - Conflicting priorities

10. When problems occur in workgroup performance, a responsible individual works with the workgroup to:

   - accurately describe the performance problem,
   - identify the causes of the performance problem,
   - decide on corrective action,
   - manage individual performance problems that contribute to problems in workgroup performance,
   - track the workgroup's implementation of corrective action,
   - provide continuing feedback on progress in correcting the performance problem, and
   - take further actions if workgroup performance does not improve.

11. Outstanding workgroup performance is recognized or rewarded.

12. Adjustments to each individual's compensation are based, in part, on their contribution to workgroup performance.

Practice 14   Workgroups are disbanded through an orderly performance of workforce activities.

1. Workgroups are made aware of the conditions under which their business activities are deemed to be complete.

2. A responsible individual discusses future assignments with each member of a disbanding workgroup.

3. When possible, future assignments are determined before a workgroup is disbanded.

4. Decisions about future assignments incorporate inputs concerning:

   - personal development plans,
   - competency development needs and activities,
   - career development issues,
   - competency needs of other workgroups or organizational entities,

- transfer of knowledge, skills, or process abilities to other individuals or workgroups in the organization, and
- the strategic workforce plan.

5. Transition among assignments is planned to minimize disruption to individuals' competency and career development activities.

> Refer to Practice 14 of the Staffing process area for information regarding transitioning between positions.

6. A responsible individual reviews workgroup performance with the members of the workgroup.

7. Performance management activities are completed before members separate from a disbanding workgroup.

> The disbanding of a workgroup may not correspond with scheduled formal performance management activities. To ensure that contemporaneous information about each individual's performance is retained, examples of individual performance management activities to be completed before the workgroup disbands include the following:
> - Recording the results of individual performance against objectives
> - Evaluating individual contribution to workgroup performance
> - Documenting accomplishments in personal development plans
> - Assessing performance against an individual's improvement plan
> - Providing rewards or recognition for outstanding performance

8. Orientation activities are planned and conducted to prepare members of disbanding workgroups for their new assignments.

Practice 15 **When workgroups disband, their assets are captured for redeployment.**

1. Prior to the completion of the workgroup's business activities, a responsible individual(s) works with the workgroup to:

- plan the process for disbanding the workgroup,
- capture and archive lessons learned about products, processes, or workforce practices, and
- prepare and archive appropriate work products.

2. The residual assets of the workgroup's activities are disposed of appropriately through such means as being:

- delivered to internal or external customers,
- deployed to other workgroups,
- returned to original owners,
- archived for future use or reference, or
- securely destroyed.

Measurement and Analysis

Measurement 1   **Measurements are made and used to determine the status and performance of Workgroup Development activities across the organization.**

Examples of measurements include the following:
- Number of workgroups and people involved in workgroups
- Average number of workgroups that individuals contribute to
- Profiles of competency mixtures across workgroups
- Time spent in training for workgroup-related skills
- Time spent developing workgroup plans and tailored processes
- Timeliness of performing workforce activities in workgroups
- Effectiveness of workgroups in meeting their milestones and other performance objectives
- Effectiveness with which dependent workgroups satisfy their dependencies
- Effectiveness in achieving the objectives of the strategic workforce plan
- Common issues and trends determined by analyzing lessons learned from disbanding workgroups

Measurement 2   **Measures of workgroup development are collected and aggregated at the organizational level.**

1. A historical database of workgroup development and performance data is maintained.

2. Workgroup development data are periodically analyzed to determine trends.

Measurement 3   **Measurements are made and used to determine the effectiveness of Workgroup Development activities.**

Verifying Implementation

Verification 1   A responsible individual(s) verifies that Workgroup Development activities are conducted according to the organization's documented policies, practices, procedures, and, where appropriate, plans; and addresses noncompliance.

These reviews verify that:

1. Workgroup development activities comply with the organization's policies and stated values.

2. Workgroup development activities comply with relevant laws and regulations.

3. Workgroup development activities are performed according to the organization's documented practices and procedures.

4. Noncompliance issues are handled appropriately.

5. Workgroup development activities are kept current and reflect existing and anticipated organizational conditions and needs.

Verification 2   Executive management periodically reviews the Workgroup Development activities, status, and results; and resolves issues.

These reviews verify:

1. The appropriateness of Workgroup Development activities.

2. Progress in performing Workgroup Development activities.

3. Results from reviews of Workgroup Development practices and activities.

> Refer to Verification 1 for practices regarding reviews of Workgroup Development activities to ensure adherence to the following:
> - Relevant laws and regulations
> - Organizational policies, practices, and procedures

4. Status of resolution of noncompliance issues.

5. Trends in workgroup development compared to objectives in the strategic workforce plan.

6. Effectiveness of Workgroup Development activities in achieving the objectives in the strategic workforce plan.

Participatory Culture
A process area at Maturity Level 3: Defined

Purpose
The purpose of a Participatory Culture is to enable the workforce's full capability for making decisions that affect the performance of business activities.

Description
The open communication established with Communication and Coordination practices at the Managed Level creates a foundation for developing a participatory culture. A participatory culture provides an environment in which competent professionals are fully able to exercise their capabilities. This participative environment ensures a flow of information within the organization, incorporates the knowledge of individuals into decision-making processes, and gains their support for commitments. Establishing a participatory culture lays the foundation for building high-performance workgroups and for empowering workgroups at the Predictable Level.

Establishing a participatory culture begins with providing individuals and workgroups with information about organizational and unit performance, and how their performance contributes. Individuals and workgroups are provided access to the information needed to perform their committed work. Information and communication systems support these information needs.

The structure of decision-making processes is analyzed across the organization and appropriate roles are defined. Based on this analysis, decisions are delegated to an appropriate location in the organization that balances competence, coordination, and speed. Once made by appropriate individuals, decisions are supported by others in the organization. Individuals participate in decisions that affect their work and work environment. Individuals and workgroups use defined processes for making decisions and resolving conflicts and disputes.

Goals

Goal 1   **Information about business activities and results is communicated throughout the organization.**

Goal 2   **Decisions are delegated to an appropriate level of the organization.**

Goal 3   **Individuals and workgroups participate in structured decision-making processes.**

Goal 4   **Participatory Culture practices are institutionalized to ensure they are performed as defined organizational processes.**

Commitment to Perform

Commitment 1   **The organization's stated values encourage open communication and participation in decision making by individuals and workgroups, when appropriate.**

> Refer to Commitment 1 of the Communication and Coordination process area for information regarding the establishment and communication of organizational values, and the types of workforce issues that might be covered in the organization's stated values.

Commitment 2   **The organization establishes and maintains a documented policy for its activities that supports the development of a participatory culture.**

Issues typically addressed in the policy include:

1. Activities that support development of a participatory culture serve the business objectives and stated values of the organization.

2. Individuals and workgroups participate in decision-making processes affecting their work.

3. Information about organizational and business performance is shared across the organization.

4. There is an environment of open communication across levels and among individuals and workgroups within the organization.

5. Open communication appropriately considers the cultural values and diversity present in the workforce.

6. Individuals and workgroups are actively encouraged and supported to assume appropriate responsibility and authority by participating in decision-making processes.

7. Activities that support development of a participatory culture comply with relevant laws, regulations, and organizational policies.

Commitment 3   **An organizational role(s) is assigned responsibility for coordinating the organization's activities for developing a participatory culture.**

> Examples of individuals who might be assigned responsibilities for activities that support development of a participatory culture include the following:
> - Executive management
> - Staff assistants
> - Committees
> - Human resources or other appropriate professionals
> - Organizational development specialists

Ability to Perform

Ability 1   Within each unit, an individual(s) is assigned responsibility and authority to ensure that the performance of business and workforce activities within the unit contributes to developing a participatory culture.

Ability 2   Adequate resources are provided for performing activities that support development of a participatory culture.

1. Strategic and operational business objectives are defined and made available.

2. Performance results are collected at the organizational and unit levels.

3. Experienced individuals who have expertise in areas such as decision analysis and communication are made available.

4. Resources that contribute to a participatory culture are made available.

> Examples of resources supporting participatory activities include the following:
> - Information
> - Information systems
> - Internal publications
> - Decision aids

5. Adequate support is made available for participatory activities.

> Examples of participatory activities include the following:
> - Decision-making processes
> - Communication processes
> - Conflict resolution processes

6. Adequate funding is made available for resources that contribute to a participatory culture.

Ability 3   Managers develop the knowledge, skills, and process abilities needed to perform their responsibilities regarding communication and participatory management.

> Examples of relevant topics in which managers may be trained include the following:
> - Commitment processes
> - Consensus-building skills
> - Participatory management techniques
> - Decision-making techniques
> - Group problem-solving techniques
> - Listening skills
> - Information analysis and communication techniques
> - Work coordination techniques

Ability 4   Individuals and groups who participate in Participatory Culture activities receive the preparation in problem-solving and decision-making processes, methods, and skills appropriate to the types of decisions they will participate in making.

Ability 5   The practices and procedures for developing a participatory culture are defined and documented.

1. Practices and procedures may be defined and documented at the organizational and/or unit levels, as appropriate.

2. Guidelines for tailoring the practices and procedures for use in different circumstances are documented and made available as necessary.

3. The individual(s) assigned responsibility for coordinating activities to develop a participatory culture across the organization ensures that defined practices and procedures are:

   - maintained under version control,
   - disseminated through appropriate media,
   - interpreted appropriately for different situations, and
   - updated through orderly methods.

4. Experiences, lessons learned, measurement results, and improvement information derived from planning and performing the practices for developing a participatory culture are captured to support the future use and improvement of the organization's practices.

Practices Performed

Practice 1   Information about organizational and unit performance is made available to individuals and workgroups.

1. Management at each level of the organization identifies information about organizational and unit performance that would assist individuals, workgroups, or units in aligning their decisions and business activities with that level's business objectives or commitments.

> Examples of information on organizational performance that could be made available to individuals, workgroups, or units include the following:
> - Business objectives and strategy
> - Performance objectives of their unit, other units, and the organization
> - Financial results and projections
> - Information about costs and expenses
> - Production data and results
> - Quality objectives and results
> - Workforce attitude results
> - Customer satisfaction and related information
> - Marketing, sales, and related information

2. Designated information about organizational and unit performance is:

   - summarized at an appropriate level of detail for use by individuals, workgroups, or units,
   - communicated to individuals, workgroups, or units using methods that make the information readily accessible and useful for decision making or other business activities, and
   - revised with a frequency appropriate to the rate of change for each type of information.

3. The workforce is made aware of the extent to which different forms of performance information must be treated as confidential.

Practice 2   Individuals and workgroups are made aware of how their work performance contributes to unit and organizational performance.

1. Individual performance feedback is presented in the context of workgroup, unit, and organizational performance.

2. Workgroup performance feedback is presented in the context of unit and organizational performance.

3. Links among individual, workgroup, unit, and organizational performance are explained.

4. Links between organizational performance and the achievement of organizational business objectives are communicated and reinforced.

Practice 3   Individuals and workgroups have access to information needed to perform their committed work.

1. Individuals and workgroups identify information:

    ■ they need for performing their work, and

    ■ others need from them.

> Examples of sources for identifying needed information include the following:
> * Assigned tasks and responsibilities
> * Standard processes
> * Workgroup coordination
> * Assigned or assumed roles
> * Dependencies within a workflow

2. Individuals and workgroups identify the most effective mechanisms for transferring needed information.

3. Individuals and workgroups coordinate with information sources to ensure timely access to required information.

4. Managers and supervisors ensure that the information requirements of those they supervise are satisfied.

5. Competency-based experience and information captured within a competency community is made available to other individuals or workgroups that have a need for this information.

Practice 4   Information and communication systems support the information needs of individuals and workgroups.

> These information and communication technologies extend beyond the basic functions of the management information systems used for managing the business. The purpose of these information technologies is to make management information accessible to every individual or workgroup who can use it for making faster and more accurate decisions. The purpose of the communication technologies described in this practice is to broaden and accelerate the flow of information needed to enhance work performance and the speed and accuracy of decisions.

1. Within boundaries defined by organizational, budgetary, and relevant technical considerations, information and communication technologies are provided to individuals and workgroups to support their information and communication needs.

2. Individuals and workgroups participate in the selection and design of information and communication technologies to ensure their needs are met.

3. Information and communication technologies are:

    ■ implemented to meet the needs of individuals and workgroups,

    ■ maintained, and

    ■ enhanced over time, as appropriate.

4. Individuals and workgroups participate in decisions about improvements and upgrades to the information and communication technologies that they use.

Practice 5   **The structure of decision-making processes within the organization is analyzed.**

> Decision processes may be analyzed in numerous ways. The decision analysis described in this practice may occur through several mechanisms that are not necessarily concurrent. In addition, decision processes in different components or at different levels of the organization may be analyzed separately. Examples of how decision analysis processes may be applied in an organization include the following:
> - Through formal analysis of existing decision-making processes
> - As part of designing workflows and management controls
> - As part of defining workgroup processes
> - As part of defining competency-based processes
> - In policies or procedures
> - In defining roles and responsibilities
> - In establishing units or workgroups
> - In designing the organization or its components

1. Decisions to be analyzed are identified.

> Decisions to be analyzed are characterized by attributes such as the following:
> - Are recurrent
> - Affect work commitments or assignments
> - Affect career opportunities
> - Impact how work is done
> - Create or affect dependencies with other individuals or workgroups
> - Affect the work environment
> - Affect significant stakeholders who are not involved in the decision process

2. Identified decisions are analyzed to determine which roles or workgroups:

    ■ have the most relevant information for making the decision,

    ■ can make the most timely and accurate decision,

    ■ are in the best position to involve all relevant stakeholders,

- share dependencies affected by the decision,
- need to be involved in providing input to or reviewing the decision, and
- need to be informed of the results of the decision.

3. Individuals, workgroups, or units at each level of the organization are involved in analyzing decisions made at their level.

Examples of different types of decisions include the following:

- Independent decisions, which are decisions where the individual or group making the decision has full authority to make it without seeking advice or consent from anyone else
- Coordinated decisions, which are decisions where the individual or workgroup making the decision has the authority to make the decision, but only with input or approval from other parties
- Consensus decisions, which are decisions where the decision reached must be one that can be supported by a defined set of individuals or groups before it is announced

---

Practice 6   Decision-making processes and roles are defined.

1. The organization develops or adopts standard decision-making methods for use with different types of decisions.

A decision-making method is a specific procedure for making a decision that can be embedded in the work processes of an individual, workgroup, or unit. Examples of decision-making methods include the following:

- Consensus development
- Structured problem solving
- Hoshin planning or policy deployment
- Nominal group technique
- Force field analysis
- Voting or multi-voting techniques
- Brainstorming
- Delphi

2. Decision-making methods are embedded in defined processes that are appropriate for the situation or business activities being performed.

> Sources of defined processes in which decision-making methods can be embedded include the following:
> - Competency-based processes
> - Workgroup operating processes
> - Business or workflow-based processes
> - Customer-specified processes

3. Decision-making processes are defined within the context of the business activities and processes they affect.

> Decision-making processes are defined and represented in a format that is consistent with the definitions of processes within which they are embedded. Thus, decision making becomes a component of a standard competency-based or workgroup operating process.

> Elements of decision-making processes that may be defined include the following:
> - Conditions under which the need for the decision is triggered
> - Inputs needed for the decision and roles that provide them
> - Roles to be involved in the decision-making process
> - Methods for identifying root causes
> - Methods for identifying or clarifying the decision needed
> - Methods for generating alternative solutions
> - Methods for selecting appropriate solutions
> - Methods for planning to implement decisions
> - Requirements for coordination of the decision with other roles or processes that share dependencies
> - Review and approval procedures, if required
> - Communication requirements
> - Outputs of the decision-making process
> - Methods for evaluating decision outcomes
> - Methods for reconsidering previous decisions
> - How the decision-making process is integrated into competency-based, workgroup, or other business processes
> - Guidelines for tailoring the decision-making process or method
> - Methods for evaluating decisions to improve the accuracy or quality of future decisions

Practice 7   **Responsibilities for decisions are delegated to appropriate levels and locations in the organization.**

1. The most appropriate roles or workgroups for participating in and making various decisions are identified.

> Examples of criteria for identifying roles or workgroups to delegate decisions to at appropriate levels include the following:
> - Speed and timeliness
> - Availability and accuracy of information
> - Responsibility for results
> - Breadth of decision impact
> - Competency
> - Decision dependencies
> - Coordination of work processes
> - Legal responsibilities

2. Authority and responsibility for decision-making are delegated to lower levels of the organization when feasible and appropriate by the nature of the decision.

3. Executives initiate participatory decision processes by analyzing and delegating appropriate decisions at their level.

Practice 8   **Individuals and workgroups use defined decision-making processes.**

1. Standard decision-making methods, roles, and processes are tailored for their most effective use based on the characteristics of the situation in which they are used.

> Decision-making methods, roles, and processes may need to be tailored to ensure they are appropriate for use in a specific project or situation. As part of planning their work activities, individuals, workgroups, or units should perform any tailoring of decision-making processes required to involve all parties and to ensure that all parties have accurate expectations about how decisions will be reached.

> Examples of issues to be considered in tailoring decision-making processes include the following:
> - Who is accountable for the results of the decision
> - Who has information relevant to the decision
> - Who must support the decision
> - Whose work activities are affected by the decision
> - Whose activities the decision must be coordinated with
> - Who must approve the actions resulting from the decision
> - How quickly the decision must be implemented
> - Whether anyone will be disenfranchised by the decision

2. Roles in the decision-making process are assigned to appropriate individuals or workgroups in planning their work processes.

3. Those with management or supervisory responsibility for individuals or workgroups involved in decision-making processes ensure that they are prepared for their responsibilities.

> Examples of knowledge and skills that are prerequisites to exercising decision-making responsibility include the following:
> - Knowing information needed to make the decision
> - Being able to execute an appropriate decision-making process
> - Understanding the basis of the authority they exercise in making the decision
> - Understanding the limits of their empowerment for making decisions
> - Understanding how to implement the decision

4. Individuals or groups perform their roles as defined or tailored when participating in making decisions.

5. Data and other inputs relevant to a decision are provided to those involved in the decision-making process.

6. Decisions are communicated and coordinated as necessary.

7. When decisions are reconsidered, appropriate decision-making processes are used.

8. Decisions are evaluated to identify factors that could improve the speed or accuracy of the decisions, when appropriate in an individual, competency-based, workgroup, or unit work process.

> Examples of factors that could improve decision-making include the following:
> - Use of different decision-making methods
> - More effective tailoring of decision-making processes
> - Involving fewer or more individuals or workgroups
> - More accurate or timely inputs
> - More effective coordination of concurrent decision-making processes
> - More effective or timely review or approval of decisions when required
> - More effective or timely implementation of decisions

Practice 9 **Decisions made by those empowered to make them are supported by others in the organization.**

> Decision-making processes must be defined and understood so that expectations about authority and responsibility are not violated.

1. Individuals responsible for individuals, workgroups, or units empowered to make or participate in decisions:

   - maintain awareness of decision-making processes to ensure that conditions affecting decision-making such as accuracy of inputs, level of competence or experience, and time allotted are appropriate to support accurate and timely decisions,

   - take corrective action when conditions affecting decision-making need to be improved, and

   - ensure that necessary coordination of decisions with relevant stakeholders occurs.

2. Issues or decisions that cannot be resolved according to defined decision-making processes are raised to decision-makers at higher levels for resolution.

3. When business or other conditions suggest that decisions be altered, changed, or reversed, management communicates with and involves those empowered to make the decision(s) affected.

Practice 10   **Individuals and workgroups are involved in making decisions that affect their work.**

1. When appropriate, input is sought from the workforce on important decisions affecting the whole organization.

2. Individuals or workgroups participate in developing and reviewing organizational policies, plans, and procedures that affect them.

3. Individuals or workgroups participate in making decisions about how to organize and perform their work through involvement, where appropriate, in:

   - identifying problems or issues,

   - generating alternatives,

   - selecting a solution,

   - planning the implementation of the selected solution, and

   - evaluating the results.

4. The rationale behind a decision is communicated to those affected by the decision.

Practice 11   **Individuals and groups participate in decisions concerning their work environments.**

1. Individuals and groups provide input for:

   - the arrangement of work facilities,

   - alterations or improvements to their work environment, and

   - resources needed to perform their work.

2. To the extent reasonable, individuals and groups participate in decisions about work resources and their work environment.

3. To the extent reasonable, individuals and workgroups arrange their work environment to best support their work processes.

Practice 12   **Defined mechanisms are used for resolving conflicts and disputes.**

1. The organization defines decision-making processes through which different types of conflicts or disputes can be resolved.

> Examples of different types of conflicts or disputes that should have defined processes for deciding resolution may include the following:
> - Resource contention among units or workgroups
> - Scheduling difficulties
> - Conflicts among commitments
> - Budget or other financial issues
> - Interpersonal problems
> - Personnel matters
> - Coordination problems
> - Legal or ethical issues
> - Issues involving business strategy or tactics

2. Appropriate problem-solving opportunities are made available for individuals or workgroups to resolve problems, issues, conflicts, or disputes that affect their work.

3. Conflicts and disputes are addressed through appropriate conflict and dispute resolution processes.

> Conflict and dispute resolution processes typically address the following:
> - Initiation
> - Participants and roles
> - Presentation of arguments and information
> - Decision-making procedures
> - Methods for review and appeal, if appropriate
> - Safeguards to ensure fairness, confidentiality, respect for individuals, and alignment with the organization's objectives

4. Appropriate stakeholders are involved in conflict and dispute resolution processes.

5. Results of conflict and dispute resolution processes are communicated and implemented.

Measurement and Analysis

Measurement 1   Measurements are made and used to determine the status and performance of participatory activities and trends within the organization.

Examples of measurements include the following:
- Measures of the use and coverage of information and communication technologies
- Rate at which decisions are delegated within the organization
- Rate at which decision-making processes are defined and the workforce trained in their use
- Number of people involved in decision-making processes
- Percentage of people actively engaged in participatory decision making
- Percentage of workgroups actively engaged in participatory decision making
- Percentage of units actively engaged in participatory decision making
- Effectiveness of communication mechanisms
- Amount of business information communicated to the workforce
- Number of conflict or dispute resolutions
- Results from opinion feedback mechanisms

Measurement 2   Measurements are made and used to determine the effectiveness of the participatory practices adopted in the organization.

Examples of measurements of the effectiveness of participatory practices include the following:
- Results of decisions
- Improvements in motivation and morale
- Number of people actively seeking involvement in decision making
- The quality of the information available for decisions
- The speed of making decisions
- Improvements in timeliness or accuracy of decisions over time
- The speed of implementing decisions
- Number and extent of coordination problems
- Timeliness and success of conflict or dispute resolutions

Verifying Implementation

Verification 1   A responsible individual(s) verifies that communication and decision-making activities within the organization are conducted in an open and participative manner according to the organization's values and policies; and addresses noncompliance.

These reviews verify that:

1. Communication and decision-making activities comply with the organization's policies and stated values.
2. Communication and decision-making activities comply with relevant laws and regulations.
3. Individuals and groups are involved in communication and decision-making processes, where appropriate.
4. Noncompliance issues are handled appropriately.

Verification 2   Executive management periodically reviews the level of participatory behavior and resolves issues.

These reviews verify:

1. The level of open communication, delegation of decision-making, and participatory behavior in the organization.
2. The appropriate use of business objectives and performance information.
3. The involvement of all appropriate stakeholders in decision and commitment processes.
4. Progress in performing Participatory Culture activities.
5. Results from reviews of Participatory Culture practices and activities performed to develop a participatory culture.

> Refer to Verification 1 for information regarding reviews of Participatory Culture activities to ensure adherence to the following:
> - Relevant laws and regulations
> - Organizational policies, practices, and procedures

6. Status of resolution of noncompliance issues.
7. Trends related to the development of a participatory culture.
8. Effectiveness of Participatory Culture activities in achieving the development of a participatory culture.

The Predictable Level:
Maturity Level 4

Process Areas at the Predictable Level focus on exploiting the knowledge and experience of the workforce framework developed at Maturity Level 3 to improve performance and achieve predictable outcomes. The competency-based processes used by different workforce competencies are interwoven to create integrated, multi-disciplinary processes. Workgroups are empowered to manage their own work processes and conduct some of their internal workforce activities. The artifacts produced through the performance of competency-based processes are captured and developed for reuse. Individuals and workgroups quantitatively manage the competency-based processes that are important for achieving their performance objectives. The organization manages the capability of its workforce and of the competency-based processes they perform. The effect of workforce practices on these capabilities is evaluated and corrective actions taken if necessary. Mentors use infrastructure provided by the organization's workforce competencies to assist individuals and workgroups in developing their capability. The process areas at Maturity Level 4 include:

	Process Areas
Competency Integration	381
Empowered Workgroups	395
Competency-Based Assets	413
Quantitative Performance Management	431
Organizational Capability Management	449
Mentoring	474

Competency Integration

A process area at Maturity Level 4: Predictable

Purpose

The purpose of Competency Integration is to improve the efficiency and agility of interdependent work by integrating the process abilities of different workforce competencies.

Description

An *integrated competency-based process* is one that has been integrated from the separate competency-based processes used by different workforce competencies. At the Defined Level of the People CMM, individuals used defined interfaces between their separate competency-based processes to manage mutual dependencies. At the Predictable Level, an integrated competency-based process is formed from integrating and interweaving different competency-based processes to achieve a seamless process-based interaction among individuals possessing different workforce competencies. The various workforce competencies provide knowledge, skills, and process abilities needed to support roles within an integrated business process whose process elements are drawn from the various competency-based processes. Thus, individuals possessing different workforce competencies work together using a single, integrated, multi-disciplinary process, rather than working separately using the independent processes of their respective competencies or disciplines.

These integrated competency-based processes provide for much more tightly interlaced interactions among different competency communities that allow problems among product, service, or work dependencies to be identified and corrected much earlier. When implemented properly, integrated competency-based processes can support an integrated business process management approach that implements a "customer-focused approach to the systematic management, measurement and improvement of all company processes through cross-functional teamwork and employee empowerment" [Lee 98] and help achieve the continuous flow objectives of lean process design [Womack 03]. Competency Integration shifts the focus from mastering the flow of tasks within each workforce competency to mastering the flow of tasks in the business, production, or service process. Integrated competency-based processes are often referred to as cross-functional processes, since they integrate the activities of the workforce competencies siloed within the functional departments of an organization into a single business process workflow. In the People CMM, cross-functional situations are described as multi-disciplinary as our focus is on the integration of workforce competencies (the multiple disciplines), rather than on the functional structure of the organization.

Integrated competency-based processes are beneficial to product design teams by accelerating the processes of making design decisions and identifying and correcting design problems. They are beneficial to product production teams by increasing flexibility in designing work procedures and by avoiding problems with workflows isolated within functions. They are also beneficial to service delivery teams by integrating the workforce competencies required to satisfy a customer's needs. For simplicity of expression throughout the Predictable and Optimizing maturity levels of the People CMM, the phrase "competency-based processes" will be used to refer to both the competency-based processes defined in the Competency Analysis process area and the integrated competency-based processes defined in the Competency Integration process area. Thus, "competency-based processes" could refer either to the processes of a single workforce competency, or to processes integrated from the processes of several workforce competencies.

Competency Integration involves analyzing work to identify high leverage opportunities to integrate the processes used by different workforce competencies. These integrated competency-based processes are defined and work situations are tailored for their use. Individuals involved in multi-disciplinary activities receive the preparation needed to work in a multi-disciplinary environment. Multi-disciplinary work is reviewed with regard to status, development needs, and improvement opportunities. Workforce practices and activities such as staffing, performance management, compensation, and arranging the work environment are adjusted to support multi-disciplinary work using integrated competency-based processes.

Goals

Goal 1   **The competency-based processes employed by different workforce competencies are integrated to improve the efficiency of interdependent work.**

Goal 2   **Integrated competency-based processes are used in performing work that involves dependencies among several workforce competencies.**

Goal 3   **Workforce practices are designed to support multi-disciplinary work.**

Goal 4   **Competency Integration practices are institutionalized to ensure they are performed as defined organizational processes.**

Commitment to Perform

Commitment 1   **The organization establishes and maintains a documented policy for conducting Competency Integration activities.**

Issues typically addressed in the policy include:

1. Competency Integration activities serve the business objectives and stated values of the organization.

2. Competency Integration activities are included in the organization's strategic workforce plan and the planned workforce activities within units.

3. Competency Integration activities are conducted to improve the efficiency of committed work that involves substantial dependencies among individuals possessing different workforce competencies.

4. Procedures are developed for guiding the organization's Competency Integration activities. These procedures typically specify:

- how work is to be analyzed and designed to integrate the process abilities of different workforce competencies,

- how integrated competency-based processes are defined and maintained,

- how individuals and workgroups are prepared to use integrated competency-based processes, and

- how workforce practices and activities are adjusted to support competency integration.

5. Competency Integration practices and activities comply with relevant laws, regulations, and organizational policies.

Commitment 2   An organizational role(s) is assigned responsibility for coordinating Competency Integration activities across the organization.

Ability to Perform

Ability 1   Within relevant organizational units or other entities, an individual(s) is assigned responsibility and authority for ensuring that Competency Integration activities are performed.

> When all activities for integrating multiple workforce competencies can be conducted within a single unit, such as an engineering department or a marketing and sales department, the individual(s) in charge of that unit will usually either accept or delegate responsibility for ensuring that competency integration occurs. In some instances, the workforce competencies to be integrated report into different organizational units (an engineer, a customer service representative, and a marketing specialist). In these instances, a virtual management team composed of management delegates from the different organizational units may assume responsibility for integrating multiple workforce competencies.

Ability 2   A responsible individual(s) coordinates the activities for defining, developing, and maintaining each integrated competency-based process.

Ability 3   Adequate resources are provided for performing Competency Integration activities.

1. The work processes to support each of the organization's workforce competencies have been defined.

> Refer to Practices 2 and 5 of the Competency Analysis process area for information regarding analyzing and documenting these competency-based processes.

2. Experienced individuals with expertise in process analysis and definition are available for defining integrated competency-based processes.

> Examples of individuals with expertise in process analysis and definition include the following:
> - Process owners
> - Subject matter experts
> - Business process designers or engineers
> - Process improvement or quality assurance groups
> - Organizational effectiveness or development professionals

3. Resources for supporting Competency Integration activities are made available.

> Examples of resources to support competency integration include the following:
> - Process analysis and definition tools
> - Space for integrated activities
> - Communication equipment
> - Tools for managing process and role definitions

4. Funding to accomplish Competency Integration activities is made available.

5. Adequate time is made available for defining, training, and facilitating the adoption of integrated competency-based process abilities.

Ability 4   Those involved in defining integrated competency-based processes develop the knowledge, skills, and process abilities needed to perform process analysis and definition.

Ability 5   Affected individuals and workgroups develop the knowledge, skills, and process abilities needed to perform the integrated competency-based processes involved in their work.

1. Documentation of the organization's business activities and processes is made available for analysis.

2. Preparation in integrated competency-based processes is provided to all affected individuals and workgroups.

> Preparation in integrated competency-based processes can be planned and delivered in a number of ways, including the following:
> - As competency development activities
> - As specific training and development activities in personal development plans
> - As workgroup development activities

3. Those who manage work performed through integrated competency-based processes receive the preparation needed to manage in multi-disciplinary situations.

> Examples of topics to be covered in preparing responsible individuals to manage multi-disciplinary work include the following:
>
> - Typical management approaches and techniques appropriate to each of the workforce competencies involved
> - Management techniques appropriate for multi-disciplinary or cross-functional environments
> - Techniques for adopting, deploying, and installing integrated competency-based processes
> - Diagnosing problems and improvement opportunities in multi-disciplinary work
> - Resolving conflicts among different disciplines
> - Adjusting and performing workforce practices in multi-disciplinary situations
> - Methods for continuously improving multi-disciplinary work such as Six Sigma or lean process design

4. Individuals participating in integrated competency-based processes are cross-trained, as needed, in the competency-based processes employed by other workforce competencies so that they can:

- better understand the context of integrated competency-based processes,

- develop more accurate expectations about how those possessing other workforce competencies may react under changing conditions, and

- expand their ability to fill roles in the workgroup that they would not ordinarily undertake.

5. Additional facilitation is made available, as necessary, for workgroups deploying integrated competency-based processes.

6. Additional preparation is made available, as necessary, when integrated competency-based processes are changed.

Ability 6   The practices and procedures for performing Competency Integration are defined and documented.

1. Practices and procedures are defined and documented at the organizational or unit levels, as appropriate.

2. Guidelines for tailoring the practices and procedures for use in different circumstances are documented and made available, as necessary.

3. The individual(s) assigned responsibility for Competency Integration activities across the organization ensures that defined practices and procedures are:

- maintained under version control,

- disseminated through appropriate media,

- interpreted appropriately for different situations, and
- updated through orderly methods.

4. Experiences, lessons learned, measurement results, and improvement information derived from planning and performing Competency Integration practices are captured to support the future use and improvement of the organization's practices.

Practices Performed

Practice 1   **Business activities involving dependencies among multiple workforce competencies are identified.**

1. Business activities where individuals representing two or more workforce competencies have shared dependencies or defined interfaces between their competency-based processes are identified and evaluated on such factors as:

    - how frequently they occur in ordinary business operations,
    - the opportunity to improve operating efficiency or quality by integrating their processes more tightly,
    - the frequency with which coordination problems occur in these interactions that result in poor efficiency or reduced quality, and
    - the impact that greater efficiency or accuracy in these operations would have on improving business performance, quality, or customer satisfaction.

2. The organization selects those business activities that involve multiple workforce competencies evaluated as having the most impact on its business performance as candidates for integrating their competency-based processes.

Practice 2   **Dependencies and interfaces among multiple workforce competencies are analyzed to identify opportunities for integrating their competency-based processes.**

1. Individuals who perform business activities that involve multiple competencies are involved in analyzing and integrating competency-based processes.

2. Competency-based processes used by different workforce competencies are analyzed to identify opportunities for improved efficiency such as:

    - iterative processes within or among workforce competencies that could be reduced by tighter integration among competency-based processes,
    - sequential processes within or among workforce competencies that could be performed in parallel,
    - idle time that could be eliminated by tighter integration and improved flow,
    - sources of defects that could be reduced or eliminated, and
    - joint rather than separate activities that reduce effort, lower costs, shorten schedules, reduce errors, or improve the quality of products or services.

3. Analyses are performed to identify the most efficient methods for integrating competency-based processes for each situation selected for integration.

> The most efficient methods for introducing integrated competency-based processes may differ by situation. Some situations may benefit most from integrating the processes of all involved workforce competencies at once, while other situations may require that different workforce competencies have their processes integrated in stages. For instance, the organization could decide to integrate all of the processes from different workforce competencies involved in a product deployment into an integrated, multi-disciplinary product development process from the initiation of a product development project. Alternatively, a staged integration would initially involve integrating several engineering disciplines into a multi-disciplinary design process, while other competencies maintain defined interfaces with the team's development process. Over time, these other competencies such as field service, customer training, or marketing may have some of their competency-based processes merged into an integrated competency-based process.

4. The most efficient methods for integrating multiple competency-based processes are selected.

> Examples of options for improving the efficiency of processes performed by multiple workforce competencies include the following:
>
> - Defining an integrated competency-based process that integrates the separate, defined processes used by different workforce competencies
> - Integrating the performance of multiple competency-based processes
> - Reorganizing competency-based processes to improve the timing and coordination of dependencies among several workforce competencies that continue to work independently
> - Improving or re-engineering business processes that involve multiple workforce competencies

Practice 3   Integrated competency-based processes are defined and made available for use.

> Examples of integrated competency-based processes include the following:
>
> - An integrated product design process created by integrating the competency-based design processes used independently by software engineers, hardware engineers, usability engineers, manufacturing engineers, and product line specialists
> - An integrated customer solution sales process created by integrating the competency-based processes for market research, customer needs analysis, requirements development, solution integration, and problem-solution sales processes used independently by customer relations, marketing, product or service line specialists, and sales specialists
> - An integrated supplier management process created by integrating the competency-based processes of purchasing agents, supply chain specialists, sourcing managers, project or product managers, and financial specialists

1. Integrated competency-based processes are defined for use in multi-disciplinary organizational structures, such as multi-disciplinary workgroups.

> Examples of concerns that must be addressed in defining integrated competency-based processes include the following:
> - Accountability and authority
> - Planning to meet common objectives
> - Decision-making processes
> - Issue and conflict resolution
> - Vertical and horizontal communication
> - Efficiency of business activities and operations

2. Integrated competency-based processes are documented and made available for guiding those performing business activities involving dependencies among multiple workforce competencies.

> Integrated competency-based processes may be made available for use through a variety of media, which may include the following:
> - Documents.
> - Web pages.
> - Videos and training materials.
> - Scripts in automated tools.
> - Other knowledge assets, such as competency-based assets. Refer to the Competency-Based Assets process area for information regarding the capture and use of competency-based assets.

Practice 4   Work is designed to incorporate integrated competency-based processes, where appropriate.

When necessary or beneficial:

- existing business processes and activities that would most benefit from integrating competency-based processes are redesigned to facilitate competency integration,
- the processes defined for a specific workforce competency are enhanced or redesigned to incorporate integrated processes performed with those possessing other workforce competencies,
- the defined processes used by workgroups are enhanced with integrated competency-based processes, and
- new business processes are defined to exploit the benefits of integrated competency-based processes.

Practice 5   **Organizational structures support multi-disciplinary work that integrates competency-based processes.**

Different workforce competencies often work in different parts of the organization or report to different managers. Examples of concerns that must be addressed in adjusting organizational structures to better support integrated competency-based processes include the following:

- Accountability and authority
- Decision speed and accuracy
- Vertical and horizontal communication
- Integrity of workforce practices and activities
- Continued evolution of competency integration
- Efficiency of business activities and operations

Examples of how organizational structures can be adjusted to support integrated, multi-disciplinary work include the following:

- Redesigning organizational structures to enhance end-to-end process performance, rather than focusing solely on functional performance
- Realigning management reporting relationships to strengthen accountability for the performance of an integrated business process workflow
- Establishing empowered, multi-disciplinary workgroups
- Establishing integrated management teams that cross organizational boundaries
- Enhancing communication and coordination mechanisms among different organizational components

Practice 6   **Skills needed for performing integrated competency-based processes are developed.**

This practice focuses on development needs specific to the performance of integrated competency-based processes. This may involve the multi-disciplinary work of a single workgroup, of multiple interacting workgroups, or of other organizational structures through which multi-disciplinary work is performed. Different instances of multi-disciplinary work may have different development needs. Development needs could be identified that are related to the workforce competencies of individuals (refer to the Competency Development process area), to the workgroup's operating processes (refer to the Workgroup Development and Empowered Workgroups process areas), or to process coordination among those from different workforce competencies (the focus of this process area).

1. A responsible individual analyzes situations in which integrated, competency-based processes are performed to determine development needs.

> Examples of responsible individuals who interact with those performing multi-disciplinary processes to analyze and plan for meeting their development needs may include the following:
> - The individual(s) to whom a multi-disciplinary workgroup reports
> - A management team to which a multi-disciplinary group with members drawn from different parts of the organization reports
> - An individual from the training or development function
> - An expert in multi-disciplinary work
> - A representative from the human resources function or other appropriate professionals

2. Plans for developing skill in performing integrated, competency-based processes are documented as:

   - development objectives for the workgroup or other multi-disciplinary entity,

   - specific training and development actions to achieve these objectives,

   - input to competency development or workgroup development plans and activities, or

   - the schedule for performing the development activities.

3. Those involved in multi-disciplinary work perform their planned development activities.

4. Plans are reviewed for the accomplishment of development activities and their impact on multi-disciplinary performance.

5. Corrective action is taken when development activities do not achieve their intended objective.

Practice 7   **The work environment supports work by individuals or workgroups using integrated competency-based processes.**

1. Individuals using integrated competency-based processes for a significant portion of their committed work are collocated to the extent possible.

2. When needed, common workspaces are provided for performing integrated competency-based processes.

3. Communication and coordination tools are provided, as necessary, for performing integrated competency-based processes.

4. Joint access to information that may be specific to a given competency is provided when needed for performing integrated competency-based processes.

Practice 8   **Workforce competency descriptions are revised to incorporate integrated competency-based processes.**

> Documented descriptions of workforce competencies are revised to include the knowledge, skills, and defined processes required to fulfill business activities using integrated competency-based processes. Refer to Practices 3, 4, and 5 of the Competency Analysis process area for information regarding establishing and maintaining descriptions of workforce competencies and competency-based processes.

Practice 9   **Workforce practices and activities are defined and adjusted to support integrated competency-based activities.**

1. Recruiting and selection activities are adjusted, where appropriate, to identify candidates with the knowledge, skills, and process abilities and with the willingness to work in interdisciplinary environments and effectively use integrated competency-based processes.

2. Where appropriate, units plan their business activities to expand the use of integrated competency-based processes where they offer performance benefits.

3. Competency development plans and activities are enhanced to include preparation for performing integrated competency-based processes.

4. Communication and coordination activities are enhanced to improve integration and cooperation among different workforce competencies.

5. Performance discussions with individuals or workgroups include feedback on the performance of integrated competency-based processes, where appropriate.

6. Career planning practices and activities incorporate:

   - capability in integrated competency-based processes among the criteria for advancement, and

   - the ability to move between workforce competencies as a component of graduated career opportunities, where appropriate.

7. Adjustments to compensation and reward activities reflect capability and performance of integrated competency-based processes.

Practice 10   **Workgroups performing integrated competency-based processes tailor and use them for planning committed work.**

1. Workgroups that include members with different workforce competencies define their workgroup processes from tailored combinations of:

   - the competency-based processes defined for performing business activities unique to each workforce competency involved,

   - integrated competency-based processes for performing the business activities in which they share dependencies, and

   - common workgroup methods and procedures tailored for use with interdisciplinary situations.

2. The workgroup's integrated processes are used for:

- planning their business activities and establishing commitments,
- defining roles for workgroup members,
- guiding the performance of committed work,
- orienting new members to the workgroup,
- coordinating work dependencies with other organizational entities, and
- collecting data and developing lessons learned.

Practice 11   **Workgroups use integrated competency-based processes for work involving multiple workforce competencies.**

1. Work being performed using integrated competency-based processes is reviewed on a periodic or event-driven basis to determine status and make necessary adjustments.

2. If significant deviations of progress from the plan are observed, corrective actions are taken, which could include making adjustments or improvements to integrated competency-based processes.

3. Data on the performance of multi-disciplinary work are captured and maintained.

> Once these performance data are captured and maintained, they can be used later in a number of workforce activities. Examples of these uses of performance data and other information on integrated competency-based processes may include the following:
> - Estimating and planning multi-disciplinary work
> - Establishing benchmarks or capability baselines for integrated competency-based processes
> - Analyzing integrated competency-based processes for improvement opportunities
> - Evaluating the benefits of integrated competency-based processes

Practice 12   **The performance of integrated competency-based processes is evaluated to identify needed adjustments and updates.**

1. Those using integrated competency-based processes to perform at least part of their committed work evaluate these processes on a periodic or event-driven basis to determine needs for adjustment.

2. Adjustments to integrated competency-based processes that are specific to a situation are implemented and recorded.

3. Adjustments that may be generic across situations are recommended for incorporation into the documented integrated competency-based process.

Measurement and Analysis

Measurement 1   **Measurements are made and used to determine the status and performance of Competency Integration activities.**

> Examples of measurements include the following:
> - Number and extent of situations employing integrated competency-based processes for performing at least part of their committed work
> - Number of integrated competency-based processes defined and in use
> - Status of planned activities for defining and employing integrated competency-based processes
> - Status of updating learning materials and experiences for preparing individuals or workgroups to perform integrated competency-based processes
> - Number of individuals or workgroups trained to perform integrated competency-based processes
> - The rate at which the competency-based processes of different workforce competencies are integrated within the organization

Measurement 2   **Measurements are made and used to determine the effectiveness of Competency Integration activities.**

> Examples of measures of the effectiveness of Competency Integration activities include the following:
> - Extent to which business objectives pursued through performing integrated competency-based processes are accomplished
> - Performance-based evidence of increases in unit or organizational performance related to competency integration
> - Value of performance increases through the use of integrated competency-based processes
> - Workforce ratings of the effectiveness of integrated competency-based processes
> - Improvements in cost, schedule adherence, time to market, quality, or other performance measures related to the use of integrated competency-based processes

Verifying Implementation

Verification 1 **A responsible individual(s) verifies that the Competency Integration activities are conducted according to the organization's documented policies, practices, procedures, and, where appropriate, plans; and addresses non-compliance.**

These reviews verify that:

1. Competency Integration activities comply with the organization's policies and stated values.
2. Competency Integration activities comply with relevant laws and regulations.
3. Competency Integration activities are performed according to the organization's documented practices and procedures.
4. Noncompliance issues are handled appropriately.

Verification 2 **Executive management periodically reviews the Competency Integration activities, status, and results; and resolves issues.**

These reviews verify:

1. The appropriateness of Competency Integration activities.
2. Effectiveness of Competency Integration activities at the organizational, competency, and unit levels.
3. Progress in performing Competency Integration activities.
4. Results from reviews of Competency Integration practices and activities.

> Refer to Verification 1 for practices regarding reviews of Competency Integration activities to ensure adherence to the following:
> - Relevant laws and regulations
> - Organizational policies, practices, and procedures

5. Status of resolution of noncompliance issues.
6. Trends related to Competency Integration.
7. Effectiveness of Competency Integration activities in accomplishing multi-disciplinary work.

Empowered Workgroups

A process area at Level 4: Predictable

Purpose

The purpose of Empowered Workgroups is to invest workgroups with the responsibility and authority to determine how to conduct their business activities most effectively.

Description

An *empowered workgroup* is a workgroup that is granted considerable autonomy for managing and performing its work, and for performing selected workforce practices within the workgroup. The concept of empowered workgroups usually implies that a workgroup is responsible for a "whole work process" [Wellins 91]. In the People CMM, workgroups that are invested with the authority to determine how they will accomplish business objectives and perform some of their internal workforce practices are described as "empowered workgroups."

The term *team* has been used in the literature to describe several types of workgroup structures and attributes, many of which involve some level of empowerment. For instance, Katzenbach and Smith [Katzenbach 93, p. 45] describe a "team" as "...a small number of people [fewer than 10] with complementary skills who are committed to a common purpose, performance goals, and approach for which they hold themselves mutually accountable." Although a team is a workgroup, not all workgroups develop into empowered workgroups. Consequently, the People CMM does not distinguish between the terms *team* and *workgroup*.

Empowered workgroups can constitute a unit, can be a component of a unit, or can consist of individuals who report to different units. In this latter case, individuals may have matrixed reporting relationships that involve their home unit and the empowered workgroup. Such workgroups may overlap several entities on the organization chart.

Empowering workgroups involves preparing workgroup members to act as an independent entity within the constraints of organizational and unit(s) objectives. It involves delegating responsibility and authority for work results to the empowered workgroup and holding the members accountable as an empowered workgroup for achieving them. It involves training workgroup members in the skills required in empowered workgroups and their associated processes. Empowered workgroups are managed as an entity rather than as individuals, and workforce practices are tailored for use within the empowered workgroup. The work environment is adjusted to support optimal performance by empowered workgroups. Empowered workgroup members accept increasing responsibility for the performance of workforce practices such as recruiting, selection, performance management, reward, training, development, and compensation activities that are appropriate to the structure and function of the empowered workgroup. Empowered workgroup performance data are used to identify needs for development. Performance of each empowered workgroup and the contributions to this performance are considered in making individual compensation decisions, as well as in recognizing and rewarding outstanding performance.

Goals

Goal 1   **Empowered workgroups are delegated responsibility and authority over their work processes.**

Goal 2   **The organization's workforce practices and activities encourage and support the development and performance of empowered workgroups.**

Goal 3   **Empowered workgroups perform selected workforce practices internally.**

Goal 4   **Empowered Workgroups practices are institutionalized to ensure they are performed as defined organizational processes.**

Commitment to Perform

Commitment 1   **The organization establishes and maintains a documented policy for conducting Empowered Workgroups activities.**

Issues typically addressed in the policy include:

1. Workgroups are empowered to serve the business objectives and stated values of the organization.

2. Empowerment activities are included in the strategic workforce plan and implemented through orderly planning in units whose work can benefit from empowered workgroups.

3. The work environment and other organizational attributes are adjusted to support empowered workgroups.

4. Workforce practices are adjusted to support empowered workgroups.

5. Empowered workgroups assume increasing responsibility for performing some of their workforce practices within the workgroup.

6. Empowered Workgroups practices and activities comply with relevant laws, regulations, and organizational policies.

Commitment 2   **An organizational role(s) is assigned responsibility for coordinating empowerment activities and tailoring workforce practices to support empowered workgroups.**

Ability to Perform

Ability 1   **Each empowered workgroup has an individual(s) or organizational entity that is assigned responsibility as its sponsor and to whom it is accountable.**

1. The individual(s) or organizational entity that is assigned responsibility for an empowered workgroup assists it by:

   ■ clarifying its mission and responsibilities,

   ■ providing organizational resources or ensuring that organizational resources are made available to the workgroup,

- reviewing its progress and performance,
- providing guidance,
- facilitating the empowered workgroup, when needed, and
- addressing problems it is unable to resolve internally.

2. The individual(s) or organizational entity that is assigned responsibility for an empowered workgroup acts as its liaison to other organizational entities, when appropriate.

3. The individual(s) or organizational entity that is assigned responsibility for an empowered workgroup represents the organization's interests to the workgroup.

Ability 2   **Adequate resources are provided for performing Empowered Workgroups activities.**

1. Workgroups have been established to optimize the performance of interdependent work.

> Refer to the Workgroup Development process area for information regarding the establishment and use of workgroups to organize and accomplish work around competency-based process abilities.

2. Competency-based processes exist that can be tailored to support empowered workgroups.

> Competency-based processes, integrated competency-based processes, and methods and procedures for performing common workgroup functions used by a workgroup, as well as competency-based workforce practices may be tailored and performed by an empowered workgroup. Refer to the Competency Analysis, Competency-Based Practices, and Workgroup Development process areas at the Defined Level, and the Competency Integration process area at the Predictable Level, for a description of the establishment of these processes.

3. Defined workforce practices exist that can be tailored to support their execution by empowered workgroups.

4. Experienced individuals who have expertise are available for facilitating empowerment within workgroups.

5. Experienced individuals who have expertise in workforce practices are available to support empowered workgroups in:

- tailoring of workforce practices for use within empowered workgroups, and
- performing these tailored workforce practices within empowered workgroups.

6. Resources for supporting Empowered Workgroups activities are made available.

7. Adequate funding is available to empower workgroups and to tailor and deploy the empowered workgroup-based practices that support them.

Ability 3 **All affected parties develop the knowledge, skills, and process abilities needed to develop effective relationships with empowered workgroups.**

1. Those to whom empowered workgroups report receive the preparation needed to manage empowered workgroups.

> Those who manage empowered workgroups develop knowledge, skills, and process abilities to enable them to perform their assigned responsibilities and support the empowerment of the workgroups that they are responsible for. Examples of topics include the following:
> - Assigning responsibility and delegating authority
> - Shifting responsibility for some workforce practices into the empowered workgroup
> - Evolving the growth of empowerment and self-management in empowered workgroups
> - Tailoring self-managed workforce practices within empowered workgroups
> - Facilitative and participatory management
> - Performing workforce practices at the empowered workgroup level
> - Forming, sustaining, and disbanding empowered workgroups
> - Diagnosing and handling empowered workgroup problems
> - Managing dependencies among empowered workgroups
> - Coordinating management decisions in empowered workgroup-based organizations

2. Other individuals or organizational entities that interact with empowered workgroups receive the preparation needed to coordinate their activities with empowered workgroups.

> Empowered workgroups interact with many components of the organization whose members are not equally empowered. These affected parties need to be prepared to adjust their methods of coordination where necessary to work effectively with empowered workgroups. They need to understand how empowered workgroups work to identify appropriate mechanisms for coordination and interaction.

> Examples of issues to be addressed in working effectively with empowered workgroups may include the following:
> - Empowered decision making
> - Delegated authority for work methods
> - Integration of competency-based processes within empowered workgroups
> - Self-management
> - Inter-group communication mechanisms
> - Planning and tracking status with empowered workgroups

3. Facilitation is provided to:

- support managers or others who work with empowered workgroups, and
- assist empowered workgroups in taking responsibility for their work processes and selected workforce practices.

Ability 4   **Individuals responsible for tailoring or administering workforce practices for empowered workgroups develop the knowledge, skills, and process abilities needed to perform their responsibilities.**

1. Individuals assigned responsibility for performing workforce practices for empowered workgroups receive the preparation needed for applying these practices in a manner consistent with the development and functioning of empowered workgroups.

2. Individuals assigned responsibility for designing or tailoring workforce practices for application to empowered workgroups receive the preparation needed to perform their responsibilities.

3. Individuals within empowered workgroups who participate in applying workforce practices within the workgroup receive the preparation needed for performing these practices.

Ability 5   **The practices and procedures for performing Empowered Workgroups are defined and documented.**

1. Practices and procedures are defined and documented at the organizational or unit levels, as appropriate.

2. Guidelines for tailoring the practices and procedures for use in different circumstances are documented and made available, as necessary.

3. The individual(s) assigned responsibility for coordinating Empowered Workgroups activities across the organization ensures that defined practices and procedures are:

- maintained under version control,
- disseminated through appropriate media,
- interpreted appropriately for different situations, and
- updated through orderly methods.

4. Experiences, lessons learned, measurement results, and improvement information derived from planning and performing Empowered Workgroups practices are captured to support the future use and improvement of the organization's practices.

Practices Performed

Practice 1   Work responsibilities are designed to provide an empowered workgroup with optimal control over an integrated set of business activities.

> An integrated set of business activities to be assigned to an empowered workgroup might consist of most or all of the tasks required to:
> - Produce a product or a component of a product
> - Provide a service or a component of a service
> - Perform a business process
> - Perform a process step in the production of a product or service
> - Perform an organizational function

1. Business activities are analyzed within and across units to determine how to most efficiently:

   - optimize the collection of dependencies within a workgroup, and

   - minimize the sharing of dependencies across workgroups.

2. Business activities are periodically reviewed to determine if they can be more effectively organized to support the functioning of workgroups.

3. Empowered workgroups participate in the design of business activities.

Practice 2   Empowered workgroups are formed with a statement of their mission and authority for accomplishing it.

> The level of empowerment extended to an empowered workgroup is limited by its interdependencies with other workgroups or organizational entities. Thus, an empowered workgroup's independence in deciding commitments, work methods, etc. is bounded by its need to coordinate dependencies and ensure proper integration among workflow, work products, or business services with other organizational entities. The level of empowerment that can be achieved within an organization is limited by the design of business processes to maximize dependencies within empowered workgroups and minimize those shared with other organizational entities.

1. Empowered workgroups are established by those who:

   - have responsibility for the business activities assigned to the empowered workgroup,

   - are capable of delegating responsibility and authority to the empowered workgroup, and

   - have reporting responsibility for the individuals assigned to the empowered workgroup.

2. Empowered workgroups are chartered with a statement of their mission that describes:

    - workgroup purpose and intended contribution to organizational and business objectives,

    - strategic and operational context of the workgroup's work,

    - assigned responsibilities and expected outputs,

    - anticipated dependencies and interfaces with other organizational entities,

    - extent of the workgroup's autonomy and authority,

    - accountability and reporting relationships, and

    - initial level of self-management, if appropriate.

3. The statement of an empowered workgroup's mission should be reviewed and updated whenever necessitated by changes in business conditions, work processes, or organizational structure.

Practice 3   **The individual(s) or organizational entity to which an empowered workgroup is accountable provides business objectives and negotiates responsibilities and commitments with the empowered workgroup.**

1. The individual(s) or entity to which the empowered workgroup is accountable provides:

    - objectives and responsibilities to be accomplished by the empowered workgroup,

    - the strategy for how the empowered workgroup's activities and work products fit in with the activities and work products of other workgroups or units, and

    - objective criteria by which empowered workgroup performance is to be evaluated.

2. The empowered workgroup:

    - reviews and achieves consensus on the objectives and responsibilities assigned to it,

    - plans its business activities and commitments,

    - reviews and achieves consensus on the criteria for evaluating its performance, and

    - negotiates agreements concerning its performance objectives, responsibilities, and commitments as necessary with the individual(s) or entity to which it reports.

3. The empowered workgroup renegotiates performance objectives, responsibilities, and commitments with the individual(s) or entity to which it reports as necessitated by its performance against plan or changing business conditions.

Practice 4   **Empowered workgroups are delegated the responsibility and authority to determine the methods by which they will accomplish their committed work.**

1. Empowered workgroups tailor and integrate competency-based processes, and standard methods and procedures for performing common workgroup functions, for performing their business activities.

2. Empowered workgroups assign roles and allocate work among their members.

3. Empowered workgroups define and coordinate interfaces with other organizational entities required to satisfy their commitments and shared dependencies.

4. Empowered workgroups plan their business activities and commitments, and negotiate inconsistencies with the individual(s) to whom they are accountable and other organizational entities, as necessary.

Practice 5   **Empowered workgroups use appropriate methods for making decisions on their commitments and methods of operation.**

1. Early in the empowered workgroup's formation, members determine how they are to:

   ■ allocate authority to roles based on dependencies in the committed work,

   ■ empower individuals or small groups within the workgroup to take independent action without review or approval by the full workgroup,

   ■ achieve consensus on plans and commitments,

   ■ make decisions that arise in the performance of the workgroup's business activities, and

   ■ negotiate and represent their interests to the individual to whom they are accountable and to other organizational entities.

2. Empowered workgroups periodically review their activities and performance to determine whether changes should be made to their decision-making processes.

Practice 6   **The organization's work environment supports the development and performance of empowered workgroups.**

1. Facilities and resources that could enhance empowered workgroup performance are identified.

> Examples of work environment resources that may enhance the performance of empowered workgroups include the following:
> - Public spaces, such as workgroup rooms and conference rooms
> - Offices and spaces close to each other that allow workgroup members to be collocated, when possible
> - Groupware or other resources to support the performance of the workgroup
> - Enhanced communications capabilities

2. Where possible, the facilities and resources identified are made available to enhance empowered workgroup performance.

3. Within boundaries established by work environment policies, budgets, and regulations, empowered workgroups are given the authority to organize and arrange their work environments to best support their business activities.

4. Activities to improve the organization's work environment involve input and review from empowered workgroups.

Practice 7   **The organization's workforce practices are tailored for use with empowered workgroups.**

> There are three ways in which workforce practices can be adjusted for use with empowered workgroups. These are the following:
>
> - Practices designed for application to individuals can be redesigned for application jointly to all members of an empowered workgroup
> - Practices designed for application to a unit can be redesigned for application to an empowered workgroup
> - Guidelines can be developed for further adjusting practices used with empowered workgroups for more effective application in specific situations

1. Individuals responsible for coordinating various workforce practices and activities across the organization are involved in adjusting these practices for use by empowered workgroups.

2. Members of empowered workgroups are involved in developing guidelines for adjusting and applying workforce practices for use with empowered workgroups.

3. Human resources or other appropriate professionals are involved in ensuring that all workforce practices and activities that are adjusted for use with empowered workgroups comply with all applicable laws, regulations, and organizational policies.

Practice 8 **Responsibility and authority for performing selected workforce activities is delegated to empowered workgroups.**

> The level of responsibility and authority to be delegated to empowered workgroups for performing their own workforce activities is a design issue. Organizations generally start by delegating a minimal set of workforce practices to empowered workgroups to allow them to gain experience in performing these activities. As an empowered workgroup becomes experienced in performing some of its own workforce activities, the level of self-management delegated to the workgroup can be increased. The rate at which empowered workgroups may successfully absorb responsibility for self-management may differ among workgroups. The level of delegated self-management may also differ by the maturity and experience of each empowered workgroup. For instance, long-lived empowered workgroups that interact frequently, such as product development teams, are generally delegated greater self-management than short-lived empowered workgroups that interact only occasionally, such as problem resolution teams. Since an individual may participate in several empowered workgroups, the organization must decide the extent to which each workgroup contributes to workforce activities performed for the individual in areas such as performance management, compensation, and career development.

1. Management, in conjunction with human resources, decides how to delegate workforce activities to different empowered workgroups:

   - internally by empowered workgroup members,

   - externally by one or more individuals such as project managers, competency managers, or human resources professionals, and

   - through a combination of activities performed by individuals internal and external to the empowered workgroup.

   > The level of involvement is typically determined by criteria such as the following:
   > - The level of privacy that the organization wishes to maintain on personal information
   > - Standard organizational practice
   > - Organizational culture
   > - Laws, regulations, and organizational policies

2. Workforce practices and activities whose performance may be delegated to empowered workgroups include:

   - recruiting for open positions,

   - developing methods and criteria for selecting new members,

   - orienting new members,

   - conducting their internal performance management activities,

- determining their learning needs and ensuring that these needs, in addition to any development needed in the organization's workforce competencies, are satisfied,
- participating in compensation decisions,

Examples of empowered workgroup involvement in compensation activities include the following:

- Using the inputs of empowered workgroup performance management activities in compensation decisions
- Recommending adjustments to compensation
- Mixing responsibility where empowered workgroups have some involvement in compensation decisions
- Reviewing compensation decisions
- Providing feedback on compensation methods and decisions
- Recommending changes to the compensation strategy or the activities defined for the empowered workgroup

---

- contributing to strategic workforce planning and the planning of unit workforce activities,
- recognizing or rewarding outstanding performance, and
- performing other workforce practices and activities, as appropriate.

3. The effectiveness of self-management within each empowered workgroup is evaluated to determine:

- corrective actions to be taken with regard to the empowered workgroup's performance of one or more of the workforce practices delegated to it,
- the extent to which the empowered workgroup is ready to assume responsibility for performing more of its own workforce practices, and
- how self-management is working in empowered workgroups across the organization and whether any corrective actions should be taken at the organizational level.

4. Within guidelines established by the organization, the responsibility and authority delegated to empowered workgroups for performing workforce activities is increased over time as empowered workgroups become more experienced and effective in self-management.

- Responsible individual(s) maintain ongoing discussion with empowered workgroups about their performance of workforce activities.
- Members of empowered workgroups are involved in decisions regarding the amount of responsibility they are delegated for performing workforce practices.

Practice 9   **Empowered workgroups tailor workforce activities delegated to them and plan for their adoption.**

> Empowered workgroups determine how to conduct the workforce activities delegated to them within a context set by how the organization has adjusted its workforce practices for use by empowered workgroups. Decisions about how a specific empowered workgroup should conduct its workforce activities are reviewed by human resources or other appropriate professionals for compliance with relevant laws, regulations, and organizational policies.

1. Empowered workgroup members receive the preparation needed to perform their delegated workforce activities.

2. Empowered workgroups define and agree on how they perform their delegated workforce activities.

3. Empowered workgroups plan the integration of delegated workforce activities into their planned business activities.

4. Facilitation is made available to empowered workgroups as needed to assist in performing their delegated workforce activities.

5. When appropriate, an empowered workgroup's workforce activities are reviewed by human resources or other appropriate professionals to ensure they comply with relevant laws, regulations, and organizational policies.

6. When necessary, corrective action is taken to improve the performance of delegated workforce activities.

7. Records of an empowered workgroup's workforce activities are maintained.

Practice 10   **Empowered workgroups perform the workforce activities delegated to them.**

1. Empowered workgroups assign roles as appropriate for participating in the performance of its delegated workforce activities.

2. Empowered workgroups perform workforce activities delegated to them according to their plan and adjustments.

3. Empowered workgroups seek advice from human resources or other appropriate professionals, as necessary, to ensure their actions comply with the organization's policies, procedures, and relevant laws and regulations.

4. The performance of workforce activities by empowered workgroups is reviewed or audited, as appropriate, to ensure compliance with the organization's policies, procedures, and relevant laws and regulations.

Practice 11   **Empowered workgroups participate in managing their performance.**

1. Empowered workgroups establish their performance objectives.

> An empowered workgroup's performance objectives should be achievable within the current performance capability of the workgroup. Consequently these objectives should not include performance targets that require capability improvements beyond what can be achieved by the workgroup within the period covered by the objectives. An empowered workgroup's performance objectives are typically based on factors such as the following:
>
> - The organization's or unit's business strategies, performance objectives, and performance measures
> - Its mission and assigned responsibilities
> - The needs of its stakeholders and the deliverables or services that meet these needs
> - The individual processes or tasks that must be accomplished
> - Expected contributions of each workgroup member
> - Its effectiveness in interacting with other workgroups or organizational entities
> - Relevant schedule, cost, and quality criteria
> - Relevant performance data, including performance baselines from performing similar processes or meeting similar objectives
> - Anticipated performance improvements from competency development and related improvement activities

2. Stakeholders in the workgroup's performance contribute to establishing its performance objectives and criteria, where appropriate.

> Examples of stakeholders in an empowered workgroup's performance may include the following:
>
> - Individual members of the workgroup
> - Members of other workgroups or organizational entities affected by an empowered workgroup's performance
> - The individual(s) or organizational entity to whom the empowered workgroup reports
> - Executive management
> - Customers

3. An empowered workgroup's performance objectives are consistent with its unit and organizational performance objectives.

4. Members of empowered workgroups jointly establish their individual performance objectives by:

   - establishing and agreeing to the performance objectives of each of its members, and
   - defining their personal performance objectives to be consistent with the performance objectives of their workgroup, their unit, and the organization.

5. Empowered workgroups define and use performance measures to evaluate their effectiveness and improve their performance.

> Refer to the Quantitative Performance Management process area for practices involved in defining measures at the workgroup level.

6. Measures of the performance of an empowered workgroup are:

    ■ integrated into the performance objectives of each individual member, and

    ■ periodically reviewed to determine their appropriateness under changing business or organizational conditions and are revised, if necessary.

7. Members of empowered workgroups maintain awareness of their performance as individuals and as a workgroup.

> Examples of mechanisms for empowered workgroups to maintain awareness of team performance include the following:
> • Progress review meetings
> • Performance review meetings
> • Workgroup problem-solving sessions
> • Sessions with a mentor, coach, or facilitator

8. Workgroup performance is periodically evaluated against established performance objectives for individuals and the workgroup.

9. Empowered workgroups manage the performance of their individual members to achieve workgroup performance objectives.

> Refer to Practices 6 through 12 of the Performance Management process area for information regarding performance management practices for individual workgroup members.

10. Members of empowered workgroups openly discuss performance issues and seek solutions to these issues.

11. To the extent these responsibilities have been delegated to them, empowered workgroups:

    ■ provide formal feedback on performance for each of their members,

    ■ provide input to compensation decisions, and

    ■ manage unsatisfactory performance by their members.

Practice 12 **Adjustments to the compensation of members of empowered workgroups are based, in part, on issues related to workgroup performance.**

1. The compensation system is reviewed and adjusted, as needed, to:

   ■ optimize the relationship of empowered workgroup performance to unit and organizational performance and of individual performance to empowered workgroup performance,

   ■ ensure that workgroup-related adjustments to compensation are having their intended effect, and

   ■ ensure that compensation decisions which incorporate workgroup considerations maintain equity within the compensation system.

   Examples of the impact of the compensation system on empowered workgroup development and performance include the following:
   - Stimulating the development of empowered workgroups
   - Motivating individuals to develop workgroup-based skills
   - Motivating cohesion and coordination among members of the workgroup
   - Aligning individual and workgroup performance
   - Aligning workgroup performance with unit and organizational performance
   - Attracting and retaining appropriately qualified individuals in empowered workgroups

   ---

2. Adjustments to compensation for each member of an empowered workgroup are based, in part, on:

   ■ their individual performance compared to their performance objectives,

   ■ their overall contribution to the development, functioning, and performance of their workgroup,

   ---

   Examples of workgroup-related factors that may influence compensation decisions include the following:
   - Current capability in workgroup tasks
   - Development of additional capabilities in workgroup tasks
   - Successful completion of activities in personal development plans that are related to workgroup performance
   - Ability to translate capability in workforce competencies into enhanced workgroup performance
   - Contribution in helping or mentoring others to improve their knowledge, skills, and process abilities related to workgroup responsibilities

   ---

■ the performance of the empowered workgroup compared to its performance objectives, and

■ the empowered workgroup's contribution to the achievement of unit and organizational performance objectives.

3. Guidance and assistance for factoring individual contribution to empowered workgroup performance is provided to individuals and workgroups responsible for making compensation decisions.

> Examples of practices for factoring empowered workgroup-based incentives into individual compensation include the following:
> - Equal adjustments for all empowered workgroup members based on empowered workgroup performance against objectives
> - Equal adjustments for all empowered workgroup members based on empowered workgroup contributions to unit or organizational performance
> - Equal adjustments for all empowered workgroup members based on improvements in empowered workgroup performance
> - Differential adjustments for individual empowered workgroup members based on each of their capabilities and individual contributions to empowered workgroup performance
> - Differential adjustments for each empowered workgroup member based on their contribution to the ability of other empowered workgroup members to contribute to empowered workgroup performance

4. The basis on which contributions to empowered workgroup performance are factored into compensation decisions is discussed with each individual.

Measurement and Analysis

Measurement 1   Measurements are made and used to determine the status and performance of workforce practices for empowering workgroups.

> Examples of measurements include the following:
> - Rate at which workgroups can be developed into empowered workgroups
> - Amount of time spent in tailoring workforce activities to the organization's empowered workgroup-based practices
> - Rate or progress in tailoring the organization's workforce activities for empowered workgroup-building application
> - Indicators of the organization's increased efficiency in performing empowered workgroup-based workforce activities

Measurement 2   **Measurements are made and used to determine the effectiveness of workforce practices for empowering workgroups.**

> Examples of measurements of the effectiveness of empowered workgroup-based workforce practices include the following:
> - Individual ratings of the effectiveness of empowered workgroup-based workforce practices
> - Improved empowered workgroup coordination and functioning
> - Increased level of motivation and retention resulting from empowered workgroup-based staffing, career planning, compensation, and reward practices
> - Increased performance of empowered workgroups over workgroups that have not been empowered
> - Improvements over time in the performance of empowered workgroups
> - Increased impact of empowered workgroup performance on unit and organizational performance

Verifying Implementation

Verification 1   **A responsible individual(s) verifies that the organization's workforce practices for empowering workgroups are conducted according to the organization's documented policies, practices, procedures, and, where appropriate, plans; and addresses noncompliance.**

These reviews verify that:

1. Workforce practices for empowering workgroups comply with the organization's policies and stated values.
2. Workforce practices for empowering workgroups comply with relevant laws and regulations.
3. Workforce practices and activities for empowering workgroups are performed according to the organization's documented practices and procedures.
4. Noncompliance issues are handled appropriately.

Verification 2   **Executive management periodically reviews the organization's Empowered Workgroups activities, status, and results; and resolves issues.**

These reviews verify:

1. Appropriateness of workforce practices for empowering workgroups at the organizational and unit levels.
2. Progress in performing workforce practices for empowering workgroups.

3. Results from reviews of workforce practices and activities for empowering workgroups.

> Refer to Verification 1 for information regarding reviews of workforce practices and activities for empowering workgroups to ensure adherence to the following:
> - Relevant laws and regulations
> - Organizational policies, practices, and procedures

4. Status of resolution of noncompliance issues.

5. Trends related to workforce activities for empowering workgroups.

6. The organization's effectiveness in implementing workforce practices for empowering workgroups.

Verification 3   The definition and use of empowered workgroup performance data are periodically audited for compliance with organizational policies.

> Organizational policies which may apply could include human resource, human capital, information security, confidentiality, privacy, or data disclosure policies.

1. Definitions of workgroup performance data are reviewed for compliance with organizational policies.

> The data definitions define what data is to be collected, aggregated, and used. They are not the data values themselves. For example, performance measures or performance ratings could be a component of a data definition, but the specific measure or rating would be a specific data value for an instance of workgroup performance data.

2. Periodic audits ensure that workgroup performance data are accessed and used in accordance with organizational policies.

> These audits may be accomplished through reviews of ongoing reporting, such as system access and use monitoring reports, and auditing to ensure compliance with relevant information security standards and organizational policies.
>
> System access and use monitoring ensures that the data are accessed only by authorized individuals, while compliance auditing ensures that these individuals perform appropriate procedures in compliance with organizational policies and standards.

Competency-Based Assets

A process area at Maturity Level 4: Predictable

Purpose

The purpose of Competency-Based Assets is to capture the knowledge, experience, and artifacts developed in performing competency-based processes for use in enhancing capability and performance.

Description

A *competency-based asset* captures the knowledge, experience, or artifacts developed in performing competency-based processes within an organization. A competency-based asset is a bundle of information or an artifact that has been prepared in standard format and made available for widespread use. As an organizational asset, it becomes a component of one or more workforce competencies. The concept of a workforce competency is expanded at the Predictable Level to include not just the knowledge, skills, and process abilities of individuals and workgroups, but also the accumulated assets that can be reused by other members of their competency community. Thus, competency-based assets include many of the concepts discussed in areas such as knowledge management, learning organizations, or reusable product components. The representation of competency-based assets for future deployment is determined by standards set by the organization or within a specific workforce competency.

At lower maturity levels, competency-based knowledge is typically shared by person-to-person communication, interactions within a community of competence, training, or searching through unstructured historical records or repositories. Competency-Based Assets builds on these practices by encouraging individuals and workgroups to capture, formalize, and share the information and artifacts they develop while performing competency-based processes. Thus, Competency-Based Assets supports the transfer of knowledge and experience across communities of competence.

Selected bundles of information or artifacts, chosen for their ability to enhance performance, are organized into competency-based assets. Investments in competency-based assets are expected to produce a return by improving performance or other defined business benefits. These competency-based assets are integrated into competency-based processes for use in performing business activities. Information on the use of these assets is also captured. Competency-based assets are incorporated into competency development activities, and mentoring activities are structured to deploy them. Competency-based assets are made available for use through information and communication technology. Workforce practices and activities are adjusted to encourage the development and use of competency-based assets.

Goals

Goal 1   **The knowledge, experience, and artifacts resulting from performing competency-based processes are developed into competency-based assets.**

Goal 2   **Competency-based assets are deployed and used.**

Goal 3   Workforce practices and activities encourage and support the development and use of competency-based assets.

Goal 4   Competency-Based Assets practices are institutionalized to ensure they are performed as defined organizational processes.

Commitment to Perform

Commitment 1   The organization's stated values encourage knowledge sharing between individuals and workgroups, when appropriate.

> Refer to Commitment 1 of the Communication and Coordination process area for information regarding the establishment and communication of organizational values and the types of workforce issues that might be covered in the organization's stated values. Also refer to Commitment 1 of the Participatory Culture process area for information regarding extending these core values to address open communication and participation in decision making by individuals and workgroups.

Commitment 2   The organization establishes and maintains a documented policy for developing and using competency-based assets.

Issues typically addressed in the policy include:

1. Competency-Based Assets activities, including capturing and exploiting the competency-based assets of the organization, serve its business objectives and stated values.

2. Knowledge, experience, and artifacts gained from performing competency-based processes are captured and retained for use.

3. Competency-based knowledge, experience, and artifacts are incorporated into competency development and business activities.

4. Workforce practices are adjusted to motivate capturing and exploiting competency-based knowledge, experience, and artifacts.

5. Appropriate professionals are involved, as needed, in ensuring that activities involved in capturing and exploiting the organization's competency-based assets comply with any contracts or similar agreements with other organizations regarding any of these assets.

6. Workforce practices and activities relating to the development and use of competency-based assets comply with relevant laws, regulations, and organizational policies.

> Human resources or other appropriate professionals are consulted to ensure that the activities involved in capturing and exploiting the organization's competency-based assets comply with relevant laws, regulations, and organizational policies.

Commitment 3   **An organizational role(s) is assigned responsibility for coordinating across the organization the activities involved in capturing and reusing competency-based assets.**

> Examples of individuals who might coordinate various Competency-Based Assets activities include the following:
> - Operational managers and executives
> - Knowledge officers or managers
> - Quality, efficiency, or performance experts
> - Human resources or other appropriate professionals
> - Training or development groups
> - Competency ownership groups
> - Information technology specialists
> - Measurement or process improvement groups

Ability to Perform

Ability 1   **Within each unit, an individual(s) is assigned responsibility and authority for ensuring that members of the unit participate in capturing and using competency-based assets, as appropriate.**

> Examples of responsibilities to be performed within units include the following:
> - Ensuring that knowledge, experience, and artifacts are captured from performing competency-based or interdisciplinary processes
> - Competency-based assets are used in performing the unit's business activities
> - Workforce activities within the unit motivate the capture and exploitation of competency-based assets

Ability 2   **A responsible individual(s) coordinates the activities for capturing and using competency-based assets within each workforce competency.**

Ability 3   **Adequate resources are provided for capturing and using competency-based assets.**

1. The organization's workforce competencies have been defined.

> Refer to the Competency Analysis process area for the information regarding defining workforce competencies.

2. The competency development plans for the organization's workforce competencies are made available.

> Refer to Practices 2, 3, 4, and 5 of the Workforce Planning process area for information regarding establishing and maintaining the organization's competency development plans.

3. Experienced individuals with appropriate expertise are available to advise and assist in capturing, representing, retaining, and exploiting competency-based knowledge, experience, and artifacts.

> Examples of individuals with appropriate expertise include the following:
> - Subject matter experts
> - Knowledge management professionals
> - Professionals with expertise in the structure and components of the organization's products or services
> - Mentors or coaches

4. Adequate resources are provided for capturing and exploiting competency-based assets, including resources such as:

   - the technology needed for capturing or exploiting competency-based assets, including information technology for storing, processing, or presenting the organization's competency-based assets and communication technology for generating or sharing the organization's competency-based assets;

   - search and presentation technology for using the organization's competency-based assets in competency development and the performance of business activities;

   - tools and methods for incorporating the organization's competency-based assets into its business activities; and

   - training needed to exploit the organization's competency-based assets.

5. Adequate funding is available for capturing and exploiting competency-based assets.

6. Adequate time is made available for capturing and exploiting competency-based assets, including:

   - the effort of those whose knowledge, experience, or artifacts are being captured, and

   - the effort of those who facilitate the capture and exploitation of competency-based knowledge, experience, or artifacts.

Ability 4   Those responsible for various tasks involved in developing and deploying the organization's competency-based assets develop the knowledge, skills, and process abilities needed to perform their responsibilities.

Learning opportunities are provided in techniques for capturing and reusing the organization's competency-based assets that include topics such as:

- capturing competency-based assets,
- representing and packaging competency-based assets for reuse,
- disseminating competency-based assets,
- assisting individuals and workgroups in sharing competency-based assets,
- storing and retrieving competency-based assets,
- building repositories of competency-based assets,
- integrating competency-based assets into competency-based processes, and
- developing and exploiting the organization's intellectual capital.

Ability 5   Individuals involved in capturing or using competency-based assets develop the knowledge, skills, and process abilities needed to perform their responsibilities.

1. Individuals and workgroups are prepared in methods for capturing knowledge, experience, and artifacts that result from performing competency-based or integrated multi-disciplinary processes.

2. Individuals and workgroups are prepared in methods for sharing the knowledge, experience, and artifacts that result from performing competency-based or integrated multi-disciplinary processes with others who might benefit from them.

3. Individuals and workgroups are prepared in methods for using competency-based assets in performing their business activities.

Ability 6   The practices and procedures for capturing or using competency-based assets are defined and documented.

1. Practices and procedures are defined and documented at the organizational or unit levels, as appropriate.

2. Guidelines for tailoring the practices and procedures for use in different circumstances are documented and made available, as necessary.

3. The individual(s) assigned responsibility for coordinating Competency-Based Assets activities across the organization ensures that defined practices and procedures are:

- maintained under version control,
- disseminated through appropriate media,

- interpreted appropriately for different situations, and
- updated through orderly methods.

4. Experiences, lessons learned, measurement results, and improvement information derived from planning and performing Competency-Based Assets practices are captured to support the future use and improvement of the organization's practices.

Practices Performed

Practice 1 **Individuals and workgroups capture and retain information and artifacts that emerge from performing competency-based processes.**

1. Competency-based processes are augmented with tasks for capturing information and artifacts developed while performing business activities.

> Refer to Practice 8 of the Competency Development process area for practices that encourage the capture of competency-based experience and information. At the Defined Level, the capture of this experience and information is less formal and may not be included in the definition of competency-based processes. However, at the Predictable Level, the capture of competency-based information and artifacts is formalized and becomes an ordinary part of the competency-based processes.

> Examples of tasks that can be augmented for capturing information and artifacts include the following:
> - Postmortem reviews and analyses of projects
> - Phase-end reviews
> - Lessons learned sessions
> - Opportunities for improvement sessions
> - Process improvement or quality circle meetings
> - Debriefings
> - Shift or workgroup handoffs
> - Progress reporting mechanisms

2. Information that can contribute to the knowledge, skills, or process abilities of workforce competencies is captured and retained.

> At the end of tasks, assignments, phases, projects, or other discrete units of work, individuals and workgroups expend effort in capturing information learned through experience that may be useful in performing future business activities. Refer to Practice 15 of the Workgroup Development process area for practices relating to the capture of workgroup assets when workgroups are disbanded.
>
> Some of this information is quantitative. Refer to the Quantitative Performance Management process area for practices involving the establishment and use of process measures. Examples of qualitative information that might be captured include the following:
>
> - Unexpected events or results
> - Variation in results under different conditions
> - Factors that affect processes or their results
> - Improvements in methods or processes
> - Means for reducing variation in process or result
> - Relationships between parameters such as effort, schedule, cost, and quality
> - Opportunities for innovation in product or process
> - Rationale for decisions and their outcomes
> - Customer habits or preferences

3. Artifacts developed while performing competency-based processes are retained.

> Artifacts are retained in repositories appropriate to the type of competency-based processes that produced them. Examples of artifacts that might be retained include the following:
>
> - Design documents
> - Templates for designing solutions
> - Documentation of products or internal systems
> - Plans
> - Process descriptions
> - Notebooks
> - Presentations
> - Audit reports, lessons learned, or postmortem reports
> - Test results
> - Minutes and other records from meetings

Practice 2   **Communication vehicles are established to support the sharing of competency-based information and artifacts within and among competency communities.**

> Not all information and artifacts developed through performing competency-based processes are selected for treatment as a competency-based asset. Nevertheless, some information or artifacts may be valuable to others in a competency community. Individuals and workgroups are encouraged to capture and share information and artifacts informally when they believe others could benefit. In this case, the organization provides communications vehicles, but remains passive with regard to how information and artifacts are represented and shared. As a result, these information and artifacts are a local, rather than an organizational, asset. When a bundle of information or an artifact experiences widespread use, it becomes an organizational asset. Informal usage patterns may provide valuable guidance in setting strategies and selection standards for developing organizational competency-based assets.

> Examples of communication vehicles to support sharing include the following:
> - Email
> - Electronic bulletin boards
> - Lessons learned repositories
> - Knowledge management systems
> - Intranets
> - Video-conferencing
> - Periodic meetings or forums
> - Mentoring or coaching
> - Communication between members of a competency community

Practice 3   **A strategy for developing and deploying competency-based assets is created for each affected workforce competency.**

1. The organization identifies the workforce competencies where the capture, development, and use of competency-based assets are determined to have sufficient business benefits.

> Strategies for developing competency-based assets are generally specific to each workforce competency, but may incorporate elements related to programs, product lines, or the entire organization. Creating competency-based assets for some workforce competencies may not be judged to have sufficient business benefit to justify inclusion in the strategy. Thus, the strategies and related Competency-Based Assets activities may target selected workforce competencies to achieve specific business benefits.

Examples of business benefits to be achieved through the development of competency-based assets include:

- Improved performance of individuals, workgroups, or business units
- Enhanced development of individuals or workgroups
- Improvements to competency-based processes through their coupling with relevant competency-based assets
- Value to customers
- Contribution to the asset value of the organization

2. For each affected workforce competency, a strategy for competency-based assets is established and maintained.

Examples of issues to be covered in the strategy for competency-based assets within each affected workforce competency include the following:

- Identification of the business objectives addressed through developing competency-based assets
- How the creation of competency-based assets within this workforce competency serves organizational objectives
- Identification of the mechanisms for acquiring source material for competency-based assets
- Guidelines and criteria for selecting information and artifacts to be incorporated into competency-based assets
- Methods for developing competency-based assets
- Organization-level or workforce competency-level standards to which competency-based assets must comply
- Methods for deploying competency-based assets
- Plans for incorporating competency-based assets into competency development activities
- Approaches for using competency communities for development and deployment of competency-based assets
- How workforce practices are adjusted to motivate contribution to, and use of, competency-based assets

3. Within each workforce competency, guidelines and criteria are established for deciding which bundles of information and artifacts are sufficiently valuable to be developed into competency-based assets.

> Competency-based assets are products typically developed for users internal to the organization. Occasionally, external users may have access to competency-based assets. Since these assets are expected to produce value for the organization, they are developed with process standards similar to those used for developing products provided to customers. Quality and other standards may differ from those applied to external products or services since they must be adjusted to be appropriate for internal use.

> Examples of guidelines and criteria for selecting competency-based assets to be developed include the following:
> - A knowledge management strategy
> - Enhanced ability to achieve business objectives or competitive advantage
> - Value for increasing the knowledge, skill, or process abilities of others in the competency community
> - Ability to improve the performance of individuals or workgroups within the competency community
> - Ability to reuse assets in future business activities
> - Ability to reduce effort or increase quality
> - Value to members of the organization outside the competency community

4. Standards for representing competency-based assets are established at either the workforce competency level or the organizational level.

> Standards for representing competency-based assets include the following:
> - Standards for terminology and use
> - Requirements for completeness, correctness, and other quality attributes
> - Semantic structure and organization
> - Representation of content
> - Format for storage and presentation
> - Archiving and access methods

5. Methods and processes are defined for:
   - capturing competency-based assets,
   - sharing competency-based assets, and
   - using competency-based assets.

6. The strategy, guidelines, and standards for selecting and developing competency-based assets are communicated to each competency community.

7. Responsibilities are assigned for acquiring, developing, deploying, and maintaining competency-based assets.

Practice 4   Selected components of competency-based information and artifacts are organized into competency-based assets and made available for use.

1. Information and artifacts produced within a competency community are selected according to appropriate standards and criteria for incorporation into competency-based assets.

2. Responsible individuals or workgroups transform information and artifacts into competency-based assets using appropriate methods and complying with relevant standards.

3. Competency-based assets are made available for use.

> Refer to Practice 7 of the Competency Development process area for information regarding communication vehicles within a competency community.

> Examples of mechanisms for deploying competency-based assets for use include the following:
> - Intranets and other electronic media
> - Asset repositories containing text, graphics, video, audio, or other forms of information
> - Remote communication access methods
> - Best practices networks
> - Competency development materials
> - Integration into competency-based processes
> - Integration into product development or service delivery technology

4. Version control is established for competency-based assets.

> Examples of issues to be addressed in establishing version control include the following:
> - Identification of assets to be placed under version control
> - Methods for logging problems or defects in the assets
> - Change control procedures
> - Mechanisms for releasing assets
> - Mechanisms for tracking or auditing the status of an asset
> - Mechanisms for maintaining multiple versions of an asset for different uses

5. When competency-based information and artifacts are developed into competency-based assets, actions are taken to ensure they are consistent with workforce competency descriptions.

Practice 5   Competency-based assets are updated to reflect periodic revisions in the knowledge, skills, and process abilities constituting workforce competencies.

1. Actions are taken to ensure competency-based assets are consistent with definitions of the knowledge, skills, and process abilities constituting workforce competencies:

   ■ Competency-based assets are periodically reviewed to ensure they are consistent with workforce competency descriptions.

   ■ When revisions are made to workforce competency descriptions, related competency-based assets are revised as necessary to maintain consistency.

   ■ Information and artifacts captured from performing competency-based processes are reviewed to discover if they indicate needed revisions to workforce competency descriptions.

2. When appropriate, competency-based assets are incorporated into continuing revisions of workforce competencies.

   > Refer to Practices 4 and 5 of the Competency Analysis process area for information regarding updating workforce competency descriptions and competency-based processes. Refer also to Practice 12 of the Competency Integration process area for information regarding updating integrated competency-based processes.

3. Competency-based assets are periodically reviewed for currency and are modified or removed when appropriate.

4. When appropriate, competency communities are involved in the process of maintaining and validating for use competency-based assets relevant to their workforce competencies.

Practice 6   Competency-based assets are integrated into competency-based processes and related technologies, as appropriate.

> Examples of incorporating competency-based assets into competency-based processes and related technologies include the following:
> - Revisions to processes based on knowledge of more innovative or efficient practices
> - Use of new artifacts (e.g., decision aids, templates for planning or design, reusable product components, troubleshooting guides, customized service guides) for performing competency-based processes
> - Automatic production or coordination of artifacts in the process flow for development or service delivery
> - Immediate access to knowledge or information relevant to the performance of a competency-based or integrated competency-based process

1. Those responsible for developing and deploying competency-based assets evaluate the definition of competency-based processes to identify adjustments that will support incorporating these assets into standard work practices and business activities.

2. Workforce competency descriptions are revised to incorporate competency-based assets. These revisions may include:

   ■ revisions of competency-based processes base l on knowledge embodied in the asset or required for using the asset, or

   ■ descriptions of the knowledge and skills embodied in the assets or required for using the assets.

3. Technologies are adjusted to deploy competency-based assets. These adjustments may include:

   ■ electronically accessible repositories of competency-based assets,

   ■ search tools for finding relevant competency-based assets,

   ■ presentation media for displaying competency-based assets through means appropriate to their most effective timing and use,

   ■ communication technology for deploying competency-based assets remotely, and

   ■ security mechanisms to ensure the protection and appropriate use of the organization's competency-based assets.

4. The incorporation of competency-based assets into competency-based processes is communicated to the competency communities affected.

Practice 7   Individuals and workgroups use competency-based assets in performing their business activities.

1. Individuals and workgroups receive preparation to incorporate competency-based assets into their performance of competency-based processes.

2. Individuals and workgroups plan (or replan) their committed work to incorporate competency-based assets where appropriate.

3. Assistance or mentoring is available to individuals or workgroups using competency-based assets.

Practice 8   Information resulting from the use of competency-based assets is captured and made available.

1. Information is captured on the use of competency-based assets.

> Examples of information on the use of competency-based assets include the following:
> - How the asset was used and any tailoring needed to accommodate its use
> - New information learned or developed through using the asset
> - Extensions or new assets developed through use of the asset
> - Effort, cost, schedule, or other resource needs experienced from using the asset
> - Knowledge, skills, or process abilities gained through using the asset
> - Performance results achieved using the asset
> - Problems experienced in using the asset
> - Improvements needed to better utilize the asset

2. Information on experiences using competency-based assets is organized and made available for use.

> Information on experiences using competency-based assets can be incorporated into repositories, intranets, or other vehicles through which competency-based assets are accessed. Examples of how this information can be used include the following:
> - Guidelines for using the asset effectively
> - Sources of assistance or mentoring in using the asset
> - Accuracy of information contained in the asset
> - Evaluations of the appropriateness of an asset in different situations
> - Expectations about the benefits or results to be gained from using an asset
> - Methods for enhancing or expanding an asset
> - Limitations of an asset

3. Information characterizing the use of competency-based assets is used in revising or expanding these assets.

Practice 9   Competency development activities incorporate competency-based assets.

1. Programs of training and development in each of the organization's workforce competencies incorporate competency-based assets in the learning opportunities offered to individuals and workgroups.

2. Some learning activities are explicitly designed to impart the information contained in competency-based assets.

3. Competency-based assets are tailored as necessary to become effective components of the organization's competency development plans and activities.

Practice 10   **Mentoring or coaching activities are organized to deploy competency-based assets.**

> The basis for mentoring using competency-based assets at the Predictable Level is in making use of the process assets created in Practices 4 and 9 to support mentoring or coaching activities. Mentoring or coaching activities are organized to deploy competency-based assets. Thus, mentoring becomes a formal means of transferring a defined content of the knowledge, skills, and process abilities, typically contained in competency-based assets, to individuals and groups throughout the organization as an advanced form of competency development. Mentoring practices are more fully described in the Mentoring process area.

1. Within each workforce competency for which mentoring is appropriate, a mentoring process is defined to a level sufficient to ensure that those being mentored develop the appropriate level of competency.

> Refer to the Mentoring process area for components of a mentoring process. At the Defined Level, mentors and those they mentor are allowed to develop these relationships according to what they believe would be most effective. However, at the Predictable Level, the process is made sufficiently formal to ensure that mentors are consistent in the capabilities imparted to those being mentored.

2. Mentors receive preparation for imparting the documented knowledge, skills, and process abilities using a defined mentoring process.

3. Mentoring practices and activities are periodically reviewed to identify needed improvements or opportunities for better exploiting competency-based assets.

Practice 11   **Workforce practices and activities encourage and support the development and use of competency-based assets.**

1. Where appropriate, decisions concerning staffing and work assignments are adjusted to identify individuals with the greatest potential for contributing to and using competency-based assets.

2. Performance management practices and activities are adjusted to consider the contribution to, and use of, competency-based assets.

   - Performance objectives at both the unit and individual levels include contribution to, and use of, competency-based assets.
   - Ongoing discussions of work performance include feedback on an individual or workgroup's contribution to, or use of, competency-based assets.

- Each individual or workgroup's performance is assessed, in part, against contribution to, or use of, competency-based assets.
- Individuals and workgroups are recognized or rewarded for outstanding contribution to, or use of, competency-based assets.

3. The work environment is adjusted, as appropriate, to encourage or support the contribution to, or use of, competency-based assets.

Practice 12   **Compensation practices and activities are defined and performed to motivate the development and use of competency-based assets.**

1. The compensation system is adjusted, as needed, to motivate the development and use of competency-based assets.

2. Guidance and assistance for factoring the development and use of competency-based assets into compensation decisions is provided to individuals responsible for compensation decisions.

3. The basis on which the development and use of competency-based assets are factored into compensation decisions is discussed with each individual.

4. Individual compensation decisions affected by the development and use of competency-based assets are reviewed to ensure they maintain equity in the compensation system.

5. The compensation system is periodically reviewed and adjusted to improve its influence on the development and use of competency-based assets.

Measurement and Analysis

Measurement 1   **Measurements are made and used to determine the status and performance of activities for contributing to and using competency-based assets.**

> Examples of measurements include the following:
> - The rate and type of competency-based assets being captured
> - Progress in packaging knowledge, experience, and artifacts into forms fit for dissemination and reuse
> - The rate at which competency-based assets are disseminated through different sources
> - The rate at which different repositories of competency-based assets grow and are accessed
> - The rate at which competency-based assets are accessed
> - The rate at which competency-based assets are incorporated into competency-based processes
> - The number of times each competency-based asset has been used

Measurement 2   **Measurements are made and used to determine the effectiveness of competency-based assets on improving competencies and performance.**

> Examples of measurements of the effectiveness of competency-based assets include the following:
>
> • Their effect on improving the rate of developing workforce competencies at the individual, workgroup, or organizational levels
> • Improved performance results at the individual, workgroup, unit, or organizational levels
> • Improved performance capability at the individual, workgroup, unit, or organizational levels
> • Increased motivation or retention
> • Return on investments in competency-based assets because of improved performance results or other defined business benefits
> • Increased value of business assets

Verifying Implementation

Verification 1   **A responsible individual(s) verifies that the organization's activities for developing and using competency-based assets are conducted according to the organization's documented policies, practices, procedures, and, where appropriate, plans; and addresses noncompliance.**

These reviews verify that:

1. The capture and use of competency-based assets comply with the organization's policies and stated values.
2. The capture and use of competency-based assets comply with relevant laws and regulations.
3. Competency-Based Assets activities are performed according to the organization's documented practices and procedures.
4. Noncompliance issues are handled appropriately.

Verification 2   **Executive management periodically reviews the Competency-Based Assets activities, status, and results; and resolves issues.**

These reviews verify:

1. The appropriateness of activities for capturing and using competency-based assets at the organizational and unit levels.
2. Progress in capturing and using competency-based assets.

3. Results from reviews of Competency-Based Assets practices and activities.

> Refer to Verification 1 for information regarding reviews of Competency-Based Assets activities to ensure adherence to the following:
> - Relevant laws and regulations
> - Organizational policies, practices, and procedures

4. Status of resolution of noncompliance issues.

5. Trends related to capturing and using competency-based assets.

6. The organization's effectiveness in capturing and using competency-based assets.

Verification 3   The definition and use of competency-based assets measures and information are periodically audited for compliance with organizational policies.

> Organizational policies which may apply could include human resource, human capital, information security, confidentiality, privacy, or data disclosure policies.

1. Definitions of competency-based assets measures and information are reviewed for compliance with organizational policies.

> The data definitions define what data is to be collected, aggregated, and used. They are not the data values themselves. For example, reuse measures for competency-based assets could be a component of a data definition, but number of accesses per month or rate of growth in accesses per category would be specific data values for instances of reuse measures for competency-based assets.

2. Periodic audits ensure that competency-based assets measures and information are accessed and used in accordance with organizational policies.

> These audits may be accomplished through reviews of ongoing reporting, such as system access and use monitoring reports, and auditing to ensure compliance with relevant information security standards and organizational policies.
>
> System access and use monitoring ensures that the data are accessed only by authorized individuals, while compliance auditing ensures that these individuals perform appropriate procedures in compliance with organizational policies and standards.

Quantitative Performance Management

A process area at Maturity Level 4: Predictable

Purpose

The purpose of Quantitative Performance Management is to predict and manage the capability of competency-based processes for achieving measurable performance objectives.

Description

At the Predictable Level, the organization strengthens its management of performance, by beginning to manage its most important competency-based processes through the analysis of performance data. Quantitative Performance Management practices are consistent with programs such as Six Sigma [Harry 00, Pande 00] and Lean [Womack 03] that seek to install a discipline of quantitative process analysis into the management of an organization's business activities. Not all business activities need to be managed quantitatively, but those with the strongest influence or control over important business outcomes should be candidates for the practices of this process area.

Measurable performance objectives are established for units and are then allocated to individuals and workgroups. Workgroups establish their measurable performance objectives. Individuals and workgroups determine which competency-based processes contribute most toward achieving unit objectives and set measurable objectives for the performance of these processes. Committed work is estimated and planned using process performance baselines developed from past performance of the relevant competency-based processes.

A quantitative performance management strategy is developed for identifying, measuring, and analyzing the performance of the competency-based processes that most contribute to achieving unit objectives. Performance data are collected and analyzed according to this strategy. The performance of these competency-based processes is managed quantitatively. Corrective actions are taken when the performance of competency-based processes deviates significantly from performance objectives. Performance data are captured for future use and are used in performing selected workforce practices and activities.

Goals

Goal 1   **Measurable performance objectives are established for competency-based processes that most contribute to achieving performance objectives.**

Goal 2   **The performance of competency-based processes is managed quantitatively.**

Goal 3   **Quantitative Performance Management practices are institutionalized to ensure they are performed as defined organizational processes.**

Commitment to Perform

Commitment 1   The organization establishes and maintains a documented policy for conducting Quantitative Performance Management activities.

Issues typically addressed in the policy include:

1. The organization is committed to continuous improvement by measuring and managing performance results at the individual, workgroup, and unit levels.

2. The organization's Quantitative Performance Management activities serve the business objectives and stated values of the organization.

3. Measurable and achievable objectives are established for those aspects of performance at the individual, workgroup, and unit levels that are most closely related to the organization's business objectives.

4. Performance against measurable objectives is analyzed and reported.

5. Responsibilities for Quantitative Performance Management activities are defined and assigned to appropriate roles.

6. Results of Quantitative Performance Management analyses are used in managing performance and adjusting workforce activities.

7. Quantitative Performance Management practices and activities comply with relevant laws, regulations, and organizational policies.

> Human resources or other appropriate professionals are consulted to ensure that collection, use, and access to performance data comply with relevant laws, regulations, and organizational policies.

Commitment 2   An organizational role(s) is assigned responsibility for coordinating Quantitative Performance Management activities across the organization.

> Performance is a management responsibility. The responsibility for coordinating performance across the organization is a responsibility of executive management. The organizational role assigned responsibility for coordinating performance across the organization must either be an executive role, or be a role acting on behalf of, and in close coordination with, executive management.

Ability to Perform

Ability 1   **Within each unit, an individual(s) is assigned responsibility and authority for ensuring that Quantitative Performance Management activities are performed.**

> This responsibility should be coordinated with performance management responsibilities assigned in Ability 1 of the Performance Management process area.

Ability 2   **Adequate resources are provided for performing Quantitative Performance Management activities.**

1. The organization makes available business objectives that can be decomposed to establish measurable performance objectives at the unit level.

> Examples of the business objectives that might be a source for Quantitative Performance Management activities include the following:
> - Improving quality as measured or perceived by the customer
> - Reducing maintenance or service costs
> - Shortening delivery schedules or response times
> - Improving productivity, yield, or profits
> - Accelerating innovation
> - Improving coordination or efficiency among organizational units

2. Measurements of performance are collected and made available for analysis.

> The initial measurements required to support this practice were defined in the Performance Management, Workgroup Development, Competency Integration, and Empowered Workgroups process areas. As Quantitative Performance Management activities mature, additional or refined measures may be defined.

3. Process performance baselines for critical competency-based processes are made available for use in performing quantitative management activities.

> Refer to Practice 7 of the Organizational Capability Management process area for information regarding developing process performance baselines for critical competency-based processes.

4. Experienced individuals with appropriate expertise are available to help individuals, workgroups, and those responsible for unit performance analyze and use quantitative performance results to:

   - understand and predict performance,
   - improve performance, and
   - adjust performance-based practices and activities.

5. Resources for supporting Quantitative Performance Management activities are made available.

> Examples of resources to support Quantitative Performance Management activities include the following:
> - Plotting and graphing tools
> - Statistical analysis packages
> - Spreadsheets
> - Performance assessment instruments
> - Databases and other repositories
> - Textual and graphical reporting tools

6. Funding to accomplish Quantitative Performance Management activities is made available.

7. Adequate time is made available for performing Quantitative Performance Management activities.

Ability 3   **Individuals who participate in Quantitative Performance Management activities develop the knowledge, skills, and process abilities needed to perform their responsibilities.**

1. Those who provide performance data receive orientation on the definitions of performance data and the use of these performance data in analyses.

2. Those who receive quantitative performance management analyses receive orientation in how the results were generated and how to interpret them.

3. All individuals who are responsible for adjusting performance-related workforce practices receive preparation in how to make such adjustments.

4. All individuals or workgroups who use performance data to understand or improve their performance receive orientation in the proper interpretation and use of these data.

Ability 4   **The practices and procedures for performing Quantitative Performance Management are defined and documented.**

1. Practices and procedures are defined and documented at the organizational or unit levels, as appropriate.

2. Guidelines for tailoring the practices and procedures for use in different circumstances are documented and made available, as necessary.

3. The individual(s) assigned responsibility for coordinating Quantitative Performance Management activities across the organization ensures that defined practices and procedures are:

- maintained under version control,
- disseminated through appropriate media,

- interpreted appropriately for different situations, and
- updated through orderly methods.

4. Experiences, lessons learned, measurement results, and improvement information derived from planning and performing Quantitative Performance Management practices are captured to support the future use and improvement of the organization's practices.

Practices Performed

Practice 1 **The quantitative performance objectives required to achieve organizational business objectives are defined.**

> The organization may define two types of performance objectives for achieving business objectives. Under challenging circumstances, the business objectives set by executive management may be beyond the current performance capability of the organization's units, workforce competencies, and competency-based processes. When there is a gap between current capabilities and the capabilities required to achieve business objectives, the organization must determine whether they can be achieved through near-term improvements during the performance period. If near-term improvements cannot close capability gaps, then these performance objectives should be established as improvement objectives to be addressed by process areas at the Optimizing Level rather than as targets for quantitative performance management at the Predictable Level.
>
> The process areas at the Optimizing Level are designed to close gaps between current performance capabilities and the greater performance capabilities required to achieve strategic performance objectives that are beyond the current capabilities of individuals, workgroups, or the organization. In essence, the Optimizing Level focuses on implementing the improvements necessary to achieve the organization's strategic competitive business objectives. Quantitative Performance Management is designed to establish quantitative control over the current performance capabilities of organizational units, workforce competencies, and competency-based processes. When individuals, workgroups, or work units are held accountable for performance objectives that exceed their capability and reasonable expectations for near-term improvement, they have been set up for failure. In extreme cases their performance can devolve back to that at lower maturity levels because they sacrifice disciplined competency-based processes in an attempt to satisfy unachievable objectives. For this reason the organization's quantitative performance objectives that are to be passed to units or workgroups should be achievable within current performance capabilities or the capabilities that can be achieved by near-term improvements.
>
> Performing within current capability is the responsibility of individuals, workgroups, and work units. Taking the actions required to achieve near-term performance improvements is also the responsibility of individuals, workgroups, and work units. Closing gaps between current and required future organizational capability is the responsibility of executive management and should be addressed using the process areas at the Optimizing Level. When business conditions necessitate that executive management set organizational performance objectives that are beyond the capabilities of organizational units, workforce competencies, and competency-based processes, then executive management must accept responsibility for risks involved.

1. The organization's business objectives are analyzed to identify the quantitative performance objectives required to achieve them.

> Performance objectives that are beyond the current performance capabilities of the organization's units, workforce competencies, and competency-based processes, even when enhanced by near-term improvements, are established as improvement objectives to be addressed by Level 5 process areas.

2. The organization sets quantitative performance objectives that are:

   - achievable within the current or near-term capability of the organization's units, workforce competencies, and competency-based processes;
   - decomposed as necessary to allocate them to units, workgroups, workforce competencies, or other organizational entities;
   - revised, when necessitated by business strategy or conditions; and
   - communicated to units.

3. Feedback is obtained from units on their ability to translate organizational performance objectives into measurable unit performance objectives.

4. Methods for establishing more effective quantitative performance objectives are improved using feedback from units.

Practice 2   Each unit establishes measurable performance objectives whose achievement most contributes to organizational business objectives.

> Refer to Practices 1 and 2 of the Performance Management process area for information regarding how units establish, update, and allocate performance objectives. Refer to Ability 2 of this process area for information regarding making business objectives available to units and the workforce to support establishing measurable performance objectives. To support practices and activities in this process area, these measurable performance objectives must be defined at a level of specificity that they can be decomposed into quantifiable results for each unit. At lower levels of maturity, the requirement was only for objectives whose performance could be evaluated objectively.

1. Units define their measurable performance objectives based on:

   - business objectives established by the organization;
   - organizational performance objectives;
   - performance capabilities of the workforce competencies and competency-based processes relevant to the unit's committed work;
   - current performance capabilities of the individuals and workgroups within the unit; and
   - anticipated performance capabilities that can be achieved through near-term competency development and related improvement activities.

2. Units inform higher level management when they cannot define measurable and achievable performance objectives that contribute to meeting organizational performance objectives.

> When informed of issues regarding these performance objectives, examples of actions higher level management may take include the following:
> - Accept the unit's performance objectives and adjust organizational performance objectives or other performance factors to reflect the impact of the unit's current or near-term capability
> - Take corrective action such as assigning the work to other work units whose current capability is sufficient to achieving organizational performance objectives or providing extra improvement resources or development time to make it possible for the unit to achieve the required capability
> - Accept the risk of requiring the unit to achieve the performance objectives that are beyond their current or near-term capabilities
> - Work with the unit to establish improvement objectives or capability development objectives, and the necessary actions to achieve these objectives
> - Review the business objectives relevant to the unit's committed work

3. Units identify the business activities most critical to the achievement of their measurable performance objectives and establish methods for measuring the performance and effectiveness of these activities.

4. The unit reaches consensus with individuals and workgroups about methods for measuring the performance and effectiveness of critical business activities allocated to them.

Practice 3   Individuals and workgroups establish measurable performance objectives for competency-based processes that most contribute to their achieving unit performance objectives.

> Measurable performance objectives for units were established in the Performance Management process area. Refer to Practices 1 and 2 of the Performance Management process area for information regarding how units establish, update, and allocate performance objectives.
>
>   It may not always be possible for a unit to establish measurable performance objectives for its processes, as all individuals or workgroups within the unit may not use common processes. Several competencies, each having their own defined processes, may exist within a single unit. For example, a software development unit may be composed of software architects, designers, programmers, and testers who work in independent workgroups to perform their own competency-based processes.

This practice focuses on establishing measurable performance objectives for those competency-based processes that contribute most to achieving desired performance. The kinds of processes for which measurable objectives may be established include the following:

- Defined processes, which are those competency-based processes defined in each workforce competency. Refer to Practices 2 and 5 of the Competency Analysis process area for information regarding the identification and definition of defined, competency-based processes.
- The workgroup's operating processes, which include both methods and procedures for performing common workgroup functions and competency-based processes tailored for use by workgroups. Refer to Practices 4 and 7 of the Workgroup Development process area and to Practices 4 and 5 of the Empowered Workgroups process area for information regarding the definition and tailoring of the workgroup's operating processes.
- Integrated competency-based processes, which are those processes that have been integrated from the separate defined processes used by different workforce competencies. Refer to Practice 3 of the Competency Integration process area for information regarding the definition of integrated competency-based processes.

Individuals and workgroups:

1. Determine the business activities that must be completed to achieve the unit's measurable performance objectives.

2. Identify the competency-based processes required to accomplish these business activities.

3. Select from the identified processes those competency-based processes that most contribute to the achievement of the unit's measurable performance objectives.

4. Establish measurable objectives for the performance of these selected competency-based processes to ensure that the unit's measurable objectives are achieved.

5. Evaluate whether each competency-based process can contribute to achieving the unit's measurable performance objectives by analyzing relevant process performance baselines, as well as individual and workgroup capabilities.

6. Take action when a competency-based process is determined not to be capable of contributing to the achievement of the unit's measurable performance objectives by:

   - adjusting the performance objectives to reflect the current capability of the competency-based process involved,

   - identifying improvements in the capability of competency-based processes required to achieve measurable performance objectives, and

   - communicating the capability improvements needed to those responsible for improving the capability of competency-based processes.

   > Refer to Practice 12 of the Continuous Capability Improvement process area for information regarding identifying opportunities for improving the capability and performance of competency-based processes.

7. Take action when the capability of an individual or workgroup is not sufficient for contributing to the unit's measurable performance objectives by:

   - adjusting the performance objectives for an individual or workgroup to reflect their current or near-term capability to contribute,

   - identifying improvements in the capability of an individual or workgroup required to achieve the unit's measurable performance objectives and assigning development or improvement activities to improve their capability,

   - adjusting the performance objectives or assigned work of other individuals or workgroups if necessary to ensure the overall capability of the work unit is sufficient to achieve its measurable performance objectives, or

   - acquiring resources or development actions to improve the capabilities of individuals or workgroups to the level required to achieve the unit's measurable performance objectives.

8. Incorporate measurable performance objectives for competency-based processes into individual and workgroup performance objectives, as appropriate.

9. Reevaluate measurable performance objectives when necessitated by changes in business conditions or process capability results, and revise individual or workgroup performance objectives, as appropriate.

Practice 4   Individuals and workgroups plan their committed work using process performance baselines for competency-based processes.

> A *process performance* baseline is a documented characterization of the actual results achieved by following a process. Refer to Practice 7 of the Organizational Capability Management process area for more information regarding process performance baselines and their construction.

Individuals and workgroups:

1. Identify the competency-based processes required to accomplish their business activities.

2. Identify conditions that may affect their performance of competency-based processes.

3. Identify relevant process performance baselines for the competency-based processes to be performed in accomplishing their business activities.

> Individuals or workgroups may have established process performance baselines from their own previous performance that are more accurate or relevant than organizational baselines. Under such circumstances individuals or workgroups may choose to substitute their documented process performance baselines when they have proven to be more accurate for planning and managing the performance of competency-based processes.

4. Develop work estimates and plans based on analyses using the relevant process performance baselines and information about the conditions that may affect their performance of competency-based processes.

> When individuals perform their business activities as members of a workgroup, capability-based estimating may be performed in two stages. In the first stage, individuals estimate and plan their own work based on personal process performance baselines. In the second stage, these personal estimates and plans are integrated at the workgroup level in estimating and planning workgroup performance.

5. Evaluate the planned performance of competency-based processes to determine if they are capable of achieving measurable individual and workgroup performance objectives.

6. Make recommendations for adjustments in measurable performance objectives when competency-based processes are not capable of achieving them.

7. Establish and negotiate work commitments based on capability-based estimates and plans.

Practice 5   Individuals and workgroups define quantitative methods for managing the competency-based processes that most contribute to achieving their performance objectives.

> Competency-based processes are quantitatively managed to ensure they are capable of achieving measurable performance objectives and that their performance makes predicted progress toward planned outcomes. Not all processes need to be quantitatively managed. Primarily those competency-based processes believed to most contribute to or control the achievement of measurable performance objectives are subjected to quantitative management. The outcomes of quantitative management are predictable results obtained through predictable performance.

1. A quantitative performance management strategy is developed for each competency-based process selected for quantitative management.

> Competency-based processes can be quantitatively managed at the individual level, at multiple points of performance within the workgroup, or at the workgroup level. The level at which competency-based processes are quantitatively managed may differ across processes. Individuals or workgroups may have different quantitative performance management strategies, based on having different measurable performance objectives or different contexts for the performance of their competency-based processes. In some cases, processes that are performed across workgroups may be quantitatively managed. Some processes may be managed through performance measures such as effort, duration, or cost; while others may be managed from measured attributes of their products or services such as amount, user satisfaction, defects, or other quality measures. Generally, a specific quantitative performance management strategy is defined for each competency-based process selected for quantitative management.

> Examples of issues to be covered in the quantitative performance management strategy include the following:
> - Measurable performance objectives that establish the context for quantitative management
> - Identification of the competency-based processes to be quantitatively managed
> - Measures to be used in the analyses
> - Appropriate level of data aggregation (individual, workgroup, etc.) for the measures and analyses defined
> - Methods and frequency of data collection
> - Methods for data validation, storage, and retrieval
> - Data analyses to be performed
> - Guidance and limitations for evaluating results
> - Reports to be distributed
> - Methods and tools to support using results
> - Safeguards to ensure the privacy and security of data and results

2. Measures of competency-based processes are defined and agreed to.

> Examples of sources for defined measures of competency-based processes include the following:
> - Definitions of competency-based processes
> - Existing process performance baselines for relevant processes
> - Standard business, product, or service measures

3. Procedures for analyzing data on competency-based processes are defined.

> Examples of analyses that might be performed include the following:
> - Curve-fitting or trend analyses
> - Statistical process control
> - Bayesian-based techniques
> - Regression or multivariate predictive techniques
> - Stochastic or time-series techniques
> - Classification analyses (e.g., defect or problem types)
> - Analyses of leading indicators

4. The quantitative performance management strategy is:
   - reviewed and agreed to by all individuals or groups affected by it,
   - reviewed and approved by unit management, and
   - periodically reviewed to ensure its consistency with performance objectives and revised, as necessary, to improve the value of the analyses performed.

Practice 6   **Individuals and workgroups quantitatively manage the performance of the competency-based processes that most contribute to achieving their performance objectives.**

1. Quantitative performance management activities are conducted according to the quantitative performance management strategies.

2. The performance of competency-based processes by individuals or workgroups is measured and analyzed for use in such activities as:
   - tracking progress,
   - predicting outcomes,
   - assessing risks,

- making decisions, or
- identifying needed actions.

> Examples of how quantitative analyses might be used include the following:
>
> - Establishing process performance baselines from the performance of individuals and workgroups to determine if they are capable of achieving the measurable performance objectives set for them, and whether they differ from organizational baselines established within their workforce competency
> - Using interim performance results to predict future outcomes and determine the likelihood that measurable performance objectives will be achieved
> - Analyzing variations in process results to understand and control process performance, and to identify the causes of variation and needs for corrective action
> - Evaluating trends or comparing predicted to actual results to determine whether current progress or results deviate from those planned or expected
> - Analyzing factors that affect performance to improve the validity of process performance baselines, and to establish appropriate baselines for different situations

3. The capabilities of competency-based processes that most contribute to achieving performance objectives are:

- computed using parameters from organizational process performance baselines, where appropriate,
- compared to organizational process performance baselines, and
- recomputed for use by individuals and workgroups when their capability levels differ significantly from organizational process performance baselines.

4. The capabilities of competency-based processes that most contribute to achieving performance objectives are managed quantitatively.

> Performance may be quantitatively managed at the individual or workgroup level. Thus, managing the capability of a competency-based process may imply actions to be taken by individuals, by workgroups, by managers, or by some combination of these. Examples of attributes of processes being managed quantitatively include the following:
>
> - Process performance and variation are under statistical control
> - Process performance and results are predictable within acceptable confidence limits
> - Assignable causes of performance variation have been identified and their effects have been controlled or eliminated
> - Variations in process performance can be predicted using knowledge of the effects of assignable causes that cannot be eliminated, such as differences in individual capability
> - Process performance or results can be intentionally altered by making known changes to processes or factors that control them
> - Process performance or results fit known patterns in quantitative models

5. Individuals, workgroups, and management base decisions on performance data.

6. Results of data collection and analyses are reviewed to determine if corrective actions need to be taken in the quantitative performance management strategy.

Practice 7   **Individuals or workgroups take corrective actions when the performance of their competency-based processes differs from the quantitative results required to achieve their performance objectives.**

1. The results of quantitative management activities are evaluated for their implications regarding achievement of measurable individual and workgroup performance objectives.

> Examples of conditions under which corrective actions may be indicated include the following:
> - Performance trends that differ significantly from performance objectives
> - Predictions of outcomes that differ significantly from expectations or objectives
> - Large variations in process performance that introduce risk in achieving objectives
> - Deviations from acceptable capability levels

2. The performance of competency-based processes is analyzed to identify factors that cause results to deviate from measurable performance objectives.

3. Individuals or workgroups take corrective actions to align the performance of competency-based processes with measurable performance objectives.

> Examples of corrective actions may include the following:
> - Removing or adjusting factors that inhibit competency-based processes from performing at their established level of capability
> - Eliminating or controlling factors that affect process performance (i.e., controlling assignable causes of process variation)
> - Engaging in individual or workgroup development activities that increase their performance capability
> - Making improvements that improve the capability of competency-based processes
> - Adjusting measurable performance objectives to reflect the capability results observed in performing competency-based processes
> - Informing management of the risk incurred by the capability results observed in performing competency-based processes
> - Identifying and performing actions that can compensate for performance below expected capability levels

4. When the performance of competency-based processes has been aligned with measurable performance objectives, individuals and workgroups:

    ■ continue to monitor performance results according to the quantitative performance management strategy,

    ■ manage the performance of competency-based processes to ensure they exhibit stable or predictable performance,

    ■ manage the effects of assignable causes or other factors that inhibit competency-based processes from maintaining the level of capability established in their current use, and

    ■ take additional corrective actions, as needed, to maintain the alignment of process performance results with measurable performance objectives.

Practice 8   **Quantitative records of individual and workgroup performance are retained.**

1. Individuals and workgroups retain data on their performance of competency-based processes for their future use in estimating, planning, and managing their performance.

2. Performance data that are appropriate for characterizing the capability of competency-based processes are submitted for use in organizational capability analyses.

> Refer to the Organizational Capability Management process area for information regarding organizational capability analyses.

3. Information regarding needed improvements in the capability of competency-based processes is communicated to those responsible for continuous improvement activities in each competency community.

> Refer to the Continuous Capability Improvement process area for information regarding continuous improvement activities for competency-based processes.

4. Privacy and security are established for quantitative performance management data and information at the individual, workgroup, and organizational levels.

Practice 9   **Where appropriate, quantitative performance results are used in performing workforce practices and activities.**

> The use of quantitative performance management data in performing workforce activities must be governed by policies regarding appropriate uses and levels of confidentiality for performance data at the individual and workgroup levels.

> Examples of ways in which quantitative performance management data might be used in performing workforce activities include the following:
> - Identifying learning and development needs
> - Aiding mentors in providing improvement advice and guidance
> - Guiding career development discussions and decisions
> - Aiding selection and other staffing decisions
> - Supporting ongoing communication about performance of committed work
> - Documenting accomplishments against performance objectives
> - Guiding performance improvement plans and actions
> - Providing a basis for recognition and rewards
> - Supporting adjustments and other compensation decisions
> - Improving competency development activities
> - Improving competency integration activities
> - Improving competency-based processes and/or competency-based assets
> - Improving the development or empowerment of workgroups
> - Incorporating capability levels into workforce planning

Measurement and Analysis

Measurement 1   **Measurements are made and used to determine the status and performance of the organization's Quantitative Performance Management activities.**

> Examples of measurements include the following:
> - The completeness and timeliness of the data collected
> - The accuracy of the data collected
> - Frequency with which individuals and workgroups collect and analyze performance data
> - Number or extent of changes made in competency-based and integrated competency-based processes, based on performance results
> - Number of process performance baselines produced by individuals and workgroups
> - Number of process performance baselines submitted for use in organizational capability analyses

Measurement 2   Measurements are made and used to determine the effectiveness of Quantitative Performance Management activities.

> Examples of measures to determine the value and effectiveness of Quantitative Performance Management activities at the individual, workgroup, or unit levels include the following:
> - Improvements in capability and performance
> - Extent to which measurable performance objectives are achieved
> - Improved ability to identify and manage factors that affect performance
> - Improved accuracy of predicting performance results

Verifying Implementation

Verification 1   A responsible individual(s) verifies that Quantitative Performance Management activities are conducted according to the organization's documented policies, practices, procedures, and, where appropriate, plans; and addresses noncompliance.

These reviews verify that:

1. Quantitative Performance Management activities comply with the organization's policies and stated values.
2. Quantitative Performance Management activities comply with relevant laws and regulations.
3. Quantitative Performance Management activities are performed according to the organization's documented practices and procedures.
4. Noncompliance issues are handled appropriately.

Verification 2   Executive management periodically reviews the Quantitative Performance Management activities, status, and results; and resolves issues.

These reviews verify:

1. The appropriateness of Quantitative Performance Management activities at the individual, within the workgroup, at the workgroup, and at the unit levels.
2. Progress in performing Quantitative Performance Management activities.
3. Results from reviews of Quantitative Performance Management practices and activities.

> Refer to Verification 1 for information regarding reviews of Quantitative Performance Management activities to ensure adherence to the following:
> - Relevant laws and regulations
> - Organizational policies, practices, and procedures

4. Status of resolution of noncompliance issues.

5. Trends related to Quantitative Performance Management.

6. The organization's effectiveness of Quantitative Performance Management activities in achieving quantitative performance objectives.

Verification 3   The definition and use of performance measures at the individual, workgroup, and unit levels are periodically audited for compliance with the organization's policies.

> Organizational policies which may apply could include human resource, human capital, information security, confidentiality, privacy, or data disclosure policies.

1. Definitions of performance measures and information are reviewed for compliance with organizational policies.

> The data definitions define what data is to be collected, aggregated, and used. They are not the data values themselves. For example, annual performance rating could be a component of a data definition, but "3" would be a specific data value for an instance of annual individual performance rating.

2. Periodic audits ensure that performance measures and information are accessed and used in accordance with organizational policies.

> These audits may be accomplished through reviews of ongoing reporting, such as system access and use monitoring reports, and auditing to ensure compliance with relevant information security standards and organizational policies.
>
> System access and use monitoring ensures that the data are accessed only by authorized individuals, while compliance auditing ensures that these individuals perform appropriate procedures in compliance with organizational policies and standards.

Organizational Capability Management
A process area at Maturity Level 4: Predictable

Purpose
The purpose of Organizational Capability Management is to quantify and manage the capability of the workforce and of the critical competency-based processes it performs.

Description
The *capability of the workforce* refers to the level of knowledge, skills, and process abilities available to the organization in each critical workforce competency for performing committed work. The organization's capability in a specific workforce competency is assessed from the number of individuals in a competency community and the level of knowledge, skill, and process ability that each of them possesses.

The organization identifies the workforce competencies most critical to its business strategy and objectives. The organization quantitatively manages the capability of these critical workforce competencies to ensure that critical competency-based processes can be performed with sufficient capability to achieve the organization's quantitative performance and business objectives. The organization determines its capability and related quantitative trends in each of its critical workforce competencies relative to objectives established in its strategic workforce plan. Data regarding competency development trends are defined and collected, and trends are analyzed. The organization determines the quantitative impact that its competency development and related workforce activities have on capability in each of its workforce competencies. These analyses are focused on changes in behavior and results, the highest two levels in Kirkpatrick's framework for evaluating training [Kirkpatrick 98].

The *capability of a process* typically refers to statistically based descriptions of the performance or results of a process that has been performed repeatedly. In the People CMM, we use the term *process performance baseline* to refer to these documented characterizations of the actual results achieved by following a process. Process performance baselines are typically developed by aggregating performance data across individuals, workgroups, units, or workforce competencies. However, separate process performance baselines may have to be developed for different situations whose circumstances cause predictable process performance differences. This may be necessary as it may be inappropriate to aggregate process performance baselines when competency-based processes are performed under circumstances that result in different performance characteristics. In such situations, the organization may develop and maintain several process performance baselines describing typical results under the differing circumstances where the competency-based process is performed. Thus, a process performance baseline describes the typical result that will occur when a competency-based process is performed under specific conditions. Process performance baselines provide an organization with the ability to predict future performance and results based on past experience and to control progress toward achieving these results while the process is being performed.

Organizational Capability Management defines methods for establishing process performance baselines and quantitative performance models for predicting the performance of critical competency-based processes. The products of Organizational Capability Management are used as inputs in performing Quantitative Performance Management activities in units and workgroups. The impact of workforce practices on the capability and performance of competency-based processes is quantified and managed and the results of these analyses are used in organizational decisions. The results of these analyses are used in adjusting workforce practices to improve their impact on performance and results.

Goals

Goal 1   **Progress in developing the capability of critical workforce competencies is managed quantitatively.**

Goal 2   **The impact of workforce practices and activities on progress in developing the capability of critical workforce competencies is evaluated and managed quantitatively.**

Goal 3   **The capabilities of competency-based processes in critical workforce competencies are established and managed quantitatively.**

Goal 4   **The impact of workforce practices and activities on the capabilities of competency-based processes in critical workforce competencies is evaluated and managed quantitatively.**

Goal 5   **Organizational Capability Management practices are institutionalized to ensure they are performed as defined organizational processes.**

Commitment to Perform

Commitment 1   **The organization establishes and maintains a documented policy for conducting Organizational Capability Management activities.**

Issues typically addressed in the policy include:

1. The organization's capability management practices and activities serve the business objectives and stated values of the organization.

2. The organization identifies the workforce competencies that are critical to its business strategy and objectives.

3. The organization identifies the competency-based processes within each critical workforce competency that are critical to achieving defined performance objectives and business results.

4. Measures are defined and collected for characterizing:

   ▪ the capability of each of the organization's critical workforce competencies, and

   ▪ the performance of critical competency-based processes.

5. Progress toward achieving measurable capability objectives for each of the organization's critical workforce competencies is managed quantitatively.

6. The capability of competency-based processes is analyzed and used in managing these processes to achieve performance objectives.

7. Workforce practices and activities are evaluated for their impact on:

   - the organization's capability in its critical workforce competencies, and
   - the capability and performance of competency-based processes.

8. Results of quantitative analyses of impact are used in managing and improving workforce practices and activities.

9. Responsibilities for the organization's capability management activities are defined and assigned to appropriate roles.

10. Organizational Capability Management practices and activities comply with relevant laws, regulations, and organizational policies.

> Human resources or other appropriate professionals are consulted to ensure that the collection, use, and access to competency and performance data comply with relevant laws, regulations, and organizational policies.

Commitment 2   An organizational role(s) is assigned responsibility for coordinating Organizational Capability Management activities across the organization.

> Examples of organizational roles that might be assigned responsibility for coordinating capability management activities include the following:
> - Competency center managers
> - Competency ownership teams
> - Quality, efficiency, or performance experts
> - Measurement or process improvement groups
> - The human resources function
> - Managers responsible for units requiring a unique competency

Ability to Perform

Ability 1   **Within each unit, an individual(s) is assigned responsibility and authority for ensuring the unit's involvement in Organizational Capability Management activities, as appropriate.**

> Examples of responsibilities performed within units include the following:
> - Providing competency and performance capability data to an organizational group for storage and analysis
> - Obtaining and using organizational capability baselines in planning and other activities within the unit
> - Providing data on competency development activities within the unit and performance data relevant to improved capability
> - Providing information or data on workforce activities performed within the unit for use in analyzing the impact of workforce practices and activities on performance
> - Ensuring appropriate security and use of performance data

Ability 2   **A responsible individual(s) coordinates the quantitative capability management activities within each critical workforce competency.**

Ability 3   **Adequate resources are provided for performing Organizational Capability Management activities.**

1. Measures of the performance of competency-based processes are made available for analysis.

> The initial measurements required to support this practice were defined in the Performance Management, Competency-Based Practices, Workgroup Development, Empowered Workgroups, and Quantitative Performance Management process areas. As the organization's quantitative capability management activities mature, additional or refined measures may be defined.

2. Experienced individuals who have expertise in analyzing competency-based data are available to assist in quantitative analyses of the organization's workforce competency trends and development activities and in using the results in improvement activities.

3. Experienced individuals with appropriate expertise are available to help individuals, workgroups, and those responsible for unit performance to analyze and use quantitative performance results to:

   - understand and predict the performance of competency-based processes,
   - improve their performance, and
   - adjust practices and activities as needed to enhance the performance of competency-based processes.

4. Resources for supporting the organization's capability management activities are made available.

> Examples of resources to support the organization's capability management activities include the following:
> - Capability assessment tools, such as tests or work samples
> - Plotting and graphing tools
> - Statistical analysis packages
> - Spreadsheets
> - Performance assessment instruments
> - Databases and other repositories
> - Textual and graphical reporting tools

5. Funding to accomplish the organization's capability management activities is made available.

6. Time and methods for data collection are built into workforce activities.

7. Adequate time is made available for performing the organization's quantitative capability management activities.

Ability 4   **Those responsible for Organizational Capability Management activities develop the knowledge, skills, and process abilities needed to perform their responsibilities.**

1. Those who collect capability data and process performance data receive orientation on the definitions and use of these data in analyses.

2. Those who analyze and report capability data, process performance baselines, and related results receive preparation in statistics, data analysis, presentation methods, and other activities related to performing their responsibilities.

Ability 5   **Individuals who participate in Organizational Capability Management activities receive appropriate orientation in the purposes and methods for the organization's quantitative capability management activities.**

Individuals and workgroups receive the orientation required to interpret and use capability data and process performance baselines if they have responsibilities for:

- using this information in performing workforce activities,
- using this information in evaluating and managing competency development practices and activities,
- using this information for planning and managing the performance of competency-based processes,
- adjusting workforce practices based on this information, and
- using this information to understand or improve the performance of competency-based processes.

Ability 6   **The practices and procedures for performing Organizational Capability Management are defined and documented.**

1. Practices and procedures are defined and documented at the organizational or unit levels, as appropriate.

2. Guidelines for tailoring the practices and procedures for use in different circumstances are documented and made available, as necessary.

3. The individual(s) assigned responsibility for Organizational Capability Management activities across the organization ensures that defined practices and procedures are:

   ■ maintained under version control,

   ■ disseminated through appropriate media,

   ■ interpreted appropriately for different situations, and

   ■ updated through orderly methods.

4. Experiences, lessons learned, measurement results, and improvement information derived from planning and performing Organizational Capability Management practices are captured to support the future use and improvement of the organization's practices.

Practices Performed

Practice 1   **The organization identifies the workforce competencies that are critical to its business strategies and objectives.**

> *Critical workforce competencies* are those most crucial to sustaining an organization's capability in its core competence [Prahalad 90]. Their growth and development are critical to the viability of strategic business objectives and plans. Consequently, the organization's capability in each of its critical workforce competencies is managed quantitatively to ensure that its competency-based processes can be performed with sufficient capability to achieve the organization's quantitative performance objectives.

1. The organization evaluates its strategic business and workforce plans to identify workforce competencies that are critical to achieving its business strategies and objectives.

2. The organization periodically reevaluates its business and workforce plans to identify additions or deletions to its list of critical workforce competencies.

Practice 2 **The organization quantifies its capability in each of its critical workforce competencies.**

1. Trends to be analyzed for each critical workforce competency are based on capability objectives established in the strategic workforce plan.

> Refer to Practice 2 of the Workforce Planning process area for information regarding setting capability objectives for workforce competencies and to Practice 8 of the Competency Analysis process area for information regarding determining the current resource profiles for each of the organization's workforce competencies. These resource profiles present the overall capability in the workforce for accomplishing business activities requiring knowledge, skills, or process abilities in a specific workforce competency.

> Examples of measurable objectives for capability in each of the organization's workforce competencies include the following:
> - The level of capability available in each critical workforce competency
> - The rate at which capability is developed in each critical workforce competency
> - The deployment of critical workforce competencies across the organization
> - Trends relating competency development and business performance
> - The rate at which new workforce competencies can be developed and deployed across the organization

2. For each critical workforce competency, a quantitative capability management strategy is established and maintained.

> Examples of issues to be covered in the quantitative capability strategy for each critical workforce competency include the following:
> - Capability objectives, trends, and issues to be subjected to analysis
> - Strategy for performing, validating, and revising analyses
> - Definition of measures to be used in the analysis
> - Analyses to be performed
> - Methods and frequency of data collection, validation, and storage
> - Schedule for performing and reporting the analyses
> - Guidance and limitations for evaluating results
> - Reports to be distributed
> - Incorporation of results into other workforce activities, such as Competency Analysis and Workforce Planning
> - Safeguards to ensure data privacy and security

> The initial measurements required to support this practice were defined in the Competency Analysis, Competency Development, and Competency-Based Practices process areas. As quantitative analyses of organizational competency mature, additional or revised measures can be defined.

3. Quantitative analyses of capability are conducted according to the quantitative capability management strategy for each critical workforce competency.

> Quantitative analyses of capability can be performed at the organizational level for all critical workforce competencies, or in a more decentralized fashion at the level of one or more competency communities. The level at which these analyses are performed reflects the organization's strategy (e.g., centralized vs. decentralized) for managing its workforce competencies.

4. The organization develops quantitative models of capability in its critical workforce competencies for use in workforce planning and management.

> Quantitative models of capability can range from simple quantitative projections based on historical trends to sophisticated stochastic or multivariate statistical models. The purpose of these models is to predict future capability levels based on historical experience, industry trends, current conditions, and/or future expectations. The organization may begin with industry standard models and over time refine them to reflect the organization's business conditions and unique characteristics. Quantitative models may differ in purpose, sophistication, analytic foundation, parameters, predictability, or use among the various critical workforce competencies.

> Examples of quantitative models may include:
> - Growth curves for projecting future capability in critical workforce competencies
> - Demographic models of labor supply for projecting availability and level of skills of entrants to critical workforce competencies in the future
> - Models relating hiring and retention success with various recruiting sources and methods
> - Models estimating rates at which individuals can progress through competency development activities and successfully achieve higher levels of capability in workforce competencies
> - Predictive models of characteristics most closely associated with capability and success in different workforce competencies
> - Models for evaluating tradeoffs in breadth vs. depth of individual experience on career performance at the individual level and on workforce capability at the organizational level
> - Models of the effect of increasing capability in various critical workforce competencies on performance at the individual, workgroup, unit, and/or organizational levels
> - Models relating the compensation strategy to hiring, retention, and career growth in various workforce competencies

5. Capability results for each critical workforce competency are:

- reported to responsible individuals,

- incorporated into workforce planning and other workforce practices as appropriate, and

- updated on a periodic or event-driven basis consistent with the quantitative capability management strategy.

Practice 3   **The organization's capability in each of its critical workforce competencies is managed quantitatively.**

1. Quantitative analyses of capability in each critical workforce competency are used by responsible individuals to:

- evaluate progress in achieving capability objectives,

- predict future capability levels,

- identify factors that affect capability levels,

- evaluate the effects of workforce practices and activities on capability levels, and

- identify needs for corrective action.

> Examples of conditions under which needs for corrective action may be identified include the following:
>
> - Trends in a workforce competency differ significantly from the measurable objectives established for the competency
> - The impact of competency development activities on a workforce competency is below expectations
> - Variation in results of competency development activities is too great
> - Deviations from the capability level of a workforce competency that the organization believes it must maintain

2. Corrective actions are taken when capability results deviate significantly from capability objectives for a critical workforce competency.

> Examples of corrective actions may include the following:
>
> - Improving the performance of workforce practices and activities that have been demonstrated as being capable of achieving the targeted capability results
> - Tailoring, replacing, or terminating workforce practices or activities that are not achieving intended capability results
> - Altering capability objectives for a critical workforce competency or adjusting the workforce activities performed to meet these objectives

Practice 4   **Measurable objectives for contributing to capability growth in critical workforce competencies are established for workforce practices and activities.**

1. Measurable objectives for contributing to capability growth are established for workforce practices and activities based on such factors as:

    ■ the capability development objectives for the critical workforce competency established in the strategic workforce plan,

    ■ the nature of how specific workforce practices affect capability in each critical workforce competency,

    ■ the capability of the individuals participating in the workforce activities related to the practice, and

    ■ how capability will be measured.

Refer to Practice 2 of the Workforce Planning process area for information regarding setting measurable capability objectives for workforce competencies. Examples of these measurable objectives include the following:

*   The effectiveness in recruiting candidates in different workforce competencies
*   The effectiveness of selection techniques in predicting work performance and development of capability in workforce competencies
*   The effectiveness of performance feedback in motivating and guiding capability development
*   The effectiveness of different competency development activities, such as training or mentoring, on increasing capability in critical workforce competencies
*   The effectiveness of the compensation strategy in attracting and retaining individuals in different workforce competencies
*   The effectiveness of the compensation strategy on developing capability in different workforce competencies
*   The effectiveness of career development activities in motivating and guiding capability growth
*   The effectiveness of formal and informal mechanisms for transferring capability among members of a competency community

---

2. Measurable objectives for contributing to capability growth are:

    ■ developed through the involvement of those responsible for coordinating or managing each affected workforce practice across the organization,

    ■ reviewed by responsible individuals with expertise in performing the relevant workforce practices, and

    ■ communicated to all affected parties.

Practice 5   **The organization quantitatively evaluates the impacts of workforce practices and activities on capability in each of its critical workforce competencies.**

The organization should analyze the impact of the workforce activities considered most important for increasing the capability in a critical workforce competency. Examples of effects of workforce practices and activities on the capability of a workforce competency that the organization might evaluate quantitatively include the following:

- Impact of recruiting activities on the mix and level of workforce competencies entering the organization
- Success of selection methods in identifying individuals with capabilities in the organization's workforce competencies
- Impact of performance management activities on identifying needs for development activities in the organization's workforce competencies
- Impact of training and competency-development activities on increasing the level of workforce competencies in the organization
- Impact of training, competency development, and career development activities on the rates at which individuals are progressing through graduated career levels
- Impact of career development and other competency-based practices on motivating and increasing the level and optimal mix of workforce competencies in the organization
- Effect of compensation, performance management, and recognition and reward practices and activities on capability within each critical workforce competency

1. An evaluation strategy is established and maintained for evaluating the impact of workforce practices and activities on capability in critical workforce competencies.

Examples of issues to be covered in the evaluation strategy include the following:

- Measurable objectives for contributing to the capability growth to be analyzed
- Measures to be used in the analyses
- Methods and frequency of data collection
- Methods for data validation, storage, and retrieval
- Data analyses to be performed
- Guidance and limitations for evaluating results
- Reports to be distributed
- Methods and tools to support using results
- Other uses for the data in performing workforce activities
- Safeguards to ensure the privacy and security of data and results

2. Measures of capability improvement are defined in each critical workforce competency for use in developing capability baselines and evaluating the impact of workforce practices and activities.

> Examples of capability improvement measures may include the following:
> - Knowledge tests or skill demonstrations
> - Measures of work performance or on-the-job behavior
> - Baselines for the capability of competency-based processes
> - Measures of coordination or team performance
> - Capability profiles for workforce competencies

3. Analysis methods are defined for evaluating the impact of workforce practices and activities on the capability of critical workforce competencies.

> An analysis method must be defined for each workforce practice to be evaluated that provides appropriate sensitivity to the impact of the practice on capability in relevant workforce competencies. Analyses can be conducted at several levels of analysis, based on the capability objectives to be evaluated and the evaluation strategy. Examples of different levels of analysis for evaluating the impact of competency development practices and activities might include the following:
> - The improvements associated with a single occurrence of a competency development activity
> - The improvements associated with multiple occurrences of the same competency development activity, such as a course
> - The improvements associated with a type of competency development activity, such as mentoring
> - The improvements associated with a collection of competency development activities, such as a sequence of different courses
> - The improvements achieved by different individuals based on completing their personal development plans
> - The improvements associated with a particular form of delivery (e.g., classroom vs. intranet)
> - The improvement in workforce capability within each workforce competency resulting from the full set of competency development activities

4. Data on the impact of workforce practices and activities are collected from appropriate sources and prepared for analysis.

5. The impacts of workforce practices and activities on capability baselines are evaluated quantitatively.

6. Evaluation results are reported to responsible individuals in accordance with the evaluation strategy.

> Examples of individuals or entities that would receive evaluation results include:
> - Those responsible for coordinating workforce activities across the organization
> - Those responsible for performing and reporting workforce activities
> - Those responsible for competency analysis and competency development activities
> - Those involved in workforce planning
> - Executive management

Practice 6   **The impacts of workforce practices and activities on the organization's capability in each of its critical workforce competencies are managed quantitatively.**

1. Responsible individuals use quantitative analyses to:

   - evaluate the impact of workforce practices and activities on the capability baselines of selected workforce competencies,

   - identify conditions under which these impacts vary,

   - predict future capability levels based on anticipated future impacts of workforce practices and activities, and

   - identify needs for corrective action.

2. Results that differ significantly from expectations or capability objectives for each of the organization's critical workforce competencies are analyzed for their causes, and corrective actions are proposed, if appropriate.

> Examples of conditions under which needs for corrective action may be identified include the following:
> - The impact of workforce activities on a workforce competency differs from expectations.
> - Variation in results of workforce activities is too great.
> - Significant deviations from the capability level that the organization believes it must maintain in a workforce competency.

3. Proposed actions are reviewed, approved, and taken, and completion is tracked.

> Examples of proposed actions include the following:
> - Correcting problems in the performance of workforce activities
> - Adjusting the capability objectives for the workforce competency
> - Redesigning or adjusting workforce practices to improve their impact
> - Altering the performance of workforce practices and activities under different conditions to improve their impact
> - Collecting additional data or designing other analyses to correct misleading results

4. When appropriate or beneficial to capability results, the performance of workforce practices is managed quantitatively.

> Examples of workforce practices being managed quantitatively for a critical workforce competency may include the following:
> - Using predictive models to track and adjust the flow of qualified applications from recruiting activities and targeted sources in order to match anticipated staffing needs
> - Using valid statistical predictors of capability or future performance used in selection and career guidance activities
> - Controlling variation in capability levels across organizational units through assignment and career development strategies and activities
> - Predicting, tracking, and managing shifts in capability among workforce competencies based on motivating development of new competencies through compensation and reward practices
> - Evaluating the modules or phases of a training or competency development program to take any corrective action required to ensure each module or phase achieves its planned competency development objectives

5. Evaluation results for the impact of workforce practices and activities on competency baselines are used in performing other workforce activities.

> Evaluation results might be used in strategic workforce planning to evaluate or predict such factors as:
> - The rate and effectiveness with which the organization can increase capability in various critical workforce competencies
> - The rate at which capability in new workforce competencies can be developed
> - The probability of achieving strategic capability objectives in different workforce competencies
> - The effectiveness with which increases in capability can lead to improved business performance
> - The return on investment for expenditures of time or financial resources on various workforce practices and activities

Practice 7   **Process performance baselines are developed and maintained for critical competency-based processes.**

Critical competency-based processes are those competency-based processes within each critical workforce competency that are most crucial to achieving defined performance objectives and business results.

A *process performance baseline* is a documented, statistical characterization of the actual results achieved by following a process. Such baselines can be used as benchmarks for comparing actual process performance against the process performance that would be expected under normal circumstances. The organization's process performance baselines measure performance for selected competency-based processes within the organization's set of standard processes at various levels of detail, as appropriate. Process performance baselines may be established at various levels of process detail, including the following:

- Individual process elements (e.g., specific process elements within a competency-based process)
- Sequences of individual process elements (e.g., a specific sequence of process elements within a competency-based process)
- Selected competency-based processes
- A competency-based process that may be part of a larger workflow, such as developing individual work products
- Sequences of connected processes whose elements are performed by different workforce competencies that constitute part of a larger workflow
- An integrated competency-based process
- A complete process for developing or delivering a product or service

There may be several process performance baselines that characterize performance for individuals and workgroups within the organization, stratified by conditions under which performance might be expected to differ. The organization may construct several process performance baselines for a competency-based process if its performance results differ substantially under different conditions. Thus, rather than having a single process performance baseline with excessively large variation, the process performance data are disaggregated to produce process performance baselines that are specific to the different conditions under which the competency-based process is performed. From the perspective of statistical process control, these sets of conditions would represent different common cause systems that require different baselines. Examples of conditions that may affect the performance of competency-based processes and justify the creation of separate process performance baselines include the following:

- The level of experience or proficiency of the individuals performing the processes
- Organizational or business conditions
- Specific method(s) used in performing the processes
- The nature of the product or service for which the processes are performed

> Examples of statistics used to characterize process performance baselines include the following:
> - Expected performance as measured by mean, median, mode, or other measures of central tendency
> - Performance variability as measured by standard deviation, interquartile range, range, or other measures of variation
> - Shape of the distribution as measured by such statistics as skewness or kurtosis
> - How performance parameters vary under different conditions
> - Performance trends over time

1. Performance measures are defined for critical competency-based processes.

> The initial measurements required to support this practice were defined in the Performance Management, Competency-Based Practices, Workgroup Development, Competency Integration, Empowered Workgroups, and Quantitative Performance Management process areas. As quantitative analyses of performance capability mature, additional or revised measures are defined.

> Examples of sources for defined performance measures of competency-based processes include the following:
> - Definitions of competency-based processes
> - Existing process performance baselines for relevant processes
> - Standard business, product, or service measures

2. An analysis strategy is established and maintained for computing and analyzing process performance baselines for each critical competency-based process selected for analysis.

> Examples of issues to be covered in the strategy for analyzing the process performance baseline for each critical competency-based process selected for analysis include the following:
> - Measures to be used in the analysis
> - Frequency and methods of data collection
> - Methods for data validation, storage, and retrieval
> - Data analyses to be performed and reported
> - Guidance and limitations for evaluating results
> - Mechanisms for reporting results
> - Methods and tools to support using results
> - Safeguards to ensure data privacy and security

Examples of analyses that might be performed include the following:
- Curve-fitting or trend analyses
- Statistical process control techniques
- Regression or multivariate predictive techniques
- Stochastic or time-series techniques
- Classification analyses (e.g., defect or problem types)
- Analyses of leading indicators

3. Quantitative analyses of capability of each critical competency-based process are conducted according to the analysis strategy to determine:

   - the current capability of each critical competency-based process,
   - how the capability of each critical competency-based process relates to unit and organizational performance,
   - factors that affect the capability of each critical competency-based process, and
   - capability levels of a competency-based process under different conditions or factors that affect it, if relevant.

4. Process performance baselines for critical competency-based processes are reported to appropriate individuals and incorporated into:

   - planning and tracking,
   - predicting performance,
   - understanding the factors that affect the performance of competency-based processes,
   - identifying opportunities for improving the performance of competency-based processes, and
   - evaluating the capability of competency-based processes compared to the capability required to achieve the organization's performance objectives.

5. Process performance baselines are incorporated into the unit's Quantitative Performance Management activities.

6. Process performance baselines are continually updated, adjusted, and re-computed based on new performance data.

Practice 8   The capability of critical competency-based processes is managed quantitatively.

> Refer to the Quantitative Performance Management process area for information regarding the quantitative management of competency-based processes by individuals, workgroups, and units.

1. The results of performing competency-based processes are compared to process performance baselines for critical competency-based processes within each critical workforce competency.

2. Process performance baselines are used by responsible individuals to:

   - monitor and predict the performance of business activities,
   - identify conditions under which the capability of a competency-based process varies,
   - identify how the capability of the workforce affects the capability of competency-based processes,
   - identify needs for improvement of competency-based processes,
   - identify factors that affect business performance,
   - evaluate the effects of workforce practices and activities on the capability of competency-based processes, and
   - identify needs for corrective action.

3. Corrective action is taken when the results of performing competency-based processes deviate significantly from their process performance baselines.

> Examples of corrective actions include the following:
> - Solving problems or removing barriers that inhibit a competency-based process from being performed at its potential capability
> - Improving the capability of individuals or workgroups that perform the competency-based process
> - Tailoring, replacing, or terminating workforce practices that inhibit a competency-based process from being performed at its potential capability
> - Adjusting performance objectives to match the capability of the competency-based process through which they will be achieved
> - Reorganizing business activities to reduce the impact of variations in the capability of the competency-based process on the achievement of performance objectives

> Refer to Practice 12 of the Continuous Capability Improvement process area for information regarding improvement actions to take when process performance baselines deviate significantly from the capability objectives established for each critical competency-based process.

Practice 9   **The organization uses its capability data and process performance baselines in developing quantitative models of performance.**

> Quantitative models of performance can range from simple descriptive statistics concerning capability to sophisticated Bayesian, stochastic, or multivariate predictive models. Such models may be used to predict individual, workgroup, unit, or organizational performance from the current capability of competency-based processes and the conditions that affect them. An organization may begin with standard models from related industries and over time refine their algorithms or parameters with internal data and experience. Quantitative models may differ in purpose, sophistication, analytic foundation, parameters, predictability, and use among the various competency-based processes.

> Examples of quantitative models include the following:
> - Growth curves for projecting the effect of learning and other factors on future capability and performance
> - Models for predicting the achievement of organizational performance objectives from the aggregated performance results of individuals, workgroups, units, or workforce competencies
> - Predictive models of characteristics most likely to affect capability and performance at the individual, workgroup, unit, workforce competency, or organizational levels in order to select appropriate process performance baselines and adjust performance expectations
> - Models of the effect of variations in workforce practices and activities on the resulting capability and performance of competency-based processes
> - Models for evaluating decisions involving performance tradeoffs
> - Models of the effect of competency at the individual and workgroup levels on the performance of competency-based processes
> - Models for assessing how changes or variations in the capability of the individuals composing a workgroup or unit will affect workgroup and unit performance
> - Models for assessing the effect of capability and performance of competency-based processes at the individual and workgroup levels on unit and organizational performance

1. Data are analyzed to develop quantitative models of capability and performance such as:

   - the effect of learning and competency development on the capability of competency-based processes,

   - differences in the capability of competency-based processes across individuals at different skill levels, workgroups, units, or under varying conditions,

   - the effect of aggregating capability results across individuals at different skill levels, workgroups, units, or the organization,

- how the capabilities of competency-based processes interact to affect the performance of business activities,
- the impact of overall performance among alternate ways of organizing business activities or competency-based processes, and
- the effects of workforce practices on the capability of competency-based processes.

2. Quantitative models of the capability of competency-based processes are used in:

- planning and tracking committed work,
- predicting performance and results at the individual, workgroup, unit, and organizational levels, and
- strategic business and workforce planning.

Practice 10   **The impact of workforce practices and activities on the capability and performance of competency-based processes is evaluated and managed quantitatively.**

> Examples of the effects of workforce practices and activities on the capability of competency-based processes that the organization might evaluate quantitatively include the following:
>
> - Improved capability and performance of competency-based processes
> - Reduced variation in the capability and performance of competency-based processes
> - Impact that workforce practices and activities have when adjusted to achieve their most effective application in different areas of competency-based processes or under different organizational conditions
> - Reduced variation in the application or performance of workforce activities
> - Increased predictability in the capability and performance of competency-based processes

1. Methods and associated measures are defined for evaluating the impact of workforce practices and activities on the capability and performance of competency-based processes.

> Examples of capability measures that may be affected by workforce practices and activities include the following:
> - Improvements in mean
> - Reduction in performance variation
> - Rate of change in capability parameters
> - Reduced need for different process performance baselines reflecting differences in performing competency-based processes by different levels of capability in a competency community
> - Improved predictability
> - Improved performance in data aggregated to higher organizational levels
> - Improved business performance or results

2. Data on the impact of workforce practices and activities are collected from appropriate sources and prepared for analysis.

3. The impact of workforce practices on capability baselines and process performance baselines is evaluated.

> Analyses may be conducted either at the level of workforce practices or at the level of competency-based processes. For example, analyses may be conducted for the effects of one or more workforce practices across a range of competency-based processes. This approach would be appropriate to determine whether the effects of one or more workforce practices differ across various competency-based processes. For instance, this approach would be helpful in identifying how a bonus program is motivating improved performance in some competency communities but not others.
>
> Alternatively, analyses could be conducted within each competency-based process to determine how the organization's collection of workforce practices affects these processes. For instance, this approach would be helpful in identifying which workforce practices do not appear to improve performance in a specific workforce competency.

4. Quantitative analyses of the impact of workforce practices and activities are used by responsible individuals to evaluate:

   - their impact on the capability and performance of various competency-based processes,
   - conditions under which their impact varies, and
   - needs for corrective action.

5. Corrective actions are taken when quantitative evaluations indicate that the actual impact of workforce practices and activities deviates significantly from expectations. These actions may include:

- correcting problems in the performance of workforce activities,
- adjusting expectations regarding the impact of workforce practices and activities on the capability and performance of competency-based processes,
- redesigning or adjusting workforce practices to improve their impact, and
- altering the performance of workforce practices and activities under different conditions to improve their impact.

Practice 11   **Evaluations of the impact of workforce practices and activities on the capability and performance of competency-based processes are used in performing other business and workforce activities, as appropriate.**

1. Evaluation results are used in strategic business and workforce planning.

> Evaluation results might be used to evaluate or predict such factors as:
> - The rate at which the capability of competency-based processes can be improved
> - The probability of achieving strategic capability levels for competency-based processes and quantitative performance objectives
> - The effectiveness with which increases in the capability of competency-based processes can lead to improved business performance
> - The return on investment for expenditures of time or financial resources on improving the capability of competency-based processes

2. Evaluation results are used to guide such actions as:

- designing more effective workforce practices for motivating, improving, and sustaining performance,
- redesigning, replacing, or eliminating ineffective workforce practices, or
- setting or allocating more realistic or effective quantitative performance objectives.

> Refer to Practice 6 of the Continuous Workforce Innovation process area for information regarding setting improvement objectives for the organization's workforce practices and activities, based on a quantitative understanding of the process performance of these workforce activities.

Measurement and Analysis

Measurement 1   Measurements are made and used to determine the status and performance of Organizational Capability Management activities.

> Examples of measurements include the following:
>
> - The number of workforce competencies or competency-based processes for which capability analyses are performed
> - The completeness, accuracy, and timeliness of the data collected
> - Frequency with which data is collected and analyzed on the capability of critical workforce competencies
> - Length of time between data collection and the presentation of analysis results
> - Frequency with which capability baselines are updated
> - Number and extent of corrective actions taken
> - Number or extent of changes made in workforce activities, based on analysis results

Measurement 2   Measurements are made and used to determine the effectiveness of Organizational Capability Management activities.

> Examples of measures to determine the effectiveness of the organization's capability management activities include the following:
>
> - Predictability of the organization's capability in its critical workforce competencies
> - Improvements in the capability achieved through competency development activities
> - Increases in the effectiveness with which competency development activities increase the organization's capability in each of its workforce competencies
> - Increases in the speed with which the organization or its units can increase the level of workforce competencies
> - Increases in the speed with which the organization or its units can deploy a new workforce competency
> - Increases in the organization's ability to achieve quantitative objectives in the growth of its workforce competencies over time
> - Predictable relationships between business performance trends and improvements in the organization's capability in critical workforce competencies
> - Improvements in the capability and performance of competency-based processes
> - Improvements in the prediction or achievement of quantitative performance and business objectives
> - Improved correlation between workforce practices and performance results
> - Improved ability to identify and manage factors that affect performance
> - Increases in the organization's ability to identify areas of competency development activities needing corrective action
> - Increases in the organization's ability to identify areas of workforce activities needing corrective action

Verifying Implementation

Verification 1   A responsible individual(s) verifies that Organizational Capability Management activities are conducted according to the organization's documented policies, practices, procedures, and, where appropriate, plans; and addresses noncompliance.

These reviews verify that:

1. Organizational Capability Management activities comply with the organization's policies and stated values.

2. Organizational Capability Management activities comply with relevant laws and regulations.

3. Organizational Capability Management activities are performed according to the organization's documented practices and procedures.

4. Noncompliance issues are handled appropriately.

Verification 2   Executive management periodically reviews the Organizational Capability Management activities, status, and results; and resolves issues.

These reviews verify:

1. The appropriateness of Organizational Capability Management practices and activities.

2. Progress in improving performance-related workforce practices and activities.

3. Progress in achieving capability objectives for each critical workforce competency.

4. Results from reviews of Organizational Capability Management practices and activities.

> Refer to Verification 1 for information regarding reviews of Organizational Capability Management activities to ensure adherence to the following:
> - Relevant laws and regulations
> - Organizational policies, practices, and procedures

5. Status of resolution of noncompliance issues.

6. Trends related to Organizational Capability Management activities.

7. Trends related to capability baselines.

8. Effectiveness of Organizational Capability Management activities in achieving quantitative management of:

- the capability of critical workforce competencies,
- workforce practices and activities in developing the capability of critical workforce competencies, and
- the capabilities of competency-based processes in critical workforce competencies.

Verification 3   The definition and use of measures at the individual, workgroup, and unit levels are periodically audited for compliance with organizational policies.

> Organizational policies which may apply could include human resource, human capital, information security, confidentiality, privacy, or data disclosure policies.

1. Definitions of capability measures and information at the individual, workgroup, unit, and organizational levels are reviewed for compliance with organizational policies.

> The data definitions define what data is to be collected, aggregated, and used. They are not the data values themselves. For example, current organizational capability at each competency level within a given workforce competency could be a component of a data definition, but the organizational resource profile showing the numbers of individuals at each level of capability would be a specific data value for current organizational capability.

2. Periodic audits ensure that competency description and competency information are accessed and used in accordance with organizational policies.

> These audits may be accomplished through reviews of ongoing reporting, such as system access and use monitoring reports, and auditing to ensure compliance with relevant information security standards and organizational policies.
>
> System access and use monitoring ensures that the data are accessed only by authorized individuals, while compliance auditing ensures that these individuals perform appropriate procedures in compliance with organizational policies and standards.

Mentoring

A process area at Maturity Level 4: Predictable

Purpose

The purpose of Mentoring is to transfer the lessons of greater experience in a workforce competency to improve the capability of other individuals or workgroups.

Description

The organization develops objectives for its mentoring activities. Appropriate types of mentoring relationships are designed for accomplishing different mentoring objectives. Criteria are developed for selecting mentors and those chosen are trained for their assignments. Individuals or workgroups being mentored are provided orientation on how they can best take advantage of a mentoring relationship. Criteria are developed and used for assigning mentors to individuals or workgroups. The mentor and the individual or workgroup being mentored establish agreements on how their relationship will be conducted. Mentors meet periodically and occasionally evaluate whether they are achieving their objectives. Advice is available to improve the effectiveness of the mentoring relationship. Mentoring activities are evaluated against their objectives to identify needed improvements.

At the Defined Level, mentoring and coaching are informal, and the knowledge and skills imparted by the mentor are defined more by their experience and judgment than by a documented combination of knowledge, skills, and process abilities to be imparted. The purposes for mentoring were to support competency development, but the specific content to be imparted was not defined. At the Predictable Level, mentoring and coaching activities are organized around, and guided by, a defined content of the knowledge, skills, and process abilities to be imparted. This content is defined to a level sufficient for guiding mentors and coaches to achieve common and consistent competency development results with individuals or workgroups. At the Predictable Level, mentoring or coaching activities are organized to make use of, and to deploy, competency-based assets. Thus, mentoring becomes a formal means of transferring a defined content of the knowledge, skills, and process abilities, typically contained in competency-based assets, to individuals and groups throughout the organization as an advanced form of competency development.

Goals

Goal 1   **Mentoring programs are established and maintained to accomplish defined objectives.**

Goal 2   **Mentors provide guidance and support to individuals or workgroups.**

Goal 3   **Mentoring practices are institutionalized to ensure they are performed as defined organizational processes.**

Commitment to Perform

Commitment 1   **The organization establishes and maintains a documented policy for conducting Mentoring activities.**

Issues typically addressed in the policy include:

1. Mentoring activities serve the business objectives and stated values of the organization.
2. Mentoring activities are encouraged but not imposed on individuals.
3. Mentoring activities are included in the strategic workforce plans of the organization.
4. Mentoring activities are instituted, where appropriate, to provide support to individuals or workgroups.
5. Documented procedures are developed and used to guide mentoring activities. These procedures typically specify:

   - requirements for the selection, training, and assignment of mentors;
   - conditions under which mentoring relationships may be established, changed, or terminated; and
   - requirements for periodic evaluation of mentoring activities to ensure their effectiveness and to identify improvements.

6. Mentoring practices and activities comply with relevant laws, regulations, and organizational policies.

Commitment 2   **An organizational role(s) is assigned responsibility for coordinating Mentoring activities across the organization.**

The role(s) coordinates and helps to:

1. advise on how to organize and conduct mentoring activities,
2. communicate general information about mentoring activities,
3. conduct training or orientation sessions for mentors and individuals or workgroups,
4. advise and counsel mentors and individuals or workgroups during their mentoring relationships, and
5. provide feedback on the progress of mentoring activities to executive management.

Ability to Perform

Ability 1   **Within each unit, an individual(s) is assigned responsibility and authority for ensuring that members of the unit participate in Mentoring activities, as appropriate.**

Ability 2   **Adequate resources are provided for performing Mentoring activities.**

1. Experienced individuals are made available to act as mentors.
2. Resources to support mentoring activities are made available.

> Examples of resources needed to support the mentoring program include the following:
> - Training for mentors
> - Orientation for individuals or workgroups to be mentored
> - Availability of an advisor for mentors, individuals, or workgroups
> - Support for evaluation of the mentoring program

3. Adequate funding is made available to support Mentoring activities.
4. Time is made available for mentors and individuals or workgroups to engage in Mentoring activities.

Ability 3   **Individuals selected to act as mentors develop the knowledge, skills, and process abilities needed in relevant mentoring objectives, techniques, and skills to perform their responsibilities.**

1. Mentors receive preparation in techniques and skills to accomplish their mentoring objectives.

> Examples of techniques and skills in which mentors are trained include the following:
> - How to accomplish mentoring program objectives
> - How to conduct a mentoring relationship
> - Interviewing and active listening
> - Providing guidance and advice
> - Providing a role model
> - Problem solving
> - Performance improvement methods
> - Principles of knowledge and skill development
> - Career opportunities and development methods
> - Advising workgroups
> - Team building
> - Methods for integration with the organizational culture
> - Roles to be fulfilled
> - How to evaluate mentoring success

2. For mentoring activities focused on competency development, mentors receive preparation for imparting documented knowledge, skills, and process abilities using defined mentoring processes.

3. Guidance is made available to mentors and those they mentor on how to improve their mentoring relationship.

> Examples of guidance provided on mentoring relationships include the following:
> - How to initiate the relationship
> - When and how frequently to have meetings
> - Potential topics to be discussed
> - How to determine the mentoring needs of those being mentored
> - Methods for pursuing mentoring objectives
> - How to track progress in the mentoring relationship
> - How to handle job or career problems
> - How to overcome problems in the mentoring relationship

4. An advisor is available to mentors or coaches to discuss how to make mentoring relationships more effective.

Ability 4 **Affected individuals receive appropriate orientation in Mentoring practices.**

1. Individuals or workgroups to be mentored receive orientation in the mentoring relationship.

> Those to be mentored can include the following:
> - Individuals
> - Groups of individuals
> - Workgroups

> Examples of topics covered in orientation regarding mentoring activities include the following:
> - Objectives of the mentoring relationship
> - Attributes of an effective mentoring relationship
> - Problem-solving skills
> - Expectations for mentoring relationships
> - Roles to be fulfilled in mentoring
> - How to handle problems or inefficiencies in the mentoring relationship

2. When appropriate, orientation is provided to other individuals affected by mentoring activities.

> Orientation to the mentoring program is typically focused on the individual or workgroup being mentored. Other orientation activities may include the following:
> - A combined session for mentors and individuals or workgroups being mentored
> - An orientation session for managers of those being mentored to make them familiar with the mentoring process and encourage their cooperation with the mentoring program

Ability 5   **The practices and procedures for performing Mentoring are defined and documented.**

1. Practices and procedures are defined and documented at the organizational or unit levels, as appropriate.

2. Guidelines for tailoring the practices and procedures for use in different circumstances are documented and made available, as necessary.

3. The individual(s) assigned responsibility for coordinating Mentoring activities across the organization ensures that defined practices and procedures are:

   - maintained under version control,
   - disseminated through appropriate media,
   - interpreted appropriately for different situations, and
   - updated through orderly methods.

4. Experiences, lessons learned, measurement results, and improvement information derived from planning and performing Mentoring practices are captured to support the future use and improvement of the organization's practices.

Practices Performed

Practice 1   **Opportunities for using the experience of the workforce to improve performance or achieve other organizational objectives are identified.**

1. Potential opportunities for mentoring activities are identified.

> Examples of sources through which potential opportunities for mentoring might be identified include the following:
> - Periodic review by competency ownership teams of opportunities to use mentoring in competency development activities
> - Periodic review by responsible individuals of mechanisms for more rapidly transferring knowledge across the organization
> - Recommendations for mentoring or requests for mentors from the workforce
> - Identified needs for addressing knowledge shortfalls in segments of the workforce
> - Periodic organizational assessment of opportunities by a knowledgeable person
> - Support mechanism for a new program, technology, or change in some segments of the organization

2. Opportunities to benefit from mentoring are evaluated and prioritized.

> Mentoring programs can be evaluated at the organizational or unit level, or within ownership teams for workforce competencies. The evaluation and prioritization would ordinarily be performed by the entity with the authority and budget to initiate a specific type of mentoring program.

3. Mentoring programs are initiated based on relevant criteria, such as budget or availability of qualified mentors.

Practice 2   **The objectives and structure of each mentoring program are defined.**

1. Each mentoring program addresses specific competencies, positions, individuals, or workgroups within the organization that can be involved in its mentoring activities.

2. Each mentoring program establishes a set of objectives that its mentoring activities are to accomplish.

> Examples of objectives for mentoring activities include providing:
> - Orientation and adjustment to the organization
> - Support for the acquisition of knowledge, skills, and process abilities
> - Support for the development of workforce competencies
> - Preparation of specific management or executive skills
> - Support to individuals or workgroups
> - Support for sharing the knowledge, experience, and artifacts that result from performing competency-based processes with others who might benefit from them
> - One-on-one personal attention
> - Support for attaining improved workgroup effectiveness
> - Workgroup development
> - Performance improvement guidance and support
> - Career advice and development
> - Counseling and advice concerning problems

3. Each mentoring program defines a mentoring process to a level of detail sufficient to ensure that those who receive mentoring develop the appropriate level of competency.

> At the Defined Level, mentors and those they mentor are allowed to develop their relationships according to what they believe would be most effective. However, at the Predictable Level, the process is made sufficiently formal to ensure that mentors are consistent in the capabilities imparted to those being mentored.

- Procedures for mentoring activities are tailored to each set of objectives.

> Different types of mentoring relationships may be defined for different sets of objectives. For instance, mentoring activities may differ by position or tenure in the organization such as those designed for new employees versus those designed for new executives.

> Examples of elements that could be defined for each type of mentoring relationship include the following:
> - The roles and responsibilities of the mentor and the individual or workgroup
> - How mentors are selected and trained
> - How individuals or workgroups receive orientation on mentoring
> - How mentoring relationships are established
> - How objectives of the relationship are accomplished
> - How the mentoring relationship is monitored for effectiveness
> - How the mentoring relationship is evaluated
> - The expected duration of the mentoring relationship

■ Roles are defined for mentors to fulfill.

> Examples of roles that mentors might fulfill include the following:
> - Role model
> - Personal or workgroup advisor
> - Career counselor or sponsor
> - Knowledge and skill developer
> - Performance advisor
> - Problem solver
> - Expert

4. The knowledge, skills, and process abilities that are imparted through mentoring are:

■ documented as competency-based assets,

> Refer to Practice 10 of the Competency-Based Assets process area for information regarding the use of mentoring or coaching activities to deploy competency-based assets.

■ drawn from or based on the content of documented workforce competency descriptions,

■ organized for use according to levels of capability represented in graduated career opportunities,

■ complete enough to ensure that those being mentored have the competency required to perform at the intended level,

■ described at a level of detail sufficient to create a common understanding among mentors or coaches of the specific knowledge, skills, and process abilities to be imparted at different points in the mentoring relationship,

- sufficiently thorough to ensure that any individual or workgroup who has worked with a mentor or coach has achieved a minimum capability for performing competency-based processes, and
- reviewed and updated, as necessary.

5. Alternative structures for providing the types of benefits achieved through mentoring are considered when appropriate.

> Examples of alternate approaches to mentoring include the following:
> - Mentoring circles
> - Local professional groups
> - A process group or improvement group
> - Other support groups or networks, such as a local software and systems process improvement network (SPIN) group

6. Feedback on each mentoring program is collected by a responsible individual(s) to support evaluation of mentoring activities.

> Examples of feedback data used to evaluate mentoring programs include the following:
> - Feedback received from mentors or those being mentored
> - The evaluation of mentoring activities by those being mentored
> - Reports from advisors who are available to support mentors or coaches
> - Results of meetings conducted from time to time to allow mentors, individuals, or workgroups to express concerns or improvements that should be considered in improving the mentoring programs or mentoring relationships
> - Measurements regarding the status, performance, and effectiveness of mentoring activities

7. Each mentoring program is periodically evaluated to ensure that it is achieving its set of objectives, and revised or terminated when necessitated by feedback on the mentoring program, levels of workforce capability, or changes in business strategy or conditions, to improve the value of the mentoring performed.

Practice 3 **Each mentoring program is communicated to affected individuals and workgroups.**

> Information about each mentoring program to be communicated may include the following:
> - Program objectives and structure
> - The positions, individuals, or workgroups covered in the program
> - Procedures for volunteering to act as a mentor
> - Procedures for being included as an individual or workgroup receiving mentoring
> - Orientation or training requirements

1. Methods are selected to invite participation in the mentoring program based on the objectives established for the mentoring program.

> Examples of methods that could be used to invite participation in the mentoring program range from active personal solicitation to passive announcements of the program's availability.

2. Individuals or workgroups are invited to participate in the mentoring program.

3. A responsible individual is available to answer questions about each mentoring program.

Practice 4   **Mentors are selected and matched with individuals or workgroups to be mentored.**

1. Criteria are defined for selecting mentors.

> Examples of criteria for selecting mentors include the following:
> - Commitment to developing knowledge, skills, and process abilities in others
> - Commitment to developing and guiding others
> - Interpersonal and communication skills, such as the ability to listen, trustworthiness, and objectivity
> - Ability to provide a successful role model
> - Experience required to mentor various competencies, positions, individuals, or workgroups
> - Knowledge required to mentor various competencies, positions, individuals, or workgroups
> - Business and organizational judgment
> - Availability requirements
> - Ability to assess development or career needs
> - Ability to provide guidance on performance or career enhancement
> - Ability to provide personal support
> - Ability to work with workgroups
> - Commitment to initial and ongoing mentor training

2. Candidates who have applied for mentoring assignments are evaluated against the criteria, and those who are qualified are selected to act as mentors.

3. Selected mentors are prepared to perform their mentoring responsibilities.

> Refer to Ability 3 of this process area for information regarding preparation of mentors.

4. Selected mentors are assigned to individuals or workgroups, based on defined criteria for:

- maintaining organizational or managerial distance between the mentor and the individual or workgroup to be mentored,
- matching mentors with individuals or workgroups,

> Examples of criteria for matching mentors with individuals or workgroups include the following:
> - Task, position, or career experiences
> - Knowledge and skill needs of the individual or workgroup to be mentored
> - Personal development needs of the individual to be mentored
> - Workgroup or team development needs
> - Common backgrounds
> - Career aspirations of the individual or workgroup to be mentored
> - Ability to match schedules for meetings
> - Personalities or interests
> - Level of mentoring involvement
> - Exposure to the breadth of the organization
> - Geographical considerations

- ensuring successful transfer of competency-based assets to the individual or workgroup being mentored,

> Refer to the Competency-Based Assets process area for information regarding the use of competency-based assets.

- handling requests for specific mentoring assignments, and
- having the necessary preparation in relevant mentoring objectives, techniques, and skills.

Practice 5   **Mentors and those they mentor establish a mentoring relationship.**

1. Both mentors and those they mentor receive appropriate training or orientation before establishing their mentoring relationship.

2. During their initial meetings, mentors and the individual or workgroup establish the basic agreements on which their relationship will develop.

Examples of issues that they should reach agreement on include the following:
- What they both expect to achieve from the mentoring relationship
- Whether they will meet on a periodic or event-driven basis
- Whether they will build and track a plan for their mentoring activities
- A schedule for their meetings
- Expected duration of the mentoring relationship
- Specific exit criteria, related to the achievement of specific objectives for the mentoring relationship
- How they will evaluate their progress
- How they will conduct their meetings
- How they will communicate between meetings

---

3. Mentors and the individual or workgroup determine the specific objectives to be accomplished through the mentoring relationship.

4. If competency development is a focus of the mentoring relationship, they evaluate and agree on what knowledge, skills, and process abilities the individual or workgroup needs to develop.

5. When establishing a relationship where competency development is an objective, mentors or coaches arrange their responsibilities to ensure that the documented knowledge, skills, and process abilities are:

- learned sufficiently to allow those being mentored to perform competency-based activities at the intended level of capability,

- imparted on a timely schedule, and

- demonstrated in performing business activities.

6. The mentor provides feedback and guidance to those they mentor in a timely manner.

7. The mentor and those they mentor continually discuss the job performance or behavior of the individual or workgroup, and plan for future development needs.

> Examples of issues that might be handled during mentoring sessions include the following:
> - Evaluation of current performance and behaviors
> - Use of time
> - Setting priorities
> - Self management
> - Interpersonal style and skills
> - Replaying the handling of situations or the making of decisions
> - Identifying strengths and areas needing development
> - Analyzing barriers to job performance or career growth
> - Identifying needed changes in attitude or style
> - Analyzing the processes, resources, and operations of the organization relevant to the individual or workgroup being mentored
> - Analyzing career options and needed skills
> - Identifying actions and plans to support development needs

Practice 6   Mentors assist individuals or workgroups in developing capability in workforce competencies.

1. Mentors maintain awareness of developments in the workforce competencies relevant to the individuals or workgroups they mentor.

2. Mentors evaluate gaps between the current capability and the capability levels established in the mentoring objectives of the individuals or workgroups they mentor.

3. Mentors assist individuals or workgroups in improving their capability relative to their:

   ■ mentoring objectives,

   ■ individual development objectives, if appropriate, and

   ■ workgroup development objectives, if appropriate.

4. Mentors assist individuals or workgroups in adopting and improving their capability in using competency-based processes.

> An example of a mentor assisting a workgroup in adopting a competency-based process would be the use of a TSP Launch Coach to help a software team initiate a project using the software development processes incorporated in the Team Software Process (TSP) [Humphrey 00]. This example of mentoring involves a person who has been certified by an external entity (the Software Engineering Institute at Carnegie Mellon University authorizes TSP Launch Coaches) to assist individuals or workgroups in developing or improving their capability in specific competency-based processes.

5. Mentors provide feedback to those they mentor on their capability and rate of development in workforce competencies and other skills relevant to their mentoring objectives.

6. Mentors use competency-based assets in conducting their mentoring activities.

7. Mentors assist those they mentor in learning how to leverage or benefit from competency-based assets in performing their business activities.

8. When appropriate, mentors can assist individuals or workgroups in using and interpreting data during quantitative management activities.

> Mentors are especially valuable to individuals or workgroups who are attempting to manage their competency-based processes quantitatively. The concept of mentor used in the People CMM is broad, and one form of mentor would be a Six Sigma Blackbelt or similarly qualified expert in quantitative process analysis and improvement who assists individuals or workgroups in analyzing and improving their operating processes. Refer to the Quantitative Performance Management process area for information regarding quantitative management practices.

Practice 7   **Mentoring relationships are reviewed to ensure that they satisfy their intended objectives.**

1. The mentor and those they mentor review the progress they are making toward their agreed-upon objectives on a periodic or event-driven basis.

> Examples of reasons for conducting this review could include the following:
> - Normal period for review, as established in the basic agreements on the mentoring relationship that were established between the mentor and those they mentor
> - A change in the competency of those being mentored
> - Change in work assignments that cause mentoring to be difficult
> - Problems in the mentoring relationship
> - Attainment of the intended objectives of the mentoring relationship
> - Assigning a new mentor to the individual or workgroup being mentored

2. When problems with mentoring relationships are identified, corrective action is taken to resolve the problem.

> Examples of corrective actions include the following:
> - Reestablishing the basis for the specific mentoring relationship
> - Planning more effective meetings or actions
> - Getting additional advice or training on conducting an effective mentoring relationship
> - Assigning a new mentor to the individual or workgroup

3. The mentor and individual or workgroup can agree to discontinue their mentoring relationship at any time.

Practice 8   Mentors support the development and improvement of competency-based assets.

1. Mentors identify opportunities to capture lessons from their mentoring activities that can be incorporated into developing or improving competency-based assets.

> Examples of contributions that mentors can make to developing or improving competency-based assets include additions or improvements to the following:
> - Competency-based processes
> - Competency development materials or methods
> - Lessons learned or other information in a knowledge repository
> - Measures of competency-based processes
> - Any competency-based asset(s) relevant to a workforce competency

2. Mentors contribute to the development or improvement of competency-based assets through mechanisms that are appropriate for the specific type of asset.

> Refer to Practices 4, 5, and 6 of the Competency-Based Assets process area for information regarding the development and maintenance of competency-based assets.

Practice 9   Mentors participate in performance management and related workforce activities, as appropriate.

1. Mentors hold continuing discussions with the individuals or workgroups they coach on the performance of their work.

2. For the individuals or workgroups they mentor, mentors may provide input for:

  ■ formal performance feedback,

  ■ training and development needs,

  ■ personal development plans,

  ■ performance improvement plans,

  ■ workgroup staffing and composition,

  ■ decisions regarding adjustments to compensation, or

  ■ decisions regarding promotion or career advancement.

Practice 10   **The organization's workforce practices support mentoring activities, as needed.**

1. Workforce practices are adjusted, as necessary, to achieve the objectives of the organization's mentoring programs.

Examples of areas where workforce practices may need to be adjusted to support mentoring activities include the following:
- Performance management
- Training and development
- Recognition and rewards
- Compensation
- Competency analysis and development
- Career development
- Work environment
- Workgroup development and role definitions
- Quantitative performance management
- Organizational capability management

---

2. Objectives of the mentoring relationship are confidential and should not be revealed without the agreement of the individual.

3. Objectives and progress in individuals' mentoring relationships are not used in performing any workforce activities without the agreement of the individuals affected.

4. Mentors are recognized for successful mentoring activities.

> Examples of recognition for successful mentors include the following:
> - Awards
> - Public recognition in meetings or newsletters
> - Privileges
> - Financial considerations
> - Acknowledgment for success in mentoring-related performance or career objectives

Measurement and Analysis

Measurement 1 **Measurements are made and used to determine the status and performance of Mentoring activities.**

> Examples of measurements include the following:
> - The number of mentoring relationships established
> - The rate at which candidates apply to become mentors
> - The rate at which new mentors are trained and assigned
> - The efficiency with which new mentoring relationships are established
> - The frequency with which mentors and those they mentor interact
> - The evaluation of mentoring activities by those being mentored
> - The number of problems identified and improvements made in mentoring relationships

Measurement 2 **Measurements are made and used to determine the effectiveness of Mentoring activities.**

> Examples of measurements to determine the effectiveness of Mentoring activities include the following:
> - The growth of workforce competencies in individuals or workgroups being mentored
> - The ability of individuals or workgroups being mentored to use the resources of the organization
> - The performance of individuals or workgroups being mentored on their tasks
> - The career development of individuals being mentored
> - The alignment of individual and workgroup motivations with the objectives of the organization

Verifying Implementation

Verification 1   A responsible individual(s) verifies that Mentoring activities are conducted according to the organization's documented policies, practices, procedures, and, where appropriate, plans; and addresses noncompliance.

These reviews verify that:

1. Mentoring activities comply with the organization's policies and stated values.
2. Mentoring activities comply with relevant laws and regulations.
3. Mentoring activities are performed according to the organization's documented practices and procedures.
4. Noncompliance issues are handled appropriately.

Verification 2   Executive management periodically reviews Mentoring activities, status, and results; and resolves issues.

These reviews verify:

1. The appropriateness of Mentoring activities.
2. Progress in performing Mentoring activities.
3. Results from reviews of Mentoring practices and activities.

> Refer to Verification 1 for practices regarding reviews of Mentoring activities to ensure adherence to the following:
> - Relevant laws and regulations
> - Organizational policies, practices, and procedures

4. Status of resolution of noncompliance issues.
5. Trends related to Mentoring.

The Optimizing Level: Maturity Level 5

Process Areas at the Optimizing Level focus on continually improving the organization's capability and workforce practices. Individuals continually improve the personal work processes they use in performing competency-based processes. Workgroups continuously improve their operating processes through improved integration of the personal work processes of their members. The organization evaluates and improves the alignment of performance among its individuals, workgroups, and units both with each other and with the organization's business objectives. The organization continually evaluates opportunities for improving its workforce practices through incremental adjustments or by adopting innovative workforce practices and technologies. The process areas at Maturity Level 5 include:

	Process Areas
Continuous Capability Improvement	495
Organizational Performance Alignment	522
Continuous Workforce Innovation	538

Continuous Capability Improvement

A process area at Maturity Level 5: Optimizing

Purpose

The purpose of Continuous Capability Improvement is to provide a foundation for individuals and workgroups to continuously improve their capability for performing competency-based processes.

Description

Continuous Capability Improvement involves enterprise-wide support for individuals and workgroups as they focus on improving their capability in the performance of competency-based processes. The organization establishes a voluntary framework for continuously improving personal work processes and workgroup operating processes. Within each competency community, actions are taken to continually improve the capability and performance of competency-based processes.

Individuals focus on the capability of their personal methods for performing competency-based processes. Individuals analyze the capability of their personal work processes, identify opportunities for improvement, and establish measurable improvement objectives. Individuals engage in learning activities to continuously improve the capability and performance of their personal work processes.

Workgroups focus on improving the capability and performance of their operating processes by continuously improving the integration of the personal work processes performed by workgroup members. Workgroups analyze the capability of their operating processes to identify opportunities for improvement. Workgroups set measurable objectives for improvement and continuously improve their capability and performance. The organization adjusts the application of workforce practices to support continuous competency improvement.

Within competency communities, recommendations from improvements in personal work processes or workgroup operating processes are reviewed to determine if they should be incorporated into defined competency-based processes. Capability objectives are established for competency-based processes based on the organization's business objectives. Improvement objectives are established for competency-based processes whose capability is insufficient to achieve these capability objectives. Within some competency communities, responsible individuals identify opportunities for improving competency-based processes and evaluate potential improvements. Improvements that demonstrate their value are incorporated into competency-based processes and made available for use. The organization's workforce practices are adjusted to support continual improvement at all levels of the organization.

Goals

Goal 1   The organization establishes and maintains mechanisms for supporting continuous improvement of its competency-based processes.

Goal 2   Individuals continuously improve the capability of their personal work processes.

Goal 3   Workgroups continuously improve the capability of their workgroup's operating processes.

Goal 4   The capabilities of competency-based processes are continuously improved.

Goal 5   Continuous Capability Improvement practices are institutionalized to ensure they are performed as defined organizational processes.

Commitment to Perform

Commitment 1   The organization establishes and maintains a documented policy for continuously improving individual and workgroup capability.

Issues typically addressed in the policy include:

1. Continuous Capability Improvement activities serve the business objectives and stated values of the organization.

2. Individuals and workgroups are encouraged to continuously improve their capability.

3. Individuals and workgroups set measurable objectives for improving their capability.

4. Support is provided for assisting individuals and workgroups in continuously improving their capability.

5. All individuals and workgroups are able to voluntarily participate in continuously improving their capability.

6. The organization proactively investigates improvements to competency-based processes and deploys those that prove most promising.

7. Continuous Capability Improvement practices and activities comply with relevant laws, regulations, and organizational policies.

Commitment 2   **An organizational role(s) is assigned responsibility for coordinating Continuous Capability Improvement activities across the organization.**

> Examples of individuals who might coordinate Continuous Capability Improvement activities across the organization include the following:
> - Operational managers and executives
> - Human capital officers or human capital managers
> - Knowledge officers or managers
> - Quality, efficiency, or performance experts
> - Human resources or other appropriate professionals
> - Training or development groups
> - Competency ownership groups
> - Measurement or process improvement groups

Ability to Perform

Ability 1   **Within each unit, an individual(s) is assigned responsibility and authority for ensuring that members of the unit participate in Continuous Capability Improvement activities, as appropriate.**

Ability 2   **Within selected workforce competencies, responsible individual(s) coordinate activities to improve its competency-based processes.**

> Refer to Ability 1 in the Competency Analysis process area and Ability 2 in the Competency-Based Assets process area for information regarding those who are involved in maintaining and improving competency-based processes and competency-based assets.

> Examples of individuals who might coordinate Continuous Capability Improvement activities within a workforce competency include the following:
> - Competency ownership group, or an organizational competency definition or competency management group, for the workforce competency
> - Knowledge officers or managers
> - Human resources or other appropriate professionals
> - Training or development groups
> - Committee of representatives from ownership teams for each workforce competency
> - Measurement or process improvement groups

Ability 3   **Adequate resources are provided for continuously improving individual and workgroup capabilities.**

1. Experienced individuals who have expertise in capability improvement are available for coaching individuals and workgroups.

> Examples of individuals with appropriate expertise include the following:
> - Subject matter experts
> - Process improvement professionals
> - Professionals experienced in Six Sigma techniques
> - Measurement experts
> - Mentors or coaches

2. Funding and resources for supporting Continuous Capability Improvement activities are made available.

> Examples of resources to support Continuous Capability Improvement activities include the following:
> - Data collection tools
> - Statistical analysis packages
> - Tools to support representation and analyses of workflow and processes
> - Competency-based assets or repositories
> - Databases and other repositories
> - Intranet and other means of electronic access
> - Knowledge management tools
> - Reporting and communication tools

3. The organization's strategic workforce plan provides guidance to units for individual and workgroup participation in continuous capability improvement activities.

4. Each unit's workforce planning allocates a portion of each individual's time for participation in continuous capability improvement activities.

Ability 4   **Mentoring support is offered to improve the capability and performance of individuals and workgroups.**

> In the context of Continuous Capability Improvement, mentoring is provided primarily in the form of detailed coaching in the knowledge, skills, and process abilities involved in the personal and workgroup processes undergoing improvement. Although some authors distinguish between mentoring and coaching, the People CMM treats coaching as a special form of mentoring that focuses on detailed expertise in the knowledge, skills, or process abilities of one or more workforce competencies. The use of mentors in Continuous Capability Improvement implies using an experienced individual(s) with expert capability in the competency-based processes on which these personal and workgroup processes are based. Refer to the Mentoring process area for information regarding selecting and preparing mentors and for information regarding establishing and maintaining a mentoring relationship.

1. Improvement opportunities are evaluated to determine whether the individual or workgroup could benefit from mentoring support.

> Mentors providing detailed coaching are made available in situations where performance improvements are expected to contribute most strongly to achieving unit or organizational performance objectives. Examples of factors to be considered in evaluating the benefits of providing a mentor include the following:
> - The impact of the processes being coached on meeting unit or organizational performance objectives
> - The marginal improvement in work performance to be achieved through coaching
> - The number of individuals and workgroups affected
> - The rate at which capability can be increased
> - The opportunity to transfer unique knowledge, skill, or process abilities
> - The ability to increase unit and organizational capability or performance

2. Opportunities to provide detailed coaching are prioritized and selected.

> Examples of factors to be considered in prioritizing mentoring opportunities include the following:
> - Magnitude of the expected enhancement in performance
> - Potential value of mentoring to achieving individual, unit, or organizational performance objectives
> - The number of people available qualified to provide detailed coaching
> - The balance between performing work and coaching
> - The value of raising staff capability in targeted areas

3. Mentoring relationships are established in those selected situations to support individuals or workgroups in improving their capability and performance.

> Mentoring relationships are established where the enhancement in performance will justify the investment in coaching support. Refer to Practices 4, 5, 6, and 7 of the Mentoring process area for information regarding selecting and assigning mentors and establishing and maintaining a mentoring relationship.

Ability 5   Individuals and workgroups develop the knowledge, skills, and process abilities needed to perform their responsibilities in applying techniques for continuously improving their capabilities.

> Examples of learning opportunities to support Continuous Capability Improvement include the following:
> - Measurement and analysis of personal work processes and performance
> - Measurement and analysis of workgroup processes and performance
> - Process engineering techniques
> - Advanced knowledge, skills, or process abilities underlying relevant competencies
> - Statistical analysis
> - Change management

Ability 6   The practices and procedures for performing Continuous Competency Improvement are defined and documented.

1. Practices and procedures are defined and documented at the organizational or unit levels, as appropriate.

2. Guidelines for tailoring the practices and procedures for use in different circumstances are documented and made available, as necessary.

3. The individual(s) assigned responsibility for coordinating Continuous Competency Improvement activities across the organization ensures that defined practices and procedures are:
   - maintained under version control,
   - disseminated through appropriate media,
   - interpreted appropriately for different situations, and
   - updated through orderly methods.

4. Experiences, lessons learned, measurement results, and improvement information derived from planning and performing Continuous Capability Improvement practices are captured to support the future use and improvement of the organization's practices.

Practices Performed

Practice 1   **Individuals and workgroups are empowered to continuously improve their capability for performing competency-based processes.**

1. Support for individuals and workgroups to participate in continuous capability improvement is communicated throughout the organization.

2. Units include support for continuous capability improvement in planning their workforce activities.

3. Participation in continuous capability improvement is voluntary.

4. Where appropriate, activities for continuous capability improvement are supported in the personal development plans of those participating in improvement activities.

Practice 2   **Individuals characterize the capability and performance of their personal work processes.**

> *Personal work processes* refer to how single individuals perform the elementary tasks constituting the competency-based processes involved in their work.
>
> The purpose of this practice is for individuals to characterize these personal work processes at a more detailed level than provided in the definitions of the competency-based processes included in the organization's set of standard processes. Refer to the Competency Analysis, Workgroup Development, and Competency Integration process areas for information regarding defining competency-based and workgroup processes.

1. Individuals identify competency-based processes to provide a framework for describing their personal work processes.

> Competency-based processes are typically defined at a level of abstraction higher than the elementary tasks performed by individuals when participating in these processes. In many cases, competency-based processes are defined only to the level of the interactions among people required to accomplish a business activity. Individuals may differ substantially in how they perform the elementary tasks that constitute a component of a competency-based process. For instance, salespeople may use different techniques in closing a sale or designers may perform their activities in different orders based on their preferred design philosophy, experience, or area of greatest knowledge.

2. Individuals analyze their work activities and describe how they uniquely perform the competency-based processes involved.

> Examples of process descriptions include the following:
> - Textual listings of work activities
> - Flowcharts or other graphical depictions of work activities
> - Procedural descriptions of work activities
> - Highlighted points of contribution in processes at the workgroup, unit, or organizational levels

3. Individuals use measures defined during Quantitative Performance Management activities as a basis for measuring the capability and performance of their personal work processes.

> Refer to the Quantitative Performance Management process area for information regarding defining measures of performance at the unit and workgroup level. If the measures used in quantitatively managing performance have been defined at the workgroup level, then measures characterizing the capability of personal work processes will have to be defined. However, if performance is being quantitatively managed at the individual level, these measures may be sufficient if they provide the insight required to continuously improve the capability of personal work processes.

4. Individuals define measures that can be used in analyzing their personal work processes.

> To the extent that individuals can tailor standard measures of competency-based processes, they can benefit from the comparison of existing capability baselines and results. However, the primary purpose of the measures established in this practice is to gain insight into personal performance and guide personal improvement actions. The most important attribute of these measures is their accuracy in characterizing individual capability in performing competency-based processes. Examples of issues to consider in defining measures of personal work processes may include the following:
> - Relationship to individual, workgroup, or unit performance objectives
> - Relationship to measures of competency-based, integrated competency-based, or workgroup operating processes
> - Ability to characterize individual contribution to the workgroup or unit
> - Accuracy of characterizing unique aspects of assigned responsibilities
> - Relationship to personal development or improvement objectives
> - Likelihood of providing insight into personal styles, habits, or sources of mistakes
> - Difficulty of collection or interpretation

5. Individuals collect and retain measures characterizing the capability and performance of their personal work processes.

> The capability of a personal work process is the range of outcomes that occur when an individual performs it repeatedly. Examples of capability measures may include the following:
> - Time to perform the process
> - Mistakes made in performing the process
> - Effectiveness of coordination with processes performed by others
> - Number of work products produced per unit of time
> - Quality of work products produced by the process

Practice 3   Individuals evaluate the capability of their personal work processes to identify opportunities for improvement.

1. Individuals review strategies and methods employed in Quantitative Performance Management activities as a basis for evaluating the capability of their personal work processes.

> If the unit of analysis for Quantitative Performance Management activities is the workgroup, then additional quantitative analysis methods will have to be defined for analyzing the capability of personal work processes. However, if quantitative performance management has been implemented at the individual level, then these measures and analyses may be sufficient if they provide the insight needed to support continuous capability improvement.

2. Individuals define the strategies and methods that can be used in evaluating the capability of their personal work processes.

> Typically, capability is described quantitatively, most often using statistics. Examples of statistical representations for the capability of a work process include the following:
> - Descriptive statistics of central tendency and dispersion
> - Frequency distributions or probability density functions
> - Statistical process control charts
> - Curve-fitting techniques

4. Individuals identify the root causes of inefficiency or defects in their personal work processes.

5. The capabilities of personal work processes are analyzed to determine their potential for improvement.

6. Individuals continuously refine measures of their personal work processes to improve their analyses and insight.

7. Individuals maintain records of their capability and performance.

Practice 4   **Individuals establish measurable improvement objectives and plans for improving the capability of their personal work processes.**

1. Personal work processes are prioritized according to the potential they present for improving work performance.

2. Individuals set measurable improvement objectives for the personal work processes most likely to improve the performance of their committed work.

3. Individuals identify the knowledge, skills, or process abilities that need to be improved to accomplish their improvement objectives.

4. Individuals plan the improvement actions that will be taken to improve the capability and performance of their personal work processes.

> Examples of issues to be resolved in planning to achieve measurable improvement objectives include the following:
> - What knowledge needs to be acquired
> - Which skills need to be improved
> - What process abilities need to be developed
> - Which competency-based assets can be used to improve capability
> - How these knowledge, skills, process abilities, or competency-based assets relate to the performance of their personal work processes
> - The order in which different skills or process abilities will be addressed
> - How improvement will be measured
> - How much capability needs to be developed and at what rate

> Planned improvement activities would normally be recorded in the individual's personal development plan. Refer to the Career Development process area for information regarding the development and use of personal development plans.

5. Individuals review their measurable improvement objectives and planned improvement actions with their workgroup, mentor, career counselor, manager, or other appropriate individuals.

Practice 5   **Individuals continuously improve the capability and performance of their personal work processes.**

1. Individuals engage in timely learning activities to improve the capability and performance of their personal work processes.

> The learning activities employed to continuously improve individual capability extend beyond the typical competency development activities referred to in the Competency Development process area at the Defined Level. The learning activities that are appropriate for capability development are focused much more closely on understanding and improving an individual's personal work processes. Examples of learning activities that would support continuous capability improvement for individuals include the following:
> - Six Sigma-type activities performed on personal work processes
> - Personal Software Process (PSP) [Humphrey 95, Humphrey 97b]
> - Working with a personal mentor or coach on improved methods for performing personal work processes

2. When appropriate, individuals use mentors to guide improvements in their capability and performance.

> Examples of how mentors or coaches can assist individuals include the following:
> - Defining their work processes and performance measures
> - Evaluating the capability of their personal work processes
> - Identifying sources of inefficiency or defects in their personal work processes
> - Providing detailed guidance and advice for improving their personal work processes
> - Evaluating the effectiveness of their improvement activities
> - Making continued improvements
> - Taking corrective actions when improvement activities do not have their intended effect

> Refer to Ability 4 for information regarding mentoring support to improve the capability and performance of individuals.

3. Individuals eliminate the sources of inefficiency or defects from their personal work processes.

4. When appropriate, individuals use competency-based assets to improve the capability of their personal work processes.

> Refer to the Competency-Based Assets process area for information regarding using the organization's competency-based assets.

5. When appropriate, individuals practice the skills and process abilities that will improve the capability and performance of their personal work processes.

6. Individuals apply their improved personal work processes to their committed work and measure the results.

7. Individuals continuously evaluate the performance of their personal work processes to assess improvements in capability and progress against improvement objectives and planned improvement actions.

8. When improvement progress deviates significantly from improvement objectives or planned improvement actions, individuals take corrective actions as appropriate.

> Examples of actions to address deviations from expected improvement progress include the following:
> - Evaluating the effectiveness of the improvement activities
> - Evaluating whether sufficient time has been committed to improvement activities
> - Identifying and engaging in alternate improvement activities that may be more appropriate
> - Pursuing expert advice or coaching
> - Revising improvement objectives or plans

9. When individuals achieve their improvement objectives, they:

   - capture lessons learned from the improvement activities,

   - propose improvements to competency-based processes or their integration across workforce competencies, if appropriate,

   - contribute material for inclusion in competency-based assets, if appropriate, and

   - establish new improvement objectives or planned improvement actions.

> The repeated performance of Practices 3, 4, and 5 form a continuous improvement cycle.

10. Individuals use the capability of their personal work processes as the basis for estimating and planning their committed work.

> Individuals continuously improve their ability to estimate and plan their personal work processes by evaluating their estimates against improved capability and performance results.

Practice 6   **Workgroups evaluate the capability and performance of their operating processes to identify opportunities for improvement.**

1.   Workgroups identify the personal work processes through which individuals perform competency-based processes in accomplishing the workgroup's operating process.

> This identification of the personal work processes that are performed as part of the workgroup's operating process provides a framework for improving the workgroup's capability for performing competency-based processes. Workgroups typically tailor competency-based processes for use in their work settings. A *workgroup's operating process* refers to all the tailored versions of competency-based processes, integrated competency-based processes, and common workgroup methods and procedures used within a workgroup. Since individuals have their own personal work processes by which they perform these competency-based processes, each workgroup will find differences in how these personal work processes are most effectively integrated. Workgroup performance will be enhanced to the extent the workgroup can capitalize on individual strengths, compensate for individual weaknesses, and blend individual styles and characteristics into a smooth workgroup process. For a workgroup that is relatively long-lived, continuous improvement of its capability for performing these processes may substantially benefit unit and organizational performance objectives. The workgroup-related practices in this process area build on the practices established in the Quantitative Performance Management process area.

2.   Workgroups analyze how their members perform and integrate their personal work processes.

> This practice builds on the analysis of personal work processes accomplished in Practice 2 of this process area. The workgroup analyzes how to integrate the personal work processes of its members to form its workgroup operating process. The operating processes of workgroups may be slightly different based on their tailoring of competency-based processes, and each workgroup's unique integration of the personal work processes of its members.

3.   Workgroups use measures defined during Quantitative Performance Management activities as a basis for measuring the capability and performance of the workgroup's operating process.

> Refer to the Quantitative Performance Management process area for practices involved in defining measures of performance at the unit and workgroup level.

4. Workgroups define additional measures needed to analyze and improve how the workgroup integrates personal work processes into the workgroup's operating process.

> The primary purpose of the measures established in this practice is to gain insight into how workgroup performance emerges from the integration of personal work processes, and into how to use this insight to guide improvements at the workgroup level. The most important attribute of these measures is the insight they provide into the factors that determine the workgroup's capability in performing competency-based processes. Examples of issues to consider in defining measures of workgroup processes may include the following:
> - Relationship to individual, workgroup, or unit performance objectives
> - Relationship to measures of competency-based, integrated competency-based, or workgroup processes
> - Ability to characterize the integration of individual work processes into a workgroup operating process
> - Likelihood of providing insight into workgroup characteristics, inefficiencies, or sources of mistakes
> - Difficulty of collection or interpretation

5. Workgroups determine the capability and performance of their workgroup's operating processes.

6. Workgroups identify the root causes of inefficiency or defects in their operating processes.

> In addition to improvements resulting from the integration of personal work processes and a deep understanding of the workgroup's capability and performance measures, workgroups also focus on evaluating current work for causes of inefficiency, while Practice 7 uses this information to set improvement targets for future work.

7. The workgroup evaluates its capability in performing competency-based processes to determine opportunities for improvement.

> Measures regarding integration of personal work processes may be collected and retained in addition to workgroup capability and performance measures from the Quantitative Performance Management process area. Refer to the Quantitative Performance Management process area for practices involved in determining and evaluating the capability of the competency-based processes performed by a workgroup.

Practice 7   **Workgroups establish measurable improvement objectives and plans for improving the capability of their operating processes.**

1. The processes performed by the workgroup are prioritized according to the potential they present for improving workgroup performance.

2. The workgroup sets measurable improvement objectives for the processes most likely to improve the performance of the workgroup.

> These high-priority processes were identified as having the greatest potential for improving the capability and performance of the workgroup. Refer to Practice 10 for information regarding defining capability objectives for critical competency-based processes. These capability objectives for competency-based processes represent the improvement targets necessary to meet the performance capability required for each of these critical competency-based processes to satisfy the organization's performance objectives. Workgroups should be aware of these organizational capability objectives when setting measurable improvement objectives for their high-priority processes.

3. Workgroups identify the knowledge, skills, or process abilities of their members that need to be improved to accomplish their improvement objectives.

> This practice extends the training and development needs analysis activities initiated in the Training and Development, Competency Development, and Workgroup Development process areas.

4. Workgroups identify improvements that need to be made to how personal work processes are organized and integrated into an overall workgroup process.

> Workgroups may be capable of accurately analyzing their own performance. However, this analysis is often best performed by an outside party, such as a coach, who can provide impartial analysis of how effectively personal work processes are being integrated into a workgroup process, and what adjustments need to be made to personal work processes to improve workgroup coordination and performance.

5. Workgroups plan the improvement actions that will be taken to meet their improvement objectives and incorporate these actions into their workgroup and personal development plans.

> Workgroups need to add an element into their planning for completing the tasks required to improve their capability and performance. Individuals, who need to undertake specific improvement activities to either improve their performance or adjust their personal work processes to improve workgroup coordination, should incorporate these actions into their personal development plans.

6. Workgroups review their measurable improvement objectives and planned improvement actions with:

   ■ other workgroups with whom they share dependencies,

   ■ mentors or coaches, as appropriate, and

   ■ those responsible for their performance.

Practice 8   Workgroups continuously improve their capability and performance.

1. Workgroups engage in timely improvement activities that satisfy their improvement objectives and planned improvement actions.

2. When appropriate, workgroups use mentors to guide improvements in their capability and performance.

> Examples of how mentors or coaches can assist workgroups include the following:
> - Defining their work processes and performance measures
> - Analyzing the coordination of their work processes
> - Evaluating the capability of their operating processes
> - Identifying sources of inefficiency or defects in their operating processes
> - Providing detailed guidance and advice for improving their operating processes
> - Evaluating the effectiveness of their improvement activities
> - Making continued improvements
> - Taking corrective actions when improvement activities do not have their intended effect

> Although the coaching provided to a workgroup may be provided by the individual(s) who is responsible for its performance, coaching will more often be provided by an expert in the competency-based processes performed by the workgroup. A workgroup may have several mentors, especially if its members are involved in performing or integrating competency-based processes from several different workforce competencies. Refer to the Mentoring process area for information regarding preparing for and establishing a mentoring or coaching relationship.

3. Workgroups eliminate the sources of inefficiency or defects in their work.

4. When appropriate, workgroups use competency-based assets to improve their capability and performance.

> Refer to the Competency-Based Assets process area for information regarding using the organization's competency-based assets.

5. When appropriate, workgroups practice performing the improved processes that will improve their capability and performance.

6. Workgroups apply their improvements to their committed work and measure the results.

7. Workgroups continuously evaluate their capability and performance to assess progress against improvement objectives and planned improvement actions.

8. When improvement progress deviates significantly from improvement objectives or planned improvement actions, workgroups take corrective actions as appropriate.

> Examples of actions to address deviations from expected improvement progress include the following:
> - Evaluating the effectiveness of the improvement activities
> - Evaluating whether sufficient time has been committed to improvement activities
> - Identifying and engaging in alternate improvement activities that may be more appropriate
> - Pursuing expert advice or coaching
> - Revising improvement objectives or plans

9. When workgroups achieve their improvement objectives, they:

   - capture lessons learned from the improvement activities,

   - propose improvements to competency-based processes or their integration across workforce competencies, if appropriate,

   - contribute material for inclusion in competency-based assets, if appropriate,

   - adjust capability baselines and other quantitative models that characterize their capability or predict their performance, and

   - establish new improvement objectives or planned improvement actions.

> The repeated performance of Practices 6, 7, and 8 form a continuous improvement cycle.

10. Workgroups continuously improve their ability to estimate and plan their operating processes by evaluating their estimates against improved capability and performance results.

> Refer to Practice 4 of the Quantitative Performance Management process area for information regarding the use of process performance baselines for competency-based processes in establishing work commitments.

Practice 9   Recommendations resulting from improvements in personal work processes or workgroup operating processes are reviewed to determine if they should be incorporated into competency-based processes.

1. Individuals and workgroups are encouraged to recommend improvements to competency-based processes that result from their efforts to improve capability.

> Refer to Practice 5 of this process area for information regarding capturing lessons learned and proposing improvements to competency-based processes by individuals participating in Continuous Capability Improvement activities. Refer to Practice 8 of this process area for information regarding capturing lessons learned and proposing improvements to competency-based processes by workgroups participating in Continuous Capability Improvement activities.

2. Individuals with responsibility for making improvements to competency-based processes evaluate improvement recommendations from individuals and workgroups.

> Refer to Practices 13 and 14 of this process area for information regarding evaluating and implementing improvements to the organization's critical competency-based processes.

3. Individuals and workgroups are informed of the disposition of their improvement recommendations.

Practice 10   Within each critical workforce competency, capability objectives are defined for critical competency-based processes.

> Refer to Practice 7 of the Organizational Capability Management process area for information regarding identifying the critical competency-based processes in each critical workforce competency. *Critical competency-based processes* are those competency-based processes within each critical workforce competency that are most crucial to achieving defined performance objectives and business results. Consequently, the organization quantitatively manages the organization's performance in these workforce competencies, as well as the impact of the organization's workforce practices and activities, to ensure that these critical competency-based processes can be performed with sufficient capability to achieve the organization's quantitative performance objectives and intended business results.

1. The organization's performance objectives are analyzed to determine:

   ■ the business activities that must be performed to achieve them,

   ■ the quantitative results required of these business activities if they are to achieve the organization's performance objectives,

- which competency-based processes are most critical to achieving these quantitative results and how they interact, and
- the performance capability required for each of these critical competency-based processes to satisfy the organization's performance objectives.

2. The capability objectives for each critical competency-based process are defined, based on the analysis of capability and performance data.

> Capability objectives for a competency-based process represent the improvement targets necessary to meet the performance capability required for each of these critical competency-based processes to satisfy the organization's performance objectives.

> Capability objectives for competency-based processes should be based on analysis of capability and performance data. Examples of factors to be considered in developing quantitative objectives include the following:
> - Capability compared to industry benchmarks
> - Customer-specified capability levels
> - Cost-benefit tradeoffs for levels of improvement
> - Required capability for improving integration or coordination with other competency-based processes
> - Capability required to support business objectives

3. The capability required of each competency-based process and defined capability objectives to achieve this level of capability are communicated to those:

- responsible for managing or developing the affected workforce competencies, and
- in the affected competency communities.

4. The capability objectives to achieve this level of capability for each critical competency-based process are:

- incorporated into the organization's quantitative performance management activities, and
- used in setting performance objectives for individuals, workgroups, and units performing the competency-based process, as appropriate.

> Refer to the Quantitative Performance Management process area for information regarding using process capability objectives in setting performance objectives for performing competency-based processes.

5. The capability objectives for competency-based processes are refined and adjusted, as necessary, based on:

- changes in business strategy, conditions, or objectives,
- the results of capability analyses, or
- improvements in the performance of competency-based processes.

Practice 11   **Within each critical workforce competency, capability objectives for competency-based processes are compared to process performance baselines to identify improvement objectives.**

> Refer to Practice 7 of the Organizational Capability Management process area for information regarding establishing process performance baselines.

1. Capability objectives for critical competency-based processes are compared to their process performance baselines to identify gaps between current capability and the capability required to satisfy business objectives.

2. Significant gaps between current and required capability levels for critical competency-based processes are used to establish improvement objectives for competency-based processes.

> Refer to Practices 7 and 8 of the Organizational Capability Management process area for information regarding quantifying organizational capability in each of the organization's critical competency-based processes and the quantitative management of capability in each of the organization's critical competency-based processes.

3. Improvement objectives for critical competency-based processes are prioritized and submitted to those involved in improving relevant competency-based processes.

Practice 12   **Within each critical workforce competency, responsible individuals identify opportunities for improving the capability and performance of competency-based processes.**

1. The organization identifies the workforce competencies where committing responsible individuals to proactive continuous improvement of competency-based processes is determined to have sufficient business benefit.

> Committing proactive resources for improving competency-based processes for some workforce competencies may not be judged to have sufficient business benefit to justify the commitment of effort and funds. Thus, proactive activities for continuous improvement may be targeted to selected workforce competencies where continual improvement activities are determined to have sufficient business benefit. In each of these affected workforce competencies, responsible individuals coordinate continual improvement activities.

> Continual improvement activities for competency-based processes are generally specific to each workforce competency, but may also involve improvement of multidisciplinary, integrated competency-based processes among several workforce competencies.

2. Data on the capability and performance of competency-based processes are analyzed to determine which competency-based processes are most in need of improvement.

> Refer to Practices 7 and 8 of the Organizational Capability Management process area for information regarding quantifying organizational capability in each of the organization's critical competency-based processes and the quantitative management of capability in each of the organization's critical competency-based processes.

3. Root cause and similar analytic techniques are applied to identify systems of causes that affect the capabilities of critical competency-based processes with the highest priorities for improvement.

4. The causal systems underlying these critical competency-based processes are analyzed to identify the types of improvements from which these processes would most benefit, including candidate improvements to:

   - the method by which the competency-based process is performed,
   - the structure or sequencing of tasks within the competency-based process,
   - the integration of the competency-based process with other competency-based or business processes,
   - the workforce practices and activities which have an impact on the performance of the competency-based process,
   - technologies that would support or automate the process, or
   - the preparation of individuals or workgroups to perform the process.

5. The results of these analyses are used to guide investigations of potential improvements to critical competency-based processes.

6. When these analyses indicate that the actual impact of workforce practices and activities on the capability and performance of critical competency-based processes deviates significantly from expectations or capability objectives, corrective actions are taken.

> Refer to Practices 10 and 11 of the Organizational Capability Management process area for information regarding the measurement and analysis activities on which analyses of the impact of workforce practices on performance alignment can be built.

These actions may include:

- correcting problems in the performance of workforce activities,
- adjusting capability objectives for competency-based processes,
- adjusting expectations regarding the impact of workforce practices and activities on the capability and performance of competency-based processes,
- redesigning or adjusting workforce practices to improve their impact, and
- altering the performance of workforce practices and activities under different conditions to improve their impact.

Practice 13   **Within selected workforce competencies, responsible individuals identify, evaluate, and select improvements to competency-based processes.**

> In addition to improvements that emerge from continuous improvement of individual or workgroup capability and performance, an individual(s) within each selected workforce competency should proactively investigate improvements in methods or technologies that can be adopted from sources outside the organization.

1. Responsible individuals investigate methods or technologies that have the potential to approach or achieve quantitative improvement objectives.

> Examples of sources of improved methods or technologies include the following:
> - Best practices from industry-leading companies
> - New offerings from technology or method vendors
> - Recent developments at universities
> - Demonstrations at trade and industry conferences
> - Results from research laboratories
> - Prototypes from advanced development groups
> - Lessons learned from continuously improving individual or workgroup capability

2. Candidate improvements to competency-based processes are evaluated to determine their anticipated benefits.

> Examples of techniques for evaluating improvements to competency-based processes include the following:
> - Analytic studies of the method or technology's anticipated change in a competency-based process's performance or results
> - Data from uses external to the organization
> - Simulations

3. When appropriate, trial implementations are conducted to determine the suitability of improvements to competency-based processes.

> Examples of reasons for conducting trial implementations include the following:
> - Validate anticipated improvements in the capability or performance of competency-based processes
> - Evaluate conditions under which capability results differ from those expected
> - Identify the learning and support necessary to successfully deploy the improvement

4. Improvements to competency-based processes are selected for deployment based on appropriate criteria.

> Criteria for evaluating and selecting improvements to competency-based processes may differ among workforce competencies. Examples of criteria that may be used in evaluating improvement recommendations include the following:
> - Results from an analytic study, simulation, or implementation trial
> - Anticipated impact on the capability of competency-based processes
> - Breadth of individuals or workgroups that would benefit from the improvement
> - Extent to which the improvement can be applied to situations other than the one in which it was first applied
> - Cost or difficulty of implementing the improvement
> - Extent to which the improvement provides a reasonable alternative to standard competency-based processes
> - Extent to which the improvement contains elements that are specific to the individual or workgroup making the recommendation

Practice 14   Selected improvement recommendations are incorporated into competency-based processes and made available for use.

1. Improvements selected for inclusion are incorporated into the descriptions of competency-based processes.

> Refer to Practice 5 in the Competency Analysis process area for practices involved in defining and updating competency-based processes.

2. Improvements selected for inclusion are incorporated into the relevant competency-based assets.

> Refer to Practices 5 and 6 in the Competency-Based Assets process area for practices involved in updating competency-based assets and their integration into competency-based processes and related technologies.

3. Individuals and workgroups are informed of improvements to competency-based processes.

4. Improved competency-based processes are deployed for use by individuals and workgroups.

> Examples of issues to be handled in deploying improvements to competency-based processes include the following:
> - Updating descriptions of competency-based processes
> - Updating competency-based assets
> - Incorporating changes into competency development activities
> - Adjusting or redefining measures of competency-based processes, as required
> - Ensuring other workforce competencies engaged in integrated competency-based processes are made aware of potential changes or impacts, if they are anticipated
> - Adjusting individual or workgroup performance objectives, if appropriate
> - Adjusting workforce practices or activities, if appropriate

5. Information is gathered and evaluated on the use and benefits of improved competency-based processes.

6. Lessons learned in improving competency-based processes are incorporated into the criteria for evaluating and selecting improvement recommendations.

Practice 15   **The organization's workforce practices are adjusted, as needed, to accommodate continuous improvement activities by individuals and workgroups.**

> Examples of areas where workforce practices may need to be adjusted, based on continuous improvement activities, include the following:
> - Performance management
> - Training and development
> - Recognition and rewards
> - Compensation
> - Competency analysis and development
> - Career development
> - Work environment
> - Workgroup development and role definitions
> - Mentoring
> - Quantitative management of performance
> - Quantitative management of capability

1. Individual improvement objectives and data on personal work processes are confidential and should not be revealed without the agreement of the individual.

2. Objectives and data for improving personal or workgroup performance are not used in performing any workforce activities without the agreement of the individuals affected.

Measurement and Analysis

Measurement 1   Measurements are made and used to determine the status and performance of activities for Continuous Capability Improvement.

> Examples of measurements include the following:
> - Trends in participation in Continuous Capability Improvement activities
> - Number of individuals trained in techniques for continuously improving personal work processes
> - Number of individuals and workgroups actively engaged in Continuous Capability Improvement activities
> - The number of coaching relationships established
> - The rate at which coaches have helped the individuals and workgroups that they coach achieve performance objectives or improvement objectives
> - Number and types of adjustments made to workforce practices
> - Rate at which individual or workgroup improvement objectives are being accomplished
> - Number of methods and technologies selected for evaluation
> - Number, level of effort, and results for trial implementations of new methods and technologies
> - Number of improvements made to competency-based processes
> - Schedule adherence and level of effort for deploying improvements to competency-based processes

Measurement 2   Measurements are made and used to determine the effectiveness of activities for Continuous Capability Improvement.

Examples of measurements for determining the effectiveness of Continuous Capability Improvement activities include the following:

- Improvements in individual performance
- Growth in workforce competencies of individuals
- Improvements in workgroup or unit performance
- Improvements in workgroup capability
- Quality improvements in the products or services to which individuals and workgroups contribute
- Improvement in the coordination within workgroups
- Improvements to the capability of competency-based processes
- Improvements reported by customers
- Enhanced accomplishment of the performance objectives for individuals, workgroups, units, or the organization

Verifying Implementation

Verification 1   A responsible individual(s) verifies that the activities for Continuous Capability Improvement are conducted according to the organization's documented policies, practices, procedures, and, where appropriate, plans; and addresses noncompliance.

These reviews verify that:

1. The activities for Continuous Capability Improvement comply with the organization's policies and stated values.
2. The activities for Continuous Capability Improvement comply with the relevant laws and regulations.
3. Continuous Capability Improvement activities are performed according to the organization's documented practices and procedures.
4. Noncompliance issues are handled appropriately.

Verification 2   Executive management periodically reviews the Continuous Capability Improvement activities, status, and results; and resolves issues.

These reviews verify:

1. The appropriateness of the activities for continuous capability improvement.
2. Progress in performing the activities for continuous capability improvement.

3. Results from reviews of Continuous Capability Improvement practices and activities.

> Refer to Verification 1 for information regarding reviews of Continuous Capability Improvement activities to ensure adherence to the following:
> - Relevant laws and regulations
> - Organizational policies, practices, and procedures

4. Status of resolution of noncompliance issues.

5. Trends related to Continuous Capability Improvement.

6. Effectiveness of Continuous Capability Improvement activities in achieving improvements in capability of individual or workgroup processes.

7. Effectiveness of Continuous Capability Improvement activities in achieving improvements in capability of competency-based processes.

Organizational Performance Alignment

A process area at Maturity Level 5: Optimizing

Purpose

The purpose of Organizational Performance Alignment is to enhance the alignment of performance results across individuals, workgroups, and units with organizational performance and business objectives.

Description

Organizational Performance Alignment builds on the analyses of competency-based processes initiated in the Quantitative Performance Management and Organizational Capability Management process areas. Where those analyses focused narrowly on process performance, analyses of performance alignment expand this focus to evaluate how the various components of performance fit together across workgroups, units, and the entire organization. Practices within this process area knit together a complete picture of performance within the organization and how the integration of its various business activities are affected by workforce practices and activities. These analyses allow management to integrate the entire enterprise and use workforce activities strategically to achieve organizational business objectives.

Workgroups improve the alignment of performance among their members. Units improve performance alignment among the individuals and units that compose it. Organizations improve performance alignment among their units with organizational business objectives. The organization evaluates the impact of its workforce practices and activities on performance alignment and manages these impacts quantitatively.

Goals

Goal 1   The alignment of performance among individuals, workgroups, units, and the organization is continuously improved.

Goal 2   The impact of workforce practices and activities on aligning individual, workgroup, unit, and organizational performance is continuously improved.

Goal 3   Organizational Performance Alignment practices are institutionalized to ensure they are performed as defined organizational processes.

Commitment to Perform

Commitment 1 **The organization establishes and maintains a documented policy for aligning performance across individuals, workgroups, units, and the organization.**

This policy typically specifies that:

1. The organization is committed to continuously aligning performance results at the individual, workgroup, unit, and organizational levels.

2. The organization's performance alignment activities serve the business objectives and stated values of the organization.

3. Measurable objectives are defined for aligning performance at the individual, workgroup, unit, and organizational levels.

4. Measurable objectives for aligning performance are reviewed and revised, if necessary, based on changes in the organization's stated values or strategic business objectives.

5. Performance measures are defined and collected at the individual, workgroup, unit, and organizational levels.

6. Progress toward performance alignment objectives is quantitatively analyzed, reported, and monitored.

7. Responsibilities for performance alignment activities are defined and assigned to appropriate organizational roles.

8. Results of performance alignment analyses are used in managing performance and adjusting workforce practices and activities.

9. Organizational Performance Alignment practices and activities comply with relevant laws, regulations, and organizational policies.

> Human resources or other appropriate professionals are consulted to ensure that collection, use, and access to the data and analyses from performance alignment activities comply with all relevant laws, regulations, and organizational policies.

Commitment 2 **An organizational role(s) is assigned responsibility for coordinating performance alignment activities across the organization.**

> Examples of individuals who might coordinate performance alignment activities include the following:
>
> - Operational managers and executives
> - Quality, efficiency, or performance experts
> - Human resources or other appropriate professionals
> - Competency ownership groups
> - Measurement or process improvement groups

Ability to Perform

Ability 1   **Within each unit, an individual(s) is assigned responsibility and authority for ensuring the unit's involvement in the organization's performance alignment activities.**

> Examples of responsibilities to be performed within units include the following:
> - Providing performance capability data to an organizational group for storage and analysis
> - Obtaining and using organizational capability baselines in planning and other relevant workforce activities within the unit
> - Providing information or data on workforce activities performed within the unit for use in analyzing the impact of workforce practices and activities on performance
> - Ensuring appropriate security for, and use of, performance data

Ability 2   **Adequate resources are provided for performing Organizational Performance Alignment activities.**

1. Strategic and operational business objectives are made available for performance alignment activities.

2. Measures of performance are collected and made available for analysis.

> The initial measures required to support this practice were defined in the Performance Management, Competency-Based Practices, Workgroup Development, Empowered Workgroups, Quantitative Performance Management, and Organizational Capability Management process areas at the Managed, Defined, and Predictable maturity levels. As performance alignment activities mature, additional or refined measures can be defined.

3. Experienced individuals who have expertise in analyzing performance data are available to assist with analyses of performance alignment.

4. Experienced individuals with appropriate expertise are available to help use the results of performance alignment analyses to adjust performance-based practices and activities.

5. Funding and resources for supporting performance alignment activities are made available.

> Examples of resources to support performance alignment activities include the following:
> - Statistical analysis packages
> - Spreadsheets
> - Performance assessment instruments
> - Databases and other repositories
> - Textual and graphical reporting tools

6. The organization's strategic workforce plan and planned workforce activities in each unit allocate resources for Organizational Performance Alignment activities.

Ability 3   **Individuals performing Organizational Performance Alignment activities develop the knowledge, skills, and process abilities needed to perform their responsibilities.**

1. Those who collect performance data receive orientation on the definitions and use of performance data in analyses.

2. Those who analyze and report performance results have developed the knowledge, skills, and process abilities needed to apply statistics, data analysis and reporting, and other relevant topics needed to perform their responsibilities.

Ability 4   **Individuals and workgroups participating in Organizational Performance Alignment activities receive appropriate orientation in Organizational Performance Alignment practices.**

Individuals and workgroups receive the orientation required to interpret and use performance alignment results if they have responsibilities for:

- using performance alignment results for planning and managing business activities,

- adjusting workforce practices and activities based on performance alignment results, and

- using performance alignment results to understand or improve performance among individuals, workgroups, units, or the organization.

Ability 5   **The practices and procedures for performing Organizational Performance Alignment are defined and documented.**

1. Practices and procedures are defined and documented at the organizational or unit levels, as appropriate.

2. Guidelines for tailoring the practices and procedures for use in different circumstances are documented and made available, as necessary.

3. The individual(s) assigned responsibility for Organizational Performance Alignment activities across the organization ensures that defined practices and procedures are:

- maintained under version control,

- disseminated through appropriate media,

- interpreted appropriately for different situations, and

- updated through orderly methods.

4. Experiences, lessons learned, measurement results, and improvement information derived from planning and performing Organizational Performance Alignment practices are captured to support the future use and improvement of the organization's practices.

Practices Performed

Practice 1   **Workgroups continuously improve the alignment of performance among individuals and across the workgroup.**

1. Workgroups define their methods for evaluating performance alignment, including:

   ■ adjustments to Quantitative Performance Management practices required to evaluate performance alignment,

   ■ analyses to be conducted,

   ■ methods for using the results, and

   ■ additional performance data required to support the analyses.

> Examples of performance data to be analyzed include the following:
> • Individual performance results
> • Performance results for competency-based and interdisciplinary processes
> • The quality of intermediate or final products and services
> • Performance against commitments
> • Contribution to the unit's measurable performance objectives

2. Workgroups analyze performance data to identify misaligned performance among individuals or across the workgroup.

> Examples of misaligned performance to be managed at the workgroup level include the following:
> • Conflicts among individual or workgroup performance objectives or commitments
> • Performance problems caused by those processes whose performance impedes the performance of other processes
> • Timing and coordination problems among individuals or across the workgroup
> • Work products that satisfy the exit criteria of processes that produced them, but do not satisfy the needs of other individuals, workgroups, or units to whom they are delivered
> • Effort that exceeds the requirements for achieving performance objectives, yet fails to add value
> • Conflicts between self-managed workforce activities within the workgroup and workgroup performance objectives
> • Improvements or corrective actions that have unintended side effects on other aspects of performance

> Refer to the Quantitative Performance Management process area for information regarding establishing quantitative control over competency-based processes to achieve a unit's measurable performance objectives.

3. The root causes of misaligned performance are identified.

4. Measurable objectives for aligning performance are included in the performance objectives of misaligned individuals and workgroups.

> Examples of measurable objectives for aligning performance include the following:
> - Individual performance against workgroup performance objectives
> - Contributions by individuals or workgroups to the achievement of performance objectives of other individuals or workgroups
> - Contributions by individuals or workgroups to improvements in the work environment or culture of workgroups
> - Individual or workgroup development against capability development objectives
> - Individual or workgroup performance against continuous improvement objectives

5. Improvement actions for aligning performance among individuals or within the workgroup are identified and implemented.

6. Performance data are monitored and evaluated to determine if performance:

   ■ has become more aligned,

   ■ satisfies the alignment objectives, or

   ■ requires additional actions to improve alignment.

Practice 2   Units align performance among individuals, workgroups, and other entities within the unit.

1. Units define their methods for evaluating performance alignment, including:

   ■ adjustments to Quantitative Performance Management practices required to evaluate performance alignment,

   ■ analyses to be conducted,

   ■ methods for using the results, and

   ■ additional performance data required to support the analyses.

> Examples of performance data to be analyzed include the following:
> - Performance results for competency-based and interdisciplinary processes
> - Performance results aggregated across workgroups or units
> - The quality of intermediate or final products and services
> - Performance against commitments
> - Contribution to the unit's measurable performance objectives

2. Units analyze performance data to identify misaligned performance among individuals, workgroups, or other entities composing the unit.

> When individuals work independently and are not part of a workgroup, misalignments in their performance must be managed at the unit level by a responsible individual(s) at the unit level. A unit may be composed of other units and is therefore responsible for aligning performance among these subordinate units.

> Examples of misaligned performance to be managed at the unit level include the following:
> - Individuals working independently whose performance is not sufficiently synchronized with the performance of other individuals, workgroups, or units with whom they share dependencies
> - Timing and coordination problems among workgroups or units
> - Workgroups whose commitments or business activities interfere with the business activities or commitments of other workgroups or units
> - Timing and coordination problems that develop among individuals or workgroups who are achieving their measurable performance objectives
> - Work products that satisfy the exit criteria of processes that produced them, but do not satisfy the needs of other individuals, workgroups, or units to whom they are delivered
> - Work that fails to add value
> - Conflicts between workforce activities and unit performance objectives
> - Improvements or corrective actions that have unintended side effects on other workgroups or units

> Refer to Practice 2 of the Quantitative Performance Management process area for information regarding establishing measurable performance objectives that most contribute to organizational business objectives.

3. The root causes of misaligned performance are identified through methods that involve all misaligned individuals, workgroups, and units.

4. Measurable objectives for aligning performance are included in the performance objectives of misaligned individuals, workgroups, and units.

> This subpractice builds on practices already established in the Performance Man-
> agement process area at the Managed Level, the Competency-Based Practices and
> Workgroup Development process areas at the Defined Level, and the Empowered
> Workgroups and Quantitative Performance Management process areas at the Pre-
> dictable Level.

> Examples of measurable objectives for aligning performance include the following:
> - Individual performance against workgroup, unit, and organizational perfor-
>   mance objectives
> - Workgroup performance against unit and organizational performance objectives
> - Unit performance against organizational performance objectives
> - Contributions by individuals, workgroups, or units to the achievement of perfor-
>   mance objectives of other individuals, workgroups, or units
> - Contributions by individuals, workgroups, or units to improvements in the
>   overall work environment or culture of workgroups, units, or the organization
> - Individual and workgroup development against workgroup, unit, and organiza-
>   tional objectives for capability development
> - Individual, workgroup, unit, and organizational performance against continuous
>   improvement objectives

5. Actions for aligning performance among individuals, workgroups, or units
are identified and implemented. These actions may involve:

   - improving the performance of one or more individuals, workgroups, or
     units,

   - improving coordination among several individuals, workgroups, or units,

   - tailoring existing processes or defining new processes to improve align-
     ment in the performance of several workgroups or units,

   - changing or adjusting performance objectives or commitments at the
     individual, workgroup, or unit level, or

   - clarifying confusing or conflicting processes or objectives.

6. Performance data are monitored and evaluated to determine if performance:

   - has become more aligned,

   - satisfies the alignment objectives, or

   - requires additional actions to improve alignment.

Practice 3   **The organization aligns performance across units and with the organization's business objectives.**

> Examples of misaligned performance to be managed at the organizational level include the following:
> - Misalignment of performance or objectives among units
> - Misalignment of unit performance or objectives with organizational business strategies and objectives
> - Mismatches between current or strategic levels in workforce competencies and organizational business objectives
> - Conflicts between workforce practices or activities and organizational business objectives
> - Mismatches between organizational process performance capabilities and business objectives
> - Products or services that are misaligned across units or with organizational objectives

1. Responsible individuals define methods for evaluating performance alignment at the organizational level, including:

   ▪ adjustments to Organizational Capability Management practices required to evaluate performance alignment,

   ▪ analyses to be conducted,

   ▪ methods for using the results, and

   ▪ additional performance data required to support the analyses.

2. Organizational performance data is analyzed to identify misaligned performance among units.

> Refer to Practice 10 of the Continuous Capability Improvement process area for information regarding establishing the organization's capability objectives for critical competency-based processes. Also refer to Practices 1, 2, and 3 of the Quantitative Performance Management process area for information regarding establishing measurable performance objectives at individual, workgroup, unit, and organizational levels.

Examples of performance data or measures to be analyzed include the following:
- Performance against commitments
- Contribution to the unit's measurable performance objectives
- Performance results aggregated across units or at the organizational level
- Trends in capability baselines and process performance baselines
- Quality measures or customer response to products and services
- Performance in meeting organizational business objectives
- Measures related to customers, the organization's workforce, the organization, or the community and society in which the organization operates
- Financial measures, such as Return on Capital Employed (ROCE), Residual Income (RI), or cash flow return on investment (CFROI)
- Balanced Scorecard [Kaplan 92] measures
- Value-based metrics, such as Economic Value Creation (EVC), Economic Value Added (EVA) [Ehrbar 98], or shareholder value analysis (SVA)

3. The root causes of misaligned performance are identified through methods that involve all misaligned units and other affected parties.

This subpractice builds on practices already established in the Workgroup Development process area at the Defined Level and the Organizational Capability Management process area at the Predictable Level. That is, performance objectives and capabilities for individual units need to be evaluated for the effect of their interactions and coordination on mutual business objectives. Performance data from within and across units is analyzed to identify root causes for misaligned performance.

Examples of other affected parties may include the following:
- Customers
- Labor unions or other organizations representing the workforce
- Directors or stockholders
- Professional or regulatory organizations
- Executive management

4. Actions for aligning performance among units and with organizational business objectives are identified and implemented. These actions may involve:

   - improving the performance of one or more units,
   - improving coordination among several units,
   - tailoring existing processes or defining new processes to improve alignment in the performance of units,
   - changing or adjusting performance objectives or commitments at the unit or organizational level, or
   - clarifying confusing or conflicting processes or objectives.

   > This subpractice builds on practices already established in the Performance Management process area at the Managed Level, the Competency-Based Practices and Workgroup Development process areas at the Defined Level, and the Quantitative Performance Management process area at the Predictable Level.

5. Performance data are monitored and evaluated to determine if performance:

   - has become more aligned,
   - satisfies the alignment objectives, or
   - requires additional actions to improve alignment.

Practice 4   **The impact of the organization's workforce practices and activities on aligning performance is understood quantitatively.**

1. Performance alignment results at the workgroup, unit, and organizational levels are quantified and recorded, based on analyses of performance data.

   > These results serve as baselines (or recurring observations) for performing trend analyses. Refer to subpractices 1 and 2 in Practices 1, 2, and 3 for the analyses from which these baselines can be established.

2. Trends in the impact of workforce activities on aligning performance at the individual, workgroup, unit, and organizational levels are established quantitatively.

   > Refer to Practices 10 and 11 of the Organizational Capability Management process area for information regarding the measurement and analysis activities on which analyses of the impact of workforce practices on performance alignment can be built.

Examples of analyzing the impact of workforce practices and activities may include the following:

- The impact of performance management activities on aligning performance
- The impact of mentoring on understanding how to align performance
- The impact of salary adjustment criteria and bonus determinations, if applicable, on aligning performance
- The impact of individual, workgroup, unit, and organizational rewards for aligning performance
- The impact of strategies for career development on aligning performance
- The impact of including performance alignment material in training and competency development
- The impact of participatory commitment procedures on reducing over-commitment
- The impact of work environment factors on aligning performance
- The impact of workgroup factors, such as development or empowerment of the workgroup, on aligning performance

3. Results of these analyses are made available for use in managing and improving performance-related workforce activities.

Examples of individuals or entities who receive analyses of the impact of workforce practices and activities on organizational performance alignment could include the following:

- Those responsible for coordinating workforce practices and activities across the organization
- Those responsible for performing and reporting workforce activities
- Those with management responsibilities for units
- Executive management

Practice 5   The impact of workforce practices and activities on performance alignment is managed quantitatively.

1. Responsible individuals use quantitative analyses of the impact of workforce practices and activities to evaluate:

   - the impacts of workforce practices and activities on aligning performance across individuals, workgroups, units, and the organization,

   - conditions under which the impacts of workforce practices and activities vary, and

   - needs for corrective action.

2. Corrective actions are taken when quantitative evaluations indicate that the actual impact of workforce practices and activities on performance alignment deviates significantly from expectations or performance objectives. These actions may include:

   - correcting problems in the performance of workforce activities,
   - redesigning or adjusting workforce practices to improve their impact on alignment,
   - altering the performance of workforce practices and activities under different conditions to improve their impact, or
   - altering the performance or capability objectives that workforce practices and activities were intended to support.

Practice 6 **Evaluations of the impact of workforce practices and activities on performance alignment are used in performing other business and workforce activities.**

1. Evaluation results are used in strategic business and workforce planning.

Evaluation results might be used in strategic business and workforce planning to evaluate or predict such factors as:

- The potential of workforce practices and activities to improve performance alignment at the individual, workgroup, unit, or organizational levels
- The rate at which the organization can approach and achieve strategic performance objectives for the business
- The return on investment for expenditures of time or financial resources on performance alignment activities

---

2. Evaluation results are used to guide such actions as:

   - designing more effective workforce practices for aligning performance,
   - redesigning, replacing, or eliminating workforce practices that cause misaligned performance, or
   - setting or allocating more realistic or effective quantitative performance objectives.

Measurement and Analysis

Measurement 1   Measurements are made and used to determine the status and performance of the organization's performance alignment activities.

Examples of measurements include the following:

- The number and frequency of analyses being conducted at the workgroup, unit, and organizational levels
- The number of instances of misaligned performance identified in these analyses
- Frequency distributions of the types or causes of misaligned performance
- Number and type of corrective actions taken to remedy misaligned performance
- Number and type of adjustments made to workforce practices and activities to improve performance alignment

Measurement 2   Measurements are made and used to determine the effectiveness of the organization's performance alignment activities.

Examples of measurements to determine the effectiveness of performance alignment activities include the following:

- Improvements in performance at the individual, workgroup, unit, or organizational levels
- Improvements in the process performance baseline results for competency-based processes
- Increases in the organization's ability to correct misaligned performance or other results needing corrective action
- Increases in the speed with which the organization or its units can deploy and align new performance objectives
- Increases in the organization's ability to align its performance objectives and results over time

Verifying Implementation

Verification 1   A responsible individual(s) verifies that the organization's performance alignment activities are conducted according to the organization's documented policies, practices, procedures, and, where appropriate, plans; and addresses noncompliance.

These reviews verify that:

1. Organizational Performance Alignment activities comply with the organization's policies and stated values.
2. Organizational Performance Alignment activities comply with relevant laws and regulations.

3. Organizational Performance Alignment activities are performed according to the organization's documented practices and procedures.

4. Noncompliance issues are handled appropriately.

Verification 2 **Executive management periodically reviews the organization's performance alignment activities, status, and results; and resolves issues.**

These reviews verify:

1. The appropriateness of performance alignment activities at the individual, workgroup, unit, and organizational levels.

2. Progress in performing Organizational Performance Alignment activities.

3. Results from reviews of Organizational Performance Alignment practices and activities.

> Refer to Verification 1 for information regarding reviews of Organizational Performance Alignment activities to ensure adherence to the following:
> - Relevant laws and regulations
> - Organizational policies, practices, and procedures

4. Status of resolution of noncompliance issues.

5. Trends related to Organizational Performance Alignment.

6. Effectiveness of the organization's performance alignment activities in achieving alignment of performance across the individual, workgroup, unit, and organizational levels.

Verification 3 **The definition and use of measures of individual, workgroup, unit, and organizational performance are periodically audited for compliance with organizational policies.**

> Organizational policies which may apply could include human resource, human capital, information security, confidentiality, privacy, or data disclosure policies.

1. Definitions of individual, workgroup, unit, and organizational performance measures and information are reviewed for compliance with organizational policies.

> The data definitions define what data is to be collected, aggregated, and used. They are not the data values themselves. For example, unit performance measures could be a component of a data definition, but the specific unit results would be a specific data value for an instance of unit performance information.

2. Periodic audits ensure that individual, workgroup, unit, and organizational performance measures and information are accessed and used in accordance with organizational policies.

> These audits may be accomplished through reviews of ongoing reporting, such as system access and use monitoring reports, and auditing to ensure compliance with relevant information security standards and organizational policies.
>
> System access and use monitoring ensures that the data are accessed only by authorized individuals, while compliance auditing ensures that these individuals perform appropriate procedures in compliance with organizational policies and standards.

Continuous Workforce Innovation

A process area at Maturity Level 5: Optimizing

Purpose

The purpose of Continuous Workforce Innovation is to identify and evaluate improved or innovative workforce practices and technologies, and implement the most promising ones throughout the organization.

Description

Continuous Workforce Innovation involves establishing mechanisms for proposing improvements in workforce activities, identifying needs for new practices, surveying and evaluating innovative practices and technologies, conducting exploratory trials of new practices and technologies, and implementing the most beneficial ones across the organization.

Innovative workforce practices and technologies include new channels for recruiting, new selection techniques, innovative ways to manage performance, innovative technologies for communication, creative compensation schemes, introducing new media and methods for developing knowledge and skills, alternative career choices, and new ways of organizing and empowering the workforce.

Effort toward implementing innovative workforce practices is included in the strategic workforce plans. The group assigned responsibility for coordinating continuous workforce innovation stays aware of the current effectiveness of the organization's workforce activities. A procedure for proposing improvements to workforce activities is developed and communicated to the workforce. Recommendations for adopting innovative or improved workforce practices can result from suggestions from the workforce or from analyzing best practices at other organizations. The coordinating group continually reviews internal proposals and external developments in workforce practices and technology to determine which innovations offer the greatest opportunity to improve the competency and performance of the organization. The most promising innovations can be tried and, if successful, they are implemented across the organization. The effectiveness of these improved practices is evaluated quantitatively and the results are communicated to the workforce.

Goals

Goal 1   **The organization establishes and maintains mechanisms for supporting continuous improvement of its workforce practices and technologies.**

Goal 2   **Innovative or improved workforce practices and technologies are identified and evaluated.**

Goal 3   **Innovative or improved workforce practices and technologies are deployed using orderly procedures.**

Goal 4   **Continuous Workforce Innovation practices are institutionalized to ensure they are performed as defined organizational processes.**

Commitment to Perform

Commitment 1   **The organization establishes and maintains a documented policy for conducting Continuous Workforce Innovation activities.**

> This policy establishes organizational expectations for identifying improvements in workforce practices and technology innovations that measurably improve the organization's workforce capability and process performance.

Issues typically addressed in the policy include:

1. The continuous improvement and innovation of workforce practices:

   - serves the business objectives and stated values of the organization, and
   - complies with all relevant laws, regulations, and organizational policies.

2. The organization sets and tracks measurable objectives for improvement to be achieved through the adoption of innovative workforce practices.

3. Improvements in workforce activities are directed toward:

   - improving the organization's capability in its workforce competencies;
   - aligning performance at the individual, workgroup, unit, and organizational levels; or
   - improving the efficiency of workforce activities.

4. The organization maintains an awareness of:

   - new developments in workforce practices and technologies, and
   - trends in workforce attitudes and needs.

5. The organization evaluates promising new workforce practices and technologies and adopts the most effective ones for ordinary use.

6. All members of the workforce are able to participate in continuously improving workforce activities.

Commitment 2   **An organizational role(s) is assigned responsibility for coordinating the continuous innovation and improvement of workforce practices across the organization.**

> Although everyone in the organization may submit improvement proposals (and broad participation should be encouraged), the responsibility and authority for collecting, evaluating, selecting, and coordinating the deployment of innovative improvements is usually assigned to a group having responsibility for coordinating continuous improvement activities. Several such groups may exist within the organization, with each group focused on a different area of workforce practices.

Examples of how continuous innovation and improvement of workforce practices might be coordinated across the organization include the following:

- A committee reviewing improvement recommendations submitted by individuals or groups
- Specialists in each area of workforce practices working to improve practices or adopt innovations in their area
- A team of experts working together to develop or deploy innovative practices in their area of expertise
- Workforce experts working independently or as a team with technologists to develop innovative workforce technologies in such areas as training or work-group communication

The role(s) coordinates and helps to:

1. Review suggested improvements in workforce practices submitted by individuals or groups.
2. Identify needed improvements in workforce practices.
3. Explore potential applications of innovative workforce practices and technology.
4. Select and plan for the implementation of innovative or improved workforce practices and technologies.
5. Acquire, customize, install, and evaluate new workforce practices and technologies.
6. Communicate and coordinate with researchers on new developments in workforce practices and technologies that may have potential benefit within the organization.
7. Communicate with suppliers of workforce technology on problems and enhancements.

Ability to Perform

Ability 1   **Within each unit, a responsible individual(s) coordinates actions regarding proposals for improving workforce practices and activities and manages deployment of improvements or innovations.**

Ability 2   **Adequate resources are provided for continuously improving workforce practices and activities.**

1. Data are available for evaluating the needs for continuous workforce improvements or innovations.

Refer to the Communication and Coordination, Quantitative Performance Management, Organizational Capability Management, Organizational Performance Alignment, and Continuous Capability Improvement process areas regarding sources of data that can be used to evaluate the needs for continuous improvement.

2. Experienced individuals with expertise in specialized areas are available to help in evaluating, planning, and supporting initiatives for innovating or improving workforce practices and technologies.

> Examples of specialized areas for continuous workforce innovation include the following:
> - Traditional workforce functions, such as selection or training
> - Resources to support ongoing work, such as computers and software
> - Advanced communication technology
> - Computer-aided training and learning technologies
> - Groupware and team coordination technologies
> - Knowledge assessment and knowledge management methods
> - Performance enhancement methods
> - Computer-supported cooperative work
> - Organizational design strategies

3. Resources for supporting continuous improvement of workforce practices and activities are made available.

> Examples of resources to support continuous improvement include the following:
> - Workstations and software
> - Workgroup software and other groupware technologies
> - Instructional design technology
> - Communication technology
> - Resources to support scanning the external environment for improvement opportunities, such as benchmarking or subscriptions to online databases and external research services

4. Funding and resources are available for:

   - acquiring advanced workforce technologies for evaluation and for running trial projects,

   - supporting the facilities and infrastructure needed to install and maintain advanced workforce practices and technology, and

   - establishing the knowledge, skills, and process abilities needed to use improved workforce practices.

5. Time and support are made available for evaluating suggestions and conducting trial implementations.

Ability 3 **Those responsible for continuously innovating and improving workforce practices and activities develop the knowledge, skills, and process abilities needed to perform their responsibilities and to apply relevant evaluation methods and continuous improvement techniques.**

> Examples of relevant methods and techniques include the following:
> - Advanced workforce practices
> - Continuous improvement techniques
> - Change management
> - Field experimentation
> - Technology evaluation
> - Usability analysis
> - Workforce performance analysis

Ability 4 **Individuals receive orientation or preparation in the innovative or improved workforce practices and technologies adopted by the organization.**

1. Individuals who are responsible for performing new workforce activities have developed the knowledge, skills, and process abilities needed to perform their new responsibilities.

2. Individuals who will be subject to new workforce practices and activities are provided orientation to the new activities.

3. Individuals who will use new workforce technologies receive required training in the use of these technologies.

4. Consulting support is available on a continuing basis in the use of new workforce practices and technologies.

Ability 5 **The practices and procedures for performing Continuous Workforce Innovation are defined and documented.**

1. Practices and procedures are defined and documented at the organizational or unit levels, as appropriate.

2. Guidelines for tailoring the practices and procedures for use in different circumstances are documented and made available, as necessary.

3. The individual(s) assigned responsibility for coordinating Continuous Workforce Innovation activities across the organization ensures that defined practices and procedures are:

   - maintained under version control,
   - disseminated through appropriate media,
   - interpreted appropriately for different situations, and
   - updated through orderly methods.

4. Experiences, lessons learned, measurement results, and improvement information derived from planning and performing Continuous Workforce Innovation practices are captured to support the future use and improvement of the organization's practices.

Practices Performed

Practice 1   **The organization establishes a framework for continuously improving its workforce practices and activities.**

1. The organization identifies a group of responsible individuals with organization-wide responsibility for continuous improvement within each area of workforce practices and activities.

> Examples of those with organization-wide responsibility for continuous improvement of workforce practices include the following:
> - Staff functions, such as human resources or training, that incorporate continuous improvement responsibilities into their committed work
> - Competency ownership teams
> - Task forces composed of those responsible for specific workforce practices and those who represent other relevant areas of the organization

2. Those with organizational responsibility for continuous improvement within an area of workforce practices and activities, establish for their area:

- organizational priorities for improvements, if any,
- approaches and guidance for identifying and implementing improvements,
- high-level plans for pursuing improvement activities,

> At a high level, Continuous Workforce Innovation activities may be planned as part of the organization's strategic workforce plan. Planning for Continuous Workforce Innovation activities is based on the units' and the organization's measurable objectives. Refer to Practice 6 for information regarding establishing quantitative improvement objectives. Action teams should also develop plans for specific improvement planning, piloting, and deployment activities focused on improving the organization's capability. Deployment planning is addressed in Practice 10 of this process area.

- funding and other resources required to support planned improvement activities, and
- how improvement activities will incorporate both suggestions from the workforce and structured improvement activities guided by quantitative objectives and analyses.

Practice 2   Individuals and workgroups are empowered to continuously improve their performance of workforce activities.

1. The workforce is informed of:

    ■ their ability to continuously improve the competency-based processes that they perform,

    > Refer to Practices 9, 12, 13, and 14 of the Continuous Capability Improvement process area for information regarding continual improvement of competency-based processes.

    ■ their ability to continuously improve the workforce activities that they perform, and

    ■ methods available to them for participating in improvement activities.

2. Those who perform workforce practices and activities are encouraged to identify improvements in performing their responsibilities.

3. When they begin performing an improved practice or activity, individuals or workgroups record evidence for evaluating whether the new practice represents an improvement over previous methods.

Practice 3   A continuous improvement program is established to encourage individuals and workgroups to propose improvements to workforce practices and activities.

1. Based on their experience in implementing improved workforce practices or activities, individuals and workgroups are encouraged to submit improvement proposals for possible adoption across their units or across the organization.

    > Refer to Practices 5 and 8 of the Continuous Capability Improvement process area for information regarding capturing lessons learned from continuous improvement of personal and workgroup processes.

2. Improvement proposals can:

    ■ be submitted by any individual or workgroup, and

    ■ address any area of workforce practices or activities.

3. Proposals concerning workforce practices or activities at the organizational level are reviewed by those coordinating improvements in the relevant area of workforce practices for the organization.

4. Proposals concerning workforce activities within a unit are reviewed by the person(s) responsible for workforce activities within the unit, with advice from an appropriate person at the organizational level, if appropriate.

5. Improvement proposals are evaluated by appropriate individuals or groups responsible for improving the area of workforce practices relevant to the proposal.

6. When the implementation of a proposal is localized to a unit and does not require changes to policies or procedures at the organizational level, the unit is empowered to implement the improvement with appropriate review and guidance.

7. Decisions regarding proposals that affect practices and activities at the organizational level are evaluated in the context of other proposed improvements or innovations.

8. Individuals and workgroups are informed of decisions regarding their improvement proposals.

Practice 4   Workforce opinions about their working conditions are periodically evaluated to identify areas that would most benefit from innovative or improved practices.

1. Based upon data collected regarding employee opinions about their working conditions, identify and document employee needs, requirements, and priorities.

> Refer to Practice 4 of the Communication and Coordination process area for information regarding the gathering of employee opinions.
> Example techniques for gathering employee opinions include the following:
> - Focus groups
> - Interviews
> - Surveys
> - Satisfaction feedback
> - Exit interviews

2. The employee needs, requirements, or priorities emerging from these analyses provide inputs for use in:

    - identifying workforce practices needing improvement, and
    - selecting among improved workforce practices for trial use and deployment.

Practice 5   Data regarding the impact of the organization's workforce practices and activities are analyzed to identify areas that would most benefit from innovative or improved practices.

1. Data on the capability of the organization's competency development activities are analyzed to determine:

- which of the organization's workforce competencies would most benefit from innovative or improved competency development practices or activities,

> Refer to Practices 2 and 3 of the Organizational Capability Management process area for practices quantifying organizational capability in each of the organization's critical workforce competencies and the quantitative management of capability in each of the organization's critical workforce competencies.

- within each workforce competency, which competency development activities have been most effective and which are most in need of improvement, and

> Refer to Practices 5 and 6 of the Organizational Capability Management process area for information regarding quantitative management of those competency development activities that have impacts on the capability of critical workforce competencies.

- within each workforce competency, which workforce practices have been most effective and which are most in need of improvement.

> Refer to Practices 5 and 6 of the Organizational Capability Management process area for information regarding quantitative management of those workforce practices and activities that have impacts on the capability of critical workforce competencies.

2. Data on the impact of workforce practices and activities on the capability of competency-based processes are analyzed to determine:

- which competency-based processes are most in need of improvement, and

> Refer to Practices 7 and 8 of the Organizational Capability Management process area for information regarding quantifying organizational capability in each of the organization's critical competency-based processes and the quantitative management of capability in each of the organization's critical competency-based processes.

- within each area of competency-based processes, which workforce practices have had the most beneficial impact and which are most in need of improvement.

> Refer to Practice 10 of the Organizational Capability Management process area for information regarding quantitative management of those workforce practices and activities that have an impact on the capability and performance of competency-based processes.

3. Data on the impact of workforce practices and activities on the alignment of performance are analyzed to determine:

    ■ which areas of performance are most in need of improved alignment, and

    > Refer to Practices 1, 2, and 3 of the Organizational Performance Alignment process area for information regarding analysis of data on the alignment of performance across the organization.

    ■ within each area of misaligned performance, which workforce practices have had the most beneficial impact and which are most in need of improvement.

    > Refer to Practices 4 and 5 of the Organizational Performance Alignment process area for information regarding analysis of data concerning the impact of workforce practices and activities on the alignment of performance across the organization.

Practice 6   **Quantitative objectives are established for improving the impact of workforce practices and activities.**

> Quantitative objectives for improving workforce practices may be established at several levels. They may be established globally across all workforce practices, or they may be established separately for each area of workforce practices, such as staffing practices, compensation practices, and competency development practices. They may be established for specific needs within each workforce competency, or they may be established at the organizational level to affect all workforce competencies. They may be established separately within an organizational unit based on the need to address specific business conditions within that unit.

> Quantitative objectives should be set at a level where sufficient control is exercised over the performance of the workforce practice to achieve the targeted result. Quantitative objectives are typically based upon needs for:
> * Improving capability in workforce competencies
> * Aligning performance
> * Anticipated current and future workforce needs

1. Quantitative objectives for improving the impact of competency development practices and activities are based on:

    ■ the organization's strategic objectives for developing capability in each of its workforce competencies compared to the impact of its competency development practices and activities, and

    ■ the opportunities for improvement identified in analyzing data on the impact of competency development practices and activities.

2. Quantitative objectives for improving the impact of workforce practices and activities on competency-based processes are based on:

- the current capability of competency-based processes compared to the capability required to achieve organizational business objectives, and

- the opportunities for improvement identified in analyzing data on the impact of workforce practices and activities on the capability and performance of competency-based processes.

3. Quantitative objectives for improving the impact of workforce practices and activities on the alignment of performance are based on:

- the current level of performance alignment across individuals, workgroups, and units compared to that needed to achieve organizational business objectives, and

- the opportunities for improvement identified in analyzing data on the impact of workforce practices and activities on the alignment of performance.

Practice 7   The organization continuously investigates innovative workforce practices and technologies.

Those responsible for coordinating the continuous innovation and improvement of workforce practices and technologies across the organization:

1. Maintain awareness of:

- quantitative objectives for improving the impact of competency development practices and activities,

- quantitative objectives for improving the impact of workforce practices and activities on competency-based processes,

- quantitative objectives for improving the impact of workforce practices and activities on the alignment of performance,

- analyses of the organization's competency and capability management data,

- evaluations of the organization's proposals for improvements to workforce practices,

- results of appraisals of the organization's workforce practices and activities,

- opinions, concerns, needs, requirements, and priorities of the workforce, and

- other relevant information about the business conditions affecting the organization.

2. Search for innovations and other developments in workforce practices and technologies through such means as:

- reading relevant journals and periodicals,

- attendance at relevant seminars and conferences,

- benchmarking with other organizations known to innovate in relevant areas of workforce practices, and

- use of consultants or other external sources of expertise in the state of the art.

3. Determine the feasibility of implementing promising workforce practices and technologies by:

- gathering information from vendors and consultants on previous implementation and maintenance costs,

- estimating the cost of implementing and maintaining any communication, information, or other technology required to support the innovative practice,

- evaluating the training and other implementation and maintenance costs involved, and

- assessing the potential disruption and learning curve associated with introducing the innovative practice.

4. Recommend which innovations in workforce practices and technologies would provide the greatest potential benefit to the organization.

Practice 8   Innovative and improved workforce practices and technologies are evaluated and selected for implementation.

1. Those responsible for coordinating the continuous innovation and improvement of workforce practices and technologies review improvement proposals and information on innovative practices or technologies in their area and select the most promising for further evaluation.

2. Preliminary cost-benefit analyses are performed for the anticipated impact of proposed innovations or improvements and those with the highest potential benefits are selected for implementation.

3. The potential risks to effective implementation or potential benefits of selected innovations or improvements are evaluated.

4. Innovative and improved workforce practices and technologies that are evaluated to have few risks to effective implementation or expected benefits are approved for organization-wide implementation.

> For an innovative or improved practice or technology to be evaluated as having few risks, its effective implementation or expected benefits should have already been demonstrated within a unit or in other organizations whose conditions are similar to those under which it will be implemented. When there is uncertainty about a practice or technology, it is evaluated in a trial before being implemented throughout the organization.

5. When significant risks to effective implementation or potential benefits are identified, the innovation or improvement is proposed for trial implementation.

Practice 9   **When appropriate, innovative or improved workforce practices or technologies are evaluated in trials to evaluate their benefits and most effective methods for implementation.**

> The trial is designed to show the strengths and weaknesses that an innovative or improved practice or technology would exhibit in use throughout the organization. Therefore, the trial should identify risks to successful implementation and expected benefits by exposing the practice or technology to the typical conditions under which it will be implemented throughout the organization.

1. The objectives and evaluation criteria for the trial implementation are documented.

2. A plan for conducting one or more trial implementations is developed which covers:

   - the unit(s) to be involved in the trial implementation,
   - resources needed to conduct the trial implementation,
   - the schedule of activities involved in the trial implementation,
   - the training for those who will implement the practice or use the technology,
   - the orientation of those who are affected by the trial implementation,
   - the criteria for evaluating the trial implementation,
   - the data and other information that will be collected for evaluating the trial implementation,
   - how the evaluation will be performed, and
   - the steps to be taken if the trial implementation demonstrates that the practice or technology is beneficial.

3. The plan for the trial implementation is reviewed by all affected parties.

> Examples of affected parties for trials include the following:
> - Those responsible for administering innovative or improved workforce practices
> - Those affected by innovative or improved workforce practices or technologies
> - Those who must use innovative or improved workforce practices or technologies
> - Those who must provide support for innovative or improved workforce practices or technologies

4. Those responsible for innovative or improved workforce practices or technologies provide consultation and assistance to the trial implementation.

5. The trial implementation is conducted and evaluated according to the plan for the trial implementation.

6. The results of the trial implementation are collected, analyzed, and documented, including:

   - documentation of any lessons learned and problems encountered during the trial period,
   - estimates of the benefits and impacts of broader use in the organization, and
   - assessment of risks in moving to broader implementation.

7. Adjustments to a proposed workforce practice or technology are made and documented during the trial period to optimize its effective implementation and benefits.

8. Based on trial results, a decision is made to either:

   - terminate the further work with the practice or technology because it has proven ineffective,
   - proceed with full implementation, or
   - make adjustments to the practice or technology, based on lessons learned, and then replan and continue with additional trials.

Practice 10   The deployment of innovative or improved workforce practices or technologies is planned and prepared.

1. The scope of the organization to which the innovative or improved practice or technology is to be deployed is identified.

   > The scope to which an innovative or improved practice or technology may be applied can include the entire organization or it may be restricted to a specific component of the organization, such as the following:
   > - Specific workforce competencies
   > - Specific segments of the workforce
   > - Specific units
   > - Specific locations

2. A plan is developed for deploying innovative or improved workforce practices or technologies that have been approved for organization-wide use. The plan typically covers:

   - resources needed for deployment,
   - the schedule for deployment across units,
   - the activities involved in deployment within a unit,
   - the training or other preparation for those who will deploy the practice or use the technology,

- the orientation of those who are affected by the practice or technology,
- how to mitigate risks involved in the deployment,
- steps in reviewing deployment status and effectiveness, and
- any changes required for deploying the practice or technology.

> Examples of actions that should be taken in implementing an innovative or improved workforce practice or technology might include changes to the following:
> - Organizational policies or procedures
> - The measurement or verification of workforce practices and activities
> - Descriptions of workforce competencies
> - Competency development methods
> - Competency or capability management activities

3. Before implementing a workforce practice or activity, those responsible for deploying it should review it with:

   - those affected by the practice or activity to identify unanticipated problems or effects,
   - those who have expertise in the area of the practice to determine if the improvement is likely to prove beneficial,
   - a human resources professional, if they believe the improvement may conflict with organizational policies or procedures, or
   - a human resources or legal professional, if the practice or activity is governed by laws or regulations.

> Examples of those with whom innovative or improved workforce practices or technologies can be discussed include the following:
> - Those responsible for coordinating specific workforce practices and activities across the organization
> - Human resources or other appropriate professionals
> - Trainers in the relevant area
> - Experts in performing the activity

4. The strategy for collecting data to measure and track the impact of an innovative or improved workforce practice or technology is documented, reviewed by all affected parties, and agreed to.

5. Training and other methods for preparing responsible individuals to perform innovative or improved workforce practices or to use new technologies are developed.

Practice 11   Innovative or improved workforce practices and technologies are implemented according to their deployment plans.

1. Innovative or improved workforce practices and technologies are implemented across all segments of the organization within the deployment scope.

2. Consulting and other facilitative support is provided to those implementing innovative or improved workforce practices and technologies.

3. Progress in deploying innovative or improved practices or technologies is tracked against the plan.

4. When progress in deploying innovative or improved practices or technologies deviates significantly from plan, corrective actions are taken, which may include:

   - replanning the deployment,

   - resolving shortfalls in resources, training, or other preparations for deployment,

   - correcting inefficiencies in the method of deployment, or

   - adjusting innovative or improved workforce practices and technologies to improve their integration into unit activities.

5. Problems in deploying innovative or improved workforce practices and technologies are identified and adjustments are defined for use in future deployments.

Practice 12   The effectiveness and benefits of innovative or improved workforce practices and technologies are evaluated quantitatively.

1. A strategy for evaluating the effectiveness and benefits of innovative or improved workforce practices and technologies is developed.

2. Appropriate methods for evaluating the effectiveness and benefits of innovative or improved workforce practices and technologies are identified, and analyses are planned.

3. Data concerning the effectiveness and benefits of innovative or improved workforce practices and technologies are collected, analyzed, and reported.

4. Results of these analyses are used to improve the selection and implementation of innovative or improved workforce practices and technologies.

> Refer to the Organizational Capability Management process area for practices regarding the evaluation of the effectiveness and benefits of workforce practices and technologies.

Practice 13   **The status and results of the organization's Continuous Workforce Innovation activities are periodically reviewed and communicated across the organization.**

1. Responsible individuals periodically review the progress in implementing improved or innovative workforce practices and technologies.

> Examples of issues to be covered in status reviews include the following:
> - Level of suggestions or improvement proposals being made and accepted for broader implementation
> - Progress in achieving quantitative objectives for improvement in different areas of workforce practices
> - Alternatives considered and those selected for implementation
> - Progress or results of trial implementations
> - Progress against deployment plans
> - Effectiveness and benefits of improved practices and technologies

2. The workforce is kept informed of the organization's activities for continuously innovating or improving its workforce practices and activities.

> Refer to Practice 2 of the Communication and Coordination process area for examples of organizational communications mechanisms. Examples of information that are to be communicated include the following:
> - The organization's plans and schedules for deploying improved workforce practices and technologies
> - Status and disposition of deployment efforts
> - Status of the improvement proposals and associated workforce practice improvements
> - Significant accomplishments, innovations, and actions taken for workforce practice improvement
> - Measured results of deploying the workforce practice improvements
> - Recognition of the contributions of the people and teams who are involved in improvement or deployment activities
> - Summary information describing the organization's improvement and deployment activities and their results

Measurement and Analysis

Measurement 1   Measurements are made and used to determine the status and performance of activities for continuously innovating and improving workforce practices and activities.

Examples of measurements include the following:

- The number of improvement proposals submitted in total and for each area of workforce practices
- The response time for handling improvement proposals
- The percentage of workforce improvement proposals accepted
- The number of innovative workforce practices and technologies evaluated in total and for each area of workforce practices
- The number of innovations or improvements in workforce practices and technologies evaluated in trial implementations
- The number of improved or innovative workforce practices and technologies implemented across the organization

Measurement 2   Measurements are made and used to determine the effectiveness of continuously innovating and improving workforce practices and technologies.

Examples of measurements to evaluate the effectiveness of innovative or improved workforce practices and technologies include the following:

- Their impact on individual, team, unit, or organizational performance
- The impact of each workforce innovation or improvement on the efficiency of workforce activities
- The impact of each workforce innovation or improvement on increasing the organization's capability in one or more of its workforce competencies
- The impact of each innovation or improvement on aligning performance
- The effect of implementing each workforce innovation or improvement compared to its defined improvement objective
- The effect of workforce innovations or improvements on team, unit, or organizational performance

Verifying Implementation

Verification 1   A responsible individual(s) verifies that the activities for continuously innovating and improving workforce practices are conducted according to the organization's documented policies, practices, procedures, and, where appropriate, plans; and addresses noncompliance.

These reviews verify that:

1. The activities for Continuous Workforce Innovation comply with the organization's policies and stated values.

2. The activities for Continuous Workforce Innovation comply with relevant laws and regulations.

3. All innovative or improved workforce practices and their implementations are reviewed to ensure they comply with relevant laws and regulations.

4. Continuous Workforce Innovation activities are performed according to the organization's documented practices and procedures.

5. Noncompliance issues are handled appropriately.

Verification 2   Executive management periodically reviews the Continuous Workforce Innovation activities, status, and results; and resolves issues.

These reviews verify:

1. The appropriateness of the continuous evaluation, innovation, or improvement activities.

2. Progress in evaluating or implementing continuous improvements.

3. Results from reviews of Continuous Workforce Innovation practices and activities.

Refer to Verification 1 for information regarding reviews of Continuous Workforce Innovation activities to ensure adherence to the following:
- Relevant laws and regulations
- Organizational policies, practices, and procedures

---

4. Status of resolution of noncompliance issues.

5. Trends related to Continuous Workforce Innovation.

6. Effectiveness of Continuous Workforce Innovation activities in continuously innovating and improving workforce practices and technologies.

PART THREE

Appendices

Appendix A

References

Accenture 08   Accenture. *Accenture Global Delivery Network: Certifications.* 2008. Available WWW <URL: www.accenture.com/Global/Services/Global_Delivery_and_Sourcing/AccentureCertifications.htm>.

Amit 99   Amit, R. & Belcourt, M. "Human Resources Management Processes: A Value-Creating Source of Competitive Advantage." *European Management Journal 17*, 2 (1999): 174–181.

Anderson 05   Anderson, J. & Snyder, C. "Customized People CMM Assessment Leads to ISTG Improvements." *SEPG 2005*. Pittsburgh: Software Engineering Institute, Carnegie Mellon University, 2005.

Appleby 00   Appleby, A. & Mavin, S. "Innovation Not Imitation: Human Resource Strategy and the Impact on World-Class Status." *Total Quality Management 11*, 4–6 (2000): S554–S561.

Athey 99   Athey, T. R. & Orth, M. S. "Emerging Competency Methods for the Future." *Human Resource Management 38*, 3 (Fall 1999): 215–226.

BAE SYSTEMS 01   BAE SYSTEMS Mission Solutions. *Certifications.* 2001. Available WWW <URL: www.marconi-is.com/about/certifications.html>.

Baldrige 01   Baldrige National Quality Program. *2001 Criteria for Performance Excellence—Business*. Gaithersburg, MD: Baldrige National Quality Program, National Institute of Standards and Technology, Technology Administration, U.S. Dept. of Commerce, 2001.

Becker 96   Becker, B. & Gerhart, B. "The Impact of Human Resource Management on Organizational Performance: Progress and Prospects." *Academy of Management Journal 39*, 4 (1996): 779–801.

Becker 98   Becker, B. E. & Huselid, M. A. "High Performance Work Systems and Firm Performance: A Synthesis of Research and Managerial Implications." In *Research in Personnel and Human Resources Management, Vol. 16,* Gerald R. Ferris (ed.). Greenwich, CT: JAI Press (1998): 53–101.

Becker 01   Becker, B. E.; Huselid, M. A.; & Ulrich, D. *The HR Scorecard: Linking People, Strategy, and Performance*. Boston: Harvard Business School Press, 2001.

Billings 94   Billings, C.; Clifton, J.; Kolkhorst, B.; Lee, E.; & Wingert, W. B. "Journey to a Mature Software Process." *IBM Systems Journal 33*, 1 (1994): 46–61.

Birdi 08   Birdi, K.; Clegg, C.; Patterson, M.; Robinson, A.; Stride, C. B.; Wall, T. D.; & Wood, S. J. "The Impact of Human Resource and Operational Management Practices On Company Productivity: A Longitudinal Study." *Personnel Psychology 61*, 3 (2008): 467–501.

Boehm 81   Boehm, B. *Software Engineering Economics*. Englewood Cliffs, NJ: Prentice-Hall, 1981.

Boehm 87   Boehm, B. "Increasing Software Productivity." *IEEE Computer 20*, 9 (1987): 43–57.

Boehm 00   Boehm, B., et al. *Software Cost Estimation with COCOMO II.* Upper Saddle River, NJ: Prentice-Hall, 2000.

Boudreau 07   Boudreau, J. W. & Ramstad, P. M. *Beyond HR: The New Science of Human Capital.* Boston: Harvard Business School Press, 2007.

Bontis 02   Bontis, N. & Fitz-enz, J. "Intellectual capital ROI: a causal map of human capital antecedents and consequents." *Journal of Intellectual Capital 3*, 3 (2002): 223–247.

BNY Mellon 07   The Bank of New York Mellon. *The Bank of New York Mellon's Pershing Unit Assessed at P-CMM® Level 3 for People Management Processes.* Jersey City, NJ: The Bank of New York Mellon, 2007. Available WWW <URL: www.bnymellon.com/ pressreleases/2007/pdf/ pr120607b.pdf>.

Brown 00   Brown, J. S. & Duguid, P. *The Social Life of Information.* Boston: Harvard Business School Press, 2000.

Buckingham 99   Buckingham, M. & Coffman, C. *First, Break All the Rules: What the World's Greatest Managers Do Differently.* New York: Simon & Schuster, 1999.

Business Line 02   Bureau. *IBM Global assessed for PCMM.* The Hindu Business Line, November 29, 2002. Available WWW <URL: www.thehindubusinessline.com/2002/11/29/ stories/ 2002112901000703.htm>.

Buttles 08   Buttles-Valdez, P.; Svolou, A.; & Valdez, F. "A Holistic Approach to Process Improvement Using the People CMM and the CMMI-DEV: Technology Process, People, & Culture, The Holistic Quadripartite." *SEPG North America 2008.* Pittsburgh: Software Engineering Institute, Carnegie Mellon University, 2008.

Byrnes 04   Byrnes, P.; Glover, M.; Hayes, W.; & Ryan, C. "Best Practice Panel for CMMI Class B and Class C." *CMMI Technology Conference 2004.* Pittsburgh: Software Engineering Institute, Carnegie Mellon University, 2004. Available WWW <URL: www.dtic.mil/ ndia/2004cmmi/ CMMIT3WedPM/Glover_PanelBestPractices.pdf>.

Carnegie Mellon University 95   Carnegie Mellon University, Software Engineering Institute (Principal Contributors and Editors: Mark C. Paulk, Charles V. Weber, Bill Curtis, and Mary Beth Chrissis), *The Capability Maturity Model: Guidelines for Improving the Software Process.* Reading, MA: Addison-Wesley, 1995.

Cascio 00   Cascio, W. F. *Costing Human Resources: The Financial Impact of Behavior in Organizations (4th ed.).* Cincinnati: South-Western College Publishing, 2000.

Cascio 08   Cascio, W. & Boudreau, J. *Investing in People: Financial Impact of Human Resource Initiatives.* Upper Saddle River, NJ: FT Press, 2008.

CEPAA 97   CEPAA—Council on Economic Priorities Accreditation Agency. *SA 8000: International Standard: Social Accountability 8000.* New York: Council on Economic Priorities Accreditation Agency, 1997.

Chaffee 96   Chaffee, M. & Gunning, K. "Putting the People CMM into Practice." *The SEI Software Engineering Symposium: Achieving Maturity Through Technology Adoption* (September 9–12, 1996, Pittsburgh). Pittsburgh: Software Engineering Institute, Carnegie Mellon University, 1996.

Chand 07   Chand, M. & Katou, A. A. "The impact of HRM practices on organizational performance in the Indian hotel industry." *Employee Relations 29*, 6 (2007): 576–594.

Chrissis 06   Chrissis, M. B.; Konrad, M.; & Shrum, S. *CMMI®: Guidelines for Process Integration and Product Improvement (2nd Edition).* Boston: Addison-Wesley, 2006.

CIPD 06   Human Capital Panel, CIPD. *Human Capital Evaluation: Getting Started*. London: Chartered Institute of Personnel and Development, 2006.

CMMI 00   CMMI Product Development Team. *CMMI^{SM} for Systems Engineering/Software Engineering/Integrated Product and Process Development, Version 1.02, Staged Representation* (CMMI-SE/SW/IPPD, V1.02, Staged. Technical Report CMU/SEI-2000-TR-030). Pittsburgh: Software Engineering Institute, Carnegie Mellon University, 2000.

Crane 01   Crane, S. "India's Most Wanted: As the Global War for IT Talent Heats Up, CFOs on the Subcontinent Are Fighting to Stem Their Losses." *CFO Asia,* December 2000–January 2001. Available WWW <URL: www.cfoasia.com/archives/200012-38.htm>.

Crosby 79   Crosby, P. B. *Quality Is Free: The Art of Making Quality Certain*. New York: McGraw-Hill, 1979.

Curley 04   Curley, M. G. *Managing Information Technology for Business Value: Practical Strategies for IT and Business Managers*. Hillsboro, OR: Intel Press, 2004.

Curtis 81   Curtis, B. "Substantiating Programmer Variability." *Proceedings of the IEEE 69*, 7 (1981): 846.

Curtis 88   Curtis, B.; Krasner, H.; & Iscoe, N. "A Field Study of the Software Design Process for Large Systems." *Communications of the ACM 31*, 11 (1988): 1268–1287.

Curtis 90   Curtis, B. "Managing the Real Leverage in Software Productivity and Quality." *American Programmer 4* (August 1990): 4–14.

Curtis 95   Curtis, B.; Hefley, W. E.; & Miller, S. *People Capability Maturity Model, Version 1* (CMU/SEI-95-MM-002). Pittsburgh: Software Engineering Institute, Carnegie Mellon University, September 1995.

Curtis 00   Curtis, B. & Thorhauge, T. "People CMM: Current Benefits and Future Directions." *Proceedings of the European SEPG 2000 Conference*. Milton Keynes, UK: ESPI Foundation, 2000.

Curtis 02a   Curtis, B.; Hefley, W.E.; & Miller, S. *The People Capability Maturity Model: Guidelines for Improving the Workforce*. Boston: Addison-Wesley, 2002.

Curtis 02b   Curtis, B.; Hefley, W.E.; & Miller, S. *The People Capability Maturity Model: Guidelines for Improving the Workforce* (ISBN 81-297-0018-2). Delhi, India: Pearson Education, 2002.

Curtis 03   Curtis, B.; Hefley, W. E.; & Miller, S. A. "Experiences Applying the People Capability Maturity Model." *Crosstalk: The Journal of Defense Software Engineering*, April 2003, 9–13.

Curtis 03a   Curtis, B.; Hefley, W. E.; Miller, S.; & Maeda, T. *People CMM: Capability Maturity Model for Motivating People and Improving the Organization*. (ISBN: 4526052175). Tokyo: Nikkan Kogyo Shimbunsha, 2003.

Curtis 03b   Curtis, B.; Hefley, W. E.; & Miller, S. *The People Capability Maturity Model: Guidelines for Improving the Workforce. Chinese Edition* (ISBN 730207044X), 2003.

Curtis 07   Curtis, B.; Hefley, W. E.; & Miller, S. *The People Capability Maturity Model: Guidelines for Improving the Workforce* (ISBN 81-317-0798-9). Delhi, India: Dorling Kindersley (India) Pvt. Ltd., 2007.

Dahmann 03   Dahmann, F. D. *Correlation Between Quality Management Metric and People Capability Maturity Model* (Master's thesis). Naval Postgraduate School, Monterey, CA, 2003.

Davenport 99 Davenport, T. O. *Human Capital: What It Is and Why People Invest It*. San Francisco: Jossey-Bass, 1999.

Delaney 96 Delaney, J. T. & Huselid, M. A. "The Impact of Human Resource Management Practices on Perceptions of Organizational Performance." *Academy of Management Journal 39*, 4 (1996): 949–969.

Deming 86 Deming, W. E. *Out of the Crisis*. Cambridge, MA: MIT, 1986.

D'Monte 08 D'Monte, L. "BPOs finally emerging out of IT shadow." *Business Standard* (Mumbai edition, February 15, 2008). Available WWW <URL: http://businessstandard .co.in/india/storypage.php? autono=313877>.

DTI 03 Task Force on Human Capital Management, Department of Trade and Industry. *Accounting for People Consultation Paper*. London: Department of Trade and Industry, 2003.

EFQM 99 European Foundation for Quality Management. *The EFQM Excellence Model*. Brussels, Belgium: European Foundation for Quality Management, 1999.

Ehrbar 98 Ehrbar, A. *EVA: The Real Key to Creating Wealth*. New York: John Wiley & Sons, 1998.

Embar 01 Embar, C. "The State of Software Development in India." *Crosstalk 14*, 8 (2001): 9–11.

Ericsson 08 Ericsson Nikola Tesla d. d. "Business results of joint stock company Ericsson Nikola Tesla in Q1 2008." Available WWW <URL: www.ericsson.hr/investors/actual_2008/ results_q1.shtml>.

Eskildsen 00 Eskildsen, J. K. & Dahlgaard, J. J. "A Causal Model for Employee Satisfaction." *Total Quality Management 11,* 8 (2000): 1081–1094.

Ferguson 99 Ferguson, P.; Leman, G.; Perini, P.; Renner, S.; & Seshagiri, G. *Software Process Improvement Works!* (Technical Report CMU/SEI-99-TR-027). Pittsburgh: Software Engineering Institute, Carnegie Mellon University, 1999.

Fitz-enz 95 Fitz-enz, J. *How to Measure Human Resources Management*. New York: McGraw-Hill, 1995.

Fitz-enz 09 Fitz-enz, J. *The ROI of Human Capital: Measuring the Economic Value of Employee Performance (2nd edition)*. New York: ANACOM, 2009.

Foster 05 Foster, K. "Utilizing the People CMM to Leverage Organizational Success." *SEPG 2005*. Pittsburgh: Software Engineering Institute, Carnegie Mellon University, 2005.

GAO 02 United States General Accounting Office. *A Model of Strategic Human Capital Management* (Publication No. GAO-02-373SP). Washington, DC: United States General Accounting Office, 2002.

Gates 02 Gates, S. *Value at Work: The Risks and Opportunities of Human Capital Measurement and Reporting* (Research Report No. R-1316-02-RR). New York: Conference Board, 2002.

Gates 03 Gates, S. *Linking people measures to strategy: from top management support to line management buy-in* (Research Report No. R-1342-03-RR). New York: Conference Board, 2003.

Gates 08 Gates, S. *Strategic Human Capital Measures: Orientation, Accountability, and Communication* (Research Report No. R-1417-08-WG). New York: Conference Board, 2008.

Gremba 97 Gremba, J. & Myers, C. "The IDEAL[SM] Model: A Practical Guide for Improvement." *Bridge*, 3 (1997): 19–23. Available WWW <URL: www.sei.cmu.edu/ideal/ ideal.bridge.html>.

GRI 06   Global Reporting Initiative. *Sustainability Reporting Guidelines.* Amsterdam, the Netherlands: Global Reporting Initiative, 2006.

Griffin 00   Griffin, S. "Boeing's Continuous Improvement Journey." Keynote address at *12th Annual Software Engineering Process Group Conference, SEPG 2000.* Pittsburgh: Software Engineering Institute, Carnegie Mellon University, 2000.

Hannon 96   Hannon, J. M. & Milkovich, G. T. "The Effect of Human Resource Reputation Signals on Share Prices: An Event Study." *Human Resources Management 35,* 3 (1996): 405–424.

Hansen 89   Hansen, G. S. & Wernerfelt, B. "Determinants of Firm Performance: Relative Importance of Economic and Organizational Factors." *Strategic Journal of Management 10* (1989): 399–411.

Harry 00   Harry, M. & Schroeder, R. *Six Sigma: The Breakthrough Management Strategy Revolutionizing the World's Top Corporations.* New York: Currency, 2000.

Hassan 06   Hassan, M.; Hagen, A.; & Daigs, I. "Strategic Human Resources as a Strategic Weapon for Enhancing Labor Productivity: Empirical Evidence." *Academy of Strategic Management Journal 5,* (2006): 75–96.

HCL 07   HCL Technologies Ltd.–BPO Services. *Achieving Organizational Excellence through People CMM®.* Noida, U. P., India: HCL Technologies Ltd. – BPO Services, 2007.

Hefley 98   Hefley, W. E. & Curtis, B. *People CMM®-Based Assessment Method Description* (Technical Report CMU/SEI-98-TR-012). Pittsburgh: Software Engineering Institute, Carnegie Mellon University, 1998.

Hefley 03   Hefley, W. & Miller, S. A. "Software CMM® or CMMI®? The People CMM® supports them both." *Software Engineering Process Group (SEPG) 2003.* Pittsburgh: Software Engineering Institute, Carnegie Mellon University, 2003.

Holbeche 01   Holbeche, L. *Aligning Human Resources and Business Strategy.* Oxford: Butterworth-Heinemann, 2001.

Humphrey 89   Humphrey, W. S. *Managing the Software Process.* Reading, MA: Addison-Wesley, 1989.

Humphrey 95   Humphrey, W. S. *A Discipline for Software Engineering.* Reading, MA: Addison-Wesley, 1995.

Humphrey 97a   Humphrey, W. S. *Managing Technical People.* Reading, MA: Addison-Wesley, 1997.

Humphrey 97b   Humphrey, W. S. *Introduction to the Personal Software Process^{SM}.* Reading, MA: Addison-Wesley, 1997.

Humphrey 00   Humphrey, W. S. *Introduction to the Team Software Process^{SM}.* Boston: Addison-Wesley, 2000.

Huselid 95   Huselid, M. A. "The Impact of Human Resource Management Practices on Turnover, Productivity, and Corporate Financial Performance." *Academy of Management Journal 38* (1995): 635–672.

Intel 03   Intel. *People Capability Maturity Model: How Intel uses the P-CMM model to improve workforce practices* (Intel Information Technology White Paper 0203\IT\TU\PDF-001). Intel, 2003.

Intelligroup 00   PR Newswire. *Intelligroup Global Development Center Achieves SEI Certification for Continuous Improvement of Software and People Development.* New York, 2000.

Josko 04   Josko, J. M. B. *Management of People in Information Technology: A Perspective View of Approaches* (Master's thesis). Universidade Estadual de Campinas. Instituto de Computação, 2004.

Kaplan 92   Kaplan, R. S. & Norton, D. P. "The Balanced Scorecard—Measures That Drive Performance." *Harvard Business Review 70*, 1 (1992): 71–79.

Katzenbach 93   Katzenbach, J. R. & Smith, D. K. *The Wisdom of Teams*. Boston: Harvard Business School Press, 1993.

Keeni 00a   Keeni, G. "Benefits Accrued from Moving Up CMM Levels and Continuous Process Improvement." *Proceedings of the European SEPG 2000 Conference*. Milton Keynes, UK: ESPI Foundation, 2000.

Keeni 00b   Keeni, G. "The Evolution of Quality Processes at Tata Consultancy Services." *IEEE Software 17*, 4 (2000): 79–88.

Kingsmill 03   Kingsmill, D. (Chair) and The Task Force on Human Capital Management. *Accounting for People Report (Report of the Task Force on Human Capital Management)*. London: Accounting for People Task Force, Dept. of Business, Enterprise & Regulatory Reform, 2003. Available WWW <URL: www.berr.gov.uk/files/file38839.pdf>.

Kirkpatrick 98   Kirkpatrick, D. L. *Evaluating Training Programs (2nd ed.)*. San Francisco: Berrett-Koehler, 1998.

Kishore 08   Kishore, S. & Naik, R. *Aligning Ferret, How an Organization Meets Extraordinary Challenges*. Bangalore: Postscript Impressions, 2008.

Kling 95   Kling, J. "High-Performance Work Systems and Firm Performance." *Monthly Labor Review 118*, 5 (1995): 29–36.

Kravetz 88   Kravetz, D. *The Human Resources Revolution*. San Francisco: Jossey-Bass, 1988.

Kumar 01   Kumar, A. *Hughes Route to Quality*. 2001. Available WWW <URL: www.softwaredioxide.com/Channels/Corporate_Space/HSS/Arun_Kumar.htm>.

Labor 93   U.S. Dept. of Labor, Office of the American Workplace. *High-Performance Work Practices and Firm Performance*. Washington, DC: U. S. Department of Labor, 1993.

Lawler 01   Lawler, E., III; Mohrman, S.; & Benson, G. *Organizing for high-performance: Employee involvement, TQM, reengineering, and knowledge management in the Fortune 1000*. San Francisco: Jossey-Bass, 2001.

Lawler 03   Lawler, E., III & Mohrman, S. *Creating a Strategic Human Resources Organization: An Assessment of Trends and New Directions*. Stanford, CA: Stanford University Press, 2003.

Lawler 06   Lawler, E., III; Boudreau, J.; & Mohrman, S. *Achieving Strategic Excellence: An Assessment of Human Resource Organizations*. Stanford, CA: Stanford Business Books, 2006.

Lee 98   Lee, R. G. & Dale, B. G. "Business process management: a review and evaluation." *Business Process Management Journal 4*, 3 (1998): 214–225.

Lockheed 99   PR Newswire. *Lockheed Martin Mission Systems Ranked Highly for Workforce Practices*. New York: 1999. [Also available online]. Available WWW <URL: www.lockheedmartin.com/news/press_releases/1999/LockheedMartinMissionSystemsRankedH.html>.

Major 98   Major, J.; Pellegrin, J. F.; & Pittler, A. W. "Meeting the Software Challenge: Strategy for Competitive Success." *Research-Technology Management 41*, 1 (1998): 48–56.

Mallick 05   Mallick, K. "Achieving People CMM Level 3 at Club Mahindra Varca Beach." *Human Capital*, October 2005.

Martin 07   Martin, K. *The Global War for Talent: Getting What You Want Won't Be Easy.* Boston: Aberdeen Group, 2007.

Martin 08   Martin, K. & Saba, J. *The 2009 HR Executive's Agenda.* Boston: Aberdeen Group, 2008.

Martín-Vivaldi 99   Martín-Vivaldi, M. & Berg, U. "Influencing the People Perspective at Ericsson Using the People CMM." *Proceedings of the European SEPG 1999 Conference.* Milton Keynes, UK: ESPI Foundation, 1999.

Mastek 01   Mastek. *Mastek Is an SEI-CMM Level 5 Company and the World's First P-CMM Level 3 IT Company,* 2001. Available WWW <URL: www.mastek.com/art2.asp>.

Mavrinac 95   Mavrinac, S. C.; Jones, N. R.; & Meyer, M. W. *Competitive Renewal through Workplace Innovation: The Financial and Non-Financial Returns to Innovative Workplace Practices* (CBI Working Paper 15). Boston: Ernst & Young Center for Business Innovation (CBI), 1995.

Mayo 01   Mayo, A. *The Human Value of the Enterprise: Valuing People as Assets – Monitoring, Measuring, Managing.* London: Nicholas Brealey International, 2001.

McClure 02   McClure, D. L. "Human Capital: Attracting and Retaining a High-Quality Information Technology Work Force." Testimony Before the Subcommittee on Technology and Procurement Policy, Committee on Government Reform, U.S. House of Representatives (GAO-02-113T). Washington, DC: GAO, 2002.

McKinsey 08a   Guthridge, M.; Komm, A. B.; & Lawson, E. "Making talent a strategic priority." *The McKinsey Quarterly,* 1 (2008): 49–59.

McKinsey 08b   McKinsey. "Realigning the HR function to manage talent." *The McKinsey Quarterly Chart Focus Newsletter,* August 2008. Available WWW <URL: www.mckinseyquarterly.com/newsletters/chartfocus/2008_08.html>.

Miller 06   Miller, S. A. "Destination Human Capital Management: You better get a map!" *SEPG 2006.* Pittsburgh: Software Engineering Institute, Carnegie Mellon University, 2006.

Mirvis 97   Mirvis, P. H. "Human Resource Management: Leaders, Laggards, and Followers." *Academy of Management Executive 11,* 2 (1997): 43–56.

Mohrman 95   Mohrman, S. A.; Cohen, S. G.; & Mohrman, A. M., Jr. *Designing Team-Based Organizations.* San Francisco: Jossey-Bass, 1995.

Muralidharan 04   Muralidharan, S. & Subramanian, G. "Process Performance Improvements Through People CMM L5." Asia-Pacific SEPG Conference, 2004. Available WWW <URL: www.innovation-is-free.com/SEPG Paper.pdf>.

Nandyal 03   Nandyal, R. S. *People CMM: Interpreting People CMM for Software Organizations.* New Delhi: Tata Mc-Graw Hill, 2003.

Nandyal 06   Nandyal, R. S, "Shoehorning CMMI Initiatives With People CMM." *Proceedings of the 18th SEPG 2006 Conference.* Pittsburgh: Software Engineering Institute, Carnegie Mellon University, 2006.

NelsonHall 08   NelsonHall. *Global BPO Market Forecast: 2008-2012* (Report BGCQ1836168). Bracknell, Berkshire, UK: NelsonHall, 2008.

Newman 96   Newman, K. L. & Nollen, S. D. "Culture and Congruence: The Fit between Management Practices and National Culture." *Journal of International Business Studies 27,* 4 (1996): 753–779.

Pande 00   Pande, P. S.; Neuman, R. P.; & Cavanagh, R. R. *The Six Sigma Way: How GE, Motorola, and Other Top Companies Are Honing Their Performance.* New York: McGraw-Hill, 2000.

Paulk 93a   Paulk, M. C.; Curtis, B.; Chrissis, M. B.; & Weber, C. V. "The Capability Maturity Model for Software, Version 1.1." *IEEE Software 10,* 4 (1993): 18–27.

Paulk 93b   Paulk, M. C.; Weber, C. V.; Garcia, S. M.; Chrissis, M. B.; & Bush, M. *Key Practices of the Capability Maturity Model, Version 1.1* (Technical Report CMU-SEI-93-TR-25). Pittsburgh: Software Engineering Institute, Carnegie Mellon University, 1993.

Paulk 01a   Paulk, M. C. & Chrissis, M. B. *The 2001 High Maturity Workshop* (Technical Report CMU/SEI-2001-SR-014). Pittsburgh: Software Engineering Institute, Carnegie Mellon University, 2001.

Paulk 01b   Paulk, M.C.; Goldenson, D.; White, D.M.; & Zuccher, M. *The 2001 Survey of High Maturity Organizations* (Technical Report CMU/SEI-2001-SR-013). Pittsburgh: Software Engineering Institute, Carnegie Mellon University, 2001.

PCMM 08   People CMM Team. *People Capability Maturity Model Product Suite Maturity Profile, January 2008.* Pittsburgh: Software Engineering Institute, Carnegie Mellon University, 2008.

Pfeffer 94   Pfeffer, J. *Competitive Advantage through People.* Boston: Harvard Business School Press, 1994.

Pfeffer 98   Pfeffer, J. *The Human Equation: Building Profits by Putting People First.* Boston: Harvard Business School Press, 1998.

Pfeffer 01   Pfeffer, J. "Fighting the War for Talent Is Hazardous to Your Organization's Health." *Organizational Dynamics 29,* 4 (2001): 248–259.

Porter 01   Porter, B. L. "Starting People CMM without an Assessment, Lessons Learned." *Software Engineering Process Group Conference (SEPG 2001)* (March 12–15, New Orleans). Pittsburgh: Software Engineering Institute, Carnegie Mellon University, 2001.

Poulston 08   Poulston, J. "Hospitality workplace problems and poor training: a close relationship." *International Journal of Contemporary Hospitality Management 20,* 4 (2008): 412–427.

Prahalad 90   Prahalad, C. K. & Hamel, G. "The Core Competence of the Corporation." *Harvard Business Review 68,* 3 (1990): 79–91.

Radice 85   Radice, R. A.; Harding, J. T.; Munnis, P. E.; & Phillips, R. W. "A Programming Process Study." *IBM Systems Journal 24,* 2 (1985): 79–90.

Radice 05a   Radice, R.; Chandrasekaran, N.; Hefley, B.; Modi, N.; & Chawla, A. "Results of an Enterprise Appraisal." *Proceedings of SEPG 2005 Conference.* Pittsburgh: Software Engineering Institute, Carnegie Mellon University, 2005.

Radice 05b   Radice, R.; Chawla, A.; & Sokhi, R. "Return on Investment (ROI) from OID and CWI." *Proceedings of SEPG 2005 Conference.* Pittsburgh: Software Engineering Institute, Carnegie Mellon University, 2005.

Radice 05c   Radice, R.; Hefley, W. E.; Curtis, B.; Ferguson, J.; Hayes, W.; Miller, S.; & Wemyss, G. *Interpreting SCAMPI for a People CMM Appraisal at Tata Consultancy Services* (Special Report CMU/SEI-2005-SR-001). Pittsburgh: Software Engineering Institute, Carnegie Mellon University, 2005.

Rao 07   Rao, A. P.; Maitra, A.; & Tarnacha, N. *Achieving Organizational Excellence through People CMM.* Noida, India: HCL Technologies BPO Services, 2007.

Reich 08   Reich, R. "Finding and Keeping Talent." Keynote address at the SSPA/TSPA Services Leadership Conference, Las Vegas, NV, October 22, 2008.

Ringo 08   Ringo, T.; Schweyer, A.; DeMarco, M.; Jones, R.; & Lesser, E. *Integrated talent management: Part 1—Understanding the opportunities for success* (Publication GBE03071-USEN-01). Somers, NY: IBM Institute for Business Value & the Human Capital Institute, 2008.

Rothman 01   Rothman, J. "Crisis? What Crisis? A Contrarian Perspective." *Cutter IT Journal: The Journal of Information Technology Management 14*, 6 (2001): 19–25.

RS 01   RS Software (India) Ltd. *P-CMM Level III—Our Achievement,* 2001. Available WWW <URL: www.rssoftware.com/general/html/pcmm_ini.html>.

SA8000 08   Social Accountability International (SAI). *SA8000®: 2008, Social Accountability 8000*. New York: Social Accountability International (SAI), 2008.

Sackman 68   Sackman, H.; Ericsson, W. J.; & Grant, E. E. "Exploratory Experimental Studies Comparing Online and Offline Performance." *Communications of the ACM 11*, 1 (1968): 3–11.

SCAMPI 06a   SCAMPI Upgrade Team. *Appraisal Requirements for CMMI, Version 1.2 (ARC, V1.2)* (Technical Report CMU/SEI-2006-TR-011). Pittsburgh: Software Engineering Institute, Carnegie Mellon University, 2006.

SCAMPI 06b   SCAMPI Upgrade Team. *Standard CMMI® Appraisal Method for Process Improvement (SCAMPI^SM) A, Version 1.2: Method Definition Document* (Handbook CMU/SEI-2006-HB-002). Pittsburgh: Software Engineering Institute, Carnegie Mellon University, 2006.

Seshagiri 00   Seshagiri, G. "Aligning Measurements to Strategy in a Small/Medium Enterprise: The AIS (Advanced Information Services Inc.) Balanced Scorecard." *Proceedings of the European SEPG 2000 Conference*, Milton Keynes, UK: ESPI Foundation, 2000.

Shih 06   Shih, H.; Chiang, Y.; & Hsu, C. "Can high performance work systems really lead to better performance?" *International Journal of Manpower 27*, 8 (2006): 741–763.

Siemens 01   Siemens Information Systems Ltd., India. *Strategic Structure,* 2001. Available WWW <URL: www.sislindia.com/strat2.htm>.

Spencer 93   Spencer, L. M. & Spencer, S. M. *Competence at Work: Models for Superior Performance*. New York: John Wiley, 1993.

Staples 08   Staples, M. & Niazi, M. "Systematic review of organizational motivations for adopting CMM-based SPI." *Information and Software Technology 50*, 7–8 (2008): 605–620.

Subramanyam 04   Subramanyam, V.; Deb, S.; Krishnaswamy, P.; & Ghosh, R. *An Integrated Approach to Software Process Improvement at Wipro Technologies: veloci-Q* (Technical Report CMU/SEI-2004-TR-006). Pittsburgh: Software Engineering Institute, Carnegie Mellon University, 2004.

Sutherland 08   Sutherland Global Services. *Sutherland Global Services Becomes First BPO Worldwide to Achieve Maturity Level 5 P-CMM® Assessment.* Rochester, NY: Sutherland Global Services, 2008. Available WWW <URL: www.suth.com/company_pressrel_mar18_2008.htm>.

Tondon 00   Tondon, A.; Narayan, S.; & Gulati, S. "P-CMM Impacts on SW-CMM Implementation." *SEPG India 2000*, Bangalore, India, February 22–26, 2000.

Tzafrir 06   Tzafrir, S. S. "A universalistic perspective for explaining the relationship between HRM practices and firm performance at different points in time." *Journal of Managerial Psychology 21*, 4 (2006): 109–130.

Ulrich 97   Ulrich, D. "Measuring Human Resources: An Overview of Practice and a Prescription for Results." *Human Resource Management 36*, 4 (1997): 303–320.

Ulrich 98   Ulrich, D. "A New Mandate for Human Resources." *Harvard Business Review 76*, 1 (1998): 124–134.

US 02   "Chief Human Capital Officers Act of 2002." (P.L. 107–296, November 25, 2002). *United States Statutes at Large* 116 Stat. 2135.

Valett 89   Valett, J. D. & McGarry, F. E. "A Summary of Software Measurement Experiences in the Software Engineering Laboratory." *Journal of Systems and Software 9*, 2 (1989): 137–148.

Vaz 04   *Vaz, L. C. Proposta De Fusão Dos Modelos P-CMM e PSP Em Busca Da Melhoria Da Capacitação Da Força De Trabalho De Uma Organização* (Master's thesis). Universidade de São Paulo, 2004.

Verburg 07   Verburg, R. M.; den Hartog, D. N.; & Koopman, P. L. "Configurations of human resource management practices: a model and test of internal fit." *The International Journal of Human Resource Management 18*, 2 (2007): 184–208

Vu 01   Vu, J. D. "Process Improvement Journey (From Level 1 to Level 5)." *The Sixth Annual European Software Engineering Process Group Conference (SEPG 2001)* (June 11–14, Amsterdam). Milton-Keynes, UK: ESPI Foundation, 2001.

Wademan 05   Wademan, M. R. *Utilizing Development Research to Guide People Capability Maturity Model Adoption Considerations* (Ph.D. thesis) Syracuse University, Syracuse, NY, 2005.

Walker 01   Walker, D. M. "Human Capital: Building the Information Technology Work Force to Achieve Results." Testimony before the Subcommittee on Technology and Procurement Policy, Committee on Government Reform, U.S. House of Representatives (GAO-01-1007T). Washington, DC: GAO, 2001.

Wall 05   Wall, T. D. & Wood, S. J. "The romance of human resource management and business performance, and the case for big science." *Human Relations 58*, 4 (2005): 429–462.

Welbourne 96   Welbourne, T. M. & Andrews, A. O. "Predicting the Performance of Initial Public Offerings: Should Human Resource Management Be in the Equation?" *Academy of Management Journal 39*, 4 (1996): 891–919.

Wellins 91   Wellins, R. S.; Byham, W. C.; & Wilson, J. M. *Empowered Teams: Creating Self-Directed Work Groups That Improve Quality, Productivity, and Participation*. San Francisco: Jossey-Bass, 1991.

Wemyss 07   Wemyss, G. & Svolou, A. "People CMM and CMMI Synergy: Maintaining Long-Term CMMI-Based Improvement through Enhanced Workforce Practices." *SEPG North America 2007*. Pittsburgh: Software Engineering Institute, Carnegie Mellon University, 2007.

Wemyss 08   Wemyss, G. & Ryan, C. *Guidance for Use of SCAMPI with People CMM* (Technical Report CMU/SEI 2009-TN-002). Pittsburgh: Software Engineering Institute, Carnegie Mellon University, 2008.

Wenger 98   Wenger, E. *Communities of Practice: Learning, Meaning, and Identity*. New York: Cambridge University Press, 1998.

Wenger 00   Wenger, E. C. & Snyder, W. M. "Communities of Practice: The Organizational Frontier." *Harvard Business Review 78*, 1 (January–February 2000): 139–146.

Wheeler 06   Wheeler, C. R. *Implementation of the People Capability Maturity Model With Technical Support Personnel in Volusia County School District (Florida)* (Ph.D. thesis). Nova Southeastern University, Ft. Lauderdale, FL, 2006.

Wigle 99   Wigle, G. B. & Yamamura, G. "SEI CMM[SM] Level 5: Boeing Space Transportation Systems Software" (Chapter 13). In Schulmeyer, G. G. & McManus, J. I. (eds.), *Handbook of Software Quality Assurance (3rd ed.).* Upper Saddle River, NJ: Prentice-Hall PTR, 1999.

Wilson 00   Wilson, D. D. & Collier, D. A. "An Empirical Investigation of the Malcolm Baldrige National Quality Award Causal Model." *Decision Sciences 31*, 2 (2000): 361–390.

Womack 03   Womack, J. P. & Jones, D. T. *Lean Thinking.* New York: Free Press, 2003.

Yamamura 99   Yamamura, G. "Process Improvement Satisfies Employees." *IEEE Software 16*, 5 (1999): 83–85.

Yeung 97   Yeung, A. K. & Berman, B. "Adding Value Through Human Resources: Reorienting Human Resource Measurement to Drive Business Performance." *Human Resource Management 36*, 3 (Fall 1997): 321–335.

Yochum 96   Yochum, D. S.; Laws, E. P.; & Barlow, G. K. "An Integrated Human Resources Approach to Moving Information Technology Professionals Toward Best in Class." *AT&T Technical Journal 75*, 1 (1996): 46–53.

Appendix B

Acronyms

AB	Ability to Perform
ADA	Americans with Disabilities Act
AHT	average call handling time or average hold time
AIS	Advanced Information Services Inc.
ARC	Appraisal Requirements for CMMI
BPO	business process outsourcing
BRS	Business Resources Support (Boeing)
CA	Competency Analysis (process area)
CBA	Competency-Based Assets (process area)
CBP	Competency-Based Practices (process area)
CCI	Continuous Capability Improvement (process area)
CD	Competency Development (process area)
CEF	Colleague Engagement Framework (Pfizer)
CFROI	cashflow return on investment
CI	Competency Integration (process area)
CMM	Capability Maturity Model
CMMI	Capability Maturity Model Integration
CMMI-DEV	CMMI for Development
CMP	Compensation (process area)
CO	Commitment to Perform
COBRA	Consolidated Omnibus Budget Reconciliation Act
CoE	center of excellence
COM	Communication and Coordination (process area)
CRD	Career Development (process area)
CWI	Continuous Workforce Innovation (process area)
DoD	Department of Defense
EEO	Equal Employment Opportunity
EFQM	European Foundation for Quality Management
EPG	enterprise process group

ESAT	employee satisfaction
eSCM-SP	eSourcing Capability Model for Service Providers
EVA	Economic Value Added
EVC	Economic Value Creation
EWG	Empowered Workgroups (process area)
GPTW	Great Place to Work
HCLT	HCL Technologies
HCM	human capital management
HEP	Holiday Experience Profile (Club Mahindra)
HIPAA	Health Insurance Portability and Accountability Act
HR	Human Resources
HRM	human resource management
IDEAL	Initiating, Diagnosing, Establishing, Acting, Learning
IEEE	Institute of Electrical and Electronics Engineers
IPPD	Integrated Product and Process Development
IQA	Intel Quality Award
iQMS	Integrated Quality Management System (TCS)
IT	information technology
ITIL	Information Technology Infrastructure Library
IVI	Innovation Value Institute
KRA	Key Result Area
MBNQA	Malcolm Baldrige National Quality Award
MBWA	management by walking around
MDD	Method Definition Document
ME	Measurement and Analysis
MHRIL	Mahindra Holidays & Resorts India Ltd.
ML	Maturity Level
MTR	Mentoring (process area)
MTS	Member of the Technical Staff
NNIT	Novo Nordisk IT A/S
OCA	Organizational Capability Assessment (Intel)
OCM	Organizational Capability Management (process area)
OPA	Organizational Performance Alignment (process area)
OSHA	Occupational Safety and Health Administration
P	Practice (as in *Practices Performed*)
P-CMM	See *People CMM*

PC	Participatory Culture (process area)
People CMM	People Capability Maturity Model
PM	Performance Management (process area)
PSP	Personal Software Process
QPM	Quantitative Performance Management (process area)
QWL	quality of work life
RI	Residual Income
ROCE	Return on Capital Employed
ROI	return on investment
SAM	Self-Assessment Methodology (Intel)
SCAMPI	Standard CMMI Appraisal Method for Process Improvement
SDMM	Service Delivery Maturity Model (Ericsson)
SEI	Software Engineering Institute (http://sei.cmu.edu)
SEIR	Software Engineering Information Repository (http://seir.sei.cmu.edu)
SEPM	Software Engineering Process Management
SFIA	Skills Framework for the Information Age
SPA	Software Process Achievement
SPIN	Software and Systems Process Improvement Network
STF	Staffing (process area)
SVA	shareholder value analysis
SW-CMM	Capability Maturity Model for Software
TCS	Tata Consultancy Services
TD	Training and Development (process area)
TQM	total quality management
TSP	Team Software Process
TUPE	Transfer of Undertakings (Protection of Employment)
VE	Verifying Implementation
WARN	Worker Adjustment and Retraining Notification
WE	Work Environment (process area)
WFP	Workforce Planning (process area)
WGD	Workgroup Development (process area)
WT	Worldwide Technology (Pfizer)

Appendix C

Glossary of Terms

Ability to Perform   A category of institutionalization practices in a process area that describes the preconditions that must exist in the unit or organization to implement practices competently. Ability to Perform typically involves resources, organizational structures, and preparation to perform the practices of the process area.

activity   Actions taken by responsible individuals or workgroups to implement workforce practices. (See also *practices*.)

activities   See *workforce activities*.

adequate   This word is used so that you can interpret goals and practices in light of your organization's business objectives. When using the People CMM, you must interpret the practices so that they work for your organization. This term is used in goals and practices where certain activities may not be done all of the time. (See also *appropriate* and *as needed*.)

affected individuals   The people affected by the performance of a workforce activity or by a decision. Also may imply that a workforce practice is conducted only with individuals in selected positions, job types, or units.

alternative practice   A practice that is a substitute for one or more practices contained in the People CMM that achieves an equivalent effect toward satisfying the goal associated with these People CMM practices. Alternative practices are not necessarily one-for-one replacements for specific People CMM practices.

appraisal   An examination of one or more processes by a trained team of professionals using an appraisal reference model as the basis for determining, as a minimum, strengths and weaknesses. The appraisal reference model for People CMM appraisals is the People CMM. (See also *assessment* and *capability evaluation*.)

appraisal findings   The results of an appraisal that identify the most important issues, problems, or opportunities for improvement within the appraisal scope. Appraisal findings are inferences drawn from corroborated objective evidence.

appraisal method class   A family of appraisal methods that satisfy a defined subset of requirements in the Appraisal Requirements for CMMI (ARC). These classes are defined so as to align with typical usage modes of appraisal methods.

appraisal modes of usage   The contexts in which an appraisal method might be utilized. Appraisal modes of usage identified for the SCAMPI method include internal process improvement, supplier selection, and process monitoring.

appraisal objectives   The desired outcome(s) of an appraisal process.

appraisal participants   Members of the organizational unit who participate in providing information during the appraisal.

appraisal rating   The value assigned by an appraisal team to a People CMM goal or process area or the maturity level of an organizational unit. The rating is determined by enacting the defined rating process for the appraisal method being employed.

appraisal record   An orderly, documented collection of information that is pertinent to the appraisal and adds to the understanding and verification of the appraisal findings and ratings generated.

appraisal reference model   As used in SCAMPI appraisal materials, the reference model to which an appraisal team correlates implemented process activities. In a SCAMPI with People CMM appraisal, the appraisal reference model is the People CMM.

appraisal scope   The definition of the boundaries of the appraisal encompassing the organizational limits and the People CMM model limits within which the processes to be investigated operate.

appraisal sponsor   The individual who requires the appraisal to be performed and provides financial or other resources to carry it out.

appraisal tailoring   Selection of options within the appraisal method for use in a specific instance. The intent of tailoring is to assist an organization in aligning application of the method with its business needs and objectives.

appraisal team leader   The person who leads the activities of an appraisal and has satisfied the qualification criteria for experience, knowledge, and skills defined by the appraisal method.

appropriate   This word is used so that you can interpret goals and practices in light of your organization's business objectives. When using the People CMM, you must interpret the practices so that they work for your organization. This term is used in goals and practices where certain activities may not be done all of the time. (See also *adequate* and *as needed.*)

artifact   A tangible form of objective evidence indicative of work being performed that is a direct or indirect result of implementing a People CMM model practice.

as needed   This phrase is used so that you can interpret goals and practices in light of your organization's business objectives. When using the People CMM, you must interpret the practices so that they work for your organization. This term is used in goals and practices where certain activities may not be done all of the time. (See also *adequate* and *appropriate.*)

assessment   An appraisal that an organization does internally for the purposes of process improvement. The word *assessment* is also used in the People CMM in an everyday English sense (e.g., performance assessment). (See also *appraisal.*)

assignable cause of process variation   An extraordinary event outside the bounds of the normal execution of the process.

assignment   The tasks involved in one or more roles whose performance constitutes an individual's committed work.

capability baseline   A statistically based description of the performance or results of a process that has been performed repeatedly. Capability baselines can quantify attributes of the process (e.g., effort or duration) or of the product produced by the process (e.g., amount or quality).

Control charts used in statistical process control are one form of capability baseline. However, other statistical representations may be more appropriate, depending on the nature of the data being characterized. The purpose of a capability baseline is to predict outcomes and to interpret the results of process performance. (See also *process performance baseline*.)

capability evaluation   An appraisal by a trained team of professionals used as a discriminator to select suppliers, to monitor suppliers against the contract, or to determine and enforce incentives. Evaluations are used to gain insight into the process capability of a supplier organization and are intended to help decision makers make better acquisition decisions, improve subcontractor performance, and provide insight to a purchasing organization. (See also *appraisal* and *assessment*.)

Capability Maturity Model   A Capability Maturity Model (CMM) is an evolutionary roadmap for implementing the vital practices from one or more domains of organizational process. It contains the essential elements of effective processes for one or more disciplines. It describes an evolutionary improvement path from an ad hoc, immature process to a disciplined, mature process with improved quality and effectiveness.

capability of the workforce   See *workforce capability*.

coaching   The use of an experienced and capable individual(s) to increase the knowledge, skills, and process abilities of individuals or workgroups. Coaching is a form of mentoring that involves expert knowledge and skill in the subject matter being coached.

commitment   A pact that is freely assumed, visible, and expected to be kept by all parties involved.

Commitment to Perform   A category of institutionalization practices in a process area that describes the actions an organization must take to ensure that the activities constituting a process area are established and will endure. Commitment to perform typically involves establishing organizational policies (to set expectations for performance), executive management sponsorship, and assigned responsibilities for advising on and coordinating the implementation of workforce practices.

committed work   An agreement concerning the scope of work to be performed and the work products or services to be produced.

common workgroup methods and procedures   Common methods and procedures for performing standard activities that occur in most workgroups, such as problem solving and conducting meetings.

compensation   All forms of inducements or remuneration offered to employees for work performed, most commonly pay and guaranteed benefits. Pay includes any guaranteed fixed rate of salary or hourly wages provided to individuals, plus any variable amounts that are provided based on an agreement between the organization and the individual on how it is administered.

compensation strategy   An organization's philosophy and method for compensating its workforce.

competency   An underlying characteristic of an individual that is causally related to effective or superior performance, as determined by measurable, objective criteria, in a job or situation [adapted from Spencer 93, p. 9]. See also *workforce competency*.

competency-based asset   A bundle of information or an artifact that has been prepared in a standard format and made available for widespread use. It captures knowledge, experience, or artifacts developed in performing competency-based processes in an organization. As an organizational asset, it becomes a component of one or more workforce competencies.

competency-based process   Defines how individuals within a specific workforce competency apply their knowledge, perform their skills, and apply their process abilities in the context of an organization's defined work processes. At Maturity Levels 4 and 5 of the People CMM, "competency-based processes" also may include integrated competency-based processes (or multidisciplinary processes). The organization's defined processes are often described in terms of the processes performed by different workforce competencies, such as the software development process, the sales process, or the customer training process. Competency-based processes are documented, trained, performed, enforced, measured, and improved over time. The competency-based processes associated with a single workforce competency may represent only part of a defined organizational process; other elements of the defined process may be performed by individuals with different workforce competencies.

competency community   Members of a workforce who share and practice a workforce competency; those who share the knowledge, skills, and process abilities of a particular workforce competency. They are also sometimes referred to as "communities of practice" [Brown 00, Wenger 98, Wenger 00].

competency development plan   Identifies the current and future needs of a workforce competency. These plans can either be produced as separately documented plans for each workforce competency, or be integrated in the organization's strategic workforce plan.

competency information   Typically describes an individual's level of capability in relation to the list of knowledge, skills, and process abilities in relevant workforce competency descriptions.

competency management   A collection of workforce practices used to enhance the capability of the workforce to perform assigned tasks and responsibilities, and to achieve specific competency growth objectives.

concern   An issue, state of affairs, condition, complaint, or grievance that an individual or workgroup wants the organization to address and resolve.

core competency   The combination of technology and production skills that creates an organization's products and services and provides its competitive advantage in the marketplace. A workforce competency is different from the concept of a core competency of the organization, as formulated by Prahalad and Hamel [Prahalad 90]. One or more workforce competencies must be present in the workforce so that they can execute a core competency of the organization.

corrective action   Acts or deeds used to remedy a situation, remove an error, or adjust a condition.

corroboration   The activity of considering multiple pieces of objective evidence in support of a judgment regarding an individual People CMM model practice.

critical competency-based processes   The competency-based processes in each critical workforce competency that are most crucial to achieving defined performance objectives and business results. Consequently, critical competency-based processes are managed quantitatively at Maturity Level 4 to ensure that they can be performed with sufficient capability to achieve the organization's quantitative performance objectives and intended business results.

critical positions   Critical to the accomplishment of the organization's business objectives; such positions include more than just executive and other senior management positions. Certain technical, operational, or business positions may also be designated as critical positions because of the difficulty in finding or developing individuals with the knowledge, skills, and process abilities to perform successfully in these positions. The organization organizes the development and career activities required to provide qualified candidates to fill critical positions.

critical skills   Skills that, if not performed effectively, could jeopardize the successful performance of assigned tasks.

critical task   A task that is important for accomplishing an individual's or unit's performance objectives. A task that could jeopardize the successful performance of an assignment, if it is not performed well according to task-related criteria.

critical workforce competency   Critical workforce competencies are those most crucial to sustaining an organization's capability in its core competence [Prahalad 90]. Their growth and development are critical to the viability of the organization's strategic business objectives and plans. Consequently, at Maturity Level 4, the organization's capability in these workforce competencies is managed quantitatively to ensure their competency-based processes can be performed with sufficient capability to achieve the organization's quantitative performance objectives.

defined process   A managed process that documents a set of tasks, contributes to the production of a work product or the delivery of a service, and provides appropriate measurements of performance.

development objectives   An individual's intentions to satisfy needs for critical skills required to perform assigned work and for development to prepare for future assignments and career options.

discovery-based appraisal   An appraisal in which limited objective evidence is provided by the appraised organization prior to the appraisal, and the appraisal team must probe and uncover a majority of the objective evidence necessary to obtain sufficient coverage of People CMM model practices. Discovery-based appraisals typically involve substantially greater appraisal team effort than verification-based appraisals, in which much of the objective evidence is provided by the appraised organization. See *verification-based appraisal* for contrast.

document   A collection of data, regardless of the medium on which it is recorded, that generally has permanence and can be read by humans or machines. Documents can be work products reflecting the implementation of one or more People CMM model practices. These documents typically include work products such as organizational policies, procedures, and implementation-level work products. Documents may be available in hard copy or soft copy, or accessible via hyperlinks in a Web-based environment.

empowered workgroup   A workgroup granted considerable autonomy in managing and performing its work that may perform selected workforce practices within the workgroup.

establish and maintain   In goal and practice statements in a CMM, this phrase means to define, document, make available for use, and periodically update.

equity   A state wherein a market-adjusted balance exists between an individual's remuneration and his or her value to the organization as measured by capability and performance.

evidence See *objective evidence*.

executive management Management roles whose primary focus is the long-term vitality of the organization, rather than short-term production or service concerns. Executive management provides and protects resources for long-term improvement of workforce practices.

As used in the People CMM practices, the term *executive management* should be interpreted in the context of the process area and the projects and organization under consideration. The intent is to include specifically those executive managers who are needed to fulfill the leadership and oversight roles essential to achieving the goals of the process area.

expected model component A model component that explains what may be done to satisfy a required model component. The expected model components are meant to guide in implementing improvements or performing appraisals. Either the practices, as described, or acceptable alternative practices to them must be present with a frequency appropriate to a reasonable implementation of the practice before goals can be considered achieved.

finding (See *appraisal findings*.)

goal A required model component in the People CMM. When you see the word *goal* in the People CMM, it always refers to a model component. In the People CMM, the word *goal* is used only when referring to the model component. A goal in the People CMM represents an organizational state to be achieved by implementing the practices of a process area. Goals are requirements for implementing People CMM-based improvements. Each process area contains one or more implementation goals and one institutionalization goal. The organizational state described by each goal in a process area must be achieved to consider the process area to be successfully implemented and institutionalized. (See also *objective*, *implementation goal*, and *institutionalization goal*.)

graduated career opportunities An arrangement of positions or work responsibilities that require increasing levels of capability in one or more workforce competencies. Graduated career opportunities include not only promotion opportunities in the organization such as career ladders or paths, but also career lattices that provide broadening or lateral assignments to gain experience or increase the individual's capabilities in additional workforce competencies.

group A cluster of individuals organized into a structure that is convenient for managing. This term is used only at Maturity Level 2, and makes no assumption about the level of dependency among the work activities of individuals within the group. A high level of interdependency among people in a group might justify their being developed into a workgroup at Maturity Level 3.

human capital management An approach to people management (or workforce management) that treats it as a high-level strategic issue and seeks systematically to analyze, measure, and evaluate how workforce policies and practices contribute to value creation. [Kingsmill 03] suggests that this approach should be treated as a high-level strategic issue rather than an operational matter "to be left to the HR people."

Human Resources The collection of individuals (both managers and staff) comprising the unit(s) within an organization that focuses on devising practical, effective ways to manage employer-employee relations. Their responsibility is directed toward, but not limited to, the recruitment, selection, hiring, training, compensation, and well-being of employees and the formulation of policies, practices, and procedures that affect employees.

IDEAL   The IDEAL model is an organizational improvement model that serves as a roadmap for initiating, planning, and guiding improvement actions. It is called the IDEAL model after the first letters in each of its five phases: Initiating, Diagnosing, Establishing, Acting, and Learning.

implementation goal   A required model component within a process area of the People CMM. An implementation goal constitutes requirements an organization should satisfy in implementing the workforce practices in a process area. Implementation goals in each process area are accomplished through its implementation practices. (See *institutionalization goal* for contrast. See also *implementation practices*.)

implementation practices   The practices and procedures implemented by the organization to satisfy the implementation goals of a process area. These are the practices that collectively constitute the area of practice denoted by the title of the process area. Each implementation practice within a process area supports accomplishment of a single implementation goal. Implementation practices are categorized as Practices Performed. (See *institutionalization practices* for contrast.)

individual competency   The combination of knowledge, skills, and process abilities an individual possesses, which may be related to performing tasks or roles for the organization. See also *competency* and *workforce competency*.

individual development objectives   An individual's intentions for meeting training and development needs to develop critical skills required by the current assignment or to prepare for future assignments and career opportunities.

individuals   People who perform assignments required to execute the business activities of the organization. The term *individuals* normally refers to those affected by the performance of a workforce practice or activity.

informative model component   A model component that provides details that help explain or elaborate approaches to implementing and institutionalizing a practice or goal. These components help model users understand the required and expected components of the People CMM. These components can contain examples, detailed explanations, or other helpful information. Subpractices, notes, and references are informative model components.

institutionalization   The building and reinforcement of an organizational culture that sustains the performance of workforce practices as standard, ongoing business activities, even after those who originally defined them are gone. Institutionalization results in an ingrained way of doing business that an organization follows routinely as part of its corporate culture.

institutionalization goal   A required model component within a process area of the People CMM. An institutionalization goal constitutes requirements an organization should satisfy in institutionalizing the workforce practices in a process area. The institutionalization goal in each process area is accomplished through its institutionalization practices. (See *implementation goal* for contrast. See also *institutionalization practices*.)

institutionalization practices   The practices and procedures implemented to ensure that the organization has a continuing commitment to and capability for performing the organization's workforce practices and activities. Institutionalization practices support accomplishment of an institutionalization goal in each process area. Institutionalization practices can be categorized as Commitment to Perform, Ability to Perform, Measurement and Analysis, and Verifying Implementation. (See *implementation practices* for contrast.)

instruments   Artifacts used in an appraisal for the collection and presentation of data (e.g., questionnaires, organizational unit information packets). In SCAMPI appraisals, instruments can be used to collect written information relative to the organizational unit's implementation of People CMM model practices. This can include assets such as questionnaires, surveys, or an organizational mapping of People CMM model practices to its corresponding processes.

integrated competency-based processes   Processes that have been interwoven from separate competency-based processes to achieve a more seamless, process-based interaction among people who possess different workforce competencies; for instance, the interweaving of a mechanical design process and a manufacturing design process into a single product design process. Also called a multidisciplinary process. Throughout Maturity Levels 4 and 5, the use of the term *competency-based processes* implies the inclusion of integrated competency-based processes.

integrated product and process development   A systematic approach to product development that achieves a timely collaboration of relevant stakeholders throughout the product life cycle to satisfy customer needs.

internal process improvement (IPI)   An appraisal mode of usage in which organizations appraise internal processes, generally to baseline their process capability, to establish or update a process improvement program, or to measure progress in implementing such a program.

interviews   A meeting of appraisal team members with appraisal participants for the purpose of gathering information relative to work processes in place. In SCAMPI, this includes face-to-face interaction with those implementing or using the processes within the organizational unit. Interviews are typically held with various groups or individuals. A combination of formal and informal interviews may be held and interview scripts or exploratory questions developed to elicit the information needed.

knowledge   An individual's understanding of facts or information. Knowledge provides the basis for performing a skill that an individual must have to perform a task successfully.

Lead Appraiser   A person who has achieved recognition from an authorizing body to perform as an appraisal Team Leader for a particular appraisal method.

managed process   A performed process that is planned and executed in accordance with policy, employs skilled people having adequate resources to produce controlled outputs, involves relevant stakeholders, and is reviewed and evaluated for adherence to relevant procedures.

maturity level   Degree of process improvement across a predefined set of process areas in which all goals in the set are attained. A maturity level represents a level of organizational capability created by the transformation of one or more domains of an organization's processes. It is an evolutionary plateau on an organization's improvement path from ad hoc practices to a state of continuous improvement. The People CMM contains five levels of maturity. (See also *process area.*)

maturity level rating   See *appraisal rating.*

measurable objective   See *quantitative objective.*

Measurement and Analysis   A category of institutionalization practices in a process area that describes the actions the organization must take to ensure that workforce practices are evaluated for performance and effectiveness. Measurement and Analysis typically involves measuring the status of the practices performed, aggregating some measures from the unit to the organizational level, and evaluating the effectiveness of the practices performed.

mentoring   The process of transferring the lessons of greater experience in a workforce competency to improve the capability of other individuals or workgroups.

method   A reasonably comprehensive set of rules and criteria that establish a precise and repeatable way of performing a task or practice and arriving at a desired result.

multidisciplinary process   A process that has been interwoven from separate competency-based processes to achieve a more seamless, process-based interaction among people who possess different workforce competencies. One example of a multidisciplinary process is the interweaving of a mechanical design process and a manufacturing design process into a single product design process. Also called an integrated competency-based process. Throughout Maturity Levels 4 and 5, the use of the term *competency-based processes* implies the inclusion of multidisciplinary processes.

objective   When used as a noun in the People CMM, the term *objective* replaces the word *goal* as used in its common everyday sense, since the word *goal* is reserved for use when referring to the People CMM model component called goals. (See also *goal*.)

objective evidence   As used in SCAMPI with People CMM appraisal materials, documents or interview results used as indicators of the implementation or institutionalization of model practices. Sources of objective evidence can include instruments, presentations, documents, and interviews.

observation   As used in SCAMPI with People CMM appraisal materials, a written record that represents the appraisal team members' understanding of information either seen or heard during the appraisal data collection activities. The written record may take the form of a statement or may take alternative forms as long as the information content is preserved.

optimizing process   A quantitatively managed process that is continually improved to increase its capability. These continuous improvements can be made through both incremental and innovative improvements. (See *quantitatively managed process* and *defined process* for contrast.)

organization   A collection of units for which an executive manager is responsible. An organization could constitute an entire company or agency, or it could constitute only a component of a larger organizational entity, such as a division or branch.

organization's business objectives   Strategies devised by executive management to ensure an organization's continued existence, and to enhance its profitability, market share, and other factors that influence the organization's success.

organization's set of standard processes   The definition of the basic processes used as the basis for establishing common processes across the organization. It describes the fundamental process elements that are expected to be incorporated into the defined processes. It also describes the relationships (e.g., ordering and interfaces) among these process elements. (See also *defined process* and *process element*.)

organizational maturity   The extent to which an organization has explicitly and consistently deployed workforce practices or processes that are documented, managed, measured, controlled, and continually improved. Organizational process maturity may be measured via appraisals.

organizational policy   A principle typically established by executive management that is adopted by an organization to guide behavior and influence decisions.

organizational role   One or more individuals who coordinate and advise people throughout the organization on the implementation of practices in a process area. Those who might fill organizational roles are usually found in staff positions such as human resources, training, process engineering, and so on.

organizational unit   The part of an organization that is the focus of an appraisal. An organizational unit deploys one or more processes that have a coherent process context and operates within a coherent set of business objectives. An organizational unit operates within a coherent workforce context, a coherent process context, and a coherent set of business objectives. An organizational unit is typically part of a larger organization, although in a small organization, the organizational unit may be the whole organization.

participatory culture   An environment in which information is made available to support individuals in making appropriate decisions, and where decisions are shifted to the most appropriate location in the organization so that those affected by a decision participate in, or are represented in, the process of making it.

People CMM Steward   The Software Engineering Institute (SEI) is the Steward of the People CMM Product Suite. The People CMM Steward supports and facilitates the maintenance and evolution of the People CMM Product Suite.

performance alignment   The congruence of performance objectives and the consistency of performance results across the individuals, workgroups, units, and organization. Therefore, the process of aligning performance results across individuals, teams, and units with the organization's performance objectives, and quantitatively assessing the effectiveness of workforce practices in achieving alignment.

performance improvement plan   A document describing the detailed actions and expected results for correcting identified performance problem(s).

performance management   The process of establishing objective criteria against which unit and individual performance can be measured, providing performance feedback, managing performance problems, rewarding and recognizing outstanding performance, and enhancing performance continuously.

performance objective   A measurable attribute or result of work behavior that can be used to evaluate the performance of a unit, workgroup, or individual.

perquisites   A privilege or profit beyond regular pay that is provided as a component of overall compensation. A benefit provided only to specified individuals or positions in the organization.

personal development plan   Specification of the actions to be taken by an individual for developing additional capability in workforce competency, and for applying this capability to his or her work. The plan usually contains objectives for completing development activities, and may contain objectives for capability or performance improvement.

personal work processes   The work processes used by an individual to perform his or her portion of a business process; the ways that individuals perform the elementary tasks constituting the competency-based processes involved in their work. Thus, personal work processes reflect unique, individual characteristics that differ among people performing the same competency-based process. Through Continuous Capability Improvement, these personal work processes mature to become a "customized set of orderly, consistently practiced, and high-quality personal practices" [Humphrey 95].

policy   A guiding principle, typically established by executive management, that is adopted by an organization or project to influence and determine decisions.

position   A post of employment, an assignment of duty, a job.

practice   Description of an activity essential to, in part or in whole, accomplish a goal of the process area. A practice is a subprocess of a process area that contributes to achieving a process area goal. (See also *process area* and *goal*.)

practices   Used throughout the People CMM to refer to standard workforce processes. (See *workforce practices*. See also *activities*, which refers to actions taken to implement these practices.)

Practices Performed   The implementation practices in a process area that describes the practices and procedures that an organization would ordinarily be expected to perform to achieve the implementation goals of a process area. These practices constitute the area of concern represented in the title of the process area. (See *implementation practices*. See also *process area*.)

preparation   Activities undertaken to ensure that individuals have the skills required to perform their responsibilities. Preparation could involve mentoring, classroom training, self-study, or any other activity that ensures the affected individual has the required level of knowledge and skill to perform the assigned practices and activities.

procedure   A written description of a course of action to be taken in performing a task or workforce practice.

process   A set of tasks or activities performed to achieve a given purpose or a specified result.

process ability   The capacity to perform individual skills in the specific sequencing or method used in the organization to coordinate activities among individuals or groups, and to adjust the performance of skills, as necessary, to maintain an orderly flow of work.

Process abilities represent an individual's capacity to apply knowledge and perform skills in the context of the organization's defined, competency-based processes. It includes the ability to adjust the performance of skills in ways that maintain an orderly flow of work. Possession of a process ability indicates that an individual is able to perform the competency-based processes appropriate for someone at his or her level of development in the workforce competency.

process area   A cluster of related practices that, when performed collectively, satisfy a set of goals that contribute to the capability gained by achieving a maturity level.

process area goal   See *goal*.

process area profile   See *process profile*.

process asset   Anything that the organization considers useful in attaining the goals of a process area.

process capability   The range of expected results that can be achieved by following a process. The ability of a process to meet its objectives or requirements or to perform within specified limits.

process capability baseline   A documented characterization of the range of expected results that would normally be achieved by following a specific process under typical circumstances.

process description   A documented expression of a set of activities performed to achieve a given purpose that provides an operational definition of the major components of a process. The documentation specifies, in a complete, precise, and verifiable manner, the requirements, design, behavior, and other characteristics of a process. It also may include procedures for determining whether these provisions have been satisfied. Process descriptions may be found at the activity, personal, workgroup, unit, or organizational levels.

process element   The fundamental unit of a process. A process can be defined in terms of subprocesses or process elements. A subprocess can be further decomposed into subprocesses or process elements; a process element cannot. A process element can be an activity or task that would not be defined into more elementary components or finer-grained descriptions.

process group   A collection of specialists who facilitate the definition, maintenance, and improvement of the process(es) used by the organization.

process improvement   A program of activities designed to improve the performance and maturity of the organization's processes, and the results of such a program.

process maturity   The extent to which an organization's processes are defined, managed, measured, controlled, and continually improved. Process maturity implies continued improvement in the organization's capability for performing its business activities, and indicates consistency in performing its processes throughout the organization.

process monitoring   An appraisal mode of usage in which appraisals are used to monitor process implementation (e.g., after contract award by serving as an input for an incentive/award fee decision or a risk management plan). The appraisal results are used to help the sponsoring organization tailor its contract or process monitoring efforts by allowing it to prioritize efforts based on the observed strengths and weaknesses of the organization's processes. This usage mode focuses on a long-term teaming relationship between the sponsoring organization and the development organization (buyer and supplier).

process owner   The person responsible for defining and maintaining a process. At the organizational level, the process owner is the individual(s) responsible for the description of a standard process or set of related practices. Within a workforce competency, the process owner is the individual(s) responsible for defining and maintaining the competency-based processes associated with that workforce competency. A process may have multiple owners at different levels of responsibility. (See also *defined process*.)

process performance   A measurement of the actual results achieved by performing or following a process.

process performance baseline   A documented characterization of the results achieved by following a process that is used as a benchmark for comparing actual process performance against expected process performance. (See also *process performance*.)

process profile   The set of goal ratings assigned to the process areas in the scope of the appraisal. (See also *process area profile*.)

process tailoring   To make, alter, or adapt a process description to make it fit for use in a particular situation. For example, the organization tailors its defined processes to adapt them for use with different competencies at Maturity Level 3. Similarly, competency-based processes may be tailored for use within a specific workgroup. (See also *process description*, *competency-based process*, and *defined process*.)

quantitative objective   Desired target value expressed as quantitative measures.

quantitatively managed process   A defined process that is evaluated and controlled using statistical and other quantitative techniques. The product quality, service quality, or process performance are measured to determine if results are within expected or predicted bounds, and needs for corrective action are assessed. (See *optimizing process* and *defined process* for contrast.)

rating   See *appraisal rating*.

recognition   Special acknowledgments of an individual or group for accomplishments of value to the organization.

reference   An informative model component that points to additional or more detailed information in related process areas.

reference model   A model that is used as a benchmark for measuring some attribute.

required model component   People CMM components that are essential to achieving process improvements in a given process area. These required model components are used in appraisals to determine organizational workforce capability. Goals are required model components within a process area that are considered essential contributors to the organizational workforce capability achieved at the maturity level of the process area.

resource profile   A quantitative representation of the capability of the workforce within a selected workforce competency. At a minimum, a resource profile presents the number of individuals available to the organization at each level of capability in the workforce competency.

reward   Special recognition outside of the compensation system for accomplishments of significant value to the organization. Usually consists of variable amounts of money, stock, or other considerations provided to individuals or groups at appropriate times without prior agreement as to conditions of receipt. Rewards are distinguished from recognition in that rewards typically involve financial considerations.

role   A defined set of work tasks, dependencies, and responsibilities that can be assigned to an individual as a work package. A role describes a collection of tasks that constitute one component of a process, and would normally be performed by an individual.

root cause   A source of a defect such that if it is removed, the defect is decreased or removed.

skills   The behaviors that an individual must be able to perform in order to accomplish committed work. Skills may involve behaviors that directly accomplish the task or that provide the support of, or coordination with, others involved in accomplishing tasks.

staffing   The process by which talent is recruited, selected, and transitioned into assignments in the organization.

staged representation   A Capability Maturity Model structure wherein attaining the goals of a set of process areas establishes a maturity level; each level builds a foundation for subsequent levels. (See also *process area* and *maturity level*.)

stakeholder   A group or individual that is affected by or is in some way accountable for the outcome of an undertaking.

stated values   A set of documented principles intended to guide behaviors or decisions about how the organization conducts its business, how it treats its workforce, how it interacts with its environment, and other important issues.

strategic workforce plan   Identifies the current and future workforce competency needs of the organization, based on current and anticipated future developments in the business and its products, services, markets, technologies, and business processes. This plan integrates the planned development activities for the organization's workforce competencies that are necessary to provide the needed competencies over time. The strategic workforce plan sets long-term objectives for workforce activities at the organizational and unit levels.

strength   Exemplary or noteworthy implementation of a People CMM model practice.

subpractice   An informative model component that provides guidance for interpreting and implementing a practice. Subpractices may be worded as if prescriptive, but are actually meant only to provide ideas that may be useful for process improvement. Subpractices are the elements of a numbered practice in a process area that are elaborated to guide its effective implementation. Subpractices describe tasks or activities that may be included in implementing the practice. Subpractices are provided for informational purposes only (i.e., are informative model components), and are intended to provide clarification of the practice or ideas for guiding implementation.

subprocess   A process that is part of a larger process. A subprocess can be decomposed into subprocesses and/or process elements. (See also *process, process description*, and *process element*.)

succession plans   Plans produced for critical positions in the organization to ensure that individuals with the required knowledge, skills, and process abilities are always available to perform a position's responsibilities. (See also *critical positions*.)

supplier selection   An appraisal mode of usage in which appraisal results are used as a high value discriminator to select suppliers. The results are used in characterizing the process-related risk of awarding a contract to a supplier.

tailoring   The activity of elaborating, adapting, or completing the details of a practice, process, or role for use in a particular situation or set of circumstances. (See also *appraisal tailoring*.)

team   The People CMM does not use the term *team* in order not to confuse the reader with the many meanings that have been attached to this word in the literature on team building. The People CMM uses the term *workgroup* and describes some workgroups as *empowered workgroups*.

training   Activities undertaken to ensure that all individuals have the knowledge and skills required to perform their assignments.

turnover   In a human capital context, the term *turnover* (or employee turnover) refers to the loss (or attrition) of individuals from the organization. Sometimes turnover is addressed as the turnover rate, which is the characteristic of a given organization or industry which describes the rate at which the organization or industry gains and loses staff, typically expressed as the ratio of the number of individuals that left the organization in a given time period to the average number of individuals in the organization's workforce. Turnover is frequently categorized as either voluntary (such as personal choice, resignation to accept other employment, resignation for continued education, or retirement) or involuntary (such as termination for cause or a reduction in force). Voluntary turnover is frequently also referred to as attrition.

unit   A single, well-defined organizational component (e.g., a department, section, or project) of an organization. The term *unit* is used to refer to any organizational entity that is accountable to a specified individual(s) (usually a manager) responsible for accomplishing a set of performance objectives that can be met only through collective action. A workgroup may constitute the lowest-level unit, but the lowest-level units often consist of several workgroups. "Unit" is a recursive concept; units may be composed from other units cascading down the organization. For instance, a division may be a unit consisting of departments, each of which may be a unit consisting of programs, each of which may be a unit consisting of projects, and so on.

unit training needs   The aggregated requirements for development of knowledge, skills, and process abilities among the individuals in a unit. These are typically documented in the unit training plan.

values   Ideas held by individuals about ethical behavior or appropriate behavior, what is right or wrong, desirable or undesirable.

verification-based appraisal   An appraisal in which the focus of the appraisal team is on verifying the set of objective evidence provided by the appraised organization in advance of the appraisal, in order to reduce the amount of probing and discovery of objective evidence during the appraisal on-site period. (See *discovery-based appraisal* for contrast.)

Verifying Implementation   A category of institutionalization practices in a process area that describes the actions the organization must take to ensure that it is complying with its policies regarding workforce practices. Verifying Implementation typically involves ensuring that practices are being performed in compliance with policies, stated values, plans, laws, and regulations; and that executive management maintains awareness of the level of compliance.

weakness   The ineffective, or lack of, implementation of one or more People CMM model practices.

work commitment   An agreement concerning work to be accomplished. The commitment is made to the responsible individual for whom the work is being performed or to whom the result is being delivered.

workforce   The people an organization needs to perform its business activities. Used especially when workforce practices and activities are to be applied to the people in the organization collectively rather than as individuals.

workforce activities   Actions taken to implement a workforce practice. Therefore, workforce activities are what responsible individuals actually do when performing a workforce practice. These actions are taken by individuals, in workgroups or units, or by the organization to implement workforce practices.

workforce capability   The readiness or preparedness of an organization's workforce to perform its business activities. Specifically, the level of knowledge, skills, and process abilities available to the organization in each critical workforce competency for performing committed work. The capacity of the workforce for performing work or for achieving specified levels of performance. Workforce capability is often measured for each workforce competency.

workforce competency   The People CMM refers to workforce competencies as a cluster of knowledge, skills, and process abilities that an individual should develop to perform a particular type of work in the organization. A workforce competency can be stated at a very abstract level, such as a workforce competency in software engineering, financial accounting, or technical writing. Workforce competencies can also be decomposed to more granular levels, such as competencies in designing avionics software, testing switching-system software, managing accounts receivable, preparing consolidated corporate financial statements, or writing user manuals and training materials for reservation systems.

workforce improvement activities   Activities that improve the level of knowledge, skills, process abilities, motivation, and coordination of an organization's workforce.

workforce improvement proposal   A documented suggestion for change to a workforce process or practice that will improve workforce capability and performance.

workforce planning   The process of matching workforce capability with business needs by planning the workforce activities required to meet current and future business needs at both the organizational and unit levels.

workforce practices   Processes, procedures, or guidelines for implementing the organization's workforce policies. Practices provide guidance for complying with the organization's workforce policies. A workforce practice specifies documented procedures, guidelines, and content for performing workforce activities in any people-related area (e.g., compensation, performance management, workgroup development, coaching). Workforce practices are typically documented and maintained by the human resources function or another appropriate group.

workgroup   A collection of people who work closely with each other on highly interdependent tasks to achieve shared objectives.

workgroup's operating process   All the tailored versions of competency-based processes, integrated competency-based processes, and common workgroup methods and procedures used by a workgroup.

A workgroup's operating processes at the Defined Level are composed from the collection of tailored competency-based processes and common workgroup methods and procedures selected for use in the workgroup. A workgroup's operating processes at the Predictable Level are composed from the collection of tailored competency-based processes, integrated competency-based processes, and common workgroup methods and procedures selected for use in the workgroup. A workgroup's operating processes at the Optimizing Level refer to all the tailored versions of competency-based processes, integrated competency-based processes, and common workgroup methods and procedures.

The operating processes of workgroups may be slightly different based on their tailoring of competency-based processes, and each workgroup's unique integration of the personal work processes of its members.

Appendix D

Practice-to-Goal Mappings for People CMM Process Areas

Purpose

This appendix describes the People CMM, the maturity levels, and the process areas that correspond to each maturity level of the People CMM, and the goals and practices in each process area.

Structure of the People CMM

The People CMM consists of five maturity levels that lay successive foundations for continuously improving talent, developing an effective workforce, and successfully managing the human assets of the organization. Each *maturity level* is a well-defined evolutionary plateau that institutionalizes a level of capability for developing the organization's workforce.

Each maturity level provides a layer in the foundation for continuous improvement of an organization's workforce practices. In maturing from the Initial to the Managed Level, the organization installs the discipline of performing basic workforce practices. In maturing to the Defined Level, these practices are tailored to enhance the particular knowledge, skills, and work methods that best support the organization's business. In maturing to the Predictable Level, the organization develops competency-based, high-performance empowered workgroups, and empirically evaluates how effectively its workforce practices are meeting objectives. In maturing to the Optimizing Level, the organization looks continually for innovative ways to improve its workforce capability and to support the workforce in its pursuit of professional excellence.

Process Areas

Figure A.1 displays the 22 process areas in the five maturity levels in the People CMM. Each *process area* identifies a cluster of related activities that, when performed collectively, achieve a set of goals considered important for enhancing workforce capability. Process areas have been defined so that each resides at a single maturity level.

Process areas identify both

- the capabilities that must be institutionalized to achieve a maturity level and
- the practices that an organization should implement to improve its workforce capability.

The process areas at the Managed Level (Maturity Level 2) focus on instilling basic discipline into workforce activities. At Maturity Level 2, managers take responsibility for managing and developing their people. The process areas at Maturity Level 2 are Staffing, Communication and Coordination, Work Environment, Performance Management, Training and Development, and Compensation.

The process areas at the Defined Level (Maturity Level 3) address issues surrounding the identification of the organization's primary competencies and aligning its people management activities with them. At Maturity Level 3, the organization identifies and develops the workforce competencies required to accomplish its business strategy and objectives. The process areas at Maturity Level 3 are Competency Analysis, Workforce Planning, Competency Development, Career Development, Competency-Based Practices, Workgroup Development, and Participatory Culture.

The process areas at the Predictable Level (Maturity Level 4) focus on stabilizing predictable workforce capability. Opportunities enabled by developing workforce competencies are exploited. Workforce capability and performance become predictable through quantitative management. The process areas at Maturity Level 4 are Competency Integration, Empowered Workgroups, Competency-Based Assets, Quantitative Performance Management, Organizational Capability Management, and Mentoring.

The process areas at the Optimizing Level (Maturity Level 5) focus on continuous improvement of workforce capability and practices. These practices cover issues that address continuous improvement of methods for developing competency, at both the organizational and the individual level. The process areas at Maturity Level 5 are Continuous Capability Improvement, Organizational Performance Alignment, and Continuous Workforce Innovation.

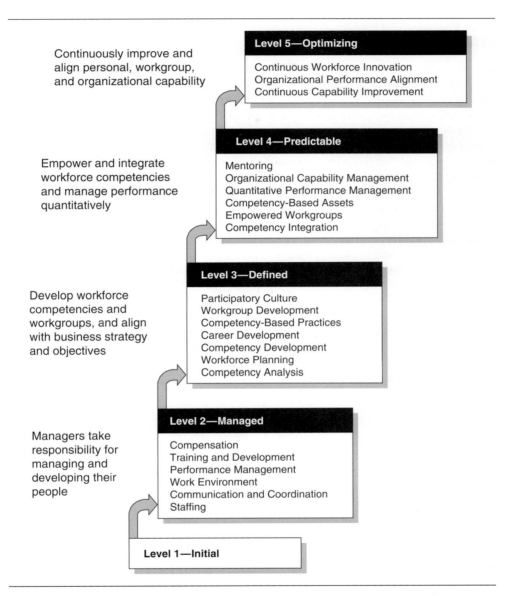

FIGURE A.1
People CMM process areas

Practices

This appendix contains an abridged version of the People CMM practices, which provides a high-level overview of the practices within each process area. This appendix contains the purpose of each process area, its goals, and the practice statements from the process area. These items are extracted verbatim from the detailed descriptions of each process area.

Each process area lists the implementation practices mapped to their respective goals. Institutionalization practices (i.e., Commitment to Perform, Ability to Perform, Measurement and Analysis, and Verifying Implementation) are mapped to an institutionalization goal in each process area. Commitment to Perform typically involves establishing organizational policies, executive management sponsorship, and assigned responsibilities for advising on and coordinating the implementation of workforce practices. Ability to Perform typically involves resources, organizational structures, and preparation to perform the practices of the process area. Measurement and Analysis typically involves measuring the status of the workforce practices performed, aggregating some measures from the unit to the organizational level, and evaluating the effectiveness of the workforce practices performed. Verifying Implementation typically involves ensuring that practices are being performed in compliance with policies, stated values, plans, laws, and regulations; and that executive management maintains awareness of the level of compliance.

These practices must be in place to ensure that the process area is implemented appropriately and effectively, is solidly established, will be maintained and not erode over time, and can be applied effectively in future situations. To establish a process area appropriately, the full set of practices should be used.

Goal Mappings

The following process area tables map the practices to the relevant process area goals in each of the 22 process areas in the People CMM. The *goals* of a process area summarize the states that must exist for that process area to have been implemented in an effective and lasting way. The extent to which the goals have been accomplished is an indicator of how much capability the organization has established at that maturity level. The goals signify the scope, boundaries, and intent of each process area.

These practice-to-goal mappings can be used for comprehending the structure of the model, for guiding the implementation of improvement activities, and for evaluating the satisfaction of goals during an appraisal. These mappings suggest the strongest relationships between practices and goals. However, relationships may exist between practices and goals to which they are not mapped in these tables. SEI-authorized SCAMPI with People CMM Lead Appraisers must use their professional judgment in guiding appraisal team members to make appropriate mappings of practices to goals under the organizational circumstances being appraised.

Staffing

The purpose of Staffing (STF) is to establish a formal process by which committed work is matched to unit resources and qualified individuals are recruited, selected, and transitioned into assignments.

Staffing		
Goal 1 Individuals or workgroups in each unit are involved in making commitments that balance the unit's workload with approved staffing.	**P1**	Responsible individuals plan and coordinate the staffing activities of their units in accordance with documented policies and procedures.
	P2	Each unit analyzes its proposed work to determine the effort and skills required.
	P3	Individuals and workgroups participate in making commitments for work they will be accountable for performing.
	P4	Each unit documents work commitments that balance its workload with available staff and other required resources.
Goal 2 Candidates are recruited for open positions.	**P6**	Position openings within a unit are analyzed, documented, and approved.
	P7	Position openings within the organization are widely communicated.
	P8	Units with open positions recruit for qualified individuals.
	P9	External recruiting activities by the organization are planned and coordinated with unit requirements.
Goal 3 Staffing decisions and work assignments are based on an assessment of work qualifications and other valid criteria.	**P10**	A selection process and appropriate selection criteria are defined for each open position.
	P11	Each unit, in conjunction with its human resources function, conducts a selection process for each position it intends to fill.
	P12	Positions are offered to the candidate whose skills and other qualifications best fit the open position.
	P15	Representative members of a unit participate in its staffing activities.
Goal 4 Individuals are transitioned into and out of positions in an orderly way.	**P5**	Individual work assignments are managed to balance committed work among individuals and units.
	P13	The organization acts in a timely manner to attract the selected candidate.
	P14	The selected candidate is transitioned into the new position.

	Staffing

Goal 4 *Continued*	**P16**	Workforce reduction and other outplacement activities, when required, are conducted according to the organization's policies and procedures.
	P17	Discharges for unsatisfactory performance or other valid reasons are conducted according to the organization's policies and procedures.
	P18	Causes of voluntary resignation from the organization are identified and addressed.
Goal 5 Staffing practices are institutionalized to ensure they are performed as managed processes.	**CO1**	The organization establishes and maintains a documented policy for conducting its Staffing activities.
	CO2	An organizational role(s) is assigned responsibility for assisting and advising units on Staffing activities and procedures.
	AB1	Within each unit, an individual(s) is assigned responsibility and authority for ensuring that Staffing activities are performed.
	AB2	Adequate resources are provided for performing Staffing activities.
	AB3	Individuals performing Staffing activities receive the preparation in methods and procedures needed to perform their responsibilities.
	AB4	Individuals participating in Staffing activities receive appropriate orientation in Staffing practices.
	ME1	Measurements are made and used to determine the status and performance of Staffing activities.
	ME2	Unit measures of Staffing activities are collected and maintained.
	VE1	A responsible individual(s) verifies that Staffing activities are conducted according to the organization's documented policies, practices, procedures, and, where appropriate, plans; and addresses noncompliance.
	VE2	Executive management periodically reviews the Staffing activities, status, and results; and resolves issues.

Communication and Coordination

The purpose of Communication and Coordination (COM) is to establish timely communication throughout the organization and to ensure that the workforce has the skills to share information and coordinate activities efficiently.

	Communication and Coordination		
Goal 1	Information is shared across the organization.	P1	The workforce-related policies and practices of the organization are communicated to the workforce.
		P2	Information about organizational values, events, and conditions is communicated to the workforce on a periodic and event-driven basis.
		P3	Information required for performing committed work is shared across affected units in a timely manner.
Goal 2	Individuals or groups are able to raise concerns and have them addressed by management.	P4	Individuals' opinions on their working conditions are sought on a periodic and event-driven basis.
		P5	Individuals or groups can raise concerns according to a documented procedure.
		P6	Activities related to the resolution of a concern are tracked to closure.
Goal 3	Individuals and workgroups coordinate their activities to accomplish committed work.	P7	The interpersonal communication skills necessary to establish and maintain effective working relationships within and across workgroups are developed.
		P8	Interpersonal problems or conflicts that degrade the quality or effectiveness of working relationships are handled appropriately.
		P9	Individuals and workgroups coordinate their activities to accomplish committed work.
		P10	Individuals and workgroups monitor and coordinate the dependencies involved in their committed work.
		P11	Meetings are conducted to make the most effective use of participants' time.

Communication and Coordination

Goal 4 Communication and Coordination practices are institutionalized to ensure they are performed as managed processes.

CO1 Executive management establishes and communicates a set of values for the organization regarding the development and management of its workforce.

CO2 The organization establishes and maintains a documented policy for conducting its Communication and Coordination activities.

CO3 An organizational role(s) is assigned responsibility for assisting and advising units on Communication and Coordination activities and procedures.

AB1 Within each unit, an individual(s) is assigned responsibility and authority for ensuring that Communication and Coordination activities are performed.

AB2 Adequate resources are provided for performing Communication and Coordination activities.

AB3 Individuals responsible for facilitating or improving Communication and Coordination activities receive the preparation needed to perform their responsibilities.

ME1 Measurements are made and used to determine the status and performance of Communication and Coordination activities.

ME2 Unit measures of Communication and Coordination activities are collected and maintained.

VE1 A responsible individual(s) verifies that the Communication and Coordination activities are conducted according to the organization's documented policies, practices, procedures, and, where appropriate, plans; and addresses noncompliance.

VE2 Executive management periodically reviews the Communication and Coordination activities, status, and results; and resolves issues.

Work Environment

The purpose of Work Environment (WE) is to establish and maintain physical working conditions and to provide resources that allow individuals and workgroups to perform their tasks efficiently without unnecessary distractions.

Work Environment		
Goal 1 The physical environment and resources needed by the workforce to perform their assignments are made available.	**P1**	The physical environment and resources required to perform committed work are identified in each unit.
	P2	The physical environment required to perform assigned work is provided.
	P3	Individual workspaces provide an adequate personal environment for performing assigned work responsibilities.
	P4	The resources needed to accomplish committed work are made a vailable in a timely manner.
	P5	Improvements are made to the work environment that improve work performance.
Goal 2 Distractions in the work environment are minimized.	**P6**	Environmental factors that degrade or endanger the health or safety of the workforce are identified and corrected.
	P7	Physical factors that degrade the effectiveness of the work environment are identified and addressed.
	P8	Sources of frequent interruption or distraction that degrade the effectiveness of the work environment are identified and minimized.

Work Environment

Goal 3 Work Environment practices are institutionalized to ensure they are performed as managed processes.

CO1 The organization establishes and maintains a documented policy for conducting its Work Environment activities.

CO2 An organizational role(s) is assigned responsibility for assisting and advising units on work environment-related activities, and for assuming appropriate organizational responsibilities for the physical work environment and work resources.

AB1 Within each unit, an individual(s) is assigned responsibility and authority for ensuring that Work Environment activities are performed.

AB2 Within prudent limits, adequate resources are provided for performing Work Environment activities, implementing the physical environment and resources necessary to perform assigned work, and making improvements to the work environment.

AB3 The workforce receives the preparation needed to maintain an effective work environment.

AB4 Those responsible for improving the work environment receive the preparation in relevant methods and procedures needed to perform their responsibilities.

ME1 Measurements are made and used to determine the status and performance of Work Environment activities.

ME2 Unit measures of Work Environment activities are collected and maintained.

VE1 A responsible individual(s) verifies that Work Environment activities are conducted according to the organization's documented policies, practices, procedures, and, where appropriate, plans; and addresses noncompliance.

VE2 Executive management periodically reviews the Work Environment activities, status, and results, including improvements to the work environment; and resolves issues.

Performance Management

The purpose of Performance Management (PM) is to establish objectives related to committed work against which unit and individual performance can be measured, to discuss performance against these objectives, and to continuously enhance performance.

Performance Management		
Goal 1 Unit and individual performance objectives related to committed work are documented.	**P1**	Measurable performance objectives based on committed work are established for each unit.
	P2	The unit's performance objectives are periodically reviewed as business conditions or work commitments change, and, if necessary, they are revised.
	P4	Performance objectives based on committed work are documented for each individual on a periodic or event-driven basis.
	P5	Performance objectives for each individual are reviewed on a periodic or event-driven basis, and, if necessary, they are revised.
Goal 2 The performance of committed work is regularly discussed to identify actions that can improve it.	**P3**	Those accountable for the accomplishment of unit performance objectives track and manage unit performance.
	P6	Those responsible for performance management activities maintain ongoing communication about the performance of committed work with those whose performance they manage.
	P7	Those responsible for managing the performance of others maintain an awareness of accomplishments against performance objectives for each individual whose performance they manage.
	P8	Potential improvements in process, tools, or resources, which could enhance an individual's performance of committed work, are identified, and actions are taken to provide them.
	P9	The accomplishments of individuals against their performance objectives are documented and discussed on a periodic or event-driven basis according to a documented procedure.
Goal 3 Performance problems are managed.	**P10**	If performance problems occur, they are discussed with the appropriate individual(s).
	P11	Performance improvement plans are developed for resolving persistent performance problems according to a documented procedure.

Performance Management

Goal 3	*Continued*	**P12**	Progress against a documented performance improvement plan is periodically evaluated, discussed, and documented.
Goal 4	Outstanding performance is recognized or rewarded.	**P13**	Guidelines for recognizing or rewarding outstanding performance are developed and communicated.
		P14	Recognition or rewards are made on an appropriate basis as events occur that justify special attention.
Goal 5	Performance Management practices are institutionalized to ensure they are performed as managed processes.	**CO1**	The organization establishes and maintains a documented policy for conducting its Performance Management activities.
		CO2	An organizational role(s) is assigned responsibility for assisting and advising units on Performance Management activities.
		AB1	Within each unit, an individual(s) is assigned responsibility and authority for ensuring that Performance Management activities are performed.
		AB2	Adequate resources are provided for performing Performance Management activities.
		AB3	Individuals conducting Performance Management activities receive the preparation needed to perform their responsibilities.
		AB4	Individuals who participate in Performance Management activities receive appropriate orientation in Performance Management practices.
		ME1	Measurements are made and used to determine the status and performance of Performance Management activities.
		ME2	Unit measures of Performance Management activities are collected and maintained.
		VE1	A responsible individual(s) verifies that the Performance Management activities are conducted according to the organization's documented policies, practices, procedures, and, where appropriate, plans; and addresses noncompliance.
		VE2	Executive management periodically reviews the Performance Management activities, status, and results; and resolves issues.

Training and Development

The purpose of Training and Development (TD) is to ensure that all individuals have the skills required to perform their assignments and are provided relevant development opportunities.

Training and Development		
Goal 1 Individuals receive timely training that is needed to perform their assignments in accordance with the unit's training plan.	**P1**	In each unit, the critical skills required for performing each individual's assigned tasks are identified.
	P2	Training needed in critical skills is identified for each individual.
	P3	Each unit develops and maintains a plan for satisfying its training needs.
	P4	Individuals or groups receive timely training needed to perform their assigned tasks.
	P5	Training is tracked against the unit's training plan.
Goal 2 Individuals capable of performing their assignments pursue development opportunities that support their development objectives.	**P6**	A development discussion is held periodically with each individual.
	P7	Relevant development opportunities are made available to support individuals in accomplishing their individual development objectives.
	P8	Individuals pursue development activities that support their individual development objectives.

Training and Development

Goal 3 Training and Development practices are institutionalized to ensure they are performed as managed processes.

CO1 The organization establishes and maintains a documented policy for conducting its Training and Development activities.

CO2 An organizational role(s) is assigned responsibility for assisting and advising units on Training and Development activities and procedures.

AB1 Within each unit, an individual(s) is assigned responsibility and authority for ensuring that Training and Development activities are performed.

AB2 Adequate resources are provided for performing Training and Development activities.

AB3 Training time is made available to each individual according to the organization's training policy.

AB4 Individuals performing Training and Development activities receive the preparation needed to perform their responsibilities.

ME1 Measurements are made and used to determine the status and performance of Training and Development activities.

ME2 Unit measures of Training and Development activities are collected and maintained.

VE1 A responsible individual(s) verifies that Training and Development activities are conducted according to the organization's documented policies, practices, procedures, and, where appropriate, plans; and addresses noncompliance.

VE2 Executive management periodically reviews the Training and Development activities, status, and results; and resolves issues.

Compensation

The purpose of Compensation (CMP) is to provide all individuals with remuneration and benefits based on their contribution and value to the organization.

Compensation		
Goal 1 Compensation strategies and activities are planned, executed, and communicated.	**P1**	An organizational compensation strategy is developed.
	P2	The organization's compensation strategy is periodically reviewed to determine whether it needs to be revised.
	P3	When appropriate, the workforce provides inputs for developing or revising components of the organization's compensation strategy.
	P4	A documented compensation plan is prepared periodically for administering compensation activities needed to execute the compensation strategy.
	P6	The organization's compensation strategy is communicated to the workforce.
Goal 2 Compensation is equitable relative to skill, qualifications, and performance.	**P5**	The compensation plan is designed to maintain equity in administering the compensation strategy.
	P10	Responsible individuals periodically review compensation packages for those whose compensation they administer to ensure they are equitable and consistent with the organization's compensation policy, strategy, and plan.
	P11	Action is taken to correct inequities in compensation or other deviations from the organization's policy, strategy, and plan.
Goal 3 Adjustments in compensation are made based on defined criteria.	**P7**	Each individual's compensation package is determined using a documented procedure that is consistent with the organization's compensation policy, strategy, and plan.
	P8	Compensation adjustments are made based, in part, on each individual's documented accomplishments against their performance objectives.
	P9	Decisions regarding an individual's compensation package are communicated to the individual.

Compensation

Goal 4   Compensation practices are institutionalized to ensure they are performed as managed processes.

CO1   The organization establishes and maintains a documented policy for conducting its Compensation activities.

CO2   An organizational role(s) is assigned responsibility for performing or coordinating Compensation practices at the organizational level and for assisting and advising units on Compensation activities.

AB1   Within each unit, an individual(s) is assigned responsibility and authority for ensuring that Compensation activities are performed.

AB2   Adequate resources are provided for Compensation activities.

AB3   Individuals performing Compensation activities receive the preparation needed to perform their responsibilities.

ME1   Measurements are made and used to determine the status and performance of Compensation activities.

ME2   Unit measures of Compensation activities are collected and maintained.

ME3   Aggregate trends in compensation activities and decisions are measured and reviewed on a recurring basis.

VE1   A responsible individual(s) verifies that Compensation activities are conducted according to the organization's documented policies, practices, procedures, and, where appropriate, plans; and addresses noncompliance.

VE2   Executive management periodically reviews the Compensation activities, status, and results; and resolves issues.

Competency Analysis

The purpose of Competency Analysis (CA) is to identify the knowledge, skills, and process abilities required to perform the organization's business activities so that they may be developed and used as a basis for workforce practices.

Competency Analysis		
Goal 1 The workforce competencies required to perform the organization's business activities are defined and updated.	**P1**	The workforce competencies required to perform the organization's business activities are identified.
	P2	Each of the organization's workforce competencies is analyzed to identify the knowledge, skills, and process abilities that compose it.
	P3	Workforce competency descriptions are documented and maintained according to a documented procedure.
	P4	Workforce competency descriptions are updated on a periodic and event-driven basis.
Goal 2 The work processes used within each workforce competency are established and maintained.	**P5**	The competency-based processes to be performed by capable individuals in each workforce competency are established and maintained.
	P6	Information about the use of competency-based processes is captured and made available.
Goal 3 The organization tracks its capability in each of its workforce competencies.	**P7**	Competency information regarding the capabilities of individuals in their workforce competencies is collected and maintained according to a documented procedure.
	P8	Current resource profiles for each of the organization's workforce competencies are determined.
	P9	Competency information is updated on a periodic and event-driven basis.

Competency Analysis

Goal 4 Competency Analysis practices are institutionalized to ensure they are performed as defined organizational processes.

CO1 The organization establishes and maintains a documented policy for conducting its Competency Analysis activities.

CO2 An organizational role(s) is assigned responsibility for coordinating Competency Analysis activities across the organization.

AB1 A responsible individual(s) coordinates the Competency Analysis activities for defining, developing, and maintaining each workforce competency.

AB2 Adequate resources are provided for performing Competency Analysis activities.

AB3 Individuals performing Competency Analysis activities develop the knowledge, skills, and process abilities needed to perform their responsibilities.

AB4 The practices and procedures for performing Competency Analysis are defined and documented.

ME1 Measurements are made and used to determine the status and performance of Competency Analysis activities within each unit and across the organization.

ME2 Measurements are made and used to determine the quality of workforce competency descriptions and competency information.

VE1 A responsible individual(s) verifies that Competency Analysis activities are conducted according to the organization's documented policies, practices, procedures, and, where appropriate, plans; and addresses noncompliance.

VE2 Executive management periodically reviews the Competency Analysis activities, status, and results; and resolves issues.

VE3 The definition and use of competency descriptions and competency information are periodically audited for compliance with organizational policies.

Workforce Planning

The purpose of Workforce Planning (WFP) is to coordinate workforce activities with current and future business needs at both the organizational and unit levels.

Workforce Planning		
Goal 1 Measurable objectives for capability in each of the organization's workforce competencies are defined.	**P1**	The current and strategic workforce needs of the organization are documented.
	P2	Measurable objectives are established for developing the organization's capability in each of its selected workforce competencies.
Goal 2 The organization plans for the workforce competencies needed to perform its current and future business activities.	**P3**	A competency development plan is produced for each of the organization's selected workforce competencies.
	P4	Competency development plans are reviewed and revised on a periodic and event-driven basis.
	P5	The organization establishes and maintains a strategic workforce plan to guide its workforce practices and activities.
	P8	The organization develops succession plans for its key positions.
	P9	The organization's performance in meeting the objectives of its strategic workforce plan is tracked.
	P10	Progress in meeting the objectives of the competency development plan for each of the organization's workforce competencies is tracked.
Goal 3 Units perform planned workforce activities to satisfy current and strategic competency needs.	**P6**	Units plan workforce activities to satisfy current and strategic competency needs.
	P7	Units review and revise plans for workforce activities on a periodic and event-driven basis.
	P11	Each unit's performance in conducting its planned workforce activities is tracked.

Workforce Planning

Goal 4 Workforce Planning practices are institutionalized to ensure they are performed as defined organizational processes.

CO1 The organization establishes and maintains a documented policy for conducting its Workforce Planning activities.

CO2 An organizational role(s) is assigned responsibility for coordinating Workforce Planning activities across the organization.

AB1 Within each unit, an individual(s) is assigned responsibility and authority for ensuring that Workforce Planning activities are performed.

AB2 A responsible individual(s) coordinates the Workforce Planning activities for each workforce competency.

AB3 Adequate resources are provided for performing Workforce Planning activities.

AB4 Individuals performing Workforce Planning activities develop the knowledge, skills, and process abilities needed to perform their responsibilities.

AB5 The practices and procedures for performing workforce planning are defined and documented.

ME1 Measurements are made and used to determine the status and performance of Workforce Planning activities.

ME2 Unit measures of workforce planning are collected and aggregated at the organizational level.

VE1 A responsible individual(s) verifies that Workforce Planning activities are conducted according to the organization's documented policies, practices, procedures, and, where appropriate, plans; and addresses noncompliance.

VE2 Executive management periodically reviews the Workforce Planning activities, status, and results; and resolves issues.

Competency Development

The purpose of Competency Development (CD) is to enhance constantly the capability of the workforce to perform its assigned tasks and responsibilities.

Competency Development		
Goal 1 The organization provides opportunities for individuals to develop their capabilities in its workforce competencies.	**P1**	Competency Development activities are based on the competency development plans within each workforce competency.
	P2	Graduated training and development activities are established and maintained for developing capability in each of the organization's workforce competencies.
	P3	The organization makes available descriptions of workforce competencies and information about development opportunities related to them.
Goal 2 Individuals develop their knowledge, skills, and process abilities in the organization's workforce competencies.	**P4**	Competency-based training and development activities are identified for each individual to support their development objectives.
	P5	Individuals actively pursue learning opportunities to enhance their capabilities in the organization's workforce competencies.
Goal 3 The organization uses the capabilities of its workforce as resources for developing the workforce competencies of others.	**P6**	Capable individuals within a competency community are used to mentor those with less capability in the competency.
	P7	The organization supports communication among those comprising a competency community.
	P8	Competency-based experience and information is captured and made available to those within a competency community.

Competency Development

Goal 4 Competency Development practices are institutionalized to ensure they are performed as defined organizational processes.

CO1 The organization establishes and maintains a documented policy for conducting its Competency Development activities to develop the core competencies required to perform its business processes.

CO2 An organizational role(s) is assigned responsibility for coordinating Competency Development activities across the organization.

AB1 Within each unit, an individual(s) is assigned responsibility and authority for ensuring that Competency Development activities are performed.

AB2 A responsible individual(s) coordinates the Competency Development activities for each workforce competency.

AB3 Adequate resources are provided for performing the planned organization-wide and unit-specific Competency Development activities.

AB4 Individuals performing Competency Development activities develop the knowledge, skills, and process abilities needed to perform their responsibilities.

AB5 Individuals who participate in Competency Development activities receive appropriate orientation in Competency Development practices.

AB6 The practices and procedures for performing competency development are defined and documented.

ME1 Measurements are made and used to determine the status and performance of Competency Development activities within each unit and across the organization.

ME2 Measurements are made and used to determine the quality of Competency Development activities.

VE1 A responsible individual(s) verifies that Competency Development activities are conducted according to the organization's documented policies, practices, procedures, and, where appropriate, plans; and addresses noncompliance.

VE2 Executive management periodically reviews the Competency Development activities, status, and results; and resolves issues.

VE3 The definition and use of data on competency development are periodically audited for compliance with organizational policies.

Career Development

The purpose of Career Development (CRD) is to ensure that individuals are provided opportunities to develop workforce competencies that enable them to achieve career objectives.

Career Development		
Goal 1 The organization offers career opportunities that provide growth in its workforce competencies.	**P1**	The organization defines graduated career opportunities to support growth in the workforce competencies required to perform its business activities.
	P2	Career promotions are made in each area of graduated career opportunities based on documented criteria and procedures.
	P3	Graduated career opportunities and promotion criteria are periodically reviewed and updated.
Goal 2 Individuals pursue career opportunities that increase the value of their knowledge, skills, and process abilities to the organization.	**P4**	Affected individuals periodically evaluate their capabilities in the workforce competencies relevant to their career objectives.
	P5	Affected individuals create and maintain a personal development plan to guide their training and career options.
	P6	Career options and development in the organization's workforce competencies are discussed with affected individuals on a periodic or event-driven basis.
	P7	Affected individuals pursue training and development opportunities that enhance their career options and capabilities in the organization's workforce competencies.
	P8	Individual development activities are tracked against personal development plans.

Career Development

Goal 3	Career Development practices are institutionalized to ensure they are performed as defined organizational processes.

CO1 The organization establishes and maintains a documented policy for conducting its Career Development activities.

CO2 An organizational role(s) is assigned responsibility for coordinating Career Development activities across the organization.

AB1 Within each unit, an individual(s) is assigned responsibility and authority for ensuring that members of the unit participate, as appropriate, in Career Development activities.

AB2 A responsible individual(s) coordinates the Career Development activities for each workforce competency.

AB3 Adequate resources are provided for implementing Career Development activities.

AB4 Individuals responsible for Career Development activities develop the knowledge, skills, and process abilities needed to perform their responsibilities.

AB5 Individuals who participate in Career Development activities receive appropriate orientation in career development opportunities and activities.

AB6 The practices and procedures for performing Career Development are defined and documented.

ME1 Measurements are made and used to determine the status and performance of Career Development activities within each unit.

ME2 Unit measures of Career Development status are collected and aggregated at the organizational level.

ME3 Measurements are made and used to determine the effectiveness of Career Development activities.

VE1 A responsible individual(s) verifies that Career Development activities are conducted according to the organization's documented policies, practices, and procedures; and addresses noncompliance.

VE2 Executive management periodically reviews the Career Development activities, status, and results; and resolves issues.

Competency-Based Practices

The purpose of Competency-Based Practices (CBP) is to ensure that all workforce practices are based in part on developing the competencies of the workforce.

	Competency-Based Practices		
Goal 1	Workforce practices are focused on increasing the organization's capability in its workforce competencies.	**P1**	Recruiting activities are planned and executed to satisfy the organization's requirements for workforce competencies.
		P2	Selection processes are enhanced to evaluate each candidate's potential for contributing to organizational and unit objectives for capability in workforce competencies.
		P3	Staffing decisions are made, in part, to achieve the competency development objectives of the organization and the career objectives of qualified candidates.
		P4	Transition activities provide orientation to workforce competencies.
		P14	As the definition or requirements of its workforce competencies change, the organization reevaluates its workforce policies and practices and adjusts them, as needed.
Goal 2	Workforce activities within units encourage and support individuals and workgroups in developing and applying the organization's workforce competencies.	**P5**	Work assignments are designed, in part, to enhance personal and career development objectives.
		P6	Each unit documents performance objectives for developing workforce competencies.
		P7	Each individual documents performance objectives for developing additional capability in the organization's workforce competencies.
		P8	Ongoing discussions of work performance include feedback on an individual's development and application of relevant workforce competencies.
		P9	Each individual's performance is assessed, in part, against the objectives of his or her personal development plan.
Goal 3	Compensation strategies and recognition and reward practices are designed to encourage development and application of the organization's workforce competencies.	**P10**	The compensation strategy is established and maintained, in part, to increase the organization's capability in its workforce competencies.
		P11	Compensation practices are defined to support capability objectives within each workforce competency.
		P12	Adjustments to compensation are partly determined by each individual's development and application of relevant workforce competencies.

Competency-Based Practices

Goal 3	*Continued*	**P13**	Recognition and rewards for developing or applying workforce competencies are provided, when appropriate, at the individual, workgroup, or unit levels.
Goal 4	Competency-Based Practices are institutionalized to ensure they are performed as defined organizational processes.	**CO1**	Relevant organizational policies promote increased capability in the organization's workforce competencies.
		CO2	An organizational role(s) is assigned responsibility for coordinating adjustments in workforce practices designed to increase the organization's capability in its workforce competencies.
		AB1	Within each unit, an individual(s) is assigned responsibility and authority for ensuring that workforce practices and activities are designed to motivate individuals and workgroups to develop and apply workforce competencies.
		AB2	A responsible individual(s) coordinates the Competency-Based Practices and activities for each workforce competency.
		AB3	Adequate resources are provided for ensuring that workforce practices and activities are designed to increase the organization's capability in its workforce competencies.
		AB4	Those responsible for competency-based workforce activities develop the knowledge, skills, and process abilities needed to perform their responsibilities.
		AB5	The practices and procedures for performing competency-based workforce practices are defined and documented.
		ME1	Measurements are made and used to determine the status and performance of workforce practices to increase capability in the organization's workforce competencies.
		ME2	Measurements are made and used to determine how effectively competency-based workforce practices are increasing capability in the organization's workforce competencies.
		VE1	A responsible individual(s) verifies that competency-based workforce practices are conducted according to documented policies, practices, procedures, and, where appropriate, plans; and addresses noncompliance.
		VE2	Executive management periodically reviews the activities implementing competency-based workforce practices, their status, and results; and resolves issues.

Workgroup Development

The purpose of Workgroup Development (WGD) is to organize work around competency-based process abilities.

Workgroup Development		
Goal 1 Workgroups are established to optimize the performance of interdependent work.	**P1**	The committed work within a unit is analyzed to identify its process dependencies.
	P2	Committed work is structured to optimize the coordination and performance of interdependent work within workgroups.
	P3	Each workgroup is formed to perform a defined set of business activities and to accomplish defined objectives.
Goal 2 Workgroups tailor defined processes and roles for use in planning and performing their work.	**P4**	Methods and procedures for performing common workgroup functions are defined and maintained for use by workgroups.
	P7	Workgroups tailor competency-based processes for performing their business activities.
	P8	Roles for performing the workgroup's operating processes are defined and allocated to individuals.
	P10	Workgroup members establish mechanisms for communicating information and coordinating dependencies among roles.
	P11	Skills needed to perform jointly as a workgroup using the workgroup's operating processes are developed.
	P12	Workgroups that share dependencies define interfaces through which their activities and commitments are coordinated.
Goal 3 Workgroup staffing activities focus on the assignment, development, and future deployment of the organization's workforce competencies.	**P5**	The competencies required to perform a workgroup's business activities are identified.
	P6	Staffing processes are performed to ensure that workgroups are staffed with individuals whose competencies match those needed to perform the workgroup's business activities.
	P14	Workgroups are disbanded through an orderly performance of workforce activities.
Goal 4 Workgroup performance is managed against documented objectives for committed work.	**P9**	Workgroup activities and commitments are planned.
	P13	A responsible individual(s) tracks and manages workgroup performance.
	P15	When workgroups disband, their assets are captured for redeployment.

Workgroup Development

Goal 5   Workgroup Development practices are institutionalized to ensure they are performed as defined organizational processes.

CO1   The organization establishes and maintains a documented policy for conducting Workgroup Development activities.

CO2   An organizational role(s) is assigned responsibility for coordinating Workgroup Development activities across the organization.

CO3   Workgroup Development activities are incorporated into the organization's strategic workforce plan and the planned workforce activities within units.

AB1   Within each unit, an individual(s) is assigned responsibility and authority for ensuring that members of the unit participate in Workgroup Development activities, as appropriate.

AB2   Adequate resources are provided for performing Workgroup Development activities.

AB3   Responsible individual(s) to whom the members of a workgroup are accountable develop the knowledge, skills, and process abilities needed to manage workgroups.

AB4   Workgroup members receive appropriate guidance or training in workgroup skills.

AB5   The practices and procedures for performing Workgroup Development are defined and documented.

ME1   Measurements are made and used to determine the status and performance of Workgroup Development activities across the organization.

ME2   Measures of workgroup development are collected and aggregated at the organizational level.

ME3   Measurements are made and used to determine the effectiveness of Workgroup Development activities.

VE1   A responsible individual(s) verifies that Workgroup Development activities are conducted according to documented policies, practices, procedures, and, where appropriate, plans; and addresses noncompliance.

VE2   Executive management periodically reviews the Workgroup Development activities, status, and results; and resolves issues.

Participatory Culture

The purpose of a Participatory Culture (PC) is to enable the workforce's full capability for making decisions that affect the performance of business activities.

Participatory Culture		
Goal 1 Information about business activities and results is communicated throughout the organization.	**P1**	Information about organizational and unit performance is made available to individuals and workgroups.
	P2	Individuals and workgroups are made aware of how their work performance contributes to unit and organizational performance.
	P3	Individuals and workgroups have access to information needed to perform their committed work.
	P4	Information and communication systems support the information needs of individuals and workgroups.
Goal 2 Decisions are delegated to an appropriate level of the organization.	**P5**	The structure of decision-making processes within the organization is analyzed.
	P6	Decision-making processes and roles are defined.
	P7	Responsibilities for decisions are delegated to appropriate levels and locations in the organization.
	P9	Decisions made by those empowered to make them are supported by others in the organization.
Goal 3 Individuals and workgroups participate in structured decision-making processes.	**P8**	Individuals and workgroups use defined decision-making processes.
	P10	Individuals and workgroups are involved in making decisions that affect their work.
	P11	Individuals and groups participate in decisions concerning their work environments.
	P12	Defined mechanisms are used for resolving conflicts and disputes.

Participatory Culture

Goal 4   Participatory Culture practices are institutionalized to ensure they are performed as defined organizational processes.

CO1   The organization's stated values encourage open communication and participation in decision making by individuals and workgroups, when appropriate.

CO2   The organization establishes and maintains a documented policy for its activities that supports the development of a participatory culture.

CO3   An organizational role(s) is assigned responsibility for coordinating the organization's activities for developing a participatory culture.

AB1   Within each unit, an individual(s) is assigned responsibility and authority to ensure that the performance of business and workforce activities within the unit contributes to developing a participatory culture.

AB2   Adequate resources are provided for performing activities that support development of a participatory culture.

AB3   Managers develop the knowledge, skills, and process abilities needed to perform their responsibilities regarding communication and participatory management.

AB4   Individuals and groups who participate in Participatory Culture activities receive the preparation in problem-solving and decision-making processes, methods, and skills appropriate to the types of decisions they will participate in making.

AB5   The practices and procedures for developing a participatory culture are defined and documented.

ME1   Measurements are made and used to determine the status and performance of participatory activities and trends within the organization.

ME2   Measurements are made and used to determine the effectiveness of the participatory practices adopted in the organization.

VE1   A responsible individual(s) verifies that communication and decision-making activities within the organization are conducted in an open and participative manner according to the organization's values and policies; and addresses noncompliance.

VE2   Executive management periodically reviews the level of participatory behavior and resolves issues.

Competency Integration

The purpose of Competency Integration (CI) is to improve the efficiency and agility of interdependent work by integrating the process abilities of different workforce competencies.

Competency Integration		
Goal 1 The competency-based processes employed by different workforce competencies are integrated to improve the efficiency of interdependent work.	**P1**	Business activities involving dependencies among multiple workforce competencies are identified.
	P2	Dependencies and interfaces among multiple workforce competencies are analyzed to identify opportunities for integrating their competency-based processes.
	P3	Integrated competency-based processes are defined and made available for use.
	P12	The performance of integrated competency-based processes is evaluated to identify needed adjustments and updates.
Goal 2 Integrated competency-based processes are used in performing work that involves dependencies among several workforce competencies.	**P4**	Work is designed to incorporate integrated competency-based processes, where appropriate.
	P6	Skills needed for performing integrated competency-based processes are developed.
	P10	Workgroups performing integrated competency-based processes tailor and use them for planning committed work.
	P11	Workgroups use integrated competency-based processes for work involving multiple workforce competencies.
Goal 3 Workforce practices are designed to support multidisciplinary work.	**P5**	Organizational structures support multidisciplinary work that integrates competency-based processes.
	P7	The work environment supports work by individuals or workgroups using integrated competency-based processes.
	P8	Workforce competency descriptions are revised to incorporate integrated competency-based processes.
	P9	Workforce practices and activities are defined and adjusted to support integrated competency-based activities.

Competency Integration

Goal 4 Competency Integration practices are institutionalized to ensure they are performed as defined organizational processes.

CO1 The organization establishes and maintains a documented policy for conducting Competency Integration activities.

CO2 An organizational role(s) is assigned responsibility for coordinating Competency Integration activities across the organization.

AB1 Within relevant organizational units or other entities, an individual(s) is assigned responsibility and authority for ensuring that Competency Integration activities are performed.

AB2 A responsible individual(s) coordinates the activities for defining, developing, and maintaining each integrated competency-based process.

AB3 Adequate resources are provided for performing Competency Integration activities.

AB4 Those involved in defining integrated competency-based processes develop the knowledge, skills, and process abilities needed to perform process analysis and definition.

AB5 Affected individuals and workgroups develop the knowledge, skills, and process abilities needed to perform the integrated competency-based processes involved in their work.

AB6 The practices and procedures for performing competency integration are defined and documented.

ME1 Measurements are made and used to determine the status and performance of Competency Integration activities.

ME2 Measurements are made and used to determine the effectiveness of Competency Integration activities.

VE1 A responsible individual(s) verifies that the Competency Integration activities are conducted according to the organization's documented policies, practices, procedures, and, where appropriate, plans; and addresses noncompliance.

VE2 Executive management periodically reviews the Competency Integration activities, status, and results; and resolves issues.

Empowered Workgroups

The purpose of Empowered Workgroups (EWG) is to invest workgroups with the responsibility and authority to determine how to conduct their business activities most effectively.

	Empowered Workgroups		
Goal 1	Empowered workgroups are delegated responsibility and authority over their work processes.	**P1**	Work responsibilities are designed to provide an empowered workgroup with optimal control over an integrated set of business activities.
		P2	Empowered workgroups are formed with a statement of their mission and authority for accomplishing it.
		P3	The individual(s) or organizational entity to which an empowered workgroup is accountable provides business objectives and negotiates responsibilities and commitments with the empowered workgroup.
		P4	Empowered workgroups are delegated the responsibility and authority to determine the methods by which they will accomplish their committed work.
		P5	Empowered workgroups use appropriate methods for making decisions on their commitments and methods of operation.
Goal 2	The organization's workforce practices and activities encourage and support the development and performance of empowered workgroups.	**P6**	The organization's work environment supports the development and performance of empowered workgroups.
		P7	The organization's workforce practices are tailored for use with empowered workgroups.
		P12	Adjustments to the compensation of members of empowered workgroups are based, in part, on issues related to workgroup performance.
Goal 3	Empowered workgroups perform selected workforce practices internally.	**P8**	Responsibility and authority for performing selected workforce activities is delegated to empowered workgroups.
		P9	Empowered workgroups tailor workforce activities delegated to them and plan for their adoption.
		P10	Empowered workgroups perform the workforce activities delegated to them.
		P11	Empowered workgroups participate in managing their performance.

Empowered Workgroups

Goal 4   Empowered Workgroups practices are institutionalized to ensure they are performed as defined organizational processes.

CO1   The organization establishes and maintains a documented policy for conducting Empowered Workgroups activities.

CO2   An organizational role(s) is assigned responsibility for coordinating empowerment activities and tailoring workforce practices to support empowered workgroups.

AB1   Each empowered workgroup has an individual(s) or organizational entity that is assigned responsibility as its sponsor and to whom it is accountable.

AB2   Adequate resources are provided for performing Empowered Workgroups activities.

AB3   All affected parties develop the knowledge, skills, and process abilities needed to develop effective relationships with empowered workgroups.

AB4   Individuals responsible for tailoring or administering workforce practices for empowered workgroups develop the knowledge, skills, and process abilities needed to perform their responsibilities.

AB5   The practices and procedures for performing empowered workgroups are defined and documented.

ME1   Measurements are made and used to determine the status and performance of workforce practices for empowering workgroups.

ME2   Measurements are made and used to determine the effectiveness of workforce practices for empowering workgroups.

VE1   A responsible individual(s) verifies that the organization's workforce practices for empowering workgroups are conducted according to the organization's documented policies, practices, procedures, and, where appropriate, plans; and addresses noncompliance.

VE2   Executive management periodically reviews the organization's Empowered Workgroups activities, status, and results; and resolves issues.

VE3   The definition and use of empowered workgroup performance data are periodically audited for compliance with organizational policies.

Competency-Based Assets

The purpose of Competency-Based Assets (CBA) is to capture the knowledge, experience, and artifacts developed in performing competency-based processes for use in enhancing capability and performance.

Competency-Based Assets		
Goal 1 The knowledge, experience, and artifacts resulting from performing competency-based processes are developed into competency-based assets.	**P1**	Individuals and workgroups capture and retain information and artifacts that emerge from performing competency-based processes.
	P2	Communication vehicles are established to support the sharing of competency-based information and artifacts within and among competency communities.
	P3	A strategy for developing and deploying competency-based assets is created for each affected workforce competency.
	P4	Selected components of competency-based information and artifacts are organized into competency-based assets and made available for use.
	P5	Competency-based assets are updated to reflect periodic revisions in the knowledge, skills, and process abilities constituting workforce competencies.

Competency-Based Assets

Goal 2	Competency-based assets are deployed and used.	**P6**	Competency-based assets are integrated into competency-based processes and related technologies, as appropriate.
		P7	Individuals and workgroups use competency-based assets in performing their business activities.
		P8	Information resulting from the use of competency-based assets is captured and made available.
Goal 3	Workforce practices and activities encourage and support the development and use of competency-based assets.	**P9**	Competency development activities incorporate competency-based assets.
		P10	Mentoring or coaching activities are organized to deploy competency-based assets.
		P11	Workforce practices and activities encourage and support the development and use of competency-based assets.
		P12	Compensation practices and activities are defined and performed to motivate the development and use of competency-based assets.

Continued on next page

Competency-Based Assets

Goal 4   Competency-Based Assets practices are institutionalized to ensure they are performed as defined organizational processes.

CO1   The organization's stated values encourage knowledge sharing between individuals and workgroups, when appropriate.

CO2   The organization establishes and maintains a documented policy for developing and using competency-based assets.

CO3   An organizational role(s) is assigned responsibility for coordinating across the organization the activities involved in capturing and reusing competency-based assets.

AB1   Within each unit, an individual(s) is assigned responsibility and authority for ensuring that members of the unit participate in capturing and using competency-based assets, as appropriate.

AB2   A responsible individual(s) coordinates the activities for capturing and using competency-based assets within each workforce competency.

AB3   Adequate resources are provided for capturing and using competency-based assets.

AB4   Those responsible for various tasks involved in developing and deploying the organization's competency-based assets develop the knowledge, skills, and process abilities needed to perform their responsibilities.

AB5   Individuals involved in capturing or using competency-based assets develop the knowledge, skills, and process abilities needed to perform their responsibilities.

AB6   The practices and procedures for capturing or using competency-based assets are defined and documented.

Competency-Based Assets

Goal 4   *Continued*

ME1   Measurements are made and used to determine the status and performance of activities for contributing to and using competency-based assets.

ME2   Measurements are made and used to determine the effectiveness of competency-based assets on improving competencies and performance.

VE1   A responsible individual(s) verifies that the organization's activities for developing and using competency-based assets are conducted according to the organization's documented policies, practices, procedures, and, where appropriate, plans; and addresses noncompliance.

VE2   Executive management periodically reviews the Competency-Based Assets activities, status, and results; and resolves issues.

VE3   The definition and use of competency-based assets measures and information are periodically audited for compliance with organizational policies.

Quantitative Performance Management

The purpose of Quantitative Performance Management (QPM) is to predict and manage the capability of competency-based processes for achieving measurable performance objectives.

Quantitative Performance Management		
Goal 1 Measurable performance objectives are established for competency-based processes that most contribute to achieving performance objectives.	**P1**	The quantitative performance objectives required to achieve organizational business objectives are defined.
	P2	Each unit establishes measurable performance objectives whose achievement most contributes to organizational business objectives.
	P3	Individuals and workgroups establish measurable performance objectives for competency-based processes that most contribute to their achieving unit performance objectives.
Goal 2 The performance of competency-based processes is managed quantitatively.	**P4**	Individuals and workgroups plan their committed work using process performance baselines for competency-based processes.
	P5	Individuals and workgroups define quantitative methods for managing the competency-based processes that most contribute to achieving their performance objectives.
	P6	Individuals and workgroups quantitatively manage the performance of the competency-based processes that most contribute to achieving their performance objectives.
	P7	Individuals or workgroups take corrective actions when the performance of their competency-based processes differs from the quantitative results required to achieve their performance objectives.
	P8	Quantitative records of individual and workgroup performance are retained.
	P9	Where appropriate, quantitative performance results are used in performing workforce practices and activities.

Quantitative Performance Management

Goal 3 Quantitative Performance Management practices are institutionalized to ensure they are performed as defined organizational processes.

CO1 The organization establishes and maintains a documented policy for conducting Quantitative Performance Management activities.

CO2 An organizational role(s) is assigned responsibility for coordinating Quantitative Performance Management activities across the organization.

AB1 Within each unit, an individual(s) is assigned responsibility and authority for ensuring that Quantitative Performance Management activities are performed.

AB2 Adequate resources are provided for performing Quantitative Performance Management activities.

AB3 Individuals who participate in Quantitative Performance Management activities develop the knowledge, skills, and process abilities needed to perform their responsibilities.

AB4 The practices and procedures for performing quantitative performance management are defined and documented.

ME1 Measurements are made and used to determine the status and performance of the organization's Quantitative Performance Management activities.

ME2 Measurements are made and used to determine the effectiveness of Quantitative Performance Management activities.

VE1 A responsible individual(s) verifies that Quantitative Performance Management activities are conducted according to the organization's documented policies, practices, procedures, and, where appropriate, plans; and addresses noncompliance.

VE2 Executive management periodically reviews the Quantitative Performance Management activities, status, and results; and resolves issues.

VE3 The definition and use of performance measures at the individual, workgroup, and unit levels are periodically audited for compliance with the organization's policies.

Organizational Capability Management

The purpose of Organizational Capability Management (OCM) is to quantify and manage the capability of the workforce and of the critical competency-based processes it performs.

Organizational Capability Management

Goal 1	Progress in developing the capability of critical workforce competencies is managed quantitatively.	**P1**	The organization identifies the workforce competencies that are critical to its business strategies and objectives.
		P2	The organization quantifies its capability in each of its critical workforce competencies.
		P3	The organization's capability in each of its critical workforce competencies is managed quantitatively.
Goal 2	The impact of workforce practices and activities on progress in developing the capability of critical workforce competencies is evaluated and managed quantitatively.	**P4**	Measurable objectives for contributing to capability growth in critical workforce competencies are established for workforce practices and activities.
		P5	The organization quantitatively evaluates the impacts of workforce practices and activities on capability in each of its critical workforce competencies.
		P6	The impacts of workforce practices and activities on the organization's capability in each of its critical workforce competencies are managed quantitatively.
Goal 3	The capabilities of competency-based processes in critical workforce competencies are established and managed quantitatively.	**P7**	Process performance baselines are developed and maintained for critical competency-based processes.
		P8	The capability of critical competency-based processes is managed quantitatively.
		P9	The organization uses its capability data and process performance baselines in developing quantitative models of performance.
Goal 4	The impact of workforce practices and activities on the capabilities of competency-based processes in critical workforce competencies is evaluated and managed quantitatively.	**P10**	The impact of workforce practices and activities on the capability and performance of competency-based processes is evaluated and managed quantitatively.
		P11	Evaluations of the impact of workforce practices and activities on the capability and performance of competency-based processes are used in performing other business and workforce activities, as appropriate.

Organizational Capability Management

Goal 5 Organizational Capability Management practices are institutionalized to ensure they are performed as defined organizational processes.

CO1 The organization establishes and maintains a documented policy for conducting Organizational Capability Management activities.

CO2 An organizational role(s) is assigned responsibility for coordinating Organizational Capability Management activities across the organization.

AB1 Within each unit, an individual(s) is assigned responsibility and authority for ensuring the unit's involvement in Organizational Capability Management activities, as appropriate.

AB2 A responsible individual(s) coordinates the quantitative capability management activities within each critical workforce competency.

AB3 Adequate resources are provided for performing Organizational Capability Management activities.

AB4 Those responsible for Organizational Capability Management activities develop the knowledge, skills, and process abilities needed to perform their responsibilities.

AB5 Individuals who participate in Organizational Capability Management activities receive appropriate orientation in the purposes and methods for the organization's quantitative capability management activities.

AB6 The practices and procedures for performing organizational capability management are defined and documented.

ME1 Measurements are made and used to determine the status and performance of Organizational Capability Management activities.

ME2 Measurements are made and used to determine the effectiveness of Organizational Capability Management activities.

VE1 A responsible individual(s) verifies that Organizational Capability Management activities are conducted according to the organization's documented policies, practices, procedures, and, where appropriate, plans; and addresses noncompliance.

VE2 Executive management periodically reviews the Organizational Capability Management activities, status, and results; and resolves issues.

VE3 The definition and use of measures at the individual, workgroup, and unit levels are periodically audited for compliance with organizational policies.

Mentoring

The purpose of Mentoring (MTR) is to transfer the lessons of greater experience in a workforce competency to improve the capability of other individuals or workgroups.

Mentoring		
Goal 1 Mentoring programs are established and maintained to accomplish defined objectives.	**P1**	Opportunities for using the experience of the workforce to improve performance or achieve other organizational objectives are identified.
	P2	The objectives and structure of each mentoring program are defined.
	P3	Each mentoring program is communicated to affected individuals and workgroups.
	P8	Mentors support the development and improvement of competency-based assets.
	P10	The organization's workforce practices support Mentoring activities, as needed.
Goal 2 Mentors provide guidance and support to individuals or workgroups.	**P4**	Mentors are selected and matched with individuals or workgroups to be mentored.
	P5	Mentors and those they mentor establish a mentoring relationship.
	P6	Mentors assist individuals or workgroups in developing capability in workforce competencies.
	P7	Mentoring relationships are reviewed to ensure that they satisfy their intended objectives.
	P9	Mentors participate in performance management and related workforce activities, as appropriate.

Mentoring

Goal 3 Mentoring practices are institutionalized to ensure they are performed as defined organizational processes.

CO1 The organization establishes and maintains a documented policy for conducting Mentoring activities.

CO2 An organizational role(s) is assigned responsibility for coordinating Mentoring activities across the organization.

AB1 Within each unit, an individual(s) is assigned responsibility and authority for ensuring that members of the unit participate in Mentoring activities, as appropriate.

AB2 Adequate resources are provided for performing Mentoring activities.

AB3 Individuals selected to act as mentors develop the knowledge, skills, and process abilities needed in relevant mentoring objectives, techniques, and skills to perform their responsibilities.

AB4 Affected individuals receive appropriate orientation in Mentoring practices.

AB5 The practices and procedures for performing mentoring are defined and documented.

ME1 Measurements are made and used to determine the status and performance of Mentoring activities.

ME2 Measurements are made and used to determine the effectiveness of Mentoring activities.

VE1 A responsible individual(s) verifies that Mentoring activities are conducted according to the organization's documented policies, practices, procedures, and, where appropriate, plans; and addresses noncompliance.

VE2 Executive management periodically reviews Mentoring activities, status, and results; and resolves issues.

Continuous Capability Improvement

The purpose of Continuous Capability Improvement (CCI) is to provide a foundation for individuals and workgroups to continuously improve their capability for performing competency-based processes.

Continuous Capability Improvement		
Goal 1 The organization establishes and maintains mechanisms for supporting continuous improvement of its competency-based processes.	**P1**	Individuals and workgroups are empowered to continuously improve their capability for performing competency-based processes.
	P10	Within each critical workforce competency, capability objectives are defined for critical competency-based processes.
	P11	Within each critical workforce competency, capability objectives for competency-based processes are compared to process performance baselines to identify improvement objectives.
	P15	The organization's workforce practices are adjusted, as needed, to accommodate continuous improvement activities by individuals and workgroups.
Goal 2 Individuals continuously improve the capability of their personal work processes.	**P2**	Individuals characterize the capability and performance of their personal work processes.
	P3	Individuals evaluate the capability of their personal work processes to identify opportunities for improvement.
	P4	Individuals establish measurable improvement objectives and plans for improving the capability of their personal work processes.
	P5	Individuals continuously improve the capability and performance of their personal work processes.

Continuous Capability Improvement

Goal 3	Workgroups continuously improve the capability of their workgroup's operating processes.	**P6**	Workgroups evaluate the capability and performance of their operating processes to identify opportunities for improvement.
		P7	Workgroups establish measurable objectives and plans for improving the capability of their operating processes.
		P8	Workgroups continuously improve their capability and performance.
Goal 4	The capabilities of competency-based processes are continuously improved.	**P9**	Recommendations resulting from improvements in personal work processes or workgroup operating processes are reviewed to determine if they should be incorporated into competency-based processes.
		P12	Within affected workforce competencies, responsible individuals identify opportunities for improving the capability and performance of competency-based processes.
		P13	Within selected workforce competencies, responsible individuals identify, evaluate, and select improvements to competency-based processes.
		P14	Selected improvement recommendations are incorporated into competency-based processes and made available for use.

Continued on next page

Continuous Capability Improvement

Goal 5 Continuous Capability Improvement practices are institutionalized to ensure they are performed as defined organizational processes.

CO1 The organization establishes and maintains a documented policy for continuously improving individual and workgroup capability.

CO2 An organizational role(s) is assigned responsibility for coordinating Continuous Capability Improvement activities across the organization.

AB1 Within each unit, an individual(s) is assigned responsibility and authority for ensuring that members of the unit participate in Continuous Capability Improvement activities, as appropriate.

AB2 Within selected workforce competencies, responsible individual(s) coordinate activities to improve its competency-based processes.

AB3 Adequate resources are provided for continuously improving individual and workgroup capabilities.

AB4 Mentoring support is offered to improve the capability and performance of individuals and workgroups.

AB5 Individuals and workgroups develop the knowledge, skills, and process abilities needed to perform their responsibilities in applying techniques for continuously improving their capabilities.

AB6 The practices and procedures for performing Continuous Competency Improvement are defined and documented.

Continuous Capability Improvement

Goal 5 *Continued*

ME1 Measurements are made and used to determine the status and performance of activities for Continuous Capability Improvement.

ME2 Measurements are made and used to determine the effectiveness of activities for Continuous Capability Improvement.

VE1 A responsible individual(s) verifies that the activities for Continuous Capability Improvement are conducted according to the organization's documented policies, practices, procedures, and, where appropriate, plans; and addresses noncompliance.

VE2 Executive management periodically reviews the Continuous Capability Improvement activities, status, and results; and resolves issues.

Organizational Performance Alignment

The purpose of Organizational Performance Alignment (OPA) is to enhance the alignment of performance results across individuals, workgroups, and units with organizational performance and business objectives.

Organizational Performance Alignment		
Goal 1 The alignment of performance among individuals, workgroups, units, and the organization is continuously improved.	**P1**	Workgroups continuously improve the alignment of performance among individuals and across the workgroup.
	P2	Units align performance among individuals, workgroups, and other entities within the unit.
	P3	The organization aligns performance across units and with the organization's business objectives.
Goal 2 The impact of workforce practices and activities on aligning individual, workgroup, unit, and organizational performance is continuously improved.	**P4**	The impact of the organization's workforce practices and activities on aligning performance is understood quantitatively.
	P5	The impact of workforce practices and activities on performance alignment is managed quantitatively.
	P6	Evaluations of the impact of workforce practices and activities on performance alignment are used in performing other business and workforce activities.

Organizational Performance Alignment

Goal 3 Organizational Performance Alignment practices are institutionalized to ensure they are performed as defined organizational processes.

CO1 The organization establishes and maintains a documented policy for aligning performance across individuals, workgroups, units, and the organization.

CO2 An organizational role(s) is assigned responsibility for coordinating performance alignment activities across the organization.

AB1 Within each unit, an individual(s) is assigned responsibility and authority for ensuring the unit's involvement in the organization's performance alignment activities.

AB2 Adequate resources are provided for performing Organizational Performance Alignment activities.

AB3 Individuals performing Organizational Performance Alignment activities develop the knowledge, skills, and process abilities needed to perform their responsibilities.

AB4 Individuals and workgroups participating in Organizational Performance Alignment activities receive appropriate orientation in Organizational Performance Alignment practices.

AB5 The practices and procedures for performing Organizational Performance Alignment are defined and documented.

ME1 Measurements are made and used to determine the status and performance of the organization's performance alignment activities.

ME2 Measurements are made and used to determine the effectiveness of the organization's performance alignment activities.

VE1 A responsible individual(s) verifies that the organization's performance alignment activities are conducted according to the organization's documented policies, practices, procedures, and, where appropriate, plans; and addresses noncompliance.

VE2 Executive management periodically reviews the organization's performance alignment activities, status, and results; and resolves issues.

VE3 The definition and use of measures of individual, workgroup, unit, and organizational performance are periodically audited for compliance with organizational policies.

Continuous Workforce Innovation

The purpose of Continuous Workforce Innovation (CWI) is to identify and evaluate improved or innovative workforce practices and technologies, and implement the most promising ones throughout the organization.

Continuous Workforce Innovation		
Goal 1 The organization establishes and maintains mechanisms for supporting continuous improvement of its workforce practices and technologies.	**P1**	The organization establishes a framework for continuously improving its workforce practices and activities.
	P2	Individuals and workgroups are empowered to continuously improve their performance of workforce activities.
	P3	A continuous improvement program is established to encourage individuals and workgroups to propose improvements to workforce practices and activities.
	P6	Quantitative objectives are established for improving the impact of workforce practices and activities.
Goal 2 Innovative or improved workforce practices and technologies are identified and evaluated.	**P4**	Workforce opinions about their working conditions are periodically evaluated to identify areas that would most benefit from innovative or improved practices.
	P5	Data regarding the impact of the organization's workforce practices and activities are analyzed to identify areas that would most benefit from innovative or improved practices.
	P7	The organization continuously investigates innovative workforce practices and technologies.
	P8	Innovative and improved workforce practices and technologies are evaluated and selected for implementation.
	P9	When appropriate, innovative or improved workforce practices or technologies are evaluated in trials to evaluate their benefits and most effective methods for implementation.

Continuous Workforce Innovation

Goal 3	Innovative or improved workforce practices and technologies are deployed using orderly procedures.	**P10**	The deployment of innovative or improved workforce practices or technologies is planned and prepared.
		P11	Innovative or improved workforce practices and technologies are implemented according to their deployment plans.
		P12	The effectiveness and benefits of innovative or improved workforce practices and technologies are evaluated quantitatively.
		P13	The status and results of the organization's Continuous Workforce Innovation activities are periodically reviewed and communicated across the organization.
Goal 4	Continuous Workforce Innovation practices are institutionalized to ensure they are performed as defined organizational processes.	**CO1**	The organization establishes and maintains a documented policy for conducting Continuous Workforce Innovation activities.
		CO2	An organizational role(s) is assigned responsibility for coordinating the continuous innovation and improvement of workforce practices across the organization.
		AB1	Within each unit, a responsible individual(s) coordinates actions regarding proposals for improving workforce practices and activities and manages deployment of improvements or innovations.
		AB2	Adequate resources are provided for continuously improving workforce practices and activities.
		AB3	Those responsible for continuously innovating and improving workforce practices and activities develop the knowledge, skills, and process abilities needed to perform their responsibilities and to apply relevant evaluation methods and continuous improvement techniques.
		AB4	Individuals receive orientation or preparation in the innovative or improved workforce practices and technologies adopted by the organization.
		AB5	The practices and procedures for performing Continuous Workforce Innovation are defined and documented.

Continued on next page

Continuous Workforce Innovation	
Goal 4 *Continued*	**ME1** Measurements are made and used to determine the status and performance of activities for continuously innovating and improving workforce practices and activities.
	ME2 Measurements are made and used to determine the effectiveness of continuously innovating and improving workforce practices and technologies.
	VE1 A responsible individual(s) verifies that the activities for continuously innovating and improving workforce practices are conducted according to the organization's documented policies, practices, procedures, and, where appropriate, plans; and addresses noncompliance.
	VE2 Executive management periodically reviews the Continuous Workforce Innovation activities, status, and results; and resolves issues.

Book Authors

Dr. Bill Curtis is the senior vice president and chief scientist at CAST, a leader in providing technology for measuring and evaluating application software quality. He coauthored the Capability Maturity Model (CMM), the People CMM, and the Business Process MM. Until its acquisition by Borland, he was the cofounder of and chief scientist at TeraQuest, a global leader in providing CMM-based services. He is a former director of the Software Process Program in the Software Engineering Institute (SEI) at Carnegie Mellon University.
Prior to joining the SEI, Dr. Curtis worked for MCC, ITT's Programming Technology Center, GE Space Division, and Weyerhaeuser, and also taught statistics at the University of Washington. While a staff psychologist in Weyerhaeuser's Human Resources Department, he codeveloped the training for their performance appraisal system and conducted organizational effectiveness interventions in several divisions. Dr. Curtis holds a Ph.D. with emphasis in organizational psychology and statistics from Texas Christian University. He has published four books and more than 150 articles, and was recently elected a Fellow of the Institute of Electrical and Electronics Engineers for his contributions to software process improvement and measurement.

Dr. William E. Hefley is an associate teaching professor and program director of the MSIT Information Technology Service Management (MSIT-ITSM) program at Carnegie Mellon University. He is the managing principal consultant with Pinnacle Global Management, LLC, a global consulting firm. He is also associated with the Information Technology Services Qualification Center (ITSqc), whose mission is to address the emerging need for capability models and qualification methods for organizations involved in the evolving Internet economy.
He is currently working in the areas of IT-enabled sourcing from the perspectives of both the service providers (the eSCM-SP) and their clients, where he led the effort to develop the eSCM for Client Organizations (eSCM-CL). Dr. Hefley teaches IT, service science, service innovation, and sourcing management courses, and is a frequent lecturer on service innovation and global software delivery. He also supervises graduate studies and projects related

to sourcing relationships, software process management, human capital management, and knowledge management. He was a senior member of the technical staff at the SEI from 1987 to 1996, where he led the team that developed the People CMM and its assessment method. Dr. Hefley received his Ph.D. in organization science and information technology from Carnegie Mellon University. He also received an M.S. in engineering and public policy from Carnegie Mellon University and an M.S.S.M. from the University of Southern California. He also received a B.S. in computer science and political science, and a B.A. (with distinction) in psychology. He is currently on the editorial boards of several journals and is series editor for the Springer book series on Service Science: Research and Innovations in the Service Economy.

Sally A. Miller, coauthor of the People CMM, is currently a visiting scientist at the SEI. Previously, she managed the SEI's People CMM effort, including the completion of the product suite and the transition to SCAMPI with People CMM. Ms. Miller has more than 23 years of service to the SEI as a human resources professional, senior member of the technical staff, and People CMM interface to major organizations. She has led People CMM assessments and consulting engagements across the United States. Before joining the SEI, she worked for Pittsburgh-based Fortune 500 organizations focusing on marketing, training, and development. She is a guest lecturer at Carnegie Mellon University and a graduate of Grove City College with concentrations in business administration and psychology.

Index

A

Ability to Perform
  defined, 575
  as institutionalization practice, 50
  practices related to, 62–63
Accenture, 137–141
  achieving high performance, 137
  commitment to high performance, 141
  factors influencing People CMM achievements, 138–139
  reasons for adopting People CMM, 137–138
Accomplishments
  compensation based on, 253–254
  monitoring/documenting, 221–224
Acronyms, defined, 571–573
Acting phase, IDEAL life cycle model, 86, 100
Activities
  business. *See* Business activities
  communication and coordination activities, 185–186
  competency development, 426–427
  defined, 575
  development activities, 300–301, 320
  evaluating impact on competency-based processes, 468–470
  evaluating impact on critical workforce competencies, 459–461
  learning, 505–506
  managing impact on critical workforce competencies, 461–462
  mentoring or coaching, 427
  outplacement, 176–178
  recruiting, 327–328
  staffing, 163–164
  transition, 173, 329–330
  workforce. *See* Workforce activities
  workgroups planning, 352–353
Adequate
  defined, 575
  use in interpretation of practices, 61
Adoption of People CMM
  benefits of, 114–117
  benefits varying by maturity level achieved, 117–120
  overview of, 113–114
  rates of, 84–85, 87
Advanced Information Services, Inc. (AIS), 84, 87, 89–91
Advisors. *See* Mentoring
Affected individuals
  defined, 575
  use in interpretation of practices, 61
Aggregate trends in compensation, measurement of, 256
Aggregation, of unit measures, 65
AIS (Advanced Information Services, Inc.), 84, 87, 89–91
Alignment, of personal development plan, 319
Alignment objectives, 523, 527, 529, 532. *See also* Organizational Performance Alignment
Alternative practices
  for achieving goals, 48, 110
  defined, 575
Analysis. *See also* Appraisals; Competency Analysis; Measurement and Analysis
  baseline, 94–95
  gap analyses, 111, 133
  organizational, 92–93
  questionnaire-based, 95–97
Appraisals
  defined, 103
  discovery-based, 108, 579
  in low-maturity organizations, 21
  multimodel, 112
  SCAMPI Class A, 106–110
  SCAMPI Class B, 110–111
  SCAMPI Class C, 111–112
  SCAMPI with People CMM method, 92–93, 103–106
  uses of People CMM, 84–85
  verification-based, 109, 589
Apprenticeship. *See* Mentoring
Architecture, People CMM
  model components. *See* Model components
  structural components. *See* Structural components of People CMM

The SEI Partner Network:
Helping hands with a global reach.

Do you need help getting started with People CMM adoption in your organization? Or are you an experienced professional in the field who wants to join a global network of People CMM service providers? Regardless of your level of experience with People CMM tools and methods, the SEI Partner Network can provide the assistance and the support you need to make your People CMM adoption a success.

The SEI Partner Network is a world-wide group of licensed organizations with individuals qualified by the SEI to deliver SEI services. SEI Partners can provide you with training courses, People CMM adoption assistance, proven appraisal methods, and teamwork and management processes that aid in implementation of the SEI's tools and methods.

To find an SEI Partner near you, or to learn more about this global network of professionals, please visit the SEI Partner Network website at
http://www.sei.cmu.edu/partners

ESSENTIAL GUIDES TO CMMI®

CMMI®, Second Edition: Guidelines for Process Integration and Product Improvement

Mary Beth Chrissis, Mike Konrad, and Sandy Shrum

978-0-321-27967-5

The definitive guide to CMMI—now updated for CMMI v1.2! Whether you are new to CMMI or already familiar with some version of it, this book is the essential resource for managers, practitioners, and process improvement team members who to need to understand, evaluate, and/or implement a CMMI model.

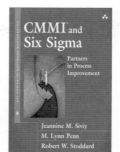

CMMI® and Six Sigma: Partners in Process Improvement

Jeannine M. Siviy, M. Lynn Penn, and Robert W. Stoddard

978-0-321-51608-4

Focuses on the synergistic, rather than competitive, implementation of CMMI and Six Sigma—with synergy translating to "faster, better, cheaper" achievement of mission success.

CMMI® Survival Guide: Just Enough Process Improvement

Suzanne Garcia and Richard Turner

978-0-321-42277-4

Practical guidance for any organization, large or small, considering or undertaking process improvement, with particular advice for implementing CMMI successfully in resource-strapped environments.

CMMI® Distilled, Third Edition: A Practical Introduction to Integrated Process Improvement

Dennis M. Ahern, Aaron Clouse, and Richard Turner

978-0-321-46108-7

Updated for CMMI version 1.2, this third edition again provides a concise and readable introduction to the model, as well as straightforward, no-nonsense information on integrated, continuous process improvement.

CMMI®-ACQ: Guidelines for Improving the Acquisition of Products and Services

Brian P. Gallagher, Mike Phillips, Karen J. Richter, and Sandy Shrum

978-0-321-58035-1

The official guide to CMMI-ACQ—an extended CMMI framework for improving product and service acquisition processes. In addition to the complete CMMI-ACQ itself, the book includes tips, hints, and case studies to enhance your understanding and to provide valuable, practical advice.

Also Available

CMMI® Assessments: Motivating Positive Change

Marilyn Bush and Donna Dunaway

978-0-321-17935-7

CMMI® SCAMPI Distilled: Appraisals for Process Improvement

Dennis M. Ahern, Jim Armstrong, Aaron Clouse, Jack R. Ferguson, Will Hayes, and Kenneth E. Nidiffer

978-0-321-22876-5

For more information on these and other books in The SEI Series in Software Engineering, please visit informit.com/seiseries